A-Z CORNW

CONTENTS

Key to Map Pages	2-5
Map Pages	6-162
Large Scale Looe Town Centre	81
Large Scale St. Ives Town Centre	137
Large Scale Plymouth City Centre	163

Road Map (Reference

Index to Streets etc.

Index to Hospitals etc. — 224

REFERENCE

Primary Route	A30
A Road	A389
B Road	B3284
Dual Carriageway	
One-way Street Traffic flow on A Roads is also indicated by a heavy line on the driver's left	
Road Under Construction Opening dates are correct at the time of publication	
Proposed Road	
Restricted Access	
Pedestrianized Road	
Track / Footpath	
Residential Walkway	
Railway	Station Heritage Station Level Crossing Tunnel
Built-up Area	BARNS ROAD
Beach	
Local Authority Boundary	
Posttown Boundary	
Postcode Boundary (within Posttown)	
Map Continuation	Large Scale Centres 74 137 Road Map Pages 165

Airport	✈
Car Park (selected)	P
Church or Chapel	†
Cycleway (selected)	🚲
Fire Station	■
Hospital	H
House Numbers (A & B Roads only)	21 40
Information Centre	i
National Grid Reference	³05
Park & Ride	Truro P+R
Police Station	▲
Post Office	★
Speed Camera with Speed Limit Fixed cameras and long term road works cameras. Symbols do not indicate camera direction	30
Toilet	▽
Viewpoint	☀
Educational Establishment	
Hospital or Healthcare Building	
Industrial Building	
Leisure or Recreational Facility	
Place of Interest	
Public Building	
Shopping Centre or Market	
Other Selected Buildings	

SCALE

Map Pages 6-162

1:16,896   3¾ inches (9.52 cm) to 1 mile   5.9cm to 1km

0   ¼   ½ Mile

0   250   500 Metres

Large Scale Map Pages

1:8,448   7½ inches (19.05 cm) to 1 mile   11.8cm to 1km

0   ⅛   ¼ Mile

0   100   200   300   400 Metres

Copyright of Geographers' A-Z Map Company Limited

Fairfield Road, Borough Green, Sevenoaks, Kent TN15 8PP
Telephone: 01732 781000 (Enquiries & Trade Sales)
01732 783422 (Retail Sales)

www.az.co.uk
Copyright © Geographers' A-Z Map Co. Ltd.
EDITION 2 2012

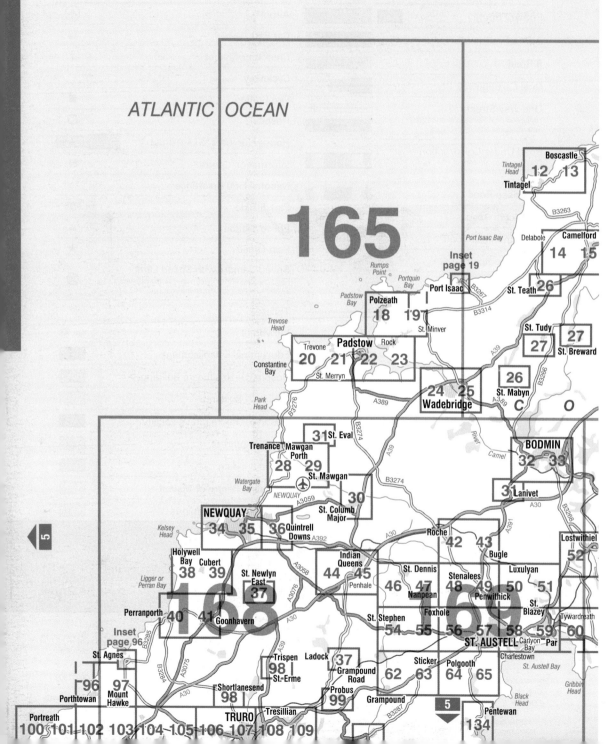

ATLANTIC OCEAN

165

168

69

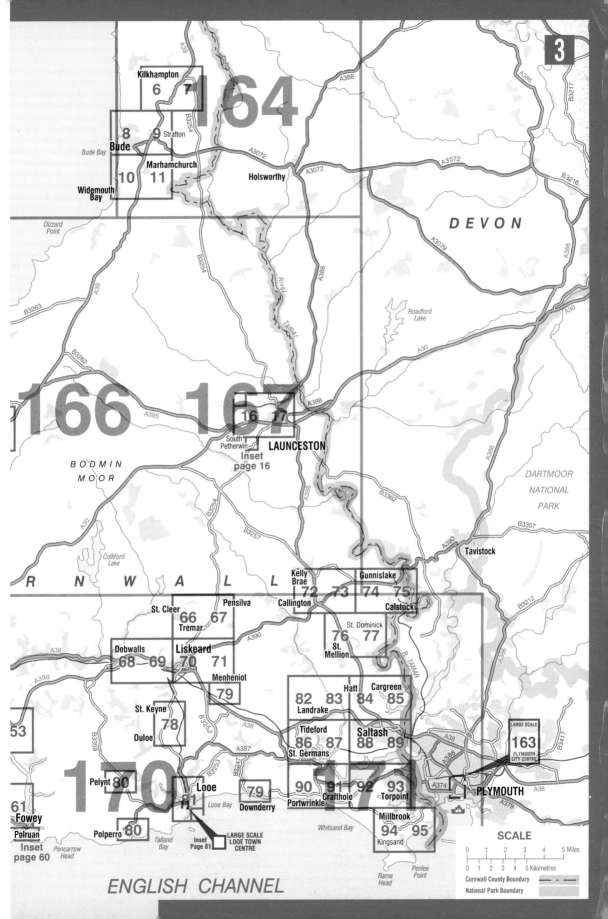

3

Kilkhampton
6 7

164

8 9
Stratton
Bude
Bude Bay
10 11
Marhamchurch
Widemouth
Bay

Holsworthy

Dizzard Point

D E V O N

Roadford Lake

166 **167**

South
Petherwin
LAUNCESTON
Inset
page 16

B O D M I N
M O O R

Colliford Lake

DARTMOOR
NATIONAL
PARK

Tavistock

R   N   W   A   L   L   L

Kelly
Brae
Gunnislake
72 73 74 75
Callington
Calstock
St. Cleer
66 67
Tremar
Pensilva
76 77
St. Dominick
St.
Mellion
Dobwalls
68 69
Liskeard
70 71
Menheniot
79

St. Keyne
78
Duloe

82 83
Landrake
Hatt
84 85
Cargreen

Tideford
86 87
St. Germans
Saltash
88 89

LARGE SCALE
163
PLYMOUTH
CITY CENTRE

Pelynt 80

170

Looe
81 *Looe Bay*
79
Downderry

90 91 92 93
Portwrinkle Crafthole Torpoint

171

PLYMOUTH

61
Fowey
Polruan
Inset
page 60

Pencarrow Head

Polperro 80
Talland Bay

Inset
Page 81

LARGE SCALE
LOOE TOWN
CENTRE

Millbrook
94 95
Kingsand

Whitsand Bay

Rame Head

Penlee Point

SCALE

0   1   2   3   4   5 Miles
0 1 2 3 4 5 Kilometres

Cornwall County Boundary — · — · —
National Park Boundary

ENGLISH CHANNEL

ATLANTIC OCEAN

DEVON

Ligger or Perran Bay

Perranporth

St. Agnes Head

Inset page 96

St. Agnes

96 **97**
Mount Hawke

Porthtowan

LARGE SCALE ST. IVES TOWN CENTRE | Inset Page 137

Portreath | Cambrose | Blackwater

100 **101** **102** **103** **104**
Chacewater

Navax Point

Illogan | **REDRUTH**

The Carracks

St. Ives Bay

110 **111** **112** **113** **114**
Lanner | Carharra

St. Ives

Gwithian

136 **137** **138** **139**
Carbis Bay | Hayle | Connor Downs

A30

Camborne

118 **119** **120** **121** **122**
Four Lanes | Stithians

Gurnard's Head

B3306

Lelant

140 **141**
St. Erth

Reawla
142 **143**
Praze-an-Beeble
Leedstown

Stithians Lake

B3280 | B3297

126
Longdown

Pendeen Watch

Pendeen
144

B3318 | A3071 | B3311

Crowlas
Ludgvan **551**

B3280

B3302 | B3303

Cape Cornwall
The Brisons

St. Just
145

B3306 | A30

Madron
148 **149**
PENZANCE

Longrock
150 **151** **152** **153**
Marazion
St. Michael's Mount

Goldsithney

Germoe

Helston

Constantine
159

Whitesand Bay

Longships

LAND'S END

146
Sennen

147
Porthcurno

Gwennap Head

St. Buryan
147

B3315

Newlyn
154
Mousehole

172

Cudden Point

Praa Sands
155

Breage
156 **157** **158**
Porthleven

173

Inset page 156

Gweek
159

B3293

Cribba Head

Runnel Stone

Trevavas Head

Poldhu Point

Mullion
161

Mullion Island

Vellan Head

Lizard **161**
LIZARD POINT

Hot Point

A3083

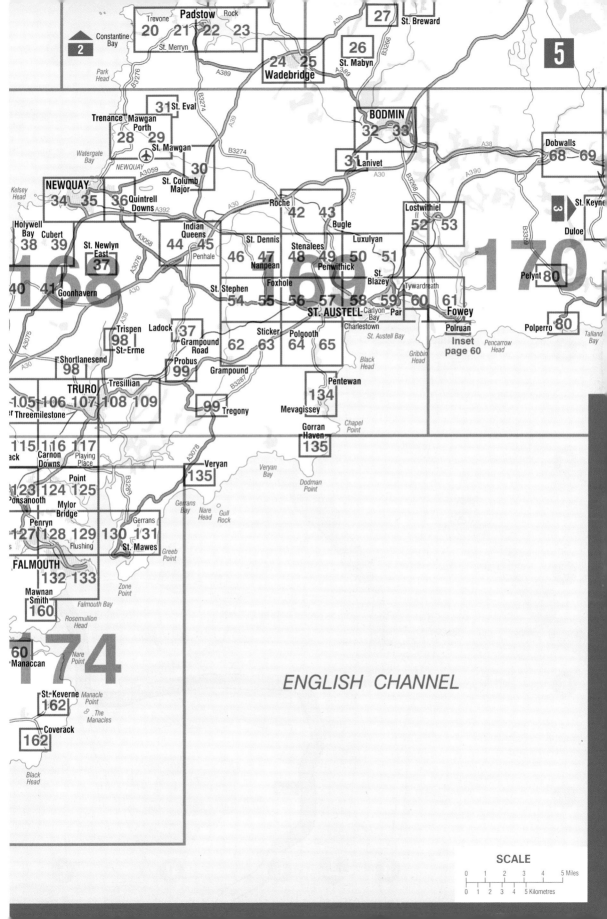

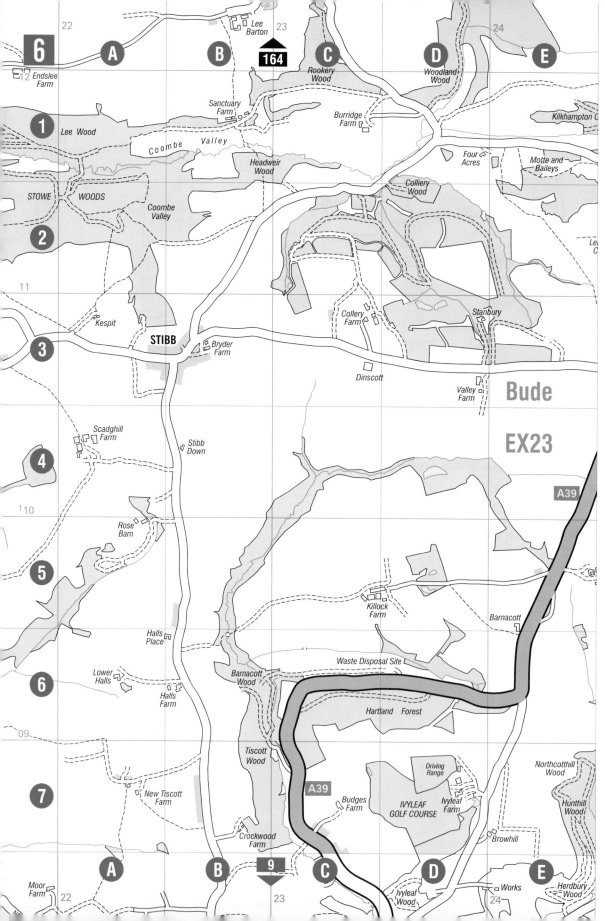

6

A   22   B   23   ▲ 164   C   D   24   E

Endslee Farm 12

Lee Barton

Rookery Wood

Woodland Wood

Kilkhampton C

1 Lee Wood

Sanctuary Farm

Burridge Farm

Coombe Valley

Four Acres

Motte and Baileys

Headweir Wood

Colliery Wood

STOWE WOODS

Coombe Valley

11

2

Kespit

Colliery Farm

Stanbury

3 STIBB

Bryder Farm

Dinscott

Valley Farm

Bude

EX23

Scadghill Farm

Stibb Down

4

110

Rose Barn

A39

5

Killock Farm

Barnacott

6 Halls Place

Lower Halls

Halls Farm

Barnacott Wood

Waste Disposal Site

Hartland Forest

09

Tiscott Wood

Driving Range

Northcotthill Wood

7

New Tiscott Farm

A39

Budges Farm

IVYLEAF GOLF COURSE

Ivyleaf Farm

Hunthill Wood

Crockwood Farm

Browhill

Moor Farm 22

A   B   23   ▼ 9   C   D   24   E

Ivyleaf Wood

Works

Herdbury Wood

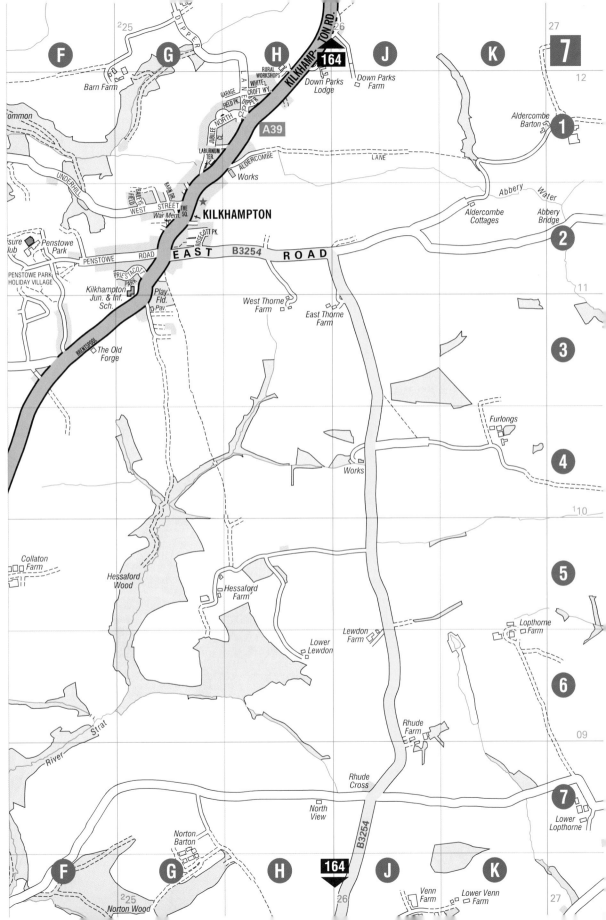

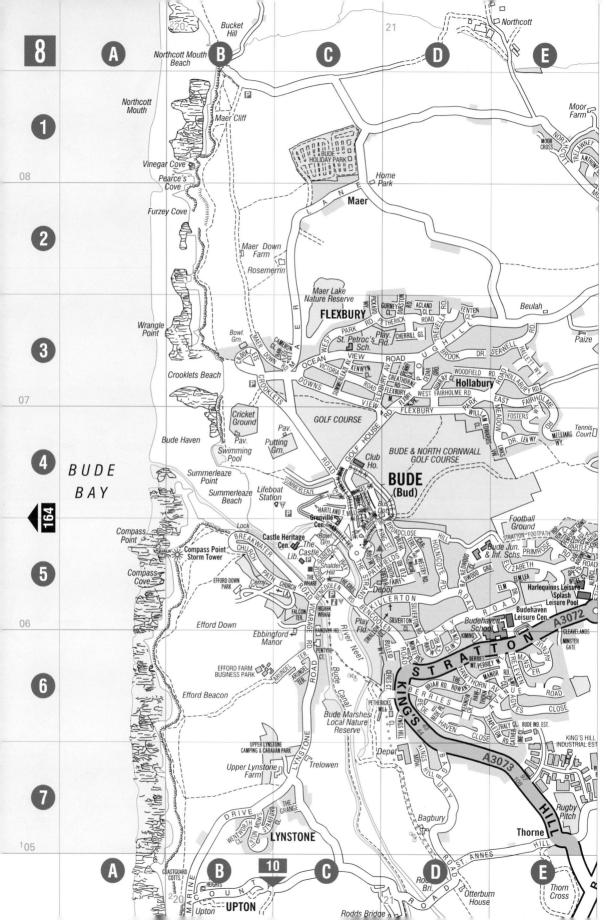

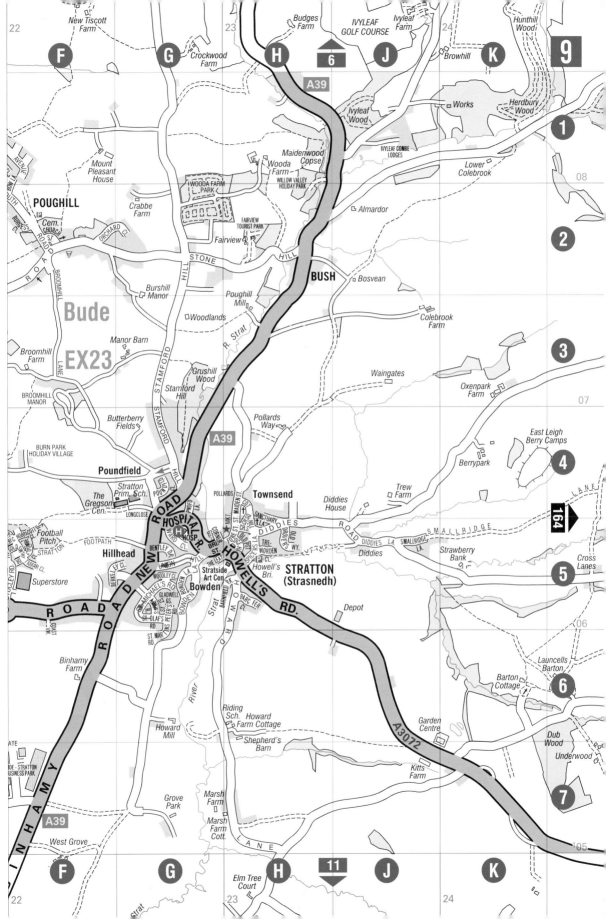

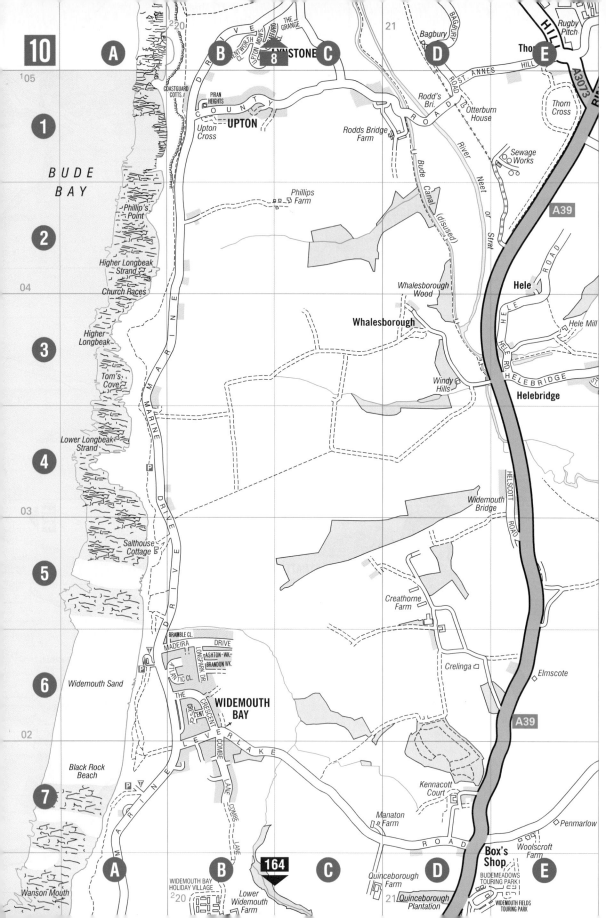

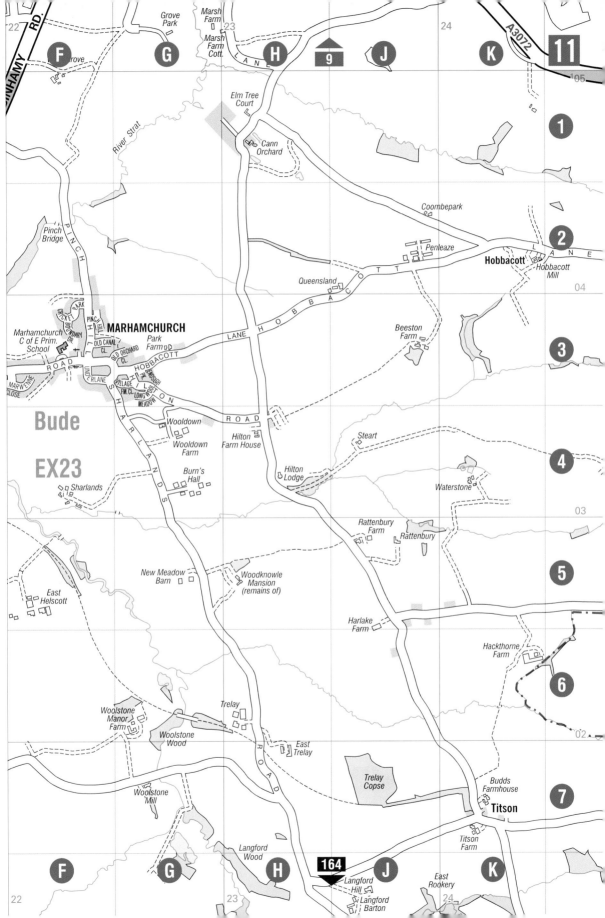

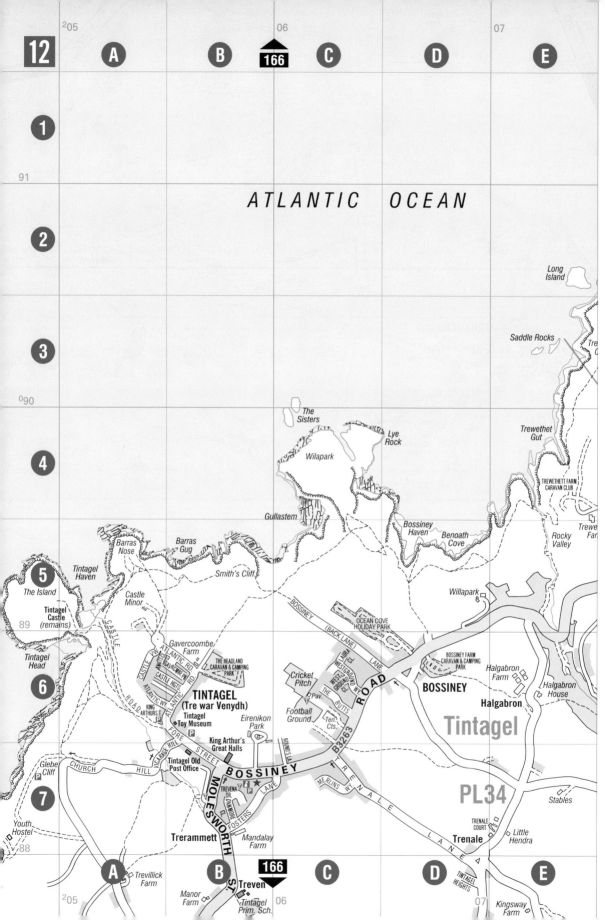

12

1

91

ATLANTIC OCEAN

2

Long Island

3

Saddle Rocks

Trewe

90

The Sisters

Lye Rock

Trewethet Gut

4

Wilapark

Trewethel

TREWETHETT FARM CARAVAN CLUB

Trewe Far

Gullastem

Bossiney Haven

Benoath Cove

Rocky Valley

Trewe

Barras Nose

Barras Gug

Smith's Cliff

Willapark

Tintagel Haven

5

The Island

Castle Minor

BOSSINEY (BACK LANE)

OCEAN COVE HOLIDAY PARK

Tintagel Castle (remains)

89

CASTLE

Gavercoombe Farm

THE HEADLAND CARAVAN & CAMPING PARK

LAURA CL.

BOSSINEY FARM CARAVAN & CAMPING PARK

Halgabron Farm

Halgabron House

6

Tintagel Head

ATLANTIC RD

CASTLE VW.

GAVERCOMBE PK.

CASTLE HGTS.

ATLANTIC WY.

KING ARTHUR'S T.

ROAD

TINTAGEL
(Tre war Venydh)

Tintagel Toy Museum

Eirenikon Park

Cricket Pitch

Pav.

Football Ground

Ten. Cts.

WESTGROUND WY.

WEST CL.

THE BUTTS

LANE

ROAD

B3263

BOSSINEY

Halgabron

Tintagel

King Arthur's Great Halls

Glebe Cliff

CHURCH HILL

VICARAGE HILL

FORE STREET

Tintagel Old Post Office

BOSSINEY

ROUND'S LA.

MERLIN'S WY.

TRENALE

LANE

PL34

Stables

7

P

MOLESWORTH ST.

TREVENA DR.

DINMORE CL.

LANE

FOSTERS

TRENALE COURT

Little Hendra

Youth Hostel

88

Trerammett

Mandalay Farm

Trenale

Manor Farm

Tintagel Prim. Sch.

Kingsway Farm

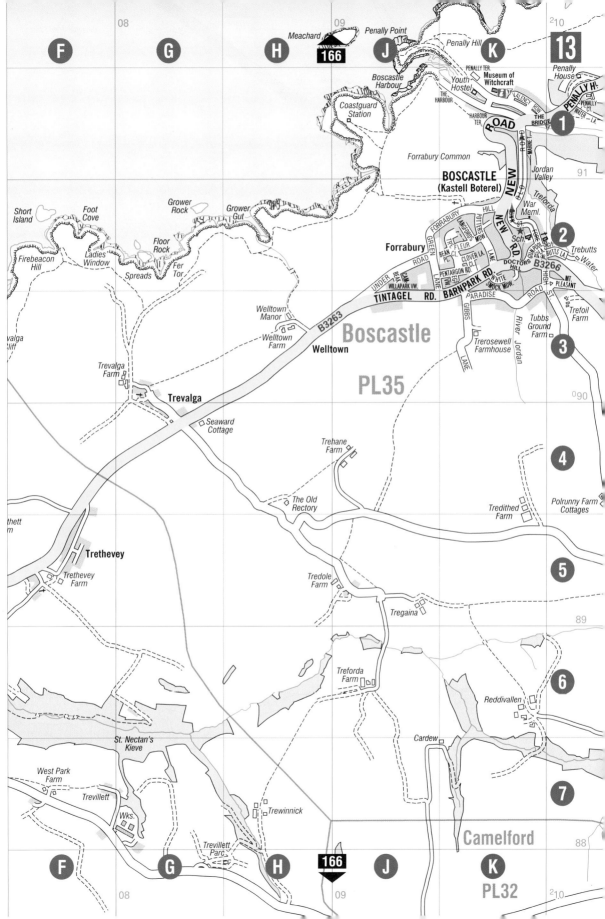

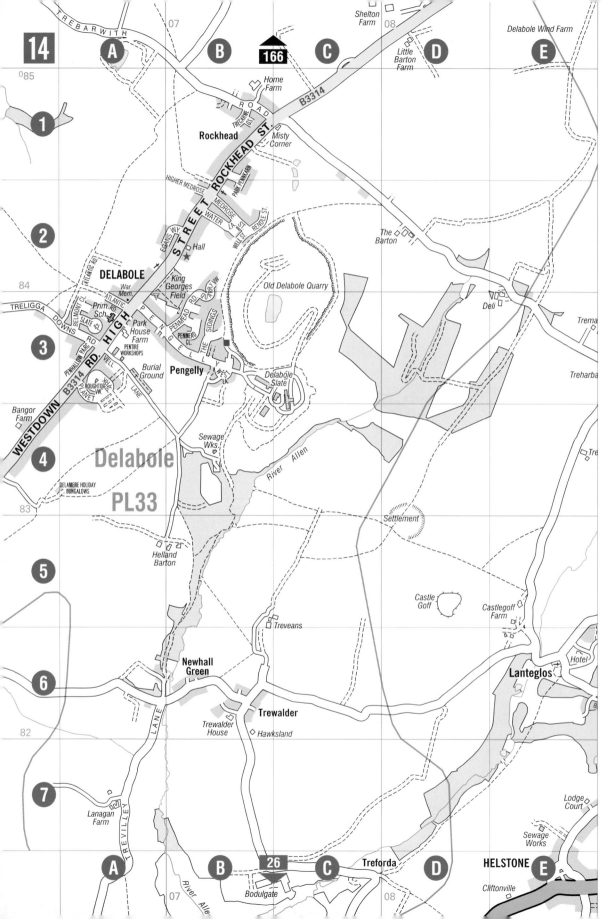

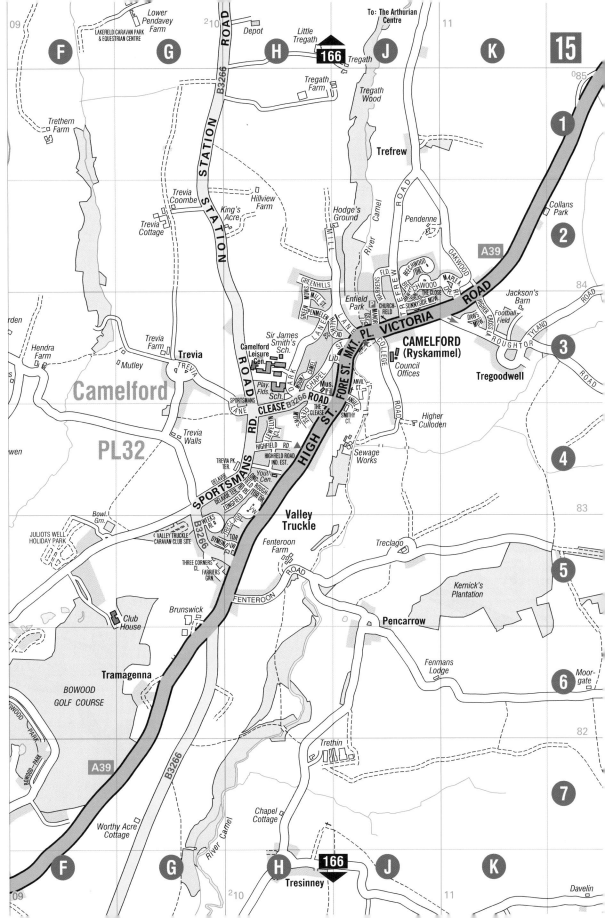

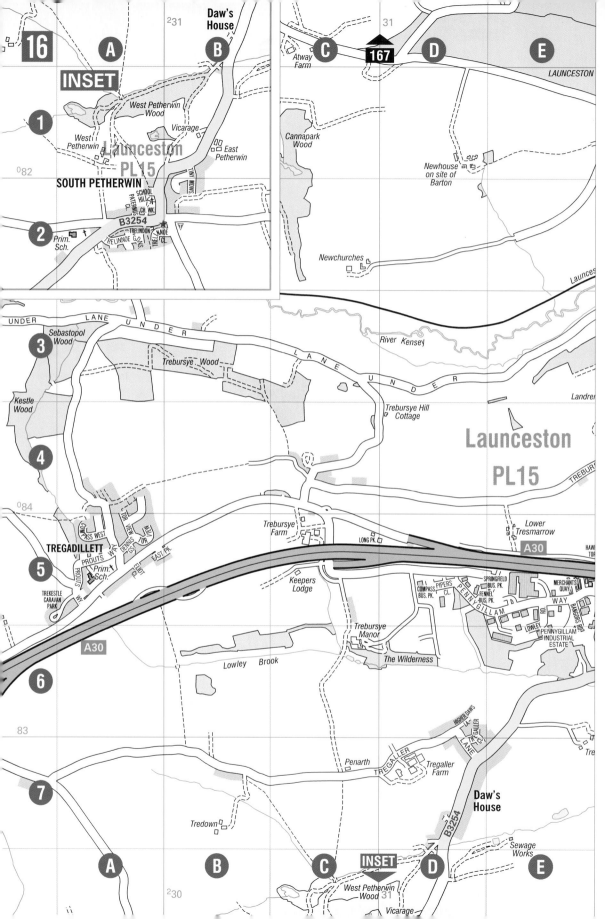

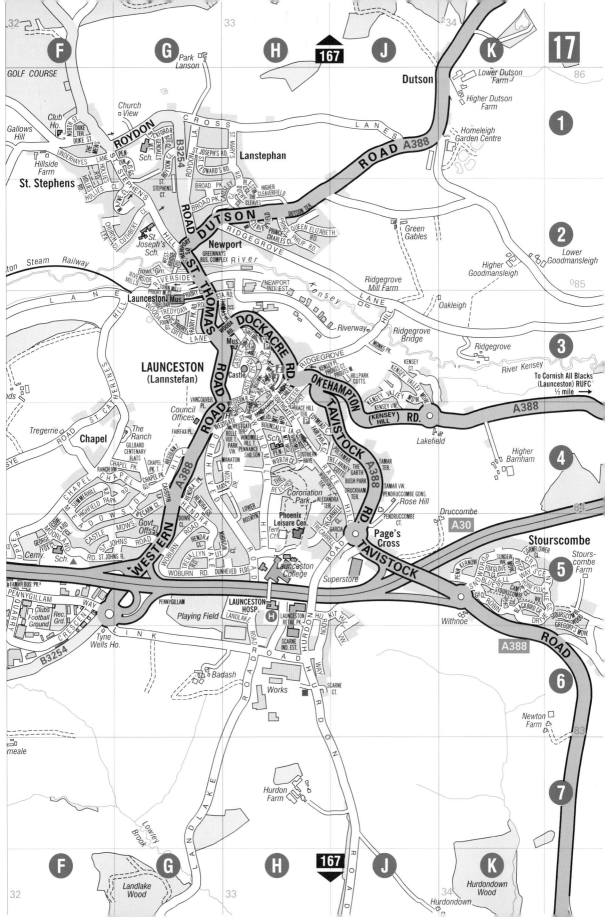

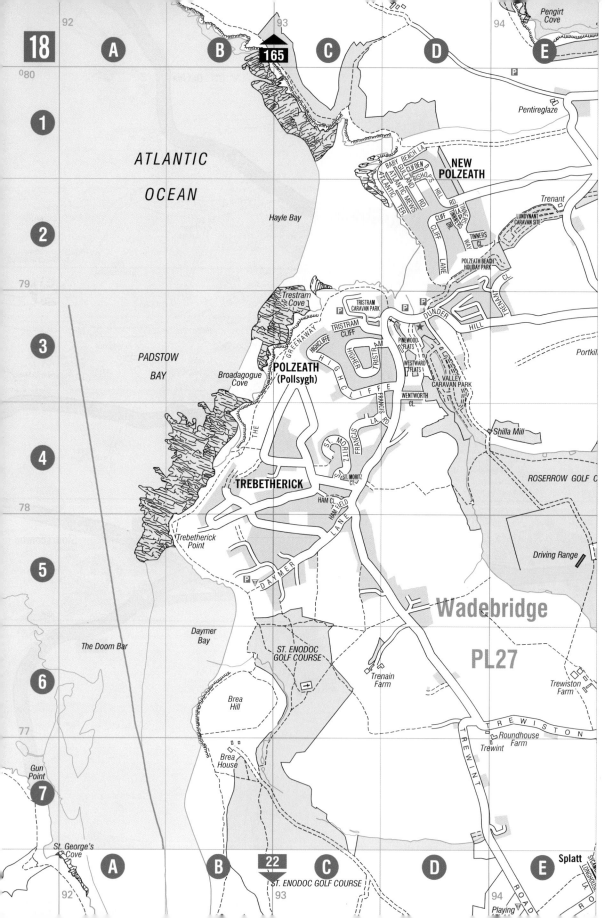

ATLANTIC

OCEAN

Hayle Bay

PADSTOW
BAY

NEW POLZEATH

Pengirt Cove

Pentireglaze

Trenant

LUNDYNANT CARAVAN SITE

BABY BEACH LA.
CLIFDEN
ATLANTIC MEWS
BISHOP'S HILL
CLIFF RD.
TINNERS DR.
CLIFF LANE
TINNERS WAY
TINNERS CL.

POLZEATH BEACH HOLIDAY PARK

TRENANT CL.

Portkil

Trestram Cove

TRISTRAM CARAVAN PARK

DUNDER HILL

Shilla Mill

Broadagogue Cove

POLZEATH (Pollsygh)

GREENAWAY
HIGHCLIFFE
TRISTRAM CLIFF
HIGHER TRISTRAM
HIGH CLIFFE

PINEWOOD FLATS
WESTWARD FLATS
VALLEY CARAVAN PARK

ROSERROW GOLF C

FRANCIS RD.
WENTWORTH CL.

THE

TREBETHERICK

ST. MORITZ CL.
ST. MORITZ CT.
FRANCIS LA.
HAM CL.
HAMFIELD
LANE

Trebetherick Point

Driving Range

DAYMER

Daymer Bay

The Doom Bar

Wadebridge

PL27

Brea Hill

ST. ENODOC GOLF COURSE

Trenain Farm

Trewiston Farm

Brea House

TREWISTON ROAD

TREWINT

Roundhouse Farm

Trewint

Gun Point

St. George's Cove

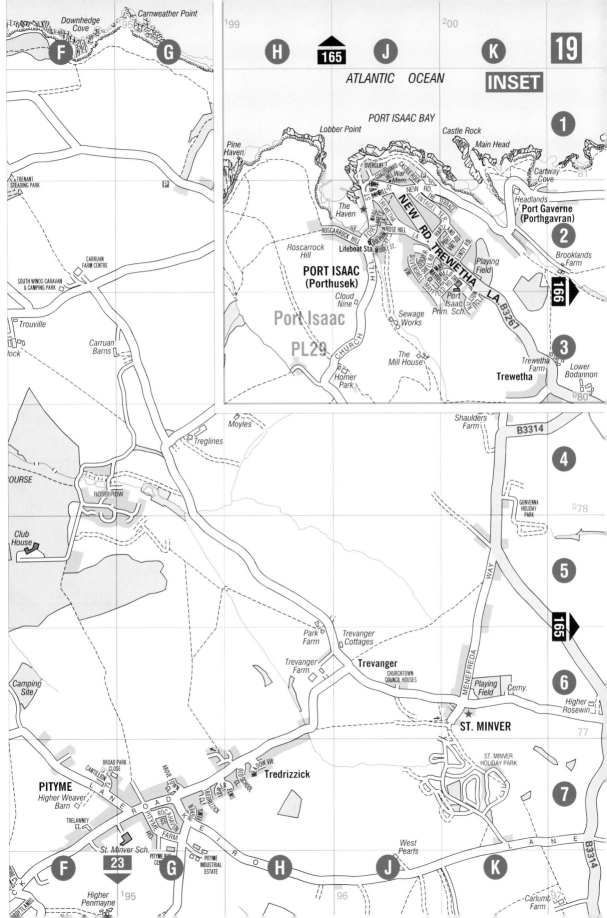

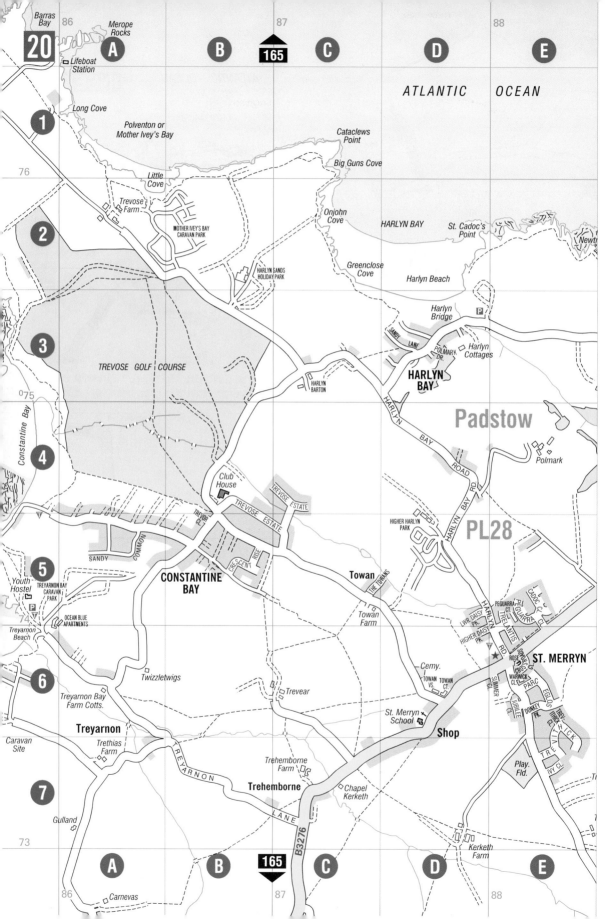

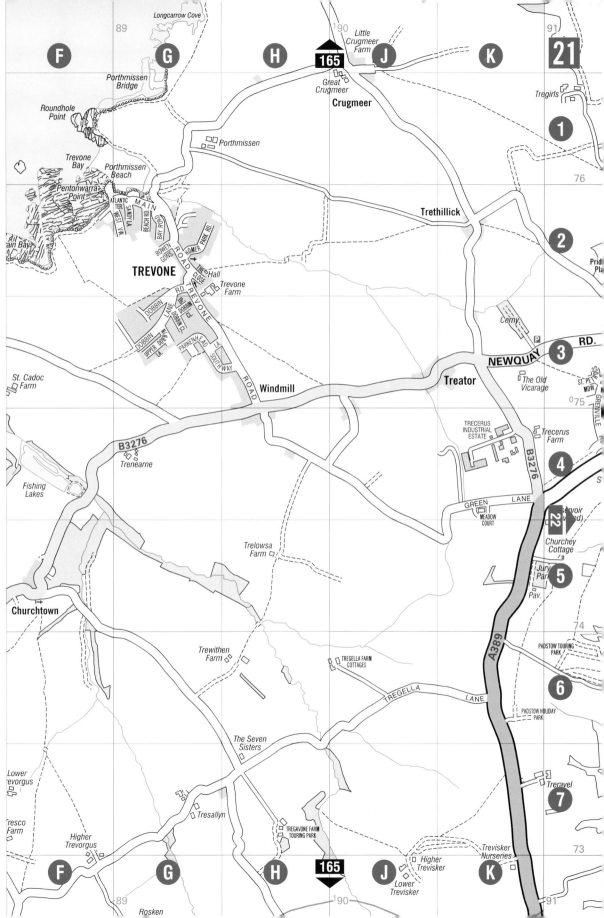

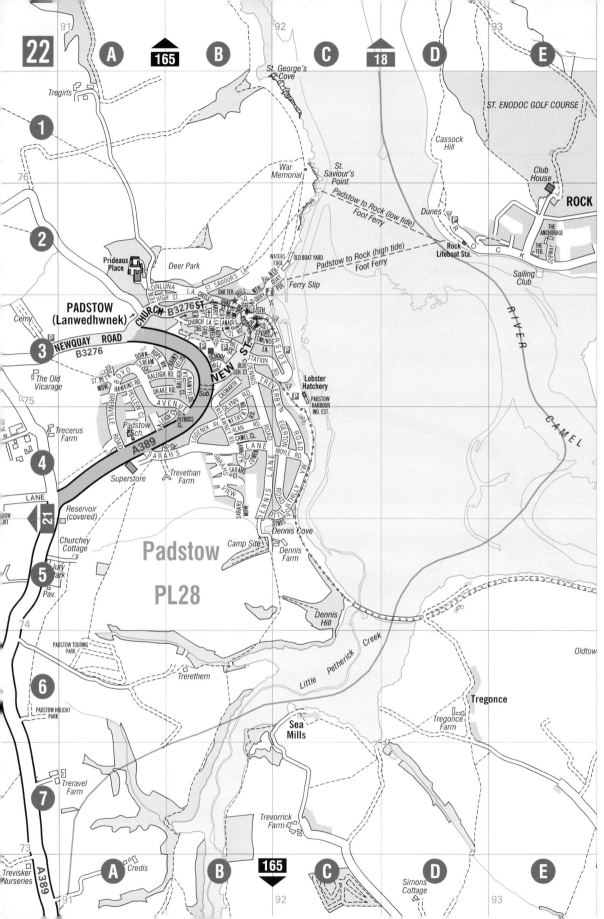

Higher Weaver Barn

PITYME

Trelawney Ct.

St. Minver School

Pityme Bus Centre

PITYME INDUSTRIAL ESTATE

West Pearls

Splatt

Higher Penmayne

Penmayne Vs.

D/NGLES WY.

Penmayne

CROFTLANDS

SYCAMORE CL.

LONGHOUSE LA.

TREWINT ROAD

Playing Fields

MONAGUE LA.

LOWENNA MANOR

LONG AGRES CL.

BREA RD.

SHORES LANE

CROER

DRO

CRICKETERS HOLLOW

LWR. GREEN BANKS

GREENBANKS CT.

LITTLE TRELYN

GREEN LANE

FORTAZE RD.

ROCK VS.

KEN

TRURO

STILLY CLOSE

McDROSE RD.

THE PAVILION

STOPTIDE

SANDYHILLS

LITTLE TREVERROW

TREFRESA FARM CARAVAN SITE

Trefresa Farm

Little Trefresa

Porthilly Cove

PORTHILLY ROAD

Porthilly

Porthilly Farm

PORTHILLY FARM CARAVAN SITE

Treverrow Farm

Treverra Farm

Carlyon

Trevelver

Wadebridge
PL27

Sewage Works

Cant Farm

Cant Cove

Trecant

Gentle Jane

CAMEL

RIVER

Ball Hill

Oldtown Cove

Lower Halwyn

Penquean Farm

Middle Halwyn Farm

Pinkson Creek

Higher Halwyn Farm

Bodellick

Carhart

Trevilgus Farm

F **G** **H** **J** **K**

18 **19**

1
2
3
4
5
6
7

165

94 195 96

75 74 73

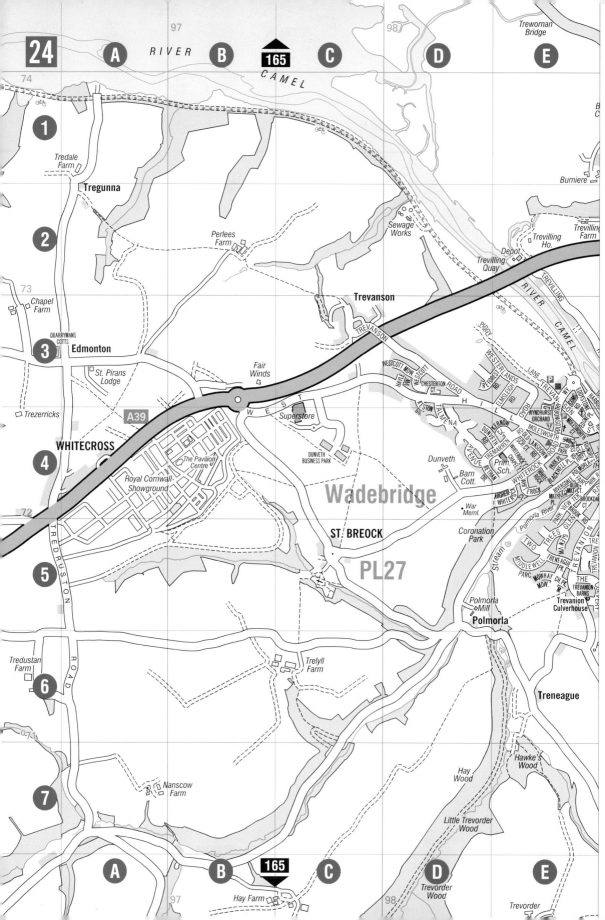

24

A B C D E

RIVER
165
CAMEL

97 · 98

Treworan Bridge

1
74
Tredale Farm
Tregunna
Burniere

2
Perlees Farm
Sewage Works
Trevilling Ho.
Trevilling Farm
Depot
Trevilling Quay

73
Chapel Farm
Trevanson
RIVER CAMEL

3
QUARRYMANS COTTS.
Edmonton
St. Pirans Lodge
Fair Winds
TREVANSON
PIGGY LANE
WESTCOTT MDW
WESTERLANDS
TREVANSON
TREWORNA RD.
ELMSLEIGH RD.

Trezerricks
A39
WEST
WESTCOTT MDW
WESTCOTT ROW
HAYLE VIEW
CHESTERTON CT.
CHESTERTON ROAD
WESTCOTT
HILL
TREVANSON RD.
MOLESWORTH
WYNDHURST ORCHARD

WHITECROSS
Superstore
KESTON GDS.
TALMENA
KERNOW
TREMARREN RD.
DUNVETH AVENUE
BETHAN
WHITECROSS RD.
BLACKWELL PL.
PARK PL.
MOLESWORTH

4
The Pavilion Centre
Royal Cornwall Showground
DUNVETH BUSINESS PARK
Dunveth
Barn Cott.
Prim. Sch.
WHITECROSS
ROCK
HIGHER WHITER.
RIVERSIDE
OLDE MKT.
BROOK
POLMORLA
BROOKDALE CT.

72
Wadebridge
War Meml.
Polmorla River
PARK VIEW TERR.
TWO TREES
GLEN RD.

5
TREDRUSTON
ST. BREOCK
PL27
Coronation Park
Stream
MIDDLEWELL
PARC
TRENEAGUE PK.
MOWHAY MDW.
THE TREVANION BARNS
TREVANION

Polmorla Mill
Polmorla
Trevanion Culverhouse

71
Tredustan Farm

6
ROAD
Trelyll Farm
Treneague

7
Nanscow Farm
Hay Wood
Hawke's Wood
Little Trevorder Wood

A B C D E
165
97 · 98
Hay Farm
Trevorder Wood
Trevorder

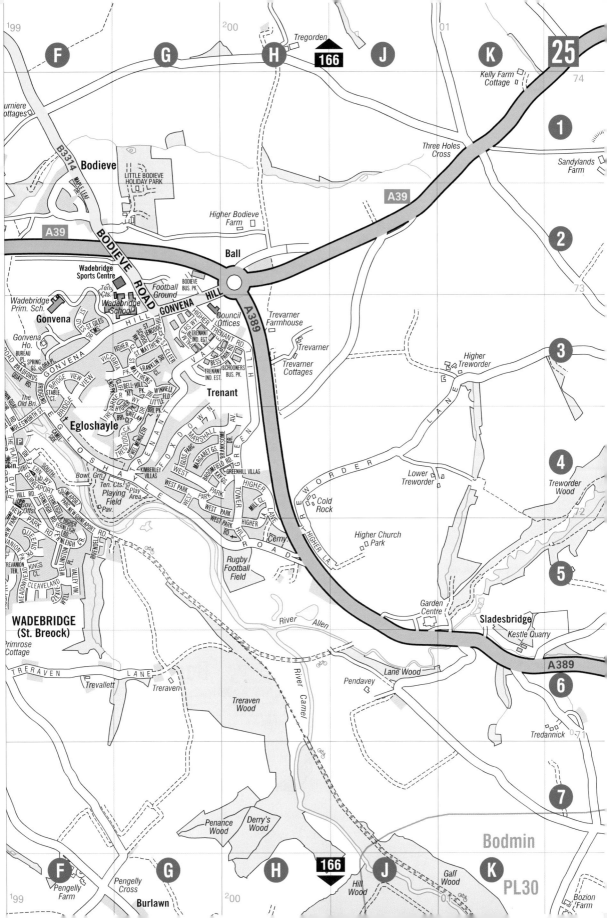

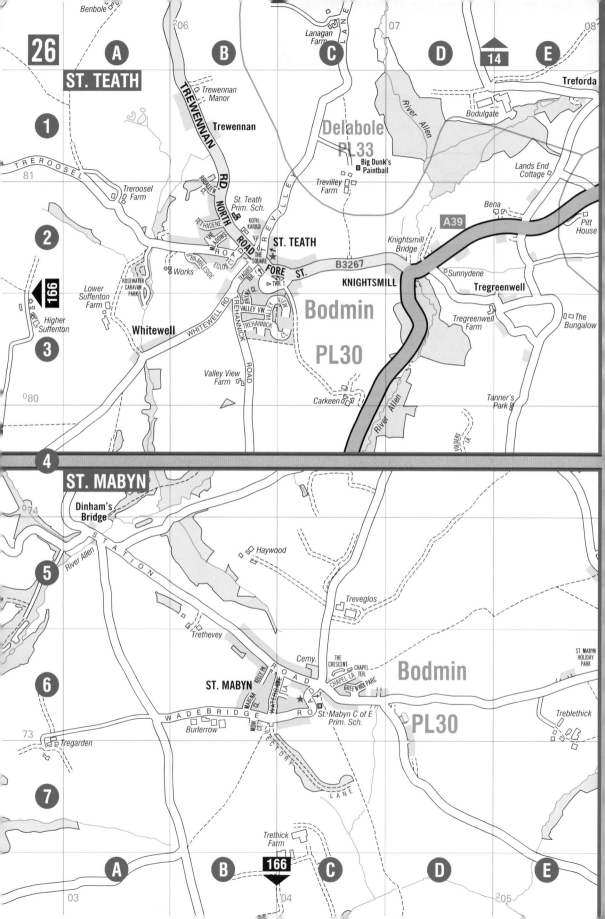

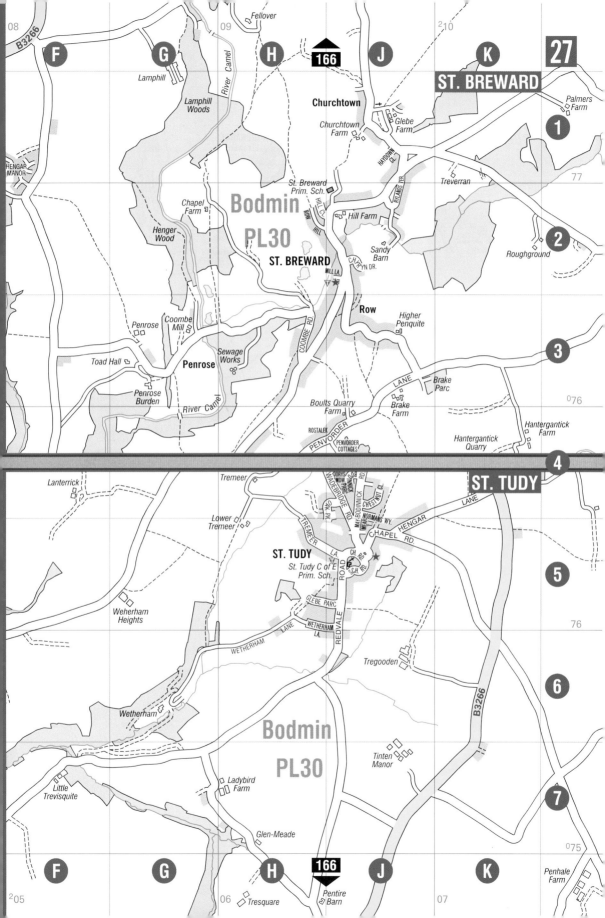

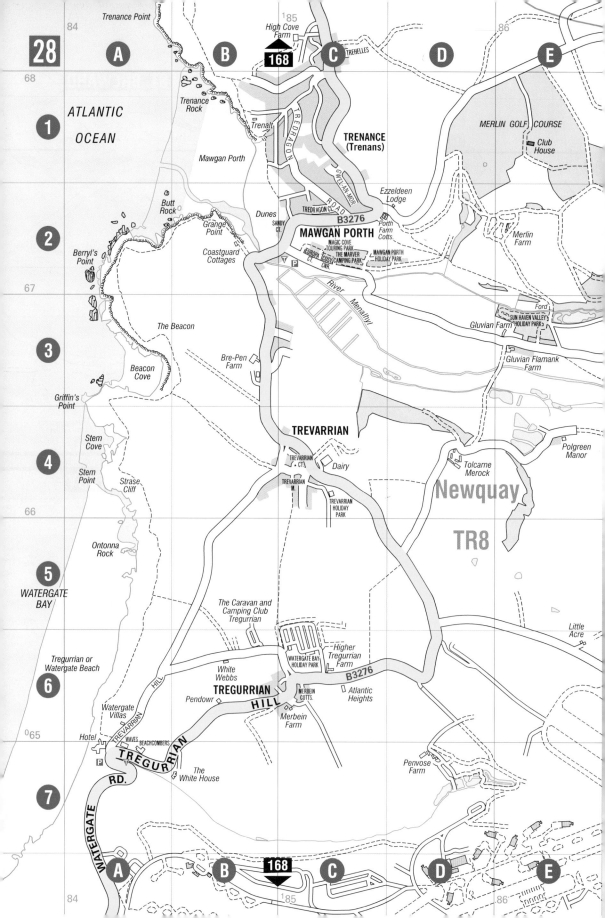

F **G** **H** **31** **J** **K**

87 88 89
68

1 TREVILLEDOR CARAVAN SITE

Higher
Lanherne

Lower
Lanherne

Dayman's
Farm

Middle
Lanherne
Cottage

2

67

Little
Lanherne

New
Farm

Higher
Lanvean
Farm

Lower
Denzell

3

RETORRICK
MILL

Trevedras

**Higher
Winsor**

River Menalhyl

FIVE
LANES
Lanvean
Farm

Bolingey

Ford

4

66

Japanese Garden
& Bonsai Nursery

Hall

Play.
Fld.

Fernleigh

**Trevenna
Cross**

Trevanna
Cottage

Oak Valley
Farm

Cemetery

Ford
Sch.

**ST. MAWGAN
(Sen Mowgan)**

Higher
Parsonage

Trevenna
Farmhouse

St. Columb

5

Hall

Rolling
Hills

Trembleath
Cottage

Springstein
House

LANVEAN AV.
CHALLIS
AV.

**Vale of Mawgan
or Lanherne**

**Higher
Tolcarne**

TR9

High Barn
Farm

Ball
Cott.

Lanett

Carloggas

Trembleath
Farm

6

• Masts

✈ Terminal
Building

Lawrey's
Mill

65

NEWQUAY CORNWALL AIRPORT

Nanskeval
Cottage

7

Carnanton

F **G** **H** **168** **J** **K**

RAF
ST. MAWGAN

87 88 89

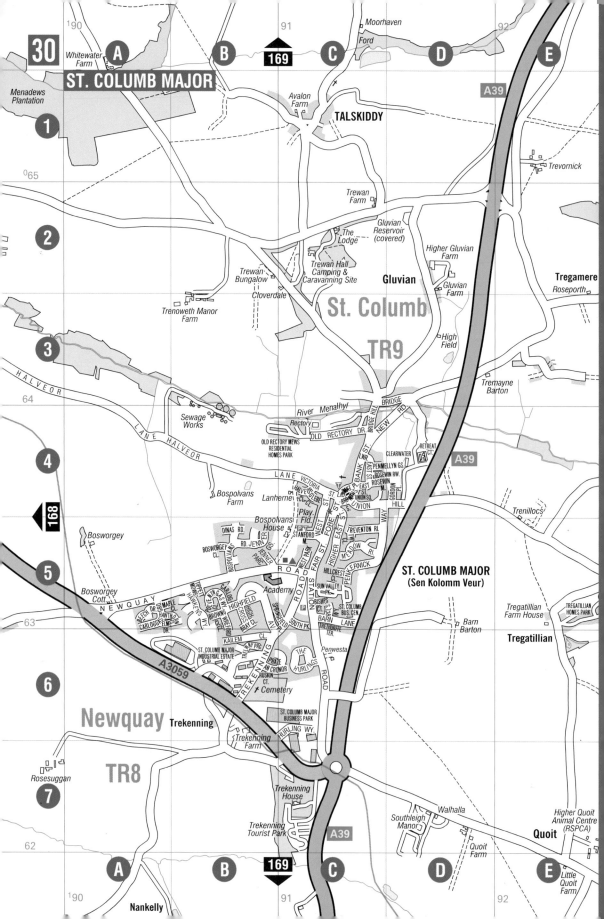

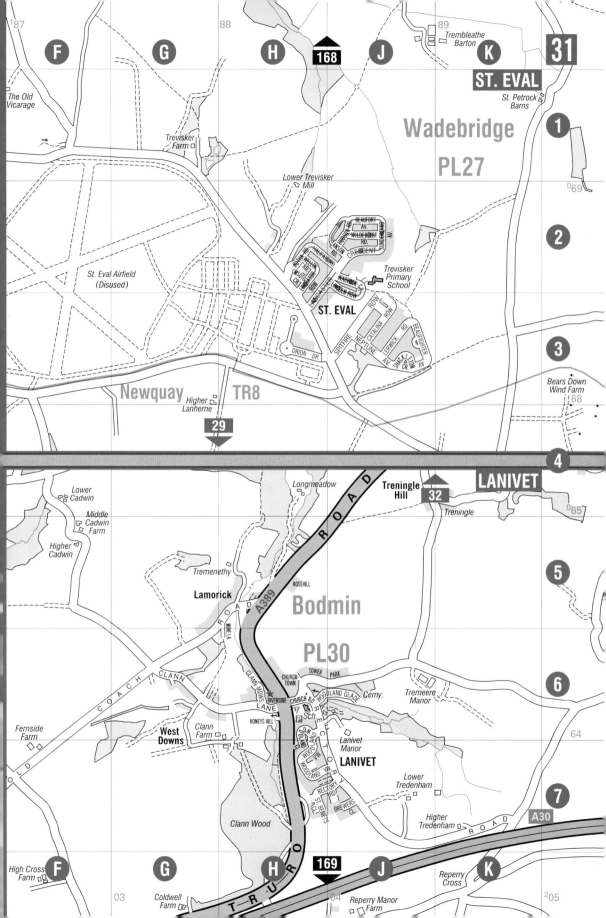

F **G** **H** ▲ **168** **J** **K**

Trembleathe
Barton

ST. EVAL

St. Petrock
Barns

The Old
Vicarage

Wadebridge

PL27

1

Trevisker
Farm

Lower Trevisker
Mill

2

BEAUFORT
AV.
WILDEBEEST
RD.
SUNDERLAND AV.
CRESCENT

St. Eval Airfield
(Disused)

NORTH HR.
HALLAMSHIRE RD.
MSQT CR.
WARWICK
LINCOLN ROW
LANCASTER
LINCOLN ROW

Trevisker
Primary
School

3

ORION DR.
ST. EVAL

ROW
CATALINA AV.
LERWICK RD.
BEAUFIGHTER AV.

Bears Down
Wind Farm

Newquay Higher
Lanherne **TR8**

SPITFIRE
NEPTUNE
SHACK. CR.
LYNX CR.

▼ **29**

4

Lower
Cadwin

Longmeadow

Treningle
Hill ▲ **32** **LANIVET**

Treningle

Middle
Cadwin
Farm

ROAD

5

Higher
Cadwin

Tremenethy

A389

ROSEHILL

Bodmin

Lamorick

ROAD
MINE LA.

PL30

TOWER
PARK

CLANN

CLANN MDWS.
LANE

CHURCH
TOWN
RIVERSIDE CHURCH RD.
WOODLAND GLADE
Cemy.

Tremeere
Manor

6

COACH

HONEYS HILL
Sch.
P

Fernside
Farm

Clann
Farm

**West
Downs**

Lanivet
Manor

64

LANIVET

RECTORY RD.
ST. BENETS RD.
BREWERS CL.

Lower
Tredenham

7

Clann Wood

Higher
Tredenham
ROAD

A30

High Cross
Farm

F **G** **H** ▼ **169** **J** **K**

Coldwell
Farm

Reperry Manor
Farm

Reperry
Cross

TRURO ROAD

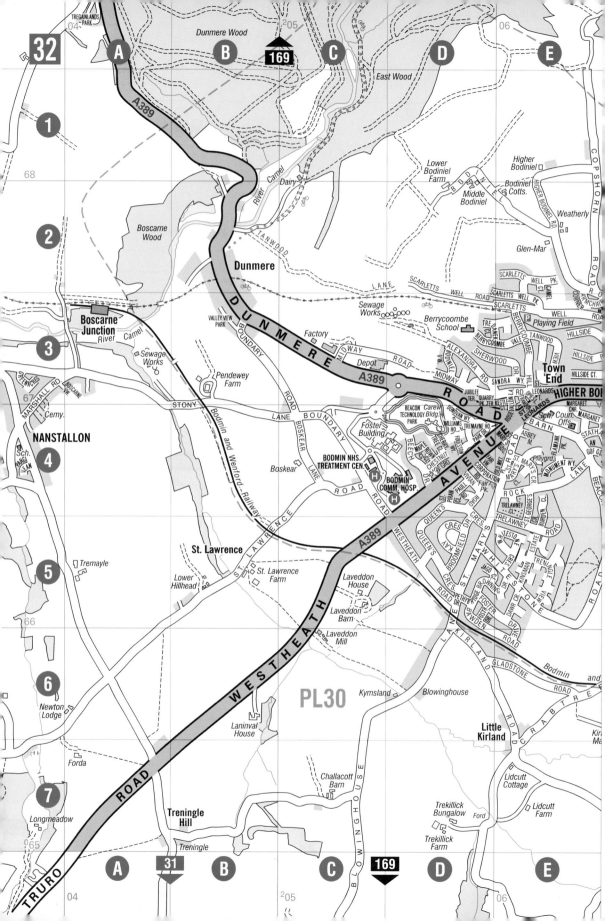

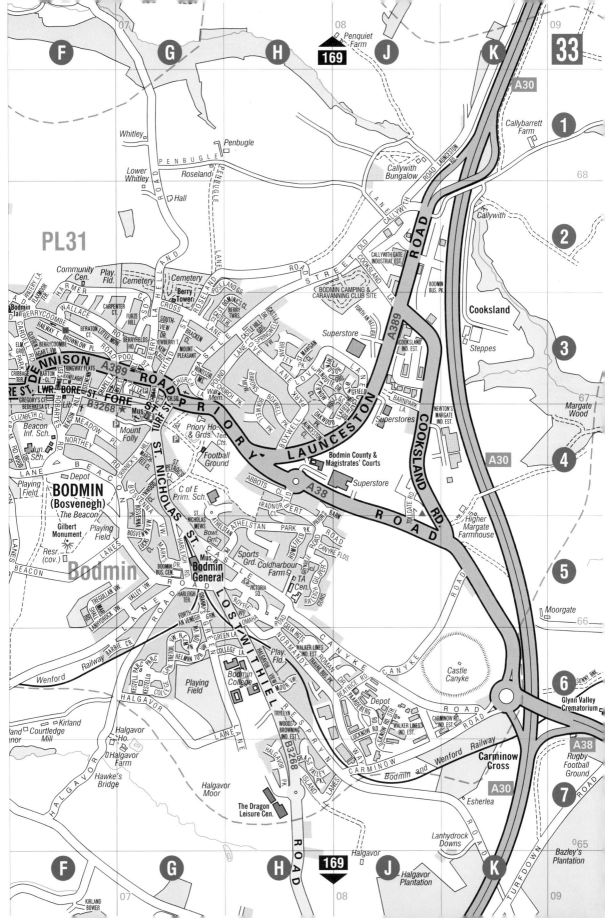

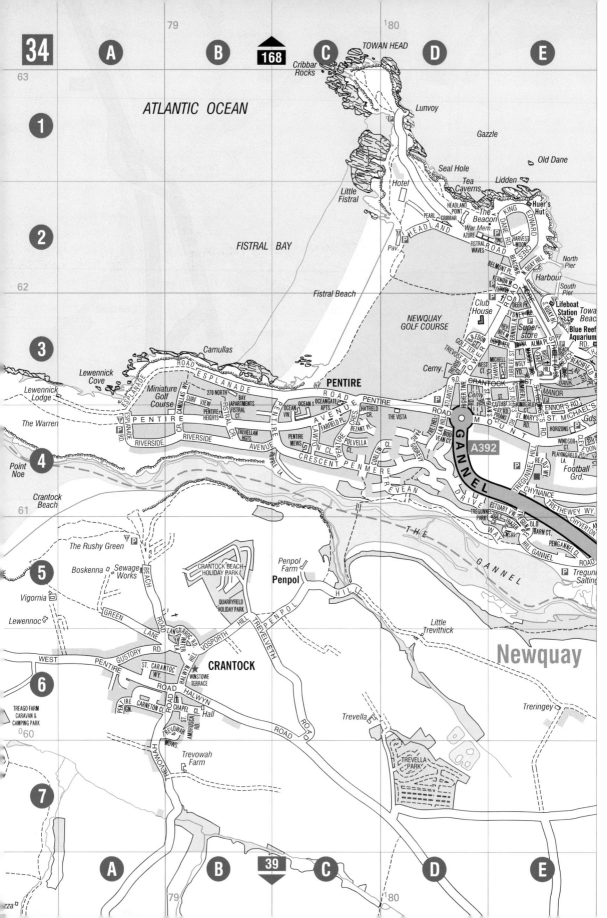

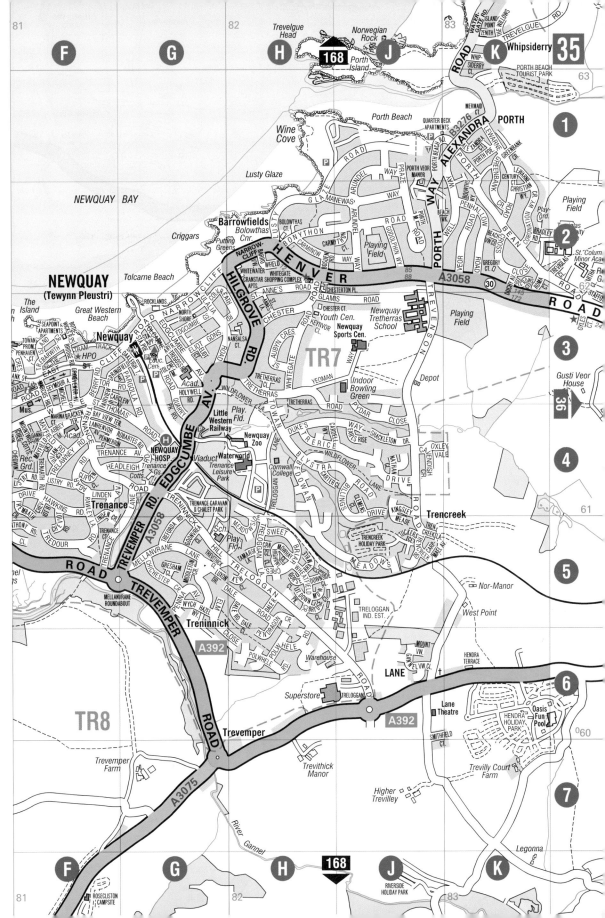

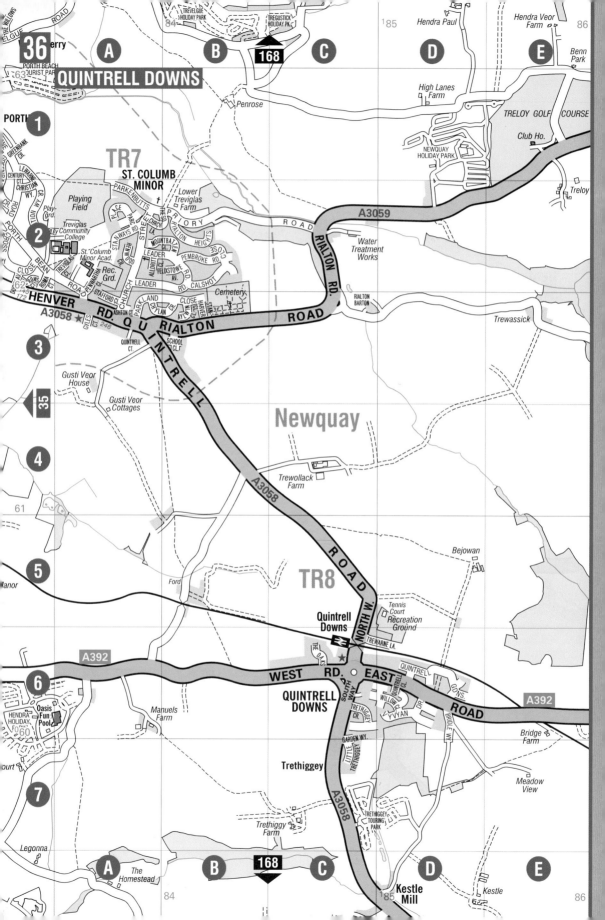

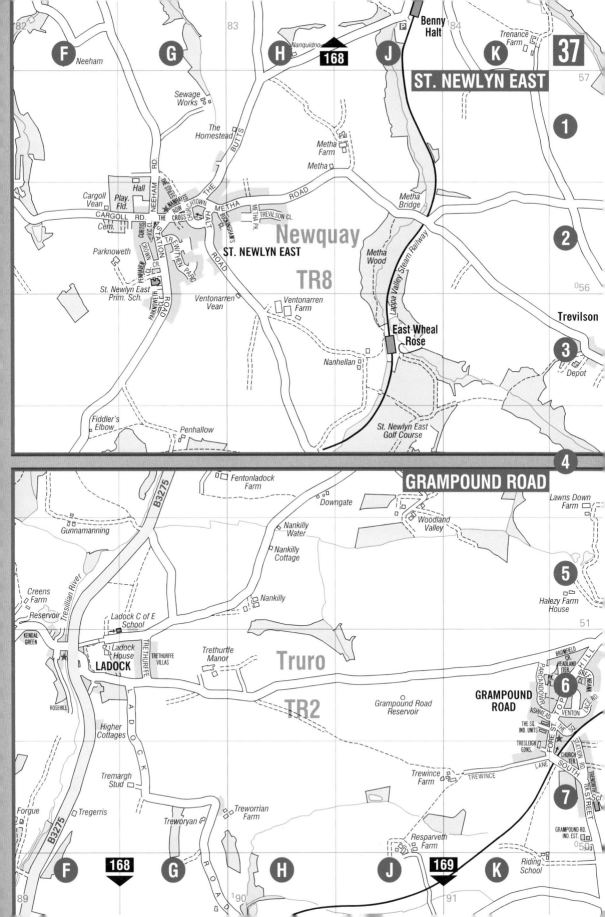

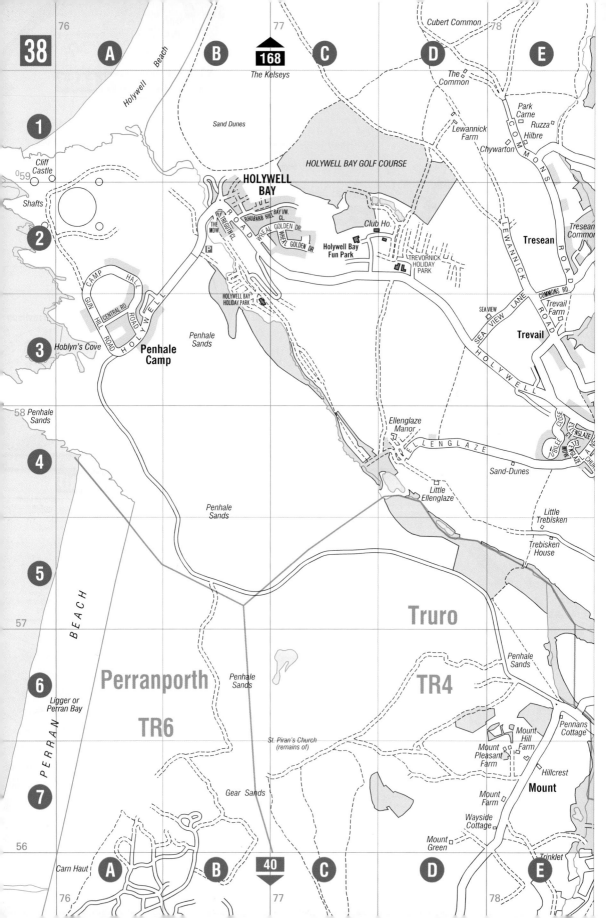

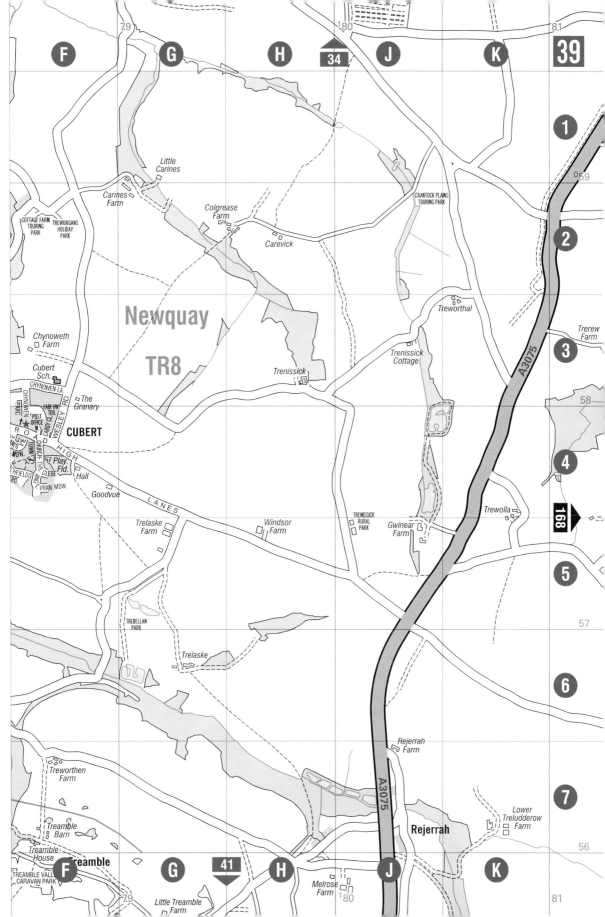

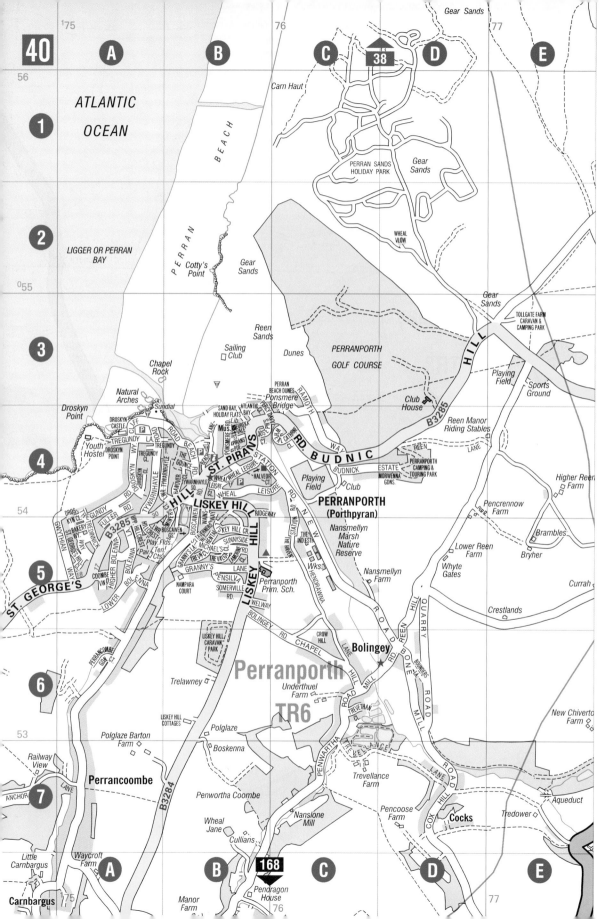

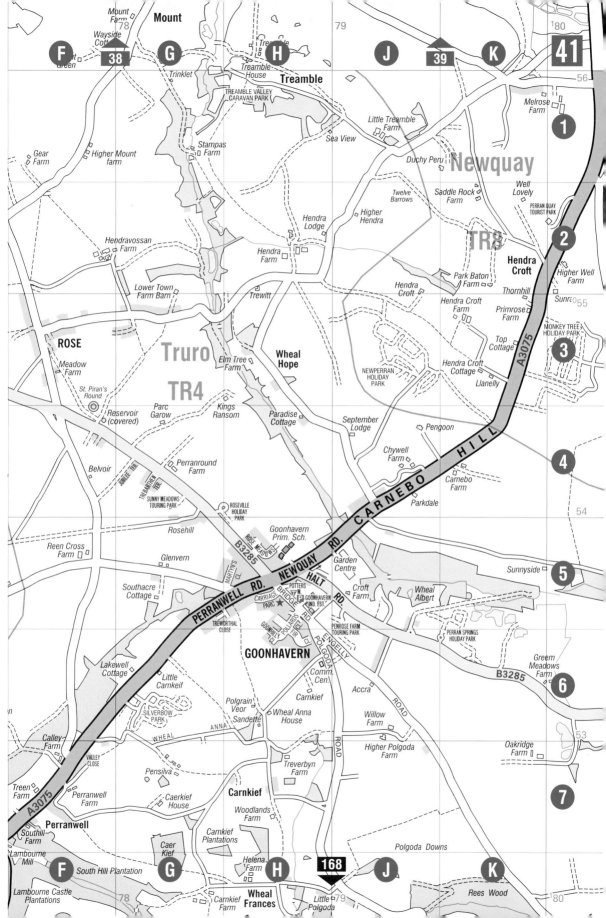

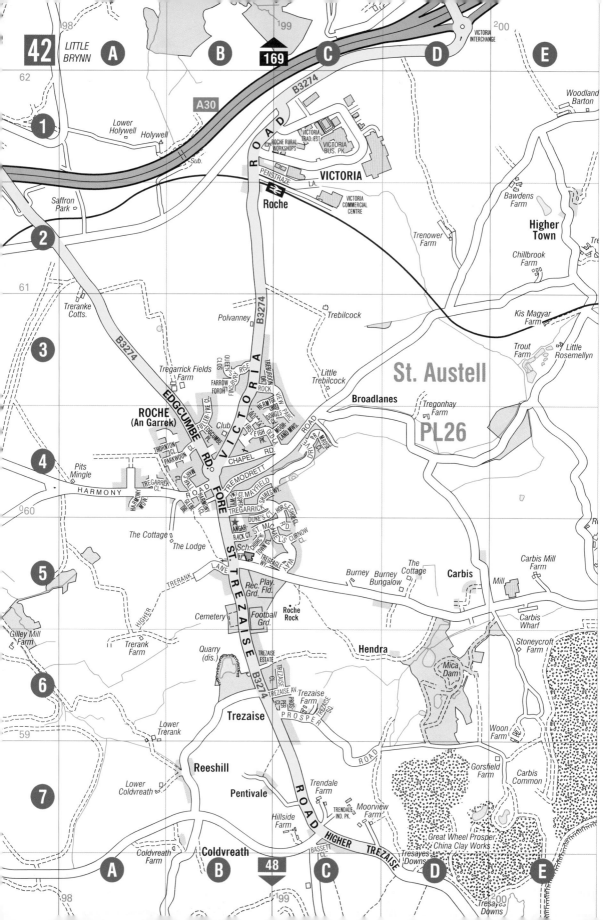

Hunters Moon
Higher Harros
Lower Harros
Lower Innis Farm
Rose Cottage

Rosevath Farm
Crift

Trescoll Farm
Kestles Farm
Trescoll   1

CRIGGAN MOORS

Outer Savath

Lockengate
Depot
Southernhay   2

emodrett Farm

Little Innisvath

Savath Farm

61

Clear View Farm

A391

Anchorage Farm
Moorview Farm

Raylside Farm

Criggan Farm

Bodwen   3

Polskeys Farm

Criggan

LANE

4

Bilberry Farm

Kents Farm
60

Tresibble Farm

Rosemellyn Farm

Bilberry

MINORCA

Rosemellyn Ho.

Caravan Park
Rocks Farm

Higher Menadew   5

Depot

WISLEY TER.
Wheal Rose Depot and Plant

Sunny Corner

Hallew

WOON MILL COTTS.

SPRINGFIELD APTS.
Bugle
Springfields

Molinnis Farm
Forkandles Farm

6

Bowling Green

Cricket Grnd.

ROCHE

VALLEY RD
VALLEY VW
ORCHARD PARK
STATION RD.
NEW RD.
PARK
NEWTOWN
ORCHARD LA.

Molinnis

LOWER MOLINNIS

59
Lavrean Farm

Goonbarrow China Clay Works

BUGLE

MOL.

Football Ground

Goonbarrow Junction

Great Lavrean Farm

Gracca

CHARLES PARK
LA.
ROAD
BEAM TER.
LOMBARDA

Bugle Sch.
NEW RD.
ST. WILLOWS
ROSEVEAR RD. IND. EST.
THE MEADOW

Wheal Henry Residue Recovery Plant

Rock Dryers

7

Lavrean

Goonbarrow Refinery
GOONBARROW WK.
NETLEY MDW.
GOONBARROW MDW.
CARNSMERRY
HIGHER BUGLE

FORE STREET

A391
ROSEVEAR ROAD
B3374

HILLSIDE CT.

Rosevear
Rocks

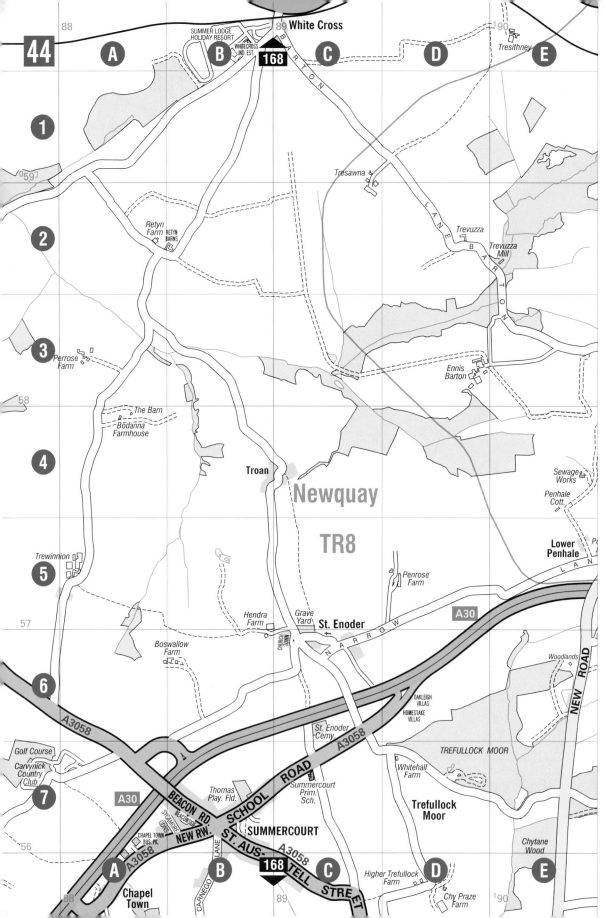

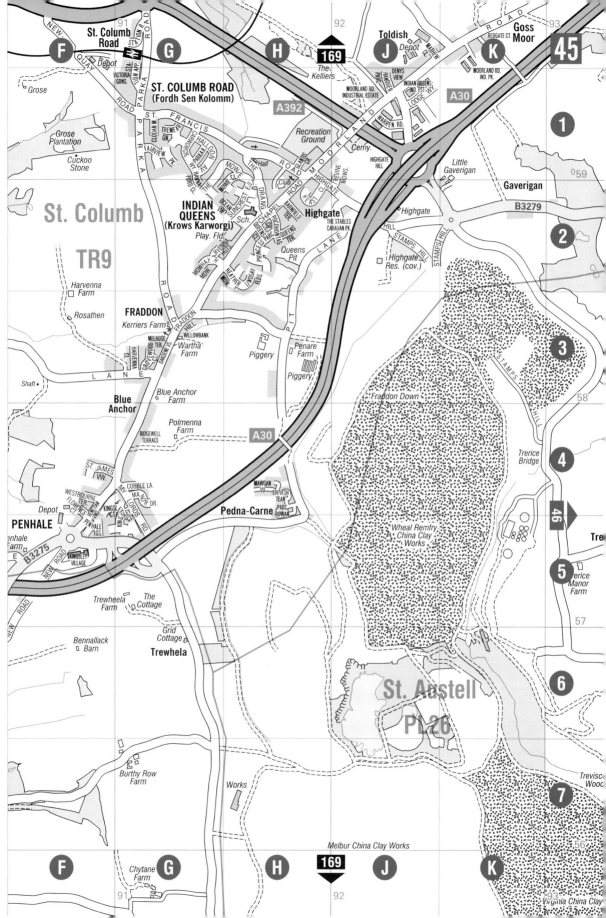

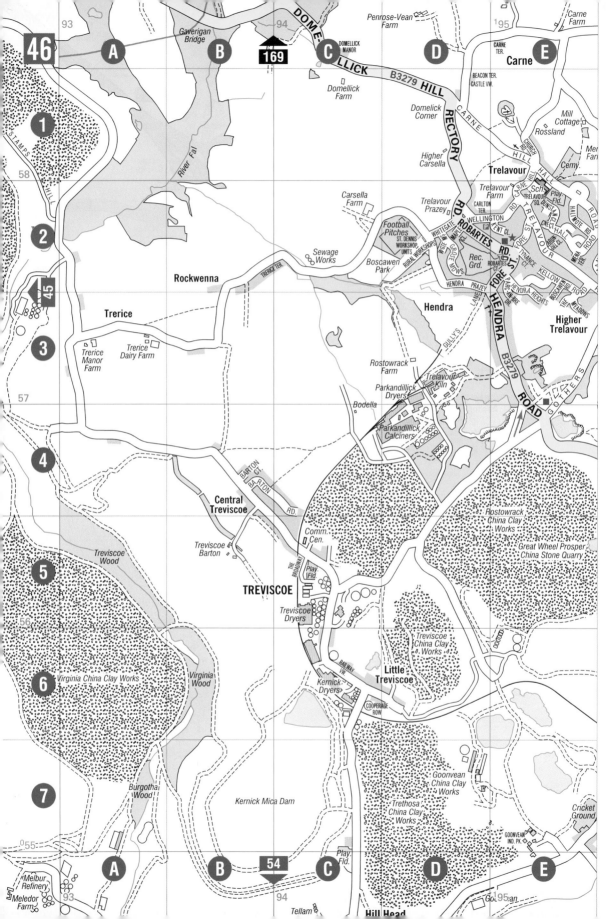

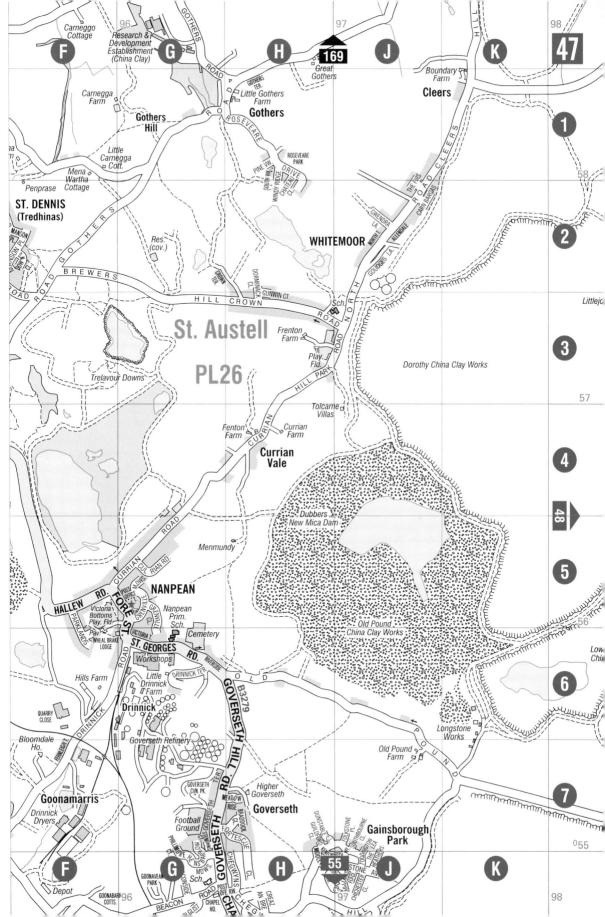

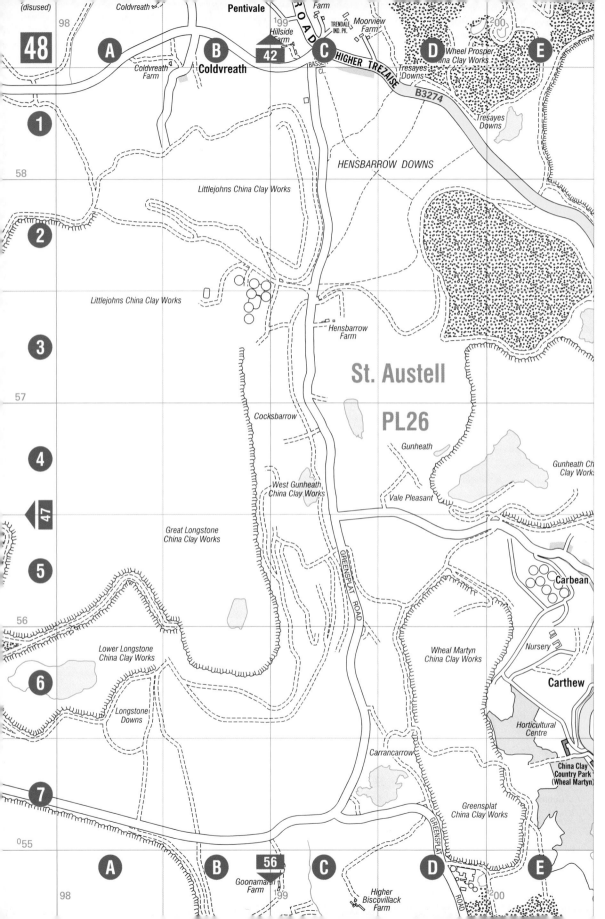

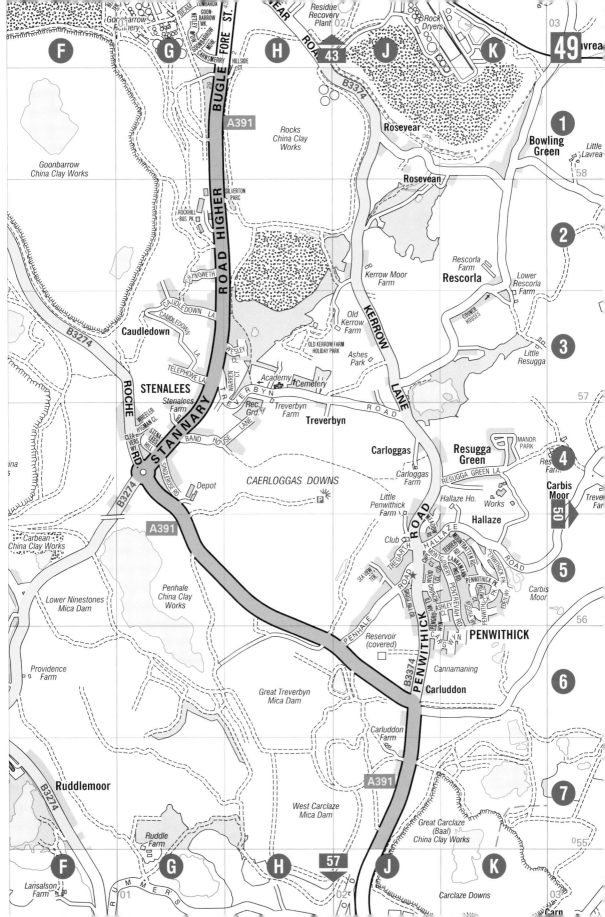

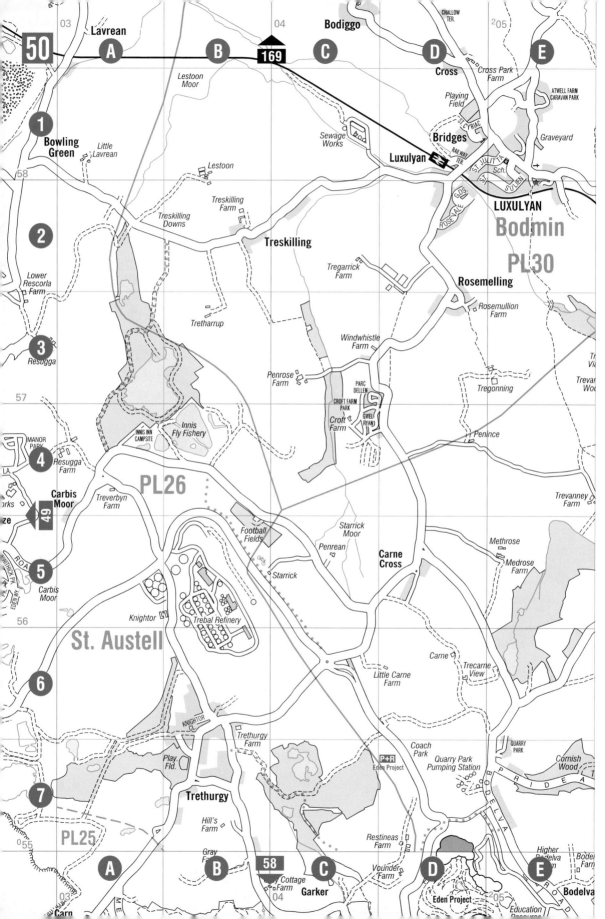

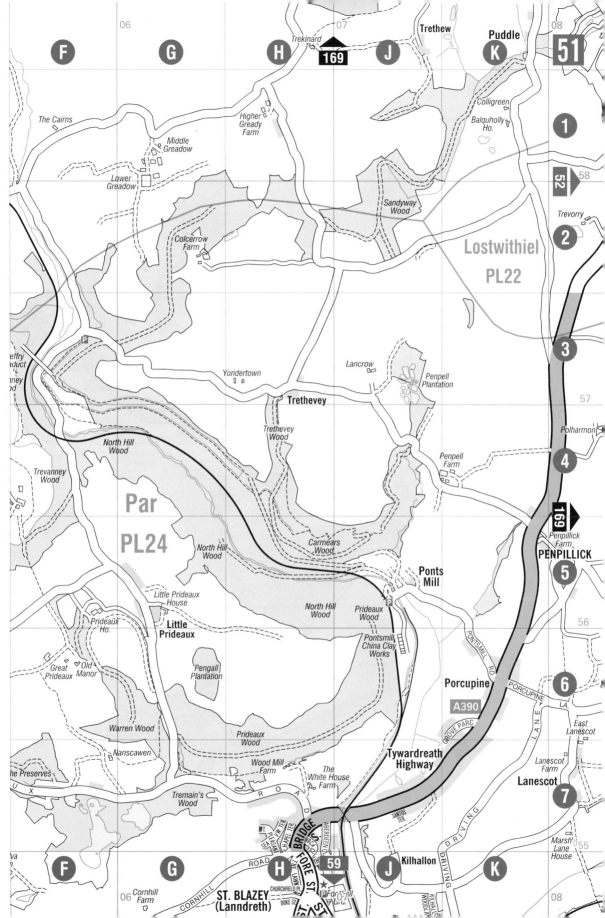

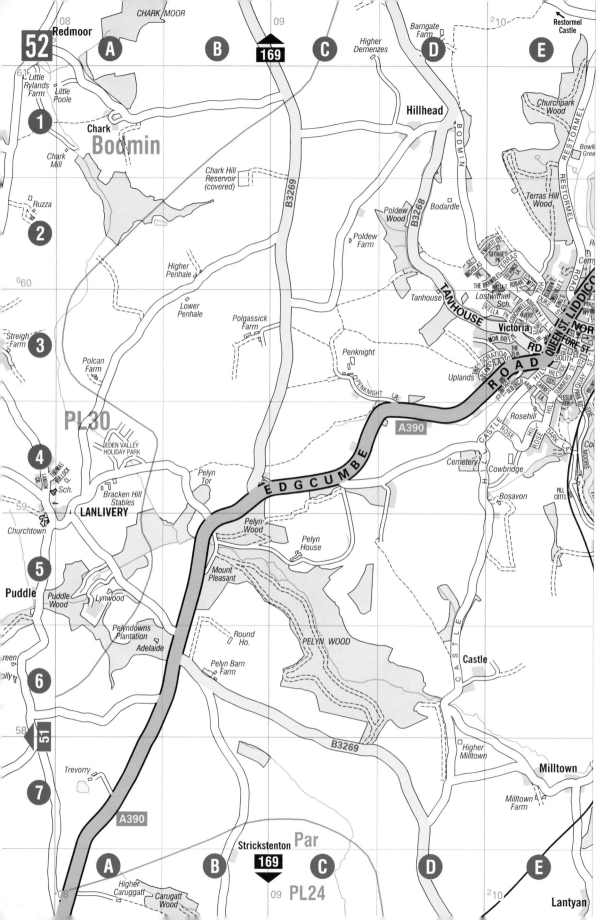

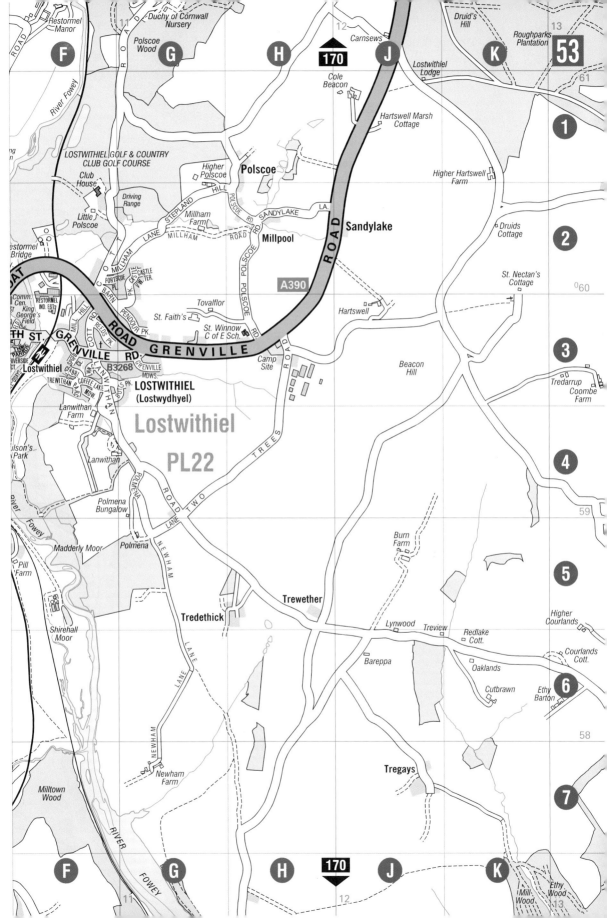

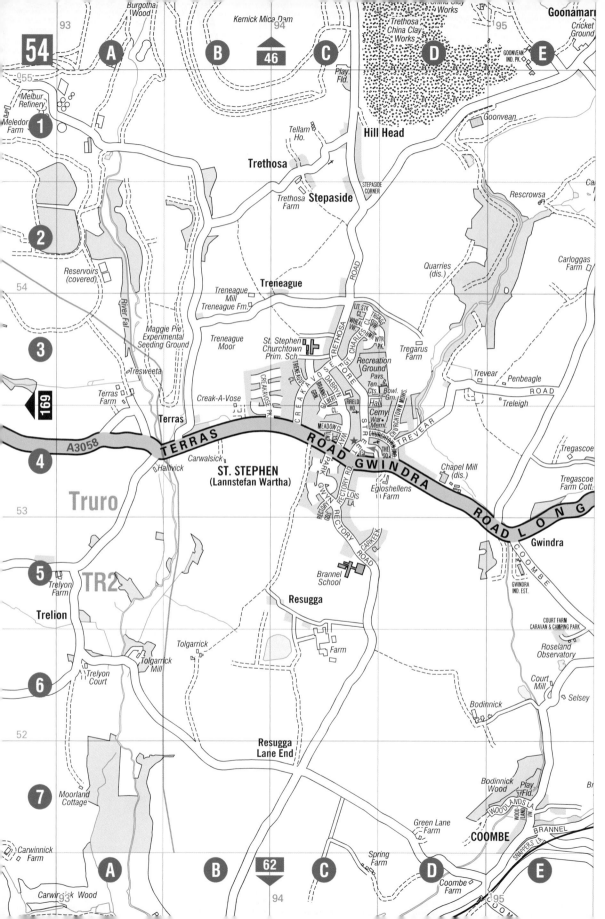

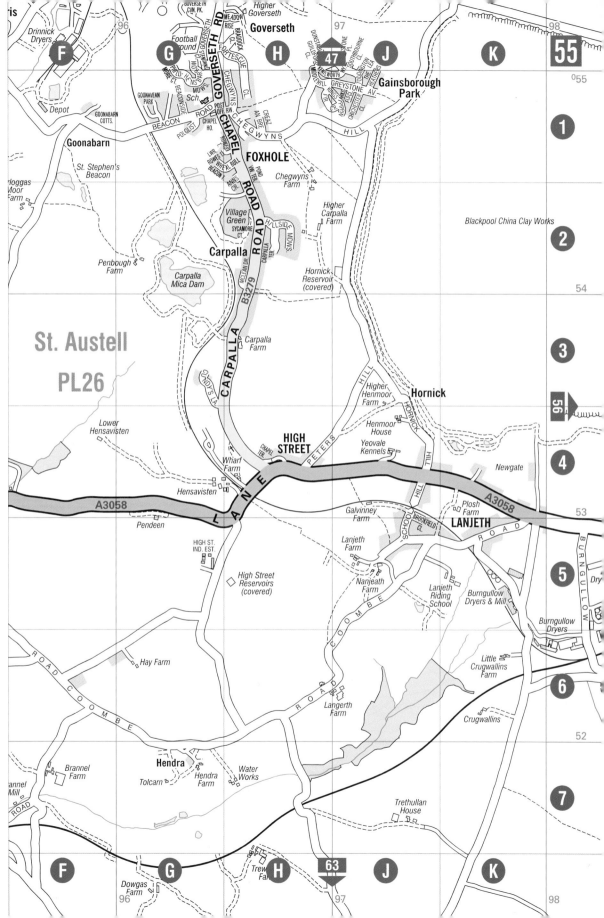

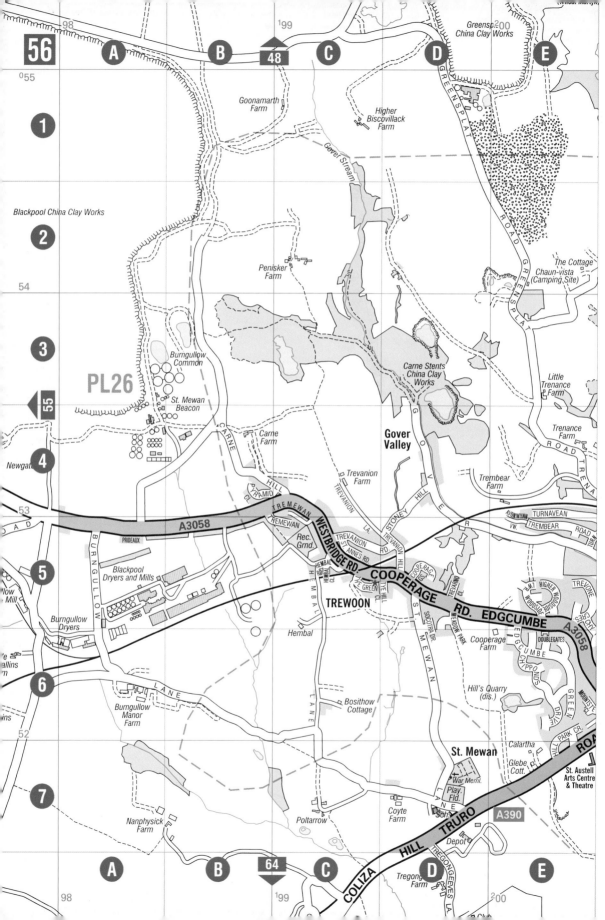

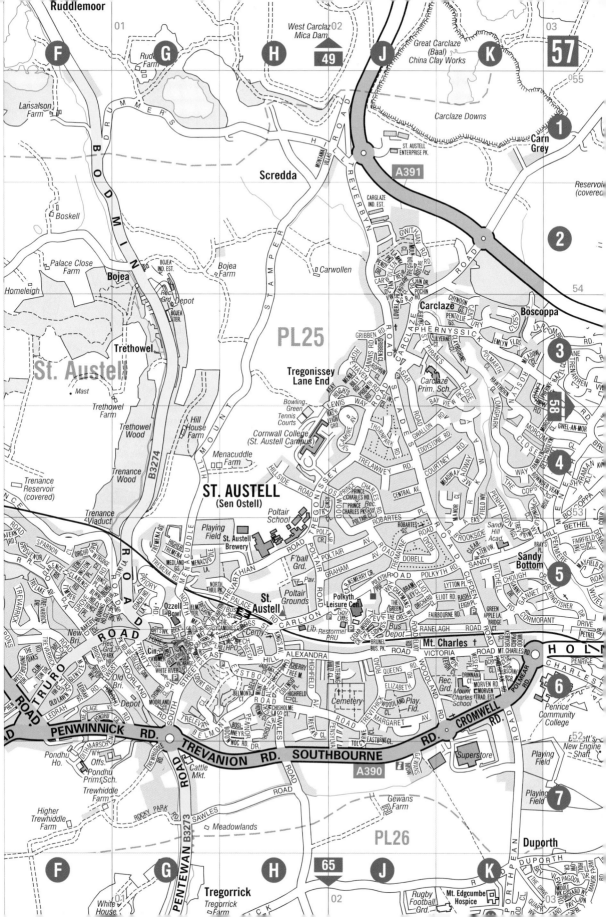

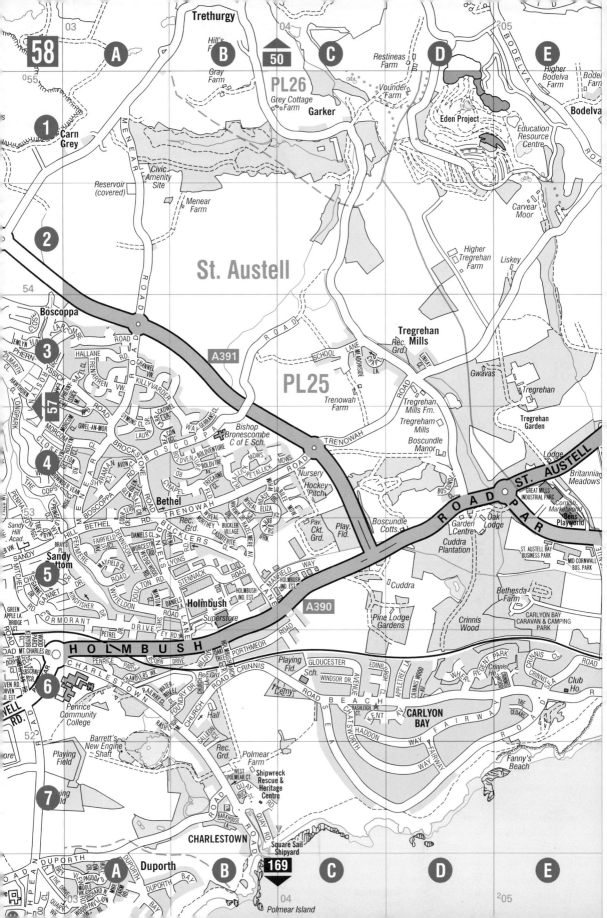

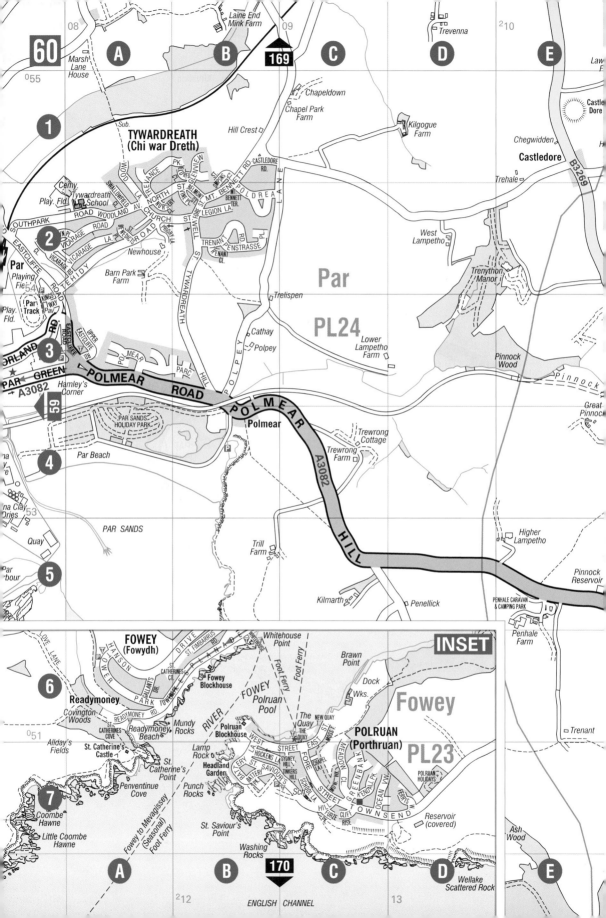

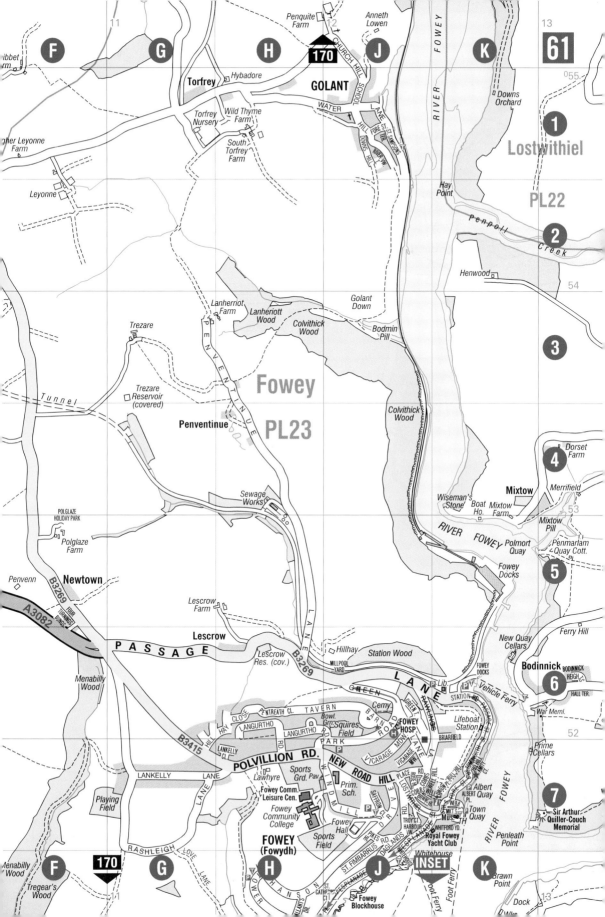

62

A · B · **54** · C · D · COOMBE · E

Moorland Cottage · 93

Wood · Play Fld. · WOODLANDS LA. · 95

Green Lane · SNAPPERS LA · TUNNEL

Carwinnick Wood · **1**

Spring Farm · Coombe Farm

River Fal · Crow Hill · Resugga Castle · Coombe Hill Farm

Trenowth Wood · 51

Sewage Works · Lower Downderry Farm

Barn Wood · **2** · Trenowth House · Little Downderry Farm

High Sheriffs House

Treway Farm

3 · Trevan Wood

Garlenick Manor

⁰50

Garlenick Wood

4 · Nantellan · Trewinnow Vean · Trewinnow

Benallack

River Fal · **Trewinnow-med**

5 · Trevillick Farm

Truro

Trevillick

Higher Trevillick · **TR2**

49

6 · Town Mills

Pengarth · BONYTHON DR.

MILL LANE · TYBESTA · NEW HILL ST · P.O.

Grampound Bri. · P.O.

OLD HILL · FORE · **GRAMPOUND**

Comm. Cen. · Sch.

7 · Recreation Ground · **STREET** · OAK VALE · Nancor

BARTLIVER · Manor Tannery · A390

River Fal · CREED LANE · BOSSILLION · Bossillian

48 · Barteliver Wood · QUARRY PARC

A · Creed Wood · B · **169** · C · Higher Tregonjohn Farm · D · E · Treswallen Farm

93 · 94 · ⁹95

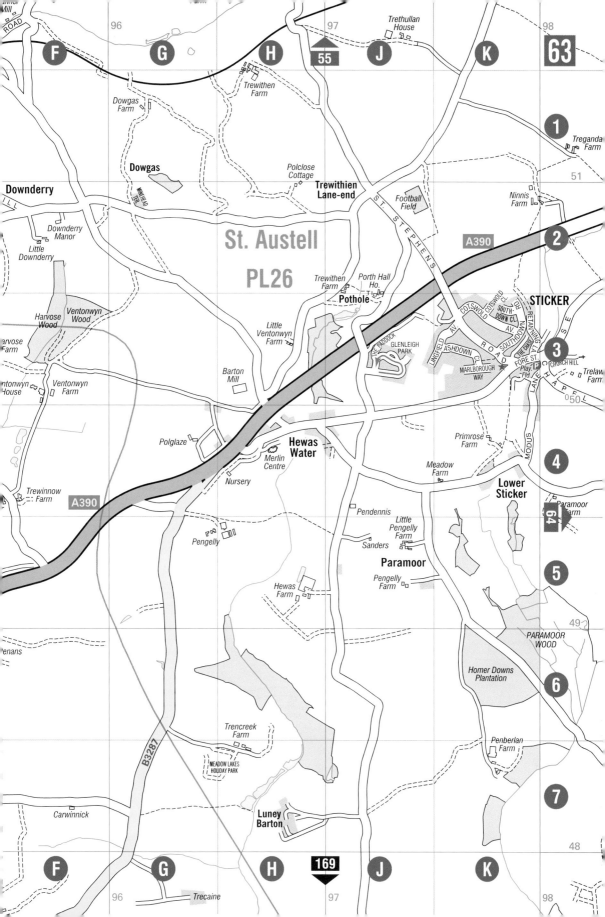

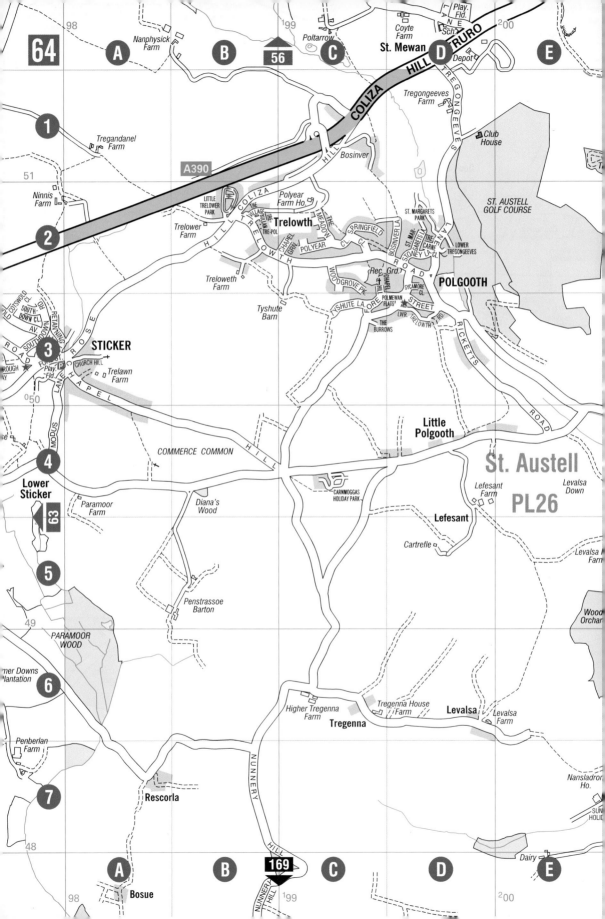

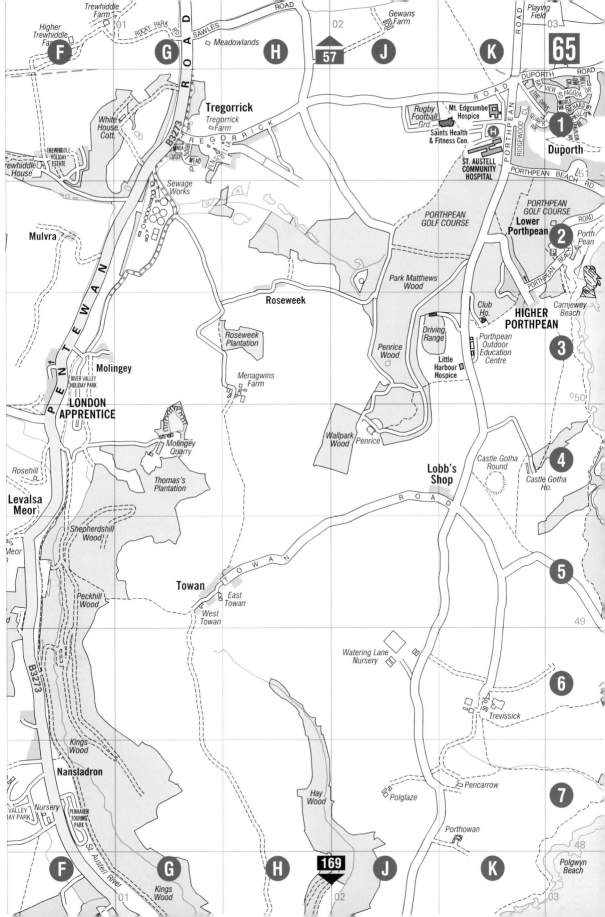

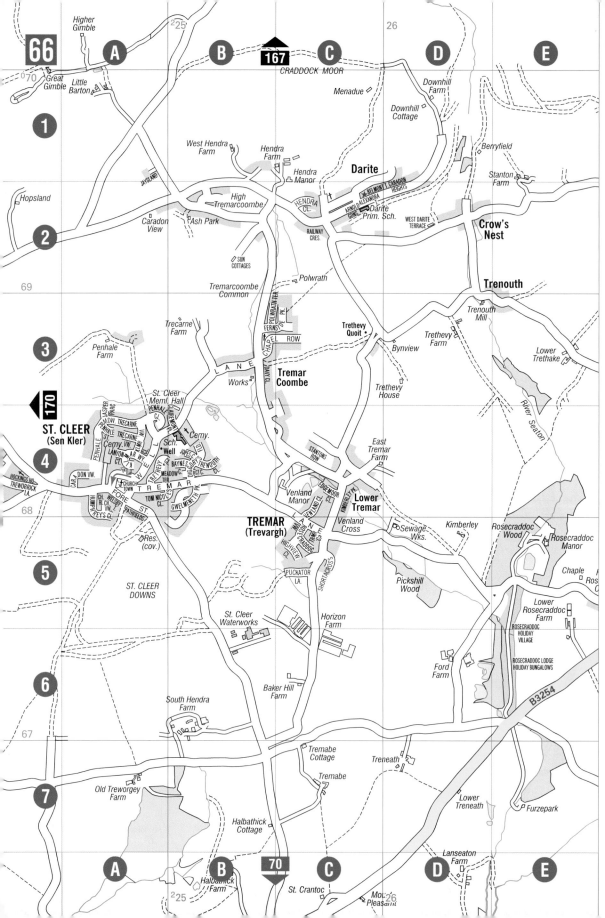

66

A   B   **167**   C   D   E

CRADDOCK MOOR

1

Higher Gimble
Great Gimble
Little Barton
Menadue
Downhill Farm
Downhill Cottage

2

Hopsland
West Hendra Farm
Hendra Farm
Hendra Manor
High Tremarcoombe
Caradon View
Ash Park
HENDRA CL.
RAILWAY CRES.
SUN COTTAGES
Darite
BELMONT CARADON HEIGHTS
ARNOLD ALEXANDRA
Darite Prim. Sch.
WEST DARITE TERRACE
Berryfield
Stanton Farm
Crow's Nest

3

Penhale Farm
Trecarne Farm
Tremarcoombe Common
Polwrath
POLWRATTH FERNS PK.
CHAPEL ROW
LANE
Works
Trethevy Quoit
Bynview
Trethevy Farm
Trethevy House
Trenouth
Trenouth Mill
Lower Trethake
River Seaton

4

170
ST. CLEER
(Sen Kler)
HOCKINGS HO.
TREWORRICK LA.
St. Cleer Meml. Hall
JASPER TRAG
PENHALE ST.
MDW. TRECARNE
CLAREMONT CL.
Cemy.
Sch.
Well
LANYON CL.
PENHALE VW.
CEMY. VW.
CAR. DON VW.
AR WY.
BAYNES
MEADOW C.
JOPES CT.
TRENOUTH CL.
Tremar Coombe
STANTONS ROW
East Tremar Farm

5

St. CLEER DOWNS
CHURCH TOWN
FORE ST.
TREY'S CL.
TOM NICOL CL.
GWELMENETH PK.
Res. (cov.)
TREMAR
(Trevargh)
Venland Manor
EDGEMOOR CL.
VENLAND LANE
HIGHVIEW CL.
CRADDOC
PUCKATOR LA.
SHORTACROSS
Lower Tremar
Venland Cross
Sewage Wks.
Kimberley
Pickshill Wood
Rosecraddoc Wood
Rosecraddoc Manor
Chaple
Lower Rosecraddoc Farm
ROSECRADDOC HOLIDAY VILLAGE
ROSECRADDOC LODGE HOLIDAY BUNGALOWS

6

St. Cleer Waterworks
Horizon Farm
Ford Farm
B3254

7

Old Treworgey Farm
South Hendra Farm
Baker Hill Farm
Tremabe Cottage
Tremabe
Treneath
Lower Treneath
Furzepark
Halbathick Cottage

A   B   **70**   C   D   E

Halbathick Farm
St. Crantoc
Mount Pleasant
Lanseaton Farm

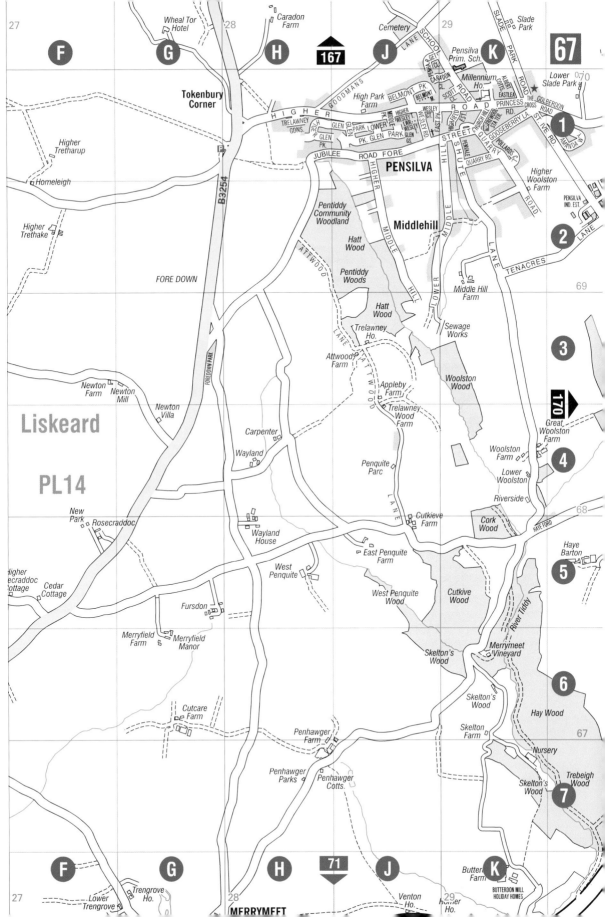

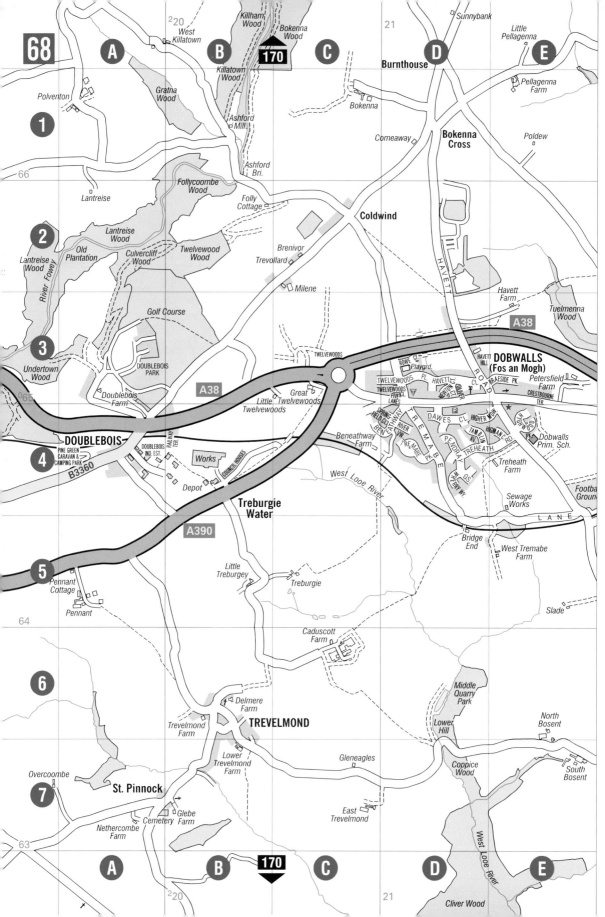

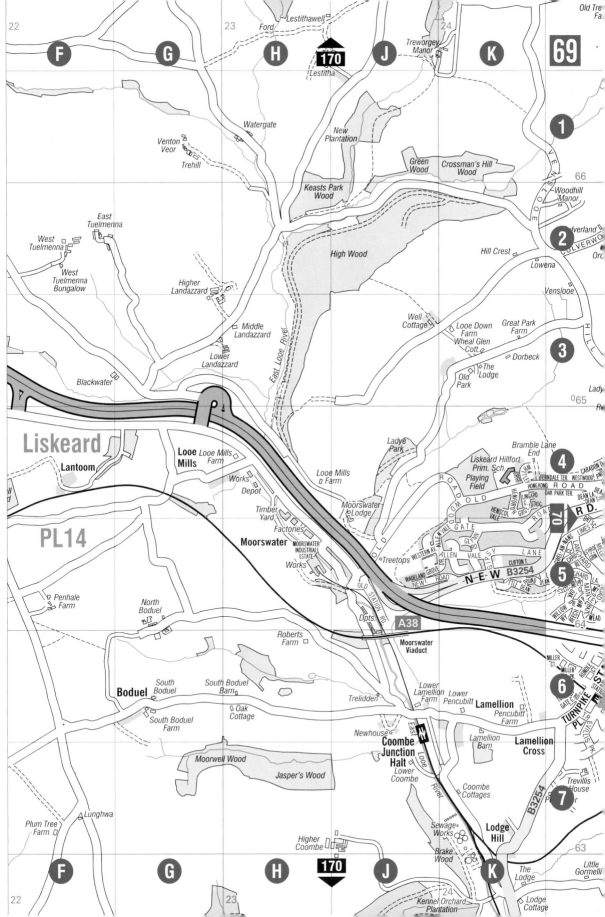

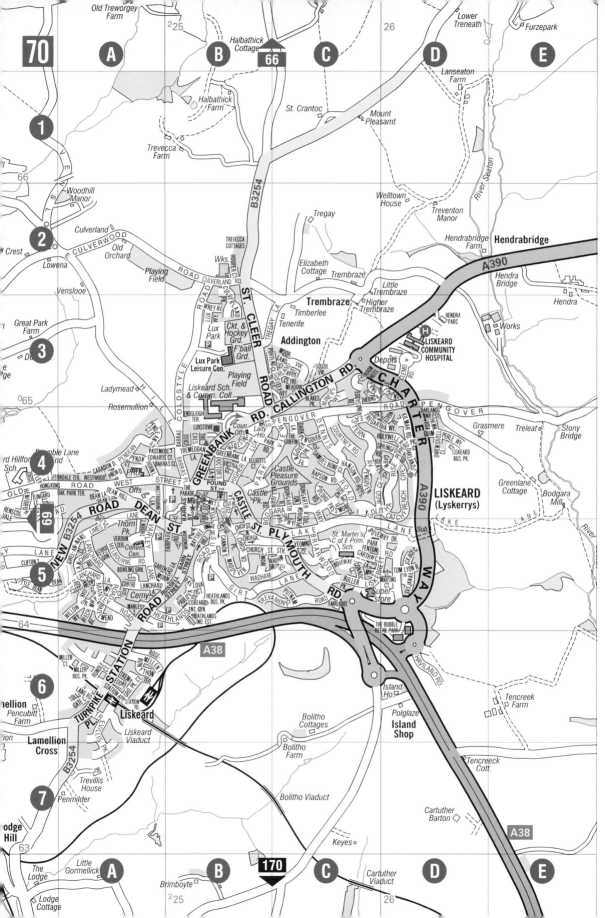

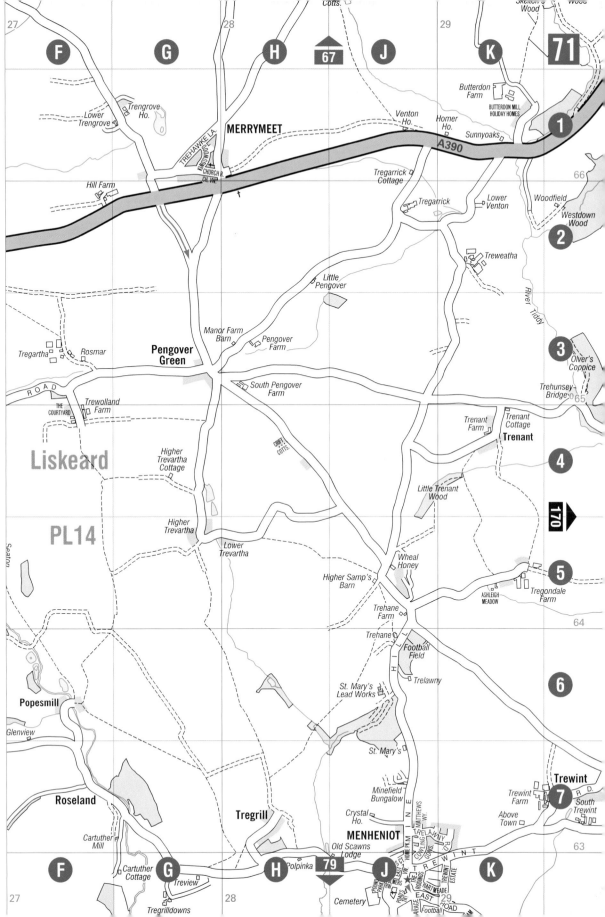

Cotts.

Skelton's Wood

Lower Trengrove

Trengrove Ho.

Hill Farm

MERRYMEET

TREHAWKE LA

KINGSWOOD

CHURCH R

CH. VW.

A390

Butterdon Farm

BUTTERDON MILL HOLIDAY HOMES

Venton Ho.

Homer Ho.

Sunnyoaks

1

Tregarrick Cottage

Tregarrick

Lower Venton

Woodfield

Westdown Wood

66

2

Treweatha

River Tiddy

Little Pengover

Tregartha

Rosmar

Manor Farm Barn

Pengover Farm

Pengover Green

3

Olver's Coppice

Trehunsey Bridge

65

ROAD

THE COURTYARD

Trewolland Farm

South Pengover Farm

Trenant Farm

Trenant Cottage

Trenant

Liskeard

Higher Trevartha Cottage

CROFT COTTS

4

170

PL14

Higher Trevartha

Lower Trevartha

Little Trenant Wood

Seaton

Higher Samp's Barn

Wheal Honey

ASHLEIGH MEADOW

Tregondale Farm

5

64

Trehane Farm

Trehane

Football Field

Trelawny

6

Popesmill

Glenview

St. Mary's Lead Works

St. Mary's

Minefield Bungalow

Crystal Ho.

MATTHEWS WY

COWLING GDNS

TRELAWNY RD

Trewint Farm

Above Town

South Trewint

Trewint

7

Roseland

Tregrill

MENHENIOT

Old Scawns Lodge

Polpinka

HOME PK M

TRE
WINT
ESTATE

Cartuther Mill

Cartuther Cottage

Treview

POUND PARK

POUND CL

PALMERS VW.

THE BODMINS

HARTMEADE

GARAGE

EAST ROAD

Football

Tregrilldowns

Cemetery

29

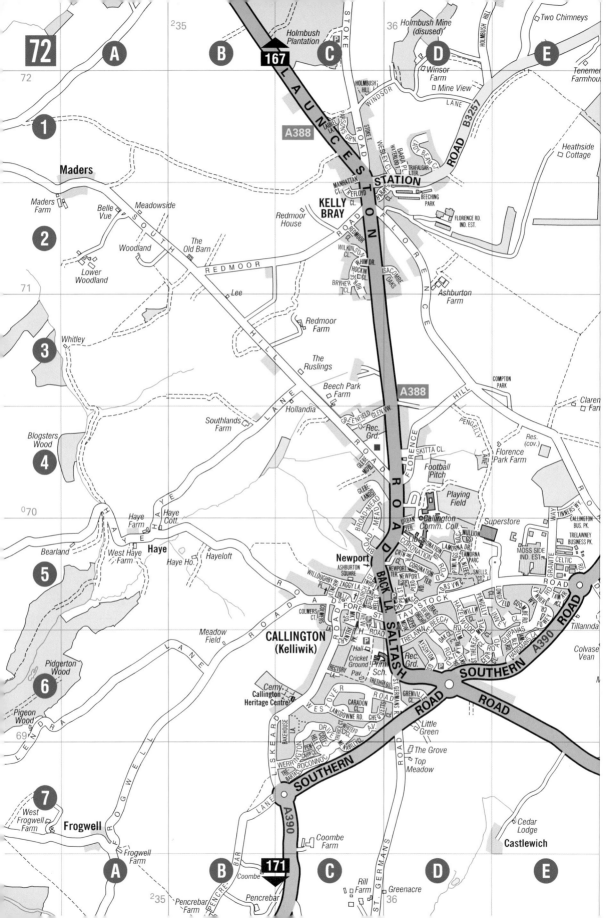

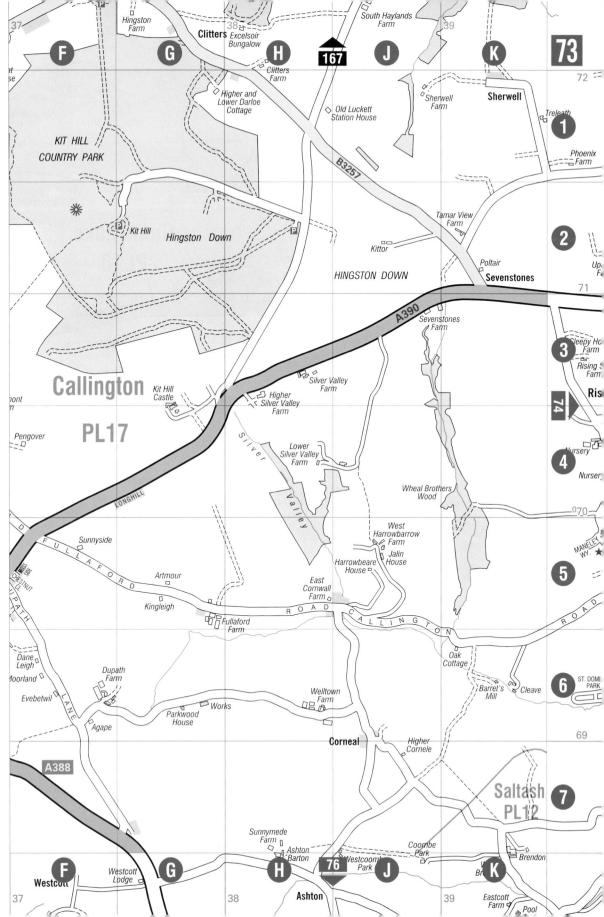

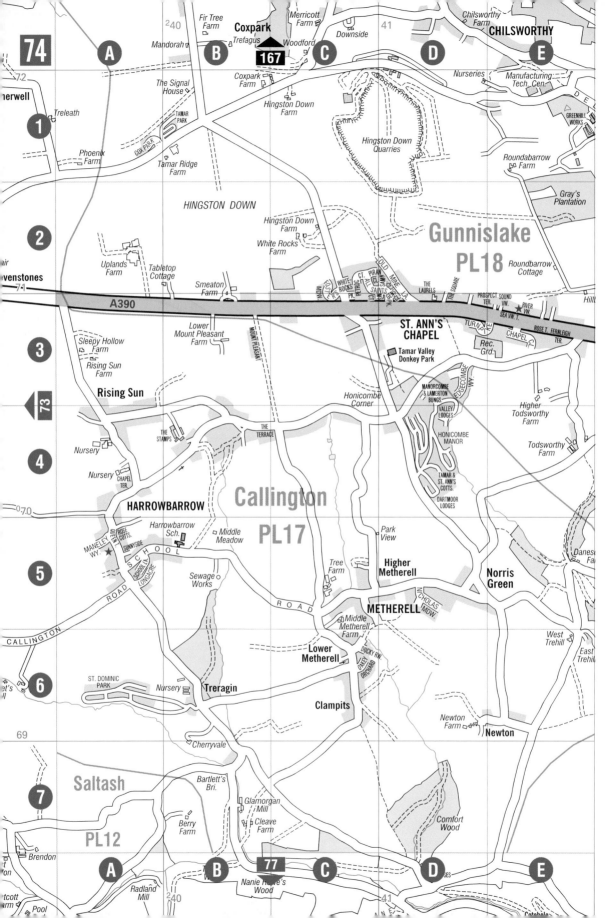

A   B   C   D   E

240   **41**

1   2   3   4   5   6   7

73

77

167

Coxpark

Trefagus
Woodford
Mandorah
Fir Tree Farm
Merricott Farm
Downside
Chilsworthy Farm
CHILSWORTHY

Treleath
The Signal House
Coxpark Farm
Nurseries
Manufacturing Tech. Cen.
GREENHILL WORKS

Phoenix Farm
TAMAR PARK
Hingston Down Farm
Hingston Down Quarries
Roundabarrow Farm

Tamar Ridge Farm
COX PARK

Gray's Plantation

HINGSTON DOWN

Hingston Down Farm
White Rocks Farm
Gunnislake PL18
Roundbarrow Cottage

Uplands Farm
Tabletop Cottage
Smeaton Farm
WHITE ROCKS PK.
PIRAN CL.
ALL SAINTS CT.
OLD MINE RD.
CT.
THE LAURELS
THE SQUARE
PROSPECT TER.
SOUND VW.
SEA VW. T.
RIVER VW.
ROSE T.
FERNLEIGH TER.
Hill

A390

ravenstones

Sleepy Hollow Farm
Lower Mount Pleasant Farm
MOUNT PLEASANT
ST. ANN'S CHAPEL
Tamar Valley Donkey Park
TURNP.
CHAPEL CL.
Rec. Grd.

Rising Sun Farm
Honicombe Corner
MANORCOMBE & LAMERTON BUNGS.
VALLEY LODGES
BUCKCOMBE VW.
Higher Todsworthy Farm

Rising Sun
THE STAMPS
THE TERRACE
HONICOMBE MANOR
Todsworthy Farm

Nursery
TAMAR & ST. ANN'S COTTS.
DARTMOOR LODGES

Nursery
CHAPEL TER.

HARROWBARROW
Callington PL17
Park View
Higher Metherell
Norris Green
Danes

070

Harrowbarrow Sch.
Middle Meadow

MANELEY WY.
GREEN
ROSE COTTS.
SUNNYSIDE
SCHOOL
LONGACRE
SCHOOL
Tree Farm
NICHOLAS MDW.
West Trehill

Sewage Works
ROAD
METHERELL
East Trehill

ROAD
Middle Metherell Farm

CALLINGTON
ST. DOMINIC PARK
Nursery
Treragin
DUCKY RW.
ORCHARD
ONSLOW

69
Lower Metherell
Newton Farm
Newton

Clampits

Cherryvale
Comfort Wood

Saltash

Bartlett's Bri.

PL12
Berry Farm
Glamorgan Mill
Cleave Farm
Brendon

Radland Mill
Nanie Howe's Wood
Pool

240   **41**

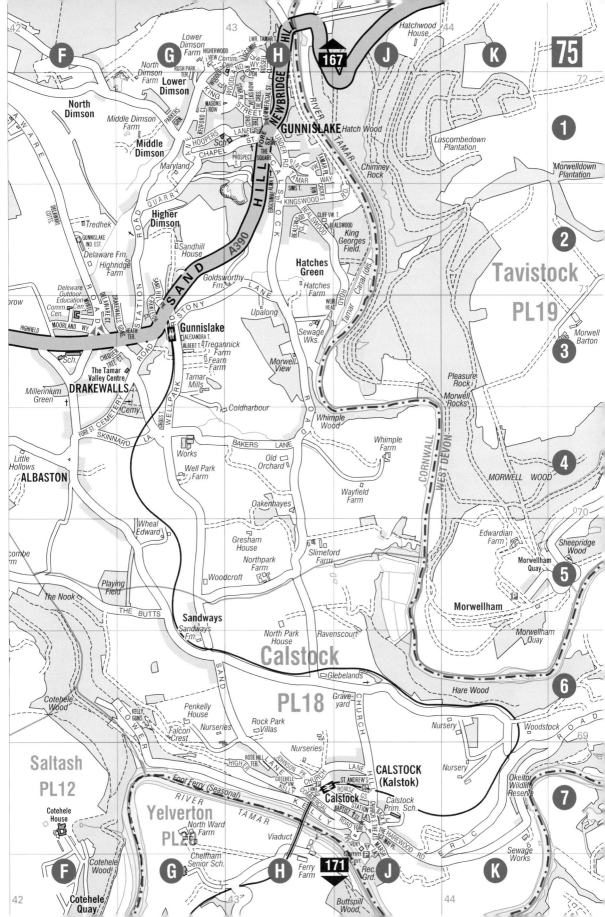

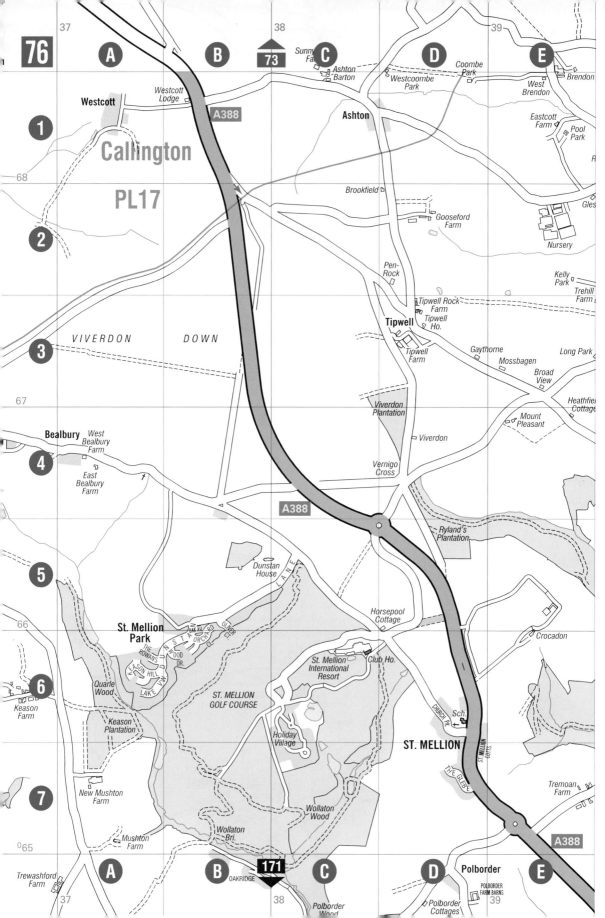

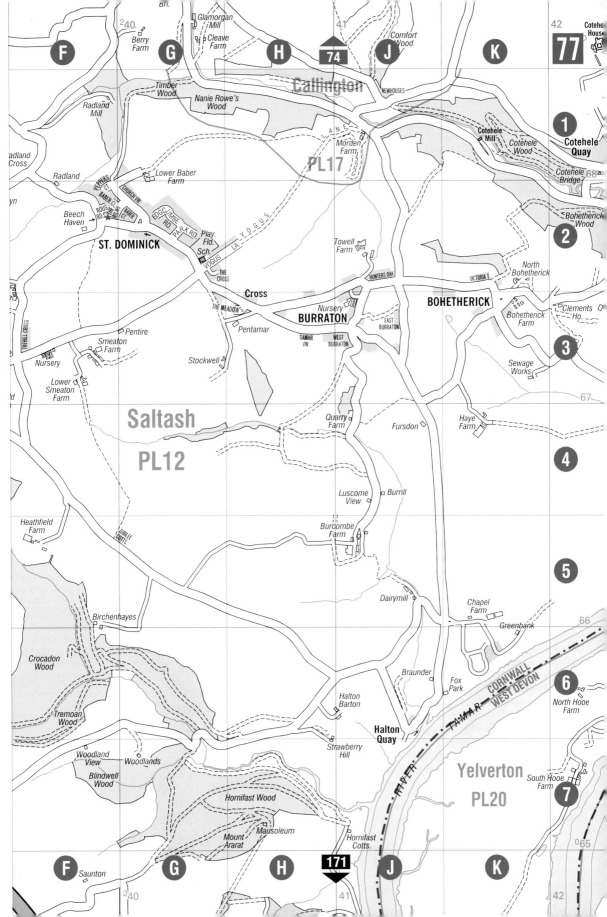

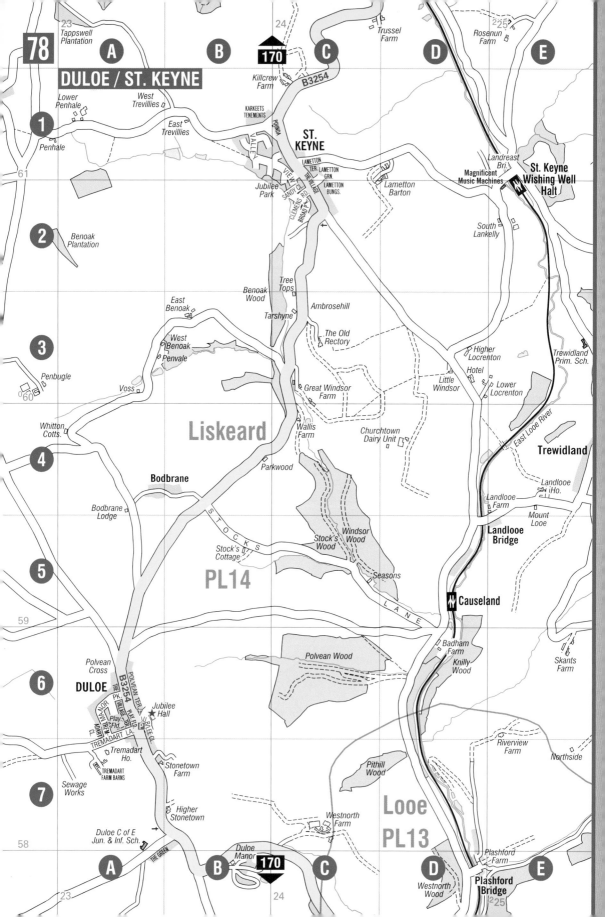

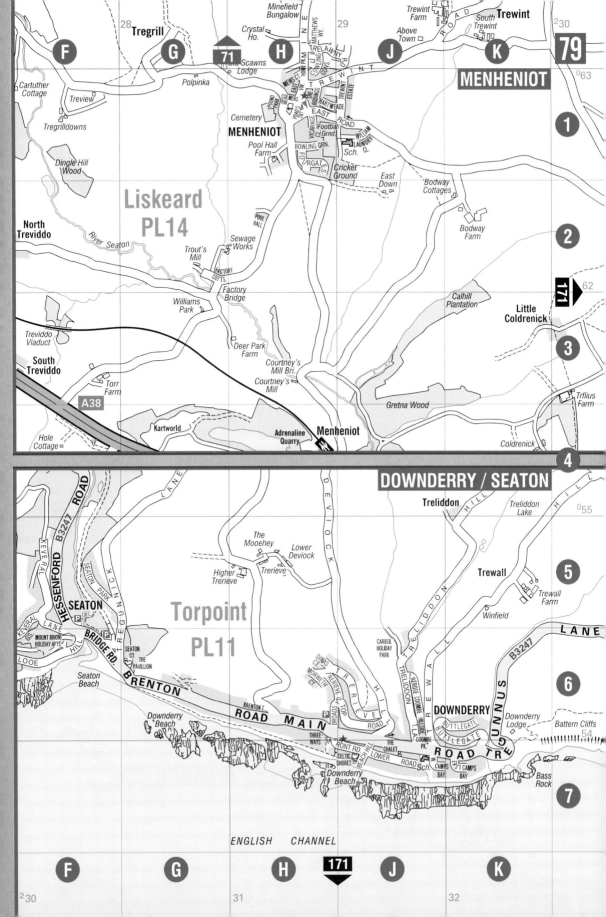

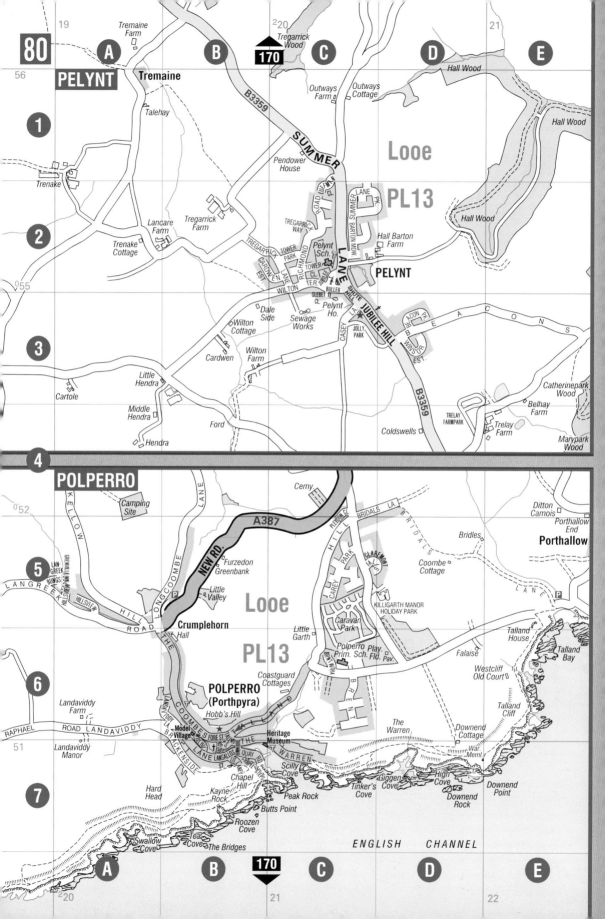

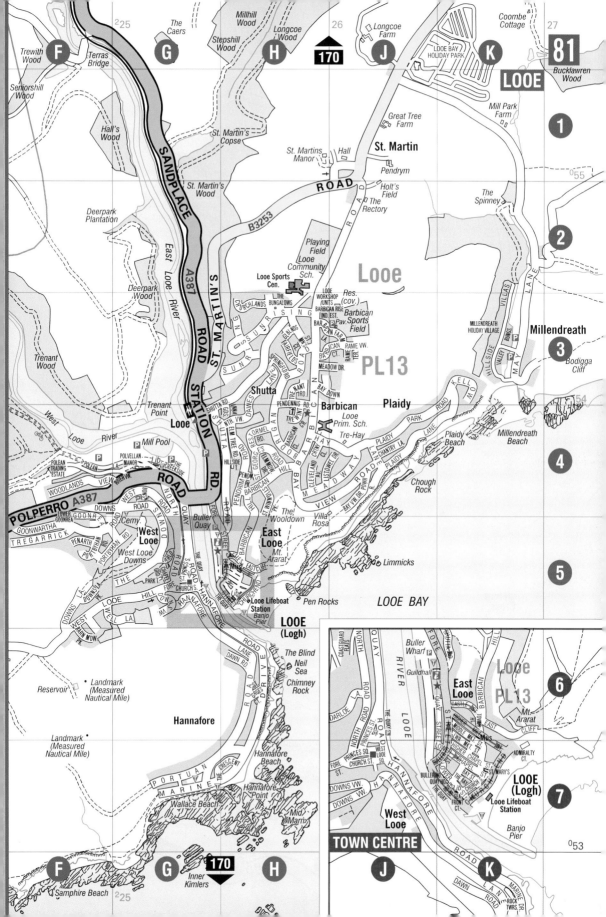

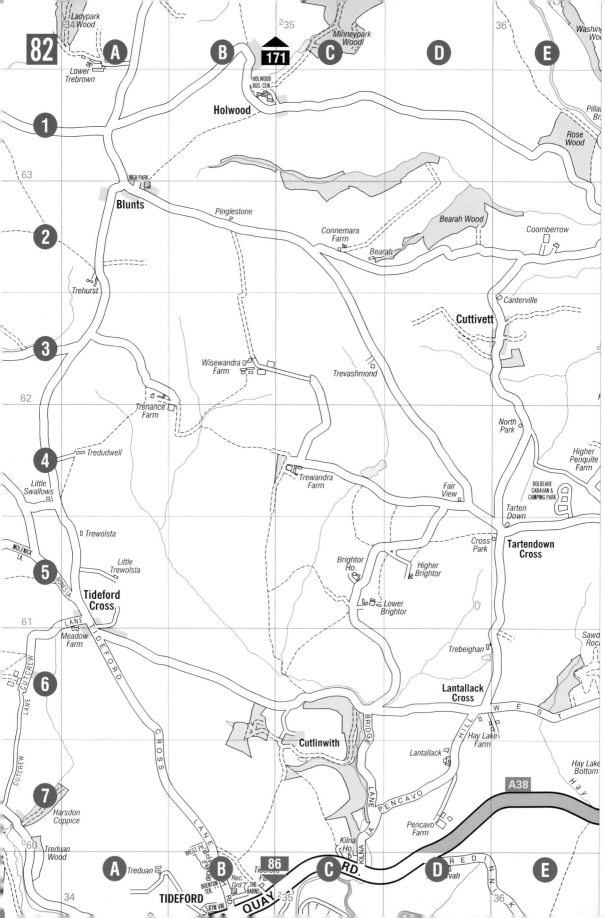

82

A　B　171　C　D　E

1

Ladypark Wood 34

Lower Trebrown

Holwood

HOLWOOD BUS. CEN.

Minneypark Wood

235

36

Washing Wood

Pillai Br

Rose Wood

63

HIGH PARK P

Blunts

Pinglestone

Connemara Farm

Bearah Wood

Bearah

Coomberrow

2

Trehurst

Canterville

Cuttivett

3

Wisewandra Farm

Trevashmond

62

Trenance Farm

North Park

Higher Penquite Farm

DOLBEARE CARAVAN & CAMPING PARK

4

Tredudwell

Trewandra Farm

Fair View

Tarten Down

Little Swallows

Cross Park

Tartendown Cross

Trewolsta

MOLENICK LA.

Little Trewolsta

Brightor Ho.

Higher Brightor

5

BONES LA.

Tideford Cross

Lower Brightor

61

LANE

Meadow Farm

TIDEFORD

Trebeighan

6

CUTCREW LANE

LANE

Lantallack Cross

Sawd Rock

Hay Lake Farm

Hay Lake Bottom

CUTCREW LA.

CROSS LANE

Cutlinwith

Lantallack

A38

7

Harsdon Coppice

BRIDGE LANE

PENCAVO LA.

Pencavo Farm

Hay

60

Treduan Wood

Kilna Ho.

KILNA LA.

REDIN

A　Treduan

WEST PK.

B　86

Tideford Fa.

C　RD.

D　vah

E

NICK

Brenton Ter.

Rec. Grd. P

THE BARNS

TIDEFORD

QUAY

235

34

36

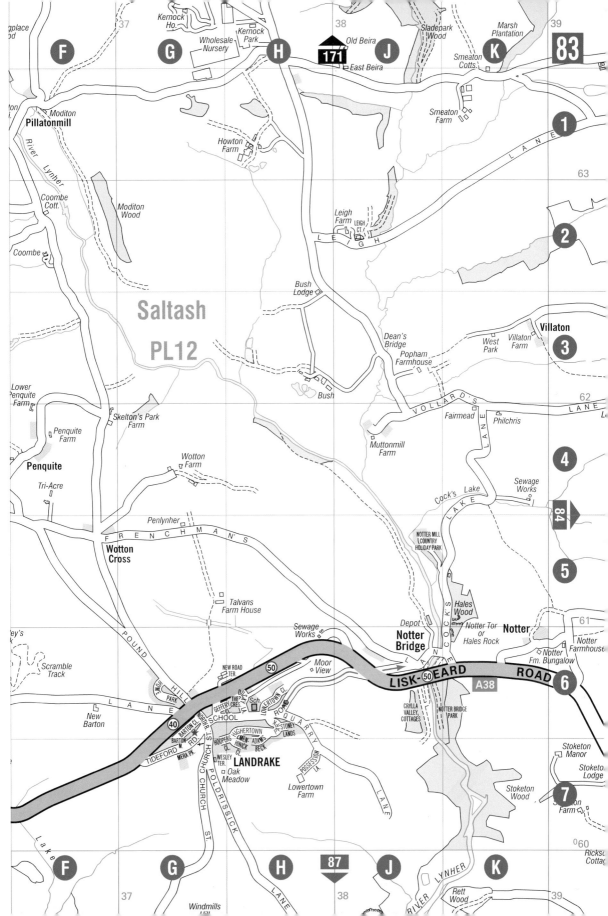

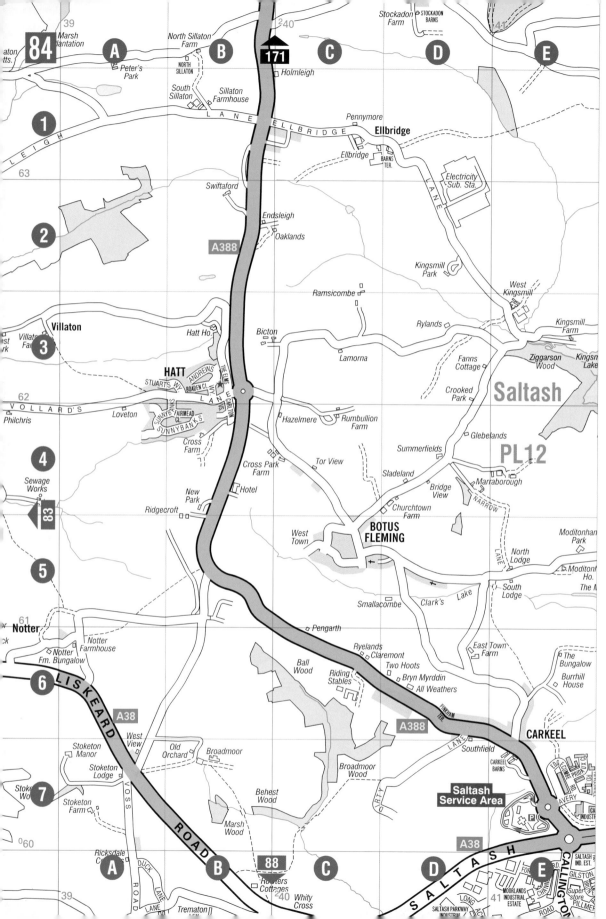

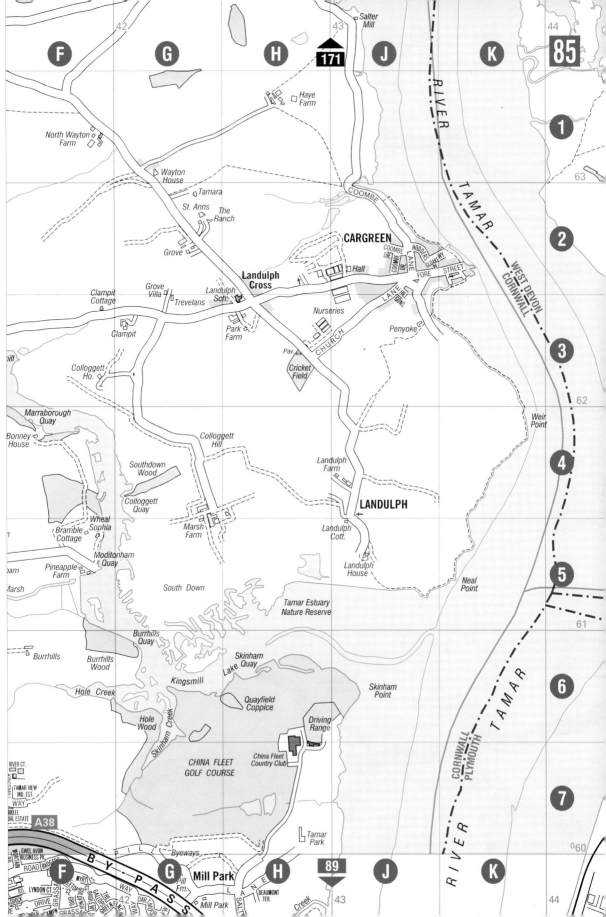

1

Salter Mill

RIVER TAMAR

WEST DEVON
CORNWALL

2

Haye Farm

North Wayton Farm

Wayton House

Tamara

St. Anns
The Ranch

Grove

COOMBE

CARGREEN

COOMBE DR.
COOMBE LANE
HOOPERS
GLOANS WY.
FORE STREET
LANE HILL GDNS.

Hall

Landulph Cross

Grove Villa
Trevelans
Landulph Sch.

Clampit Cottage

Clampit

Park Farm

Nurseries

CHURCH LANE

Penyoke

3

62

Colloggett Ho.

Colloggett Hill

Pav.
Cricket Field

Marraborough Quay

Bonney House

Southdown Wood

Colloggett Quay

Landulph Farm

Weir Point

4

Bramble Cottage

Wheal Sophia

Marsh Farm

LANDULPH

Moditonham Quay

Pineapple Farm

Marsh

South Down

Landulph Cott.

Landulph House

Neal Point

5

61

Tamar Estuary Nature Reserve

Burrhills Quay

Skinham Quay

Burrhills

Burrhills Wood

Kingsmill Lake

Skinham Point

CORNWALL
PLYMOUTH

6

TAMAR

Hole Creek

Hole Wood

Skinham Creek

Quayfield Coppice

Driving Range

7

RIVER CT.
WINDSMILL WAY

TAMAR VIEW IND. EST.

China Fleet Country Club

CHINA FLEET GOLF COURSE

ARKEEL
TRIAL ESTATE

A38

GWEL AVON
MORTAIN
ROAD BADGERS

RIVER
LYNDON CT.
PADDOCK
DRIVE

MYRTL CT.
TOP VIEW
GALLOWS
GRASS
THE
GREEN

BEECH
BROADWAY
GRASSMERE

Mill Park

Byeways

PILL

BY-PASS

WAY
DARTMOOR

Pill Fm.

Mill Park

SALT LANE

Tamar Park

BEAUMONT TER.

Creek

060

60

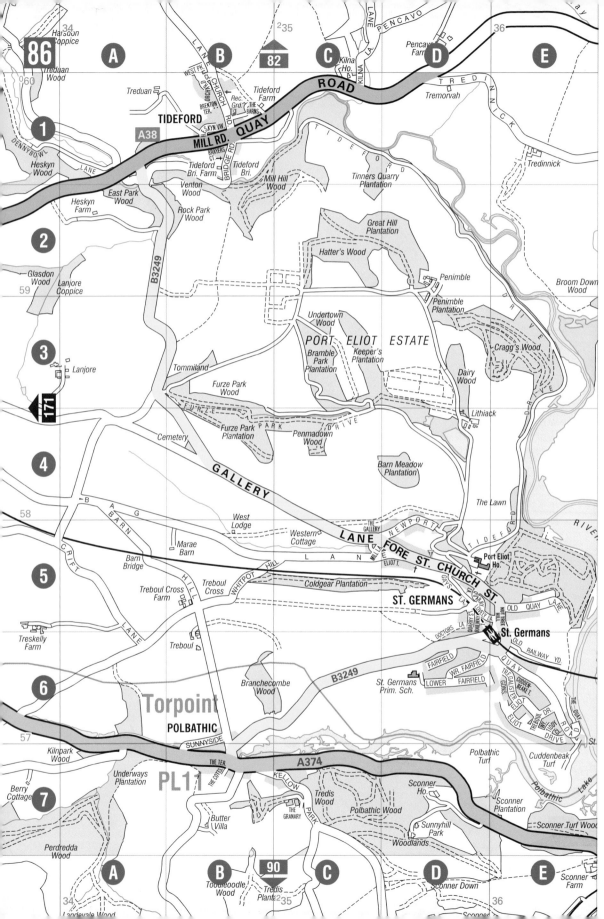

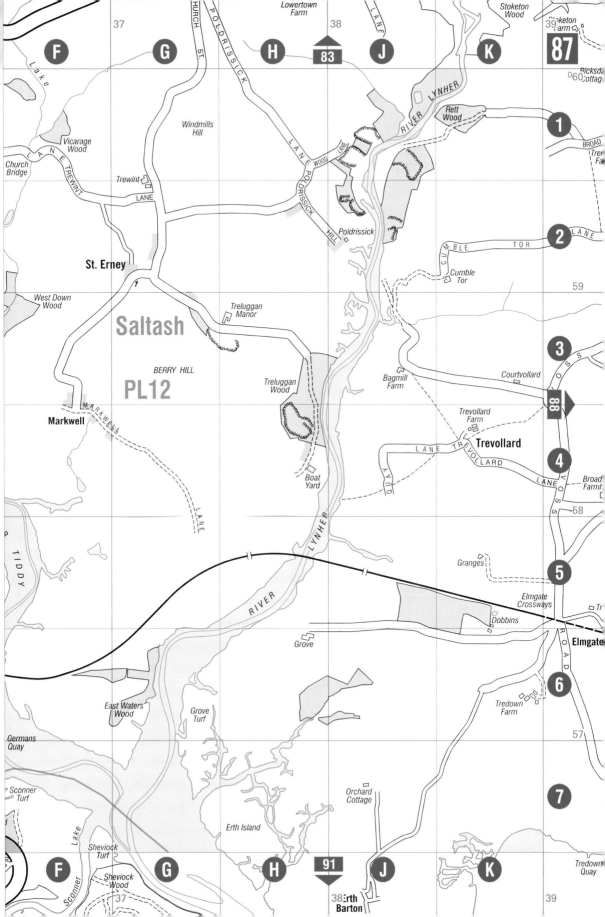

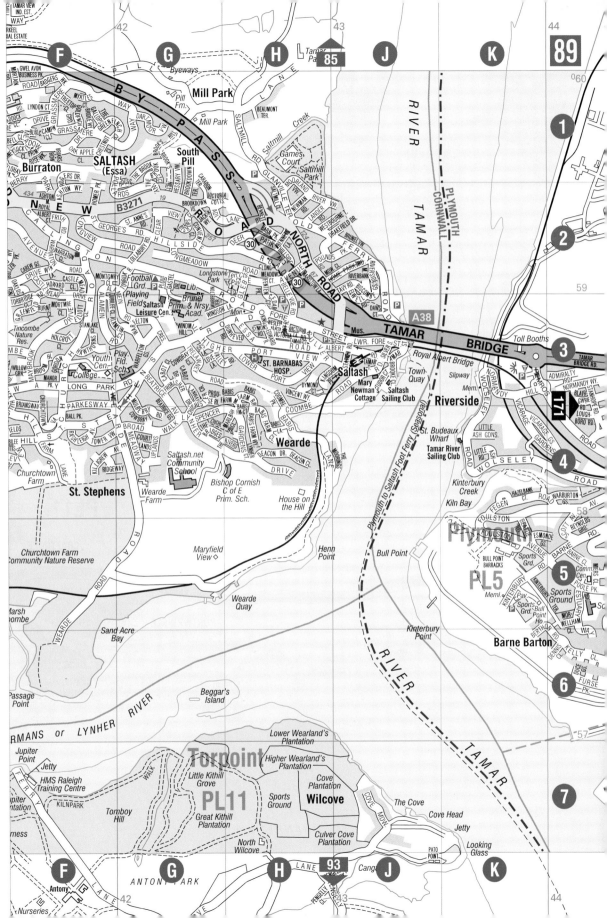

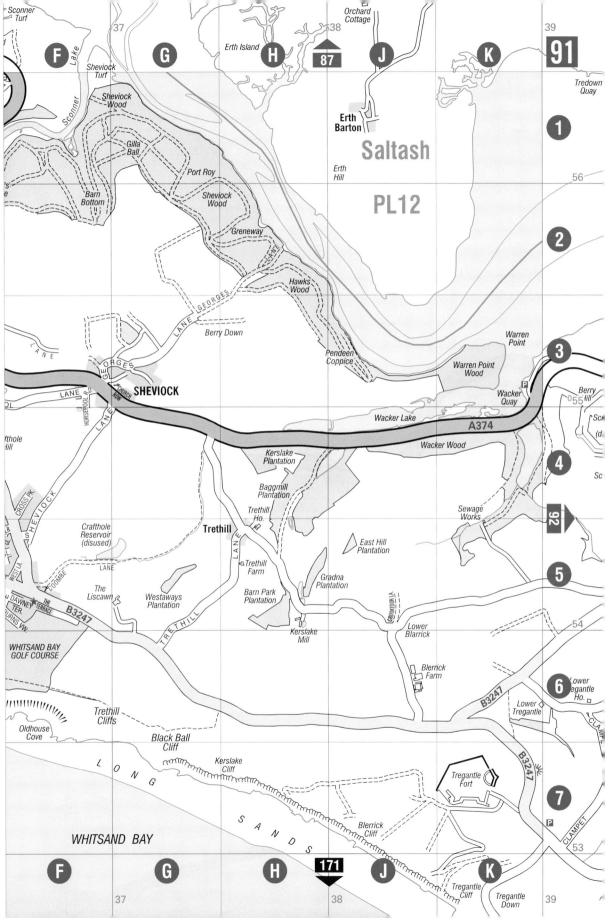

F G H J K

Sconner Turf
Sconner Lake
Erth Island
Orchard Cottage

87

Tredown Quay

1

Sheviock Turf
Sheviock Wood
Erth Barton

Saltash

Gilla Ball
Port Roy

Barn Bottom
Sheviock Wood
Erth Hill

PL12

56

Greneway

2

Hawks Wood

Warren Point

LANE GEORGES
Berry Down
Pendeen Coppice

Warren Point Wood

Warren Point Wood

3

GEORGES LANE
LANE

CHURCH ROW
SHEVIOCK
HORSEPOOL RD.

Wacker Lake
Wacker Quay
Berry Hill

55

Sc
(d

A374

Wacker Wood

LANE

Kerslake Plantation

Baggmill Plantation

Sewage Works

4

Sc

CROSS PK.
SHEVIOCK
WEST LA.

Crafthole Reservoir (disused)

Trethill Ho.
Trethill
Trethill Farm

East Hill Plantation

92

DAWNEY TER.
BURNS VW.
THE TERRACE
COOMBE

B3247
The Liscawn

Westaways Plantation

Barn Park Plantation

Gradna Plantation

CROOKEDOAK LA.

Lower Blarrick

5

54

WHITSAND BAY GOLF COURSE

TRETHILL LANE

Kerslake Mill

Blerrick Farm

Lower Blarrick

B3247
Lower Tregantle
Lower Tregantle Ho.

6

Trethill Cliffs

Oldhouse Cove

Black Ball Cliff

Kerslake Cliff

Tregantle Fort

B3247

CLAMPET

7

L O N G   S A N D S

Blerrick Cliff

WHITSAND BAY

171

Tregantle Cliff
Tregantle Down

53

F G H J K

37 38 39

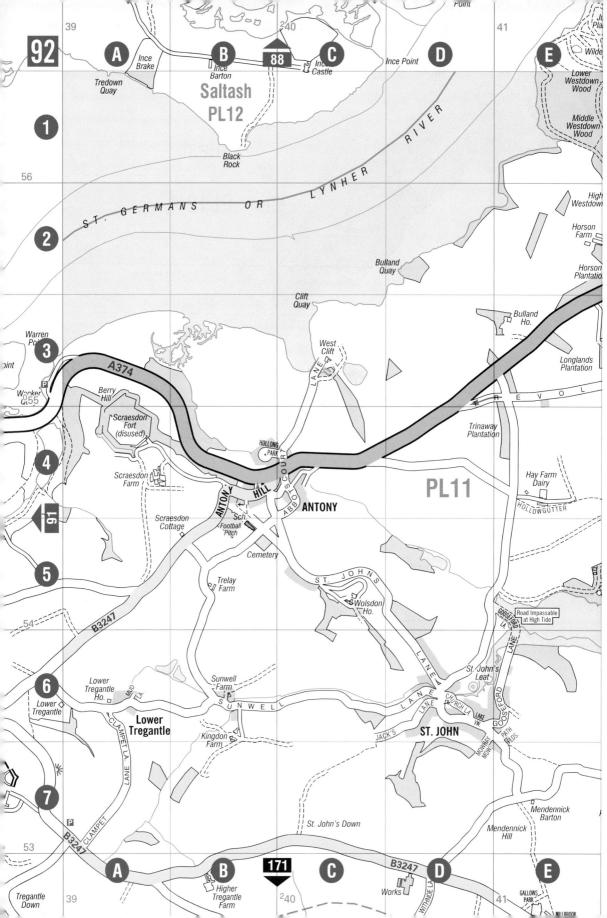

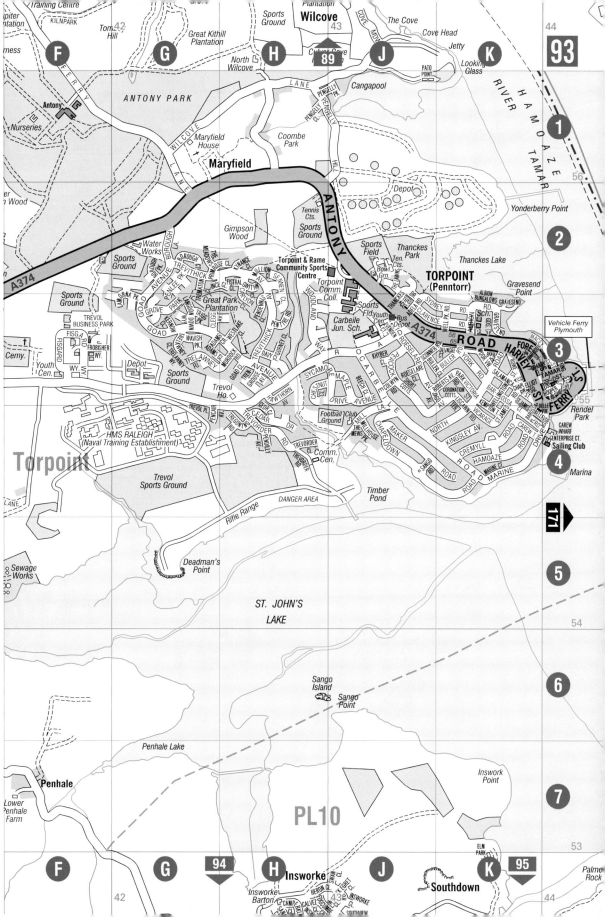

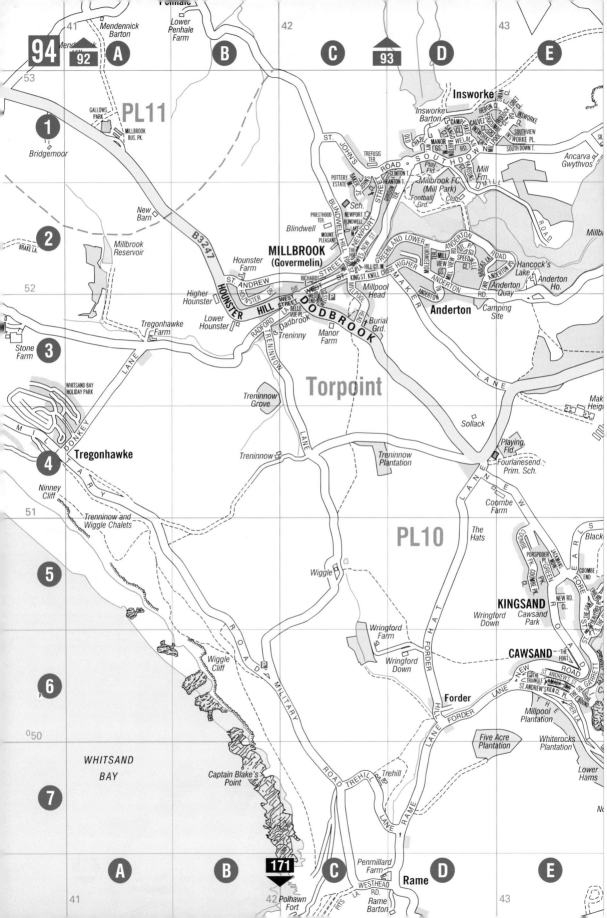

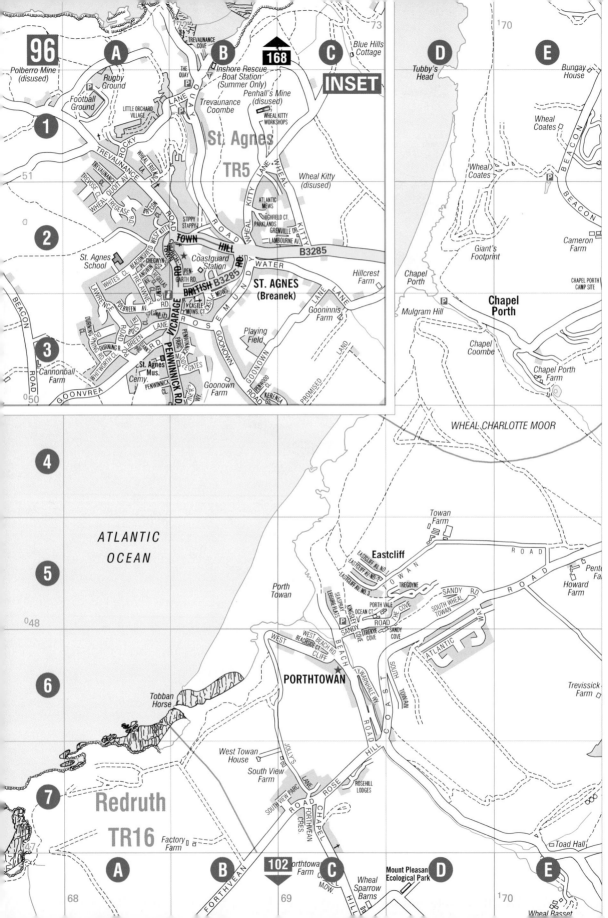

96

Polberro Mine (disused)

INSET

Rugby Ground

Football Ground

THE QUAY

Trevaunance Cove

Inshore Rescue Boat Station (Summer Only)

Trevaunance Coombe

Penhall's Mine (disused)

WHEAL KITTY WORKSHOPS

Blue Hills Cottage

Tubby's Head

Bungay House

St. Agnes

TR5

LITTLE ORCHARD VILLAGE

ATLANTIC MEWS

Wheal Kitty (disused)

Wheal Coates

Wheal Coates

St. Agnes School

TOWN HILL

Coastguard Station

HIGHFIELD CT. PARKLANDS

GRENVILLE DR.

LAMBOURNE AV.

B3285

Giant's Footprint

Cameron Farm

ST. AGNES (Breanek)

Hillcrest Farm

Chapel Porth

CHAPEL PORTH CAMP SITE

Gooninnis Farm

Mulgram Hill

Chapel Porth

St. Agnes Mus.

Cemy.

Goonown Farm

Playing Field

Chapel Coombe

Chapel Porth Farm

Cannonball Farm

WHEAL CHARLOTTE MOOR

4

ATLANTIC OCEAN

Towan Farm

5

Porth Towan

EASTCLIFF AV. NO.1

Eastcliff

EASTCLIFF AV. NO.2

EASTCLIFF AV. NO.3

Tregoyne

Pento Fa

Howard Farm

Porth Vale

KINGSLEY CT.

SANDY RD.

SOUTH WHEAL TOWAN

SEASPRAY LEISURE FLATS

THE COVE

SANDY COVE

Sandy Cove

TREKYE COVE

SANDY COVE ROAD

6

Tobban Horse

WEST BEACH RD.

BEACHSIDE CT.

WEST CLIFF

PORTHTOWAN

Trevissick Farm

BEACH

COAST ROAD

ATLANTIC WAY

7

Redruth

TR16

West Towan House

South View Farm

JOLLY'S LANE

SOUTH VIEW PARC

ROAD

CHAPEL HILL

ROSE HILL

FORTHVEAN

FORTHVEAN CRES.

ROSEHILL LODGES

Toad Hall

Factory Farm

orthtowan Farm

Wheal Sparrow Barns

Mount Pleasan Ecological Park

Wheal Basset

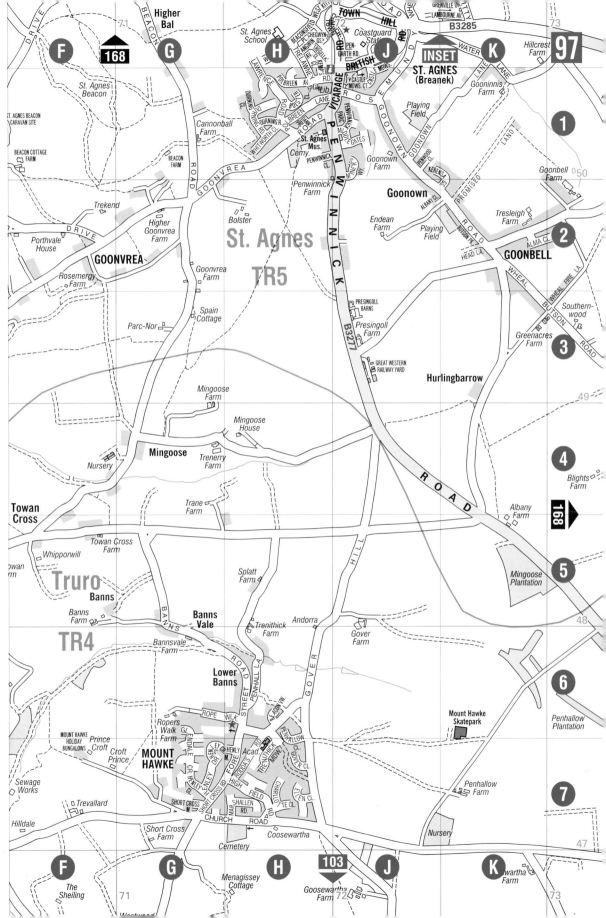

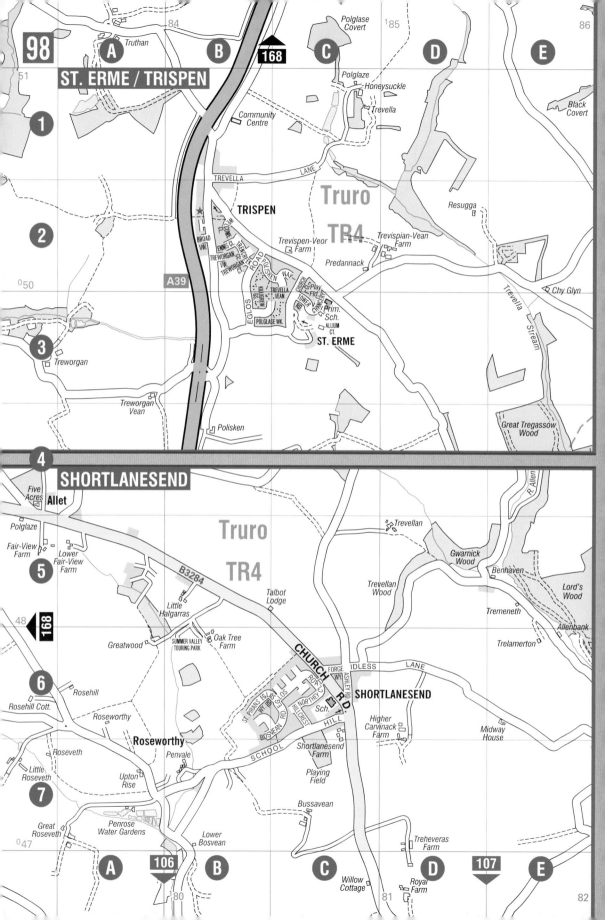

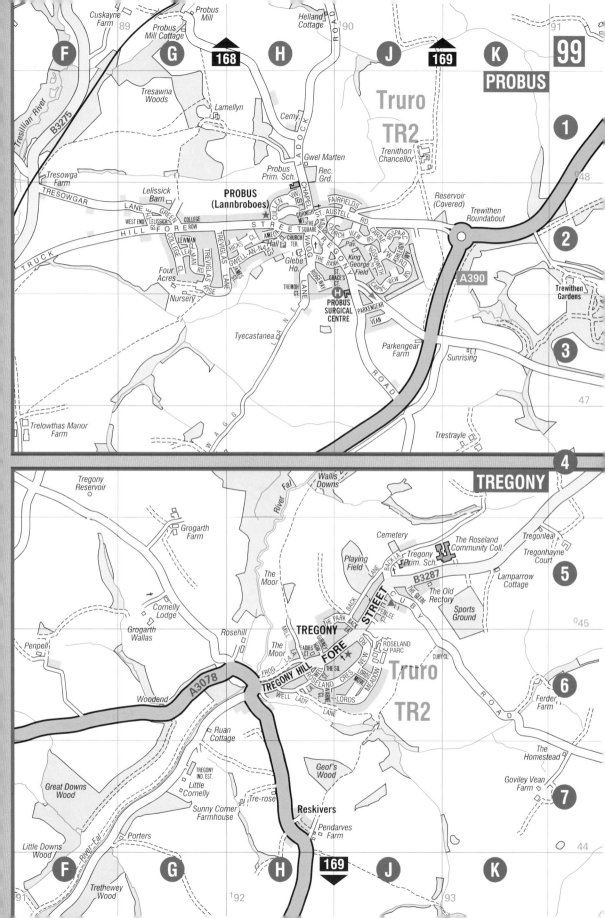

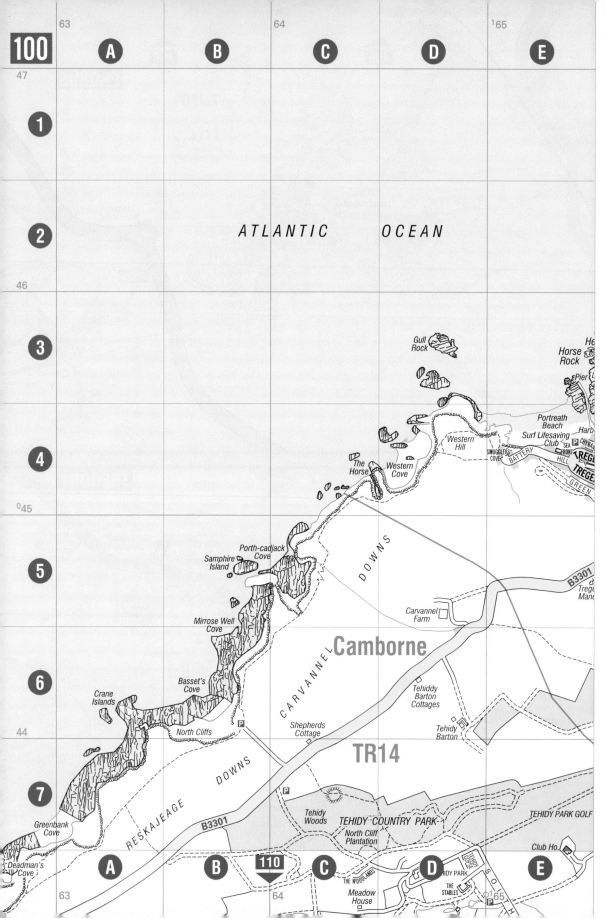

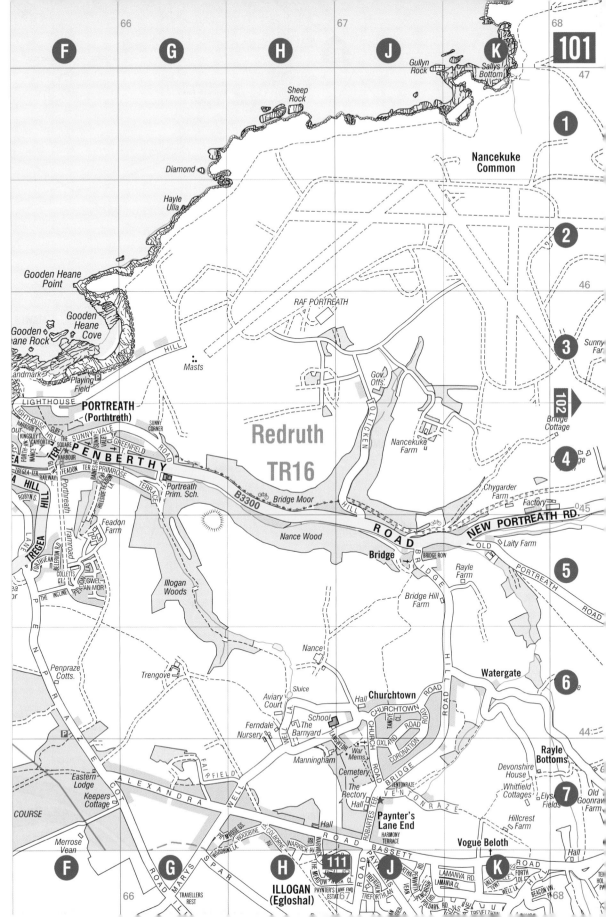

66 67 68

47

1

Gullyn Rock

Sallys Bottom

Sheep Rock

Nancekuke Common

2

Diamond

46

Hayle Ulla

Gooden Heane Point

RAF PORTREATH

3 Sunny Far

Gooden Heane Cove

Gov. Offs.

Gooden Heane Rock

Masts

Bridge Cottage

4 102

andmark

Playing Field

LIGHTHOUSE

PORTREATH
(Porthtreth)

SUNNY CORNER

HILL

Nancekuke Farm

Redruth

TR16

Chygarder Farm

Factory

045

Cottage

ea HILL

LIGHTHOUSE

KINGSLEY T.

HARBOUR

FORTH AN

NANCE

THE SQUARE

SUNNY-VALE

GREENFIELD

SUNNY CORNER

ROAD

TOLTICKEN

Laity Farm

TREGEA

PENBERTHY

PRIMROSE TER.

Portreath Prim. Sch.

B3300

Bridge Moor

HILL

ROAD

NEW PORTREATH RD.

OLD

5

PORTREATH

ROAD

CLIFF

CAYFORTH

TREGEA-TER.

RAILWAY T.

FEADON

PRIMROSE TERRACE

Nance Wood

Bridge

BRIDGE ROW

Rayle Farm

ROBYN'S

HILLSIDE FEADON

FEADON LA.

Feadon Farm

Illogan Woods

Bridge Hill Farm

TREGEA HILL

FORTH VEAN

COLLETTS CT.

FERN GWEL AN MOR

THE INCLINE

Tramroad

BELERION RD.

Penpraze Cotts.

Trengove

Nance

Watergate **6**

44

Rayle Bottoms

Sluice

Aviary Court

Hall

Churchtown

CHURCHTOWN

ROAD

TANDY

ROAD

Devonshire House

P

School

The Barnyard

OXLAND

ROAD

Whitfield Cottages

Elysii Fields

Old Goonrav Farm

Ferndale Nursery

WELL LA.

CHURCH

CHAPEL

CORONATION

ROAD

Eastern Lodge

Manningham

War Mems

Cemetery

BRIDGE

VENTONRAZE

Hillcrest Farm

7

Keepers Cottage

The Rectory Hall

ALEXANDRA

FAIRFIELD

WELL

ROAD

ROBARTES TER.

VENTONRAZE

COURSE

Merrose Vean

MARYS

SPAR

PRIMROSE GS.

COLBORNE

WARWICK AV.

WOODBINE

WOODBINE LA.

Paynter's Lane End

HARMONY TERRACE

Vogue Beloth

Hall

ROAD

FORTH

HILL

66 67 68

ILLOGAN
(Egloshal)

PAYNTER'S LANE END ESTAT

TRAVELLERS REST

BASSETT

ROAD

PAYN

THE MEADOW

TREFORTHLAN

LAMANVA RD.

LAMANVA CL.

VALL

WELL LA.

TWNT

NEW

TREVELTHAN

POLDARK RD.

BEACON VW.

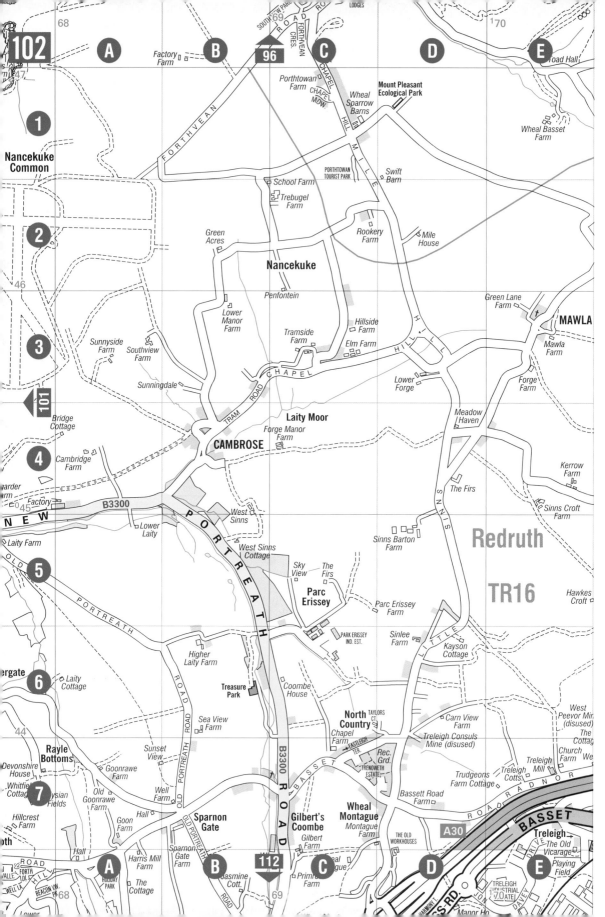

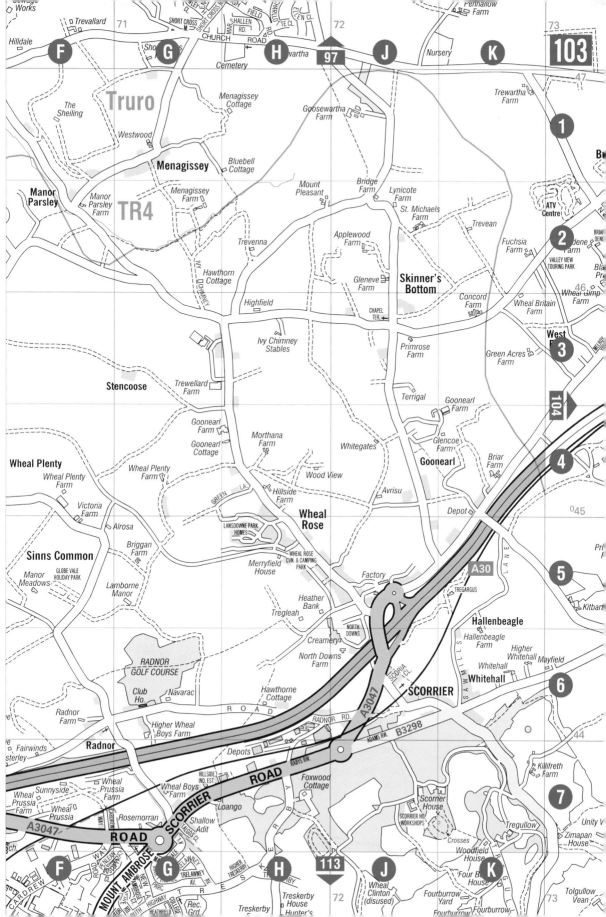

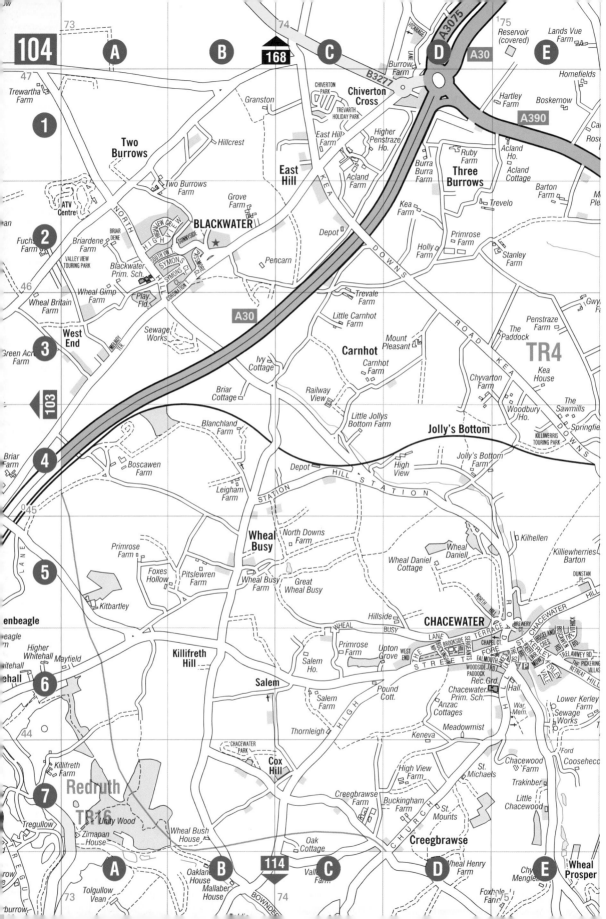

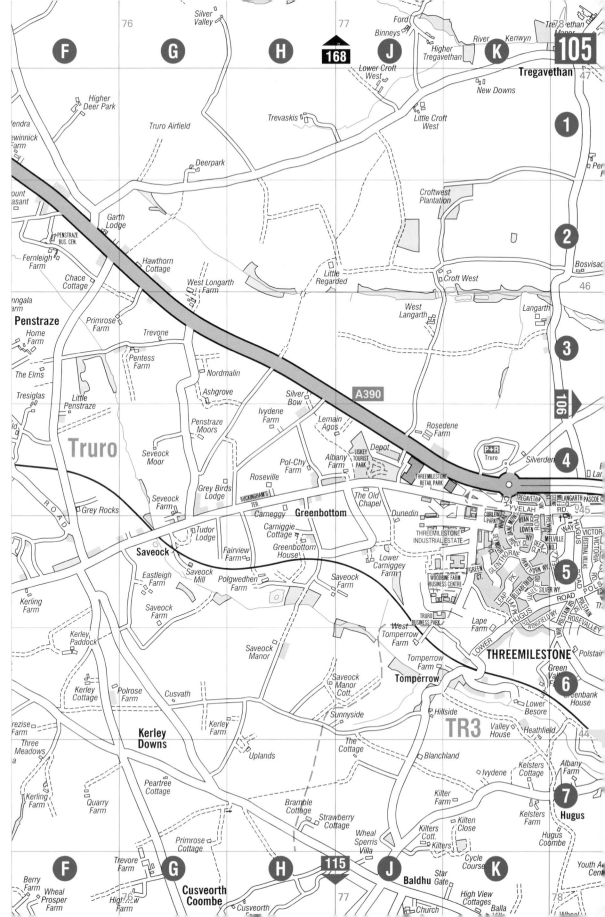

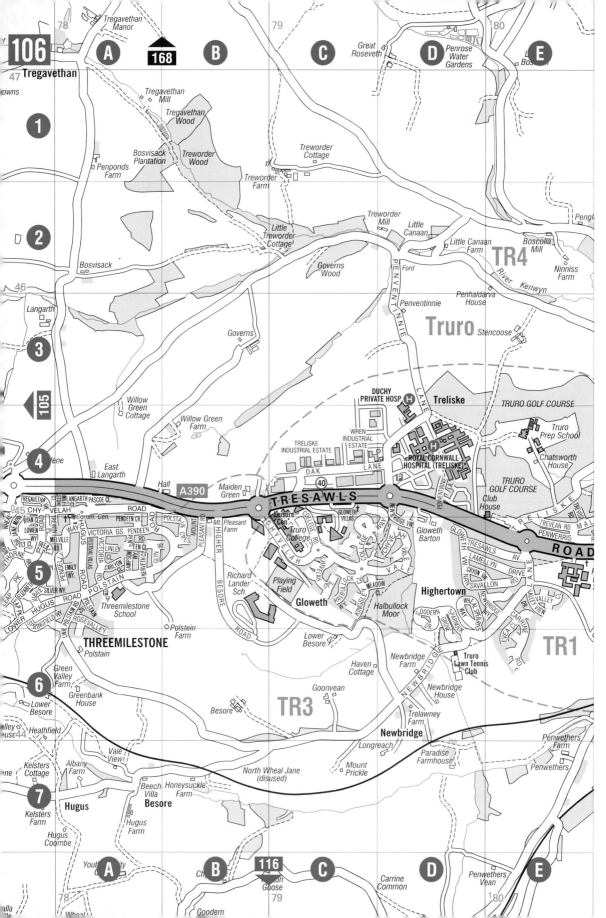

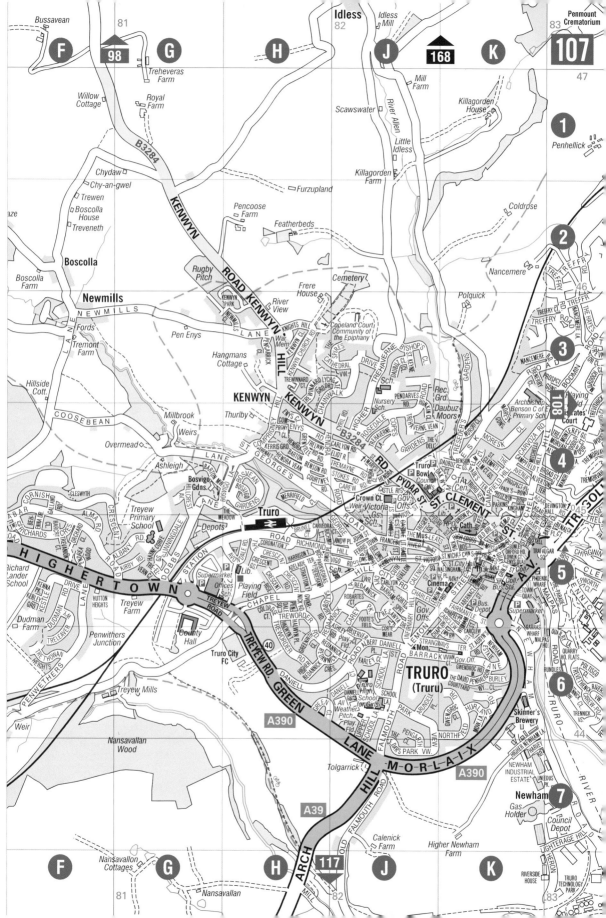

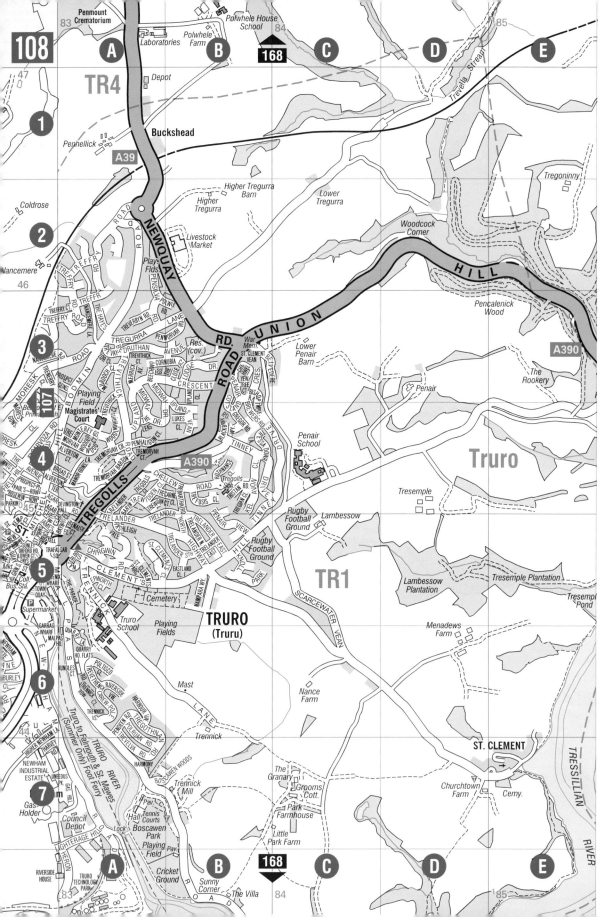

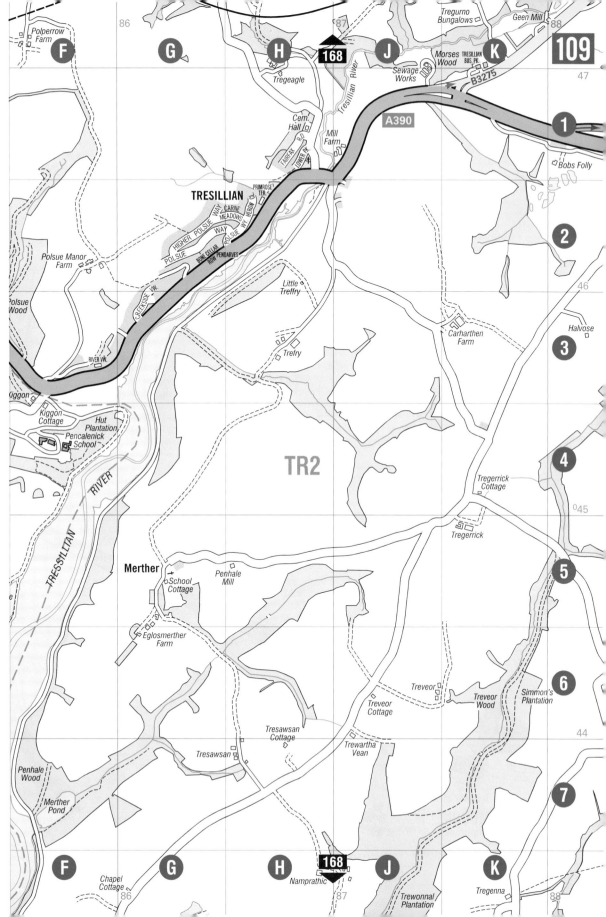

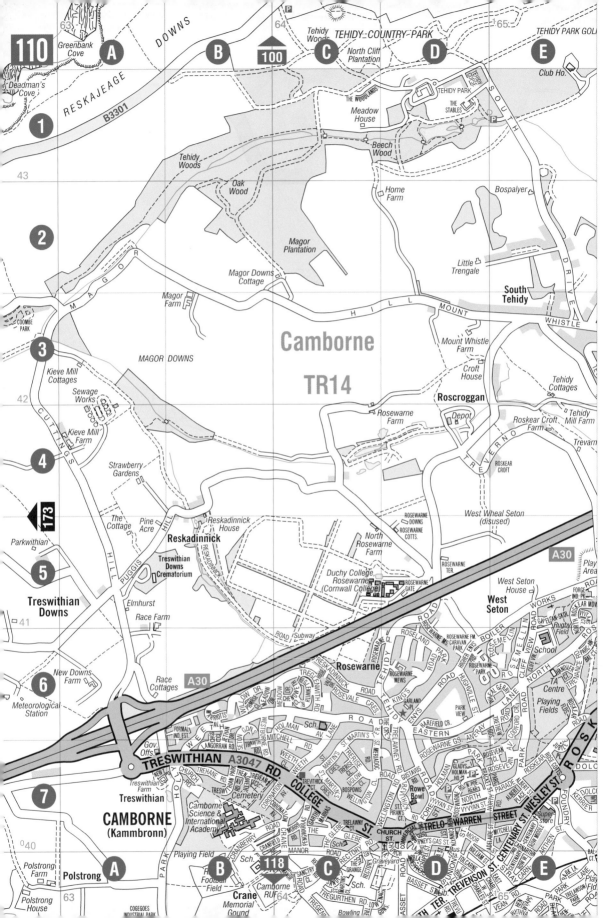

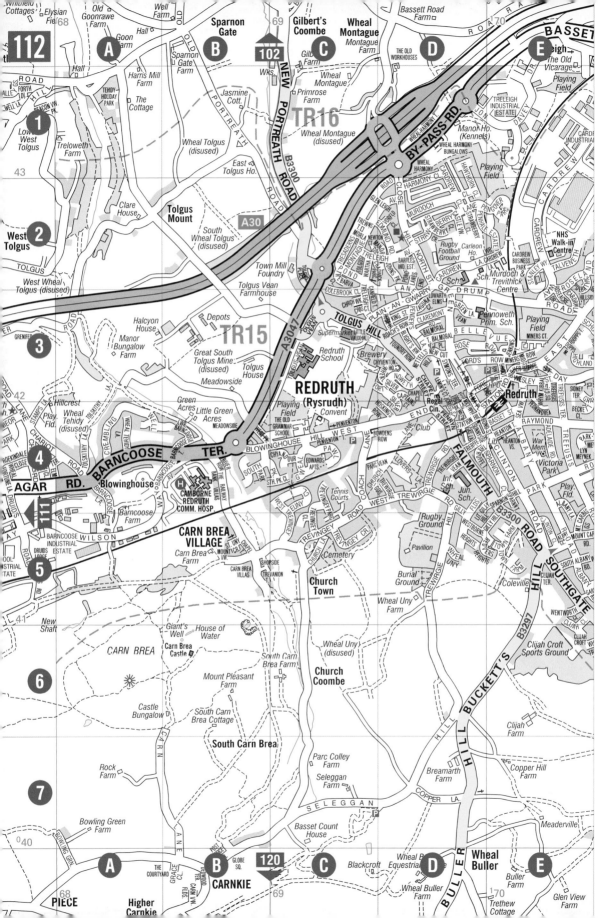

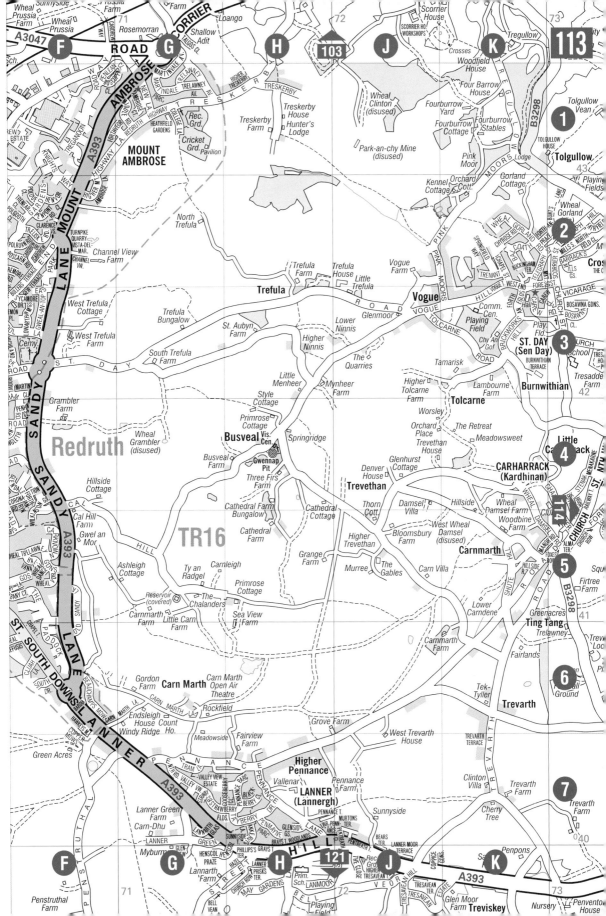

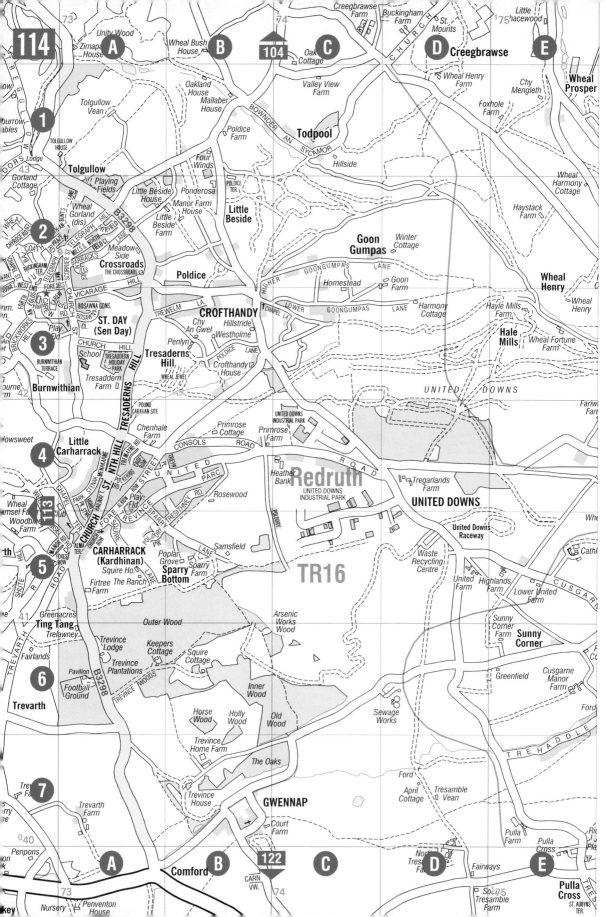

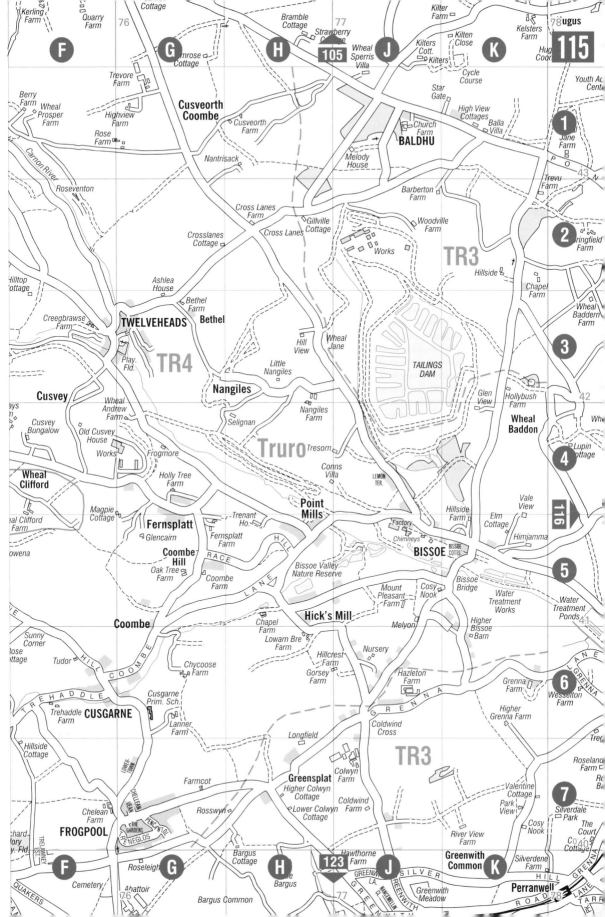

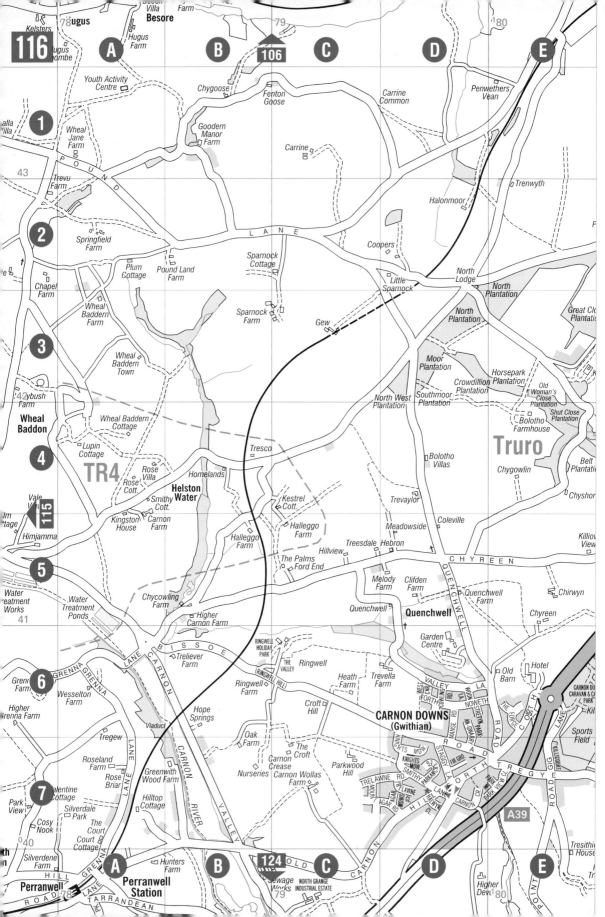

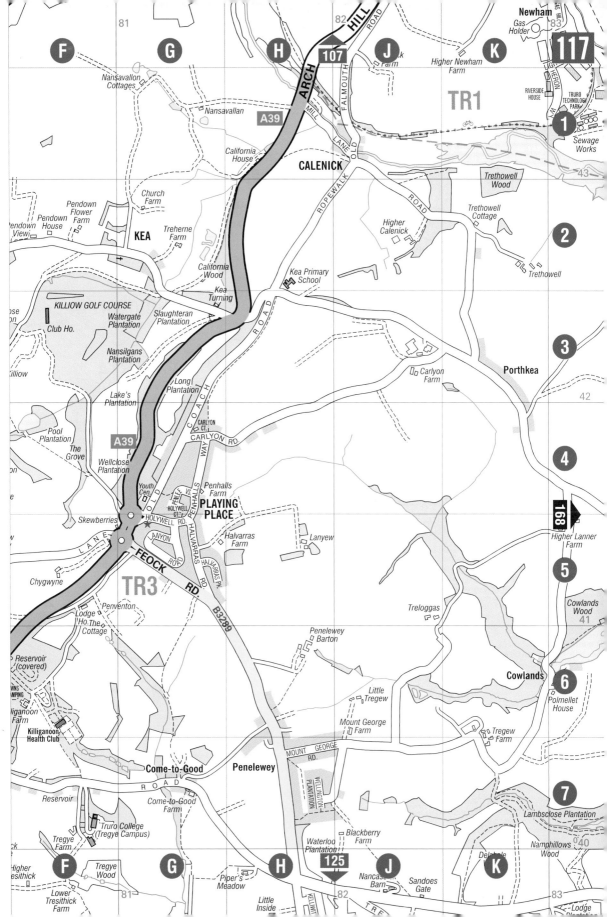

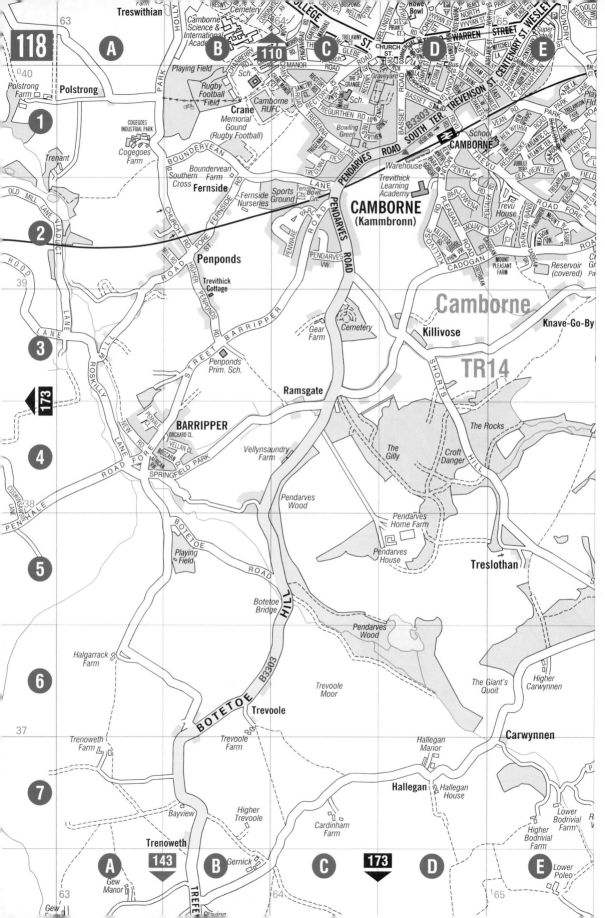

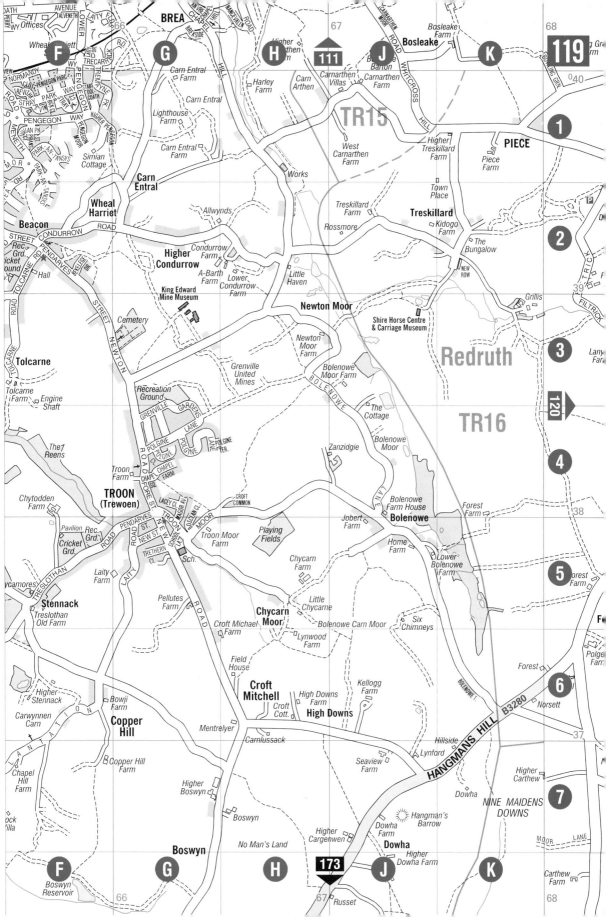

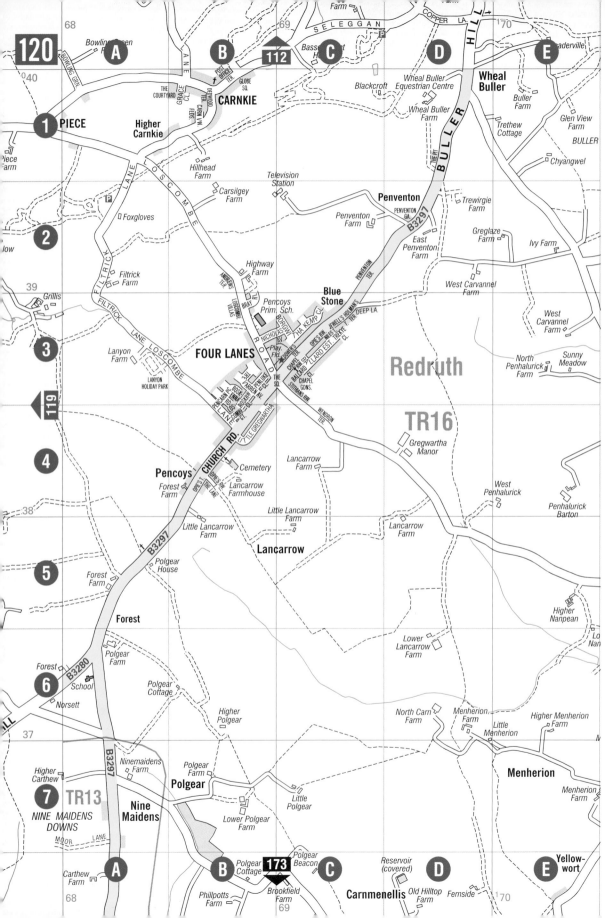

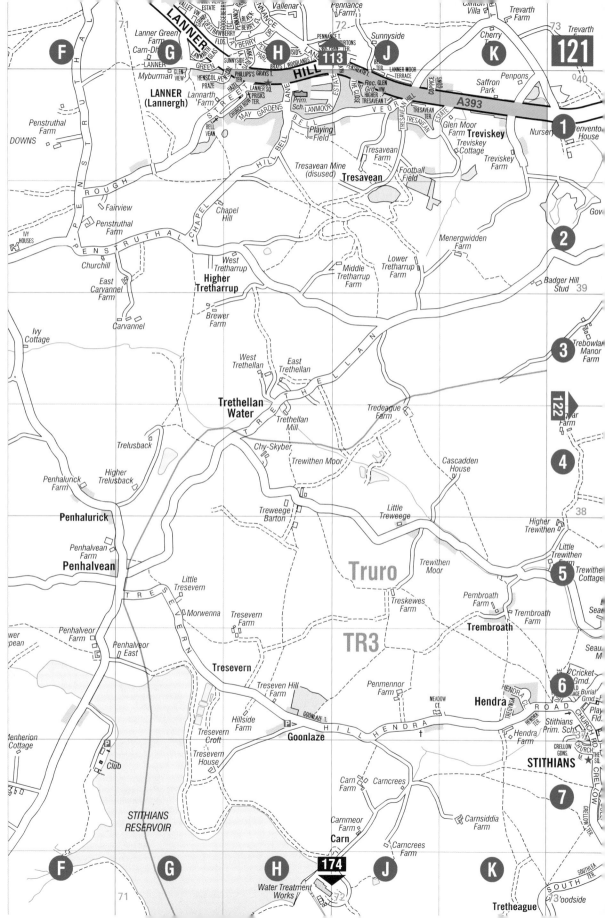

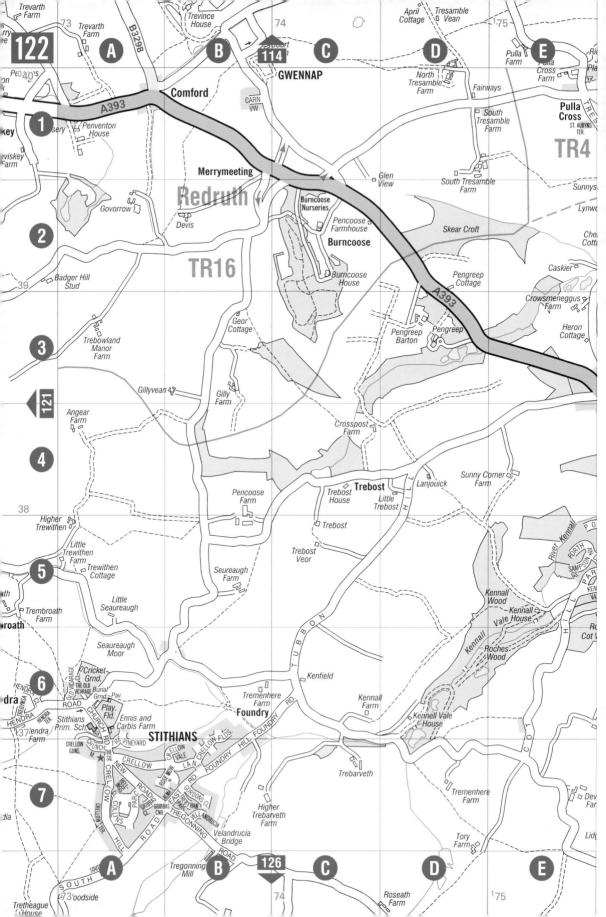

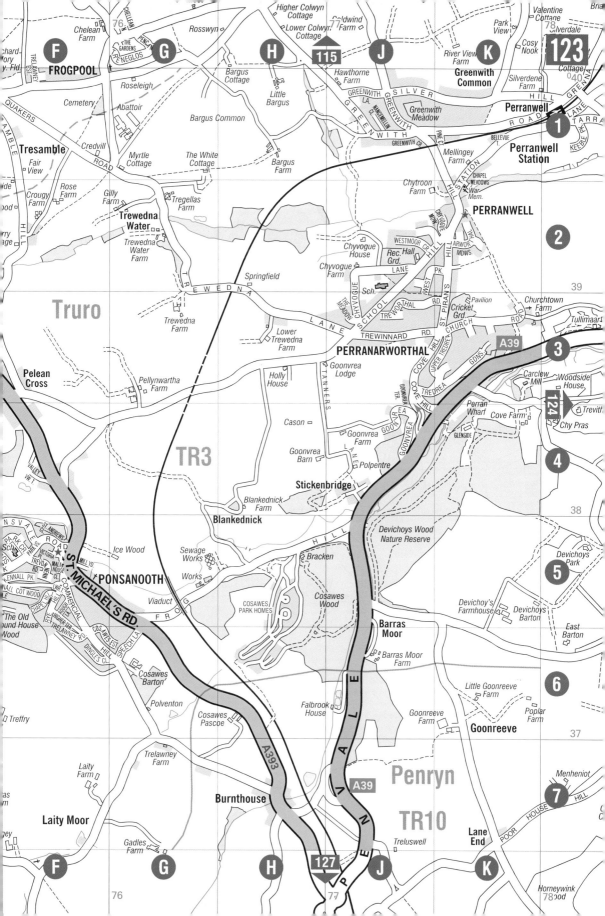

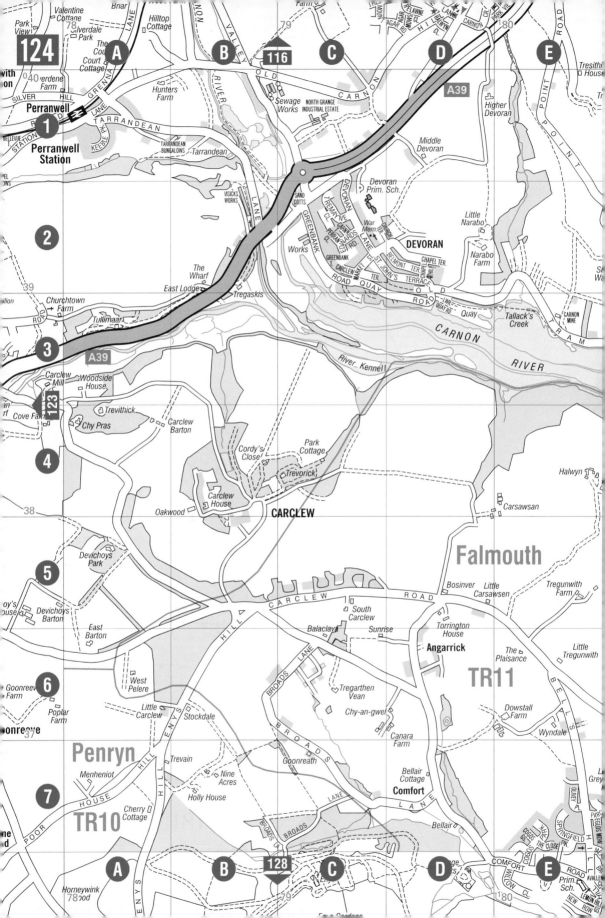

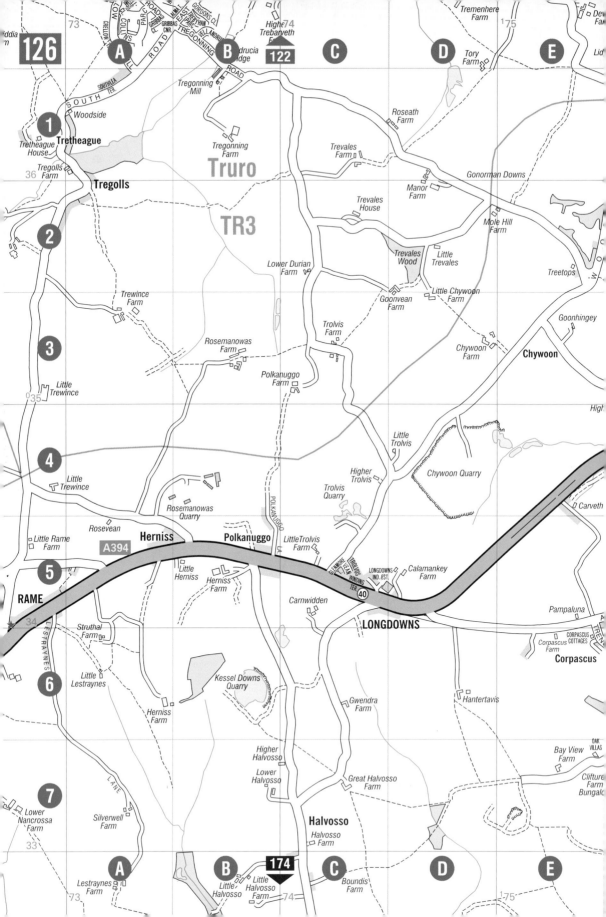

A B C D E

73 74 175

1

Woodside
Tretheague
Tretheague
House
Tregolls
Farm
36

Truro

Tregonning
Mill
Tregonning
Farm

High
Trebarveth

122

Roseath
Farm

Trevales
Farm

Gonorman Downs

Tory
Farm

Tremenhere
Farm

De
Fa

Lid

2

TR3

Trewince
Farm

Lower Durian
Farm

Trevales
House

Trevales
Wood

Little
Trevales

Manor
Farm

Mole Hill
Farm

Little Chywoon
Farm

Treetops

Goonhingey

3

Little
Trewince

035

Rosemanowas
Farm

Polkanuggo
Farm

Goonvean
Farm

Trolvis
Farm

Chywoon
Farm

Chywoon

4

Little
Trewince

Rosemanowas
Quarry

Little
Trolvis

Higher
Trolvis

Chywoon Quarry

Carveth

High

5

Rosevean
Little Rame
Farm

Herniss

A394

Little
Herniss

Herniss
Farm

Polkanuggo

Trolvis
Quarry

LittleTrolvis
Farm

LONGDOWNS
IND. EST.

Calamankey
Farm

Pampaluna

Corpascus
Farm

CORPASCUS
COTTAGES

RAME

34

Struthal
Farm

Carnwidden

LONGDOWNS

40

Corpascus

6

Little
Lestraynes

Herniss
Farm

Kessel Downs
Quarry

Gwendra
Farm

Hantertavis

7

Lower
Nancrossa
Farm

Silverwell
Farm

Higher
Halvosso

Lower
Halvosso

Great Halvosso
Farm

Bay View
Farm

OAK
VILLAS

Clifture
Farm
Bungalo

33

Lestraynes
Farm

Halvosso

Halvosso
Farm

A B C D E

174

Little
Halvosso

Little
Halvosso Farm

Boundis
Farm

73 74 175

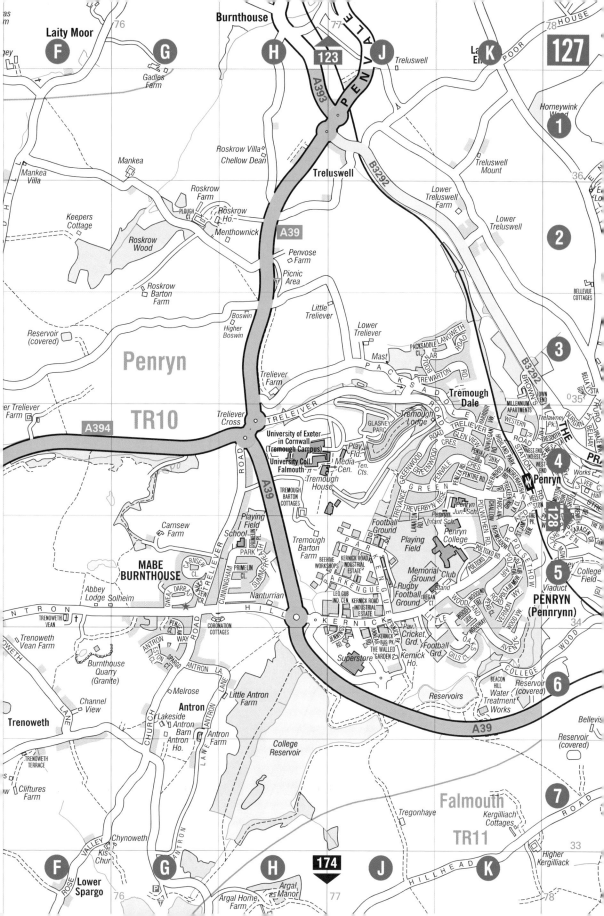

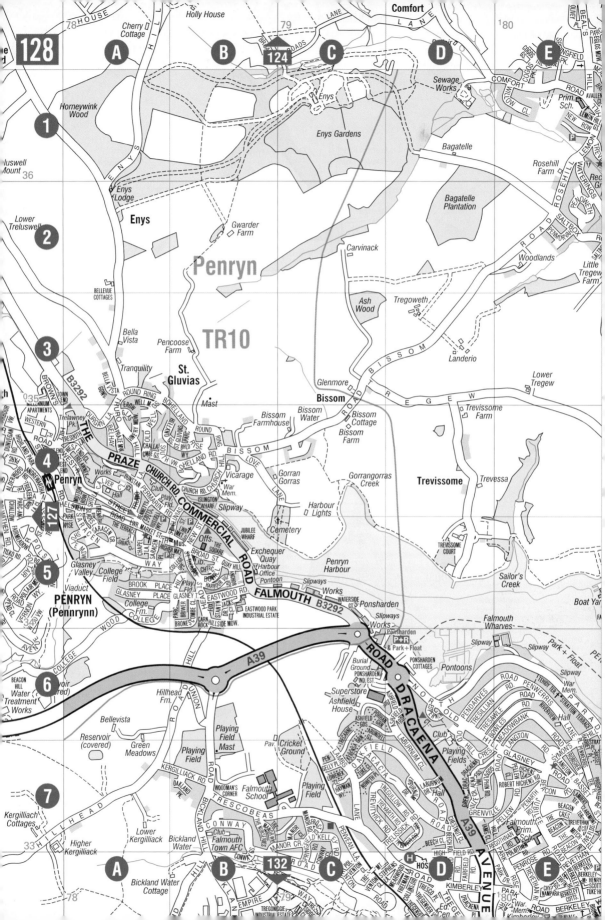

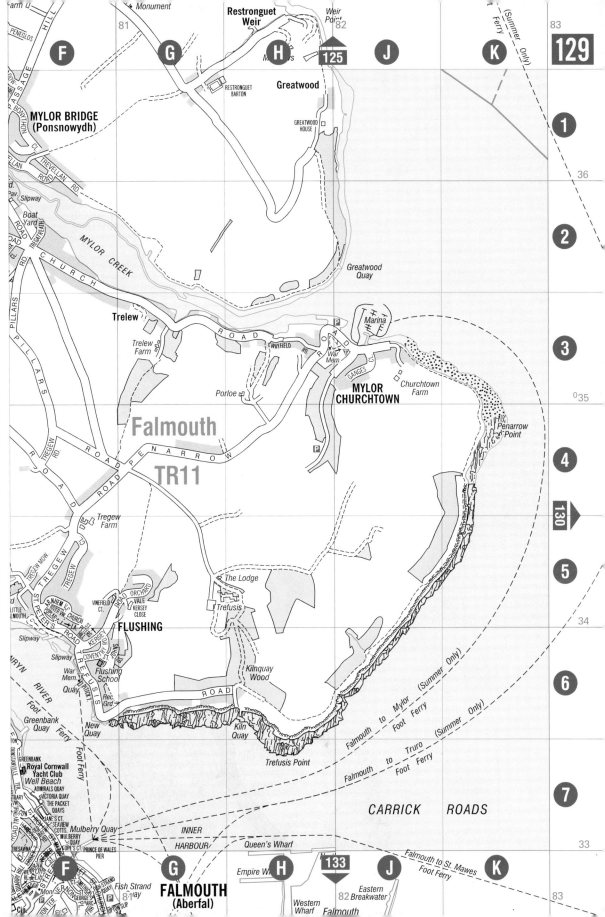

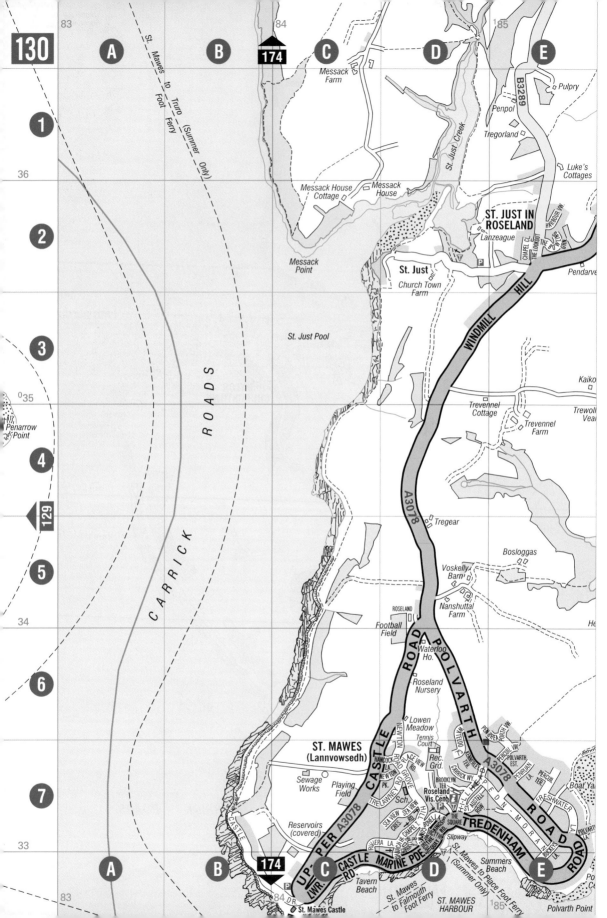

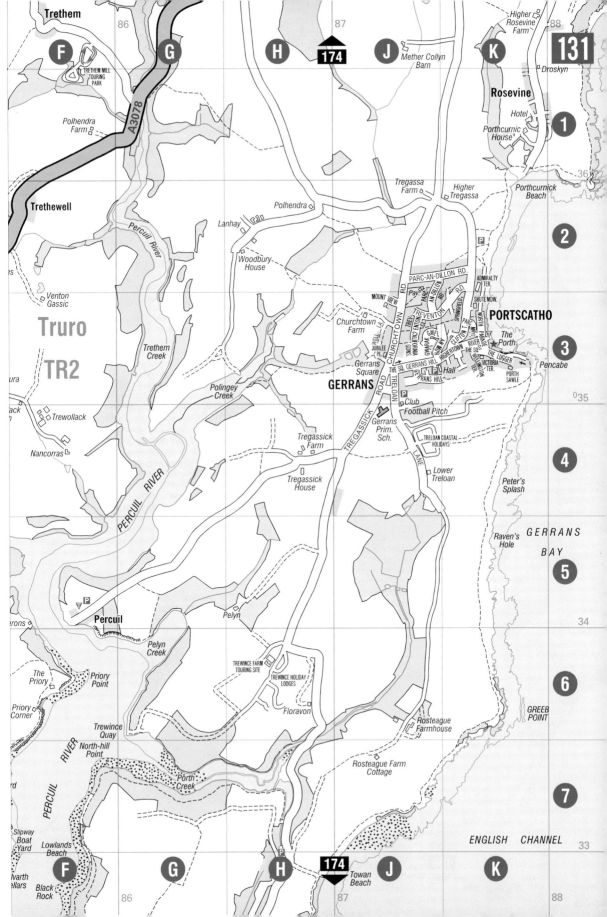

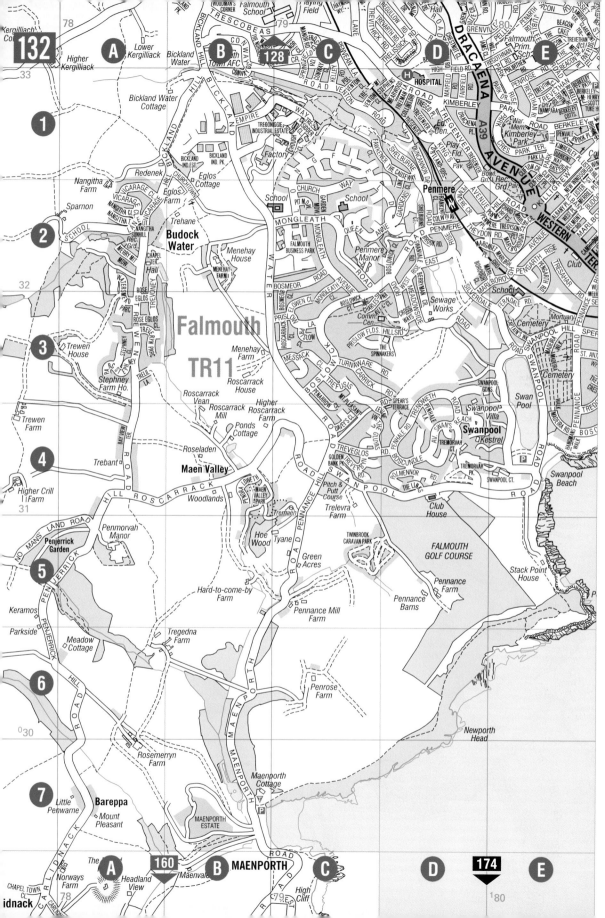

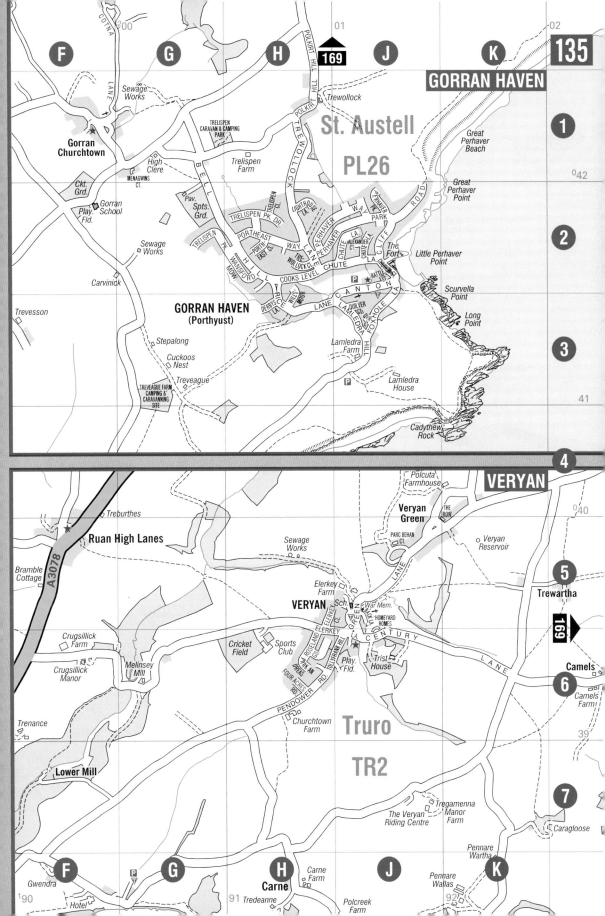

COTNA

200

01

02

Sewage Works

Trewollock

St. Austell

PL26

Great Perhaver Beach

Gorran Churchtown

Trelispen CARAVAN & CAMPING PARK

Trelispen Farm

High Clere

MENAGWINS CT.

Ckt. Grd.

Play. Fld.

Gorran School

Pav. Spts. Grd.

TRELISPEN PK. DR.

PORTHEAST WAY

PORTH EAST CL.

TRE. WOLLOCK CL.

LIGHTHOUSE LA.

PERHAVER LANE

PERHAVER WAY

PERHAVER PARK

CHUTE LA.

ALEXANDER CT.

CHUTE LA.

The Fort

Great Perhaver Point

042

Sewage Works

Carvinick

TRELISPEN PK.

HILL

WANSFORD MDW.

COOKS LEVEL

RISE LA.

DERBYSE LA.

WILLS MOOR

CHUTE LANE

CANTON

RATTLE ST.

CHURCH ST.

P

LAMLEDRA HILL

QUILVER DR.

FOXHOLE LA.

CLIFF LA.

Little Perhaver Point

Scurvella Point

Long Point

41

Trevesson

GORRAN HAVEN
(Porthyust)

Stepalong

Cuckoos Nest

Treveague

TREVEAGUE FARM CAMPING & CARAVANNING SITE

Lamledra Farm

P

Lamledra House

Cadythew Rock

4

Polcuta Farmhouse

Veryan Green

THE ROW

040

Treburthes

Ruan High Lanes

Sewage Works

PARC BEHAN CT.

Veryan Reservoir

Bramble Cottage

A3078

Elerkey Farm

VERYAN

Sch.

War Mem.

GREEN LANE

LANE

HOMEYARD HOMES

5

Trewartha

▶ 169

Crugsillick Farm

Melinsey Mill

Cricket Field

Sports Club

ELERKEY CT.

ELERKEY

ROSELAND CL.

PARK AN DREAS

FOUR ACRES RD

TULLIMAAR HILL

Play. Fld.

Trist House

CENTURY LANE

Camels

6

Camels Farm

Crugsillick Manor

PENDOWER RD.

Churchtown Farm

Truro

TR2

39

Trenance

Lower Mill

The Veryan Riding Centre

Tregamenna Manor Farm

7

Caragloose

Gwendra

190

Hotel

91

Tredeanne

Carne

Carne Farm

Polcreek Farm

Pennare Wartha

Pennare Wallas

92

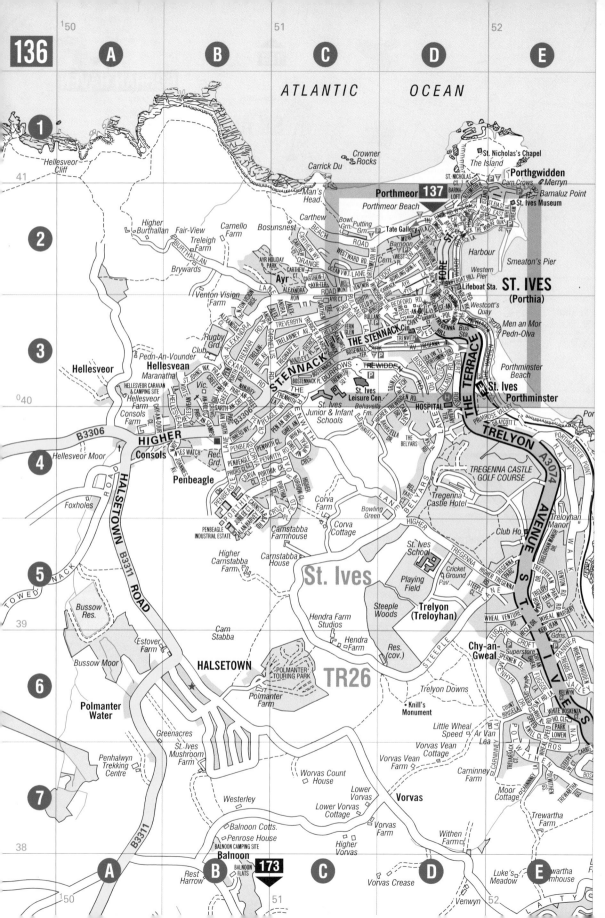

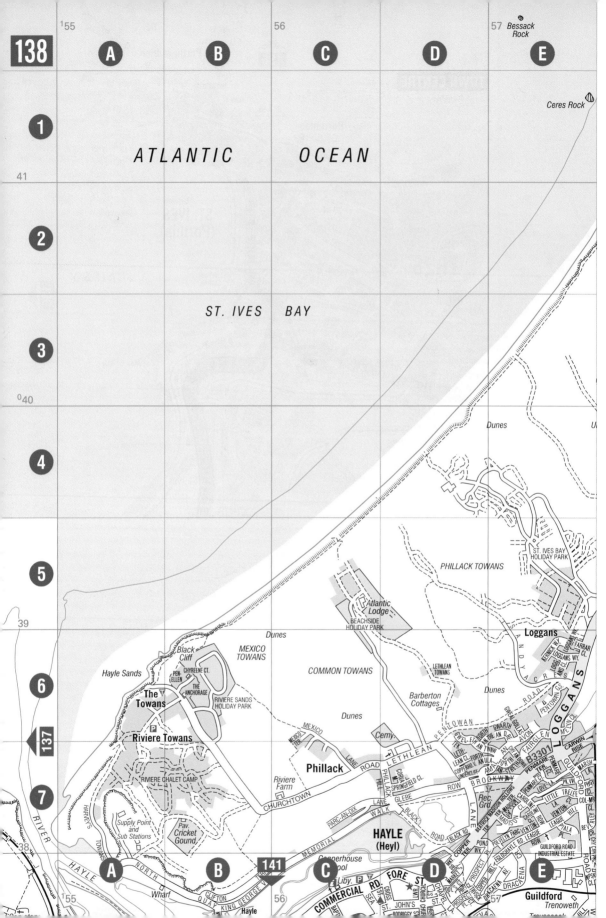

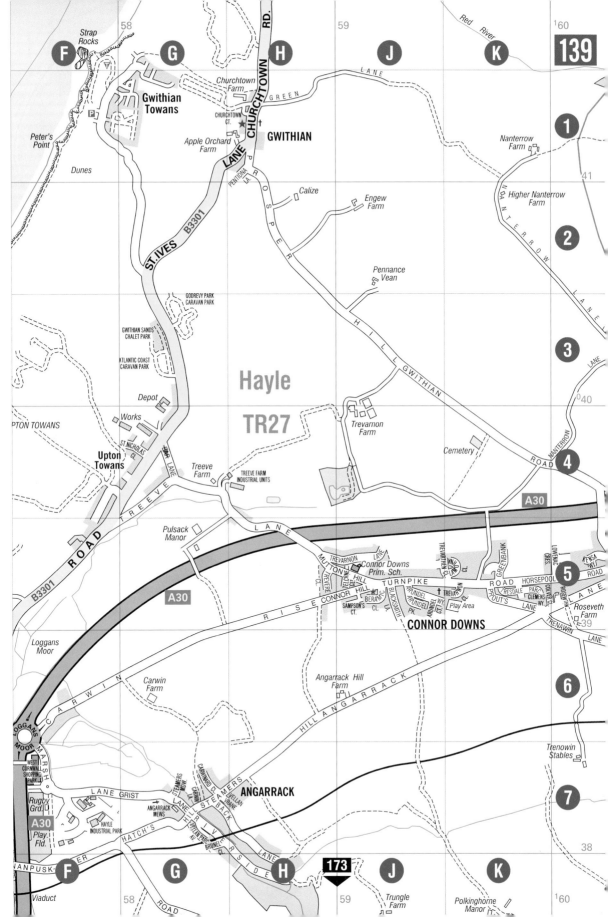

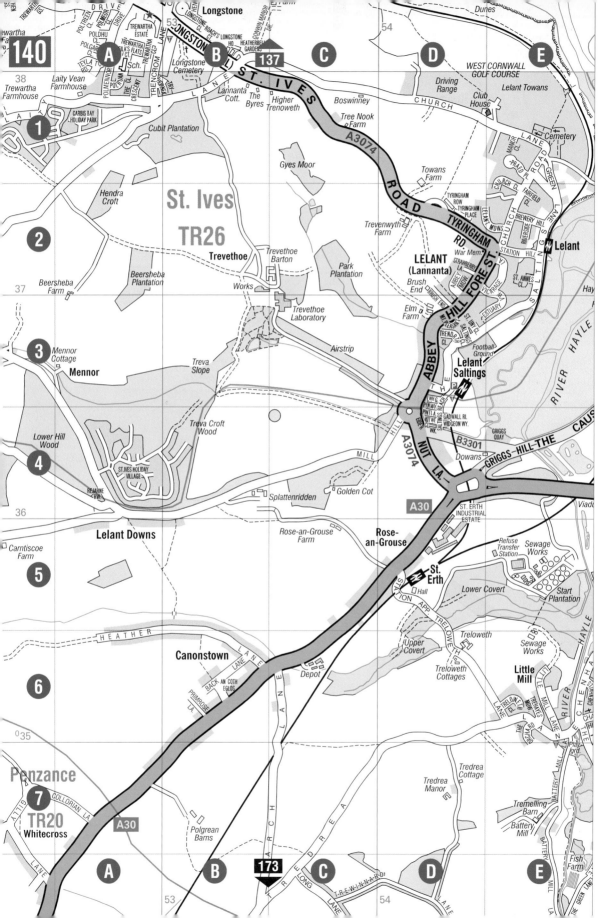

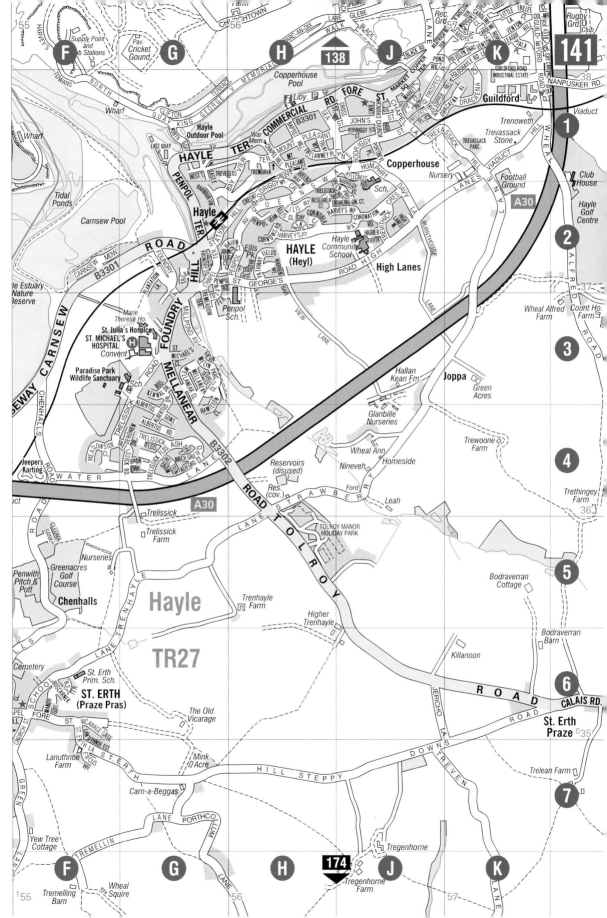

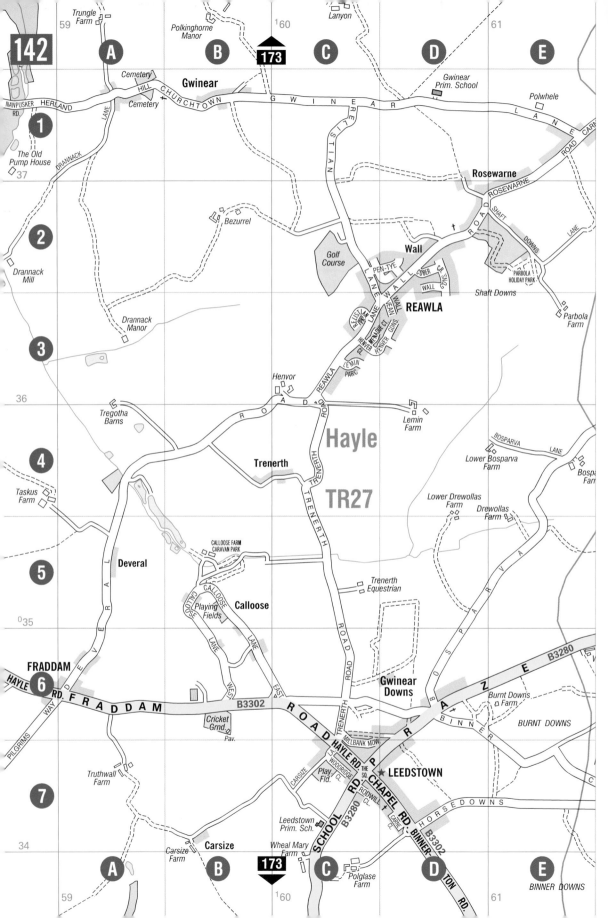

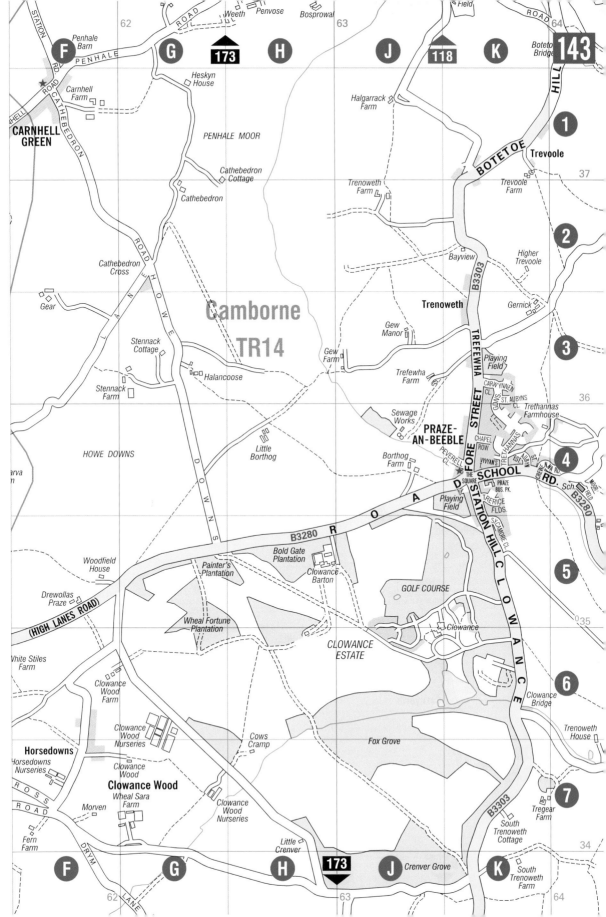

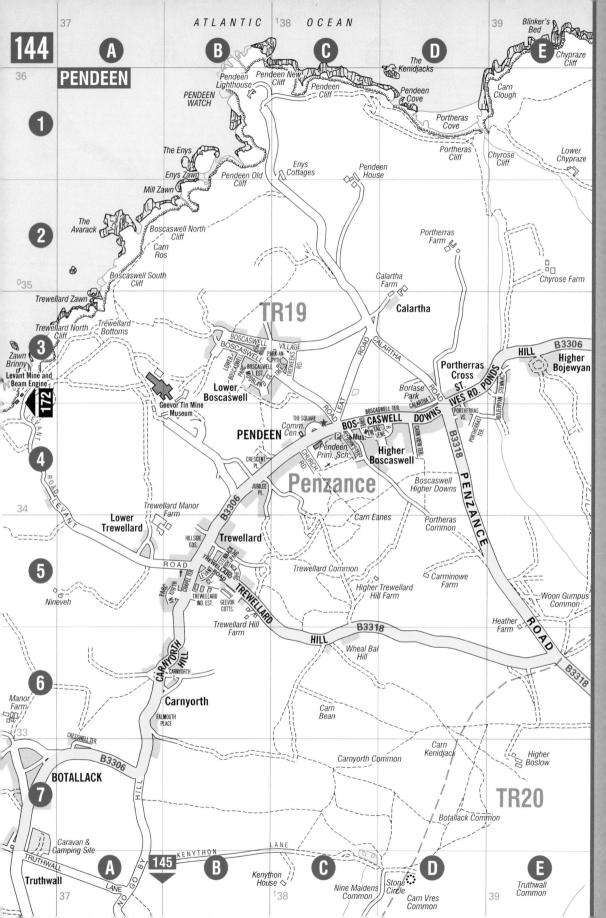

ATLANTIC OCEAN

A B C D E

37 138 39

36

1

2

035

3

34

4

5

6

33

7

A 145 B C D E

37 138 39

Penzance

PENDEEN

TR19

TR20

Blinker's Bed
Chypraze Cliff
Carn Clough
Lower Chypraze
Chyrose Cliff
Chyrose Farm

The Kenidjacks
Pendeen Cove
Porthcras Cove
Portheras Cliff

Pendeen New Cliff
Pendeen Cliff
Pendeen House
Portherras Farm

Pendeen Lighthouse
PENDEEN WATCH
Enys Cottages

The Enys
Enys Zawn
Pendeen Old Cliff
Mill Zawn

The Avarack
Boscaswell North Cliff
Carn Ros
Boscaswell South Cliff

Trewellard Zawn
Trewellard North Cliff
Trewellard Bottoms

Zawn Brinny
Levant Mine and Beam Engine
172

Geevor Tin Mine Museum

BOSCASWELL
LOWER BOSCASWELL
PARC-AN-PYTH
VILLAGE
TREWEEKS RD.
MOORLAND
BOSCASWELL EST

Lower Boscaswell

Calartha Farm
Calartha

Borlase Park

Portherras Cross
ST. IVES RD.
HILL
B3306
Higher Bojewyan
PONDS
BOJEWYAN STENNACK
PORTHERRAS VS.
PORTHERRAS TER.

THE SQUARE
Comm. Cen.
BOS CASWELL DOWNS
Higher Boscaswell
Boscaswell Higher Downs

Pendeen Prim. Sch.
Mus.
CHURCH RD.
CRESCENT PL.
JUBILEE PL.

Carn Eanes
Portheras Common
Carminowe Farm

Woon Gumpus Common

ROAD LEVANT
Lower Trewellard
Trewellard Manor Farm
HILLSIDE GDS.
Trewellard
TREWELLARD IND. EST.
GEEVOR COTTS.
CHAPEL TER.
PARC AN VORTH

Trewellard Common
Higher Trewellard Hill Farm

Heather Farm

Nineveh

Trewellard Hill Farm
TREWELLARD HILL
B3318
Wheal Bal Hill

CARNWORTH HILL
Carnworth
Carnyorth
FALMOUTH PLACE

Carn Bean
Carn Kenidjack
Carn Kenidjack
Higher Boslow

Manor Farm
CRESSWELL TER.
B3306
BOTALLACK
HILL

Carnyorth Common
Botallack Common

Caravan & Camping Site
TRUTHWALL LANE
NO GO BY LANE
KENYTHON LANE

Kenython House
Nine Maidens Common
Stone Circle
Carn Vres Common

Truthwall
Truthwall Common

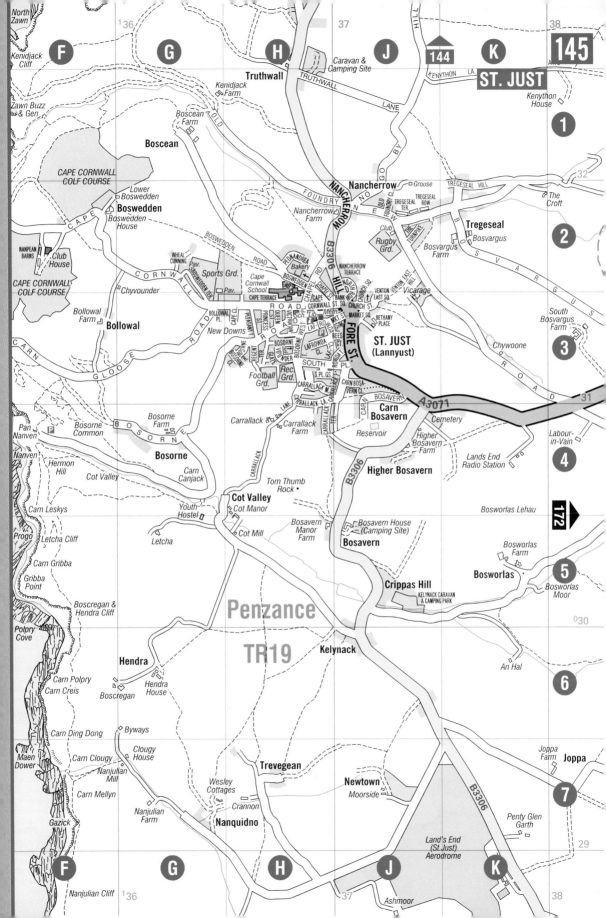

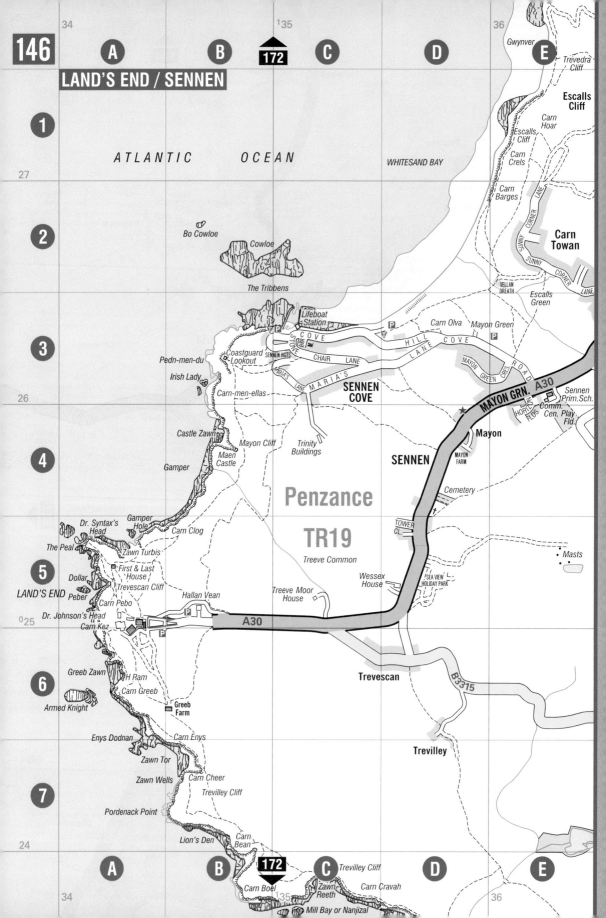

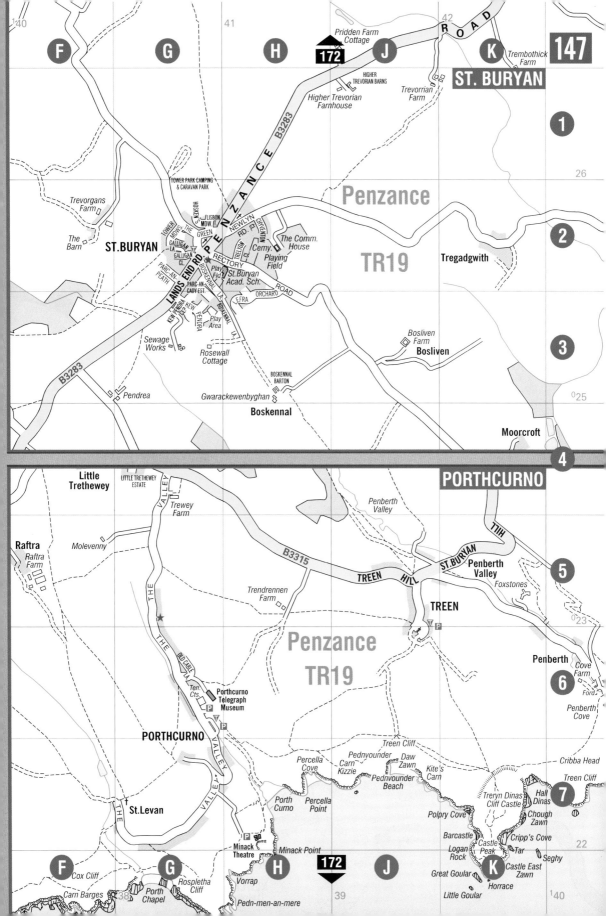

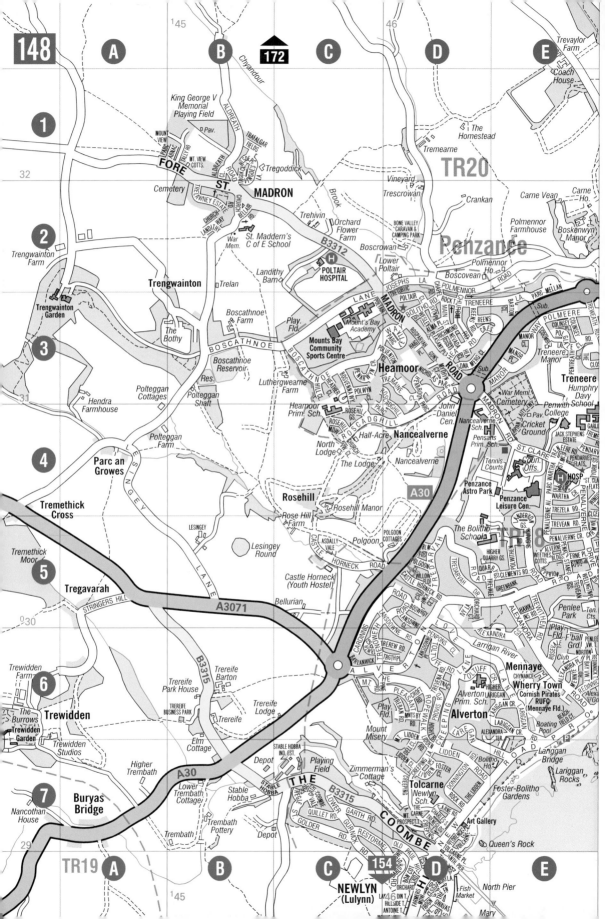

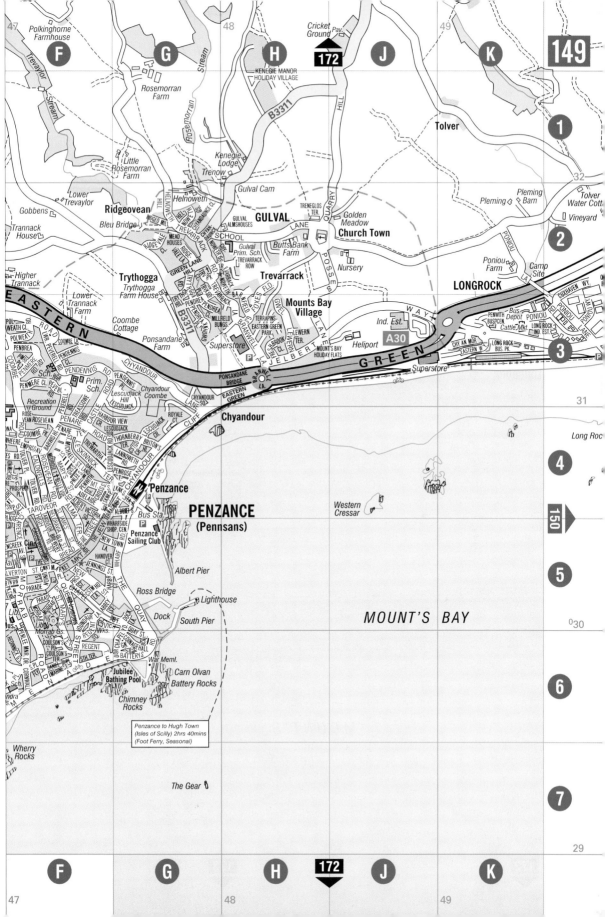

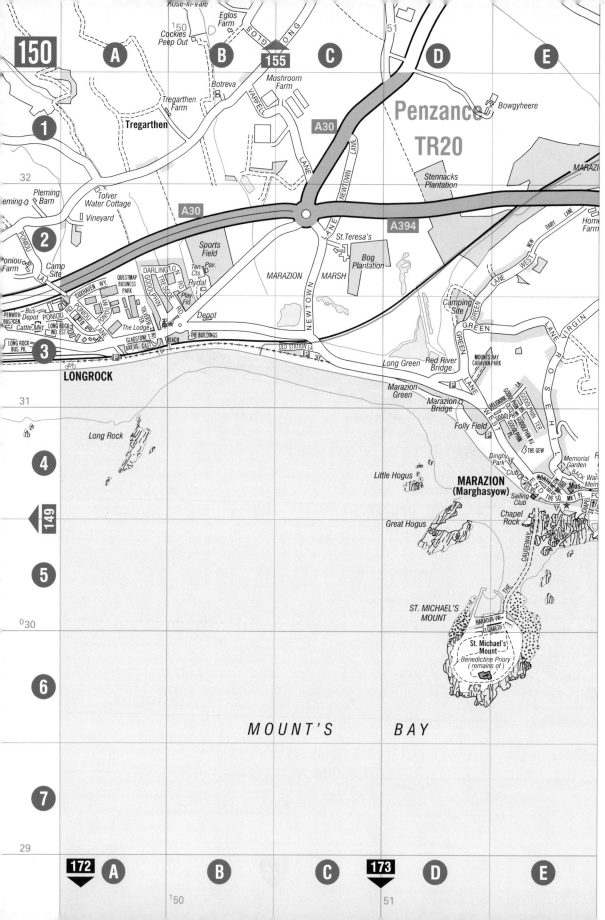

150

A B **155** C D E

1

Rose-in-Vale
Eglos Farm
Cockies Peep Out
150
Botreva
Tregarthen Farm
Tregarthen
Mushroom Farm

Penzance
TR20

Bowgyheere

A30

32

Stennacks Plantation

MARAZI

Fleming
Pleming Barn
Tolver Water Cottage
Vineyard

A30

A394

Home Farm

St.Teresa's

2

Poniou Farm
Camp Site

Sports Field

Bog Plantation

DAIRY LANE

Questmap Business Park
DARLINGTON RD
Pav.
Ten-Cts.
Rydal
Play Fld.

Camping Site

Bus Depot
PENWITH BUS GEN.
Cattle. Mkt.
The Lodge
LONG ROCK IND. EST.
Depot

MARAZION
MARSH

MOUNTS BAY CARAVAN PARK

3

LONG ROCK BUS. PK.
GLADSTONE T.
BAY.VS. CASTV
BEACH
THE BUILDINGS
OLD STATION LA.

LONGROCK

Long Green
Red River Bridge

Marazion Green
Marazion Bridge

Folly Field

THE GEW

31

Long Rock

4

Little Hogus

Dinghy Park
Club
Memorial Garden

MARAZION
(Marghasyow)
Mus

149

Sailing Club

5

Great Hogus

Chapel Rock

30

ST. MICHAEL'S
MOUNT

HARBOUR VW.
ELIZABETH T.

6

St. Michael's
Mount
Benedictine Priory
(remains of)

M O U N T ' S   B A Y

7

29

172 A B C **173** D E

150 51

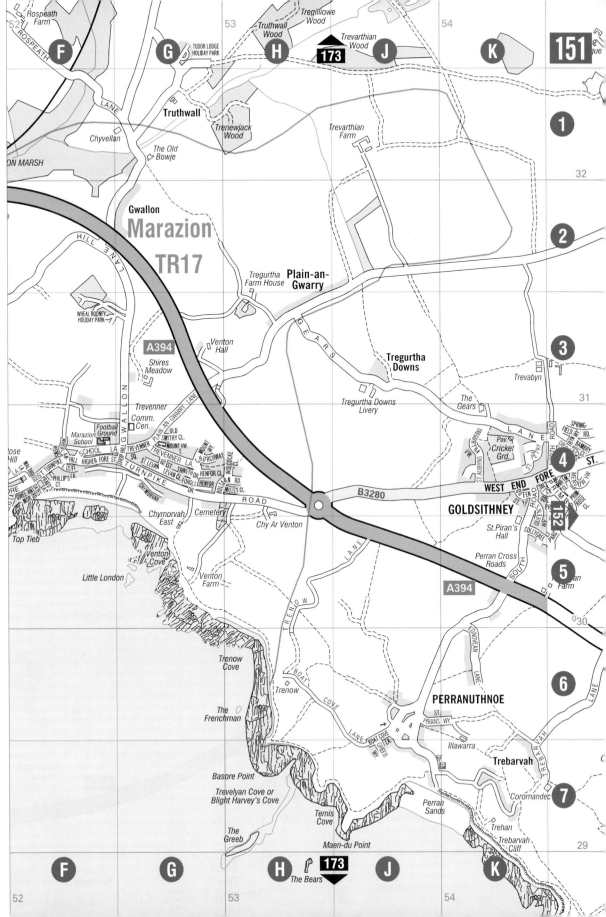

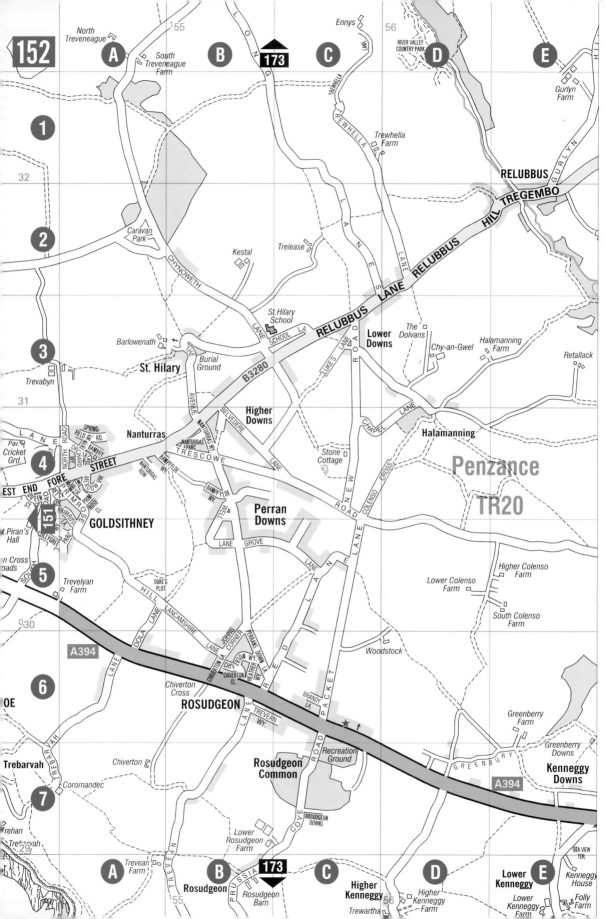

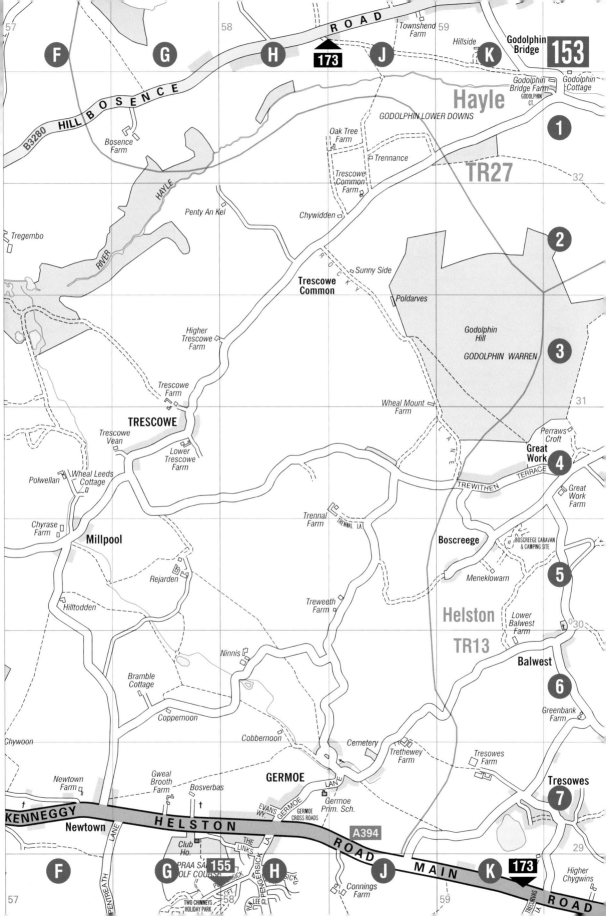

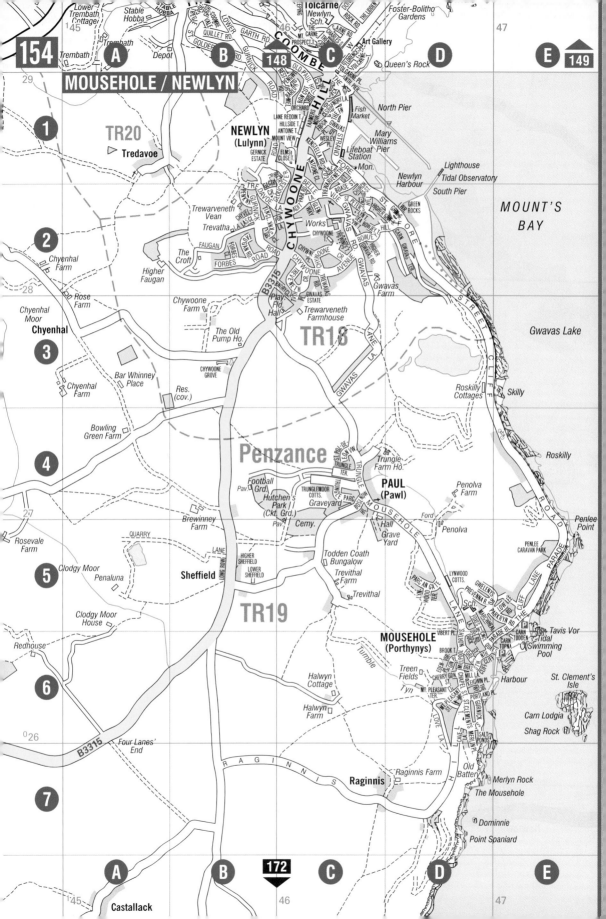

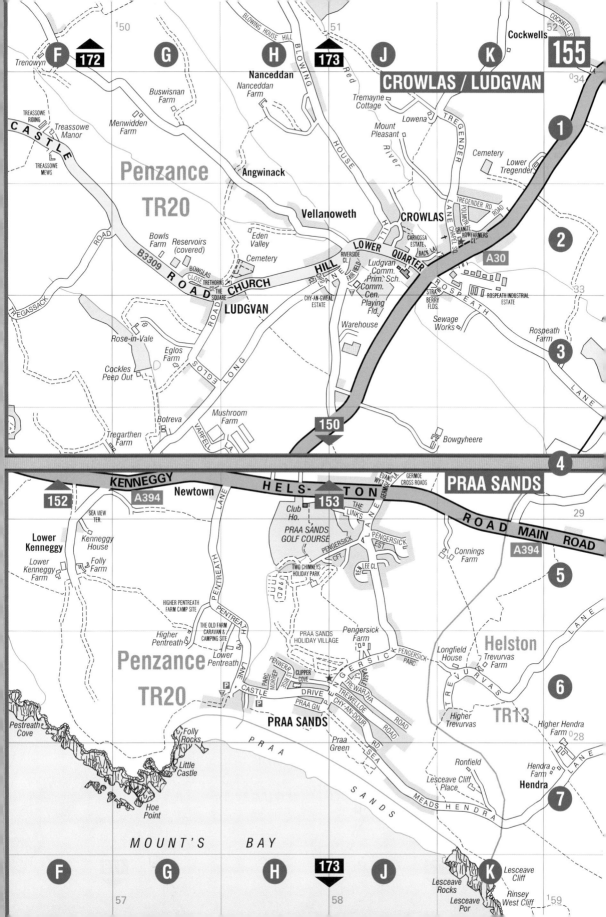

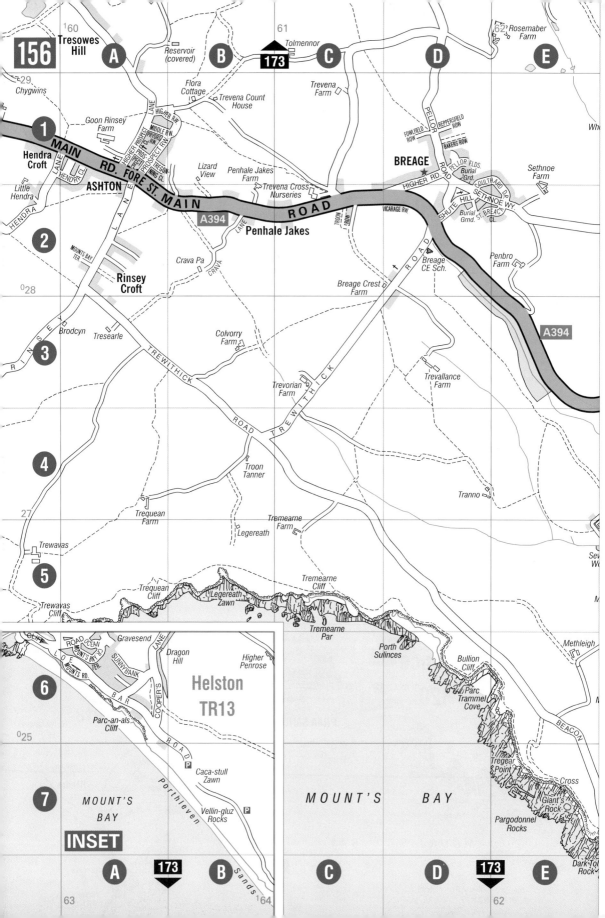

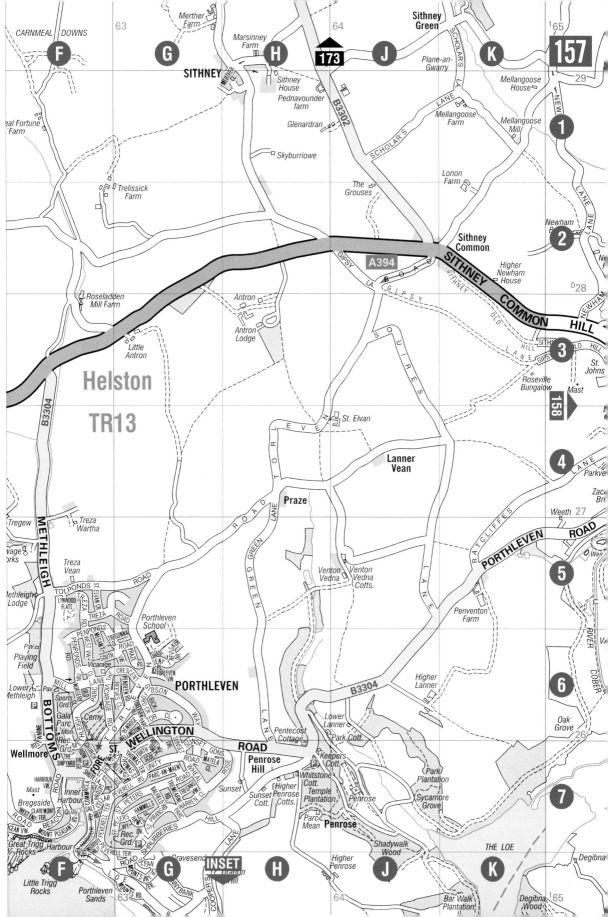

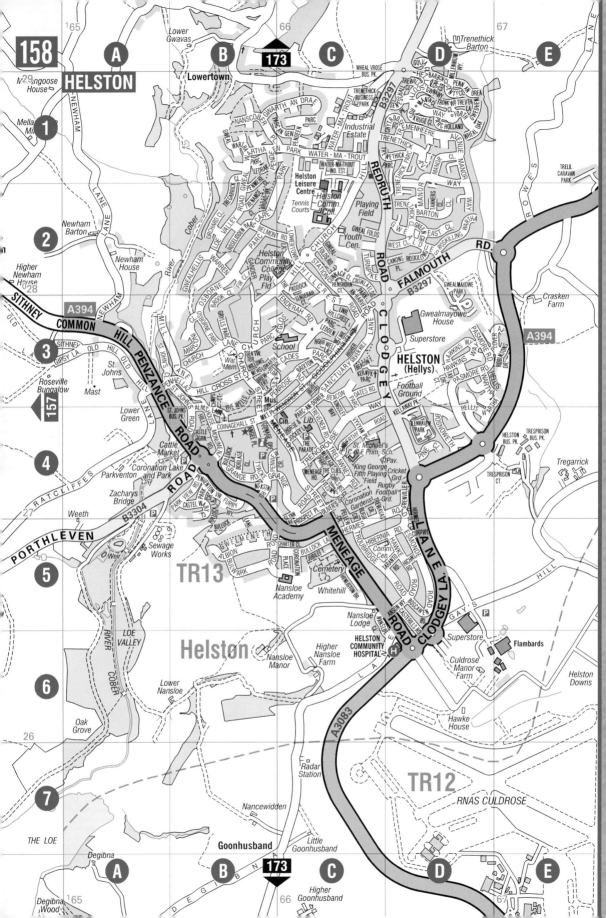

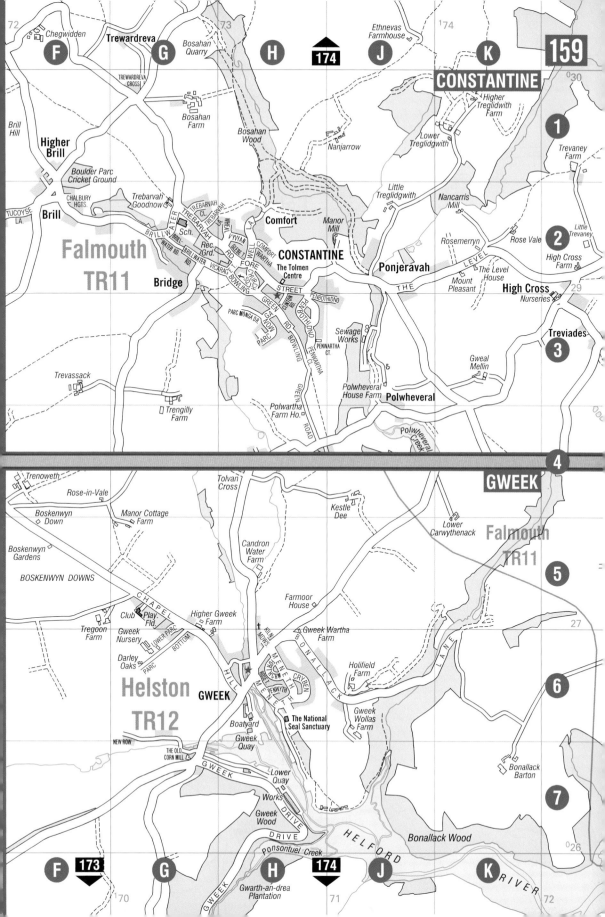

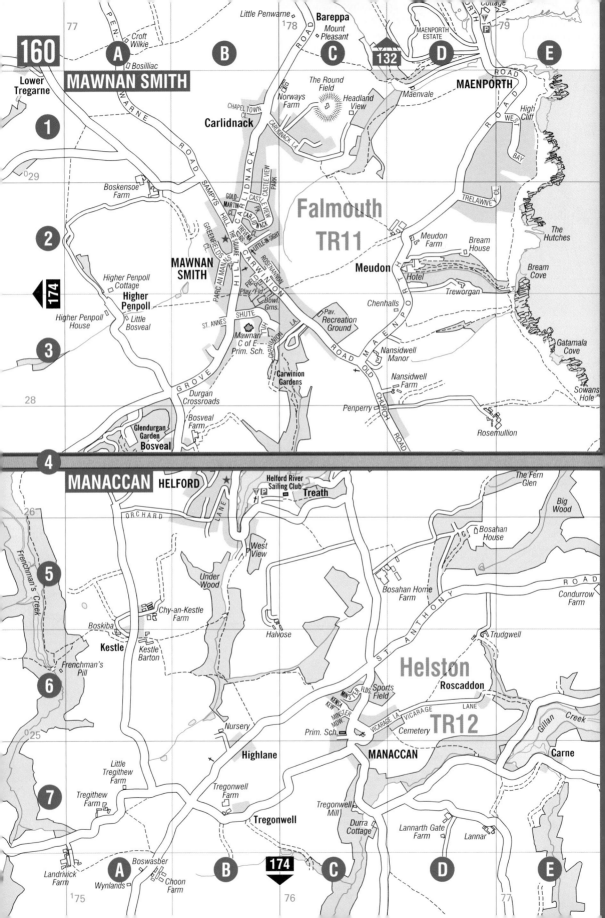

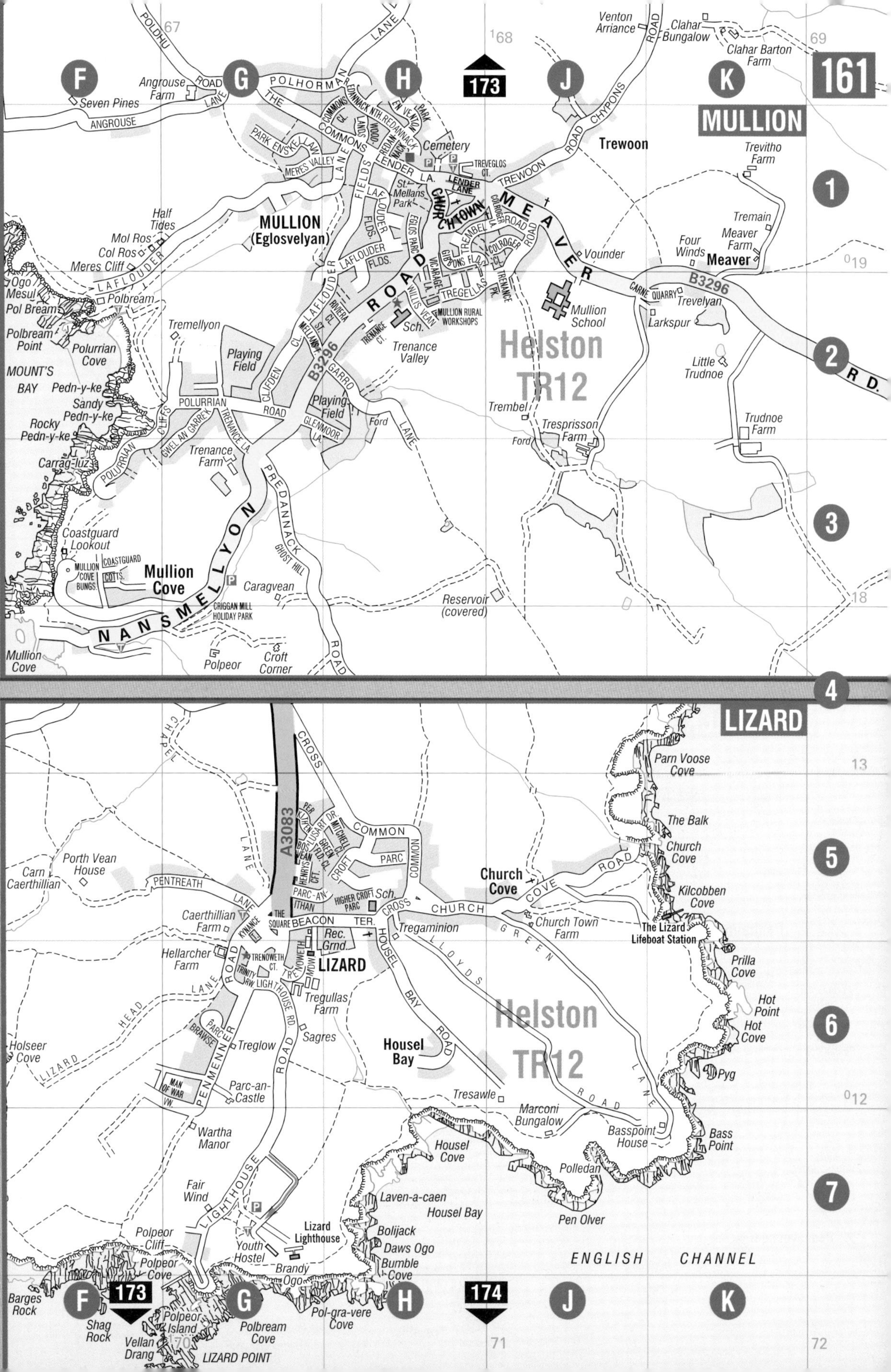

MULLION
LIZARD
173
174
Helston TR12
MULLION (Eglosvelyan)
Mullion Cove
Trewoon
Meaver
Meaver Farm
Four Winds
Tremain
Trevitho Farm
Venton Arriance
Clahar Bungalow
Clahar Barton Farm
Angrouse Farm
Seven Pines
Cemetery
Mullion School
Vounder
Trevelyan
Larkspur
Little Trudnoe
Trudnoe Farm
Trembel
Tresprisson Farm
Ford
Trenance Valley
Mullion Rural Workshops
Sch.
Playing Field
Tremellyon
Half Tides
Mol Ros
Col Ros
Meres Cliff
Ogo Mesul
Pol Bream
Polbream
Polbream Point
Polurrian Cove
MOUNT'S BAY
Pedn-y-ke
Sandy Pedn-y-ke
Rocky Pedn-y-ke
Carrag-luz
Trenance Farm
Coastguard Lookout
Mullion Cove Bungs.
Coastguard Cotts.
Caragvean
Criggan Mill Holiday Park
Reservoir (covered)
Polpeor
Croft Corner
B3296
NANSMELLYON
PREDANNACK
GHOST HILL
POLHORMAN LANE
POLDHU ROAD
ANGROUSE LANE
LAFLOUDER
CHURCHTOWN
MEAVER ROAD
CHYPONS ROAD
TREWOON
LENDER LA.
POLURRIAN ROAD
A3083
Parn Voose Cove
The Balk
Church Cove
Kilcobben Cove
The Lizard Lifeboat Station
Prilla Cove
Hot Point
Hot Cove
Pyg
Bass Point
Basspoint House
Marconi Bungalow
Tresawle
Polledan
Pen Olver
Housel Bay
Housel Cove
Laven-a-caen
Bolijack
Daws Ogo
Bumble Cove
Pol-gra-vere Cove
Brandy Ogo
Lizard Lighthouse
Youth Hostel
Polpeor Cliff
Polpeor Cove
Polpeor Island
Polbream Cove
Vellan Drang
LIZARD POINT
Shag Rock
Barges Rock
Fair Wind
Wartha Manor
Parc-an-Castle
Treglow
Man of War Vw.
Sagres
Tregullas Farm
Tregaminion
Church Town Farm
Church Cove
Rec. Grnd.
Hellarcher Farm
Caerthillian Farm
Carn Caerthillian
Porth Vean House
Holseer Cove
ENGLISH CHANNEL
LIZARD HEAD LANE
PENNENNER
LIGHTHOUSE ROAD
HOUSEL BAY ROAD
CHURCH COVE ROAD
LLOYDS ROAD
GREEN LANE
PENTREATH LANE
BEACON TER.
THE SQUARE

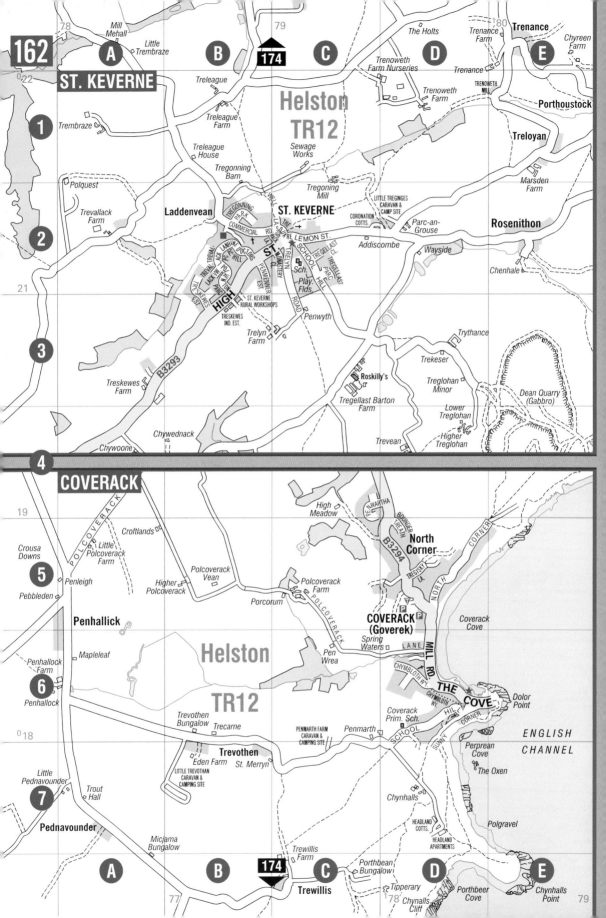

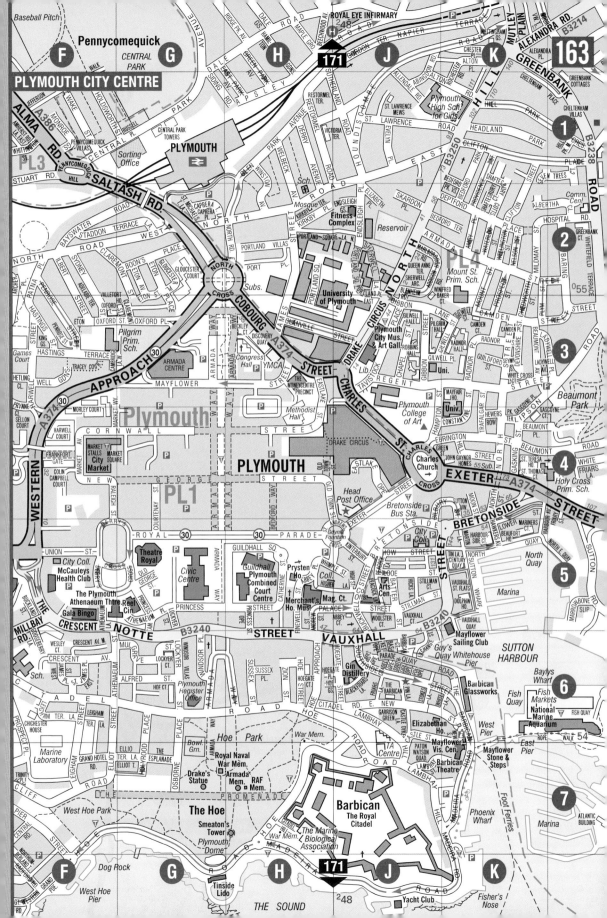

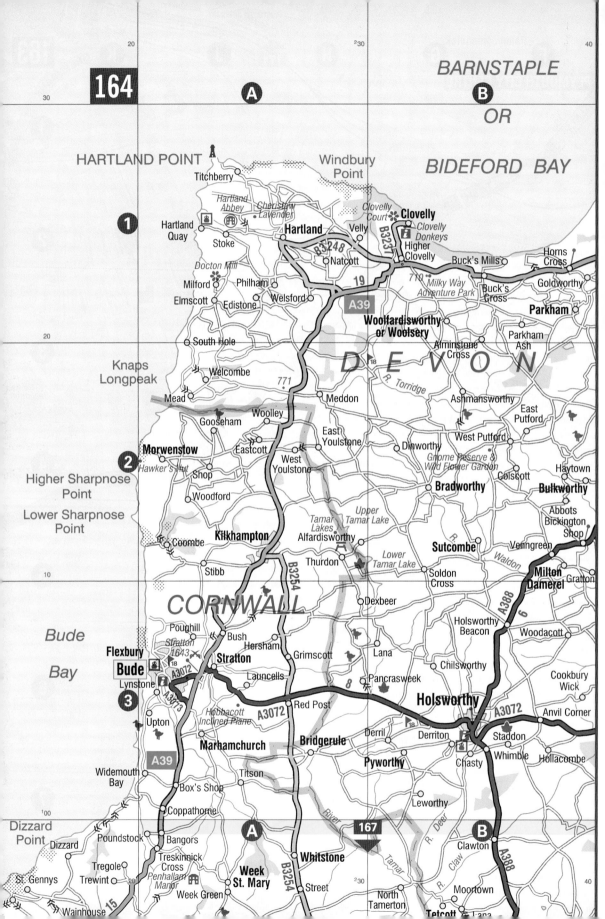

Ⓒ　　　　　　　Ⓓ

ATLANTIC　*OCEAN*

➊

90

Tintagel
Head　Bos
Tintagel
Tintagel

▶166

Treknow

*Gull
Rock*

Trebarwith

➋

Treligga　　De

*Port Isaac
Bay*　　Westdowns

Port　**Port**　Port
Quin　**Isaac**　Gaverne
*Lifeboat
Station*　　Trewetha
Long Cross　　B3314
Victorian　　geare
Porteath　　Rounds
Bee Centre　**Trelights**　Pendoggett

*Rumps
Point*　*The
Mouls*
Newland　Cliff
Castle　*Portquin
Bay*
Pentire Point

Padstow Bay　New　B3267
Polzeath
Polzeath　　St. Endellion　Trelill

*Gulland
Rock*　　Trebetherick　　18　　B3314　Chapel　St.
*Gunver
Head*　　Trevanger　　Amble　Kew
Plyme　**St.**
TREVOSE HEAD　*Lifeboat
Station*　Crugmeer　　Rock　**Minver**　Lower
Amble　　A39
Quies　Harlyn　**Trevone**　*Prideaux*　18　　➌　St. Kew
Bay　B3276　*Place*　Stoptide　　Highway
*Constantine
Bay*　Constantine
Bay　Treator　National
Lobster Hatchery　　Bodieve
Treyarnon　St.　　**Padstow**　**CORNWALL**
Merryn　Little　　Trevanson
14　Shop　Petherick　　**Wadebridge**　**St.**
Porthcothan　*Old
MacDonald's
Farm*　Trevance　Whitecross　St.　Egloshayle　**Mabyn**
St. Issey　7　Breock　　Croanford
Penrose　　Royal　Culverhouse　Pencarrow
Park Head　Treburrick　Trenance　*Cornwall
Showground*　Sladesbridge　A389
Rumford　*Mellingey Mill*　　Pawton
St.　Tredinnick　dgey　Burlawn
➤168 *Bedruthan
Steps*　Ⓒ　Ervan　*Crealy*　Ⓓ　➤169　Washaway
B3274　St. Breock
A39　Downs　Monolith　Polbrock
Berryl's Point　683　　*Camel Valley
Vineyard*
Mawgan　*Japanese*　Cornish　Nanstallon
Porth　Birds of Prey　Ruthernbridge
B327　Centre　Bodmin &
Wenford

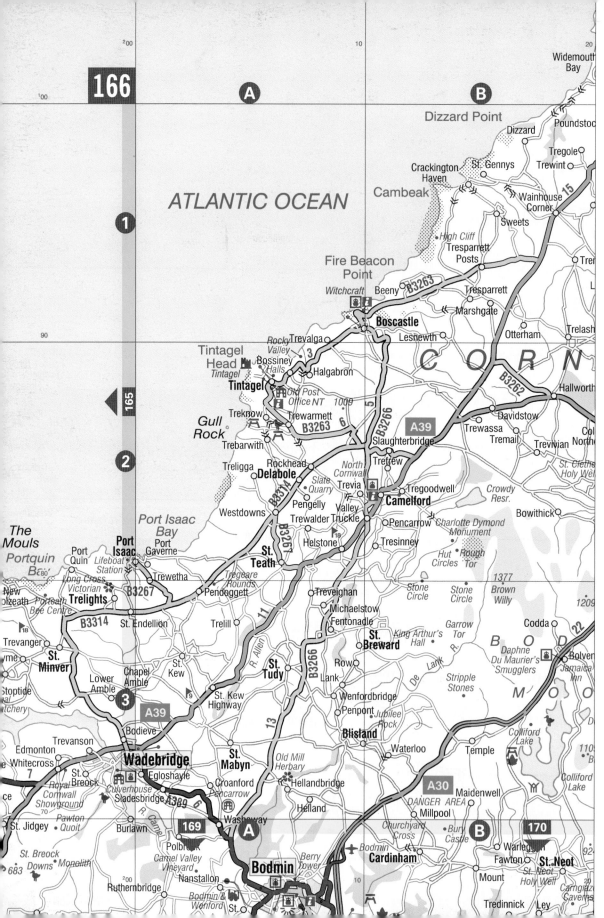

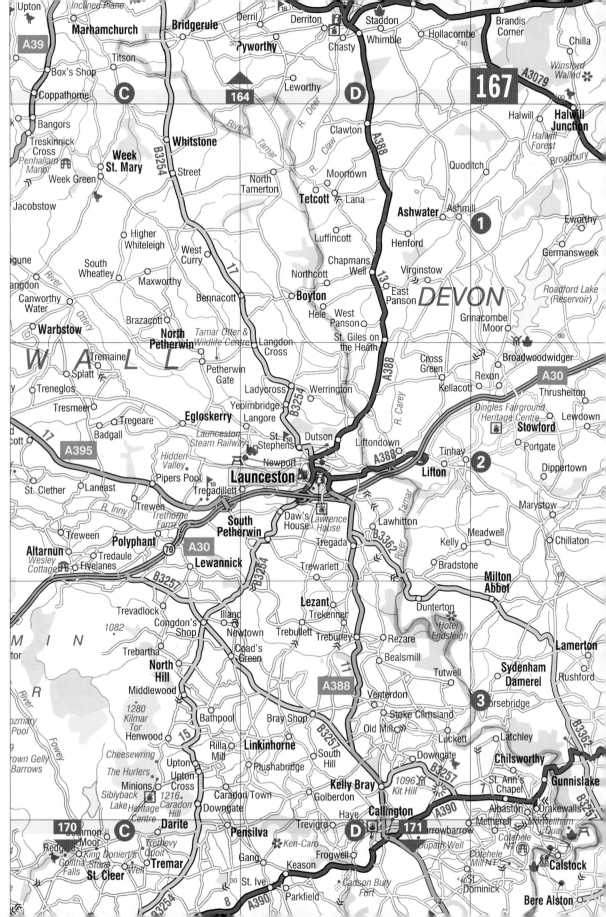

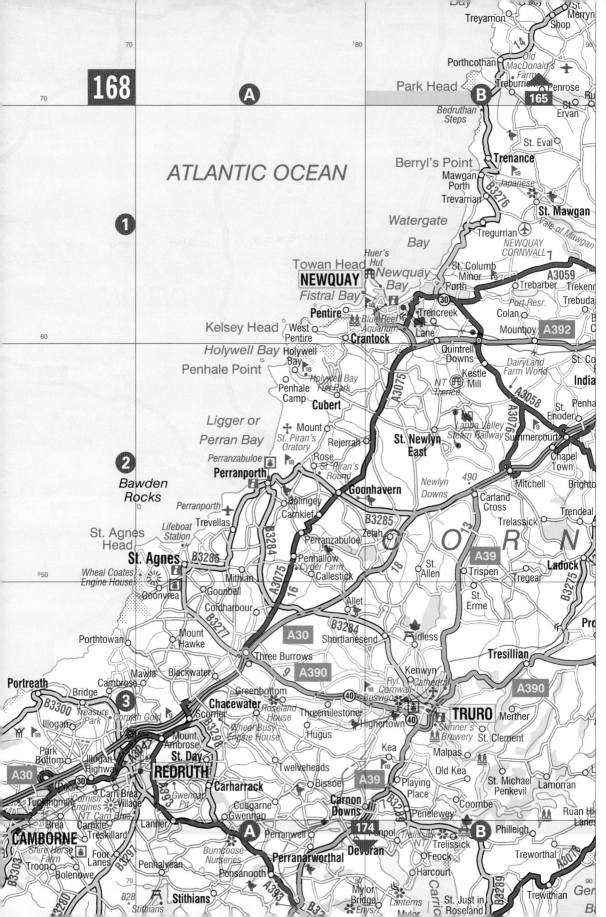

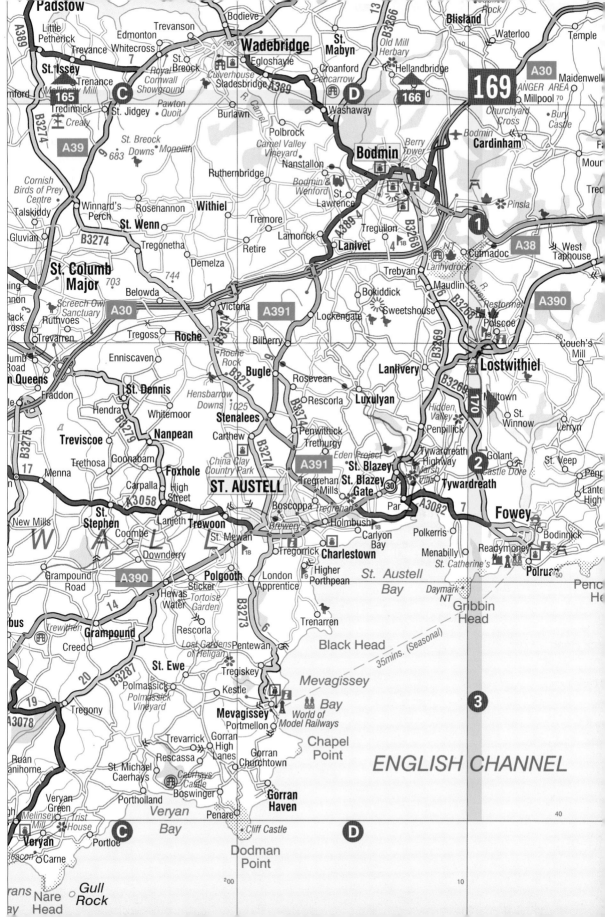

Padstow
Little Petherick
Trevance Whitecross
Edmonton
Trevanson
Bodieve
Blisland
Waterloo
Temple

A389
St. Issey
Trenance
Mellingey Mill
St. Breock
Wadebridge
Egloshayle
St. Mabyn
Croanford
Old Mill Herbary
Hellandbridge
A30
Maidenwell
Millpool 70

165
C
Tredinnick
St. Jidgey
Royal Cornwall Showground
Culverhouse
Sladesbridge
A389
Pencarrow
D
166 d
Churchyard Cross
Bury Castle

B3274
Creaty
A39
St. Breock Downs
Monolith
Burlawn
Washaway
169
ANGER AREA

Pawton Quoit
Polbrock
Camel Valley Vineyard
Nanstallon
Bodmin & Wenford
St. Lawrence
Bodmin
Berry Tower
Bodmin
Pinsla
Cardinham
Mour
Trec

Cornish Birds of Prey Centre
Winnard's Perch
Rosenannon
Withiel
Tremore
Ruthernbridge
Tregullon
NT
Lanhydrock
Cutmadoc
A38
West Taphouse

Talskiddy
Gluvian
St. Wenn
Tregonetha
Lamorick
Retire
A389
Lanivet
4 18
Trebyan
Maudlin
B3268
Restormel
A390

B3274
Demelza
744
St. Columb Major
703
Belowda
Victoria
A391
Bokiddick
Sweetshouse
Lanlivery
B3269
Polscoe
Couch's Mill

Screech Owl Sanctuary
A30
Tregoss
Roche
Bilberry
Rosevean
Rescorla
Luxulyan
Hidden Valley
Penpillick
St. Winnow
Lerryn

Ruthvoes
Trevarren
Enniscaven
Roche Rock
Bugle
Lostwithiel
170
Milltown

Queens
Fraddon
Hendra
Whitemoor
Stenalees
Carthew
Penwithick
Trethurgy
Eden Project
Tywardreath Highway
Golant
St. Veep
Penr

Treviscoe
Nanpean
China Clay Country Park
St. Blazey
Marsh Villa
Tywardreath
Castle Dore
Lante High

Trethosa
Goonabarn
Foxhole
High Street
Tregrehan Mills
St. Blazey Gate
30
Par
A3082
Fowey
Bodinnick

Menna
Carpalla
ST. AUSTELL
Boscoppa
Holmbush
Carlyon Bay
Polkerris
Readymoney
Polruan

St. Stephen
Lanjeth
Trewoon
St. Mewan
Brewery
18
Tregorrick
Charlestown
Menabilly
St. Catherine's
50

Coombe
Downderry
London Apprentice
Higher Porthpean
St. Austell Bay
Daymark NT
Gribbin Head

Grampound Road
A390
Sticker
Tortoise Garden
Trenarren
35mins. (Seasonal)

Hewas Water
Rescorla
Grampound
Creed
Pentewan
Black Head

Tregiskey
Lost Gardens of Heligan
Mevagissey Bay

St. Ewe
Polmassick
Polmassick Vineyard
Kestle
World of Model Railways
Chapel Point

Tregony
Mevagissey
Portmellon

ENGLISH CHANNEL

Trevarrick
Gorran High Lanes
Gorran Churchtown

Rescassa
St. Michael Caerhays
Caerhays Castle
Boswinger
Gorran Haven

Veryan Green
Trist House
Portholland
Veryan Bay
Penare
Cliff Castle

Veryan
Portloe
C
D
Dodman Point

Nare Head
Gull Rock

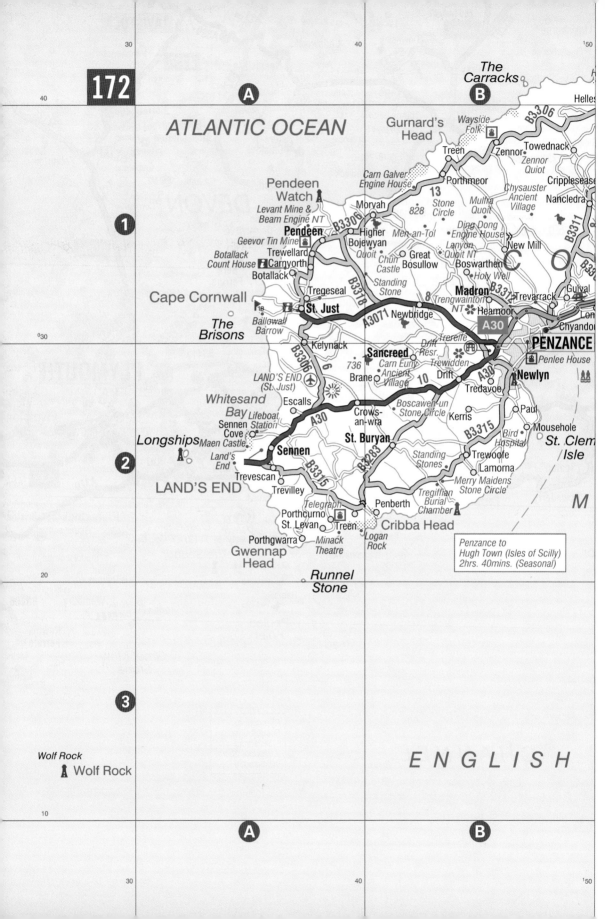

Ⓐ

Ⓑ

The
Carracks

Helles

ATLANTIC OCEAN

Gurnard's
Head

Wayside
Folk

B3306

Treen

Zennor

Towednack

Zennor
Quiot

Carn Galver
Engine House

Porthmeor

Crippleseas

Pendeen
Watch

13

Stone
Circle

Chysauster
Ancient
Village

Nancledra

Levant Mine &
Beam Engine NT

Morvah

828

Mulfra
Quiot

1

B3306

Higher
Bojewyan

Men-an-Tol

Ding Dong
Engine House

C

Pendeen

Quoit

Lanyon
Quoit NT

New Mill

O

Trewellard

Great
Bosullow

Boswarthen

Chûn
Castle

B3311

Geevor Tin Mine

Holy Well

B33

Botallack
Count House

Carnyorth

Standing
Stone

8

Madron

Trengwainton
NT

Trevarrack

Gulval

Botallack

Tregeseal

B3318

A3071

Newbridge

Heamoor

A30

Lon

Chyandor

Cape Cornwall

18

St. Just

Trereife

PENZANCE

The
Brisons

Ballowall
Barrow

B3306

Kelynack

Drift
Resr.

Trewidden

Penlee House

6

Sancreed

736

Carn Euny
Ancient
Village

Drift

Newlyn

10

LAND'S END
(St. Just)

Brane

Escalls

Boscawen-un
Stone Circle

Tredavoe

Paul

Whitesand
Bay

Crows-
an-wra

A30

Kerris

B3315

Mousehole

Longships

Lifeboat
Sennen
Cove

Maen Castle

St. Buryan

Bird
Hospital

St. Clem
Isle

2

Land's
End

Sennen

B3315

B3283

Standing
Stones

Trewoofe

Lamorna

M

LAND'S END

Trevescan

Trevilley

Merry Maidens
Stone Circle

Telegraph

Porthcurno

Penberth

Tregiffian
Burial
Chamber

St. Levan

Treen

Cribba Head

Porthgwarra

Minack
Theatre

Logan
Rock

Gwennap
Head

Runnel
Stone

Penzance to
Hugh Town (Isles of Scilly)
2hrs. 40mins. (Seasonal)

3

E N G L I S H

Wolf Rock

🚨 Wolf Rock

Ⓐ

Ⓑ

40

30

40

¹50

°30

20

30

40

50

10

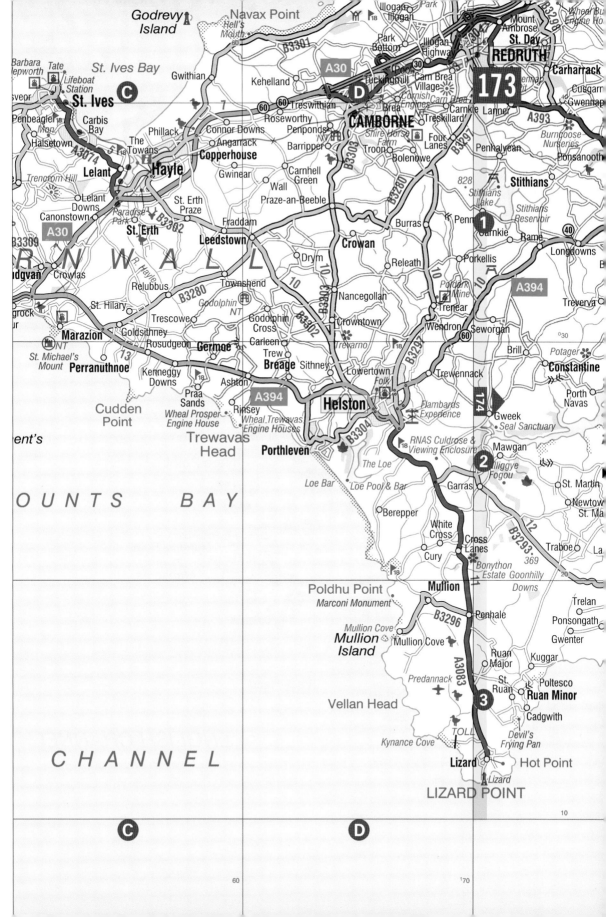

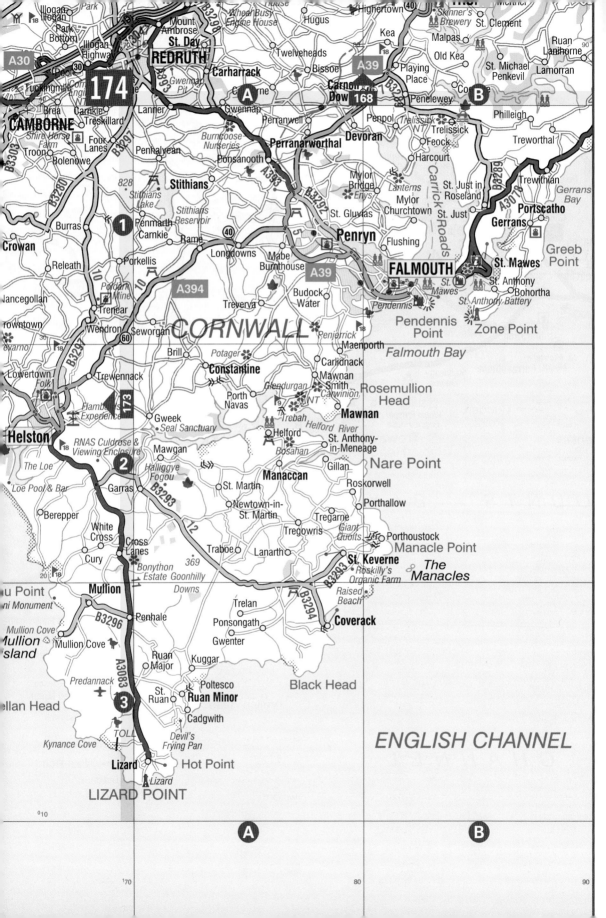

INDEX

Including Streets, Places & Areas, Industrial Estates,
Selected Flats & Walkways, Service Areas, Stations and Selected Places of Interest.

HOW TO USE THIS INDEX

1. Each street name is followed by its Postcode District, then by its Locality abbreviation(s) and then by its map reference;
   e.g. **Abbey Hill** TR26: Lel . . . .3D **140** is in the TR26 Postcode District and the Lelant Locality and is to be found in square 3D on page **140**.
   The page number is shown in bold type.

2. A strict alphabetical order is followed in which Av., Rd., St., etc. (though abbreviated) are read in full and as part of the street name;
   e.g. **Bellevue Cotts.** appears after **Belle Vue Av.** but before **Belle Vue La.**

3. Streets and a selection of flats and walkways that cannot be shown on street map pages **6-163**, appear in the index with the thoroughfare to which they are connected shown in brackets; e.g. **Abbey Pl.** *TR19: Mou* . . . . 6D **154** (off North Cliff)

4. Addresses that are in more than one part are referred to as not continuous.

5. Places and areas are shown in the index in **BLUE TYPE** and the map reference is to the actual map square in which the town centre or area is located and not to the place name shown on the map. Map references for entries that appear on street map pages **6-163** are shown first, with references to road map pages **164-174** shown in brackets;
   e.g. **CALENICK** 1J **117**

6. An example of a selected place of interest is **Bodmin Mus.** 4G **33**

7. An example of a station is **Bugle Station (Rail)** . . . . 6H **43**. Included are Rail **(Rail)**, Park & Float and Park & Ride.
   e.g. **Eden Project (Park & Ride)** 7D **50**

8. Service Areas are shown in the index in **BOLD CAPITAL TYPE**; e.g. **SALTASH SERVICE AREA** 7E **84**

9. Map references for entries that appear on large scale pages **81**, **137** & **163** are shown first, with small scale map references shown in brackets;
   e.g. **Ayr La.** TR26: St Ives 2H **137** (2D **136**)

GENERAL ABBREVIATIONS

All. : Alley	**Cft.** : Croft	**Lit.** : Little	**Rdbt.** : Roundabout
App. : Approach	**Dr.** : Drive	**Lwr.** : Lower	**Shop.** : Shopping
Arc. : Arcade	**E.** : East	**Mnr.** : Manor	**Sth.** : South
Av. : Avenue	**Ent.** : Enterprise	**Mkt.** : Market	**Sq.** : Square
Bk. : Back	**Est.** : Estate	**Mdw.** : Meadow	**Sta.** : Station
Bri. : Bridge	**Fld.** : Field	**Mdws.** : Meadows	**St.** : Street
Bldg. : Building	**Flds.** : Fields	**M.** : Mews	**Ter.** : Terrace
Bldgs. : Buildings	**Gdn.** : Garden	**Mt.** : Mount	**Twr.** : Tower
Bungs. : Bungalows	**Gdns.** : Gardens	**Mus.** : Museum	**Trad.** : Trading
Bus. : Business	**Ga.** : Gate	**Nth.** : North	**Up.** : Upper
Cen. : Centre	**Gt.** : Great	**No.** : Number	**Va.** : Vale
Chu. : Church	**Grn.** : Green	**Pal.** : Palace	**Vw.** : View
Cir. : Circus	**Gro.** : Grove	**Pde.** : Parade	**Vs.** : Villas
Cl. : Close	**Hgts.** : Heights	**Pk.** : Park	**Vis.** : Visitors
Comn. : Common	**Ho.** : House	**Pas.** : Passage	**Wlk.** : Walk
Cnr. : Corner	**Ho's.** : Houses	**Pl.** : Place	**W.** : West
Cotts. : Cottages	**Ind.** : Industrial	**Prom.** : Promenade	**Yd.** : Yard
Ct. : Court	**Info.** : Information	**Ri.** : Rise	
Cres. : Crescent	**La.** : Lane	**Rd.** : Road	

LOCALITY ABBREVIATIONS

Alb : **Albaston**	Carn : **Carnkie**	Fow : **Fowey**	I Hig : **Illogan Highway**
Allet : **Allet**	C Mar : **Carn Marth**	Fox : **Foxhole**	I Que : **Indian Queens**
Ang : **Angarrack**	C Dow : **Carnon Downs**	Fr'ham : **Fraddam**	Kea : **Kea**
Ant : **Antony**	Caws : **Cawsand**	Fr'don : **Fraddon**	K Bray : **Kelly Bray**
Ash : **Ashton**	Chac : **Chacewater**	Ger : **Germoe**	Ken : **Kenwyn**
Baldh : **Baldhu**	Char : **Charlestown**	Gerr : **Gerrans**	Kil : **Kilhallon**
Barr : **Barripper**	Chils : **Chilsworthy**	Glo : **Gloweth**	Kilkh : **Kilkhampton**
Bea : **Beacon**	Cleer : **Cleers**	Gola : **Golant**	Kill : **Killivose**
B'vey : **Biscovey**	Cocks : **Cocks**	Gold : **Goldsithney**	King : **Kingsand**
Biss : **Bissoe**	Cockw : **Cockwells**	Goona : **Goonabarn**	Lad : **Ladock**
Black : **Blackwater**	Con D : **Connor Downs**	Goonb : **Goonbell**	Land : **Landrake**
B'lva : **Bodelva**	Const : **Constantine**	G Gump : **Goon Gumpas**	Lane : **Lane**
B'eve : **Bodieve**	Cons B : **Constantine Bay**	Goonh : **Goonhavern**	L'scot : **Lanescot**
B'ick : **Bodinnick**	Coomb : **Coombe**	Goonm : **Goonmarris**	L'ock : **Lanhydrock**
B'min : **Bodmin**	Cover : **Coverack**	Gorr : **Gorran**	Lani : **Lanivet**
Bol : **Bolingey**	Cox : **Coxpark**	G Hav : **Gorran Haven**	Lanj : **Lanjeth**
Bosc : **Boscastle**	Craft : **Crafthole**	Goth : **Gothars**	Lanl : **Lanlivery**
Bosl : **Bosleake**	Cran : **Crantock**	G Val : **Gover Valley**	L'ner : **Lanner**
Boss : **Bossiney**	Crof : **Crofthandy**	Gram : **Grampound**	I'los : **Lansallos**
Bota : **Botallack**	Crow : **Crowlas**	Gram R : **Grampound Road**	Laun : **Launceston**
Bot F : **Botus Fleming**	C Nes : **Crows Nest**	Green : **Greensplat**	Leeds : **Leedstown**
Bre : **Brea**	Cube : **Cubert**	Gul : **Gulval**	Lel : **Lelant**
Breag : **Breage**	Curr V : **Currian Vale**	G'thy : **Gulworthy**	L Dow : **Lelant Downs**
Brid : **Bridge**	Cusg : **Cusgarne**	Gun : **Gunnislake**	Lisk : **Liskeard**
Bud : **Bude**	Dar : **Darite**	Gweek : **Gweek**	Lizar : **Lizard**
B Wat : **Budock Water**	Dela : **Delabole**	Gwen : **Gwennap**	Log : **Loggans**
Bugl : **Bugle**	Devi : **Deviock**	Gwinn : **Gwinnear**	Lon A : **London Apprentice**
Burr : **Burras**	Devo : **Devoran**	Gwith : **Gwithian**	Longd : **Longdowns**
Bus : **Bush**	Dob : **Dobwalls**	Hal : **Halsetown**	L Roc : **Long Rock**
Cale : **Calenick**	Doubl : **Doublebois**	H Bay : **Harlyn Bay**	Loo : **Looe**
Call : **Callington**	Downd : **Downderry**	Harr : **Harrowbarrow**	Los : **Lostwithiel**
Cals : **Calstock**	Downg : **Downgate**	Hatt : **Hatt**	L'twn : **Lowertown**
Camb : **Camborne**	Dra : **Drakewalls**	Haye : **Haye**	Ludg : **Ludgvan**
Came : **Camelford**	Duloe : **Duloe**	Hayl : **Hayle**	Lux : **Luxulyan**
Can : **Canonstown**	Dun : **Dunmere**	Hea : **Heamoor**	Lyn : **Lynstone**
C Bay : **Carbis Bay**	Dup : **Duporth**	Helf : **Helford**	M Bur : **Mabe Burnthouse**
Carg : **Cargreen**	Edmon : **Edmonton**	Helst : **Helston**	Mad : **Madron**
Carh : **Carharrack**	Eglo : **Egloshayle**	H Cft : **Hendra Croft**	Maen : **Maenporth**
Cark : **Carkeel**	Fal : **Falmouth**	Hern : **Hernis**	Mae : **Maer**
Carl : **Carlyon Bay**	Feo : **Feock**	Hew W : **Hewas Water**	Mal : **Malpas**
Carm : **Carminow Cross**	Flex : **Flexbury**	H St : **High Street**	Mana : **Manaccan**
C Bre : **Carn Brea**	Flu : **Flushing**	Hol B : **Holywell Bay**	Mar : **Marazion**
C Grn : **Carnhell Green**	Four L : **Four Lanes**	I'gan : **Illogan**	March : **Marhamchurch**

A-Z Cornwall Atlas 175

Locality Abbreviations

M Por : **Mawgan Porth**
Mawn S : **Mawnan Smith**
Menh : **Menheniot**
Merry : **Merrymeet**
Meth : **Metherell**
Mev : **Mevagissey**
Mill : **Millandreath**
M'brk : **Millbrook**
Moo : **Moorswater**
Mt Ed : **Mount Edgcumbe**
Mt Hwk : **Mount Hawke**
Mou : **Mousehole**
Mull : **Mullion**
M Bri : **Mylor Bridge**
M Chu : **Mylor Churchtown**
Nanc : **Nancekuke**
Nanp : **Nanpean**
Nans : **Nanstallon**
Nark : **Narkurs**
Newb : **Newbridge**
Newl : **Newlyn**
Newm : **Newmills**
N Pol : **New Polzeath**
Newq : **Newquay**
Nott : **Notter**
Pad : **Padstow**
Par : **Par**
P Bot : **Park Bottom**
Pau : **Paul**
Pely : **Pelynt**
Penb : **Penberth**
Pend : **Pendeen**
Pen Gn : **Pengover Green**
P'ale : **Penhale**
Penp : **Penpillick**
P'nds : **Penponds**
P'ose : **Penrose**
P'ryn : **Penryn**
Pens : **Pensilva**
Pent : **Pentewan**
Penw : **Penwithick**
Penz : **Penzance**
P'hal : **Perranarworthal**
P'mbe : **Perrancoombe**
P'rth : **Perranporth**
Perran : **Perranuthnoe**
P Sta : **Perranwell Station**
Phil : **Phillack**
Piece : **Piece**
Pilla : **Pillaton**
Pity : **Pityme**
P Pla : **Playing Place**
Plym : **Plymouth**
Polb : **Polbathic**
Polg : **Polgooth**
Polp : **Polperro**
Polr : **Polruan**
Polz : **Polzeath**
Pons : **Ponsanooth**
Pool : **Pool**
P'cno : **Porthcurno**
P'ven : **Porthleven**
P'ean : **Porthpean**
P'twn : **Porthtowan**
P Isa : **Port Isaac**
P'melln : **Portmellon**
P'ath : **Portreath**
P'stho : **Portscatho**
P'wkle : **Portwrinkle**
Pou : **Poughill**
Pra S : **Praa Sands**
Praze : **Praze-an-Beeble**

Pro : **Probus**
Q Dow : **Quintrell Downs**
Rame : **Rame**
Reaw : **Reawla**
Red : **Redruth**
Relu : **Relubbus**
Resc : **Rescorla**
Res : **Reskadinnick**
Roch : **Roche**
Rock : **Rock**
Rose : **Rose**
Rosu : **Rosudgeon**
Rudd : **Ruddlemoor**
S Agn : **St Agnes**
S An Cpl : **St Ann's Chapel**
S Aus : **St Austell**
S Bla : **St Blazey**
S Bl G : **St Blazey Gate**
S Bre : **St Breock**
S B'wd : **St Breward**
St Bury : **St Buryan**
S Cle : **St Cleer**
St C'mt : **St Clement**
S Maj : **St Columb Major**
S Mino : **St Columb Minor**
S Roa : **St Columb Road**
S Da : **St Day**
S Den : **St Dennis**
S Dom : **St Dominick**
S Eno : **St Enoder**
S Erm : **St Erme**
S Ern : **St Erney**
S Er : **St Erth**
S Pra : **St Erth Praze**
S Eval : **St Eval**
S Ewe : **St Ewe**
S Ger : **St Germans**
S Hil : **St Hilary**
S Ive : **St Ive**
S Ives : **St Ives**
S John : **St John**
S Jus R : **St Just in Roseland**
S Jus : **St Just**
S Kev : **St Keverne**
S Keyn : **St Keyne**
S Lev : **St Levan**
S Mab : **St Mabyn**
S Mar : **St Martin**
S Mawe : **St Mawes**
S Mawg : **St Mawgan**
S Mel : **St Mellion**
S Mer : **St Merryn**
S Mew : **St Mewan**
S Minv : **St Minver**
S New E : **St Newlyn East**
S Ste : **St Stephen**
S Teat : **St Teath**
S Tud : **St Tudy**
Salt : **Saltash**
Scor : **Scorrier**
Scre : **Scredda**
Seat : **Seaton**
Senn : **Sennen**
Senn C : **Sennen Cove**
Shev : **Sheviock**
Short : **Shortlanesend**
S Cmn : **Sinns Common**
Sithn : **Sithney**
Sk Btm : **Skinner's Bottom**
Sth P : **South Petherwin**
Sth T : **South Tehidy**
Sten : **Stenalees**

Stib : **Stibb**
Stick : **Sticker**
Stith : **Stithians**
Stra : **Stratton**
Sum : **Summercourt**
T Bay : **Talland Bay**
Thre : **Threemilestone**
Tide : **Tideford**
Tide C : **Tideford Cross**
Tin : **Tintagel**
Todp : **Todpool**
Tol D : **Tolvaddon Downs**
Tor : **Torpoint**
Towns : **Townshend**
Treb : **Trebetherick**
Tred : **Tredrizzick**
Treen : **Treen**
Tref : **Trefula**
Treg : **Tregadillett**
T'gvrh : **Tregavarah**
Tregon : **Tregony**
Treg : **Tregorrick**
T Mil : **Tregrehan Mills**
Tr'grn : **Tregurrian**
Treg'y : **Tregurthy**
Treh : **Trehan**
Trel : **Treliske**
T'lwth : **Trelowth**
Trem : **Tremar**
T'ton : **Trematon**
Tren : **Trenale**
T'nce : **Trenance**
Tresc : **Trescowe**
Tr'sln : **Tresillian**
Tres : **Treskillard**
Tresl : **Treslothan**
Tres D : **Treswithian Downs**
T'thvy : **Trethevey**
Treth : **Trethosa**
T'thwl : **Trethowel**
Trev : **Trevanson**
T'ren : **Trevarren**
Trev'rn : **Trevarrian**
T'rth : **Trevarth**
Trevem : **Trevemper**
T'via : **Trevia**
T'vsce : **Treviscoe**
T'one : **Trevone**
T'vose : **Trevose**
Trew : **Trewellard**
T'oon : **Trewoon**
Trey : **Treyarnon**
Trez : **Trezaise**
Trisp : **Trispen**
Tro : **Troon**
Tru : **Truro**
Tyw : **Tywardreath**
Tyw H : **Tywardreath Highway**
U'ton : **Upton**
Very : **Veryan**
V Grn : **Veryan Green**
Vict : **Victoria**
Vog : **Vogue**
Wade : **Wadebridge**
Wash : **Washaway**
W Cros : **White Cross**
White : **Whitecross**
W'moor : **Whitemoor**
Wid B : **Widemouth Bay**
Wilc : **Wilcove**
Win : **Windmill**

270 North TR7: Newq 3B **34**

A

Abbey Ct. PL1: Plym 5J **163**
Abbey Hill TR26: Lel 3D **140**
Abbey Mdw. TR26: Lel 2D **140**
Abbey M. PL31: B'min 4E **32**
 TR7: Newq 4F **35**
Abbey Pl. PL1: Plym 5H **163**
 TR19: Mou 6D **154**
 (off North Cliff)
Abbey St. TR18: Penz 5F **149**
ABBOTS BICKINGTON 2B **164**
Abbots Cl. PL31: B'min 4H **33**
Abbotscourt La. PL11: Ant 4C **92**
Aberdeen Cl. PL24: S Bla 7H **51**
ABERFAL 2G **133**
Abingdon Rd. PL4: Plym 1J **163**
Above Town Cl. PL27: Pity 7G **19**
Acacia Rd. TR11: Fal 7C **128**

Academy Pl. TR26: S Ives 2J **137**
Academy Ter. TR26: S Ives 2J **137**
Acland Cl. EX23: Flex 3D **8**
Acland Gdns. *TR7: Newq* *3E 34*
 (off Tower Rd.)
Acorn Dr. PL25: S Aus 6A **58**
Adams Beck PL12: Land 7H **83**
Adams Cl. PL11: Tor 3G **93**
Adams Cres. PL11: Tor 3G **93**
Adams Row TR16: Scor 6J **103**
ADDINGTON 3C **70**
Addington Nth. *PL14: Lisk* *4C 70*
 (off Callington Rd.)
Addington Sth. *PL14: Lisk* *4C 70*
 (off Pengover Rd.)
Addison Rd. PL4: Plym 2J **163**
Addison Ter. PL22: Los 3E **52**
Adelaide Rd. TR15: Red 4E **112**
Adelaide St. TR14: Camb 7D **110**
 TR18: Penz 4F **149**
Adelaide Ter. PL1: Plym 2F **163**
 TR1: Tru .5H **107**
Adela Rd. PL11: Tor 3J **93**
Adit La. PL12: Salt 2G **89**
 TR18: Newl 2C **154**

Adits, The PL18: Cals 7J **75**
Admirals Quay TR11: Fal 7F **129**
Admiralty Ct. PL13: Loo 7K **81**
Admiralty Rd. PL5: Plym 3K **89**
Admiralty Ter. TR2: P'stho 2K **131**
Adrenaline Quarry 4H **79**
African Row TR14: Barr 4A **118**
Agar Ct. TR1: Tru 4K **107**
Agar Cres. TR15: I Hig 4K **111**
Agar Mdws. TR3: C Dow 7D **116**
Agar Rd. PL25: S Aus 3J **57**
 TR1: Tru .4K **107**
 TR7: Newq 4F **35**
 TR15: I Hig 4J **111**
Agar Ter. PL31: B'min 3F **33**
Agar Way TR15: Red 5J **111**
Agnes Cl. EX23: Bud 6E **8**
Alamein Cl. PL12: Salt 3F **89**
Alamein Rd. PL12: Salt 3F **89**
Alan Harvey Cl. TR26: S Ives 5B **136**
Alan Rd. PL28: Pad 4B **22**
Albany Cl. TR5: S Agn 2J **97**
 TR15: Red 5E **112**
Albany Ct. TR15: Red 5F **113**
Albany Gdns. TR15: Red 5E **112**

Albany La. TR15: Red 4E 112
Albany Pl. TR11: Fal 2E 132
Albany Rd. TR1: Tru 5G 107
   TR7: Newq 3G 35
   TR11: Fal 2E 132
   TR15: Red 4E 112
Albany Ter. TR26: S Ives 4D 136
ALBASTON 4F 75 (3D 167)
Albert Bldgs. TR18: Penz 4F 149
                  (off Taroveor Rd.)
Albert Cotts. PL14: Pens 1K 67
   TR11: Fal 1F 133
                  (off Minnie Pl.)
Albertha Cl. PL4: Plym 2K 163
Albert Pier 5G 149
Albert Pl. PL23: Fow 7K 61
   TR1: Tru 6J 107
   TR14: Camb 7E 110
   TR26: S Ives 3J 137
Albert Quay PL23: Fow 7K 61
Albert Rd. PL12: Salt 3H 89
   PL25: S Aus 6H 57
   TR26: S Ives 4J 137 (3D 136)
Alberts La. TR2: S Mawe 7D 130
             (off St Austell Row)
Albert St. TR14: Camb 7E 110
   TR18: Penz 4G 149
Albert Ter. PL18: Dra 3G 75
   PL22: Los 3E 52
             (off Liddicoat Rd.)
   TR18: Penz 4F 149
   TR26: S Ives 3H 137
Albertus Dr. TR27: Hayl 4G 141
Albertus Gdns. TR27: Hayl 3G 141
Albertus Rd. TR27: Hayl 4G 141
Albion Bungs. PL11: Tor 3K 93
Albion Ct. PL11: Tor 3K 93
           (off Gravesend Gdns.)
Albion Rd. PL11: Tor 3K 93
   TR13: Helst 5B 158
Albion Row TR16: Carh 4A 114
Aldercombe La. EX23: Kilkh 1H 7
Alderwood Parc TR10: P'ryn 4K 127
Aldreath Cl. TR20: Mad 1B 148
Aldreath Rd. TR20: Mad 1B 148
Alexander Ct. PL26: G Hav 2J 135
Alexander Gro. PL24: Par 4H 59
Alexandra Cl. TR16: I'gan 1H 111
   TR26: S Ives 3B 136
Alexandra Ct. TR7: Newq 1K 35
Alexandra Gdns. TR18: Penz 6D 148
Alexandra Pl. PL4: Plym 1K 163
   PL10: M'brk 2C 94
             (off Blindwell Hill)
   TR18: Penz 6E 148
   TR26: S Ives 3B 136
Alexandra Rd. PL4: Plym 1K 163
   PL25: S Aus 6H 57
   PL31: B'min 3D 32
   TR7: Newq 1K 35
   TR16: I'gan 7G 101
   TR18: Penz 5E 148
   TR26: S Ives 3B 136
Alexandra Row TR26: S Ives 2C 136
Alexandra Sq. PL12: Salt 3J 89
               (off Fore St.)
Alexandra Ter. PL14: Dar 2C 66
   PL15: Laun 4H 17
   PL18: Dra 3G 75
   TR1: Tru 5H 107
             (off Richmond Hill)
   TR18: Penz 6D 148
   TR26: S Ives 3C 136
ALFARDISWORTHY 2A 164
Alford Cl. EX23: Bud 5E 8
Alfred St. PL1: Plym 6G 163
Alldritt Cl. TR7: S Mino 2A 36
Allendale PL26: W'moor 2J 47
Allendale Rd. PL4: Plym 1J 163
Allen Va. PL14: Lisk 5J 69
ALLET 4A 98 (3A 168)
Allium Ct. TR4: S Erm 3C 98
All Saints Pk. PL18: S An Cpl 2C 74
Alma Cl. TR5: Goonb 2K 97
Alma Pl. PL28: Pad 3B 22
             (off Middle St.)
   TR7: Newq 3E 34
   TR15: Red 3D 112
   TR18: Hea 3D 148
Alma Rd. PL3: Plym 1F 163
   TR1: Tru 4F 107
Alma Ter. PL18: Gun 2H 75
   TR3: Stith 7B 122
   TR16: Carh 5A 114
   TR18: Penz 4F 149
   TR26: S Ives 3H 137
ALMINSTONE CROSS 1B 164
Almshouse Hill TR13: Helst 4B 158
ALTARNUN 2C 167

Alton Pl. PL4: Plym 1K 163
Alton Rd. PL4: Plym 1J 163
Alverne Bldgs. TR18: Penz 5E 148
ALVERTON 6D 148
Alverton Ct. TR1: Tru 4A 108
Alverton Gdns. TR1: Tru 4A 108
             (off Alverton Ct.)
Alverton La. TR1: Tru 4A 108
             (off Alverton Ter.)
Alverton Pl. TR18: Penz 5E 148
Alverton Rd. TR18: Penz 6C 148
Alverton St. TR18: Penz 5F 149
Alverton Ter. TR1: Tru 4K 107
   TR18: Penz 5E 148
             (off Alverton Rd.)
Amal an Avon TR27: Phil 7E 138
Amanda Way PL14: Pens 1K 67
Amble Rd. PL17: Call 6E 72
Ambrose Ct. TR15: Red 1G 113
Amelia Cl. TR2: Pro 2H 99
Amherst Rd. La. East
   PL3: Plym 1F 163
Amity Ct. PL23: Fow 7K 61
Amity Pl. PL4: Plym 2K 163
Ancarva TR18: Penz 6E 148
             (off Alexandra Rd.)
Anchorage, The TR27: Rock 2E 22
   TR27: Phil 6B 138
Anchor La. TR6: P'mbe 7A 40
Anchor Quay TR10: P'ryn 5B 128
Anchor Ter. TR10: P'ryn 5B 128
             (off Quay Hill)
An Coth Eglos TR27: Can 6B 140
ANDERTON 2D 94
Anderton Ri. PL10: M'brk 2D 94
Andrewartha Rd. TR10: P'ryn 4K 127
Andrew Pl. TR1: Tru 5J 107
Andrews Ter. TR16: Four L 2B 120
Andrews Way PL12: Hatt 3B 84
Aneray Rd. TR14: Camb 6D 110
ANGARRACK 7G 139 (1C 173)
Angarrack Ct. PL26: Roch 5B 42
Angarrack La. TR27: Con D 6J 139
Angarrack M. TR27: Ang 7G 139
AN GARREK 5B 42
ANGARRICK 6D 124
Angel Hill PL15: Laun 3H 17
Angel Pl. TR13: Helst 4B 158
Angevran Mdw. TR8: Cube 4F 39
An Gof Gdns. PL31: B'min 4E 32
Angrouse La. TR12: Mull 1F 161
ANGWINACK 1H 155
Angwin Av. TR5: S Agn 2A 96
Anjardyn Pl. PL24: Tyw 2K 59
Ankervis La. TR16: L'ner 7H 113
Annear Rd. TR10: P'ryn 6J 127
Annethy Lowen PL28: Pad 4B 22
Anns Cres. PL26: Fox 1H 55
Anson Rd. PL27: S Eval 2J 31
Anson Way PL13: Helst 5D 158
Anthony Cl. EX23: Pou 1E 8
Anthony Rd. TR7: Newq 5F 35
Antoine Cl. TR18: Newl 1C 154
Antoine Ter. TR18: Newl 1C 154
ANTONY 4B 92 (2D 171)
Antony 1F 93
Antony Hill PL11: Ant 4B 92
ANTONY PASSAGE 6E 88
Antony Rd. PL11: Tor 2J 93
ANTRON 6G 127
Antron Hill TR10: M Bur 5F 127
Antron La. TR10: M Bur 6G 127
Antron Way TR10: M Bur 6G 127
ANVIL CORNER 3B 164
Anvil Ct. PL32: Came 3J 15
Anvil Rd. PL32: Came 3J 15
An Vownder TR16: I'gan 1J 111
Appin Gdns. PL15: I Hig 3J 111
Appletree La. PL25: Carl 6D 58
Apsley Rd. PL4: Plym 1H 163
Arcade, The TR2: S Mawe 7D 130
             (off The Square)
   TR18: Penz 5F 149
Archer Pl. PL1: Plym 2F 163
Arch Hill TR1: Tru .1H 117
   TR3: Kea 1H 117
Arch La. TR27: Can, S Er 7C 140
Arena Cres. PL25: S Aus 5A 58
Armada Cen. PL1: Plym 3G 163
Armada Memorial .7H 163
Armada Rd. PL10: Caws 6E 94
Armada St. PL4: Plym 2J 163
Armada Way PL1: Plym 7G 163
            (not continuous)
Armchair Cnr. PL31: B'min 3E 32
Arnhem Vs. TR11: Flu 5F 129
Arnold Gdns. PL14: Dar 2C 66
Art Gallery Ter. TR18: Newl 7D 148
             (off New Rd.)

Arthurian Centre, The 1J 15
Arthur Ter. PL11: Tor 4K 93
             (off Bellevue Sq.)
Arundel Cl. PL26: S Den 2E 46
Arundel Ct. TR27: Con D 5J 139
Arundell Gdns. TR9: S Maj 4C 30
             (off Union Hill)
   TR11: Fal 6C 128
Arundell Pl. TR1: Tru 6J 107
Arundel Pk. TR27: Con D 5J 139
Arundel Ter. EX23: Bud 6C 8
   TR27: Con D 5J 139
Arwenack Av. TR11: Fal 2G 133
Arwenack St. TR11: Fal 1F 133
Arworthal Mdws. TR3: P Sta 2K 123
Arwyn Cotts. TR11: Fal 2G 133
             (off Avenue Rd.)
Arwyn Pl. TR11: Fal 2G 133
             (off Bar La.)
Asdally Va. TR20: Penz 5C 148
Ashburgh Parc PL12: Salt 2D 88
Ashburton Sq. PL17: Call 5C 72
Ashbury Cl. PL14: Lisk 3C 70
Ash Cl. PL24: B'vey 4G 59
Ashdown Cl. PL26: Stick 3K 63
Asher Ct. TR7: Newq 4F 35
             (off Mount Wise)
Ashfield Gdns. TR11: Fal 6C 128
Ashfield Rd. TR11: Fal 6D 128
Ashfield Vs. TR11: Fal 6D 128
Ash Gro. PL24: B'vey 4G 59
   TR27: Hayl 4G 141
Ashleigh Mdw. PL14: Menh 5K 71
Ashleigh Way TR2: Pro 2J 99
Ashley Cl. PL26: Penw 5K 49
Ashley Rd. TR1: Tru 5J 107
   TR4: Short 6C 98
ASHMANSWORTHY 2B 164
Ashmead TR2: Gram R 6K 37
ASHMILL 1D 167
Ash Pk. Ter. PL14: Lisk 5A 70
             (off Station Rd.)
ASHTON
   Callington 1C 76
   Helston 1A 156 (2D 173)
Ashton Ct. TR7: Newq 3A 36
Ashton M. PL12: Salt 2F 89
Ashton Wlk. EX23: Wid B 6B 10
Ashton Way PL12: Salt 2F 89
ASHWATER 1D 167
Athelstan Pk. PL31: B'min 5G 33
Athenaeum La. PL1: Plym 5F 163
Athenaeum Pl. PL1: Plym 5G 163
Athenaeum St. PL1: Plym 6F 163
Atlantic Bay TR6: P'rth 4B 40
Atlantic Bldg. PL4: Plym 7K 163
Atlantic Cl. EX23: Wid B 6B 10
   TR14: Camb 1E 118
Atlantic Coast Caravan Pk.
   TR27: Gwith 3G 139
Atlantic M. PL27: N Pol 1D 78
   TR5: S Agn 2B 96
Atlantic Rd. PL33: Dela 2A 14
   PL34: Tin 6B 12
   TR7: Newq 3D 34
Atlantic Ter. PL27: N Pol 2D 78
   PL28: T'one 2G 21
   TR14: Camb 1E 118
   TR26: S Ives 2H 137
Atlantic Way PL34: Tin 6A 12
   TR4: P'twn 6D 96
Attwood La. PL14: Pens 2H 67
ATV Centre 2A 104
Atwell Farm Caravan Pk.
   PL30: Lux 1E 50
Audierne TR10: P'ryn 5A 128
             (off The Terrace)
Ava Est. PL26: Mev 5C 134
Avallen Cl. TR11: M Bri 1E 128
Avenue, The TR1: Tru 4K 107
   TR20: S Hil 3B 152
Avenue Rd. TR11: Fal 2G 133
Avery's Row PL28: Pad 3B 22
Avery Ter. PL22: Los 3E 52
Avery Way PL12: Salt 7F 89
Avon Cl. PL25: S Aus 4A 58
Avondale Rd. TR1: Tru 5H 107
Avonwynn Vw. PL25: S Aus 4E 56
Aylmer Pl. PL25: S Aus 6G 57
Aylmer Sq. PL25: S Aus 6G 57
Aylwin Cl. TR7: S Mino 3B 36
AYR 2G 137 (2C 136)
Ayr Ct. TR26: S Ives 3C 136
Ayr Holiday Pk.
   TR26: S Ives 2B 136
Ayr La. TR26: S Ives 2H 137 (2D 136)
Ayr Ter. TR26: S Ives 2G 137 (2C 136)

Aysshton Gdns. PL17: Call 6D 72
Azure TR7: Newq 2D 34

B

Baber Cl. PL12: S Dom 2F 77
Baber Ct. PL12: S Dom 2G 77
Babis Farm Cl. PL12: Salt 4H 89
Babis Farm Ct. PL12: Salt 4H 89
Babis Farm M. PL12: Salt 3H 89
Babis Farm Row PL12: Salt 3H 89
Babis Farm Way PL12: Salt 4H 89
Babis La. PL12: Salt 4H 89
Baby Beach La. PL27: N Pol 1D 18
Back Hill PL12: Salt 3E 88
    PL29: P Isa 2J 19
Back La. PL17: Call 5C 72
    PL34: Tin 6C 12
    TR2: Tregon 5J 99
    TR2: Very 5J 135
    TR12: S Kev 2C 162
    TR17: Mar 4E 150
    TR20: Crow 2J 155
    TR26: S Ives 1J 137 (2D 136)
    TR27: Ang 7G 139
    TR27: Can 6B 140
Back La. W. TR15: Red 4D 112
Back Quay TR1: Tru 5K 107
Back Rd. PL18: Cals 7J 75
Back Rd. E. TR26: S Ives 1J 137 (2D 136)
Back Rd. W. TR26: S Ives 1J 137 (2D 136)
Back St. TR26: S Ives 2J 137 (2D 136)
BADGALL 2C 167
Badgers Wlk. PL12: Salt .1F 89
Bagbury Rd. EX23: Bud 7D 8
Bag La. PL12: S Ger 4A 86
Bahavella TR26: S Ives 4C 136
Bahavella Dr. TR26: S Ives 4D 136
Baileys Fld. EX23: Kilkh 2G 7
Baileys La. TR26: S Ives 1J 137
Baines Hill TR16: P'ath 4F 101
Bakehouse La. PL17: Call 6C 72
Bakers La. PL18: Alb, Gun 4H 75
Bakers Row TR13: Breag .1D 156
Bakery Cl. PL25: S Aus 5F 57
Bakery Way TR6: P'rth 5A 40
Balcoath TR16: S Da 2K 113
BALDHU 1J 115
Balfield Rd. TR13: P'ven .7G 157
Bal-Jinjy Cl. PL24: B'vey .4H 59
Balkin Way TR15: I Hig 3J 111
BALL 2H 25
Ball TR8: S Mawg 6G 29
Ballard Cl. TR16: Four L .3C 120
Ballard Est. TR16: Four L 3C 120
Ball Pk. PL12: Salt 4F 89
Balmoral Pl. TR15: Red 3D 112
Balmoral Ter. TR15: Red .3D 112
BALNOON 7B 136
Balnoon Camping Site
    TR26: Lel 7B 136
Balnoon Flats TR26: Lel .7B 136
Bal Vw. Ct. TR14: Camb .1E 118
BALWEST 6K 153
Bambry Cl. TR20: Gold 4A 152
Bampfylde Way TR20: Gold 4A 152
    (not continuous)
Band Ho. La. PL26: Sten .4G 49
BANGORS 1C 167
Bangors Rd. PL15: Laun .5E 16
Bank, The TR2: Pro 2H 99
    TR15: I Hig 4B 112
Bank Pl. TR11: Fal 2G 133
Bank Sq. TR19: S Jus 3J 145
Bank St. PL26: Mev 6C 134
    (off Bank Ter.)
    TR7: Newq 3E 34
    TR9: S Maj 4C 30
Bank Ter. PL26: Mev 6C 134
BANNS 5F 97
Banns Rd. TR4: Mt Hwk .5G 97
BANNS VALE 5G 97
Baptist Hill TR27: Hayl 1H 141
Baptist St. PL18: Cals 7J 75
Bara Pl. PL17: K Bray 1D 72
Barbara Hepworth Museum & Sculpture Garden
    . . . . .2H 137

BARBICAN
    Looe 4H 81
    Plymouth 7J 163
Barbican, The PL1: Plym .6J 163
    (New St.)
    PL1: Plym 6K 163
    (Quay Rd.)
Barbican Cl. PL13: Loo 4H 81
    TR13: Helst 1D 158
Barbican Ct. PL4: Plym 6J 163
    PL13: Loo 3H 81

Barbican Farm La. PL13: Loo 3H 81
Barbican Glassworks 6K 163
Barbican Hill PL13: Loo 6K 81 (5H 81)
Barbican La. TR18: Penz .6G 149
Barbican Rise Ind. Est.
    PL13: Loo 3H 81
Barbican Rd. PL13: Loo, S Mar 4H 81
Barbican Theatre 7K 163
Barbican Way TR13: Helst 1D 158
Bardia TR15: Red 6F 113
BAREPPA 7A 132
Baring St. PL4: Plym 2K 163
Barkers Grn. PL25: S Aus .5B 58
Barker's Hill PL12: Salt 3E 88
Barkhouse La. PL25: Char .7B 58
Barlandhu TR18: Newl 1C 154
Barlowena TR14: Camb 2D 118
Barnaloft TR26: S Ives 1J 137 (2D 136)
Barncoose Av. TR15: I Hig 4A 112
Barncoose Ind. Est.
    TR15: I Hig 5K 111
Barncoose La. TR15: I Hig 4A 112
Barncoose Ter. TR15: I Hig 4A 112
Barn Dr. EX23: Kilkh 2G 7
BARNE BARTON 5K 89
Barne Cl. PL5: Plym 5K 89
Barnecut Cl. PL14: S Cle .4B 66
Barne Rd. PL5: Plym 5K 89
Barnfield Gdns. TR18: Gul 3H 149
Barnfield Pk. EX23: Stra 5H 9
Barnfield Ter. PL14: Lisk .6A 70
    (off Station Rd.)
    TR9: I Que 2H 45
Barn Hill PL12: S Ger 5A 86
Barn La. PL31: B'min 4E 32
    TR9: S Maj 5C 30
Barn Mdw. Pk. PL13: Loo .6F 81
Barnoon TR26: S Ives 2H 137 (2D 136)
Barnoon Hill TR26: S Ives 2H 137 (2D 136)
Barnoon Ter. TR26: S Ives 2H 137 (2D 136)
Barn Pk. PL12: Salt 2H 89
    PL22: Los 3F 53
Barnpark La. PL31: B'min .3J 33
Barnpark Rd. PL35: Bosc .3K 13
Barns, The PL12: Tide 1B 86
Barns Ter. PL12: Hatt 1D 84
Barn St. PL14: Lisk 5B 70
Barons Mdw. PL31: B'min 3H 33
Barossa Pl. PL11: Tor 4K 93
Barossa Rd. PL11: Tor 3K 93
Barrack La. TR1: Tru 6J 107
Barrack's La. TR16: S Da .2A 114
Barras Cl. PL14: Lisk 4A 70
Barras Cross PL14: Lisk 4B 70
BARRAS MOOR 6J 123
Barras Pl. PL14: Lisk 4B 70
Barras St. PL14: Lisk 4B 70
Barrepta Cl. TR26: C Bay .7F 137
Barrie Cres. PL31: B'min .6F 33
BARRIPPER 4A 118 (1D 173)
Barripper Rd. TR14: Camb, P'nds 3B 118
Barrow Down PL12: Salt .2D 88
BARROWFIELDS 2H 35
Barrowfield Vw. TR7: Newq 2H 35
Barry's La. PL28: Pad 3B 22
Bartles Ct. TR15: I Hig 4J 111
Bartles Ind. Est. TR15: Red 2D 112
Bartles Row TR14: Camb .5G 111
Bartlett Av. EX23: Bud 5E 8
Bartliver Hill TR2: Gram 7A 62
Barton Cl. PL12: Land 6G 83
    PL31: B'min 3F 33
    TR13: Helst 2D 158
    TR18: Hea 3E 148
Barton Ct. PL26: T'vsce 4B 46
Barton La. TR8: W Cros 1C 44
    TR9: Fr'don 2D 44
Barton Mdw. PL13: Pely 2C 80
    TR1: Tru 4G 107
Barton M. PL10: M'brk 1D 94
    PL12: Land 7G 83
Barton Rd. PL26: T'vsce 4B 46
Bar Vw. La. TR27: Hayl 2H 141
Barwis Hill TR18: Penz 4F 149
Barwis Ter. TR18: Penz 4F 149
    (off Barwis Hill)
Basawna Cl. TR16: S Da .3A 114
Basket Ope PL4: Plym 6J 163
Basset Pl. TR11: Fal 7E 128
Basset Rd. TR14: Camb 1D 118
    TR15: Red 7E 102
    TR16: Red 7C 102
    (not continuous)

Basset St. TR11: Fal 7E 128
    TR14: Camb 1D 118
    TR15: Red 4E 112
Bassett Cl. PL26: Trez 7C 42
Bassett Rd. TR16: I'gan 7J 101
Bassett Wlk. TR1: Tru 5J 107
    (off Tresawya Dr.)
BATHPOOL 3C 167
Batter St. PL4: Plym 5J 163
Battery, The TR7: Newq 2E 34
    (off King Edward Cres.)
Battery Hill TR16: P'ath 4E 100
Battery La. PL23: Polr 7B 60
Battery Mill La. TR27: S Er 7E 140
Battery Pk. PL23: Polr 7B 60
Battery Rd. TR18: Penz 6G 149
Battery Ter. PL26: Mev 6D 134
Bawden Rd. PL31: B'min .5D 32
Bay, The PL13: Loo 7K 81
Bay Apartments TR7: Newq 3B 34
Bay Ct. TR11: Fal 3G 133
Bay Down PL13: Loo 3H 81
Bay Flats TR20: L Roc 3A 150
    (off Bay Vs.)
Baynards Cl. TR1: Tru 5A 108
Baynes Cl. PL14: S Cle 4B 66
Bay Rd. PL28: T'one 2G 21
Bay St. PL13: Loo 7K 81
Bayswater Rd. PL1: Plym .2F 163
    PL3: Plym 2F 163
Baytree Hill PL14: Lisk 5B 70
Bayview PL24: Par 4J 59
Bay Vw. Cl. TR8: Hol B 2C 38
Bay Vw. Cres. TR11: Fal .2H 133
Bay Vw. Dr. PL13: Loo 4J 81
Bay Vw. Pk. PL25: S Aus .3K 57
Bay Vw. Rd. PL13: Loo 4H 81
    PL26: Dup 1K 65
Bay Vw. Ter. TR7: Newq 4F 35
    TR11: B Wat 4A 132
    TR13: P'ven 7F 157
    (off Harbour Rd.)
    TR18: Newl 1C 154
    (off Chywoone Hill)
    TR18: Penz 6E 148
    TR27: Hayl 2H 141
Bay Vs. TR20: L Roc 3A 150
Beachcombers TR8: Newq 7A 28
Beach Ct. TR26: S Ives 1K 137
Beachfield Av. TR7: Newq .3E 34
Beachfield Ct. TR18: Penz .6E 148
Beach Hill PL11: Downd 7J 79
Beach Ho., The TR7: Newq 1J 35
    (off Porth Beach Rd.)
Beach La. TR6: P'rth 4B 40
Beach Pde. TR7: Newq 3E 34
Beach Rd. PL25: Carl 6C 58
    PL26: Mev 5D 134
    PL28: T'one 2G 21
    TR4: P'twn 6C 96
    TR6: P'rth 4B 40
    TR7: Newq 3E 34
    TR8: Cran 5A 34
    TR26: C Bay 6F 137
    TR26: S Ives 1G 137 (2C 136)
Beachside Ct. TR4: P'twn .6C 96
Beachside Holiday Pk.
    TR27: Phil 5C 138
Beach Ter. TR20: L Roc 3B 150
Beach Vw. Cl. TR7: Newq .2K 35
Beach Wlk. TR7: Newq 2J 35
BEACON 2F 119
Beacon, The TR11: Fal 7E 128
    (not continuous)
Beacon Cl. PL25: S Aus 4A 58
Beacon Cottage Farm TR5: S Agn 1F 97
Beacon Cres. TR11: Fal 7E 128
Beacon Dr. TR5: S Agn 1E 96
Beacon Farm TR5: S Agn .1G 97
Beacon Flds. TR14: Camb .1E 118
Beacon Hill PL31: B'min 4F 33
    TR10: P'ryn 6K 127
Beacon Hill M. PL31: B'min 4F 33
    (off Beacon Hill)
Beacon Lanes PL31: B'min 4E 32
Beacon Parc TR13: Helst .3C 158
Beacon Pk. PL13: Pely 3D 80
Beacon Pk. Rd. PL26: Fox .1G 55
    PL31: B'min 4F 33
    TR5: S Agn 1G 97
    TR7: Newq 2E 34
    TR8: Sum 7B 34
    TR11: Fal 7E 128
    TR13: P'ven 6E 157
    TR17: Mar 4E 150
Beacons PL13: Pely 3D 80
Beaconsfield Pl. TR5: S Agn 2A 96
Beaconsfield Ter. PL31: B'min 4E 32
    (off St Leonards)

Beaconside PL26: Fox 1G 55
TR8: Sum .7B 44
Beacon St. TR11: Fal 7E 128
Beacon Technology Pk. PL31: B'min 4D 32
Beacon Ter. PL26: Fox 1G 55
PL26: S Den 1D 46
TR11: Fal 7E 128
(off Beacon Rd.)
TR12: Lizar 5G 161
TR13: Helst 3C 158
TR14: Camb 2E 118
Beacon Vw. TR4: Mt Hwk 6H 97
Beacon Vw. Pk. TR16: I'gan 1K 111
BEALBURY 4A 76
BEALSMILL 3D 167
Bealswood Cl. PL18: Gun 2H 75
Bealswood Rd. PL18: Gun 2H 75
Bealswood Ter. PL18: Gun 2J 75
Beam Rd. PL26: Bugl 7G 43
Beam Ter. PL26: Bugl 7F 43
Bears Ter. TR16: L'ner 7J 113
Beatrice Av. PL12: Salt 3G 89
Beatrice Gdns. PL12: Salt 3G 89
Beatrice Rd. PL31: B'min 3J 33
Beatrice Ter. TR27: Hayl 7D 138
Beattie Rd. PL5: Plym 5K 89
Beauchamps Mdw. TR15: Red 6F 113
Beaufighter Av. PL27: S Eval 3J 31
Beaufort Av. PL27: S Eval 2J 31
Beaufort Ho. PL4: Plym 5K 163
Beaufort Pl. TR18: Newl 7D 148
(off The Coombe)
Beaumont Av. PL4: Plym 3K 163
Beaumont Park 3K 163
Beaumont Pl. PL4: Plym 4K 163
Beaumont Rd. PL4: Plym 4K 163
Beaumont Ter. PL12: Salt 1H 89
Beckett Cl. TR15: Red 4E 112
Beckley Ct. PL1: Plym 3H 163
Bede Haven Cl. EX23: Bud 6D 8
Bederkesa Ct. PL31: B'min 4F 33
Bedford Cl. PL18: Gun 1G 75
Bedford Pk. PL4: Plym 2K 163
Bedford Pk. Vs. PL4: Plym 1K 163
Bedford Pl. PL26: S Ives 3H 137
Bedford Rd. TR26: S Ives 3H 137 (3D 136)
Bedford Ter. PL4: Plym 2J 163
Bedford Way PL1: Plym 5H 163
Bedowan Mdws. TR7: Newq 4H 35
TR8: Newq .4H 35
Bedruthan Av. TR1: Tru 3A 108
Bedruthan Steps 1B 168
Beech Av. PL14: Lisk 5A 70
Beech Cl. PL11: Tor 3J 93
TR11: Fal 7D 128
TR9: S Maj .5A 30
Beech Dr. PL31: B'min 4D 32
Beeches, The PL15: Laun 4H 17
Beeching Pk. PL17: K Bray 2D 72
Beech La. PL25: S Aus 6H 57
Beech Rd. PL17: Call 5D 72
PL25: S Aus 6H 57
TR11: Fal 7D 128
Beech Ter. PL13: Loo 4G 81
(off West Rd.)
Beechwood Av. PL4: Plym 1H 163
Beechwood Dr. PL32: Came 2J 15
Beechwood Gdns. TR1: Tru 3A 108
Beehive Workshops TR10: P'ryn 5H 127
BEENY 1B 166
Behenna Dr. TR1: Tru 5F 107
Bekelege Dr. TR14: Bea 2F 119
Belerion Rd. TR16: P'ath 5F 101
Belgrave Ter. PL14: Lisk 3C 70
(off Callington Rd.)
Belgravia St. TR18: Penz 4F 149
Belhay TR10: P'ryn 4A 128
Bellair Rd. TR20: Mad 2B 148
Bellair Ter. TR26: S Ives 2H 137
Bellatt PL27: Wade 3G 25
Bella Vista Gdns. TR10: P'ryn 3A 128
Bellever Cl. TR14: Camb 7F 111
Bellever Parc TR14: Camb 7F 111
Belle Vue EX23: Bud 4C 8
PL11: Tor 3K 93
PL14: Lisk 4A 70
(off Dean Hill)
TR18: Newl 2C 154
Bellevue TR15: Red 3D 112
Belle Vue Av. EX23: Bud 4C 8
Bellevue Cotts. TR10: P'ryn 2A 128
Belle Vue La. EX23: Bud 4C 8
Belle Vue Pl. PL10: M'brk 3C 94
Belle Vue Rd. PL12: Salt 2H 89
Bellevue Sq. PL11: Tor 4K 93
Belle Vue Ter. PL15: Laun 4H 17
PL18: Gun .1H 75
(off Calstock Rd.)
TR18: Penz 4F 149

Bellevue Ter. TR3: P Sta 1K 123
Bell Hill PL26: G Hav 1G 135
Belliers Rd. TR26: S Ives 4J 137 (3D 136)
Bell La. PL31: B'min 3G 33
TR16: L'ner 1H 121
Bell's Ct. TR11: Fal 1F 133
Bell's Hill TR11: M Bri 6E 124
Bell Vean TR16: L'ner 1G 121
Bell Veor TR16: L'ner 1H 121
Belmont Cl. PL33: Dela 3A 14
Belmont Ct. PL25: S Aus 6H 57
PL27: Wade 4E 24
(off Fairpark Rd.)
Belmont M. PL14: Pens 1J 67
Belmont Pk. PL14: Pens 1J 67
Belmont Pl. TR7: Newq 2E 34
TR26: S Ives 2G 137
Belmont Rd. PL25: S Aus 6G 57
TR11: Fal 2E 132
TR13: Helst 2B 158
Belmont St. PL24: Tyw 2B 60
Belmont Ter. PL14: Dar 2C 66
TR3: Devo 2D 124
TR26: S Ives 2G 137 (2C 136)
BELOWDA 1C 169
Belvedere TR1: Tru 3B 108
Belvedere La. TR20: S Hil 4B 152
Belyars, The TR26: S Ives 4D 136
Belyars Ct. TR26: S Ives 4D 136
Belyars La. TR26: S Ives 4J 137 (4D 136)
Benallack Ct. TR1: Tru 5A 108
Bencoolen Rd. EX23: Bud 5C 8
Beneathway PL14: Dob 4D 68
BENNACOTT 1D 167
Bennets La. PL12: Salt 2H 89
Bennett Gdns. PL12: Salt 2H 89
Bennetts Cotts. TR10: P'ryn 4A 128
Benny Halt Station
Lappa Valley Steam Railway 1J 37
Benson Gdns. TR1: Tru 4K 107
Benson Rd. TR1: Tru 4H 107
Bens Playworld 4E 58
Bentley Dr. EX23: Stra 5G 9
Beramic Cl. TR27: Con D 5J 139
Beraton Ct. PL31: B'min 3F 33
BERE ALSTON 1D 171
BERE FERRERS .1D 171
BEREPPER 2D 173
Berkeley Cl. EX23: Stra 5F 9
Berkeley Cotts. TR11: Fal 1E 132
Berkeley Ct. TR11: Fal 1F 133
(off Berkley Vale)
Berkeley Hill TR11: Fal 1E 132
Berkeley M. TR11: Fal 1E 132
Berkeley Path TR11: Fal 1E 132
Berkeley Vale TR11: Fal 1E 132
Berries Av. EX23: Bud 6D 8
Berries Mt. EX23: Bud 6D 8
Berrycoombe Hill PL31: B'min 3E 32
Berrycoombe Rd. PL31: B'min 3F 33
Berrycoombe Va. PL31: B'min 3D 32
Berrycoombe Vw. PL31: B'min 3F 33
Berry La. PL31: B'min 3G 33
Berryman Cres. TR11: Fal 2D 132
Berry Pk. PL12: Salt 1F 89
Berry Rd. TR7: Newq 3F 35
Berry Tower 2G 33
Berry Towers PL31: B'min 3H 33
Berthon Rd. PL5: Plym 6K 89
Berveth Cl. TR3: Thre 5A 106
Bess Pk. Rd. PL27: Wade 3G 25
Bethan Dr. PL27: Wade 4D 24
Bethany Homes TR14: Camb 1C 118
(off Tregenna La.)
Bethany Pl. TR19: S Jus 3J 145
BETHEL
St Austell 4A 58
Truro 3G 115
Bethel Rd. PL25: S Aus 5A 58
Bethesda Hill TR26: S Ives 1K 137
Bethesda Pl. TR26: S Ives 1J 137
Beverley Cres. TR27: Hayl 7E 138
Beweys Pk. PL12: Salt 3E 88
Bezant Pl. PL7: Newq 4C 34
Bickern Rd. PL11: Tor 3K 93
Bickford Cres. TR13: P'ven 6G 157
Bickford Rd. PL15: Laun 1G 17
Bickland Hill TR11: Fal 7B 128
Bickland Ind. Est. TR11: Fal 1B 132
Bickland Ind. Pk. TR11: Fal 1B 132
Bickland Water Rd. TR11: Fal 1B 132
BICKLEIGH 1D 171
Biddick's Ct. PL25: S Aus 6G 57
Big Dunk's Paintball 1C 26
Big Green PL13: Polp 7B 80
BILBERRY 5J 43 (1D 169)
Bilbury St. PL4: Plym 4J 163

Billings Dr. TR7: Newq 4J 35
Binhamy Cl. EX23: Bud 6E 8
Binhamy Rd. EX23: Stra 1F 11
Binner Cross TR14: Praze 6D 142
TR27: Leeds 6D 142
Binnerton Rd. TR27: Leeds 7D 142
Birch Gro. TR27: Hayl 4G 141
Birkdale Cl. PL12: Salt 3E 88
Biscombe Gdns. PL12: Salt 2J 89
Biscombes La. PL17: Call 5C 72
(off New Rd.)
BISCOVEY 4G 59
Biscovey Rd. PL24: B'vey 4F 59
Bishops Cl. PL12: Salt 2G 89
TR1: Tru 3J 107
Bishops Ct. TR9: S Maj 5C 30
Bishop's Hill Rd. PL27: N Pol 1D 18
Bishop's Rd. TR26: S Ives 4H 137 (3D 136)
Bishop Temple Rd. TR1: Tru 3B 108
BISSOE 5K 115 (3A 168)
Bissoe Cotts. TR4: Biss 5K 115
Bissoe Rd. TR3: C Dow 6B 116
Bissoe Valley Nature Reserve 5H 115
BISSOM 3C 128
Bissom Rd. TR10: P'ryn 4B 128
TR11: M Bri 3D 128
Blackberry Cl. TR16: L'ner 7H 113
Blackberry Way TR1: Tru 4B 108
Blackbird Cres. PL15: Laun 5K 17
BLACK CROSS 1C 169
Blackfriars La. PL1: Plym 6J 163
Blackfriars Ope PL1: Plym 6J 163
Black Rd. TR27: Phil 7D 138
Blacksmith La. TR27: Con D 5J 139
BLACKWATER 2B 104 (3A 168)
Blackwell Pl. PL27: Wade 4E 24
Blairgowrie Rd. PL5: Plym 3K 89
Blakes Pk. PL14: Lisk 3C 70
Blanchminster Rd. EX23: Bud 5D 8
BLANKEDNICK 4H 123
Blenheim Rd. PL4: Plym 2J 163
Bligh Cres. TR13: Helst 4C 158
Blight's Row TR15: Red 3D 112
Blindhole PL15: Laun 3H 17
(off Southgate St.)
Blindwell Hill PL10: M'brk 2C 94
Blindwell Ter. PL10: M'brk 2C 94
BLISLAND 3A 166
Bloom Flds. TR18: Penz 5D 148
BLOWINGHOUSE .4B 112
Blowing Ho. Cl. PL25: S Aus 5F 57
Blowing Ho. Hill PL25: S Aus 5F 57
(not continuous)
TR20: Ludg 1H 155
Blowinghouse Hill TR15: Red 4B 112
Blowinghouse La. PL25: S Aus 5F 57
Blowinghouse La. PL30: B'min 7C 32
PL31: B'min 7C 32
BLUE ANCHOR 3G 45
Bluebell Cl. PL12: Salt 1F 89
Bluebell Way PL15: Laun 5K 17
Blue Reef Aquarium 3E 34
BLUE STONE 3C 120
BLUNTS 2A 82 (1C 171)
Boaden Cl. PL12: Hatt 3B 84
Boase St. TR18: Newl 2C 154
Boat Cove La. TR20: Perran 6H 151
Bobs Rd. PL24: S Bla 3G 59
BOCADDON 2A 170
Boconnoc Av. PL17: Call 7C 72
Boconnoc Rd. PL25: S Aus 6H 57
BODBRANE 4A 78
BODELLICK 7J 23
BODELVA 1E 58
Bodelva Rd. PL24: B'lva 7E 50
Bodgara Way PL14: Lisk 5B 70
BODIEVE 2F 25 (3D 165)
Bodieve Bus. Pk. PL27: Wade 2G 25
Bodieve Rd. PL27: B'eve, Wade 2F 25
BODIGGO 1C 50
Bodinar Rd. TR10: P'ryn 3J 127
Bodiniel Rd. PL31: B'min 2D 32
Bodiniel Vw. PL31: B'min 3D 32
BODINNICK 6K 61 (2A 170)
Bodinnick Hgts. PL23: B'ick 6K 61
Bodinnick Parc PL30: S Tud 4J 27
Bodinnick Rd. PL30: S Tud 4J 27
BODMIN 4G 33 (1D 169)
Bodmin & Wenford Railway
Bodmin General Station 5G 33
Boscarne Junction Station 3A 32
Bodmin Bus. Cen. PL31: B'min 5G 33
Bodmin Bus. Pk. PL31: B'min 2J 33
Bodmin Camping & Caravanning Club Site
PL31: B'min 2H 33
Bodmin General Station
Bodmin & Wenford Railway 5G 33
Bodmin Hill PL22: Los 1D 52
Bodmin Jail 3F 33

Bodmin Moor 3B 166
Bodmin Mus. .4G 33
Bodmin Rd. PL25: S Aus, T'thwl 1F 57
   PL26: Rudd 1F 57
   TR1: Tru 3A 108
BODRANE 1B 170
Bodrigan Rd. PL13: Loo 4H 81
Bodriggy Ct. TR27: Hayl 1J 141
Bodriggy Cres. TR27: Hayl 2H 141
Bodriggy St. TR27: Hayl 1J 141
Bodriggy Vs. TR27: Hayl 2J 141
Bodrugan Hill PL26: P'melln 7C 134
BODUEL 6G 69
Bodvean Ct. TR7: Newq 4D 34
BODWEN 3K 43
Bohelland Ri. TR10: P'ryn 3A 128
Bohelland Rd. TR10: P'ryn 4B 128
Bohelland Way TR10: P'ryn 4B 128
Bohella Rd. TR2: S Mawe 7D 130
BOHETHERICK 3K 77
Bohill TR10: P'ryn 5B 128
BOHORTHA 1B 174
Boiler Works Rd. TR14: Camb 6E 110
BOJEA 2G 57
Bojea Ind. Est. PL25: T'thwl 2G 57
Bojea Ter. PL25: T'thwl 3G 57
Bojewyan Stennack
   TR19: Pend 4E 144
BOKENNA CROSS 1D 68
BOKIDDICK 1D 169
Boldventure Av. PL25: S Aus 4B 58
Boldventure Cl. PL25: S Aus 4B 58
Boldventure Rd. PL25: S Aus 4B 58
Bolenna La. TR6: P'rth 5A 40
BOLENOWE 5J 119 (1D 173)
Bolenowe La. TR14: Tro 3H 119
Bolenowe Ter. TR14: Tro 6K 119
BOLINGEY 6D 40 (2A 168)
Bolingey Rd. TR6: P'rth 5B 40
Bolitho Rd. TR18: Hea 3D 148
BOLLOWAL 3F 145
Bollowal Pl. TR19: S Jus 3G 145
Bolowthas Ct. TR7: Newq 2H 35
Bolowthas Way TR7: Newq 2K 35
Bolster Cl. TR5: S Agn 3A 96
Boltern Rd. TR17: Mar 4G 151
BOLVENTOR 3B 166
Bonallack La. TR12: Gweek 6H 159
Bon Cot Rd. TR18: Newl 1C 154
Bond St. TR15: Red 4D 112
Bone Cellar Row TR2: Tr'sln 2G 109
Bone Mill Rd. TR6: Bol 6D 40
Bones La. PL12: Tide C 5A 82
Bone Valley Caravan & Camping Pk.
   TR20: Hea 2D 148
Bonson Cl. PL13: Loo 4G 81
Bonython Cl. TR11: M Bri 1F 129
Bonython Dr. TR2: Gram 6B 62
Bonython Estate Gardens 2D 173
Bonython Rd. TR7: Newq 2H 35
Bonython Ter. PL14: Lisk 6A 70
Boon's Pl. PL1: Plym 2G 163
Borgwitha TR16: Four L 3C 120
Borlase Cl. TR13: Helst 4B 158
Borough Cl. PL11: Tor 2G 93
Borough La. PL11: Tor 2G 93
Borough Pk. PL11: Tor 2G 93
BOSAVERN 5J 145
Bosawna Gdns. TR16: S Da 3A 114
Boscarn Cl. TR14: Barr 4B 118
Boscarne Cres. PL25: S Aus 6K 57
Boscarne Junction Station
   Bodmin & Wenford Railway 3A 32
Boscarnek TR27: S Er 6F 141
Boscarne Vw. PL30: Nans 3A 32
Boscarn Parc TR15: C Bre 6J 111
Boscarn Rd. TR15: Red 2F 113
BOSCASTLE 2K 13 (1A 166)
Boscastle Visitor Cen. *1K 13*
          (within Tourist Info. Cen.)
Boscaswell Downs TR19: Pend 4C 144
Boscaswell Est. TR19: Pend 3B 144
Boscaswell Rd. TR19: Pend 4C 144
Boscaswell Ter. TR19: Pend 4C 144
Boscaswell Village TR19: Pend 3B 144
Boscathnoe La. TR18: Hea 3B 148
   TR20: Hea 3B 148
Boscathnoe Way TR18: Hea 3C 148
Boscawen Gdns. TR6: P'rth 5B 40
Boscawen Rd. PL26: S Den 3E 46
   TR4: Chac .6E 104
   TR6: P'rth 5B 40
   TR11: Fal 4E 132
   TR13: Helst 5D 158
Boscawen St. TR1: Tru 5K 107
Boscawen-un Stone Circle 2B 172
Boscawen Woods TR1: Tru 7A 108
BOSCEAN 1G 145
Boscean Cl. TR14: Tro 5G 119

BOSCOLLA 2F 107
BOSCOPPA 3A 58 (2D 169)
Boscoppa Cl. TR15: Red 1F 113
Boscoppa Rd. PL25: S Aus 4A 58
BOSCREEGE .5K 153
Boscreege Caravan & Camping Site
   TR13: Ash .5K 153
Boscundle Av. TR11: Fal 4D 132
Boscundle Cl. PL25: S Aus 4D 58
Boscundle Row PL12: Salt *3J 89*
             (off Albert Rd.)
Bosence Rd. TR27: Towns 1F 153
Bosillion La. TR2: Gram 7B 62
Bosinney Rd. PL25: S Aus 6H 57
Bosinver La. PL26: Polg 2D 64
Boskear La. PL31: B'min 4C 32
BOSKENNAL .3H 147
Boskennal Barton TR19: St Bury 3H 147
Boskennal Dr. TR27: Hayl 3G 141
Boskennal La. TR19: St Bury 2G 147
Boskennick TR16: Four L 3B 120
            (not continuous)
Boskenza Ct. TR26: C Bay 6E 136
Boskernick Cl. TR18: Newl 2B 154
Boskerris Cres. TR26: C Bay 6F 137
Boskerris M. TR26: C Bay 7F 137
Boskerris Rd. TR26: C Bay 6F 137
Boslandew Hill TR19: Pau 4C 154
BOSLEAKE 7J 111
BOSLIVEN 3J 147
Bosloggas M. TR11: Fal 2G 133
Boslowick Cl. TR11: Fal 2D 132
Boslowick Ct. TR11: Fal 3C 132
Boslowick Rd. TR11: Fal 3C 132
Bosmeor Cl. TR11: Fal 3C 132
Bosmeor Pk. TR15: I Hig 4K 111
Bosmeor Rd. TR11: Fal 3C 132
Bosnoweth TR2: Pro 2J 99
   TR13: Helst 4D 158
BOSORNE 4G 145
Bosorne Cl. TR19: S Jus 3H 145
Bosorne Rd. TR19: S Jus 4G 145
Bosorne St. TR19: S Jus 3H 145
Bosorne Ter. TR19: S Jus 3H 145
Bosparva La. TR14: C Grn 4E 142
   TR27: Leeds 6D 142
Bospolvans Rd. TR9: S Maj 5B 30
Bospowis TR14: Camb 7C 110
BOSSINEY 6D 12 (2A 166)
Bossiney Farm Caravan & Camping Pk.
   PL34: Boss 6D 12
Bossiney La. PL34: Tin 5C 12
Bossiney Rd. PL34: Tin 7B 12
Bostennack Pl. TR26: S Ives 3C 136
Bostennack Ter. TR26: S Ives 3C 136
BOSUE 7A 64
Bosuen Rd. TR7: Newq 2H 35
Bosvargus TR19: S Jus 2K 145
BOSVEAL 4A 160
Bos Vean TR12: Lizar 5G 161
Bosvean Gdns. TR1: Tru 4H 107
   TR16: I'gan 1J 111
Bosvean Rd. TR4: Short 6B 98
BOSVENEGH .4G 33
Bosvenna Vw. PL31: B'min 4G 33
Bosvenna Way TR18: Hea 3C 148
Bosvigo Gdns. .4H 107
Bosvigo La. TR1: Tru 4H 107
Bosvigo Rd. TR1: Tru 5H 107
BOSWEDDEN .2F 145
Boswedden Rd. TR19: S Jus 2G 145
Boswedden Ter. TR19: S Jus 2G 145
Boswednack 1B 172
Boswens Standing Stone 1B 172
Boswergy TR18: Penz 5D 148
BOSWINGER .3C 169
Boswithian Rd. TR14: Tol D 4F 111
Boswonja Cl. TR9: S Maj 5B 30
BOSWORLAS .5K 145
BOSWYN 7G 119
BOTALLACK 7A 144 (1A 172)
Botallack Count House Visitor Cen. 1A 172
Botetoe Hill TR14: Camb 1K 143
Botetoe Rd. TR14: Barr 5B 118
Botha Rd. PL27: S Eval 2H 31
Bothwicks Rd. TR7: Newq 3F 35
BOTUS FLEMING 5C 84 (1D 171)
Bound, The PL10: Caws 6E 94
Boundary Cl. TR18: Newl 2C 154
Boundary Dr. EX23: March 3F 11
Boundary Gdns. PL24: S Bla 3H 59
Boundary Rd. PL31: B'min, Dun 3B 32
Bounders La. TR6: Bol 6D 40
Bounder Treath TR12: Cover 5D 162
Boundervean La. TR14: Camb 1B 118
Bounsall's La. PL15: Laun 4H 17
Boveway Dr. PL14: Lisk 5C 70
Boveway La. PL14: Lisk 5C 70
            (not continuous)

Boveway Wlk. PL14: Lisk 5D 70
           (off Liskerrett Rd.)
BOWDEN 5G 9
Bowden La. EX23: Stra 5G 9
Bowdens Row TR15: Red 4D 112
Bowen Gdns. PL28: T'one 2G 21
Bowglas Cl. TR20: Ludg 2G 155
BOWITHICK 2B 166
Bowjey Ct. TR18: Newl *2C 154*
           (off Bowjey Hill)
Bowjey Hill TR18: Newl 2C 154
Bowjey Ter. TR18: Newl 2C 154
Bow La. EX23: Pou 2F 9
Bowles Rd. TR11: Fal 6E 128
BOWLING GREEN 1K 49
Bowling Grn. PL14: Menh 1H 79
   PL17: Call *4D 72*
          (off Florence Hill)
   TR16: Carn 7A 112
   TR26: S Ives 2H 137
Bowling Grn., The TR2: S Jus R 2E 130
Bowling Grn. Ct. PL14: Lisk 5A 70
Bowling Grn. Rd. TR11: Const 2H 159
Bowling Grn. Ter. TR26: S Ives 2H 137 (2D 136)
Bownder an Sycamor TR16: Todp 1B 114
Bownder Dowr TR27: Hayl 4G 141
Bownder Vean PL25: S Aus 4K 57
Bowood Golf Course 5G 15
Bowood Pk. PL32: Came 6F 15
           (not continuous)
BOX'S SHOP 7D 10 (3A 164)
Boxwell Pk. PL31: B'min 3H 33
Boyd Av. PL28: Pad 3A 22
BOYTON 1D 167
Bracken Cl. PL31: B'min 3G 33
Brackenside PL13: Polp 6B 80
Bracken Ter. TR7: Newq 4F 35
Braddock Cl. PL26: Fox 7H 47
Bradfords Quay Rd. PL27: Wade 3F 25
Bradley Rd. TR7: Newq 2K 35
BRADSTONE 2D 167
BRADWORTHY 2B 164
Braeside Pk. PL14: Dob 3E 68
Brake La. PL10: M'brk 2A 94
Bramble Cl. EX23: Wid B 6B 10
Bramble Ct. PL31: B'min 3G 33
Bramble Hill EX23: Bud 5D 8
Brambles, The PL14: Lisk *5D 70*
           (off Tom Lyon Rd.)
   PL22: Los .2D 52
Brambleside PL30: S Teat 2B 26
Bramley Cl. PL25: S Aus 5J 57
Bramley Pk. PL31: B'min 3H 33
BRANDIS CORNER 1D 167
Brandon Wlk. EX23: Wid B 6B 10
Brandy La. TR20: Rosu 6C 152
BRANE 2B 172
Branksome Dr. PL27: Wade 4H 25
Brannel Grn. PL26: S Ste 3C 54
Brannel Rd. PL26: Coomb 7E 54
Branscombe La. TR18: Penz 3H 149
Branwells Mill TR18: Penz *4G 149*
            (off Albert St.)
Brayers Ct. PL12: Tide 1B 86
Bray Ri. TR16: Four L 3B 120
BRAY SHOP 3D 167
Bray's Pl. PL25: S Aus 5K 57
Brays Ter. TR16: L'ner 7H 113
BRAZACOTT 1C 167
BREA 7G 111 (3A 168)
Brea Arch TR14: Bre 7G 111
Bread St. TR18: Penz 5F 149
BREAGE 1D 156 (2D 173)
Breakwater Rd. EX23: Bud 5B 8
BREANEK 2B 96
Brea Rd. PL27: Rock 2F 23
Breaside Ter. TR14: Bre 7G 111
Breaview Pk. La. TR15: Pool 5J 111
Brecon Cl. TR5: S Agn 2A 96
Bredon Ct. TR7: Newq 3D 34
Bree Shute La. PL31: B'min *3G 33*
           (off Fore St.)
Brendon PL23: Polr *7C 60*
          (off St Saviour's Hill)
Brent PL13: Polp 6C 80
Brenton Rd. PL11: Downd 6G 79
Brenton Ter. PL11: Downd 6H 79
   PL12: Tide .1B 86
Brentspool EX23: Kilkh 3F 7
Brent Wartha PL13: Polp 6C 80
Bretonside PL4: Plym 5J 163
Brewers Cl. PL30: Lani 7J 31
Brewers Hill PL26: S Den, W'moor 2F 47
Brewers Rd. TR1: Tru 4B 108
Brewery Ct. TR4: Chac 5E 104
Brewery Hill TR26: Lel 2E 140
Brewery La. TR13: Helst 3B 158
Brian Laity Way TR18: Penz 4E 148

Briansway PL12: Salt 3F 89
Briar Dene TR4: Black 2A 104
Briarfield PL23: Fow .6K 61
Briar Rd. EX23: Bud 6D 8
Briars Row PL12: Salt 1F 89
Briarwood PL14: Lisk 5C 70
Brickworks Hill TR16: S Da 3K 113
Bridals La. PL13: Polp, T Bay 4C 80
BRIDGE
 Falmouth 2G 159
 Redruth 5J 101 (3A 168)
Bridge TR9: S Maj 3D 30
Bridge, The PL35: Bosc 1K 13
Bridge Cl. TR7: Newq 5H 35
Bridge Ct. PL25: S Aus 5K 57
Bridge Hill TR9: S Maj 4C 30
 TR16: Brid, I'gan 5J 101
Bridge La. PL12: Land 6C 82
Bridgemead Cl. PL26: Treg 1G 65
Bridgend PL13: Loo .4G 81
 (off North Rd.)
 PL27: Wade 3F 25
Bridge Rd. PL11: Seat 6F 79
 PL12: Tide 1B 86
 PL25: S Aus 6F 57
 TR4: Goonh 5H 41
 TR7: Newq 3F 35
 TR16: I'gan 7J 101
Bridge Row TR16: Brid 5J 101
BRIDGERULE 3A 164
BRIDGES 1D 50
Bridges, The PL12: Salt 4G 89
Bridge St. EX23: Stra 5G 9
 PL24: S Bla 7H 51
Bridge Vw. PL27: Wade 4F 25
Bridle Way PL12: Salt 1F 89
 TR8: Q Dow 6D 36
BRIGHTON 2C 169
Brighton Ter. TR18: Penz 6F 149
 (off Morrab Rd.)
BRILL .2F 159 (2A 174)
Brillwater TR11: Const 2G 159
Brillwater Rd. TR11: Const 2G 159
Brisbane Ter. PL14: Lisk 5B 70
 (off Heathlands Rd.)
British Rd. TR5: S Agn 2B 96
Briton's Hill TR18: Penz 4G 149
BRIXTON 2D 171
Brixton Ter. TR13: Helst 3C 158
Broadclose Hill EX23: Bud 5D 8
Broad La. PL12: T'ton 1A 88
 TR15: I'gan 3J 111
BROADLANES 3C 42
Broad-Mead PL17: Call 5C 72
Broad Pk. PL14: S Keyn 2C 78
 PL15: Laun 2G 17
Broad Pk. Cl. PL27: Pity 7F 19
 TR11: M Bri .6B 124
Broads La. TR10: P'ryn 7B 124
Broad St. PL15: Laun 3H 17
 PL28: Pad 3B 22
 TR1: Tru 4K 107
 TR7: Newq 3E 34
 TR9: S Maj 4C 30
 TR10: P'ryn .5B 128
Broads Yd. PL11: Downd 6H 79
Broad Vw. TR4: Trisp 2B 98
Broad Wlk. PL12: Salt 4G 89
 TR13: Helst 2B 158
Broadway, The PL26: T'vsce 5C 46
BROADWOODWIDGER 2D 167
Brocks La. PL10: M'brk 2D 94
Brockstone Rd. PL25: S Aus 4A 58
Bromfield Cres. TR2: Gram R 6K 37
Bronescombe Cl.
 TR10: P'ryn .5B 128
Brook, The PL12: Salt 1G 89
Brook Cl. TR13: Helst 3B 158
Brook Ct. TR11: Fal 1E 132
 (off Brook St.)
Brookdale Ct. PL27: Wade 4E 24
Brookdown Ter. PL12: Salt 2G 89
Brookdown Vs. PL12: Salt 2G 89
Brook Dr. EX23: Flex 3D 8
Brooke Cl. PL12: Salt 3J 89
Brookfield Cl. PL26: Lanj 5J 55
Brooking Way PL12: Salt 2E 88
Brooklyn PL27: Wade 4F 25
 (off Jubilee Rd.)
Brooklyn Flats TR2: S Mawe 7D 130
 (off Hillhead)
Brooklyn Ter. TR2: S Mawe 7D 130
Brook Pl. TR10: P'ryn 5A 128
 TR11: Fal 1E 132
Brook Rd. PL27: Wade 4E 24
 TR11: Fal 2D 132
Brook's Hill PL12: Salt 1G 89
Brookside PL25: S Aus 5K 57
 TR4: Chac 6D 104

Brookside Cl. PL15: Laun 1G 17
Brook St. TR11: Fal 1E 132
 TR19: Mou 6D 154
Brook Ter. TR19: Mou 6D 154
Brookward Ter. TR18: Hea 3D 148
 (off Madron Rd.)
Brookway TR27: Phil 7D 138
Broomfield Dr. PL31: B'min 5D 32
Broomfield Rd. PL27: Wade 4G 25
Broomhill PL12: Salt 3F 89
Broomhill La. EX23: Pou 2F 9
Broomhill Mnr. EX23: Pou 3F 9
Brown Gelly Barrows 3B 166
Browning Cl. TR9: S Maj 5B 30
Browning Dr. PL31: B'min 5D 32
Brownlow Pl. PL31: B'min 3F 33
Browns Hill PL23: Fow 7J 61
 TR10: P'ryn 3K 127
Brown Willy 420 m (1,377 ft) 3B 166
Bruallen Cl. PL30: S Teat 2B 26
Brunel Bus. Pk. PL25: S Aus 6J 57
Brunel Cl. TR27: Ang 7G 139
Brunel Ct. TR1: Tru 5H 107
Brunel Hgts. PL12: Salt 3H 89
 (off Fore St.)
Brunel Quays PL22: Los 3E 52
Brunel Rd. PL12: Salt 1E 88
Brunel Vw. PL12: Salt 2J 89
Brush End PL26: Lel 2D 140
Bryher Cl. PL17: K Bray 2C 72
Bryny Cl. PL30: S Teat 3B 26
Bubble Retail Pk., The PL14: Lisk 5D 70
Buckett's Hill TR15: Red 6D 112
 TR16: Red 6D 112
Buckeys La. TR2: S Mawe 7E 130
Buckingham Nip TR4: Chac 6D 104
Buckingham Pl. TR16: S Da 2K 113
 (off West End)
Buckingham's Cl. TR8: S New E 2G 37
Buckingham's Ter. TR4: Chac 4H 105
Buckingham Ter. TR16: S Da 2K 113
BUCKLAND MONACHORUM 1D 171
Buckland St. PL1: Plym 5F 163
Bucklers La. PL25: S Aus 5B 58
Buckler Village PL25: S Aus 5B 58
BUCK'S CROSS 1B 164
BUCKSHEAD 1A 108
BUCK'S MILLS 1B 164
Buckwell St. PL1: Plym 5J 163
BUD 4C 8
BUDE 4C 8 (3A 164)
Bude & North Cornwall Golf Course 4C 8
Budehaven Leisure Cen. 5E 8
Bude Holiday Pk. EX23: Mae 1C 8
Bude Ind. Est. EX23: Bud 6E 8
Bude Marshes Local Nature Reserve 6C 8
Budemeadows Touring Pk. EX23: Bud 7D 10
Bude-Stratton Bus. Pk. EX23: Bud 7F 9
BUDGE'S SHOP 2C 171
Budnic Hill TR6: P'rth 4C 40
Budnick Est. TR6: P'rth 4C 40
Budock Pl. TR11: Fal 1F 133
Budock Ter. TR11: Fal 2E 132
BUDOCK WATER 2A 132 (1A 174)
BUGLE .6H 43 (2D 169)
Bugle Station (Rail) .6H 43
Buildings, The TR20: L Roc 3B 150
BULKWORTHY 2B 164
Bullans Ct. TR26: S Ives 3G 137
Bullans La. TR26: S Ives 3G 137 (3C 136)
Bullans Ter. TR26: S Ives 3G 137 (3C 136)
Bulleid Way EX23: Bud 6D 8
Bullock La. TR13: Helst 4B 158
 (Grange Rd.)
 TR13: Helst 5B 158
 (Gwelmeneth)
 TR13: Helst 5C 158
 (Meneage Rd.)
Bullock Mkt. Ter. TR18: Penz 4F 149
 (off St Clare St.)
Bull Point Barracks PL5: Plym 5K 89
Bulwark Rd. TR13: Helst 5B 158
Bungalows, The PL13: Loo 3H 81
Bunkers Hill TR26: S Ives 1J 137 (2D 136)
Bunt's La. TR16: S Da 2A 114
Burden Cl. PL31: B'min 5E 32
Bureau Pl. PL27: Wade 3F 25
Burgess Cl. EX23: Pou 2F 9
Buriton Row TR18: Penz 5E 148

BURLAWN 7G 25 (1C 169)
Burley Cl. TR1: Tru .6K 107
Burnards Ct. PL31: B'min 3F 33
 (off Berrycoombe Rd.)
Burnards La. PL31: B'min 3F 33
 (off Dennison Rd.)
BURNCOOSE 2C 122
Burncoose Nurseries 2C 122
Burnett Cl. PL12: Salt 3F 89
Burngullow La. PL26: H St 5A 56
Burn Pk. Holiday Village EX23: Stra 4F 9
Burns Vw. PL11: Craft 5F 91
BURNTHOUSE
 Liskeard 1D 68
 Penryn 7H 123
Burnthouse La. TR27: Hayl 2J 141
Burn Vw. EX23: Bud .4C 8
BURNWITHIAN 3K 113
Burnwithian Ter. TR16: S Da 3K 113
BURRAS 1D 173
BURRATON
 PL12, St Dominick 3J 77
 PL12, Saltash 2F 89 (2D 171)
BURRATON COOMBE 3D 88
Burraton Rd. PL12: Salt 1D 88
Burrow Rd. PL26: S Ives 1K 137
Burrows, The PL26: Polg 3C 64
 TR26: S Ives 4G 137 (3C 136)
Burthallan La. TR26: S Ives 2B 136
BURYAS BRIDGE 7A 148
Bury Castle 1A 170
BUSH .2H 9 (3A 164)
Bush Pk. PL15: Laun 4J 17
BUSVEAL 4H 113
Butson Pk. TR5: S Agn 2K 97
Buttercup Mdw. PL15: Laun 5K 17
Butterdon Mill Holiday Homes
 PL14: Merry 1K 71
Butterdown PL12: Salt 2D 88
Buttlegate PL11: Downd 6J 79
Butts, The PL18: Cals 5G 75
 PL34: Tin 6C 12
 TR8: S New E 2G 37
Butts La. PL35: Bosc 2K 13
Butts Pk. PL22: Los .3G 53
Byan Cl. TR3: Thre .5K 105
By-Pass Rd. TR15: Red 1D 112

C

Cabot Cl. PL12: Salt .3G 89
Cades Parc TR13: Helst 3C 158
CADGWITH 3A 174
Cadoc Cl. PL28: S Mer 5E 20
Cadogan Cl. TR14: Camb 2D 118
Cadogan Dr. TR14: Camb 2E 118
Cadogan Rd. TR14: Camb 2D 118
Cadson Bury Fort 1C 171
Caerhays Castle 3C 169
Cairn William Ter. TR18: Newl 2C 154
 (off St Peter's Hill)
Calais Rd. TR27: S Pra 6K 141
CALARTHA 3D 144
Calartha Rd. TR19: Pend 3D 144
Calartha Ter. TR19: Pend 4D 144
Caldwells Rd. TR18: Penz 4F 149
CALENICK 1J 117
Calenick St. TR1: Tru 5J 107
Cal Hill TR16: Red 4F 113
California Gdns. TR2: P'stho 3J 131
CALLESTICK 2A 168
CALLINGTON 5C 72 (1C 171)
Callington Arc. PL17: Call 5C 72
 (off New Rd.)
Callington Bus. Pk. PL17: Call 5E 72
Callington Heritage Cen. 6B 72
Callington Rd. PL12: Salt 1E 88
 PL14: Lisk 3C 70
 PL17: Call, Harr 5J 73
CALLOOSE 5B 142
Calloose Farm Carvan Pk.
 TR27: Leeds 5B 142
Calloose La. E. TR27: Leeds 5B 142
Calloose La. W. TR27: Leeds 5B 142
Callywith Gate Ind. Est. PL31: B'min 2J 33
Calshot Cl. TR7: S Mino 2B 36
CALSTOCK 7J 75 (1D 171)
Calstock Rd. PL18: Gun 1H 75
Calstock Station (Rail) 7H 75
Calver Cl. TR10: P'ryn 4A 128
Calvez Cl. PL10: M'brk 1D 94
Camaret Dr. TR26: S Ives 4D 136
Cambeak PL35: Bosc 2J 13
CAMBORNE 1D 118 (1D 173)
Camborne Retail Pk. TR15: Pool 5G 111
Camborne Station (Rail) 1D 118
Cambridge La. W. PL1: Plym 3F 163
Cambridge Pl. TR11: Fal 2E 132

Cambridge Ter. *TR15: Red* 1G *113*
    (off Redruth Highway)
CAMBROSE .4B 102 (3A 168)
Camden Ct. PL4: Plym 3K 163
Camden Rd. PL4: Plym 3K 163
Camden St. PL4: Plym 3K 163
Camel Cl. PL28: Pad .4B 22
Camel Ct. PL31: B'min 2E 32
CAMELFORD 3J 15 (2B 166)
Camelford Leisure Cen. 3H 15
CAMELS 6K 135
Camelside PL27: Wade 4F 25
Camel Trail, The (Wadebridge) 1C 169
Camel Valley Vineyard 1D 169
Cameron Cl. EX23: Flex 3C 8
Campbeltown Way TR11: Fal 2G 133
Camperknowle Cl. PL10: M'brk 1D 94
Campfield Hill TR1: Tru 4K 107
Campfield Ter. TR1: Tru 4K 107
Camp Hall Rd. TR8: Hol B 2A 38
Campion Cl. PL12: Salt 1F 89
    PL15: Laun 5K 17
Cample Haye Vs. *PL5: Plym* 4K *89*
    (off Lit. Ash Rd.)
Camullas Way TR7: Newq 4B 34
Canfield Ter. TR15: Red 3C 112
Cannamanning Rd. PL26: Penw 5K 49
Cannis Rd. PL25: S Aus 3J 57
Cannon Hill PL14: Lisk 5B 70
Cannon Ter. PL14: Lisk 5B 70
Canons Pl. TR13: Helst 2D 158
CANONSTOWN 6B 140 (1C 173)
Cantillion Cl. PL27: Pity 7F 19
Canton PL26: G Hav 2J 135
CANWORTHY WATER 1C 167
Canyke Flds. PL31: B'min 5H 33
Canyke Rd. PL31: B'min 6J 33
Cape Cl. TR19: S Jus 3H 145
Cape Cornwall Golf Course 2F 145
Cape Cornwall Rd. TR19: S Jus 2F 145
Cape Cornwall St. TR19: S Jus 3H 145
Cape Terrace TR19: S Jus 3H 145
Caprera Pl. PL4: Plym 2G 163
Caprera Ter. La. PL4: Plym 2G 163
Captains Ct. TR15: Red 3D 112
Captain's Wlk. TR11: Fal 3E 132
Caradon Cl. PL14: Pens 1J 67
    PL17: Call 6C 72
Caradon Dr. PL14: Lisk 4A 70
Caradon Hgts. PL14: Dar 2D 66
    PL14: Lisk 3C 70
Caradon Ter. PL12: Salt 1G 89
CARADON TOWN .3C 167
Caradon Vw. PL14: S Cle 4A 66
CARBEAN 5F 49
Carbeile Rd. PL11: Tor 3J 93
Carbeil Holiday Pk. PL11: Downd 6J 79
Carbes La. PL22: Los 3E 52
CARBIS 5D 42
CARBIS BAY 6F 137 (1C 173)
Carbis Bay Holiday Pk. TR26: C Bay 1A 140
Carbis Bay Station (Rail) 6F 137
Carbis Beach Apartments TR26: C Bay 6F 137
Carbis Ct. TR15: Red 3C 112
CARBIS MOOR 4A 50
Carbis Water TR26: C Bay 7E 136
Carboth La. PL15: Laun 4G 17
CARCLAZE 3J 57
Carclaze Rd. PL25: S Aus 3J 57
CARCLEW 4B 124
Carclew Av. TR7: Newq 3F 35
Carclew Rd. TR11: M Bri 5C 124
Carclew St. TR1: Tru 5K 107
Carclew Ter. TR1: Tru 6K 107
    TR3: Devo 2C 124
Cardell Rd. PL31: B'min 3F 33
Cardell Way TR7: Newq 4H 35
CARDINHAM 1A 170
Cardinham Churchyard Cross 1A 170
Cardinnis Grn. *PL14: Lisk* 4C *70*
    (off Bodgara Way)
Cardinnis Rd. TR18: Penz 6C 148
Cardrew Bus. Pk. TR15: Red 2E 112
Cardrew Cl. TR15: Red 1D 112
Cardrew Dr. TR15: Red 2F 113
Cardrew Ind. Est. TR15: Red 1E 112
Cardrew La. TR15: Red 3E 112
    (Hillside Ter.)
    TR15: Red 2D 112
    (North St.)
Cardrew Ter. TR15: Red 2F 113
Cardrew Way TR15: Red 7F 103
Cardwen Est. PL13: Pely 2B 80
Carew Cl. PL11: Craft 5E 90
    TR16: S Da 3K 113
Carew Gdns. PL12: Salt 2F 89
Carew-Pole Cl. TR1: Tru 6A 108
Carew Rd. TR1: Tru .4J 107
    TR16: S Da 3K 113

Carew Ter. PL11: Tor 4K 93
Carew Wharf PL11: Tor 4K 93
Carey Cl. PL12: Salt .1G 89
Carey Pk. PL13: Polp 5C 80
    TR1: Tru 5J 107
    TR13: Helst 2B 158
Carglaze Ind. Est. PL25: S Aus 2J 57
Cargoll Rd. TR8: S New E 2F 37
CARGREEN 2J 85 (1D 171)
Cargwyn PL26: Penw 6J 49
Cargy Cl. TR8: Cube 4F 39
CARHARRACK 5A 114 (3A 168)
Carkeek Cl. PL26: S Ste 5C 54
CARKEEL 6E 84 (1D 171)
Carkeel Barns PL12: Cark 7E 84
Carkeel Ind. Est. PL12: Salt 7F 85
Carknown Gdns. TR15: Red 5F 113
CARLAND CROSS .2B 168
CARLEEN 2D 173
Carlidnack Cl. TR11: Mawn S 2B 160
Carlidnack La. TR11: Mawn S 1B 160
Carlidnack Rd. TR11: B Wat, Mawn S 2B 160
CARLOGGAS
    Newquay 6G 29
    St Austell 4J 49
Carloggas Cl. TR8: S Mawg 6G 29
Carloggas Farm TR8: S Mawg 6G 29
Carloggas Gro. TR9: S Maj 5A 30
Carloggas Way TR9: S Maj 5B 30
Carlton Ter. PL26: S Den 2D 46
Carlton Vs. PL12: Hatt 4B 84
CARLUDDON 6J 49
CARLYON BAY 6C 58 (2D 169)
Carlyon Bay Caravan & Camping Pk.
    PL25: Carl 5E 58
Carlyon Bay Golf Course 6E 58
Carlyon Cl. PL11: Tor 2H 93
    TR1: Tru 5J 107
    TR3: Thre 5A 106
Carlyon Ct. TR3: P Pla 4G 117
Carlyon Rd. PL25: S Aus 5H 57
    TR1: Tru 4J 107
    TR3: P Pla 4G 117
Carmen Sq. *TR18: Hea* 3D *148*
    (off Madron Rd.)
CARMINOW CROSS 7K 33
Carminowe Cres. TR18: Penz 5E 148
Carminow Rd. PL31: B'min 7J 33
Carminow Rd. Ind. Est. PL31: B'min 6J 33
Carminow Way TR7: Newq 2H 35
Carmython Ct. TR7: Newq 2H 35
CARN 7J 121
Carnarthen Moor TR15: C Bre 7J 111
Carnarthen Rd. TR14: Camb 7E 110
Carnarthen St. TR14: Camb 1E 118
Carn Bargas PL26: W'moor 2J 47
CARNBARGUS 7A 40
CARN BOSAVERN .4J 145
Carn Bosavern TR19: S Jus 4J 145
Carn Bosavern Cl. TR19: S Jus 3J 145
Carn Brea 6A 112
Carn Brea Av. TR15: Pool 5J 111
Carn Brea Castle 6B 112
Carn Brea La. TR15: Pool 5J 111
Carn Brea Leisure Cen. 5J 111
CARN BREA VILLAGE 5B 112 (3A 168)
Carn Brea Vs. TR15: C Bre 5B 112
Carncrows Rd. TR26: S Ives 1K 137
Carncrows St. TR26: S Ives 1K 137
CARNE
    Helston 7E 160
    St Austell 1E 46
    Truro .7H 135 (3C 169)
Carne, The TR18: Newl 7D 148
Carnebo Hill TR4: Goonh 4J 41
Carne Cl. TR27: Leeds 7D 142
Carne Ct. PL26: S Den 2E 46
CARNE CROSS 5D 50
Carnego La. TR8: Sum 7B 44
Carne Hill PL25: T'oon 4B 56
    PL26: S Den 1D 46
Carnellis Rd. TR26: S Ives 3C 136
Carne Mdws. TR2: Tr'sln 2H 109
CARN ENTRAL 1G 119
Carne Quarry TR12: Mull 2J 161
Carne Rd. TR18: Newl 7D 148
Carnes Bldgs. *TR18: Penz* 6F *149*
    (off Queen St.)
Carnes Ct. TR11: Fal 3G 133
Carne Ter. PL26: S Den 1E 46
Carneton Cl. TR8: Cran 6A 34
Carn Euny Ancient Village 2B 172
Carne Vw. Cl. TR14: Camb 5F 111
Carne Vw. Rd. TR2: Pro 2J 99
Carnewas Point 6E 11
Carn Galver Engine House 1B 172
Carnglaze Caverns .1A 170
Carnglaze Cl. PL14: Lisk 4D 70

Carnglaze Pl. *TR26: S Ives* 1K *137*
    (off Victoria Pl.)
Carn Gloose Rd. TR19: S Jus 3F 145
CARN GREY 1A 58
Carn Gwavas Ter. TR18: Newl 2D 154
CARNHELL GREEN 1F 143 (1D 173)
Carnhell Rd. TR14: C Grn 1E 142
    TR27: Gwinn 1E 142
CARNHOT 3C 104
Carninney La. TR26: C Bay 7E 136
    (not continuous)
CARNKIE
    TR16, Four Lanes 1B 120 (1D 173)
    TR16, Penryn 1A 174
CARNKIEF .7H 41 (2A 168)
Carn La. TR16: Carn 7A 112
CARN MARTH 6G 113
CARNMARTH 5K 113
Carn Marth La. TR16: C Mar 6F 113
CARNMENELLIS 7D 120
Carnmoggas Holiday Pk. PL26: Lon A 4C 64
Carnon Cres. TR3: C Dow 7D 116
CARNON DOWNS 7D 116 (3A 168)
Carnon Downs Caravan & Camping Pk.
    TR3: C Dow 6E 116
Carnon Mine TR3: Devo 3E 124
Carnon Ter. TR3: Devo 2C 124
Carnon Valley TR3: C Dow 6A 116
Carnoustie Dr. PL12: Salt 3E 88
Carn Rock TR10: P'ryn 5B 128
Carn Ros TR19: Pend 3B 144
Carnsew Cl. TR10: M Bur 5G 127
Carnsew Cres. TR10: M Bur 5G 127
Carnsew Mdw. TR27: Hayl 2F 141
Carnsew Rd. TR27: Hayl 3F 141
Carnsmerry PL26: Bugl 7G 43
Carnsmerry Cres. PL25: S Aus 5J 57
Carnstabba Rd. TR26: S Ives 4B 136
Carn Todden TR19: Mou 6E 154
Carn Topna TR19: Mou 6E 154
CARN TOWAN 2E 146
Carn Vw. TR16: Gwen 1B 122
Carn Vw. TR16: Carn 1B 120
Carn Vw. Flds. TR16: Carn 1B 120
Carn Vw. Ter. *TR15: Red* 3E *112*
    (off Jenkins Ter.)
    TR19: Pend 4D 144
CARNYORTH 6B 144 (1A 172)
Carnyorth Hill TR19: S Jus 6A 144
Carnyorth Ter. TR19: S Jus 6B 144
Caroline Cl. TR27: Hayl 7E 138
Caroline Row TR27: Hayl 7E 138
CARPALLA 2H 55 (2C 169)
Carpalla Rd. PL26: Fox 3H 55
Carpalla Ter. PL26: Fox 2H 55
Carpenter Ct. PL31: B'min 3F 33
Carpmael Av. TR8: Newq 5J 35
Carrack Dhu TR26: S Ives 3H 137 (2D 136)
Carrack Dhu Est. TR26: S Ives 2G 137
Carrack Gladden TR26: C Bay 6F 137
Carrallack La. TR19: S Jus 4H 145
Carrallack M. TR19: S Jus 3H 145
Carrallack Ter. TR19: S Jus 4H 145
Carriage Parc TR4: Goonh 5H 41
Carrickowel Cres. PL25: S Aus 4A 58
Carrick Rd. TR11: Fal 3C 132
Carrick Way TR2: S Mawe 7D 130
Carrine Rd. TR1: Tru 5E 106
Carrisbrooke Way PL12: Salt 2D 88
Carruan Farm Cen. PL27: S Minv 2F 19
CARSIZE 7B 142
Carsize La. TR27: Leeds 7C 142
Carter Cl. TR7: Newq 4H 35
Carteret Rd. EX23: Bud 5D 8
CARTHEW 6E 48 (2D 169)
Carthew Cl. PL14: Lisk 5C 70
    TR26: S Ives 2C 136
Carthew Ct. TR26: S Ives 2C 136
Carthew Ter. TR26: S Ives 2C 136
Carthew Way TR26: S Ives 2C 136
Carvath Ho. *PL25: S Aus* 6H *57*
    (off Eastbourne Rd.)
Carvedras Ct. TR1: Tru 5H 107
Carvossa Est. TR20: Crow 2J 155
Carvoza Rd. TR1: Tru 4K 107
Carwinard Ct. TR27: Ang 7G 139
Carwinion & Grebe Rock to Porth Saxon 2A 174
Carwinion Gdns. 3C 160
Carwinion La. TR11: Mawn S 3B 160
Carwinion Rd. TR11: Mawn S 2B 160
Carwinion Ter. *PL14: Lisk* 6A *70*
    (off Station Rd.)
Carwin La. TR27: Ang 7G 139
Carwin Ri. TR27: Con D, Log 7E 138
Carwollen Rd. PL25: S Aus 2J 57
Carworgie Way TR9: S Roa 1G 45
CARWYNNEN 6E 118
Carwynnen Cl. TR14: Praze 3K 143
Casebourne M. EX23: Bud 5E 8
Casey La. PL13: Pely 3C 80

Cassiterite Cl. PL25: S Aus 5B 58
CASTALLACK 7A 154
Castel Wary Cl. TR13: Helst 4B 158
Casterills Rd. TR13: Helst 5D 158
CASTLE 6D 52
Castle Canyke Rd. PL31: B'min 5G 33
Castle Cl. TR11: Fal 2J 133
Castle Ct. PL12: Salt 3E 88
  TR20: Pra S 6J 155
CASTLEDORE 1E 60
Castle Dore 1E 60
Castledore Rd. PL24: Tyw 1B 60
Castle Dr. PL31: B'min 3H 33
  TR2: S Mawe 7B 130
  TR11: Fal 2H 133
  TR20: Pra S 6H 155
Castle Dyke PL15: Laun 3H 17
Castle Dyke La. PL1: Plym 6J 163
Castle Gdns. *PL14: Lisk* 4B 70
  (off Park Vw.)
Castle Grn. TR13: Helst 4B 158
Castle Hgts. PL34: Tin 6A 12
Castle Heritage Cen. 5C 8
Castle Hill PL14: Lisk 4B 70
  PL22: Los 6D 52
  TR13: Helst 4B 158
  (off Castle Grn.)
Castle Hill Ct. PL31: B'min 3G 33
Castle Hill Gdns. PL31: B'min 3H 33
Castle Horneck Cl. TR18: Penz 5D 148
Castle Horneck Rd. TR18: Penz 5D 148
  TR20: Penz 5C 148
Castle La. PL14: Lisk 4B 70
Castlemead Cl. PL12: Salt 2F 89
Castlemead Dr. PL12: Salt 2F 89
Castle Mdws. PL15: Laun 5F 17
  TR5: S Agn 3B 96
Castle Mdws. Ct. TR5: S Agn 3B 96
Castle Ri. PL12: Salt 4E 88
  TR1: Tru 4J 107
Castle Rd. PL34: Tin 6A 12
  TR18: Penz 4F 149
  TR20: Ludg 1F 155
Castle Rock PL29: P Isa 1J 19
Castle St. PL1: Plym 6J 163
  PL13: Loo 6K 81 (5H 81)
  PL14: Lisk 4B 70
  PL15: Laun 3H 17
  PL31: B'min 3G 33
  TR1: Tru 5J 107
Castle Vw. PL12: Salt 4E 88
  PL14: Lisk 4B 70
  (off Castle St.)
  PL22: Los 2G 53
  PL26: S Den 1D 46
  PL34: Tin 6A 12
  TR20: L Roc 3A 150
Castle Vw. Cl. TR15: Red 2D 112
Castle Vw. Pk. TR11: Mawn S 2B 160
CASTLEWICH 7E 72
Caswarth Ter. PL28: Pad 3B 22
Catalina Row PL27: S Eval 3J 31
Catchfrench Cres. PL14: Lisk 4D 70
Cathebedron Rd. TR14: C Grn 1F 143
Cathedral Cl. *TR1: Tru* 5K 107
  (off Union Pl.)
Cathedral La. *TR1: Tru* 5K 107
  (off High Cross)
Cathedral Vw. TR1: Tru 3H 107
Catherine Cl. EX23: Bud 6E 8
Catherine St. PL1: Plym 5H 163
CAUDLEDOWN 3G 49
Caudledown La. PL26: Sten 3G 49
Caunter Rd. PL14: Lisk 4C 70
Causeland Station (Rail) 5D 78
Causeway, The TR11: Fal 1D 132
  TR17: Mar 5E 150
  TR27: Hayl 4E 140
Causewayhead TR18: Penz 5F 149
Causley Cl. PL15: Laun 2H 17
Cave La. TR19: Mou 6D 154
Cavendish Cres. TR7: Newq 4J 35
CAWSAND 6E 94 (2D 171)
Cayforth TR16: P'ath 4F 101
Cedar Cl. PL11: Tor 4H 93
  PL17: Call 6D 72
Cedar Ct. PL12: Salt 3H 89
  TR14: Camb 5G 111
Cedar Dr. PL11: Tor 4H 93
Cedar Gro. EX23: Flex 3D 8
Cedar Ri. *PL14: Lisk* 5A 70
  (off Manley Rd.)
Cedars, The PL25: Carl 6E 58
  TR1: Tru 7J 107
Cedar Wood Cres. PL25: S Aus 6J 57
Celia Hgts. PL31: B'min 6H 33
Celtic Rd. PL17: Call 5E 72
Celtic Shores PL11: Downd 7J 79
Cemetery Rd. PL18: Alb, Dra 4F 75

Centenary Row Middle TR14: Camb 7E 110
Centenary Row W. TR14: Camb 1E 118
Centenary St. TR14: Camb 1E 118
Central Av. PL25: S Aus 4J 57
Central Cl. PL26: S Ste 4C 54
Central Park 1G 163
Central Pk. Av. PL4: Plym 1F 163
Central Pk. Towers PL4: Plym 1G 163
Central Rd. PL1: Plym 7F 163
  TR8: Hol B 3A 38
Central Sq. TR7: Newq 3E 34
CENTRAL TREVISCOE 4B 46
Century Cl. PL25: S Aus 3K 57
  TR13: Helst 1D 158
Century Ct. TR7: Newq 1K 35
Century La. TR2: Very 6J 135
Century Quay PL4: Plym 5K 163
Ceres Ct. EX23: Bud 6D 8
CHACEWATER 6E 104 (3A 168)
Chacewater Hill TR4: Chac 5E 104
Chacewater Pk. TR4: Chac 7B 104
Chadwick Parc TR15: Red 2D 112
Chainwalk Dr. TR1: Tru 4H 107
Chalbury Hgts. TR11: Const 2F 159
Chalet, The PL11: Downd 7J 79
Challacombe Gdns. TR10: P'ryn 4A 128
Challenger Quay TR11: Fal 2G 133
Challis Av. TR8: S Mawg 5G 29
Challow Ter. PL30: Lux 1D 50
Champions Ct. TR13: Helst 3B 158
Champions Yd. *TR18: Penz* 5F 149
  (off Causewayhead)
Chancery Cl. TR4: S Erm 3C 98
Chancery La. *TR18: Penz* 5F 149
  (off Queen St.)
Chandlers Wlk. PL25: S Aus 6A 58
Chandos Pl. PL25: S Aus 6G 57
Channel Vw. *PL23: Polr* 7C 60
  (off St Saviour's Hill)
  PL25: S Aus 3A 58
  TR15: Red 2F 113
  TR26: S Ives 2G 137
Channel Vw. Ter. *TR15: Red* 4E 112
  (off Trefusis Ter.)
Channon Rd. PL12: Salt 1E 88
Chantry La. PL13: Loo 4J 81
Chantry Pk. PL17: Call 6C 72
CHAPEL 4F 17
CHAPEL AMBLE 3D 165
Chapel Cl. PL18: S An Cpl 3E 74
  TR2: S Jus R 2E 130
  TR8: Cran 6B 34
  TR14: Camb 6G 111
  TR27: Con D 5J 139
  (off Mutton Hill)
Chapel Ct. PL26: Penw 5J 49
  PL28: Pad 3B 22
  (off Lanadwell St.)
  TR4: Dec 6D 104
  TR15: Red 3D 112
  TR27: Hayl 1J 141
  (off Chapel La.)
Chapeldown Rd. PL11: Tor 4J 93
Chapel Farm TR14: Tro 4G 119
Chapel Fld. PL25: S Aus 4B 58
Chapel Forth Camp Site
  TR5: S Agn 2E 96
Chapel Gdns. TR16: Four L 3C 120
Chapel Grn. PL26: T'lwth 2C 64
Chapel Ground PL13: Loo 5G 81
Chapel Hill PL15: Laun 4F 17
  PL26: Polg 2C 64
  PL26: Stick 3A 64
  TR1: Tru 5H 107
  TR3: Devo 2D 124
  TR3: Pons 5F 123
  TR4: P'twn 7C 96
  TR6: Bol 6C 40
  TR7: Newq 3E 34
  TR12: Gweek 5G 159
  TR14: Bre 7G 111
  TR15: C Bre 6J 111
  TR16: L'ner 2G 121
  TR16: Nanc 3C 102
  TR27: S Er 6E 140
Chapelhill TR27: Hayl 1H 141
Chapel Ho. PL26: Fox 1G 55
Chapel La. PL23: Polr 7C 60
  PL25: T Mil 3C 58
  PL27: Wade 4E 24
  PL30: S Mab 6C 26
  PL31: B'min 3F 33
  TR10: P'ryn 5A 128
  TR12: Lizar 4G 161
  TR16: Crof 3B 114
  TR20: Gold 4C 152
  TR27: Hayl 1J 141
Chapel Mdw. TR4: P'twn 1C 102
Chapel Mdws. TR3: P Sta 1K 123

Chapel Pk. PL15: Laun 4G 17
Chapel Pk. Gdns. PL15: Laun 4G 17
Chapel Pk. Ter. PL15: Laun 4G 17
Chapel Pl. TR1: Tru 5K 107
Chapel Point La. PL26: P'melln 7D 134
CHAPEL PORTH 3D 96
Chapel Rd. PL12: Salt 2D 88
  PL24: Par 3K 59
  PL26: Fox 1H 55
  PL26: Roch 4B 42
  PL30: S Tud 5J 27
  TR9: I Que 2H 45
  TR14: Camb 5G 111
  TR18: Hea 2D 148
  TR19: S Jus 3H 145
  TR27: Leeds 7D 142
Chapel Row PL11: Tor 3K 93
  PL14: Trem 3B 66
  TR1: Tru 6J 107
  TR14: Praze 4K 143
  TR16: Four L 3C 120
  TR18: Gul 2G 149
  (off Green La. Hill)
Chapel Sq. PL26: Mev 6C 134
  TR14: Tro 4G 119
  TR20: Crow 2K 155
Chapel Steps PL13: Polp 7B 80
Chapel St. PL4: Plym 3J 163
  PL17: Call 5D 72
  PL18: Gun 1G 75
  PL26: Mev 6C 134
  (off Chapel Sq.)
  PL32: Came 3H 15
  TR2: Pro 2H 99
  TR14: Camb 1D 118
  TR15: Red 3D 112
  TR16: S Da 2K 113
  TR17: Mar 4E 150
  TR18: Newl 1C 154
  TR18: Penz 5F 149
  TR19: Mou 6D 154
  TR19: S Jus 2H 145
  TR26: S Ives 3H 137 (3D 136)
Chapel Ter. PL17: Harr 4A 74
  PL18: Alb 4F 75
  (off Cemetery Rd.)
  PL24: S Bla 7H 51
  PL26: H St 4H 55
  PL27: Wade 4E 24
  PL30: S Mab 6C 26
  TR2: S Mawe 7D 130
  TR3: Devo 2D 124
  TR11: B Wat 2A 132
  TR11: Fal 1F 133
  (off Vernon Pl.)
  TR13: P'ven 7F 157
  (off Fore St.)
  TR14: Bre 7G 111
  (off Chapel Hill)
  TR15: C Bre 5B 112
  TR15: I Hig 4K 111
  (not continuous)
  TR15: Red 6F 113
  TR16: Carh 4A 114
  TR16: Sk Btm 3J 103
  TR19: Trew 5B 144
  TR27: Hayl 2G 141
CHAPEL TOWN 7A 44 (2B 168)
Chapel Town Bus. Pk.
  TR8: Sum 7A 44
Chapel Town Cl. TR11: Mawn S 1B 160
Chapman Ct. PL12: Salt 2D 88
Chapmans Way PL25: S Aus 5J 57
CHAPMANS WELL 1D 167
Chard Ter. TR11: Fal 2E 132
Chariot Rd. TR15: I Hig 4K 111
CHARK 1A 52
Charles Av. TR11: Fal 3C 132
Charles Bassett Cl. TR13: Helst 4C 158
Charles Church 4J 163
Charles Cl. PL25: S Aus 6K 57
Charles Cross PL4: Plym 4J 163
Charles St. PL1: Plym 3J 163
  PL26: Bugl 7G 43
  TR1: Tru 5J 107
  TR18: Newl 7D 148
CHARLESTOWN 7B 58 (2D 169)
Charlestown Rd. PL25: Char, S Aus 6A 58
Charlotte Cl. TR4: Mt Hwk 7H 97
Charlotte Dymond Monument 2B 166
Charter Cl. TR10: P'ryn 5B 128
  TR13: Helst 5C 158
Charter Way PL14: Lisk 3D 70
Chase, The PL26: Stick 3K 63
CHASTY 3B 164
Chateau Cl. PL26: Goth 2J 55
Chatsworth Way PL25: Carl 6C 58
Chawleigh Cl. PL18: Dra 3G 75
Chedworth St. PL4: Plym 3K 163

Cheesewring 3C 167
Chegwin Ct. TR7: Newq 4F 35
Chegwin Gdns. TR7: Newq 4F 35
Chegwyn Gdns. TR5: S Agn 2A 96
Chegwyns PL26: Fox 1H 55
Chegwyns Hill PL26: Fox 1H 55
Chellean Vean TR4: Cusg 7G 115
Chellew Rd. TR1: Tru 4A 108
   TR7: Newq 3E 34
Cheltenham Pl. PL4: Plym 1K 163
   TR7: Newq 3E 34
Cheltenham Vs. PL4: Plym 1K 163
CHENHALLS 5F 141
Chenhalls Cl. TR27: S Er 6E 140
Chenhalls Rd. TR27: Hayl, S Er 3F 141
Chenoweth Cl. TR14: Camb 6C 110
Chequer Tree Ct. PL18: Dra 3F 75
Chequetts Cl. PL17: Call 6C 72
Cherrill Gdns. EX23: Flex 3D 8
Cherry Gdns. TR18: Penz 5F 149
   (off New St.)
Cherry Gdn. St. TR19: Mou 6D 154
Cherry Tree Cl. PL31: B'min 4D 32
Cherry Tree M. PL25: S Aus 6H 57
Chester Ct. TR7: Newq 3H 35
Chester Pl. PL4: Plym 1K 163
Chester Rd. TR7: Newq 3H 35
Chesterton Ct. PL27: Wade 3D 24
Chesterton Pl. TR7: Newq 2H 35
Chestnut Cl. PL11: Tor 3H 93
   PL12: Salt 1F 89
   PL17: Call 5F 73
   PL30: S Tud 4J 27
   TR11: Fal 7D 128
Chestnut Gro. PL31: B'min 4D 32
Cheviot Rd. TR7: Newq 4F 35
   (not continuous)
Chichester Cl. PL26: Fox 1J 55
Chichester Cres. PL12: Salt 4G 89
   TR7: Newq 5G 35
Chichester Ho. PL1: Plym 6F 163
Chili Rd. TR15: I Hig 4K 111
CHILLA 1D 167
CHILLATON .2D 167
CHILSWORTHY
   Gunnislake 1D 74 (3D 167)
   Holsworthy 3B 164
China Clay Country Park (Wheal Martyn) 7E 48
China Ct. PL25: S Aus 6G 57
   (off South St.)
China Fleet Golf Course 7H 85
Chings All. PL15: Laun 3H 17
   (off Southgate St.)
Chings Ct. PL15: Laun 3H 17
   (off Southgate St.)
Chipman Strand to Pencannow Point 1B 166
Chipponds Dr. PL25: S Aus 6E 56
Chirgwin Ct. TR18: Penz 5F 149
Chirgwin Rd. TR1: Tru 5A 108
Chisholm Cl. PL25: S Aus 6H 57
Chisholme Ct. PL25: S Aus 6H 57
CHIVERTON CROSS 1C 104
Chiverton Ga. TR20: Rosu 6B 152
Chiverton Pk. TR4: Black 1C 104
Chiverton Way TR20: Rosu 6B 152
CHI WAR DRETH 2B 60
Chough Cl. PL15: Laun 5K 17
   TR11: Fal 1C 132
Chough Cres. PL25: S Aus 5K 57
Choughs Cl. TR14: Camb 6B 110
Christian Way TR7: Newq 2K 35
Chûn Castle .1B 172
Chûn Quoit .1B 172
Church Av. PL23: Fow 7K 61
   (off South St.)
Church Cl. TR4: S Erm 2C 98
   TR26: Lel 1E 140
CHURCH COOMBE 6C 112
CHURCH COVE 5J 161
Church Cove Rd. TR12: Lizar 5H 161
Churchend PL13: Loo 7K 81 (5H 81)
Churchfield PL32: Came 3J 15
Churchfield Cl. TR20: Ludg 2H 155
Churchfield Pl. PL24: S Bla 1H 59
Churchfields Rd. TR8: Cube 4E 38
Church Ga. PL14: Lisk 5B 70
Church Hill PL14: Pens 1K 67
   PL18: Cals 6J 75
   PL23: Gola 1J 61
   PL26: Stick 3A 64
   PL29: P Isa 3J 19
   PL34: Tin 7A 12
   TR2: S Mawe 7D 130
   TR4: Chac 7D 104
   TR10: P'ryn 4B 128
   TR13: Helst 3B 158
   TR16: S Da 3A 114
   TR20: Ludg 2H 155
Churchill Wlk. PL12: Salt 4G 89

Churchill Way PL26: Penw 5J 49
Churchlands PL13: Loo 3H 81
Church La. EX23: Bud 5C 8
   PL11: S John 6D 92
   PL12: Carg 3H 85
   PL18: Cals 7H 75
   PL22: Los 3E 52
   PL25: S Aus 6B 58
   PL26: Mev 5C 134
   PL28: Pad 3B 22
   PL31: B'min 3G 33
   TR7: S Mino 2A 36
   TR11: Fal 5F 129
   TR13: Helst 3B 158
   TR14: Camb 7D 110
   TR15: Red 5C 112
   (not continuous)
   TR26: Lel 1D 140
Church Lea PL15: Laun 2F 17
Church M. TR3: Stith 7A 122
Church Pk. PL12: S Mel 6D 76
   PL31: B'min 3G 33
Church Pk. M. PL27: Wade 5E 24
Church Path EX23: Bud 5B 8
   TR7: Newq 3E 34
   (off Manor Rd.)
Church Pl. PL14: Lisk 5B 70
   TR26: S Ives 1J 137 (2D 136)
Church Ri. PL14: S Cle 4A 66
Church Rd. PL12: Salt 3F 89
   PL12: Tide 1B 86
   PL14: Merry 1G 71
   PL25: Char 6B 58
   PL26: S Den 1E 46
   PL30: Lani 6H 31
   PL30: S Tud 5J 27
   TR3: P'hal 3K 123
   TR3: Stith 6A 122
   TR4: Mt Hwk 7G 97
   TR4: Short 6C 98
   TR10: M Bur 6G 127
   TR10: P'ryn 4A 128
   TR11: M Bri 2F 129
   TR14: Camb 7B 110
   TR14: P'nds 2B 118
   TR15: Pool 4H 111
   TR16: Four L 4B 120
   TR16: I'gan 6J 101
   TR18: Hea 3D 148
   TR19: Pend 4C 144
   TR20: Mad 2B 148
   TR26: Lel 2E 140
Church Row PL11: Shev 3G 91
   TR13: P'ven 7F 157
   TR16: Carh 5A 114
   TR16: L'ner 1H 121
Church Side PL23: Fow 7K 61
   (off Lostwithiel St.)
Church Sq. EX23: Stra 5H 9
   PL31: B'min 3G 33
   TR11: Const 2H 159
   TR19: S Jus 3J 145
Church Stile PL15: Laun 3H 17
   (off Market St.)
Church St. EX23: Pou 2F 9
   EX23: Stra 5H 9
   PL12: Land 7G 83
   PL12: S Ger 5D 86
   PL13: Loo 7K 81
   (Church End)
   PL13: Loo 7J 81 (5G 81)
   (Fore St.)
   PL14: Lisk 4B 70
   PL15: Laun 3H 17
   PL17: Call 5C 72
   PL18: Cals 7J 75
   PL24: S Bla 1H 59
   PL24: Tyw 2A 60
   PL25: S Aus 6G 57
   PL26: G Hav 2J 135
   PL26: Mev 5C 134
   PL28: Pad 3A 22
   TR7: S Mino 3A 36
   TR11: Fal 1F 133
   TR13: Helst 3B 158
   TR14: Camb 7D 110
   TR16: Carh 5A 114
   TR16: S Da 3A 114
   TR18: Newl 2C 154
   TR19: S Jus 3J 145
   TR27: S Er 6F 141
Church St. Nth. PL14: Lisk 5B 70
Church St. Sth. PL14: Lisk 5B 70
Church Ter. TR2: Gram R 7K 37
   TR2: Pro 2H 99
   TR3: Devo 2C 124
CHURCH TOWN
   Penzance 2J 149
   Redruth 5C 112

CHURCHTOWN
   Bodmin 1J 27
   Padstow 5F 21
   Redruth 6J 101
Church Town PL14: S Cle 4A 66
Churchtown PL30: Lani 6H 31
   TR5: S Agn 2B 96
   TR8: Cube 4F 39
   TR8: S Eno 6C 44
   TR8: S New E 2G 37
   TR11: B Wat 1B 132
   TR12: Mull 1H 161
   TR27: Gwinn 1B 142
Churchtown Cl. PL26: Roch 5B 42
Churchtown Council Ho's. PL27: S Minv 6J 19
Churchtown Ct. TR27: Gwith 1G 139
Churchtown Farm Community Nature Reserve 5F 89
Churchtown Mdws. PL26: S Ste 4D 54
Churchtown Rd. PL26: S Ste 4C 54
   TR2: Gerr 3J 131
   TR16: I'gan 6J 101
   TR27: Gwith 1H 139
   TR27: Phil 7C 138
Churchtown Va. PL12: Salt 3F 89
Church Vw. PL12: S Dom 2G 77
   PL14: Merry 1G 71
   PL14: S Cle 4A 66
Church Vw. Cl. TR20: Hea 4C 148
Church Vw. Rd. TR2: Pro 2H 99
   TR14: Camb 6F 111
Church Wlk. PL15: Sth P 2A 16
   TR1: Tru 4K 107
   (off St Clement St.)
   TR15: Red 3C 112
Church Way TR11: Fal 2C 132
Churchway TR17: Mar 4G 151
   TR20: Mad 2B 148
Chute La. PL26: G Hav 2H 135
Chy-an-Chy TR26: S Ives 1J 137 (2D 136)
Chyandaunce TR18: Gul 2G 149
Chyandaunce Cl. TR18: Gul 2G 149
Chyandaunce Ter. TR18: Gul 2G 149
   (off Trevarrack Rd.)
Chyandor Cl. PL24: S Bla 3J 59
CHYANDOUR 3G 149 (1B 172)
Chyandour TR15: Red 4C 112
Chyandour Cliff TR18: Penz 4G 149
Chyandour Coombe TR18: Penz 3G 149
Chy-an-Dour Cl. TR26: S Ives 4A 136
Chyandour La. TR18: Penz 3G 149
Chy-an-Dour Rd. TR20: Pra S 6J 155
Chyandour Sq. TR18: Penz 3G 149
Chyandour Ter. TR18: Penz 3G 149
   (off Chyandour La.)
Chy an Dowr TR27: Phil 7E 138
CHY-AN-GWEAL 6E 136
Chy an Gweal TR26: C Bay 6E 136
Chy-an-Gweal Est. TR20: Ludg 3H 155
Chy an Mor TR20: L Roc 3K 149
Chy Barham TR1: Tru 5J 107
Chy Bre TR1: Tru 5J 107
   (off Tresawya Dr.)
CHYCARN MOOR 5H 119
Chy Cober TR27: Hayl 7E 138
Chycoose TR3: Devo 3F 125
Chycoose Parc TR3: Devo 3F 125
Chycornick Ter. TR18: Gul 2G 149
   (off Trevarrack Rd.)
CHYENHAL .3A 154
Chy Hwel TR1: Tru 3B 108
Chy Kensa Cl. TR27: Hayl 2H 141
Chylan Cres. TR7: S Mino 3A 36
Chymbloth Way TR12: Cover 6D 162
Chymeddon TR7: Newq 3F 35
   (off Bank St.)
Chymorvah TR17: Mar 4G 151
Chy Nampara TR11: Fal 1E 132
Chynance TR16: P'ath 4E 100
Chynance Dr. TR7: Newq 4E 34
Chynance Rd. TR18: Penz 6E 148
Chynoon Gdns. PL25: S Aus 3K 57
Chynowen La. TR8: Cube 3F 39
Chynowen Parc TR8: Cube 3F 39
Chynoweth PL26: Sten 2G 49
Chynoweth Gdns. TR18: Gul 2G 149
Chynoweth La. TR20: S Hil 2B 152
Chy Pons PL25: S Aus 5E 56
Chypons Rd. TR12: Mull 1J 161
Chypon Ter. TR18: Newl 1C 154
   (off Clifton Hill)
Chypraze Ct. TR14: Camb 7B 110
   (off Treswithian Pk.)
Chyreene Ct. TR27: Phil 6B 138
Chyreen La. TR3: C Dow, P Pla 5D 116
Chy Rentoul TR1: Tru 5J 107
   (off Tresawya Dr.)
Chyrose Rd. TR16: S Da 2K 113
Chyryn Dr. PL30: S B'wd 2J 27
Chysauster Ancient Village 1B 172

Chytroose Cl. TR13: Helst 1D 158
Chyvelah Ope TR1: Glo 5C 106
Chyvelah Rd. TR3: Thre 4K 105
Chyvelah Va. TR1: Glo 5C 106
Chyvellas Cl. TR18: Newl 2B 154
Chyventon Cl. TR19: St Bury 2H 147
Chyventon Ho. TR15: Red 3D 112
Chyverton Cl. TR7: Newq 5E 34
Chyvogue La. TR3: P Sta 3J 123
Chyvogue Mdw. TR3: P Sta 2K 123
CHYWOON 3E 126
Chywoone Av. TR18: Newl 2C 154
Chywoone Cres. TR18: Newl 2C 154
Chywoone Gro. TR18: Newl 3B 154
Chywoone Hill TR18: Newl 2C 154
Chywoone Pl. TR18: Newl 2C 154
Chywoone Ter. TR18: Newl 2C 154
Chywoon Gdns. TR15: I Hig 3K 111
Citadel Hill PL1: Plym 7H 163
Citadel Ope PL1: Plym 6J 163
Citadel Rd. PL1: Plym 6F 163
Citadel Rd. E. PL1: Plym 6H 163
City Market 4F 163
City Rd. TR1: Tru 5J 107
Clairemont Pl. PL14: S Cle 4B 66
Clampet La. PL11: Ant 6A 92
CLAMPITS 6C 74
Clann La. PL30: Lani 6G 31
Clann Mdws. PL30: Lani 6H 31
Claremont Falls PL13: Polp 5C 80
Claremont Rd. TR15: Red 3D 112
Claremont St. PL1: Plym 2F 163
(not continuous)
Claremont Ter. TR1: Tru 4J 107
(off Castle Ri.)
TR11: Fal 7E 128
TR13: P'ven 7F 157
Clarence Pl. TR18: Penz 4E 148
Clarence Rd. PL11: Tor 3J 93
PL25: S Aus 5F 57
(not continuous)
Clarence St. TR18: Penz 5F 149
Clarence Ter. PL15: Laun 4H 17
PL27: Wade 4E 24
(off Park Rd.)
TR18: Penz 5F 149
Clarence Vs. TR15: Red 2F 113
Clare Ter. TR11: Fal 1F 133
CLAWTON 1D 167
Claybourne Cl. PL25: S Aus 3K 57
CLEARBROOK 1D 171
Clear Vw. PL12: Salt 2G 89
Clearwater TR9: S Maj 4D 30
Clearwater Vw. PL25: S Aus 5K 57
Clease, The PL32: Came 4H 15
Clease Mdws. PL32: Came 4H 15
Clease Rd. PL32: Came 4H 15
Cleave, The PL10: King 5E 94
Cleaveland PL27: Wade 5F 25
Cleavelands EX23: Bud 5E 8
Cleaverfield M. PL15: Laun 2H 17
(not continuous)
Cleavers Way PL26: Sten 4G 49
Cleaves, The PL15: Laun 2H 17
Cleavewell PL27: Wade 5F 25
Cledma Bank TR27: S Er 5F 141
CLEERS 1K 47
Cleers Hill PL26: Cleer 1K 47
Clegg Av. PL11: Tor 3G 93
Clemens Cl. TR7: Newq 4J 35
Clemens Rd. PL14: S Keyn 2C 78
Clemens Way TR27: Con D 5K 139
Clements Rd. TR18: Penz 5E 148
Clemmens Av. TR7: Newq 5E 34
Clemo Rd. PL14: Lisk 3D 70
Cleswyth TR1: Tru 4F 107
Clevedon Rd. TR7: Newq 4E 34
Cleveland Av. PL13: Looe 4H 81
Clies, The TR13: Helst 4C 158
Clifden Cl. TR7: Newq 4F 35
TR12: Mull 2G 161
Clifden Dr. PL27: N Pol 1D 18
Clifden Rd. PL25: S Aus 5K 57
Clifden Ter. PL22: Los 3E 52
PL31: B'min 3F 33
Cliff, The PL26: Mev 6D 134
Cliff End Pk. PL27: Wade 3G 25
Cliff La. PL27: N Pol 2D 18
TR19: Mou 5E 154
Cliff Pk. Ter. PL27: Wade 4F 25
(off Guineaport Rd.)
Cliff Ri. PL23: Polr 7C 60
Cliff Rd. PL1: Plym 7F 163
PL11: Craft 5E 90
PL26: G Hav 2J 135
PL26: Mev 5D 134
TR6: P'rth 4A 40
TR7: Newq 3F 35
TR11: Fal 3F 133

Cliff Rd. TR13: P'ven 6A 156
TR19: Mou, Newl 3D 154
Cliff St. PL26: Mev 6D 134
Cliff Ter. TR16: P'ath 4F 101
Cliff Vw. Rd. TR14: Camb 6E 110
Cliff Vw. Ter. PL18: Gun 2H 75
TR14: Camb 6E 110
Cliff Wlk. TR26: C Bay 6G 137
Clift Ct. TR1: Tru 5K 107
(off Mitchell Hill)
Clifton Cres. TR11: Fal 1E 132
Clifton Gdns. TR1: Tru 5H 107
(off Richmond Hill)
Clifton Hill TR18: Newl 1C 154
Clifton Pl. PL4: Plym 1K 163
TR11: Fal 1E 132
Clifton Rd. TR15: P Bot 2J 111
Clifton St. PL4: Plym 2K 163
Clifton Ter. PL14: Lisk 5K 69
TR2: P'stho 3K 131
TR11: Fal 2E 132
TR18: Newl 1C 154
(off Clifton Hill)
TR27: Hayl 1G 141
Clijah Cl. TR15: Red 5E 112
Clijah Croft TR15: Red 6E 112
Clijah La. TR15: Red 6F 113
Clijah Ter. TR15: Red 5E 112
Clinton Cl. EX23: Bud 6D 8
TR15: Red 5E 112
Clinton Dr. PL25: S Aus 6F 57
Clinton Pas. TR15: Red 4D 112
(off Station Hill)
Clinton Rd. TR11: Const 3H 159
TR15: Red 4E 112
Clinton Ter. PL10: M'brk 1D 94
Clipper Cove TR20: Pra S 6H 155
CLITTERS 1G 73
Cloake Pl. TR12: Carg 2J 85
Clodan M. TR9: S Roa 1G 45
Clodgey La. TR13: Helst 3C 158
Clodgey Way TR13: Helst 5D 158
Clodgy Vw. TR26: S Ives 2H 137 (2D 136)
Close, The PL12: Salt 2E 88
PL26: Mev 5C 134
PL28: T'one 2G 21
PL32: Came 3J 15
TR1: Tru 3B 108
TR11: M Bri 7E 124
TR16: L'ner 1J 121
TR18: Penz 3E 148
Close Hill TR15: Red 2D 112
Clos Trevithick TR14. Camb 1F 119
CLOVELLY 1B 164
Clover La. Cl. PL35: Bosc 2K 13
Clover Wlk. PL12: Salt 2D 88
Clowance Ter. TR14: Praze 5K 143
CLOWANCE ESTATE 5J 143
CLOWANCE WOOD 7G 143
Coach Ho. La. PL25: S Aus 6C 57
Coach La. TR4: Chac 6E 104
(off Fore St.)
TR15: Red 4C 112
COAD'S GREEN 3C 167
Coastguard Cotts. EX23: U'ton 1B 10
PL11: P'wkle 6C 90
TR12: Mull 3F 161
Coastguard Cres. TR18: Penz 4G 149
Coastguard Flats PL13: Loo 6J 81
Coastguard Hill PL29: P Isa 1J 19
Coastguard Sta. Mall
PL26: Mev 6D 134
Coast Rd. TR4: P'twn 6D 96
Coast Vw. EX23: Bud 5F 9
Cobble La. TR9: Fr'don, P'ale 4G 45
Cobbs Well PL23: Fow 7J 61
Cobbs Well Hill PL23: Fow 7J 61
Cober Cres. TR27: Reaw 2D 142
Cobourg St. PL1: Plym 3H 163
Cocklawelva PL27: Rock 2F 23
COCKS 7D 40
Cock's Lake La. PL12: Nott 6K 83
COCKWELLS 1K 155
Cockwells La. TR20: Cockw 1K 155
CODDA 3B 166
Codiford Cres. TR14: Camb 6E 110
Coffa Bri. Cl. PL22: Los 3F 53
Coffee Lake Mdw. PL22: Los 3F 53
Cogegoes Ind. Pk.
TR14: P'nds 1A 118
Cogos Pk. TR11: M Bri 1E 128
Coinagehall Pl. TR18: Penz 6G 149
(off Coinagehall St.)
Coinagehall St. TR13: Helst 4B 158
TR18: Penz 6G 149
Coinage Ope TR13: Helst 4B 158
COLAN 1B 168
Colborne Av. TR16: I'gan 7H 101
COLDHARBOUR 3A 168

COLD NORTHCOTT 2C 167
Coldrose Ct. TR1: Tru 5H 107
Coldstyle Rd. PL14: Lisk 4B 70
COLDVREATH 1B 48
COLDWIND 2C 68
Colebrook Cl. TR15: Red 3C 112
Colenso Cross TR20: Gold 4C 152
Colenso Pl. PL25: S Aus 6H 57
Colin Campbell Ct. PL1: Plym 4F 163
Colinsey Pl. TR18: Penz 3E 148
Colinsey Rd. TR18: Penz 3E 148
Coliza Hill PL26: S Mew, T'lwth 2B 64
College Cl. TR2: Pro 2G 99
College Grn. PL25: S Aus 6G 57
PL31: B'min 6G 33
College Hill TR10: P'ryn 5A 128
College La. PL31: B'min 6G 33
TR15: Red 1G 113
College Ope TR10: P'ryn 5B 128
College Rd. PL32: Came 3J 15
TR1: Glo 5C 106
College Row TR2: Pro 2G 99
College St. TR14: Camb 7C 110
College Way TR1: Glo 5C 106
College Wood TR10: P'ryn 6K 127
Colletts Ct. TR16: P'ath 5F 101
Colliford Lake 3B 166
Collins Parc TR3: Stith 7A 122
Collorian La. TR20: White 7A 140
Collygree Parc TR20: Gold 5K 151
Colmers Ct. PL17: Call 5C 72
Colmers La. PL17: Call 5C 72
Colmers Row PL14: Menh 1H 79
Col-Moor Cl. TR27: Hayl 7E 138
Colroger Cl. TR12: Mull 1J 161
Colroger La. TR12: Mull 1J 161
COLSCOTT 2B 164
Colver Cl. TR27: Con D 5K 139
Colvreath Rd. TR7: Newq 3G 35
Colworth Av. TR11: Fal 2D 132
Colwyn Rd. PL11: Tor 3J 93
Combe La. EX23: Wid R 7B 10
Combined Court Cen.
Plymouth 5H 163
COME-TO-GOOD 7G 117
COMFORD 1B 122
COMFORT
TR11, Constantine 2H 159
TR11, Mylor Bridge 7D 124
Comfort Rd. TR11: M Bri 1E 128
Comfort Wartha TR11: Const 2H 159
Commercial Hill TR3: Pons 5F 123
Commercial Rd. PL18: Gun. Cals 7H 75
TR2: S Mawe 7D 130
TR10: P'ryn 4B 128
TR12: S Kev 2B 162
TR13: P'ven 7F 157
TR19: Mou 6D 154
TR27: Hayl 1H 141
Commercial Sq. TR14: Camb 7D 110
Commercial St. PL18: Gun 1H 75
TR14: Camb 7D 110
Commercial Ter. PL28: Pad 3B 22
(off St Edmunds La.)
Commissioners Rd. PL27: Wade 3E 24
COMMON MOOR 1B 170
Commons, The TR12: Mull 1G 161
Commons Cl. TR12: Mull 1H 161
Commons Rd. TR8: Cube 1E 38
Compass Bus. Pk. PL15: Laun 5D 16
Compass Point TR26: C Bay 6F 137
Compass Point Storm Tower 5B 8
Compass W. PL15: Treg 5A 16
Comprigney Cl. TR1: Tru 4H 107
Comprigney Hill TR1: Tru 4H 107
Compton Pk. PL17: Call 3E 72
Compton Rd. PL17: Call 5C 72
Compton Ter. TR1: Tru 4K 107
(off Campfield Hill)
Condurrow Rd. TR14: Bea 2F 119
CONGDON'S SHOP 3C 167
Connoc Cl. PL14: Lisk 5C 70
CONNOR DOWNS 5J 139 (1C 173)
Connor Hill TR27: Con D 5H 139
CONSOLS 4A 136
Consols Rd. TR16: Carh 4B 114
CONSTANTINE 3H 159 (2A 174)
CONSTANTINE BAY 5B 20 (3C 165)
Constantine Heritage Collection, The 2H 159
(within the Tolmen Cen.)
Constantine St. PL4: Plym 4K 163
Convent Cl. PL12: Salt 2G 89
Conway Cl. TR11: Fal 1C 132
Conway Gdns. TR11: Fal 1B 132
Conway Rd. TR11: Fal 7B 128
COOKBURY WICK 3B 164
Cook Ct. PL12: Salt 2D 88
COOKSLAND 3K 33
Cooksland Ind. Est. PL31: B'min 3J 33

Cooksland La. PL31: B'min 2J 33
Cooksland Rd. PL31: B'min 4J 33
Cooks Level PL26: G Hav 2H 135
Cook's Row TR1: Tru 4K 107
  (off Paul's Ter.)
COOMBE
  Bude 2A 164
  Cusgarne 5G 115
  St Austell 7E 54 (2C 169)
  Truro 3B 168
Coombe, The TR18: Newl 7C 148
Coombe Cl. EX23: Bud 5F 9
Coombe Coastline 2A 164
Coombe Dr. PL12: Carg 2J 85
Coombe End PL10: King 5E 94
COOMBE HILL 5G 115
Coombe Hill PL26: Coomb 1E 62
Coombe Junction Halt Station (Rail) 6J 69
Coombe La. PL11: Craft 5F 91
  PL12: Carg 2J 85
  TR4: Biss, Cusg 6G 115
  TR18: Hea, Penz 3E 148
  TR18: Penz 3F 149
Coombe Pk. PL10: Caws 5E 94
  PL11: Downd 6J 79
  PL12: Salt 3H 89
  TR14: Camb 3A 110
  TR18: Penz 4F 149
Coombe Pk. Cl. PL10: Caws 5E 94
Coombe Rd. PL12: Salt 4H 89
  PL17: Call 5E 72
  PL26: Coomb, Lanj, S Ste 5E 54
  PL30: S B'wd 3H 27
  TR18: Penz 3F 149
Coombes, The PL13: Polp 6B 80
Coombes La. TR1: Tru 5J 107
  (off The Leats)
Coombe Va. TR18: Newl 7C 148
Coombe Vw. TR18: P'rth 5A 40
Cooperage Gdns. PL25: T'oon 5D 56
Cooperage Rd. PL25: T'oon 5D 56
Cooperage Row PL26: T'vsce 6C 46
Cooper Mdws. TR16: Red 6F 113
Cooper's La. TR13: P'ven 6A 156
Coosebean La. TR1: Tru 4F 107
  TR4: Tru 4F 107
Copes Gdns. TR1: Tru 4J 107
COPPATHORNE 3A 164
COPPER HILL 6F 119
Copper Hill TR27: Hayl 1J 141
COPPERHOUSE 1J 141 (1C 173)
Copperhouse Vw. TR27: Phil 7D 138
Copper La. TR16: Red 7D 112
Copper Ter. TR27: Hayl 7D 138
Coppice Gdns. TR16: L'ner 1J 121
Copse, The PL25: S Aus 4K 57
Copshorn Rd. PL31: B'min 1E 32
Cormoran Ct. TR17: Mar 4G 151
  (off Trevenner Sq.)
Cormorant Dr. PL25: S Aus 5K 57
CORNEAL 6J 73
Corner Gdns. EX23: Stra 5G 9
Cornflower Cl. PL15: Laun 5K 17
Cornhill Rd. PL24: B'lva, S Bla 1F 59
Cornish All Blacks (Launceston) RUFC 3K 17
Cornish Birds of Prey Cen. 1C 169
Cornish Cres. TR1: Tru 4F 107
Cornish Mines & Engines Industrial Discovery Cen.
  ....4J 111
Cornish Mt. TR2: Pro 2H 99
Cornish Pirates RUFC 6E 148
Cornubia Cl. TR1: Tru 3A 108
  TR27: Hayl 2H 141
Cornwall's Regimental Mus. 5G 33
Cornwall St. PL1: Plym 4F 163
  (not continuous)
Cornwall Ter. TR1: Tru 4J 107
  (off Rosedale Rd.)
  TR18: Penz 6F 149
Coronation Av. TR14: Camb 7B 110
Coronation Cl. PL17: Call 5D 72
Coronation Cotts. PL11: Tor 3K 93
  TR10: M Bur 5G 127
  TR12: S Kev 2C 162
Coronation Park 4H 17
Coronation Pl. TR13: Helst 5C 158
  (not continuous)
Coronation Rd. PL17: Call 5D 72
  TR15: Red 4F 113
  TR16: I'gan 7J 101
  TR27: Hayl 2J 141
Coronation Ter. TR1: Tru 5H 107
  TR2: Tregon 5J 99
  (off Fore St.)
  TR4: Black 3B 104
Coronation Way TR7: Newq 2K 35
CORPASCUS 5E 126
Corpascus Cotts. TR10: M Bur 6E 126
Corporation Rd. PL31: B'min 4D 32

Corte Jago TR1: Tru 5J 107
  (off Tresawya Dr.)
Corte Mear TR1: Tru 6J 107
Corte Spry TR1: Tru 5J 107
Cort Simmons TR15: Pool 4J 111
Cort Treloweth TR15: Pool 4H 111
Corva Cl. TR26: S Ives 4B 136
Corva Rd. TR26: S Ives 4B 136
Cosawes Est. TR3: Pons 6F 123
Cosawes Pk. Homes TR3: P'hal 5H 123
Coswinsawsin La. TR14: C Grn 4A 118
Cosy Cnr. TR8: M Por 2C 28
Cotehele Cl. PL17: Call 6C 72
Cotehele House 7F 75
Cotehele Mill 1K 77
COTEHELE QUAY ....7F 75 & 1K 77
Cotehele Vw. PL18: Cals 5H 75
Cot Hill EX23: Stra 4H 9
  TR3: Pons 6E 122
Cotna La. PL26: Gorr 1F 135
Cot Rd. TR15: I'gan 7F 101
  TR16: I'gan 7F 101
Cotsland Rd. TR1: Tru 3B 108
Cotswold Av. PL26: Stick 3K 63
Cotswold Cl. PL26: Stick 3K 63
Cottage Farm Touring Pk. TR8: Cube 2F 39
Cottages, The PL11: Polb 7B 86
Cott Rd. PL22: Los 3F 53
  (not continuous)
COTTS 1D 171
COT VALLEY 4H 145
Cot Wood TR3: Pons 5F 123
COUCH'S MILL 2A 170
Couchwell La. PL22: Los 3E 52
Coulson's Bldgs. TR18: Penz 6F 149
  (off Queen St.)
Coulson's Pl. TR18: Penz 6F 149
Coulson's Ter. TR18: Penz 6F 149
Coulthard Dr. TR13: Breag 1D 156
Council Houses PL14: Doubl 4B 68
  PL26: Resc 3K 49
Count Ho. La. TR26: C Bay 6E 136
County Court
  Bodmin 4H 33
County Rd. EX23: Bud, U'ton 1B 10
Court, The PL12: Salt 3E 88
  PL18: Cals 7J 75
Court Cocking TR26: S Ives 2J 137
Courtenay Cl. PL13: Loo 4H 81
Courtenay St. PL1: Plym 5G 163
Court Farm Caravan & Camping Pk. PL26: S Ste 5E 54
Court Gdns. PL25: S Aus 6G 57
Courtlands PL12: Salt 4G 89
Courtlands Cres. PL25: S Aus 4A 58
Courtney Rd. PL14: Lisk 4C 70
  PL25: S Aus 4J 57
Courtyard, The PL14: Lisk 4F 71
  TR1: Tru 6K 107
  TR16: Carn 1A 120
Cove, The TR4: P'twn 5D 96
  TR12: Cover 6D 162
Cove Hill TR3: P'hal 3J 123
  TR19: Senn C 3C 146
Cove Mdw. PL11: Wilc 7J 89
Coventry Rd. PL11: Flu 6F 129
COVERACK 6D 162 (3A 174)
Cove Rd. TR19: Senn, Senn C 3D 146
Cowdray Cl. PL12: Salt 3G 89
Cowdray Ter. PL12: Salt 4G 89
COWLANDS 6K 117
Cowland Cl. PL15: Laun 5F 17
Cowling Gdns. PL14: Menh 7J 71
Cowling Rd. TR3: C Dow 6D 116
COX HILL 7C 104
Cox Hill TR6: Cocks 7D 40
COXPARK 1B 74
Cox Pk. Ter. PL18: Cox 1A 74
Crabbtree Cl. PL14: Lisk 5A 70
Crabtree La. PL30: B'min 6E 32
  PL31: B'min 6E 32
CRACKINGTON HAVEN 1B 166
CRAFTHOLE 5F 91 (2C 171)
CRANE 1B 118
Crane Mnr. Ct. TR14: Camb 1C 118
Crane Rd. TR14: Camb 7C 110
Cranfield St. TR14: Camb 7B 110
Cranstar Apartments TR7: Newq 2H 35
CRANTOCK 6B 34 (1A 168)
Crantock Beach Holiday Pk. TR8: Cran 5B 34
Crantock Plains Touring Pk. TR8: Cran 2J 39
Crantock St. TR7: Newq 3D 34
CRAPSTONE 1D 171
Crava La. TR13: Ash 2B 156
Creakavose PL26: S Ste 4C 54
Creakavose Pk. PL26: S Ste 3B 54
Crealy (Cornwall's Great Adventure Park) 1C 169
Creathorne Rd. EX23: Flex 3D 8

Creaz an Bre PL26: Fox 1H 55
CREED 3C 169
Creed La. TR2: Gram 7A 62
CREEGBRAWSE 7D 104
Creekside, The PL13: Loo 4G 81
Creekside Vw. TR2: Tr'sln 3G 109
Creeping La. TR18: Newl, Penz 7D 148
  TR18: Penz 6D 148
Crellow Flds. TR3: Stith 7B 122
Crellow Gdns. TR3: Stith 7A 122
Crellow Hill TR3: Stith 7A 122
Crellow La. TR3: Stith 7A 122
Crellow Ter. TR3: Stith 7A 122
Crellow Va. TR3: Stith 7B 122
Crembling Well TR15: I Hig 4A 112
CREMYLL 1J 95 (2D 171)
Cremyll Rd. PL11: Tor 4K 93
Crescent, The EX23: Bud 5C 8
  EX23: Wid B 6B 10
  PL1: Plym 5F 163
  PL12: Land 6H 83
  PL13: Loo 7G 81
  PL14: Lisk 4B 70
  PL18: Gun 1H 75
  PL25: S Aus 5J 57
  (Trevail Way)
  PL25: S Aus 4B 58
  (Warwick Dr.)
  PL30: S Mab 6C 26
  TR1: Tru 5H 107
  TR7: Newq 3E 34
  TR13: P'ven 6F 157
  TR14: Camb 6D 110
  TR26: C Bay 1A 140
  TR26: S Ives 3B 136
  (off Alexandra Rd.)
Crescent Av. PL1: Plym 6F 163
Crescent Av. M. PL1: Plym 6F 163
Crescent Cl. EX23: Wid B 6B 10
  TR27: Hayl 2H 141
Crescent Gdns. TR1: Tru 5H 107
Crescent Pl. TR19: Pend 4B 144
Crescent Ri. PL28: Cons B 5B 20
  TR1: Tru 5H 107
Crescent Rd. PL26: Bugl 7H 43
  TR1: Tru 5H 107
Crescent Way TR27: Hayl 1H 141
Cresswell Ter. TR19: Bota 7A 144
Crestbourne Ter. PL14: Dob 3E 68
Crest Ct. TR7: Newq 3E 34
  (off The Crescent)
Crewenna Rd. TR14: Praze 4K 143
Cribbage Ter. PL31: B'min 3F 33
Cribbar TR7: Newq 2D 34
Cricketers Hollow PL27: Rock 1H 23
Cricket Pk. EX23: March 3F 11
Crift Cotts. PL14: Pen Gn 4H 71
CRIGGAN 3H 43
Criggan Mill Holiday Pk. TR12: Mull 4G 161
Crinnick's Hill PL31: B'min 4G 33
Crinnis Cl. PL25: Carl 6E 58
Crinnis Rd. PL25: Carl 6B 58
Crinnis Wood PL25: Carl 6E 58
Crinnis Wood Av. PL25: Carl 6D 58
CRIPPAS HILL 5J 145
CRIPPLESEASE 1C 173
CROANFORD 3A 166
Crocker's Row PL18: Gun 2H 75
Crockwell St. PL31: B'min 3G 33
Croft Comn. TR14: Tro 4H 119
Croft Farm Pk. PL30: Lux 3C 50
CROFTHANDY 3B 114
Croftlands PL27: Rock 1H 23
CROFT MITCHELL 6H 119
Croft Parc PR12: Lizar 5H 161
Croft Rd. TR18: Penz 6D 148
Croft Row TR16: Carh 4A 114
Crofty Cl. TR15: Pool 5J 111
Cromwell Rd. PL25: S Aus 6K 57
Crookedor La. PL11: Ant 5J 91
Crooklets EX23: Flex 3B 8
Crooklets Rd. EX23: Bud, Flex 3B 8
CROSS
  Bodmin 1D 50
  Saltash 3H 77
Cross, The PL12: S Dom 2G 77
  PL14: Pens 1K 67
  TR8: S New E 2G 37
Cross Cl. TR7: Newq 2K 35
Cross Comn. TR12: Lizar 4G 161
Cross Fld. Pl. TR26: S Ives 4C 136
CROSS GREEN 2D 167
Cross La. PL25: S Aus 6G 57
  PL31: B'min 3G 33
CROSS LANES 2D 173
Cross Lanes PL15: Laun 1G 17
Cross Pk. PL11: Craft 4F 91
Cross Pk. Ter. PL26: Mev 5C 134
CROSS ROADS 3G 111

CROSSROADS 2A 114
Crossroads, The TR16: S Da 2A 114
Crossroads Cl. PL28: S Mer 6E 20
Cross St. PL27: Wade 4E 24
   PL28: Pad 3B 22
   TR13: Helst .3B 158
   TR14: Camb .1D 118
   TR15: Red 4D 112
   TR18: Penz 4F 149
   TR27: Hayl 1J 141
Cross Ter. PL18: Alb 4G 75
Crosswalla Flds. TR13: Helst 2C 158
Crossways TR11: Fal 3D 132
CROWAN 1D 173
Crow Hill TR6: Bol 6C 40
CROWLAS 2K 155 (1C 173)
Crown Cl. TR7: Newq 5H 35
Crown Court
   Truro 4J 107
Crown Cres. TR8: S New E 2G 37
Crown Rd. PL26: W'moor 3H 47
Crown Ter. PL26: W'moor 2G 47
CROWNTOWN .1D 173
Crows-an-Eglos TR26: S Ives 4B 136
CROWS-AN-WRA 2A 172
CROW'S NEST .2D 66
CRUGMEER 1J 21 (3D 165)
CRUMPLEHORN 5B 80
Crun-Melyn Parc TR27: Hayl 3G 141
Crusoe Flats TR26: S Ives 1H 137
Cryben TR12: Gweek 6H 159
Crylla Valley Cotts. PL12: Nott 6J 83
Cryon Vw. TR1: Tru 5D 106
CUBERT 4F 39 (2A 168)
Cubert Common 2A 168
Cuby Cl. TR2: Tregon 6J 99
Cuby Rd. TR2: Tregon 5J 99
Cuddenbeake Ter. PL12: S Ger 6E 86
Cudden Point 2C 173
Cullen Vw. TR2: Pro 2H 99
Cul Rian Rd. PL26: Nanp 5G 47
Culver Ct. PL12: Salt 3H 89
                  (off Culver Rd.)
Culverland Pk. PL14: Lisk 2B 70
Culverland Rd. PL14: Lisk 2B 70
Culver Rd. PL12: Salt 3H 89
Culvers Mdw. PL15: Laun 1G 17
              (off Roydon Rd.)
Culverwood Rd. PL14: Lisk 2A 70
Culvery, The PL27: Wade 5E 24
Cumble Tor La. PL12: T'ton 2K 87
Cundy's La. PL26: H St 3G 55
Cunnack Cl. TR13: Helst 2C 158
Cunningham Pk. PL10: M Bur 5H 127
Cunningham Way PL12: Salt 2F 89
            (off Callington Rd.)
Curlew Cl. TR7: Newq 4C 34
Curlew Pk. TR4: Thre 4K 105
Curnow Cl. PL26: Roch 5C 42
Curnows Rd. TR27: Hayl 2H 141
Currian Hill PL26: Curr V 4H 47
Currian Rd. PL26: Nanp 5G 47
CURRIAN VALE .4H 47
Curtis V.C. Cl. TR8: S New E 2G 37
CURY 2D 173
CUSGARNE 6F 115 (3A 168)
Cusgarne Hill TR4: Cusg 5E 114
Custom Ho. Ct. TR18: Penz 5G 149
                (off Quay St.)
Custom Ho. Hill PL23: Fow 7K 61
Custom Ho. La. TR18: Penz 5F 149
Custom Ho. Quay TR11: Fal 1G 133
CUSVEORTH COOMBE 1G 115
CUSVEY 3F 115
Cutcrew La. PL12: Tide C 7A 82
Cuth Avallon TR1: Tru 5J 107
CUTLINWITH 7C 82
CUTMADOC 1D 169
Cuttings Hill TR14: Tres D 4A 110
CUTTIVETT 3D 82 (1C 171)
Cuxhaven Way TR20: L Roc 2A 150
Cypress Av. PL25: Carl 6F 59
Cyril Rd. TR1: Tru 4J 107

D

Dabryn Way PL26: S Ste 3C 54
Daglands Hill PL23: Fow 7J 61
            (off Daglands Rd.)
Daglands Rd. PL23: Fow 7J 61
DairyLand Farm World 2B 168
Dale Cl. TR7: Newq 5H 35
Dale Gdns. PL4: Plym 1H 163
Dale Rd. PL4: Plym 1G 163
   TR7: Newq .5H 35
Dane Rd. TR7: Newq 2E 34
Daniell Ct. TR1: Tru 6J 107
Daniell Gdns. TR1: Tru 6J 107

Daniell Rd. TR1: Tru 6H 107
Daniell St. TR1: Tru 6J 107
Daniell Pl. TR18: Penz 6F 149
Daniels Cl. PL25: S Aus 5A 58
Daniels La. PL25: S Aus 5A 58
Danmore Cl. PL34: Tin 7B 12
Danny's Parc TR5: S Agn 3A 96
Daphne Du Maurier Literary Cen. 7K 61
               (off South St.)
Daphne Du Maurier's Smugglers Mus. 3B 166
DARITE 2C 66 (1B 170)
Dark La. PL14: Lisk 4C 70
   PL22: Los 4E 52
   PL32: Came .3H 15
Darlington Rd. TR20: L Roc 2A 150
Darloe La. PL13: Loo 6J 81 (5G 81)
Dartmoor Lodges PL17: Harr 4D 74
Dartmoor Vw. PL12: Salt 1G 89
Darton Cotts. PL12: Salt 2E 88
              (off Thorn La.)
Daubuz Cl. TR1: Tru 3J 107
Daubuz Cl. TR1: Tru 4K 107
Davey's Cl. TR11: Fal 4C 132
David Penhaligon Way TR1: Tru 6K 107
DAVIDSTOW 2B 166
Davy Cl. PL11: Tor 3H 93
   PL14: Trem .3B 66
Dawe Cres. PL31: B'min 5E 32
Dawes Cl. PL14: Dob 4D 68
Dawes La. PL10: M'brk 2C 94
   PL13: Loo 4H 81
Dawney Ter. PL11: Craft 5F 91
Dawn Rd. PL13: Loo 7K 81 (6H 81)
Daws Ct. PL12: Salt 3J 89
DAW'S HOUSE 7D 16 (2D 167)
Daws Mdw. PL32: Came 3K 15
Daymer La. PL27: Treb 5C 18
Deacon Cl. PL12: Salt 4H 89
Deacon Dr. PL12: Salt 4H 89
Dean Hill PL14: Lisk 4A 70
Dean La. PL14: Lisk 4A 70
Dean Pl. PL14: Lisk 4A 70
               (off Dean St.)
Dean St. PL14: Lisk 4A 70
Dean Ter. PL14: Lisk 4A 70
Dedwood Ter. TR16: Carn 1B 120
Deeble Cl. TR3: Thre 5K 105
Deeble Dr. PL24: S Bla 3H 59
Deep La. TR16: Four L 3C 120
Deer Pk. PL12: Salt 2H 89
   TR7: Newq .3E 34
Degibna La. TR12: Helst 7B 158
   TR13: Helst .7B 158
DELABOLE 2B 14 (2A 166)
Delamere Holiday Bungs. PL33: Dela 4A 14
Delavue Rd. PL32: Came 4G 15
Delavue Ter. PL32: Came 4G 15
Delaware Cotts. PL18: Dra 2F 75
Delaware Ho. PL18: Dra 3F 75
Delaware Outdoor Education Cen. 2F 75
Delaware Rd. PL18: Chils, Dra 1E 74
Dell, The TR1: Tru 4J 107
Dell Cl. TR18: Penz 7D 148
Dellohay Pk. PL12: Salt 1F 89
DEMELZA 1C 169
Dennis Cl. PL5: Plym 6K 89
Dennis Gdns. PL15: Treg 5A 16
Dennis La. PL28: Pad 4B 22
Dennison Av. PL25: S Aus 5A 58
Dennison Rd. PL31: B'min 3F 33
Dennis Rd. PL14: Lisk 4C 70
   PL28: Pad 3B 22
Dennybowl La. PL12: Tide 1A 86
Denys Vw. TR9: I Que 1J 45
De Pass Dr. TR11: Fal 3G 133
De Pass Rd. TR11: Fal 3G 133
Deptford Pl. PL4: Plym 2K 163
Derbys La. PL26: G Hav 3H 135
Dereham Ter. TR1: Tru 5H 107
Derowen Dr. TR27: Hayl 4G 141
DERRIL 3B 164
DERRITON 3B 164
Derry Av. PL4: Plym 1H 163
Derry's Cross PL1: Plym 5F 163
DEVERAL 5A 142
Deveral Rd. TR27: Fr'ham 6A 142
Devichoys Wood Nature Reserve 5J 123
Deviock Hill PL11: Devi, Downd 4H 79
DEVONPORT 2D 171
Devonport Hill PL10: M'bri 5F 95
Devonport Rd. TR11: Tor 3K 93
Devonshire Ct. PL11: Tor 3K 93
Devonshire St. PL4: Plym 3K 163
Devonshire Ter. TR1: Tru 4J 107
             (off Rosedale Rd.)
DEVORAN 2C 124 (1A 174)
Devoran La. TR3: Devo 2C 124

DEXBEER 3A 164
Diana Cl. TR11: Fal 3C 132
Diddies La. EX23: Stra 5J 9
Diddies Rd. EX23: Stra 5H 9
Digey, The TR26: S Ives 1H 137 (2D 136)
Digey Flats TR26: S Ives 1H 137
               (off The Digey)
Diggory's Fld. PL14: S Cle 4B 66
Dinas Ct. PL11: Downd 6H 79
Dinas Ia Rd. TR26: S Ives 4D 136
Dinas Rd. TR9: S Maj 5B 30
Ding Dong Mine Engine House 1B 172
Dingle Ct. PL17: Call 5D 72
              (off Back La.)
Dingles Cl. TR3: Pons 6F 123
Dingle's Way PL27: Rock 1H 23
DINHAM'S BRIDGE 5A 26
DINWORTHY 2B 164
Dipper Cl. EX23: Kilkh 1H 7
Dipper La. EX23: Kilkh 1G 7
DIPPERTOWN 2D 167
Dirty La. PL12: Cark 7C 84
Discovery Quay PL1: Plym 3H 163
   TR11: Fal 2G 133
Discovery Wharf PL4: Plym 5K 163
             (off North Quay)
Dithmarschen Way PL25: S Aus 7F 57
DIZZARD 1B 166
Dobbin Cl. PL28: T'one 3G 21
Dobbin La. PL28: T'one 3G 21
Dobbin Rd. PL28: T'one 3G 21
Dobbs La. TR1: Tru 5G 107
Dobell Rd. PL25: S Aus 5J 57
DOBWALLS 3D 68 (1B 170)
Dockacre Rd. PL15: Laun 3H 17
Dockey PL15: Laun 4H 17
Dock La. PL18: Penz 5G 149
Docks, The TR11: Fal 1H 133
Doctors Hill PL35: Bosc 2K 13
   TR12: S Kev 2B 162
Doctors La. PL12: S Ger 6D 86
   PL14: Lisk 4B 70
Dodbrook PL10: M'brk 3C 94
Dodman Point 3D 169
Dodman Point Cliff Castle 3D 169
Dola La. TR20: Rosu 6A 152
Dolbeare Caravan & Camping Pk. PL12: Land 4E 82
Dolcoath Av. TR14: Camb 7E 110
Dolcoath Ind. Pk. TR14: Camb 6F 111
Dolcoath Ind. Pk. TR14: Camb 6G 111
Dolcoath Rd. TR14: Camb 7E 110
Dolphin Ho. PL4: Plym 5K 163
Dolphin St. PL29: P Isa 2J 19
Domellick Hill PL26: S Den 1C 46
Domellick Mnr. PL26: S Den 1C 46
Doniert's Cl. PL14: Lisk 5A 70
Donkey La. PL10: M'brk 4A 94
   PL11: P'wkle 5D 90
Donkey Pk. PL28: S Mer 6E 20
Donnington Rd. TR18: Penz 7D 148
Donovan Way PL31: B'min 4D 32
Dopps M. TR15: Red 3E 112
Dopps Ter. TR15: Red 3E 112
Dorminack Cl. PL26: W'moor 2H 47
DOUBLEBOIS 4A 68 (1A 170)
Doublebois Ind. Est. PL14: Doubl 4A 68
Doublebois Pk. PL14: Doubl 3A 68
Doublegates PL25: S Aus 6E 56
Doubletrees PL24: S Bla 3G 59
             (not continuous)
Doubletrees Ct. PL24: S Bla 3H 59
Douglas Cl. PL26: Roch 4B 42
Doulton Rd. PL25: S Aus 5A 58
DOUSLAND 1D 171
Dove St. TR26: S Ives 3H 137 (3D 136)
Dower's Ter. TR16: Four L 3C 120
DOWGAS 2G 63
DOWHA 7J 119
Down Cl. PL12: Salt 4E 88
DOWNDERRY
   St Austell 2F 63 (2C 169)
   Torpoint 6J 79 (2C 171)
DOWNGATE
   Callington 3D 167
   Liskeard 3C 167
Downs, The PL13: Loo 5G 81
Downs Cl. PL26: S Den 2F 47
Downs Hill PL23: Gola 1J 61
Downside Cl. TR7: Newq 5H 35
Downs La. PL13: Loo 5F 81
Downs La. Pk. PL13: Loo 5F 81
Downs Rd. PL13: Loo 4F 81
Downstream Cl. PL28: Pad 3A 22
Downs Vw. EX23: Flex 3C 8
   PL13: Loo 7J 81 (5G 81)
DOWN THOMAS 2D 171
Dowr Cl. PL15: Laun 5G 17
Dozmary Pool 3B 166
Dozmere TR3: Feo 3J 125

Dozmere Cl. TR3: Feo 3J 125
Dracaena Av. TR11: Fal 6D 128
   TR27: Hayl 1K 141
Dracaena Cres. TR27: Hayl 1K 141
Dracaena Pl. TR11: Fal 1D 132
Dracaena Vw. TR11: Fal 7D 128
Dragaena Vw. TR11: Fal 7D 128
Dragon Leisure Centre, The 7H 33
Drake Cir. PL1: Plym 4J 163
   PL4: Plym 3J 163
Drakefield Dr. PL12: Salt 2J 89
Drake Rd. PL28: Pad 3A 22
Drake's Statue 7G 163
DRAKEWALLS 3F 75 (3D 167)
Drakewalls Gdns. PL18: Dra 3F 75
Drang, The TR9: I Que 1H 45
Drannack La. TR27: Gwinn 1A 142
Draycott Ter. TR26: S Ives 4E 136
Dreysen Cl. TR15: P Bot 2J 111
DRIFT 2B 172
Drillhole La. TR26: S Ives 3H 137
Drinnan Ct. PL25: S Aus 6K 57
DRINNICK 6G 47
Drinnick Rd. PL26: Nanp 6F 47
Drinnick Ter. PL26: Nanp 6G 47
Drive, The PL26: Dup 1K 65
Driving La. PL24: Kil, L'scot 7K 51
Droskyn Castle TR6: P'rth 4A 40
Droskyn Cl. TR6: P'rth 4A 40
Droskyn Point TR6: P'rth 4A 40
Droskyn Way TR6: P'rth 4A 40
Druckham Pl. *PL15: Laun* *4J 17*
   (off Race Hill)
Druckham Ter. PL15: Laun 4J 17
Druids Lodge TR15: I Hig 5K 111
Druid's Rd. TR15: I Hig 4K 111
Drummer's Hill PL25: Scre 1F 57
   PL26: Rudd 1F 57
Drump Rd. TR15: Red 3D 112
DRYM 1D 173
Drym La. TR14: Praze 7F 143
Duchy Av. TR7: Newq 2K 35
Duchy Bus. Cen. TR15: Pool 5K 111
Duchy Cl. PL15: Laun 2H 17
   PL25: S Aus 6K 57
Duck La. PL12: T'ton 1A 88
Duck St. PL25: Char 7B 58
   TR19: Mou 6D 154
Ducky La. PL12: Land 6H 83
Ducky Row PL17: Meth 6C 74
Dudman Rd. TR1: Tru 5F 107
Dudnance La. TR15: Pool 5G 111
Duke's Ct. PL26: Roch 5B 42
Duke's Plot TR20: Gold 5A 152
Duke St. PL15: Laun 1F 17
   PL22: Los 3E 52
   PL24: S Bla 1H 59
   PL25: S Aus 6G 57
   PL28: Pad 3B 22
   TR1: Tru 5K 107
   TR18: Newl *1C 154*
   (off Jack La.)
Duke's Way TR7: Newq 4H 35
Duke Ter. PL15: Laun 1F 17
DULOE 6A 78 (2B 170)
Du Maurier Ct. *PL26: Mev* *6C 134*
   (off Tregoney Hill)
Dumbarton Ter. *TR19: Mou* *5E 154*
   (off Parade Hill)
Duncannon Dr. TR11: Fal 1D 132
Dunder Hill PL27: Polz 3D 18
Dungarth Grn. PL14: Lisk 4C 70
Dungarth Rd. PL14: Lisk 4C 70
Dunheved Flds. PL15: Laun 5G 17
Dunheved Rd. PL12: Salt 3H 89
   PL15: Laun 4G 17
DUNMERE 2B 32
Dunmere Cl. PL24: Par 3K 59
Dunmere Rd. PL31: B'min, Dun 3B 32
Dunn St. PL35: Bosc 2K 13
Dunstable Cl. PL26: Fox 7H 47
Dunstan Cl. PL26: S Den 2E 46
   TR10: P'ryn 4A 128
Dunstan La. PL12: S Mel 6A 76
Dunstan Pl. TR4: Chac 5E 104
Dunstanville Ter. TR11: Fal 7F 129
Dunstanville Vs. *TR11: Fal* *7F 129*
   (off Dunstanville Ter.)
DUNTERTON 3D 167
Dunvegan Rd. TR10: P'ryn 4K 127
Dunveth Bus. Pk. PL27: Wade 4C 24
Dunveth Rd. PL27: Wade 4D 24
Dupath La. PL17: Call 5F 73
DUPORTH 7A 58
Duporth Bay PL26: Dup 7A 58
Duporth Rd. PL25: Char, S Aus 1K 65
   PL26: S Aus 1K 65
Durgan La. TR10: P'ryn 4A 128
Durning Rd. TR5: S Agn 3A 96

Durston Rd. EX23: Flex 3D 8
DUTSON 1J 17 (2D 167)
Dutson Rd. PL15: Laun 2G 17
Dutson Ter. PL15: Laun 2H 17
Dymond Cl. PL32: Came 5G 15
Dymond Ct. PL12: Salt 3H 89

E

Eadies Ct. TR2: Tregon 6H 99
Earls Dr. PL10: King, M'brk 5E 94
Earl's Dr., The PL10: Caws 6E 94
Earls Ri. TR7: Newq .4J 35
Eastbourne Cl. PL25: S Aus 6J 57
Eastbourne Rd. PL25: S Aus 6H 57
East Bri. TR4: Chac .6E 104
East Burraton PL12: S Dom 3J 77
E. Camps Bay PL11: Downd 7K 79
E. Charles St. TR14: Camb 1E 118
EASTCLIFF 5C 96
Eastcliff PL13: Loo 6K 81 (5H 81)
Eastcliff Av. No. 1 TR4: P'twn 5C 96
Eastcliff Av. No. 2 TR4: P'twn 5C 96
Eastcliff Av. No. 3 TR4: P'twn 5C 96
Eastcliffe Rd. PL24: Par 2K 59
E. Cliff La. TR17: Mar 4F 151
East Cl. TR13: Helst .2D 158
EASTCOTT 2A 164
East Crinnis PL24: B'vey 5G 59
E. Crinnis Caravan & Camping Pk. PL24: B'vey 5G 59
East End TR15: Red .3E 112
Eastern Av. PL14: Lisk 4C 70
Eastern Grn. TR18: Penz 3F 149
   (not continuous)
Eastern Grn. Pk. TR18: Penz 3H 149
Eastern Grn. Rd. TR14: Camb 6D 110
Eastern Way TR18: L Roc 3K 149
E. Fairholme Rd. EX23: Flex 3E 8
Eastfield Way PL25: S Aus 5K 57
EAST HILL 1C 104
East Hill PL25: S Aus 6G 57
   TR14: Camb 5G 111
Eastlake Ope PL1: Plym 4J 163
Eastlake St. PL1: Plym 3H 163
Eastland Cl. TR1: Tru 5B 108
Eastlea PL14: Pens .1K 67
Eastleigh Ter. TR16: Red 7C 102
EAST LOOE 5H 81 (2B 170)
EAST PANSON 1D 167
East Pk. PL14: Pens .1J 67
   PL15: Treg 5A 16
   TR15: Red 3F 113
East Pk. Av. PL4: Plym 1H 163
East Pool Mine 4J 111
East Pool Pk. TR15: Pool 4J 111
EAST PUTFORD 2B 164
East Quay PL26: Mev 6D 134
East Ri. TR11: Fal 1G 141
East Rd. EX23: Kilkh .2G 7
   PL14: Menh 1H 79
   TR3: Stith 7B 122
   TR8: Q Dow 6C 36
E. Rosewin Row *TR1: Tru* *4K 107*
   (off Rosewin Row)
East St. PL23: Polr 7C 60
   TR7: Newq 3F 35
   TR9: S Maj 4C 30
EAST TAPHOUSE 1A 170
East Ter. *TR18: Penz* *4G 149*
   (off Chyandour Cliff)
   TR27: Hayl 1G 141
East Vw. PL14: Menh 1H 79
E. Wharf PL26: Mev .6D 134
East Wheal Rose Station
   Lappa Valley Steam Railway 3J 37
Eastwood Pk. Ind. Est. TR10: P'ryn 5B 128
Eastwood Rd. TR10: P'ryn 5B 128
EAST YOULSTONE .2A 164
Ebenezer Pl. *TR18: Newl* *2C 154*
   (off St Peter's Hill)
   TR19: Mou *6D 154*
   (off Commercial Rd.)
Ebrington St. PL4: Plym 4K 163
Eddystone Pl. PL27: Wade 4E 24
Eddystone Ri. PL14: Lisk 3C 70
Eddystone Rd. PL25: S Aus 4J 57
   PL27: Wade 3E 24
Eddystone Ter. *PL27: Wade* *4E 24*
   (off Eddystone Pl.)
Eden Cl. PL24: B'vey 4G 59
Eden Gdns. *TR18: Newl* *2C 154*
   (off St Peter's Hill)
Eden Pl. *TR18: Newl* *2C 154*
   (off St Peter's Hill)
   TR19: Mou 6D 154
Eden Project 1D 58
Eden Project (Park & Ride) 7D 50

Eden Ter. *TR18: Newl* *2C 154*
   (off St Peter's Hill)
Eden Valley Holiday Pk. PL30: Lanl 4A 52
Eden Way PL26: Penw 5K 49
Edgcumbe Av. TR7: Newq 4G 35
Edgcumbe Cl. PL18: Gun 2H 75
Edgcumbe Cres. PL10: M'brk 1D 94
Edgcumbe Gdns. TR7: Newq 3G 35
Edgcumbe Grn. PL25: S Aus 6E 56
Edgcumbe Rd. PL12: S Dom 2G 77
   PL22: Los 4C 52
   PL25: S Aus, T'oon 5E 56
   PL26: Roch 3B 42
Edgcumbe Ter. PL24: S Bl G 3G 59
Edgecombe Way PL18: S An Cpl 3D 74
Edgecumbe Rd. PL12: Salt 7E 84
Edgemoor Cl. PL14: Trem 4C 66
Edinburgh Cl. PL25: Carl 6C 58
EDISTONE 1A 164
EDMONTON 3A 24 (3D 165)
Edmund Rd. TR15: Red 2D 112
Ednovean La. TR20: Perran 6K 151
Edwards Apartments TR15: Red 4C 112
Edwards Cres. PL12: Salt 3E 88
Edwards Rd. TR3: Devo 2C 124
Edward St. TR1: Tru .5J 107
   TR14: Camb 6F 111
   (not continuous)
Edward St. Rear of *TR14: Camb* *6F 111*
   (off Edward St.)
Edymead Ct. PL15: Laun 4H 17
Efford Down Pk. EX23: Bud 5B 8
Efford Farm Bus. Pk. EX23: Bud 6B 8
Egans Way PL33: Dela 2B 14
Egerton Rd. PL28: Pad 4C 22
EGGBUCKLAND 2D 171
Eglos Ct. PL30: S Teat 2B 26
EGLOSHAL 1H 111
EGLOSHAYLE 4F 25 (3A 166)
Egloshayle Rd. PL27: Eglo, Wade 4F 25
   TR27: Hayl 1K 141
EGLOSKERRY 2C 167
Eglos Mdw. TR11: M Bri 7E 124
Eglos Parc PL27: Wade 4G 25
   TR12: Mull 1H 161
Eglos Rd. TR4: S Erm 3B 98
   TR4: Short 6B 98
   TR20: Ludg 3G 155
EGLOSVELYAN 1H 161
Eglos Vw. PL35: Bosc 2K 13
Egret Cl. PL10: M'brk 1E 94
Egyptian House *5F 149*
   (off Chapel St.)
Eider Wlk. TR27: Hayl, L Dow 4D 140
ELBURTON 2D 171
Elderfield Cl. PL24: Tyw 1B 60
Elerkey Cl. TR2: Very 5H 135
Elerkey La. TR2: Very 6H 135
Eliot Cl. PL15: Treg 5A 16
Eliot Ct. TR7: Newq .3G 35
Eliot Dr. PL12: S Ger 6E 86
Eliot Gdns. TR7: Newq 3G 35
Eliot Rd. PL25: S Aus 5J 57
   (not continuous)
   TR1: Tru 4J 107
Eliot Ter. PL12: S Ger 5D 86
Elizabethan House 6J 163
Elizabeth Cl. PL31: B'min 4F 33
   TR3: Thre 5K 105
Elizabeth Pl. PL4: Plym 2J 163
Elizabeth Rd. EX23: Bud 5E 8
   PL25: S Aus 6J 57
Elizabeth Ter. TR17: Mar 5D 150
ELLBRIDGE 1C 84 (1D 171)
Ellbridge La. PL12: Hatt 1C 84
Ellen Cl. TR4: Mt Hwk 7H 97
Ellenglaze Ct. TR8: Cube 4E 38
Ellenglaze La. TR8: Cube 4D 38
Ellenglaze Mdw. TR8: Cube 4E 38
Elliot Sq. PL11: Tor 3K 93
Elliot St. PL1: Plym 7F 163
Elliott Cl. PL12: Salt .3F 89
Elliot Ter. PL1: Plym .7G 163
Elliot Ter. La. PL1: Plym 7G 163
Elliotts Cl. PL14: Lisk 4B 70
Elliott's Store *3J 89*
   (off Lwr. Fore St.)
Ellis Cl. TR27: Hayl .2H 141
Elliston Gdns. TR13: P'ven 7G 157
Ellis Way TR27: Hayl 2H 141
Elm Cl. PL17: Call 6D 72
   TR7: Newq 5G 35
   TR15: I Hig 4K 111
Elm Cotts. *PL12: Salt* *2E 88*
   (off Thorn La.)
Elm Ct. TR1: Tru 4K 107
Elm Ct. Gdns. TR1: Tru 4K 107
Elm Dr. EX23: Bud 5E 8
   TR9: S Maj 5A 30

ELMGATE 6A 88
Elm Gro. PL31: B'min 3F 33
  TR3: Feo 4J 125
Elm Lea EX23: Bud 5E 8
Elm Mdw. TR3: Feo 4J 125
Elm Mdw. Dr. PL13: Loo 4H 81
Elm Pk. PL10: M'brk 7K 93
Elms, The PL12: Hatt 3B 84
Elms Cl. Ter. TR18: Newl 1C 154
ELMSCOTT 1A 164
Elmsleigh Rd. PL27: Wade 3E 24
Elm Ter. PL25: S Aus 5G 57
  PL26: Mev 6C 134
                            (off River St.)
  TR12: Mull 1H 161
                           (off Churchtown)
Elm Tree Rd. PL13: Loo 4H 81
Elowen Cl. TR11: Fal 3C 132
Elwell Rd. PL12: Salt 2J 89
Emlyn Flds. PL25: S Aus 3K 57
Empire Way TR11: Fal 1B 132
Empress Av. TR18: Penz 4F 149
Emslie Rd. TR11: Fal 3G 133
Endsleigh Gdns. PL4: Plym 2J 163
Endsleigh Pk. EX23: March 3G 11
Endsleigh Pl. PL4: Plym 2J 163
Endsleigh Ter. PL14: Lisk 4B 70
Engelly Rd. TR4: Goonh 6H 41
ENNISCAVEN .2C 169
Ennis Cl. TR4: S Erm 2B 98
Ennor's Rd. TR7: Newq 4E 34
Enterprise Ct. PL11: Tor 4K 93
ENYS 2A 128
Enys 1C 128
Enys Cl. TR1: Tru 4H 107
  TR26: C Bay .7F 137
Enys Gardens .1C 128
Enys Hill TR10: P'ryn 1A 128
  TR11: M Bri 1A 128
Enys Quay TR1: Tru 5K 107
Enys Redenek TR14: Camb 5F 111
Enys Rd. TR1: Tru 4H 107
  TR14: Camb .6D 110
Epworth Cl. TR1: Tru 5A 108
Ercus Way TR27: S Er 7F 141
Ergue-Gaberic Way EX23: Bud 5C 8
Eric Rd. PL18: Cals 7K 75
Erisey Ter. TR11: Fal 1F 133
ERNESETTLE .2D 171
Erow Glas TR10: P'ryn 4A 128
ERTH BARTON 1J 91
ESCALLS 2A 172
ESCALLS CLIFF 1E 146
Esmonde Gdns. PL5: Plym 5K 89
Esmonde Rd. TR13: Helst 5D 158
Esperanza Ct. TR11: Fal 6D 128
Esplanade PL23: Fow 6B 60
Esplanade, The PL1: Plym 7G 163
Esplanade Rd. TR7: Newq 3A 34
ESSA 3H 89
Essa Rd. PL12: Salt 3H 89
Essex Dr. TR15: I'gan 2H 111
Eston Cl. TR10: M Bur 6G 127
ESTOVER 2D 171
Estuary Vw. TR7: Newq 4E 34
  TR11: Fal 7F 129
  TR26: Lel 3E 140
Estuary Way PL5: Plym 5K 89
Eton Av. PL1: Plym 2G 163
Eton Pl. PL1: Plym 2G 163
Eton Rd. PL25: S Aus 4A 58
Eton St. PL1: Plym 3G 163
Eton Ter. PL1: Plym 3F 163
Euny Cl. TR15: Red 4C 112
Eureka Va. TR6: P'rth 4B 40
Europa Ct. TR8: M Por 2C 28
Eva Ct. PL17: Call 5C 72
                           (off New Rd.)
Evans Way TR20: Ger 7H 153
Evea Cl. TR1: Tru 6E 106
Evely Ct. PL14: Lisk 3C 70
Evelyn Pl. PL4: Plym 1J 163
Evenden Ct. PL11: Tor 3J 93
EWORTHY 1D 167
Exchange St. PL4: Plym 6J 163
Exeter St. PL4: Plym 5J 163
  PL15: Laun 3H 17

Factory Cotts. PL14: Menh 2G 79
Fairbourne Rd. PL25: S Aus 5J 57
Fairfax Pl. PL15: Laun 4G 17
Fairfax Rd. TR2: Tr'sln 1H 109
Fairfield PL12: S Ger 6D 86
  TR16: I'gan 7G 101
  TR16: S Da 2A 114
  TR20: Ludg 2J 155

Fairfield Cl. PL25: S Aus 5A 58
  TR26: Lel 2E 140
Fairfield Rd. EX23: Bud 5D 8
  TR11: Fal 1D 132
Fairfields PL13: Loo 3H 81
  TR2: Pro 2J 99
Fairglen TR27: Phil 7E 138
Fairlight PL14: Lisk 5C 70
Fairmantle St. TR1: Tru 5K 107
Fairmead Cl. PL12: Hatt 4B 84
Fairmead M. PL12: Salt 2E 88
Fairmeadow TR10: P'ryn 5K 127
Fairmead Rd. PL12: Salt 3E 88
Fair Pk. Cl. PL15: Laun 4H 17
Fair Pk. Rd. PL14: Lisk 5B 70
Fairpark Rd. PL27: Wade 4E 24
Fair St. TR9: S Maj 5C 30
Fair Vw. PL31: B'min 4D 32
Fairview Pk. TR9: S Roa 1G 45
Fairview Pl. TR11: Fal 1F 133
                           (off Vernon Pl.)
Fair Vw. Ter. TR8: Cube 4F 39
Fairview Ter. TR7: Newq 3F 35
Fairview Tourist Pk. EX23: Pou 2H 9
Fairway PL12: Salt 3E 88
  PL25: Carl 6D 58
Falcon Ter. EX23: Bud 5C 8
FALMOUTH 2G 133 (1B 174)
Falmouth Art Gallery 1F 133
                           (off The Moor)
Falmouth Bus. Pk. TR11: Fal 2C 132
Falmouth Docks Station (Rail) 2H 133
Falmouth Golf Course 4D 132
Falmouth Pl. TR19: S Jus 6B 144
Falmouth Rd. TR1: Tru 7J 107
  TR4: Chac 6D 104
  TR10: P'ryn 5B 128
  TR11: Fal 5B 128
  TR13: Helst 2D 158
  TR15: Red 4D 112
Falmouth Town Station (Rail) 2G 133
Farfield Pl. TR7: Newq 4C 34
Farley Cl. TR1: Tru 6J 107
Farmers Cl. TR20: Crow 2K 155
Farmer's Hill PL13: Loo 4G 81
                           (off West Rd.)
Farmers Mdw. TR18: Newl 1C 154
Farm La. PL12: Salt 4F 89
Farrar Cl. TR27: Log 6E 138
Farriers Grn. PL32: Came 5G 15
Farrow Fordh PL26: Roch 3B 42
Faugan La. TR18: Newl 2B 154
                           (not continuous)
Faugan Rd. TR18: Newl 2B 154
Fawkener Cl. TR11: Fal 1C 132
FAWTON 1A 170
Fayre Vw. PL12: Treh 4C 88
Feadon La. TR16: P'ath 5F 101
Fearnside Way PL12: Salt 2E 88
Fegen Rd. PL5: Plym 4K 89
Feliskirk La. TR17: Mar 3E 150
Felixstowe Av. TR7: S Mino 2B 36
Fennel Bus. Pk. PL15: Laun 5D 16
Fenten Cl. EX23: Flex 3D 8
Fenten Pk. PL12: Salt 2H 89
Fenteroon Rd. PL32: Came 5H 15
FENTONADLE .3A 166
Fentonluna Gdns. PL28: Pad 2A 22
                           (off High St.)
Fentonluna La. PL28: Pad 3A 22
FENWICK 3F 133
Fenwick Rd. TR11: Fal 3F 133
FEOCK 4J 125 (1B 174)
Feock Rd. TR3: P Pla 5G 117
Fernacre Stone Circle 3B 166
Ferndale Rd. TR11: Fal 1E 132
Ferndale Ter. PL14: Lisk 4K 69
Fern Glen TR26: S Ives 3G 137 (3C 136)
Fernhill Rd. TR7: Newq 3E 34
Fernlea Ter. TR26: S Ives 3J 137
Fernlea Vs. TR24: S Bla 2J 59
Fernleigh Cres. PL27: Wade 5F 25
Fernleigh Gdns. PL27: Wade 5F 25
                           (off Fernleigh Cres.)
Fernleigh La. PL27: Wade 4F 25
Fernleigh Rd. PL27: Wade 4F 25
Fernleigh Ter. PL18: S An Cpl 3E 74
  PL26: Nanp 7F 47
Fernleigh Vs. TR6: P'rth 4C 40
                           (off Budnick Est.)
FERNSIDE 2B 118
Fernside Pk. PL14: Trem 3B 66
Fernside Rd. TR14: P'nds 2B 118
FERNSPLATT 5G 115
Ferris Town TR1: Tru 5J 107
Ferris Way PL23: Polr 7D 60
Ferry La. PL11: Tor 7F 89
Ferry St. PL11: Tor 3K 93
Festival Gdns. TR1: Tru 4K 107
                           (off St Clement St.)

Festival Vs. TR3: Thre 5A 106
Field Cl. PL22: Los 3F 53
Field Pl. TR11: Mawn S 2B 160
Fifield Ho. PL26: S Ste 3C 54
Filtrick La. TR16: Piece 2A 120
Finewell St. PL1: Plym 5H 163
Finn VC Est. PL31: B'min 3F 33
Finnygook La. PL11: Craft, P'wkle 6D 90
Finsbury Ri. PL26: Roch 3B 42
Fir Cl. PL25: S Aus 6F 57
  TR4: Goonh .6H 41
  TR13: Helst 2B 158
Fir Cres. PL26: Fox 1H 55
Firs, The PL26: W'moor 2J 47
Firsleigh Pk. PL26: Roch 4B 42
First & Last House 5A 146
Fisgard Way PL11: Tor 3F 93
Fish Cellars PL11: P'wkle 6D 90
Fisher Cl. PL27: Wade 3G 25
Fishermans Sq. TR19: Mou 6D 154
                           (off The Wharf)
Fish Quay PL4: Plym 6K 163
Fish Strand Hill TR11: Fal 1F 133
                           (off Market St.)
Fish Strand Quay TR11: Fal 1F 133
Fish St. TR26: S Ives 1J 137 (2D 136)
Fistral Cl. PL11: Tor 2H 93
Fistral Ct. TR7: Newq 4B 34
Fistral Cres. TR7: Newq 4B 34
Fistral Waves TR7: Newq 2D 34
Fitzsimmons Cl. TR13: Helst 4C 158
Five Flds. La. TR11: Fal 7E 128
FIVELANES 2C 167
Five Lanes PL14: Dob 3D 68
  TR8: S Mawg .4H 29
Five Wells La. TR13: Helst 4B 158
Flamank Pk. PL31: B'min 4E 32
Flambards 6E 158
Flaxmoor Ter. PL31: B'min 3F 33
FLEXBURY 3D 8 (3A 164)
Flexbury Av. EX23: Flex 3C 8
Flexbury M. EX23: Flex 3D 8
Flexbury Pk. EX23: Flex 3D 8
Flexbury Pk. Ct. EX23: Flex 3D 8
                           (off Flexbury Pk.)
Flexbury Pk. Rd. EX23: Flex 4D 8
Flora Cinema 4C 158
Flora Gdns. TR13: Helst 3B 158
Flora Pl. PL27: Wade 3F 25
Florence Ct. TR9: P'ale 4F 45
Florence Hill PL17: Call 4D 72
Florence Pl. TR11: Fal 2F 133
  TR18: Newl 7D 148
  TR19: Mou 6E 154
                           (off Quay St.)
Florence Rd. PL17: Call, K Bray 2D 72
Florence Rd. Ind. Est.
  PL17: K Bray .2D 72
Florence Ter. TR11: Fal 2F 133
FLUSHING 6F 129 (1B 174)
Folders La. PL30: S Teat 4D 26
Folkstone Cl. PL26: Fox 7J 47
Folnamodry TR20: Mad 2B 148
                           (off Fore St.)
Foote's Fld. TR1: Tru 5J 107
Forbes Cl. TR18: Newl 2B 154
Forbes Rd. TR18: Newl 2B 154
FORD 2D 171
FORDER
  Saltash 4E 88
  Torpoint 6D 94
Forder Hill PL10: Caws, Rame 6D 94
Forder La. PL10: Caws 6D 94
FORDH SEN KOLOMM
  . . . . .1G 45
Ford's Row TR15: Red 3D 112
Foredown Pk. PL14: Pens 3G 67
FOREST 6A 120
Fore St. EX23: Stra 5H 9
  PL10: King 5E 94
  PL10: M'brk 2C 94
  PL11: Tor 3K 93
  PL12: Carg 2J 85
  PL12: S Ger 5D 86
  PL12: Salt 3H 89
  PL13: Loo 7J 81 (5G 81)
                           (Church St.)
  PL13: Loo 6J 81 (4G 81)
                           (Shutta Rd.)
  PL13: Polp 6B 80
  PL14: Lisk 5B 70
  PL14: Pens 1J 67
  PL14: S Cle 4A 66
  PL17: Call 5C 72
  PL18: Alb 4F 75
  PL18: Cals 7J 75
  PL18: Gun 1H 75
  PL22: Los 3E 52
  PL23: Fow 7K 61

Fore St. PL23: Gola 1J **61**
  PL23: Polr 7C **60**
  PL24: S Bla 1H **59**
  PL24: Tyw 2B **60**
  PL25: S Aus 6G **57**
  PL26: Bugl 7H **43**
  PL26: Mev 6C **134**
  PL26: Nanp 5G **47**
  PL26: Polg 3C **64**
  PL26: Roch 4B **42**
  PL26: S Den 2E **46**
  PL26: S Ste 3C **54**
  PL26: Stick 3K **63**
  PL29: P Isa 2J **19**
  PL30: S Teat 2B **26**
  PL31: B'min 3F **33**
  PL32: Came 3J **15**
  PL34: Tin 6B **12**
  PL35: Bosc 2K **13**
  TR2: Gram 7A **62**
  TR2: Gram R 7K **37**
  TR2: Pro 2G **99**
  TR2: Tregon 4F **149**
  TR4: Chac 6D **104**
  TR4: Mt Hwk 7H **97**
  TR7: Newq 2E **34**
  TR9: S Maj 5C **30**
  TR11: Const 2H **159**
  TR13: Ash 1A **156**
  TR13: P'ven 7F **157**
  TR14: Barr, P'nds 4A **118**
  TR14: Bea 2E **118**
  TR14: Camb 7D **110**
  TR14: P'nds 2B **118**
  TR14: Praze 4K **143**
  TR14: Tro 4G **119**
  TR15: Pool 4J **111**
  TR15: Red 3D **112**
  (not continuous)
  TR16: Carh 5A **114**
  TR16: S Da 2K **113**
  TR17: Mar 4E **150**
  TR18: Newl 1C **154**
  (not continuous)
  TR19: Mou 6D **154**
  TR19: S Jus 3J **145**
  TR20: Gold 4K **151**
  TR20: Mad 1B **148**
  TR26: Lel 2D **140**
  TR26: S Ives 2J **137** (2D **136**)
  TR27: Hayl 1J **141**
  TR27: S Er 6F **141**
Forge, The TR3: C Dow 6E **116**
Forge Ind. Pk. TR14: Camb 5E **110**
Forge La. PL12: Salt 1E **88**
Forge Way TR4: Short 6C **98**
Forlaze Rd. PL27: Rock 2F **23**
Formal Ind. Est.
  TR14: Camb 6B **110**
FORRABURY 2J **13**
Forrabury Hill PL35: Bosc 2J **13**
Forreglos Dr. TR17: Mar 4G **151**
Forsythia Dr. PL12: Salt 2D **88**
Fort, The PL10: Caws 6E **94**
Fortescue Cl. PL26: Fox 7H **47**
Fortescue Pl. PL22: Los 2F **53**
Forth an Cos TR3: Pons 5E **122**
Forth an Eglos TR16: S Da 3K **113**
Forth an Hellier PL31: B'min 3J **33**
Forth-an-Nance TR16: P'ath 4F **101**
Forth-an-Praze TR15: Red 2K **111**
  TR16: S Da 2K **113**
Forth-an-Ryn TR15: Red 4F **113**
Forth an Streth TR27: Phil 7E **138**
Forth an Tewennow TR27: Phil ..7D **138**
Forth an Tre TR27: Phil 6D **138**
Forth an Ula TR27: Phil 7D **138**
Forth an Venegh PL31: B'min ..5G **33**
Forth an Vre TR14: Bre 7G **111**
Forth Coth TR3: C Dow 7D **116**
Forthcrom TR12: Gweek 6H **159**
Forth Dall TR16: I'gan 1K **111**
Forth Gwedhen TR13: Helst 1D **158**
Forth Kegyn TR15: Pool 6H **111**
Forth Noweth TR3: C Dow 6D **116**
  TR15: Red 3D **112**
Forth Scol TR13: P'ven 7G **157**
  TR15: I Hig 3K **111**
Forth Vean TR14: Camb 2D **118**
Forthvean TR4: P'twn 7C **96**
Forthvean Cres. TR4: P'twn 7C **96**
Forthvean Rd. TR4: P'twn 1B **102**
  TR16: Nanc 1B **102**
Forthveor TR15: Red 1F **113**
Forthvras TR15: I'gan 2H **111**
FOS AN MOGH 3D **68**
Foster Dr. PL31: B'min 5D **32**
Foster Pl. *TR18: Penz* 5F **149**
  (off New St.)

Fosters La. PL34: Tin 7B **12**
Foster's Mdw. PL18: S An Cpl 2C **74**
Fosters Way EX23: Flex 4E **8**
Foulston Av. PL5: Plym 5K **89**
FOUNDRY 6B **122**
Foundry Ct. *PL27: Wade* 4E **24**
  (off Foundry Ter.)
Foundry Dr. PL25: S Aus 6B **58**
Foundry Gdns. PL15: Laun 3G **17**
Foundry Hill TR3: Stith 7B **122**
  TR27: Hayl 3G **141**
Foundry La. TR18: Newl 1C **154**
  TR27: Hayl 2G **141**
Foundry Rd. TR3: Stith 6B **122**
  TR14: Camb 7E **110**
Foundry Row TR15: Red 3D **112**
Foundry Sq. TR27: Hayl 2G **141**
Foundry St. PL27: Wade 4E **24**
Foundry Ter. PL27: Wade 4E **24**
Fountain Ct. *TR18: Penz* 4F **149**
  (off St Clare St.)
Fountain Pl. *PL17: Call* 5D **72**
  (off Back La.)
Fountain Ter. PL24: S Bla 2J **59**
Four Acres Rd. TR2: Very 6H **135**
Fourgates PL14: Menh 1H **79**
FOUR LANES 3C **120** (1D **173**)
Four Turnings Bungs.
  PL23: Fow 5F **61**
FOWEY 7K **61** (2A **170**)
Fowey Blockhouse 6B **60**
Fowey Community Leisure Cen. ..7H **61**
Fowey Cres. PL17: Call 5E **72**
Fowey Docks PL23: Fow 6K **61**
Fowey Mus. 7K **61**
Fowlfield Row TR13: Breag 1D **156**
FOWYDH 7K **61**
Foxdown PL27: Wade 4G **25**
Foxes Fld. *TR18: Penz* 3H **149**
Foxes La. TR19: Mou 5D **154**
Foxes Row TR16: Carh 5A **114**
Foxglove Cl. PL15: Laun 5K **17**
Foxglove Way PL12: Salt 2D **88**
FOXHOLE 1H **55** (2C **169**)
Foxhole La. PL26: G Hav 3J **135**
Fox's La. TR11: Fal 2F **133**
Fox Stanton Dr.
  TR10: P'ryn 5B **128**
FRADDAM 6A **142** (1C **173**)
Fraddam Rd. TR27: Fr'ham, Leeds 6A **142**
FRADDON 3G **45** (2C **169**)
Fraddon Hill TR9: Fr'don 3G **45**
Fradgan, The TR18: Newl 1C **154**
Fradgan Pl. TR18: Newl 1C **154**
Frances St. TR1: Tru 5J **107**
Francis La. PL27: Treb 4C **18**
Francis Rd. PL27: Treb 3C **18**
Frankfort Ga. PL1: Plym 4F **163**
Frankland Cl. TR11: Fal 2D **132**
Franklin Cl. PL27: Wade 3G **25**
Franklyn Cl. PL25: S Aus 4K **57**
Frazer Rd. TR7: Newq 5E **34**
FREATHY 2D **171**
Freeman Collins Dr.
  TR11: Fal 1D **132**
Frenchman's La.
  PL12: Land, Nott 7J **87**
Freshbrook Cl. TR18: Penz 3H **149**
Freshwater La. TR2: S Mawe ..7E **130**
Friars La. PL1: Plym 6J **163**
Friary St. PL4: Plym 5K **163**
Friends Pl. *PL14: Lisk* 4B **70**
  (off Doctor's La.)
Frith Rd. PL12: Salt 2F **89**
Frobisher Dr. PL12: Salt 3G **89**
Frobisher Ter. TR11: Fal 7E **128**
Frobisher Way PL11: Tor 3F **93**
Frog Hill TR3: Pons 5G **123**
Frog La. TR2: Tregon 6H **99**
FROGPOOL 7F **115**
FROGWELL 7A **72** (1C **171**)
Frogwell Rd. PL17: Call 7A **72**
Front Rd. PL11: Downd 7J **79**
Frost Ct. TR11: Fal 7C **128**
Fuggoe Croft TR26: C Bay 6E **136**
Fuggoe La. TR26: C Bay 6E **136**
Fullaford Rd. PL17: Call 5F **73**
Fuller Rd. TR6: P'rth 5A **40**
Fuller-Tre Cl. PL26: Roch 4B **42**
Fulmar Cl. *TR27: Hayl* 4D **140**
  (off Pintail Av.)
Furniss Cl. *TR1: Tru* 5K **107**
  (off St Austell St.)
Furry Way TR13: Helst 4B **158**
Furse Pk. PL5: Plym 6K **89**
Furzedown Ter. *PL13: Loo* 4G **81**
  (off Downs Rd.)
Furze Hill PL31: B'min 3G **33**
Furze Pk. PL23: Polr 7C **60**

Furze Pk. Dr. PL12: S Ger 4B **86**
Future World @ Goonhilly 2A **174**

Gabriel St. TR26: S Ives 3H **137** (3D **136**)
Gadwall Ri. TR27: Hayl 4D **140**
GAINSBOROUGH PARK 1J **55**
Gala Bingo
  Plymouth, Derry's Cross 5F **163**
Gallacher Way PL12: Salt 2D **88**
Galland Rd. TR1: Tru 4F **107**
Gallant's Dr. PL23: Fow 6A **60**
Galleon Ct. PL25: Char 6B **58**
Gallery, The *TR7: Newq* 5E **34**
  (off Tregunnel Hill)
Gallery, The PL12: S Ger 5C **86**
Gallery La. PL12: S Ger 4B **86**
Galligan Cl. TR19: St Bury 2G **147**
Galligan La. TR19: St Bury 2G **147**
Gallinas Point TR26: S Ives 4J **137**
Gallops, The PL12: Salt 1F **89**
Gallows Pk. PL11: M'brk 1A **94**
Gander La. TR13: Helst 2B **158**
GANG 1C **111**
Ganges Cl. TR11: M Chu 3J **129**
Gannel Rd. TR7: Newq 4D **34**
Gannel Vw. TR7: Newq 4F **35**
Gannel Vw. Cl. TR8: Lane 6J **35**
Gannet Dr. PL25: S Aus 5K **57**
Garage Fld. Pk. EX23: Kilkh 1H **7**
Garby La. TR15: Red 5E **112**
Garcia Ter. PL15: Laun 5J **17**
Garden Mdw. TR11: Fal 2C **132**
Gardens, The TR4: Cusg 7G **115**
Garden Way TR8: Q Dow 6C **36**
GARKER 1C **58**
Garland Pl. TR14: Camb 6D **110**
Garlidna *TR18: Penz* 4E **148**
GARRAS 2A **174**
Garras Wharf TR1: Tru 5K **107**
Garrett St. PL10: Caws 6E **94**
Garrison Grn. PL1: Plym 6J **163**
Garro La. TR12: Mull 2H **161**
Garth, The PL15: Laun 4J **17**
Garth-an-Creet TR26: S Ives 4B **136**
Garth Marhas TR14: Camb 7C **110**
Garth Morcom PL14: Lisk 5A **70**
Garth Rd. TR18: Newl 7C **148**
Gascoyne Ct. PL4: Plym 4K **163**
Gascoyne Pl. PL4: Plym 4K **163**
Gas Hill TR1: Tru 7A **108**
Gasking St. PL4: Plym 4K **163**
Gas La. PL14: Lisk 5B **70**
  TR14: Camb 5G **111**
  TR15: Red 4D **112**
Gas St. TR14: Camb 7D **110**
Gavercoombe Pk. PL34: Tin 6B **12**
GAVERIGAN 2K **45**
Gay's Hill TR13: Helst 5D **158**
Gear La. PL12: S Ger 5D **86**
Gears La. TR20: Gold 3H **151**
Geevor Cotts. TR19: Trew 5B **144**
Geevor Tin Mine Mus. 4B **144**
Geffery Cl. PL12: Land 6G **83**
Gem & Jewellery Workshop, The ..4C **144**
Gendalls Way PL15: Laun 1G **17**
Gennys Cl. PL18: S An Cpl 3D **74**
George Fox Cl. PL15: Laun 5F **17**
George Pl. *PL17: Call* 5C **72**
  (off Haye Rd.)
Georges La. PL11: Shev 3F **91**
George St. TR1: Tru 5J **107**
GERMANSWEEK 1D **167**
GERMOE 7H **153** (2C **173**)
Germoe Cross Roads TR20: Ger 7H **153**
Germoe La. TR20: Ger 7H **153**
Gernick Est. TR18: Newl 1B **154**
GERRANS 3J **131** (1B **174**)
Gerrans Cl. PL25: S Aus 4B **58**
Gerrans Hill TR2: P'stho 3J **131**
Gew, The TR17: Mar 4E **150**
Gewans Mdw. PL25: S Aus 7J **57**
Gew Ter. TR15: Red 3F **113**
Ghost Hill TR12: Mull 3G **161**
Gibbon La. PL4: Plym 3J **163**
Gibbons Flds. TR12: Mull 1H **161**
Gibbon St. PL4: Plym 3J **163**
Gibbs La. PL35: Bosc 3K **13**
Gibraltar Ter. TR2: S Mawe 7D **130**
Gibralter Sq. *EX23: Stra* 5H **9**
  (off Spicers La.)
Gibson Way TR13: P'ven 6G **157**
Gig La. TR3: C Dow 7E **116**
  (not continuous)
Gilbert Cl. PL26: S Ste 3C **54**
Gilbert Monument 5F **33**
Gilbert Rd. PL31: B'min 4H **33**

GILBERT'S COOMBE 7C 102
GILLAN 2A 174
Gill-an-Creet TR26: S Ives 3B 136
Gillbard Centenary Flats PL15: Laun 4G 17
Gills Cl. TR10: P'ryn 6K 127
Gilly Flds. TR15: Red 4D 112
Gilly Hill TR15: Red 5E 112
Gilly La. TR20: White 7A 140
Gilly's Wlk. PL18: Alb 4F 75
(off Cemetery Rd.)
Gilston Rd. PL12: Salt 1E 88
Gilwell Hall PL4: Plym 3J 163
Gilwell Pl. PL4: Plym 3J 163
Gilwell St. PL4: Plym 3K 163
Gin Distillery 6J 163
Gipsy La. PL14: Lisk 5K 69
TR13: Helst .2J 157
Gladstone Rd. PL30: B'min 6E 32
Gladstone Ter. TR15: Red 3E 112
(off Rose Row)
TR20: L Roc 3A 150
Gladwell Gdns. EX23: Stra 5G 9
Gladys Holman Ho. TR14: Camb 7D 110
Glamis Rd. TR7: Newq 3H 35
Glantis Cres. TR9: I Que 1H 45
Glanville St. PL4: Plym 3H 163
Glanville Ter. PL12: Salt 1H 89
Glasney Parc TR10: P'ryn 4J 127
Glasney Pl. TR10: P'ryn 5A 128
Glasney Rd. TR11: Fal 7E 128
Glasney Ter. TR10: P'ryn 5B 128
Glebe, The PL12: S Mel 7D 76
TR2: Tregon 5J 99
TR8: Cube 4F 39
TR14: Camb 7C 110
Glebe Av. PL12: Salt 2H 89
Glebe Cliff 7A 12
Glebe Cliff to Trebarwith Strand 2A 166
Glebe Cl. PL13: Pely 3C 80
TR9: S Maj .4C 30
Glebe Dr. PL26: Roch 4B 42
Glebelands PL13: Loo 3H 81
PL17: Call 4C 72
Glebe Mdw. PL17: Call 4C 72
Glebe Parc PL30: S Tud 5H 27
Glebe Row TR27: Phil 7D 138
Glebe Ter. TR11: Const 2H 159
Glencoe Ter. PL27: Wade 4F 25
(off Guineaport Rd.)
Glencross Ct. PL14: Lisk 4B 70
(off Doctor's La.)
Glen-Dale Cl. PL25: S Aus 4A 58
Glendale Cres. TR4: Mt Hwk 6G 97
TR15: Red 4F 113
Glen-Dale Cres. PL25: S Aus 4A 58
Glendurgan 2A 174
Glendurgan Garden 4A 160
Glenfeadon La. TR16: P'ath 4F 101
Glenfeadon Ter. TR16: P'ath 4F 101
Glen Gdns. PL14: Pens 1J 67
Glenhaven Pk. TR13: Helst 4D 158
Glen Leigh TR15: Red 2C 112
Glenleigh Pk. PL26: Stick 3J 63
Glenmoor La. TR12: Mull 2G 161
Glenmore Ter. PL14: Lisk 4C 70
(off Pengover Rd.)
TR10: Longd 5C 126
Glen Pk. PL14: Pens 1J 67
Glen Pk. Av. PL4: Plym 1H 163
Glen Rd. PL27: Wade 5E 24
Glenside TR3: P'hal 4K 123
Glenside Gdns. TR16: L'ner 7H 113
Glenthorne Rd. TR3: Thre 5K 105
Glentowan Rd. PL26: Pent 1D 134
Glenvale TR15: I Hig 1B 60
(off Chariot Rd.)
Glen Vw. PL17: Call 4C 72
PL27: Wade 5E 24
TR10: P'ryn 4K 127
TR16: L'ner .1J 121
Glenview PL24: Tyw 1B 60
PL25: S Aus 6F 57
TR16: L'ner .1G 121
Glenway TR18: Newl 2C 154
Globe Sq. TR16: Carn 1B 120
Globe Va. Holiday Pk. TR16: S Cmn 5F 103
Globe Yd. PL25: S Aus 5G 57
(off Truro Rd.)
Gloucester Av. PL25: Carl 6C 58
Gloucester Ct. PL1: Plym 2G 163
Gloucester Cres. TR18: Newl 2B 154
Gloucester Pl. PL1: Plym 2G 163
TR18: Newl .1C 154
Gloucester Rd. TR18: Newl 2C 154
Glowarth Koth TR14: Camb 6F 111
Gloweth 5C 106
Gloweth Vw. TR1: Tru 5D 106
Gloweth Vs. TR1: Glo 4C 106
GLUVIAN 2D 30 (1C 169)

Gluyas, The TR11: Fal 4C 132
Glyn Cotts. TR11: Fal 2G 133
(off Bar La.)
Glynn Av. TR13: Helst 4C 158
Glynn M. PL22: Los 3E 52
(off South St.)
Glynn Rd. PL14: Lisk 5K 69
PL28: Pad 3B 22
Glynn Valley Crematorium PL30: Carm 6K 33
Glyn Way TR3: Thre 5A 106
Gnaton Cotts. PL18: Alb 4F 75
(off Cemetery Rd.)
Gnaton Ter. PL18: Alb 4F 75
(off Cemetery Rd.)
Goad Av. PL11: Tor 3G 93
Goad Cl. PL11: Tor 3H 93
Godolphin 1D 173
Godolphin Av. TR17: Mar 4E 150
GODOLPHIN BRIDGE 1K 153
Godolphin Cl. TR17: Mar 3E 150
Godolphin Ct. TR27: Towns 1K 153
GODOLPHIN CROSS 1D 173
Godolphin Dr. TR17: Mar 4E 150
Godolphin Gdns. TR17: Mar 4E 150
(off Godolphin Dr.)
Godolphin Pk. PL17: Call 6C 72
(off Werrington Dr.)
Godolphin Pl. TR17: Mar 4E 150
Godolphin Rd. TR11: Fal 7D 128
TR13: Helst 3C 158
TR20: L Roc 2A 150
Godolphin Ter. TR17: Mar 3E 150
Godolphin Vw. TR14: Camb 2D 118
Godolphin Way TR7: Newq 2J 35
Godrevy Ct. TR26: C Bay 6F 137
Godrevy Gdns. TR26: S Ives 1H 137
Godrevy Pk. Caravan Pk. TR27: Gwith 3G 139
Godrevy Rocks to Crane Islands 1D 173
Godrevy Ter. TR26: S Ives 1H 137
GOLANT 1J 61 (2A 170)
GOLBERDON 3D 167
Golberdon Rd. PL14: Pens 1K 67
Golden Bank Pk. TR11: Fal 4C 132
Golden Bank Site 1A TR11: Fal 4D 132
(off Swanpool Rd.)
Golden Mdw. TR16: I'gan 1K 111
Golden Sands Bungalows TR27: Hayl 7E 138
(off Guilford Rd.)
Golden Sands Caravans TR27: Hayl 7E 138
(off Guilford Rd.)
Goldfinch Cl. PL15: Laun 5K 17
Goldfinch Gro. PL12: Salt 1F 89
Goldmartin Cl. TR11: Mawn S 2B 160
Goldmartin Sq. TR11: Mawn S 2B 160
(off The Square)
GOLDSITHNEY 4A 152 (1C 173)
Goldsworthy Dr. EX23: Bud 5F 9
Goldsworthy Way PL27: Wade 4E 24
GOLDWORTHY 1B 164
Golf House Rd. EX23: Bud 4C 8
Golf Ter. TR7: Newq 3D 34
Golitha Falls 1B 170
Golitha Ri. PL14: Lisk 4C 70
Golva Cl. TR13: Helst 1D 158
GOONABARN 1F 55 (2C 169)
GONVENA 3F 25
Gonvena Hill PL27: Wade 3F 25
Gonwin Mnr. Dr. TR26: C Bay 7G 137
Goodern Dr. TR1: Glo 5D 106
Goodmans La. PL14: Pens 1J 67
GOONABARN 1F 55
Goonabarn Cotts. PL26: Goona 1F 55
GOONAMARRIS 7F 47
Goonavean Pk. PL26: Fox 1G 55
Goonbarrow Mdw. PL26: Bugl 7G 43
Goonbarrow Wlk. PL26: Bugl 7G 43
GOONBELL 2K 97 (3A 168)
GOONEARL 4J 103
GOON GUMPAS 2C 114
GOONHAVERN 5H 41 (2A 168)
Goonhavern Ind. Est. TR4: Goonh 5H 41
Goonhilly Cl. TR4: Goonh 5H 41
GOONHUSBAND 7C 158
Goonlaze Ter. TR3: Stith 6H 121
GOONOWN 2J 97
Goonown La. TR5: S Agn 3B 96
Goonown Rd. TR5: S Agn 3B 96
GOONPIPER 2H 125
Goonrea PL13: Loo 4F 81
GOONREEVE 6K 123
Goonvean Ind. Pk. PL26: Goonm 7E 46
GOONVREA 2F 97 (3A 168)
Goonvrea TR3: P'hal 4J 123
Goonvrea Cl. TR7: Newq 5G 35
Goonvrea Rd. TR5: S Agn 2G 97
Goonvrea Ter. TR3: P'hal 3J 123
Goonwartha Cl. PL13: Loo 5F 81
(off Goonwartha Rd.)

Goonwartha Rd. PL13: Loo 5F 81
Gooseberry La. PL1: Plym 6F 163
PL14: Pens .1K 67
Gooseford La. PL11: S John 5E 92
GOOSEHAM 2A 164
GOOSEWELL 2D 171
Gordon Ct. PL12: Salt 3F 89
Gordon Pl. TR9: S Maj 4D 30
Gordons Cl. TR3: Stith 7B 122
Gordon Ter. PL4: Plym 1J 163
PL10: M'brk .2D 94
GORRAN CHURCHTOWN 1F 135 (3C 169)
GORRAN HAVEN 2J 135 (3D 169)
GORRAN HIGH LANES 3C 169
Gorse Cl. TR7: Newq 5H 35
GOSS MOOR 1K 45
GOTHERS 1H 47
GOTHERS HILL 1G 47
Gothers Rd. PL26: Goth, S Den 1G 47
Gothers Ter. PL26: Goth 1H 47
Goudges La. PL26: W'moor 2J 47
Gounce, The TR6: P'rth 4B 40
Gover Cl. TR4: Mt Hwk 7H 97
GOVEREK 6D 162
Gover Hill TR4: Mt Hwk 6H 97
Gover La. TR7: Newq 3E 34
GOVERMELIN 2C 94
Gover Rd. PL25: G Val, S Aus 4D 56
GOVERSETH 7G 47
Goverseth Caravan Pk. PL26: Fox 7G 47
Goverseth Hill PL26: Fox 6H 47
Goverseth Rd. PL26: Fox 1G 55
Goverseth Ter. PL26: Fox 7G 47
GOVER VALLEY 4D 56
Goyne's Fld. TR4: P'twn 5C 96
(off Sandy Rd.)
GRACCA 7G 43
Gracca Ter. PL26: Bugl 7G 43
Grace Cl. TR16: Carn 1B 120
Graham Av. PL25: S Aus 5J 57
Graham Rd. TR15: Red 3E 112
Grainstore Row TR14: Praze 4K 143
(off School Rd.)
GRAMPOUND 7B 62 (3C 169)
GRAMPOUND ROAD 6K 37 (2C 169)
Grampound Rd. Ind. Est.
TR2: Gram R 7K 37
Granary, The PL11: Polb 7C 86
Grand Hotel Rd. PL1: Plym 7F 163
Grand Pde. PL1: Plym 7F 163
Grange, The EX23: Lyn 7C 8
TR14: Camb 1C 118
Grange Rd. TR13: Helst 4B 158
Granite Row TR20: Crow 2K 155
Granite Way PL17: Call 5E 72
Granny's Grn. PL31: B'min 5G 33
Granny's La. TR6: P'rth 5B 40
Grant's Wlk. PL25: S Aus 6G 57
Granville Ct. EX23: Bud 5F 9
(off Goldsworthy Dr.)
Granville Ter. EX23: Bud 5C 8
Grassmere Way PL12: Salt 1F 89
Grass Valley Pk. PL31: B'min 7H 33
GRATTON 2B 164
Gravesend PL11: Tor 3K 93
Gravesend Gdns. PL11: Tor 3K 93
Grays Ter. TR16: L'ner 1H 121
Grays Yd. TR10: P'ryn 4A 128
(off Lower Mkt. St.)
GREAT BOSULLOW 1B 172
Gt. Charles Cl. PL26: S Ste 3C 54
Greatlands PL14: Pens 1K 67
(off Gooseberry La.)
Great Mills Industrial Parc PL25: S Bl G . . .4E 58
Great Walled Garden, The
TR4: Chac 6D 104
(off High St.)
Gt. Western Railway Yd. TR5: S Agn 3J 97
Gt. Western Rd. PL1: Plym 7F 163
Gt. Wheal Seton TR14: Camb 4F 111
GREATWOOD 1H 129
Greatwood Ho. TR11: M Bri 1H 129
GREAT WORK 4K 153
Greeb Farm 6B 146
Greeb Ho. TR2: Tregon 6J 99
(off Roseland Parc)
Greeb Point 3C 169
Greeb Way TR20: Perran 7J 151
Green, The PL10: King 5E 94
PL12: Salt 2E 88
PL14: Duloe 7A 78
PL25: S Aus 5J 57
PL25: T'oon .5C 56
TR2: Pro 2G 99
TR19: St Bury 2G 147
Greenacres PL30: Nans 3A 32
Greenacres Golf Course 5F 141
Green Apple La. PL25: S Aus 5K 57
Greenaway, The PL27: Polz, Trev 4B 18

Greenbank PL23: Polr 7C **60**
TR11: Fal .7F **129**
TR18: Penz 5E **148**
TR27: Con D 5K **139**
Greenbank Cl. TR2: Gram R 6K **37**
Greenbank Cotts. PL4: Plym 1K **163**
Greenbank Ct. PL4: Plym 2K **163**
Greenbank Cres. TR7: Newq 1K **35**
Greenbank La. PL14: Lisk 4B **70**
Greenbank Rd. PL4: Plym 1K **163**
PL14: Lisk 4B **70**
TR3: Devo 2C **124**
Greenbanks Ct. PL27: Rock 2G **23**
Greenbanks Rd. PL27: Rock 2G **23**
Greenbank Ter. *PL17: Call* 5D **72**
(off Coronation Rd.)
TR3: Devo 2C **124**
GREENBOTTOM . . . . .4H **105 (3A 168)**
Greenbury TR20: Rosu 7D **152**
Green Cl. TR1: Tru 6H **107**
TR3: Feo 4J **125**
Green Ct. TR3: Thre 5K **105**
Green Cres. TR13: Helst 2D **158**
Greendale Vw. *PL26: S Den* 2D **46**
(off Whitegate)
Green Fld. Cl. TR12: Lizar 5H **161**
Greenfield Cl. PL17: Call 4C **72**
Greenfield Rd. PL12: Salt 3F **89**
Greenfields Cl. TR11: Mawn S 2B **160**
Greenfield Ter. TR16: P'ath 4G **101**
Greenfinch Cres. PL12: Salt 1F **89**
Green Hill PL27: Wade 4H **25**
Greenhills PL32: Came 2H **15**
Greenhill Vs. PL27: Wade 4H **25**
Greenhill Works PL18: Chils 1E **74**
Greenland PL10: M'brk 2C **94**
Green La. *PL10: King* 5E **94**
(off Fore St.)
PL23: Fow .6J **61**
PL27: Rock 2F **23**
PL28: Pad .4K **21**
PL31: B'min 6G **33**
PL35: Bosc 2J **13**
TR1: Tru 6H **107**
TR2: Very .5J **135**
TR8: Cran .5A **34**
TR10: P'ryn 4J **127**
TR12: Lizar 5J **161**
TR13: Helst, P'ose 5H **157**
TR15: Red .3D **112**
TR16: P'ath 4E **100**
TR16: Scor 4G **103**
TR17: Mar .3D **150**
TR26: Lel .1E **140**
TR27: Gwith 1H **139**
Green Lane, The TR27: S Er 6E **140**
Green La. Cl. TR10: P'ryn 4K **127**
Green La. Hill TR18: Gul 2G **149**
Green La. Vean TR15: Red 3D **112**
Green La. W. TR17: Mar 3D **150**
Greenmarket, The TR18: Penz 5F **149**
Green Mdws. PL32: Came 3H **15**
Green Parc Rd. TR27: Hayl 2J **141**
Green Pk. PL10: Caws 5E **94**
Green Pk. Av. PL4: Plym 1H **163**
Green Rocks TR18: Newl 2D **154**
Greens Cotts. PL12: Treh 4C **88**
GREENSPLAT 7H **115**
Greensplat Rd. PL25: S Aus 2E **56**
PL26: Green 3H **55**
(not continuous)
Green St. PL4: Plym 4K **163**
TR1: Tru 5K **107**
TR18: Penz 6G **149**
Greenways Bus. Complex PL15: Laun 2G **17**
Greenwich Pl. *PL12: Salt* 2H **89**
(off Glebe Av.)
Greenwith Cl. TR1: Tru 6H **107**
GREENWITH COMMON 1K **123**
Greenwith Cres. TR3: P Sta 1J **123**
Greenwith Hill TR3: P Sta 1J **123**
Greenwith La. TR3: P Sta 1J **123**
Greenwith Rd. TR3: P Sta 1J **123**
Greenwix Parc PL30: S Mab 6C **26**
Greenwood Cres. TR10: P'ryn 4J **127**
Greenwood Rd. TR10: P'ryn 4J **127**
Gregor Rd. TR1: Tru 4B **108**
Gregory Ct. TR7: Newq 2K **35**
Gregory's Ct. PL31: B'min 3F **33**
Gregory's Mdw. PL15: Laun 5K **17**
Grenfell Av. PL12: Salt 2E **88**
Grenfell Gdns. PL12: Salt 2E **88**
Grenfell St. *TR19: Mou* 6D **154**
(off South Cliff)
Grenifer TR15: I'gan 3K **111**
Grenifer Rd. TR15: I'gan 3K **111**
Grenna La. TR3: P Sta 6J **115**
GRENOFEN 1D **171**
Grenville Battery 4F **95**

Grenville Cen. 5C **8**
Grenville Cl. PL17: Call 6D **72**
PL26: Nanp 5G **47**
PL31: B'min 5H **33**
Grenville Ct. *PL25: S Aus* 6G **57**
(off Moorland Rd.)
Grenville Cres. TR11: Fal 7D **128**
Grenville Dr. TR5: S Agn 2B **96**
Grenville Gdns. TR14: Tro 4G **119**
Grenville Mdws. PL22: Los 3G **53**
PL26: Nanp 5G **47**
Grenville Rd. PL22: Los 3F **53**
PL28: Pad .3A **22**
TR1: Tru 4H **107**
TR11: Fal .7D **128**
TR13: Helst 4D **158**
Grenville Wlk. PL13: Polp 5A **80**
Gresham CI. TR7: Newq 5G **35**
Greystone Av. PL26: Fox 1J **55**
Gribbas Cl. TR3: Stith 7A **122**
Gribbas Cnr. TR3: Stith 7A **122**
Gribben Cl. PL25: S Aus 3J **57**
Gribben Rd. PL25: S Aus 3J **57**
Gribbin Daymark 3D **169**
Gribbin Head 3D **169**
Gribbon Way PL24: Par 4J **59**
Griffins, The PL14: Lisk 4C **70**
Grift La. PL32: S Ger 5A **86**
Griggs Hill TR27: Hayl 4E **140**
Griggs Quay TR27: Hayl 4E **140**
GRIMSCOTT 3A **164**
GRINACOMBE MOOR 1D **167**
Grist La. TR27: Ang 7G **139**
Grose Hill Cres. PL26: Penw 5J **49**
Grose Mdws. PL26: S Den 2D **46**
Grosvenor Av. TR7: Newq 3F **35**
Grosvenor Pl. PL25: S Aus 5F **57**
Grove Dr. PL14: Lisk 5J **69**
Grove Hill TR2: S Mawe 7D **130**
TR11: Mawn S 3B **160**
Grovehill Cres. TR11: Fal 2G **133**
Grovehill Dr. TR11: Fal 2F **133**
Grove La. TR20: Gold 5B **152**
Grove Parc PL24: Tyw H 6K **51**
Grove Pk. PL11: Tor 3G **93**
Grove Pk. Ct. PL14: Lisk 6A **70**
Grove Pk. Ter. *PL14: Lisk* 6A **70**
(off Station Rd.)
Grove Pl. PL28: Pad 3B **22**
TR11: Fal .2G **133**
Grove Rd. PL24: S Bl G 3F **59**
PL25: S Aus 5F **57**
Grovewood Ct. TR9: Fr'don 3G **45**
Grylls Parc TR13: Helst 3B **158**
Gue, The TR13: P'ven 7F **157**
GUILDFORD 7E **138**
Guildford CI. PL26: Fox 7H **47**
Guildford Rd. TR27: Hayl 7E **138**
Guildford Rd. Ind. Est. TR27: Hayl 7E **138**
Guildford St. PL4: Plym 3K **163**
Guildhall *TR13: Helst* 4B **158**
(off Market Pl.)
Guildhall La. PL22: Los 3E **52**
Guildhall Rd. *TR18: Penz* 5F **149**
(off Alverton St.)
Guildhall Sq. PL1: Plym 5H **163**
PL15: Laun 4H **17**
(off Western Rd.)
Guineaport Parc PL27: Wade 4F **25**
Guineaport Rd. PL27: Wade 4F **25**
Guipavas Rd. PL17: Call 6E **72**
Guisseny Pl. TR13: P'ven 6G **157**
Gulland Rd. PL27: N Pol 1D **18**
Gully's La. PL26: S Den 3D **46**
GULVAL . . . . .2H **149 (1B 172)**
Gulval Almshouses TR18: Gul 2H **149**
Gulval Cross *TR18: Gul* 2G **149**
(off Trevarrack Rd.)
Gun Hill Rd. TR8: Hol B 3A **38**
GUNNISLAKE . . . . .1H **75 (3D 167)**
Gunnislake Ind. Est. PL18: Dra 2F **75**
Gunnislake Station (Rail) 3G **75**
Gunpool La. PL35: Bosc 2K **13**
Gunvenna Holiday Pk. PL27: S Minv 4K **19**
Gunwin Ct. PL26: W'moor 3H **47**
Gurlyn Hill TR20: Relu 1E **152**
Gurney Cl. EX23: Flex 3D **8**
PL11: Tor .3H **93**
Gurney Row TR2: Tregon 6H **99**
Gurney's La. TR14: Camb 7D **110**
Gurnick Rd. TR18: Newl 2B **154**
Gurnick St. TR19: Mou 6D **154**
Gustavus Rd. TR14: Camb 7D **110**
Gustory Rd. TR8: Cran 6A **34**
GWALLON .2F **151**
Gwallon La. TR17: Mar 4G **151**
Gwallon Rd. PL25: S Aus 4J **57**
Gwarak Gwel an Mor TR2: P'stho 3J **131**
Gwarnick Rd. TR1: Tru 5H **107**

Gwarth an Drae TR13: Helst 1B **158**
Gwarth an Dre TR27: Phil 6E **138**
Gwavas Bungs. *TR18: Newl* 2C **154**
(off Gwavas Rd.)
Gwavas Est. TR18: Newl 2C **154**
Gwavas La. TR18: Newl 2C **154**
Gwavas Quay TR18: Newl 1C **154**
Gwavas St. TR18: Penz 4F **149**
Gweal-an-Top TR15: Red 3F **113**
Gweal Darras TR10: M Bur 5G **127**
Gwealdues TR13: Helst 2D **158**
Gweal Folds TR13: Helst 2C **158**
Gwealfolds Rd. TR13: Helst 2C **158**
Gweal Gollas TR27: Phil 6E **138**
Gwealhellis Warren TR13: Helst 2B **158**
Gwealmayowe Pk. TR13: Helst 2D **158**
Gweal Pawl TR15: Red 4C **112**
Gweal Wartha TR13: Helst 1B **158**
Gwedhennek TR18: Gul 3G **149**
GWEEK . . . . .6H **159 (2A 174)**
Gweek Dr. TR12: Gweek 7G **159**
Gwel an Garrek TR12: Mull 3G **161**
Gwel an Mor TR16: P'ath 5F **101**
TR8: M Por 1C **28**
TR17: Mar .4F **151**
Gwelanmor Cl. TR26: C Bay 6F **137**
Gwelanmor Rd. TR26: C Bay 6F **137**
Gwel an-Scol TR3: Feo 3J **125**
Gwel an-Skol TR14: Camb 5E **110**
Gwel an Wheal TR26: S Ives 4C **136**
Gwel an Wheal Cres. TR26: S Ives 4C **136**
Gwel Avon Bus. Pk. PL12: Salt 7F **85**
Gwelavon Cl. PL27: Wade 4G **25**
Gwelenys Rd. TR19: Mou 5D **154**
Gwell-an-Nans TR2: Pro 2H **99**
Gwel Lewern TR18: Penz 3H **149**
Gwel Marten Flats TR26: C Bay 6G **137**
Gwelmeneth TR13: Helst 5B **158**
Gwelmeneth Pk. PL14: S Cle 4B **66**
Gwelmor TR14: Camb 1E **118**
Gwel-Mor TR19: Pend 4C **144**
Gwel Ryan PL30: Lux 4C **50**
Gwel Tek TR27: Phil 6D **138**
Gwel Trencrom TR27: Hayl 4G **141**
Gwendra La. PL26: W'moor 2J **47**
Gwendroc Cl. TR1: Tru 6K **107**
Gwendroc Ho. M. TR1: Tru 6K **107**
Gwendrona CI. TR13: Helst 1D **158**
Gwendrona Way TR13: Helst 1D **158**
GWENNAP . . . . .7B **114 (3A 168)**
Gwennap Pit 4H **113**
Gwennap Pit Vis. Cen. 4H **113**
GWENTER .3A **174**
GWINDRA .5E **54**
Gwindra Ind. Est. PL26: S Ste 5E **54**
Gwindra Rd. PL26: S Ste 4C **54**
GWINEAR . . . . .1B **142 (1C 173)**
GWINEAR DOWNS 6D **142**
Gwinear La. TR27: Gwinn 1C **142**
GWITHIAN
Hayle . . . . .1H **139 (1C 173)**
Truro 7D **116**
Gwithian Cl. PL11: Tor 2H **93**
Gwithian Rd. PL25: S Aus 2J **57**
TR27: Con D 3J **139**
Gwithian Sands Chalet Pk. TR27: Gwith 3G **139**
GWITHIAN TOWANS 1G **139**
Gwythian Way TR6: P'rth 5A **40**
Gyles Ct. TR7: Newq 3A **36**
Gyllyngdune Mnr. TR11: Fal 3G **133**
Gyllyng St. TR11: Fal 1F **133**
Gyllyngvase Hill TR11: Fal 3F **133**
Gyllyngvase Rd. TR11: Fal 3F **133**
Gyllyngvase Ter. TR11: Fal 3G **133**

H

Haddon Way PL25: Carl 6C **58**
Haig Pl. TR18: Hea 3D **148**
Hain Wlk. TR26: S Ives 4E **136**
HALAMANNING 4D **152**
Halbullock Way TR1: Glo 5C **106**
HALE MILLS 3E **114**
HALGABRON . . . . .6E **12 (2A 166)**
Halgavor La. PL31: B'min 6G **33**
Halgavor Pk. PL31: B'min 7H **33**
Halgavor Rd. PL30: B'min 7F **33**
PL31: B'min 7F **33**
Halgavor Vw. PL31: B'min 6H **33**
HALGOSS .2F **111**
Halifax PL27: S Eval 2H **31**
Halimote Rd. PL26: S Den 2E **46**
Hallane Rd. PL25: S Aus 3A **58**
HALLAZE 5K **49**

Hallaze Rd. PL26: Penw 5J **49**
HALLEGAN 7D **118**
HALLENBEAGLE 5K **103**
Hallett Cl. PL12: Salt 2D **88**
Hallett Way EX23: Flex 3E **8**
HALLEW 5G **43**
Hallew Rd. PL26: Nanp 5F **47**
Hall for Cornwall Theatre 5K **107**
Halliggye Fogou 2A **174**
Halloon Av. TR9: S Roa 1G **45**
Hall Rd. PL26: S Den 1E **46**
Hall Ter. PL23: B'ick 6K **61**
HALLWORTHY 2B **166**
HALSETOWN 6B **136** (1C **173**)
Halsetown Rd. TR26: Hal, S Ives 4A **136**
HALTON QUAY 6J **77**
Halt Rd. TR4: Goonh 5H **41**
 TR8: S New E 2G **37**
Halvana TR15: Red 5F **113**
Halvarras Pk. TR3: P Pla 5G **117**
Halvarras Rd. TR3: P Pla 5G **117**
Halveor Cl. TR9: S Maj 4C **30**
Halveor Ct. TR6: P'rth 4B **40**
Halveor La. TR9: S Maj 3A **30**
HALVOSSO 7C **126**
HALWILL 1D **167**
HALWILL JUNCTION 1D **167**
Halwyn Cl. TR3: C Dow 7D **116**
Halwyn Hill TR8: Cran 6B **34**
Halwyn Pl. TR1: Tru 5H **107**
Halwyn Rd. TR8: Cran 6B **34**
Halwyn Ter. TR1: Tru 6H **107**
HAM 2D **171**
Ham Cl. PL27: Treb 4C **18**
Ham Field PL27: Treb 4C **18**
Hamilton Cl. TR27: Hayl 4G **141**
Hamilton Gdns. PL4: Plym 1H **163**
Hammills Cl. TR13: P'ven 7G **157**
Hammills Dr. TR13: P'ven 7G **157**
Hamoaze Rd. PL11: Tor 4K **93**
Hampstead Ter. *PL31: B'min* *3E 32*
 (off Higher Bore St.)
Hampton Cl. *TR7: Newq* *3E 34*
 (off St Cuthbert's Rd.)
Hampton St. PL4: Plym 4J **163**
Hancock La. TR2: S Mawe 7D **130**
Hangmans Hill TR14: Tro 7K **119**
Hangmans La. PL17: Call 6E **72**
Hangmans Wlk. TR11: Fal 4E **132**
Hannaford Cl. TR9: S Roa 1G **45**
HANNAFORE 6H **81**
Hannafore La. PL13: Loo 7J **81** (5G **81**)
Hannafore Rd. PL13: Loo 7J **81** (5G **81**)
Hanover Cl. TR6: P'rth 4B **40**
Hanover Ct. TR14: Camb 6E **110**
 TR18: Penz 5F **149**
Hanover Ho. EX23: Bud 5C **8**
Hanover Parc TR9: I Que 1J **45**
Hanson Dr. PL23: Fow 6A **60**
Hanson Rd. PL14: Lisk 4C **70**
Harbour, The PL35: Bosc 1K **13**
Harbour Av. PL4: Plym 5K **163**
Harbour Ct. *TR11: Fal* *1F 133*
 (off New St.)
 TR16: P'ath 4F **101**
 TR18: Penz 5F **149**
Harbour Flats PL26: Pent 1D **134**
Harbour Head *TR13: P'ven* *7F 157*
 (off Fore St.)
Harbour M. TR19: Senn C 3C **146**
Harbour Rd. PL24: Par 3J **59**
 PL27: Wade 3E **24**
 PL13: P'ven 7F **157**
Harbourside Ct. PL4: Plym 5K **163**
Harbour St. PL11: Tor 3K **93**
Harbour Ter. PL35: Bosc 1K **13**
 TR11: Fal 7F **129**
 TR16: P'ath 4F **101**
Harbour Vw. *PL12: Salt* *3G 89*
 (off Higher Port Vw.)
 PL23: Fow 7J **61**
 TR1: Tru 6A **108**
 TR2: S Jus R 2E **130**
 TR7: Newq *2E 34*
 (off Nth. Quay Hill)
 TR10: P'ryn 4K **127**
 TR13: P'ven 7F **157**
 TR17: Mar 5D **150**
 TR27: Hayl 2G **141**
Harbour Vw. Cres. TR18: Penz 4F **149**
Harbour Vw. Ter. *TR18: Newl* *2C 154*
 (off Belle Vue)
Harbour Village TR10: P'ryn 5B **128**
HARCOURT 5H **125** (1B **174**)
Harcourt Cl. TR1: Tru 5F **107**
Harcourt La. TR3: Feo 3H **125**
Hardings Cl. PL12: Salt 1G **89**
Harebell Cl. PL12: Salt 1E **88**
Harefield Cres. TR14: Camb 6D **110**

Harewood Rd. PL18: Cals 7J **75**
Harleigh Rd. PL31: B'min 5G **33**
Harleigh Ter. PL31: B'min 5G **33**
Harlequinns Leisure 5E **8**
Harlequins TR26: S Ives 4H **137**
Harlyn Barton PL28: H Bay 3C **20**
HARLYN BAY 3D **20** (3C **165**)
Harlyn Bay Rd. PL28: H Bay 4D **20**
Harlyn Rd. PL28: S Mer 5D **20**
Harlyn Sands Holiday Pk. PL28: H Bay 2B **20**
Harmer Cl. PL31: B'min 2F **33**
Harmony Cl. PL26: Roch 4B **42**
 TR15: Red 2D **112**
Harmony Mdw. PL26: Roch 4A **42**
Harmony Rd. PL26: Roch 4A **42**
Harmony Ter. TR1: Tru 7A **108**
 TR16: I'gan 7J **101**
Harriet Pl. TR11: Fal 6E **128**
Harris Cl. PL17: K Bray 2C **72**
Harris Ct. *TR10: P'ryn* *5A 128*
 (off Saracen Way)
Harrison Gdns. TR15: I Hig 3K **111**
Harrison Ter. TR1: Tru 5H **107**
Harriss Hill TR3: Feo 1G **125**
HARROWBARROW 4A **74** (1C **171**)
Harry's Ct. TR26: S Ives 1H **137**
HARTLAND 1A **164**
HARTLAND QUAY .1A **164**
Hartland Rd. PL29: P Isa 2K **19**
Hartland Ter. EX23: Bud 4C **8**
Hartmeade PL14: Menh 1H **79**
Harvenna Cl. TR9: Fr'don 3G **45**
Harvenna Hgts. TR9: Fr'don 2G **45**
Harvest Moon TR7: Newq 2E **34**
Harvey Rd. TR1: Tru 7K **107**
Harvey's Towans TR27: Hayl 7A **138**
Harvey St. PL11: Tor 3K **93**
Harvey's Way TR27: Hayl 2H **141**
Harwell Ct. PL1: Plym 4F **163**
Harwell St. PL1: Plym 3F **163**
Hastings St. PL1: Plym 3F **163**
Hastings Ter. PL1: Plym 3F **163**
HATCHES GREEN .2H **75**
Hatch's Hill TR27: Ang 7G **139**
Hatfield Cres. TR7: Newq 4C **34**
Hat La. PL10: Caws 5D **94**
HATT 3B **84** (1C **171**)
Haven, The TR6: P'rth 5C **40**
Haven Ct. TR27: Hayl 2H **141**
Havett Cl. PL14: Dob 3D **68**
Havett Hill PL14: Dob 3D **68**
Havett Rd. PL14: Dob 2D **68**
Haviland Rd. PL14: Lisk 6D **70**
Hawke Cl. TR7: Newq 3E **34**
Hawkens Way TR9: S Maj 5B **30**
Hawke Rd. PL15: Helst 5D **158**
Hawkers Av. PL4: Plym 5K **163**
Hawkers Ct. EX23: Flex 3C **8**
Hawker's Hut 2A **164**
Hawkeys M. TR15: Red 6F **113**
Hawkins Rd. PL28: Pad 3A **22**
 TR7: Newq 4F **35**
 TR18: Penz 5E **148**
Hawkins Way TR11: Fal 1E **132**
 TR13: Helst 3D **158**
Hawks Pk. PL12: Salt 3E **88**
Hawks Point TR26: C Bay 6G **137**
Hawks Tor PL15: Laun 5E **16**
Hawthorn Av. EX23: Bud 6D **8**
 PL11: Tor 3H **93**
Hawthorn Cl. EX23: Bud 6D **8**
 PL25: S Aus 3K **57**
 TR9: S Maj 5A **30**
 TR15: Red 1D **112**
Hawthorne Cl. PL32: Came 3J **15**
Hawthorns PL12: Salt 3F **89**
Hawthorn Way TR3: Thre 5K **105**
Haydown Cl. PL30: S B'wd 1J **27**
HAYE .5A **72** (1C **171**)
Hayeford PL14: S Ive 5K **67**
Haye La. PL17: Call, Haye 4A **72**
Haye Rd. PL17: Call, Haye 5A **72**
Hayes, The TR1: Tru 3A **108**
Hay La. PL11: Shev 3E **90**
 PL13: Loo 4H **81**
HAYLE 2G **141** (1C **173**)
Hayle (Beginners) Golf Course 1K **141**
Hayle Estuary Nature Reserve 2E **140**
Hayle Ind. Pk. TR27: Hayl 7F **139**
Hayle Outdoor Pool 1G **141**
Hayle Rd. TR27: Fr'ham 6A **142**
 TR27: Leeds 7C **142**
Hayle Station (Rail) 2G **141**
Hayle Ter. TR27: Hayl 1G **141**
Hayle Vw. PL27: Wade 3D **24**
Hayman Way TR11: Fal 7C **128**
Hayne Corfe Gdns. TR1: Tru 5G **107**
HAYTOWN 2B **164**
Hazelbank Ct. PL5: Plym 4K **89**

Hazel Cl. PL25: S Aus 3A **58**
Hazelmead PL14: Lisk 5A **70**
Hazelmere Av. PL25: S Aus 5B **58**
Hazel Ter. TR16: L'ner 1H **121**
Hazelwood Rd. PL17: Call 5D **72**
Heabrook Parc TR18: Hea 3D **148**
Hea Cl. TR18: Hea 3D **148**
Hea Cnr. *TR18: Hea* *3D 148*
 (off Hea Rd.)
Headland Apartments TR12: Cover 7D **162**
Headland Caravan & Camping Pk., The
 PL34: Tin 6B **12**
Headland Cl. TR26: C Bay 6G **137**
Headland Cotts. TR12: Cover 7D **162**
Headland Ct. TR26: C Bay 6G **137**
Headland Garden 7B **60**
Headland Pk. PL4: Plym 1K **163**
Headland Point TR7: Newq 2D **34**
Headland Rd. TR7: Newq 2D **34**
 TR26: C Bay 6G **137**
Headland Ter. TR2: Gram R 6K **37**
Head La. TR5: S Agn 2K **97**
Headleigh Rd. TR7: Newq 4F **35**
Healey's Cornish Cyder Farm 2A **168**
HEAMOOR 3D **148** (1B **172**)
Heanton Ter. PL10: M'brk 1D **94**
 TR15: Red 4E **112**
Heanton Vs. TR15: Red 4E **112**
Hearl Rd. PL12: Salt 2D **88**
Hea Rd. TR18: Hea 3D **148**
Heartlands 5H **111**
Heatherbell Gdns. TR26: C Bay 7G **137**
Heather Cl. TR18: Hea 3C **148**
Heather La. TR27: Can 6A **140**
Heather Mdw. TR9: Fr'don 2H **45**
Heathers, The PL26: Fox 1J **55**
Heather Way TR20: Rosu 6B **152**
Heathfield Gdns. TR15: Red 1G **113**
Heathfield Ter. *TR15: Red* *1G 113*
 (off Redruth Highway)
Heathlands Bus. Pk. PL14: Lisk 5B **70**
Heathlands Ind. Est. PL14: Lisk 5B **70**
Heathlands Rd. PL14: Lisk 5A **70**
Heath Ter. PL18: Dra 3G **75**
Heavitree Rd. PL10: King 5E **94**
Hecla Dr. TR26: C Bay 5E **136**
Hedgerows, The PL12: Salt 2D **88**
HELE
 Bude 2E **10**
 Launceston 1D **167**
HELEBRIDGE 3E **10**
Helebridge Rd. EX23: March 3E **10**
Helena Cl. PL26: Penw 5K **49**
Hele Rd. EX23: March 3E **10**
HELFORD 4B **160** (2A **174**)
Helford River Sailing Club 4B **160**
Heligan Ho. PL26: Pent 3A **134**
Heligan Pk. Holiday Pk. PL26: Pent 2A **134**
HELLAND 3A **166**
HELLANDBRIDGE .3A **166**
Helland Gdns. TR10: P'ryn 4B **128**
Helland Rd. PL31: B'min 2G **33**
Hellescoth Way TR13: Helst 1D **158**
HELLESVEAN 3B **136**
Hellesvean TR26: S Ives 3B **136**
Hellesvean Cl. TR26: S Ives 4B **136**
HELLESVEOR 3A **136** (1C **173**)
Hellesveor Caravan & Camping Site
 TR26: S Ives 3A **136**
Helleur Cl. PL24: S Bla 3H **59**
Hellings Cl. TR3: Stith 7A **122**
Hellis Wartha TR13: Helst 3D **158**
 (not continuous)
Hell's Mouth 1D **173**
HELLYS 4C **158**
Helman Tor Vw. PL31: B'min 6G **33**
Helnoweth Cotts. *TR18: Gul* *2G 149*
 (off Helnoweth Gdns.)
Helnoweth Gdns. TR18: Gul 2G **149**
Helnoweth Hill TR18: Gul 2G **149**
Helscott Rd. EX23: March 4E **10**
HELSTON 4C **158** (2D **173**)
Helston Bus. Pk. TR13: Helst 4E **158**
HELSTONE 7E **14** (2A **166**)
Helston Folk Mus. .3B **158**
Helston Leisure Cen. 1C **158**
Helston Rd. PL14: P'ryn 4K **127**
 TR20: Ger 7G **153**
HELSTON WATER .4B **116**
Hembal Cl. PL25: T'oon 5C **56**
Hembal La. PL25: T'oon 5C **56**
Hembal Rd. PL25: T'oon 5C **56**
HENDRA
 Helston 7K **155**
 Penzance 6G **145**
 PL26, Lanjeth 7G **55**
 PL26, Roche 6C **42**
 PL26, St Dennis 3D **46** (2C **169**)
 Truro 6K **121**

Hendra Barton TR1: Tru 4H **107**
HENDRABRIDGE 2E **70**
Hendra Cl. PL14: Dar 2C **66**
  TR1: Tru 4J **107**
  TR3: Stith 6K **121**
  TR13: Ash 1A **156**
HENDRA CROFT
  Helston 1A **156**
  Newquay 2K **41**
Hendra Gdns. PL15: Laun 4G **17**
Hendra Hgts. PL26: S Den 2E **46**
Hendra Holiday Pk. TR8: Lane 6K **35**
Hendra La. TR1: Tru 4H **107**
  TR13: Ash . . . . .7K **155** & 2A **156**
  TR20: Pra S 7K **155**
Hendra Parc PL14: Lisk 3D **70**
Hendra Pk. PL15: Laun 4G **17**
Hendra Prazey PL26: S Den 2D **46**
Hendra Rd. PL26: S Den 3E **46**
  TR1: Tru 4H **107**
  TR3: Stith 6J **121**
Hendras Ct. TR26: C Bay 6F **137**
Hendras Parc TR26: C Bay 6F **137**
Hendra Ter. TR3: Stith 6K **121**
  TR8: Lane 6K **35**
Hendra Va. PL15: Laun 4G **17**
Hendra Vean TR1: Tru 4H **107**
  TR26: C Bay 7G **137**
Hendrawna La. TR6: Bol 5C **40**
Henfor Cl. TR17: Mar 4G **151**
HENFORD 1D **167**
Henfordh Grange PL14: Lisk 4K **69**
Henfor Ter. TR17: Mar 4G **151**
Hengar La. PL30: S Tud 5J **27**
Hengar Mnr. PL30: S Tud 1F **27**
Henley Cl. TR4: Mt Hwk 7G **97**
Henley Cres. TR4: Mt Hwk 7G **97**
Henley Dr. TR4: Mt Hwk 7G **97**
Henliston Dr. TR13: Helst 5C **158**
Henly M. TR4: Mt Hwk 7H **97**
Henry Cft. TR12: Lizar 5G **161**
Henry Scott Tuke Ho. TR11: Fal 1E **132**
Hensbarrow Mdws. PL26: Fox 1G **55**
Henscol TR16: L'ner 1H **121**
Henscol Praze TR16: L'ner 1G **121**
Henscol Va. PL14: Lisk 4K **69**
Henshorn Ct. TR13: Helst 2C **158**
Hensley Row TR14: Camb 5G **111**
Hental TR6: P'rth .5B **40**
Henver Cl. TR27: Reaw 3C **142**
Henver Gdns. TR27: Reaw 3D **142**
Henver Rd. TR7: Newq 2H **35**
Henvor Cl. TR15: Red 2F **113**
Henvor Ter. TR15: Red *1G* **113**
  (off Redruth Highway)
HENWOOD 3C **167**
Henwood Cres. TR7: S Mino 2A **36**
Hen Wythva TR14: Camb 1E **118**
Hen Wythva Parc TR14: Camb 1E **118**
Heritage Cl. PL12: Salt 2E **88**
Herland Hill TR27: Gwinn 1A **142**
Hermes Cl. TR13: Helst 4D **158**
Hermes Rd. TR13: Helst 5C **158**
Hermitage Rd. PL26: Roch 3B **42**
HERNISS 5A **126**
HERODSFOOT 1B **170**
Heron Cl. PL10: M'brk 1D **94**
  TR2: Tr'sln 2H **109**
Herons Ct. TR6: P'rth *4B* **40**
  (off The Gounce)
Heron Way TR1: Tru 7A **108**
Herring Cl. PL14: Lisk 3C **70**
Herring Rd. PL14: Lisk 3C **70**
HERSHAM 3A **164**
Heskyn Vw. PL12: Tide 1B **86**
Hessary Vw. PL12: Salt 2G **89**
HESSENFORD 2C **171**
Hessenford Rd. PL11: Seat 5F **79**
Hetling Cl. PL1: Plym 3F **163**
HEWAS WATER 4H **63** (3C **169**)
Hewers Row PL4: Plym 4K **163**
Hewitt Cl. PL12: Salt 4E **88**
HEYBROOK BAY .3D **171**
Heybrook M. TR7: Newq 3E **34**
HEYL 2G **141**
Hibernia Rd. TR13: Helst 5C **158**
Hichens La. TR11: Fal 7E **128**
Hichens Rd. TR13: Helst 5D **158**
Hicks Cl. TR2: Pro 2H **99**
Hicks Ct. TR26: S Ives 1J **137**
Hicks La. PL4: Plym 5J **163**
HICK'S MILL 5H **115**
Hidden Valley 2C **167**
Hidden Valley Gdns. 2D **169**
Highburrow Ct. TR15: Pool 5J **111**
Highburrow La. TR15: Pool 5J **111**
High Cliff 1B **166**
Highcliffe PL27: Polz 3C **18**
HIGH CROSS 2K **159**

High Cross TR1: Tru 5K **107**
  TR9: S Maj 5B **30**
High Cross St. PL25: S Aus 6H **57**
HIGH DOWNS 6H **119**
Higher Albion Row *TR16: Carh* *4A* **114**
  (off Fore St.)
Higher Anderton Rd. PL10: M'brk 2D **94**
HIGHER BAL 1G **97**
Higher Beech Ter. PL13: Loo *4G* **81**
  (off West Rd.)
Higher Besore Rd. TR3: Thre 5B **106**
Higher Bodiniel Rd. PL31: B'min 2E **32**
HIGHER BOJEWYAN 3E **144** (1A **172**)
Higher Bolenna TR6: P'rth 5A **40**
Higher Bore St. PL31: B'min 3E **32**
HIGHER BOSAVERN 4J **145**
HIGHER BOSCASWELL 4D **144**
Higher Boskerris TR26: C Bay 7F **137**
Higher Bri. Pk. PL27: Wade 4G **25**
HIGHER BRILL 1F **159**
Higher Broad La. TR15: I Hig 3K **111**
Higher Bugle PL26: Bugl 2G **49**
Higher Burrow Cl. TR26: S Ives 4C **136**
HIGHER CARNKIE .1A **120**
Higher Chapel St. PL13: Loo 7K **81**
Higher Church St. TR27: Hayl 1J **141**
Higher Cleaverfield PL15: Laun 2H **17**
HIGHER CLOVELLY 1B **164**
HIGHER COMPTON 2D **171**
Higher Cft. Pk. TR12: Lizar 5H **161**
Higher Cross La. PL32: Came 3K **15**
Higher Daisy Pk. PL28: S Mer 6D **20**
Higher Daws La. PL15: Sth P 6D **16**
HIGHER DIMSON .2G **75**
HIGHER DOWNS .4B **152**
Higher East St. TR9: S Maj 5C **30**
Higher Elms PL27: Pity 7G **19**
Higher Enys Rd. TR14: Camb 6D **110**
Higher Fernleigh Rd. PL27: Wade 5F **25**
Higher Fore St. TR15: Red 3E **112**
  TR17: Mar 4F **151**
Higher Glen Pk. PL14: Pens 1H **67**
Higher Goongumpas La.
  TR16: G Gump .2B **114**
Higher Grn. St. TR18: Newl 2C **154**
Higher Gwavas Rd. TR18: Newl 2C **154**
Higher Harlyn Pk. PL28: S Mer 5D **20**
Higher Jenkins St. TR15: Red *3E* **112**
  (off Jenkins Ter.)
Higher Kelly PL18: Cals 7H **75**
HIGHER KENNEGGY 7D **152**
Higher La. PL1: Plym 5H **163**
  PL27: Eglo 4H **25**
  (not continuous)
  TR13: Ash 1A **156**
Higher Lariggan TR18: Penz 6E **148**
Higher Lavorrick PL26: Mev 4C **134**
Higher Lidden Rd. TR18: Penz 6D **148**
Higher Lux St. PL14: Lisk 4B **70**
Higher Mkt. St. PL13: Loo 6K **81**
  TR10: P'ryn 5A **128**
Higher Mdw. PL14: Dob 4D **68**
Higher Medrose PL33: Dela 2B **14**
HIGHER MENADEW 5K **43**
HIGHER METHERELL 5C **74**
Higher Middle Hill PL14: Pens 1J **67**
Higher Mt. Ambrose La. TR15: Red 2F **113**
Higher Newham La. TR1: Tru 7K **107**
Higher Pk. Stenak TR16: Carh 4A **114**
Higher Pengegon TR14: Camb 1F **119**
HIGHER PENNANCE 7H **113**
HIGHER PENPOLL 3A **160**
Higher Penponds Rd. TR14: P'nds 2B **118**
Higher Pentreath Farm Camp Site
  TR20: Pra S 5G **155**
Higher Peverell Rd. TR18: Penz 3F **149**
Higher Polsue Way TR2: Tr'sln 2G **109**
HIGHER PORTHPEAN 2K **65** (2D **169**)
Higher Port Vw. PL12: Salt 3G **89**
Higher Pumpfield Row TR15: Pool 4H **111**
Higher Quarry Gdns. TR18: Penz 5E **148**
Higher Railway Ter. TR16: Carh *4A* **114**
  (off Church St.)
Higher Redannick TR1: Tru 6H **107**
Higher Rd. PL14: Pens 1H **67**
  TR13: Breag 1D **156**
Higher Row PL10: King *5E* **94**
  (off Devonport Hill)
  TR13: Ash 1A **156**
Higher St Clements Hill TR1: Tru *5B* **108**
  (off St Clements Hill)
Higher Sheffield TR19: Pau 5B **154**
Higher Silver Hill TR13: Helst 3C **158**
Higher Stennack TR26: S Ives 4G **137** (4A **136**)
Higher Ter. TR3: Pons 5F **123**
HIGHER TOLCARNE 6J **29**
Higher Twr. Rd. TR7: Newq 3D **34**
HIGHER TOWN 2E **42**

HIGHERTOWN 5D **106** (3B **168**)
Highertown TR1: Tru 5F **107**
  TR2: P'stho 3K **131**
Highertown Pk. PL12: Land 6H **83**
HIGHER TREGAJORRAN 6K **111**
Higher Tregenna TR26: S Ives 5D **136**
Higher Tregenna Rd. TR26: S Ives 5D **136**
Higher Trehaverne TR1: Tru 4J **107**
HIGHER TRELAVOUR 3E **46**
Higher Tremena PL25: S Aus 5G **57**
Higher Trenant Rd. PL27: Wade 3G **25**
Higher Trerank La. PL26: Roch 5A **42**
Higher Tresavean Ter. TR16: L'ner 1J **121**
Higher Treskerby TR16: Red 1H **113**
HIGHER TRETHARRUP 2G **121**
Higher Trevithick TR27: Hayl 2J **141**
Higher Trevorian Barns
  TR19: St Bury 1J **147**
Higher Trewidden Rd.
  TR26: S Ives 4H **137** (4D **136**)
Higher Trezaise PL26: Trez 7C **42**
Higher Tristram PL27: Polz 3C **18**
Higherwell Cl. TR7: Newq 5H **35**
Higher Well La. TR13: Helst 3C **158**
Higher Well Pk. PL26: Mev 7C **134**
Higher Wesley Ter. PL14: Pens 1J **67**
Higher West End PL26: Pent 1D **134**
Higher Wharf EX23: Bud 5C **8**
HIGHER WHITELEIGH 1C **167**
Higher Whiterock PL27: Wade 4E **24**
HIGHER WINSOR .3G **29**
Higher Woodside PL25: S Aus 5E **56**
Higherwood Vw. PL18: Gun 1G **75**
Highfield PL18: S An Cpl 3F **75**
Highfield Av. PL25: S Aus 6H **57**
  TR9: S Maj 5B **30**
Highfield Cl. PL25: S Aus 6H **57**
Highfield Ct. TR5: S Agn 2B **96**
Highfield Est. PL14: Pens 1K **67**
Highfield Pk. PL12: Salt 2D **88**
Highfield Rd. PL15: Laun 4F **17**
High Fld. Rd. TR4: Mt Hwk 7H **97**
Highfield Rd. PL32: Came 4H **15**
  TR11: Fal 1D **132**
Highfield Rd. Ind. Est.
  PL32: Came 4H **15**
Highfields TR18: Newl *1C* **154**
  (off Bon Cot Rd.)
HIGHGATE 2H **45**
Highgate Hill TR9: I Que 1H **45**
  (not continuous)
Highland Pk. TR10: P'ryn 4K **127**
  TR15: Red 3E **112**
HIGHLANE 7B **160**
HIGH LANES 2J **141**
High Lanes TR8: Cube 4F **39**
  TR27: Hayl 2J **141**
High Lanes M. TR27: Hayl 2J **141**
High Lanes Rd. TR14: Praze 5F **143**
High Pk. PL12: Tide 1A **82**
HIGH STREET 4H **55** (2C **169**)
High St. PL1: Plym .5J **163**
  PL15: Laun 3H **17**
  PL28: Pad 3A **22**
  PL32: Came 4H **15**
  PL33: Dela 3A **14**
  PL35: Bosc 2K **13**
  TR2: Pro 2H **99**
  TR4: Chac 6C **104**
  TR11: Fal 7F **129**
  TR12: S Kev 3B **162**
  TR26: S Ives 3J **137** (2D **136**)
High St. Ind. Est. PL26: H St 5G **55**
Highview TR4: Black 2A **104**
Highview Cl. PL14: Trem 5C **66**
Highview Cres. TR4: Black 2A **104**
Highway La. TR15: Red 1F **113**
Highwood Pk. PL14: Dob 4E **68**
Higman Cl. PL14: Dob 4E **68**
Hilgrove Rd. TR7: Newq 2H **35**
Hill Cl. PL30: S B'wd 2H **27**
  TR18: Hea 2C **148**
Hill Ct. M. PL10: M'brk 2C **94**
Hillcrest TR4: Short 6C **98**
  TR13: Helst 2C **158**
Hillcrest Av. TR1: Tru 4G **107**
Hillcrest Cl. TR9: S Maj 5C **30**
Hillcrest Rd. TR27: Hayl 1J **141**
Hill Gdns. PL12: Carg 3J **85**
Hill Hay Cl. PL23: Fow 7G **61**
HILL HEAD 1C **54**
HILLHEAD
  Bude 5G **9**
  Lostwithiel 1D **52**
Hill Head TR10: P'ryn 6B **128**
Hillhead TR2: S Mawe 7D **130**
Hillhead Gdns. PL32: Came 3J **15**
Hillhead Rd. TR11: Fal 7J **127**

Hillocks, The PL13: Loo 4H **81**
   (off Pendrim Rd.)
Hill Pk. PL27: Wade 3G **25**
Hillpark Cotts. PL15: Laun 3J **17**
Hill Pk. Cres. PL4: Plym 1K **163**
   PL25: S Aus 7E **56**
Hill Pk. M. PL4: Plym 1K **163**
Hill Rd. PL27: Wade 4F **25**
Hillside PL25: S Aus 6B **58**
   TR7: Newq 5E **34**
   (off Tregunnel Pk.)
Hillside Av. PL12: Salt 2H **89**
   PL24: B'vey 4G **59**
Hillside Ct. PL26: Bugl 7H **43**
   PL31: B'min 3E **32**
Hillside Gdns. PL22: Los 3E **52**
   TR19: Trew 5B **144**
Hillside Ind. Est. TR16: Red 7G **103**
Hillside Mdw. TR10: P'ryn 5B **128**
Hillside Mdws. PL26: Fox 2H **55**
Hillside Parc TR20: Mad 1B **148**
Hillside Pk. PL31: B'min 3E **32**
Hillside Rd. PL12: Salt 2G **89**
   PL25: S Aus 4H **57**
   TR11: Fal 3D **132**
   TR16: Carh 5K **113**
Hillside Ter. PL11: Downd 6J **79**
   PL13: Loo 4H **81**
   TR15: Red 3E **112**
   TR18: Newl 1C **154**
Hillside Vs. PL13: Mill 3K **81**
Hillson Cl. PL29: P Isa 3K **19**
Hill St. PL4: Plym 4K **163**
   PL28: Pad 3B **22**
Hillsview PL13: Polp 5A **80**
   (not continuous)
Hilton Rd. EX23: March 3G **11**
HOBBACOTT 2K **11**
Hobbacott Cl. EX23: Bud 5F **9**
Hobbacott La. EX23: March 3G **11**
Hobbs Cres. PL12: Salt 2E **88**
Hockens La. PL23: Polr 7B **60**
Hockin Cl. PL17: K Bray 2C **72**
Hockings Ho. PL14: S Cle 4A **66**
Hodders Way PL12: Carg 2J **85**
Hodge Cl. PL12: Salt 3E **88**
HOE, THE 7G **163**
Hoe App. PL1: Plym 6H **163**
Hoe Ct. PL1: Plym 6G **163**
Hoe Gdns. PL1: Plym 6H **163**
Hoegate Ct. PL1: Plym 6H **163**
Hoegate Pl. PL1: Plym 6H **163**
Hoegate St. PL1: Plym 6J **163**
Hoe Park 6G **163**
Hoe Rd. PL1: Plym 7F **163**
Hoe St. PL1: Plym 6H **163**
HOE, THE 2D **171**
Holborn Ter. PL15: Laun 4J **17**
   (off Tavistock Rd.)
Holbrook Row TR27: S Er 6F **141**
   (off Church St.)
Holcroft Cl. PL12: Salt 3F **89**
Holdsworth St. PL4: Plym 1F **163**
HOLLABURY 3E **8**
Hollabury Rd. EX23: Flex 3E **8**
HOLLACOMBE 3B **164**
Hollies Cl. PL15: Laun 2F **17**
Hollies Rd. PL15: Laun 1F **17**
   (not continuous)
Hollong Pk. PL11: Ant 4B **92**
Hollow Cres. PL26: Dup 7A **58**
Hollowgutter La. PL11: Tor 4E **92**
Hollows Ter. TR27: Hayl 7E **138**
Holly Cl. TR3: Thre 5K **105**
Holly Ter. TR18: Hea 3D **148**
   (off Madron Rd.)
Holman Av. TR14: Camb 6C **110**
Holman Pk. TR14: Camb 7D **110**
Holman Rd. PL14: Lisk 4D **70**
Holman's Pl. TR13: P'ven 7F **157**
Holman's Ter. TR16: Four L 3C **120**
HOLMBUSH 6B **58** (2D **169**)
Holmbush Arch Rd. PL25: S Aus 6B **58**
Holmbush Hill PL17: Downg 1D **72**
   PL17: K Bray 1C **72**
Holmbush Ind. Est. PL25: S Aus 5B **58**
   (not continuous)
Holmbush Rd. PL25: S Aus 6A **58**
Holm Oaks Apartments TR11: Fal 6J **133**
   (off Melvill Rd.)
Holnicote Rd. EX23: Bud 5D **8**
HOLSWORTHY 3B **164**
HOLSWORTHY BEACON 3B **164**
Holt Cres. TR7: Newq 4E **34**
HOLWOOD 1B **82**
Holwood Bus. Cen. PL12: Land 1B **82**
Holyrood Pl. PL1: Plym 7G **163**
HOLYWELL BAY 2B **38** (2A **168**)

Holywell Bay Fun Park 2C **38**
Holywell Bay Golf Course 2C **38**
Holywell Bay Holiday Pk.
   TR8: Hol B 3B **38**
Holywell Beach to Pentire Point West 1A **168**
Holywell Ct. TR3: P Pla 4G **117**
Holywell Rd. PL14: Lisk 4D **70**
   TR3: P Pla 5G **117**
   TR7: Newq 3G **35**
   TR8: Cube 3D **38**
   TR8: Hol B 3A **38**
Homefield Pk. PL31: B'min 5H **33**
Home Pk. PL12: Land 6G **83**
   PL14: Menh 1H **79**
Home Pk. Rd. PL12: Salt 2J **89**
Homer Pk. PL12: Salt 2F **89**
Homer Pk. Rd. PL28: T'one 2G **21**
Homer Water Pk. PL26: S Ste 3C **54**
Homestake Vs. TR8: Sum 6D **44**
Homeyard Homes TR2: Very 5J **135**
Honeys Hill PL30: Lani 6H **31**
Honey St. PL31: B'min 3G **33**
   (off Fore St.)
Honeysuckle Cl. PL12: Salt 1F **89**
Honeysuckle Gdns. PL15: Laun 5K **17**
Hong Kong PL14: Lisk 4K **69**
Honicombe Mnr. PL17: Harr 4D **74**
Hood La. TR14: P'nds 2A **118**
HOOE 2D **171**
Hooe Lake PL10: M'brk 3F **95**
Hooper Ct. PL14: Lisk 2B **70**
Hooper La. TR14: Camb 1D **118**
Hoopers Cl. PL12: Land 7G **83**
Hoopers La. PL18: Gun 1G **75**
Hooper St. PL11: Tor 3K **93**
Hope Ter. TR7: Newq 3E **34**
Hopton Cl. EX23: Bud 5E **8**
Horizon Flds. TR19: Senn 4E **146**
Horizons TR7: Newq 4E **34**
Hornabrook Ct. PL28: Pad 3B **22**
   (off Broad St.)
Hornabrook Pl. PL28: Pad 3B **22**
   (off Broad St.)
HORNICK 4J **55**
Hornick Hill PL26: H St 4J **55**
Horn La. PL14: Lisk 4A **70**
HORNS CROSS 1B **164**
HORRABRIDGE 1D **171**
Horse & Jockey La.
   TR13: Helst 4C **158**
HORSEBRIDGE 3D **167**
HORSEDOWNS 7F **143**
Horsedowns Rd. TR14: Praze 7D **142**
   TR27: Leeds 7D **142**
Horsepool La. PL11: Shev 3E **90**
Horsepool Rd. PL11: Shev 4F **91**
   TR27: Con D 5K **139**
Horseshoe Cl. PL26: Roch 4C **42**
Horse Whim Dr. PL25: S Aus 4B **58**
Horsewhim Dr. PL17: K Bray 2C **72**
Horsley Ri. PL25: S Aus 6H **57**
Hosken's Mdw. TR19: St Bury 2G **147**
Hosking's Row TR15: Red 4D **112**
Hospital Rd. EX23: Stra 5G **9**
   PL4: Plym 2K **163**
Houndiscombe Rd. PL4: Plym 1J **163**
Hounster Dr. PL10: M'brk 3B **94**
Hounster Hill PL10: M'brk 2B **94**
HOUSEL BAY 6H **161**
Housel Bay Rd. TR12: Lizar 6H **161**
Howard Cl. PL12: Salt 2F **89**
Howard La. EX23: Stra 5H **9**
Howards Way EX23: Bud 5C **8**
Howe Downs TR14: Praze 2G **143**
Howell's Rd. EX23: Stra 5H **9**
How St. PL4: Plym 5J **163**
Hudson Rd. PL27: S Eval 2J **31**
Huer's Hut 2E **34**
Hughville St. TR14: Camb 6D **110**
HUGUS 7A **106** (3A **168**)
Hugus Rd. TR3: Thre 5A **106**
Hull's La. TR11: Fal 2G **133**
Humphrey's Cl. PL14: S Cle 4A **66**
Humphry Davy La.
   TR27: Hayl 1J **141**
Hunkin Cl. TR1: Tru 4J **107**
Huntersfield TR14: Tol D 3F **111**
Hunters Oak TR14: S Dom 2J **77**
Huntfield Gdns. EX23: Stra 5H **9**
   (off Treworden Cl.)
Hurdon Rd. PL15: Laun 6H **17**
Hurdon Way PL15: Laun 5H **17**
Hurland Rd. TR1: Tru 6K **107**
Hurlers Ct. PL14: Lisk 5B **70**
   (off Dean St.)
Hurlers Stone Circles, The 3C **167**
HURLINGBARROW 3K **97**
Hurlings, The TR9: S Maj 6C **30**
Hurling Way TR9: S Maj 6C **30**

Huthnance Cl. TR1: Tru 4B **108**
Hutton Hgts. TR1: Tru 5F **107**

I

IDLESS 1J **107** (3B **168**)
Idless La. TR4: Short 6C **98**
Ilbert St. PL1: Plym 2F **163**
ILLAND 3C **167**
ILLOGAN 1H **111** (3A **168**)
Illogan Downs TR15: I'gan, P Bot 1G **111**
ILLOGAN HIGHWAY 4K **111** (3A **168**)
Illogan Highway TR15: I'gan 1J **111**
Illogan Vs. TR1: Tru 4J **107**
   (off Higher Trehaverne)
Ince Cl. PL11: Tor 2G **93**
Incline, The TR16: P'ath 5F **101**
INDIAN QUEENS 1H **45** (2C **169**)
Indian Queens Ind. Est. TR9: I Que 1J **45**
Industrial Est., The TR6: P'rth 5C **40**
Infirmary Hill TR1: Tru 6J **107**
Inney Cl. PL17: Call 5E **72**
Innis Fly Fishery 4B **50**
Innis Inn Campsite PL26: Penw 4A **50**
Institute Hill TR13: P'ven 7F **157**
INSWORKE 1D **94**
Insworke Cl. PL10: M'brk 1E **94**
Insworke Cres. PL10: M'brk 1D **94**
Insworke Pl. PL10: M'brk 1E **94**
Isacombe Oaks PL17: K Bray 2D **72**
Island, The 1D **136**
Island Cres. TR7: Newq 3F **35**
Island Lanes PL31: B'min 7H **33**
Island Point TR7: Newq 1K **35**
Island Rd. TR26: S Ives 1J **137** (2D **136**)
ISLAND SHOP 6D **70**
Island Sq. TR26: S Ives 1J **137**
Islington Wharf TR10: P'ryn 4B **128**
Ivey Ter. PL14: Lisk 3C **70**
Ivy Chimney TR16: Scor 2G **103**
Ivy Cl. PL28: S Mer 7E **20**
Ivydene PL14: Menh 1H **79**
   (off Trewint Rd.)
Ivy Houses TR16: Red 2F **121**
Ivy La. TR18: Penz 5D **148**
Ivyleaf Combe Lodges EX23: Bus 1J **9**
Ivyleaf Golf Course 7D **6**

J

Jacka, The 3C **169**
Jack Bice Cl. PL14: Lisk 5D **70**
Jackett Steps TR11: Fal 7F **129**
   (off The Packet Quays)
Jack La. TR18: Newl 1C **154**
Jackmans Mdw. PL10: Caws 5E **94**
Jacks Cl. TR10: P'ryn 5B **128**
Jack's La. PL11: S John 6C **92**
Jackson Way PL12: Salt 2G **89**
Jack Stephens Est. TR18: Penz 4E **148**
Jacob's Ladder TR11: Fal 1F **133**
   (off Killigrew St.)
JACOBSTOW 1B **166**
Jadeana Ct. PL25: S Aus 6H **57**
Jago Av. PL11: Tor 3J **93**
Jago Cl. PL14: Lisk 4C **70**
   PL31: B'min 5D **32**
Jagos Slip TR11: Fal 7F **129**
   (off The Packet Quays)
Jake's La. TR4: Chac 6E **104**
Jamaica Inn 3B **166**
Jamaica Pl. TR18: Hea 3D **148**
   (off Madron Rd.)
Jamaica Rd. TR18: Hea 3D **148**
   (off Madron Rd.)
Jamaica Ter. TR18: Hea 3D **148**
   (off Madron Rd.)
   TR19: Mou 6D **154**
   (off Virgin St.)
James Pl. TR1: Tru 5K **107**
James St. PL4: Plym 3H **163**
Jane's Ct. TR11: Fal 7F **129**
Janeva Ct. PL12: Salt 2E **88**
Japanese Garden & Bonsai Nursery 4G **29**
Jasper Parc PL14: S Cle 4A **66**
Jaysland PL14: Trem 1A **66**
Jeanne Rees Ct. PL14: Lisk 5A **70**
Jeepers Karting 4F **141**
Jefferson Wlk. PL3: Plym 1F **163**
Jelbert Way TR18: Penz 3H **149**
Jenkins Ct. TR7: Newq 3F **35**
   (off Grosvenor Rd.)
Jenkins Ter. TR15: Red 3E **112**
Jenner Gdns. TR9: S Maj 5B **30**
Jenner Parc TR9: S Maj 5B **30**
Jennings Rd. TR10: P'ryn 6J **127**
Jennings St. TR18: Penz 5F **149**

Jericho La. TR27: S Pra 6J 141
Jeryon Cl. PL25: S Aus 3J 57
Jethan Dr. TR14: Camb 6B 110
Jetty St. PL26: Mev 6C 134
Jewell's Ter. TR16: Four L 3C 120
Joannies Av. TR26: S Ives 4B 136
Joannies Watch TR26: S Ives 4B 136
John Betjeman Cen. 4F 25
(off Southern Way)
John Ellis Ct. TR27: Hayl 2G 141
John Gaynor Homes PL4: Plym 4K 163
Johns Cnr. TR20: Rosu 6B 152
Johnson Pk. PL18: Cals 7H 75
Johns Pk. TR15: Red 2D 112
John St. TR1: Tru 5J 107
Jolly Pk. PL13: Pely 3C 80
JOLLY'S BOTTOM 4D 104
Jolly's La. TR4: P'twn 7C 96
Jon Davey Dr. TR16: Red 1D 112
Jopes Cl. PL14: S Cle 4B 66
JOPPA
Hayle 3K 141
Penzance 7K 145
Jorys Mdw. PL30: S Tud 4J 27
Joseph's Ct. TR6: P'rth 4B 40
Josephs La. TR18: Hea 2D 148
Jubilee Bathing Pool 6G 149
Jubilee Bungs. TR18: Newl 2C 154
(off Chywoone Hill)
Jubilee Cl. EX23: Kilkh 1G 7
PL12: Salt 3F 89
PL14: Duloe 6A 78
PL28: S Mer 6E 20
TR8: Cube 4E 38
Jubilee Cotts. PL12: S Dom 5G 77
PL12: Salt 4F 89
Jubilee Ct. TR26: S Ives 4B 136
Jubilee Hill PL13: Pely 3C 80
Jubilee Mdw. PL25: S Aus 4C 58
Jubilee Pl. TR2: Gerr 3J 131
TR14: Camb 7E 110
TR19: Pend 4B 144
Jubilee Rd. PL14: Pens 1H 67
PL27: Wade 4F 25
TR3: Thre 5K 105
TR11: Fal 7E 128
Jubilee Rock 3B 166
Jubilee St. TR7: Newq 3E 34
Jubilee Ter. PL13: Pely 2C 80
PL31: B'min 3D 32
TR4: Goonh 4G 41
TR13: Helst 5C 158
TR14: Camb 1E 118
Jubilee Wharf TR10: P'ryn 5B 128
Julia's Pl. EX23: Bud 5C 8
(off The Strand)
Juliots Well Holiday Pk. PL32: Came 5F 15

K

Kailem Cl. TR9: S Maj 6B 30
KALSTOK 7J 75
KAMMBRONN 1D 118
KARDHINAN 5A 114
Karenza Ct. TR26: C Bay 6G 137
(off Headland Rd.)
Karkeets Tenements PL14: S Keyn 1B 78
KARRBONS .6F 137
Kartworld 4G 79
KASTELL BOTEREL 2K 13
Kay Cres. PL31: B'min 5D 32
Kay Gdns. PL27: Wade 4G 25
KEA 2G 117 (3B 168)
Kea Downs Rd. TR4: Black, Chac 2C 104
KEASON 1C 171
Keason Hill PL12: S Mel 6A 76
Keast Cl. TR9: I Que 2H 45
Keast M. PL12: Salt 3H 89
(off Fore St.)
Keay Hgts. PL25: S Aus 3J 57
Keeble Pk. TR3: P Sta 1A 124
Keep, The PL12: Salt 3E 88
KEHELLAND 1D 173
Keigwin Pl. TR19: Mou 6D 154
Keiro La. PL27: Pity, S Minv 7G 19
Kel Avon Cl. TR1: Tru 4B 108
KELLACOTT 2D 167
Kellaway Pk. TR13: Helst 4D 158
Kelley Rd. TR11: Fal 7C 128
KELLIWIK 5C 72
Kelliwith TR3: Feo 1H 125
Kellow Pl. PL13: Loo 3K 81
Kellow Hill PL13: L'los, Polp 4A 80
Kellow Pk. PL11: Polb 7C 86
Kellow Rd. PL26: S Den 2E 46
KELLY 2D 167
KELLY BRAY 2C 72 (3D 167)
Kelly Cl. PL5: Plym 6K 89

Kelly Gdns. PL18: Cals 6G 75
Kelly Pk. PL30: S Mab 6B 26
Kellys Gdns. TR26: S Ives 3H 137
Kelseys, The 1B 38
KELYNACK 6J 145 (1A 172)
Kelynack Caravan & Camping Pk. TR19: S Jus . .5J 145
Kemp Cl. TR1: Tru 5K 107
TR16: Four L 3C 120
Kemp's Cl. TR5: S Agn 2A 96
Kempton Ter. PL11: Tor 3K 93
Ken-Caro Garden 1C 171
Kendal Grn. TR2: Lad 6F 37
Kendall Pk. PL23: Polr 7C 60
Kenegie Mnr. Holiday Village TR20: Gul . . .1H 149
Kenidjack Cl. TR26: C Bay 7G 137
Kenilworth Way PL26: Fox 1H 55
Kennall Pk. TR3: Pons 5F 123
Kennall Va. TR3: Pons 5E 122
Kenna Pk. TR1: Tru 5F 107
Kennedy Ct. TR15: I'gan 2H 111
Kenneggy TR20: Ger 7F 153
KENNEGGY DOWNS 7E 152 (2C 173)
Kennerley Ter. TR2: S Mawe 7D 130
Kenneth Launder Ct. PL14: Lisk 5A 70
(off Manley Rd.)
Kensa Kew TR12: Mana 6C 160
Kensa Way TR27: Con D 5K 139
Kensey Ct. PL15: Laun 3J 17
Kensey Hill PL15: Laun 4J 17
Kensey Pl. PL15: Laun 3H 17
Kensey Valley Mdw. PL15: Laun 3J 17
Kensey Vw. PL15: Laun 4J 17
Kenstella Rd. TR18: Newl 1C 154
Kent Av. PL25: Carl 6C 58
Kent Cl. PL26: S Den 2E 46
KENWYN 4J 107 (3B 168)
Kenwyn Chu. Rd. TR1: Ken 3H 107
Kenwyn Cl. EX23: Flex 3C 8
TR1: Ken 3H 107
Kenwyn Hill TR1: Ken 3H 107
Kenwyn M. TR1: Tru 5J 107
(off Kenwyn St.)
Kenwyn Pk. TR1: Ken 3H 107
Kenwyn Pl. TR26: S Ives 3G 137
Kenwyn Rd. TR1: Tru 4H 107
TR4: Ken 2G 107
Kenwyn St. TR1: Tru 5J 107
Kenwyn Ter. TR1: Tru 4J 107
(off Kenwyn Rd.)
Kenython La. TR19: S Jus 1J 145
Kerensa Gdns. TR5: S Agn 3B 96
Kerensa Grn. TR11: Fal 7C 128
Kergilliack Rd. TR11: Fal 7A 128
KERLEY DOWNS 7G 105
Kerley Gro. TR1: Tru 5F 107
Kerley Hill TR4: Chac 6E 104
Kerley Va. TR4: Chac 6E 104
Kernick Bus. Pk. TR10: P'ryn 6J 127
Kernick Pk. TR10: P'ryn 5J 127
Kernick Rd. TR10: P'ryn 5J 127
Kernick Rd. Ind. Est. TR10: P'ryn 5J 127
(not continuous)
Kernick Way TR27: Log 6E 138
Kernow Cl. PL11: Tor 3G 93
PL27: Wade 4E 24
PL31: B'min 3H 33
Kernow Ct. TR7: Newq 3F 35
(off Springfield Rd.)
Kernow Cres. EX23: Bud 6D 8
Kernow M. TR7: Newq 2E 34
Kernyk Lowen TR14: Camb 5F 111
Kernyk Parc TR13: Helst 3C 158
Kerrier Way TR14: Camb 7E 110
KERRIS 2B 172
Kerris Gro. TR1: Tru 4H 107
Kerrow La. PL26: Sten 3J 49
Kersey Cl. TR11: Flu 5G 129
Kersey Rd. TR11: Flu 6F 129
Keryor Cl. PL25: S Aus 6K 57
Kestell Parc PL31: B'min 6G 33
KESTLE
Helston 6A 160
St Austell 3C 169
Kestle Cl. PL31: B'min 3E 32
Kestle Dr. TR1: Tru 5F 107
KESTLE MILL 7D 36 (2B 168)
Keston Gdns. PL27: Wade 3D 24
Kestral Way TR16: I'gan 1J 111
Kestrel Ct. TR13: P'ven 7F 157
(off Shute La.)
Keveral Gdns. PL11: Seat 6F 79
Keveral La. PL11: Seat 5F 79
Kew Cl. TR7: Newq 5H 35
Kew Klavji PL31: B'min 3G 33
Kew Noweth TR14: Camb 1D 118
Kew Pendra TR19: St Bury 3G 147
Kew Pendra Cl. TR19: St Bury 3G 147
Kew Vean TR26: C Bay 5E 136

Keynvor Cl. TR7: Newq 3H 35
Khyber Cl. PL11: Tor 3J 93
KILHALLON .1J 59
Kilhallon Woodlands PL24: Kil 1J 59
KILKHAMPTON 2G 7 (2A 164)
Kilkhampton Rd. EX23: Kilkh 1H 7
Killerton Rd. EX23: Bud 5C 8
Killicourt TR3: C Dow 7E 116
Killiers Ct. TR15: I Hig 3J 111
Killiersfield TR15: Pool 4J 111
KILLIFRETH HILL 6B 104
Killiganoon Health Club 6F 117
Killigarth Mnr. Holiday Pk. PL13: Polp . .5D 80
Killigrew Av. PL12: Salt 4F 89
Killigrew Gdns. PL4: S Erm 3B 98
Killigrew Pl. TR11: Fal 1E 132
(off Killigrew St.)
Killigrew Rd. PL14: Lisk 4C 70
Killigrew St. TR11: Fal 2E 132
Killiow Golf Course 3F 117
KILLIVOSE 3D 118
Killivose Gdns. TR14: Camb 2D 118
Killivose Rd. TR14: Camb 2D 118
Killiwerris Touring Pk. TR4: Chac 4E 104
Killyvarder Way PL25: S Aus 3A 58
Kilmar Cl. PL14: S Cle 4A 66
Kilmar Rd. PL14: Lisk 4D 70
Kilmar Way PL14: S Cle 4A 66
Kilna La. PL12: Land 1C 86
Kiln Cl. PL10: Caws 6E 94
PL26: Mev 5C 134
Kiln Mdws. TR12: Gweek 6H 159
Kilnpark Wlk. PL11: Tor 7F 89
Kimberley Cotts. PL12: Salt 2E 88
(off Thorn La.)
Kimberley Cft. TR11: Fal 1E 132
(off Trevethan Ri.)
Kimberley Foster Cl. PL11: Craft 5E 90
Kimberley Pk. PL14: Trem 4C 66
Kimberley Pk. Rd. TR11: Fal 1D 132
Kimberley Pl. TR11: Fal 1E 132
Kimberley Vs. PL27: Wade 4G 25
Kimberly Ct. TR7: Newq 3E 34
(not continuous)
Kiming EX23: Bud 6D 8
King Arthur's Great Halls 6B 12
King Arthur's Hall 3B 166
King Arthurs Ter. PL34: Tin 6A 12
King Charles Quay TR11: Fal 1G 133
Kingdom Pl. PL12: Salt 3H 89
King Doniert's Stone 1B 70
King Edward Cres. TR7: Newq 2E 34
King Edward Mine Mus. 2G 119
King Edward Rd. PL12: Salt 3H 89
Kingfisher Dr. PL25: S Aus 5A 58
King Gdns. PL1: Plym 3F 163
King George V Memorial Wlk. TR27: Hayl, Phil . .1G 141
Kingham Ter. TR1: Tru 4K 107
KINGSAND 5E 94 (2D 171)
King's Av. PL25: S Aus 6H 57
TR11: Fal 1D 132
King's Hill EX23: Bud 6D 8
Kings Hill Cl. EX23: Bud 6D 8
King's Hill Ind. Est. EX23: Bud 6E 8
Kings Hill Mdw. EX23: Bud 7D 8
Kingsley Av. PL11: Tor 4K 93
Kingsley Cl. TR1: Glo 5C 106
Kingsley Ct. TR9: P'ale 4F 45
Kingsley Cove TR4: P'twn 5C 96
Kingsley Meade TR8: Newq 4J 35
Kingsley Ter. TR16: P'ath 4F 101
Kingsley Village TR9: P'ale 5F 45
Kingsley Way PL13: Helst 3C 158
Kingsmill Rd. PL12: Salt 7F 85
Kings Pippin PL26: Fox 1J 55
Kings Rd. TR2: S Mawe 7D 130
TR14: Camb 6D 110
TR17: Mar 4B 150
TR18: Penz 5E 148
King's St. PL22: Los 3E 52
King St. EX23: Bud 5D 8
PL10: M'brk 2C 94
PL11: Tor 3K 93
PL18: Gun 1G 75
TR1: Tru 5K 107
TR7: Newq 3E 34
(off Chapel Hill)
TR15: Red 3D 112
Kingsway PL10: King 5F 95
PL24: Par 3K 59
Kingswood PL14: Merry 1G 71
Kingswood Rd. PL18: Gun 2H 75
Kinsman Est. PL31: B'min 5E 32
Kinterbury Rd. PL5: Plym 5K 89
Kinterbury St. PL1: Plym 5J 163
Kinterbury Ter. PL5: Plym 5K 89
Kirby Rd. TR1: Tru 5G 107
Kirkby Pl. PL4: Plym 2H 163
Kirkby Ter. PL4: Plym 2H 163

Kirland Bower PL30: B'min 7F **33**
Kirland Rd. PL30: B'min 6D **32**
Kit Hill Country Park .1F **73**
Kit Hill Vw. PL15: Laun 5J **17**
Kittiwake Cl. TR27: Hayl 4D **140**
Kleinfontein Ter. *PL14: Pens* 1J *67*
                             (off Wesley Rd.)
KNAVE-GO-BY 3E **118**
KNIGHTON 3D **171**
Knightor Cl. PL26: Treg'y 6B **50**
Knights Cl. PL34: Tin .6A **12**
Knights Ct. PL22: Los .2D **52**
Knights Hill TR1: Ken .3H **107**
Knights Mdw. TR3: C Dow 7D **116**
KNIGHTSMILL 2D **26**
Knights Way TR15: Red 1F **113**
Knill Cl. TR26: C Bay .6E **136**
Knill Cross PL10: M'brk 2C **94**
Knill's Monument 6D **136**
Knoll Pk. TR1: Tru 5B **108**
Koth Karrji PL30: S Teat 2B **26**
Kozy Cotts. *TR14: Camb* 7A *110*
                       (off Treswithian Rd.)
Kroon Stadt Vs. *TR13: Helst* 3C *158*
                       (off Godolphin Rd.)
KROWS KARWORGI 1H **45**
KUGGAR 3A **174**
Kynance Cl. PL11: Tor .2H **93**
Kynance Cove 3D **173**
Kynance Ter. TR12: Lizar 5G **161**

L

Laburnum Cl. TR11: Fal 6D **128**
Laburnum Dr. TR11: Fal 7D **128**
                         (not continuous)
Laburnum Row *PL17: Call* 5D *72*
                         (off Back La.)
Laburnum Ter. EX23: Kilkh 1G **7**
Lacey Cl. TR14: Tro 4G **119**
LADDENVEAN 2B **162**
LADOCK 6F **37** (2B **168**)
Ladock Rd. TR2: Lad, Pro . . . . .6G **37** & 1H **99**
Lady Beam Ct. PL17: K Bray 1D **72**
LADYCROSS 2D **167**
Lady La. TR2: Tregon .6H **99**
Lady St. TR13: Helst 4B **158**
Ladywell PL28: Pad 3B **22**
Ladywell Av. PL4: Plym 3K **163**
Ladywell Pl. PL4: Plym 3K **163**
Laflouder Flds. TR12: Mull 2G **161**
Laflouder La. TR12: Mull 2F **161**
Lafrowda Cl. TR19: S Jus 3H **145**
Lafrowda Ter. TR19: S Jus 3J **145**
Laguna Ct. TR15: Red .3D **112**
Laity Dr. TR14: Camb .7F **111**
Laity Flds. TR14: Camb 7F **111**
Laity La. TR26: C Bay .7E **136**
LAITY MOOR
  Redruth 4C **102**
  Truro 7F **123**
Laity Rd. TR14: Tro 5G **119**
Lakefield Caravan Pk. & Equestrian Cen.
  PL32: Came 1F **15**
Lake La. PL14: Lisk 5C **70**
Lake M. PL10: M'brk 2C **94**
Lake Vw. PL11: S John .6D **92**
  PL12: S Mel 6A **76**
Lamanva Cl. TR16: I'gan 1J **111**
Lamanva Rd. TR16: I'gan 1K **111**
Lambert Ter. TR11: Fal 7E **128**
Lambhay Hill PL1: Plym 6J **163**
Lambhay St. PL1: Plym 7J **163**
Lambourne Av. TR5: S Agn 2B **96**
Lamb Pk. PL24: Par 3J **59**
Lambs La. TR11: Fal 7C **128**
LAMELLION 6K **69** (1B **170**)
LAMELLION CROSS 6K **69**
Lamellyn Dr. TR1: Tru .5D **106**
Lamellyn Rd. PL24: B'vey, Par 4G **59**
LAMERTON 3D **167**
Lametton Bungs. PL14: S Keyn 2C **78**
Lametton Grn. PL14: S Keyn 1C **78**
Lametton Ter. PL14: S Keyn 1C **78**
Lamledra Hill PL26: G Hav 3J **135**
Lamorak Cl. PL26: Mev 6B **134**
Lamorak Ho. *TR15: Pool* 4J *111*
                     (off Breaview Pk. La.)
LAMORICK 5H **31** (1D **169**)
LAMORNA 2B **172**
Lamorna Cl. TR27: Con D 5K **139**
Lamorna Ct. *TR16: P'ath* 4J *101*
                     (off Greenfield Ter.)
Lamorna Dr. PL17: Call 5D *72*
Lamorna Ho. TR14: Camb 5G **111**
Lamorna Parc PL17: Call 5D *72*
Lamorna Pk. PL11: Tor .3G **93**
  PL25: S Aus 2J **57**

Lamorne Cl. TR6: P'rth .5B **40**
LAMORRAN 3B **168**
LANA
  EX22, Holsworthy .3B **164**
  EX22, Launceston .1D **167**
Lanadwell St. PL28: Pad 3B **22**
LANARTH 2A **174**
Lanaton Rd. TR10: P'ryn 5J **127**
Lancamshire La. TR20: Rosu 5B **152**
LANCARROW 5B **120**
Lancaster Cres. PL27: S Eval 3H **31**
Lanchard Grn. PL14: Lisk 5A **70**
Lanchard La. PL14: Lisk 5A **70**
                       (not continuous)
Lanchard Ri. PL14: Lisk 5A **70**
Lanchard Rd. PL14: Lisk 5A **70**
Landaviddy La. PL13: Polp 6A **80**
Lander Ct. *TR1: Tru* .6K *107*
                     (off Strangways Ter.)
Lander Monument 6J **107**
Lander Rd. PL12: Salt 2H **89**
Landeryon Gdns. TR18: Penz 5E **148**
Landithy TR20: Mad 2B **148**
Landlake Rd. PL15: Laun 5H **17**
LANDLOOE BRIDGE 5D **78**
LANDRAKE 6G **83** (1C **171**)
Landreath Pl. PL24: S Bla 2H **59**
Landrew Rd. PL25: S Aus 3K **57**
Land's End 5A **146**
Lands End Rd. TR19: St Bury 3G **147**
LAND'S END (ST JUST) AIRPORT 2A **172**
LANDULPH 4J **85** (1D **171**)
LANDULPH CROSS 2H **85**
LANE .6J **35** (1B **168**)
LANEAST 2C **167**
LANE END 7K **123**
Lane Reddin Ter. TR18: Newl 1C **154**
LANESCOT 7K **51**
Lane Theatre 6J **35**
Langarth Cl. TR3: Thre .4A **106**
LANGDON 1C **167**
LANGDON CROSS 2D **167**
Langdon Down Way PL11: Tor 3G **93**
Langerwell Cl. PL12: Salt 2E **88**
Langerwell La. *PL12: Salt* 2D *88*
                     (off Hallett Cl.)
  PL12: Salt 2E **88**
                     (Langerwell La.)
Langfords Mdw. PL35: Bosc 2K **13**
Lang Gdns. PL18: Cals .7H **75**
LANGORE 2D **167**
Langorran Rd. TR14: Camb 7B **110**
Langreek Bungs. PL13: Polp 5A **80**
Langreek Rd. PL13: Polp 5A **80**
Lang Rd. PL14: Lisk 6A **70**
Langton Rd. TR11: Fal .7E **128**
Langton Ter. TR11: Fal .7E **128**
Langurroc Rd. TR8: Cran 6B **34**
Langurtho Rd. PL23: Fow 6H **61**
Langweath Gdns. TR27: Hayl 3D **140**
Langwedh TR16: I'gan .6H **101**
Lanhenvor Av. TR7: Newq 4F **35**
Lanherne Av. TR8: S Mawg 5G **29**
Lanheverne Parc TR12: S Kev 2B **162**
Lanhydrock 1D **169**
Lanhydrock Vw. PL31: B'min 5F **33**
LANIVET 6H **31** (1D **169**)
LANJETH 5K **55** (2C **169**)
LANK 3A **166**
Lankelly Cliff to St Catherine's Point 2A **170**
Lankelly Cl. PL23: Fow .7H **61**
Lankelly La. PL23: Fow .7G **61**
LANLIVERY 4A **52** (2D **169**)
Lanlovie Mdw. TR8: Cube 4F **39**
Lanmoor Est. TR16: L'ner 1H **121**
LANNANTA 2D **140**
Lannarth Glas TR16: L'ner 7G **113**
LANNBROBOES 2H **99**
LANNDRETH 1H **59**
LANNER 1H **121** (1A **174**)
LANNERGH 1H **121**
Lanner Grn. TR16: L'ner 7G **113**
Lanner Grn. Ter. *TR16: L'ner* 1G *121*
                     (off Lanner Grn.)
Lanner Hill TR15: Red .6F **113**
  TR16: L'ner 6F **113**
Lanner Moor Ter. TR16: L'ner 7J **113**
Lanner Sq. TR16: L'ner .1H **121**
LANNER VEAN 4J **157**
Lannoweth Rd. TR18: Penz 4G **149**
Lannoweth Ter. *TR18: Penz* 4G *149*
                     (off Chyandour Cliff)
LANNSTEFAN 4H **17**
LANNSTEFAN WARTHA 4C **54**
LANNVOREK 6C **134**
LANNVOWSEDH 7D **130**
LANNYUST 3J **145**
Lanoweth TR10: P'ryn .3K **127**

LANREATH 2A **170**
LANSALLOS 2A **170**
Lansallos St. PL13: Polp 7B **80**
Lansdown Cl. EX23: Bud 5C **8**
Lansdowne Cl. TR18: Penz 5D **148**
Lansdowne Ct. *TR18: Penz* 5C *148*
                     (off Lansdowne Rd.)
Lansdowne Pk. Homes TR16: Scor 5H **103**
Lansdowne Pl. TR18: Penz 6D **148**
Lansdowne Rd. PL17: Call 6C **72**
  TR11: Fal 2G **133**
  TR18: Penz 5D **148**
Lansdown La. EX23: Bud 5C **8**
Lansdown Rd. EX23: Bud 5C **8**
  PL27: Wade 4E **24**
LANSTEPHAN 1G **17**
LANTALLACK CROSS 6D **82**
LANTEGLOS 6E **14**
LANTEGLOS HIGHWAY 2A **170**
Lanterns 6G **125**
LANTOOM 4F **69**
LANTYAN 7E **52**
Lanuthnoe Est. TR27: S Er 6F **141**
Lanvean TR8: S Mawg .5G **29**
LANWEDHWNEK 3B **22**
Lanwithan Cl. PL22: Los 3F **53**
Lanwithan Rd. PL22: Los 3F **53**
Lanxon Cres. PL30: Lanl 4A **52**
Lanyon Ct. PL14: S Cle .4A **66**
Lanyon Holiday Pk. TR16: Four L 3A **120**
Lanyon Quoit 1B **172**
Lanyon Rd. TR3: P Pla .5G **117**
Lappa Valley Steam Railway
  Benny Halt Station .1J **37**
  East Wheal Rose Station 3J **37**
Larch Cl. PL12: Salt 2E **88**
Larcombe Rd. PL25: S Aus 3K **57**
Laregan Hill TR18: Penz 6D **148**
Lariggan Cres. TR18: Penz 6E **148**
Lariggan Rd. TR18: Penz 6E **148**
Larkfield Ri. *TR2: S Mawe* 6D *130*
                     (off Newton Rd.)
Larksfield Cl. PL26: Fox .1J **55**
LATCHBROOK 2D **88**
LATCHLEY 3D **167**
LAUNCELLS 3A **164**
LAUNCESTON 4H **17** (2D **167**)
Launceston Castle 3H **17**
Launceston Cl. PL31: B'min 4H **33**
Launceston Golf Course 1F **17**
Launceston Retail Pk. PL15: Laun 5H **17**
Launceston Rd. PL17: Call, K Bray 1C **72**
  PL31: B'min 4H **33**
                     (not continuous)
Launceston Station
  Launceston Steam Railway 3G **17**
Launceston Steam Railway
  Launceston Station .3G **17**
Launceston Steam Railway Transport Mus. 3G **17**
Laura Cl. PL34: Tin 6C **12**
Laura Dr. PL25: S Aus 4A **58**
Laurel La. PL17: K Bray .1C **72**
Laurels, The PL18: S An Cpl 2D **74**
La Vague TR3: Feo 4J **125**
Lavorrick Orchards PL26: Mev 5C **134**
LAVREAN 7K **43**
LAWHITTON 2D **167**
Lawn, The PL24: S Bla 1H **59**
Lawns, The PL11: Tor 2J **93**
Lawrence House Mus. .3H **17**
Lawrence Rd. TR5: S Agn 2A **96**
Lawry Cl. PL14: Lisk 5A **70**
Lawton Cl. TR7: Newq .4C **34**
Leader Rd. TR7: S Mino .2A **36**
Leafield PL31: B'min 4J **33**
Leanway PL12: Salt 3G **89**
Leap Pk. TR3: Thre 5K **105**
Leas, The TR1: Tru 4A **108**
Leat, The EX23: Stra 5G **9**
Leatfield PL26: Mev 6C **134**
Leat Rd. TR19: Pend 4C **144**
Leats, The TR1: Tru 5J **107**
Leat Vw. PL12: Salt 2D **88**
Leat Wlk. *PL12: Salt* .1F *89*
                     (off Grassmere Way)
Lea Way EX23: Flex 4E **8**
Ledrah Gdns. PL25: S Aus 6F **57**
Ledrah Rd. PL25: S Aus .6F **57**
LEEDSTOWN 7D **142** (1D **173**)
LEFESANT 5D **64**
Lefra Orchard TR19: St Bury 3H **147**
Leggos Ct. TR15: Red 3D **112**
                     (off Symons Ter.)
Legion La. PL24: Tyw 2B **60**
LEIGHAM 2D **171**
Leigham St. PL1: Plym .7F **163**
Leigham Ter. La. PL1: Plym 6F **163**
Leigh Ct. PL12: Pilla 2J **83**
Leigh La. PL12: Pilla, S Mel 2J **83**

LELANT 2D 140 (1C 173)
LELANT DOWNS 5A 140 (1C 173)
Lelant Mdws. TR26: Lel 2D 140
Lelant Saltings Station (Rail) 3D 140
Lelant Station (Rail) 2E 140
Lelissick Gdns. TR2: Pro 2G 99
Lemin Parc TR27: Reaw 3C 142
Lemin's Ct. TR15: Red 3D 112
Lemon Hill TR11: M Bri 1E 128
Lemon Hill Gdns. TR11: M Bri 1E 128
Lemon M. Rd. TR1: Tru 5J 107
Lemon Pl. TR15: Red 3F 113
Lemon Quay TR1: Tru 5K 107
Lemon Row TR1: Tru 6K 107
Lemon St. TR1: Tru 6J 107
   TR12: S Kev 2C 162
Lemon Ter. TR4: Biss 4J 115
Lender La. TR12: Mull 1H 161
Lendra La. PL17: Call 7A 72
Leo Cub Ind. Cen. TR10: P'ryn 5J 127
LERRYN 2A 170
Lerwick Rd. PL27: S Eval 3J 31
Lesceave Rocks to Trewavas Head 2C 173
LESCROW 6G 61
Lescudjack TR18: Penz 3G 149
Lescudjack Cres. TR18: Penz 4G 149
Lescudjack Rd. TR18: Penz 4F 149
Lescudjack Ter. TR18: Penz 4F 149
Lesingey TR20: Penz 5B 148
Lesingey La. TR20: Penz 4A 148
Leskinnick Ho. TR18: Penz 4G 149
                              (off Leskinnick Pl.)
Leskinnick Pl. TR18: Penz 4F 149
Leskinnick St. TR18: Penz 4G 149
Leskinnick Ter. TR18: Penz 4F 149
Leslie Ter. PL22: Los 3E 52
LESNEWTH 1B 166
Lesnewth PL24: B'vey 4H 59
Lestraynes La. TR10: Rame 6A 126
Lethlean Cl. TR27: Phil 7D 138
Lethlean La. TR27: Phil 7D 138
Lethlean Towans TR27: Phil 6D 138
LEVALSA 6D 64
LEVALSA MEOR 5F 65
Levant Beam Engine 3A 144
Levant Cl. TR19: Trew 5B 144
Levant Rd. TR19: Trew 4A 144
Level, The TR11: Const 2J 159
Leverlake Rd. EX23: Bud, Wid B 7B 10
Levine Vw. TR11: Fal 4C 132
LEWANNICK 2C 167
Lewannick Rd. TR8: Cube 2E 38
Lewarne Cres. TR7: Newq 1K 35
Lewarne Rd. TR7: Newq 1K 35
LEWDOWN 2D 167
Lewis Way PL25: S Aus 3J 57
Lewman Cl. TR2: Pro 2G 99
Lewman Rd. TR2: Pro 2G 99
LEWORTHY 3B 164
LEY 1A 170
Leys La. TR17: Mar 4F 151
LEZANT 3D 167
Liberator Row PL27: S Eval 2H 31
Lidden, The TR18: Penz 7D 148
Lidden Cl. TR18: Penz 7D 148
Lidden Cres. TR18: Penz 7D 148
Lidden Rd. TR18: Penz 7D 148
Liddicoat Rd. PL22: Los 3E 52
Lifeboat Hill TR26: S Ives 2J 137 (2D 136)
Lifeboat Station
   Falmouth Docks 2H 133
   Looe 7K 81 (5H 81)
   Newquay 3E 34
   Port Isaac 2J 19
   Rock 2D 22
   St Ives 2J 137 (2D 136)
   Sennen Cove 3C 146
   The Lizard 5K 161
LIFTON 2D 167
LIFTONDOWN 2D 167
Lighterage Hill TR1: Tru 7A 108
Lighthouse Hill TR16: P'ath 3F 101
Lighthouse La. PL26: G Hav 2H 135
Lighthouse Rd. TR12: Lizar 6G 161
Lilyerne Ct. PL25: S Aus 3K 57
Limes La. PL14: Lisk 5A 70
Lincoln Row PL27: S Eval 2J 31
Linden Av. TR7: Newq 4F 35
Linden Cres. TR7: Newq 5F 35
Lindsay Flds. TR9: Fr'don 2H 45
Lingard Cl. PL14: Lisk 4K 69
Lingfield Av. PL26: Stick 3K 63
Linhay Cl. PL25: T Mil 3D 58
Link Cl. TR11: Fal 2D 132
LINKINHORNE 3D 167
Link Rd. PL15: Laun 6G 17
Links, The TR11: Fal 4D 132
   TR20: Pra S 7H 153
Links Vw. EX23: Flex 4E 8

Linley Cl. TR3: Thre 5A 106
Linnet Ct. PL12: Salt 3E 88
Lipson Rd. PL4: Plym 4K 163
Lisbon Ter. TR19: St Bury 2G 147
Liscawn Ter. PL11: Tor 3K 93
Liscombe Cl. PL18: Gun 1H 75
LISKEARD 4B 70 (1B 170)
Liskeard and District Mus. 4B 70
Liskeard Bus. Pk. PL14: Lisk 4D 70
Liskeard Ent. Cen. PL14: Lisk 5B 70
Liskeard Gymnasium Cen. 5B 70
                              (off Church Pl.)
Liskeard Rd. PL12: Nott, Salt, T'ton 6J 83
   PL17: Call 7B 72
Liskeard Station (Rail) 6A 70
Liskerrett Rd. PL14: Lisk 5C 70
Liskey Hill TR6: P'rth 4B 40
Liskey Hill Caravan Pk. TR6: P'rth 6B 40
Liskey Hill Cotts. TR6: P'rth 6B 40
Liskey Hill Cres. TR6: P'rth 5B 40
Liskey Tourist Pk. TR4: Chac 4J 105
Lister Hill TR11: Fal 1E 132
Lister St. TR11: Fal 1E 132
Listowel Dr. PL13: Loo 4H 81
Listry Rd. TR7: Newq 4F 35
Lit. Ash Gdns. PL5: Plym 4K 89
Lit. Ash Rd. PL5: Plym 4K 89
LITTLE BESIDE 2B 114
Lit. Bodieve Holiday Pk. PL27: B'eve 1G 25
Little Bri. Pk. PL27: Wade 3G 25
LITTLE CARHARRACK 4A 114
Lit. Castle St. TR1: Tru 5J 107
LITTLE COLDRENICK 3K 79
Little Dean PL14: Lisk 5K 69
Little Dinas PL28: Pad 4C 22
Lit. Down Pk. TR7: Newq 5H 35
Little Falmouth TR11: Flu 5F 129
Lit. Gilly Hill TR15: Red 5D 112
Little Green PL13: Polp 7B 80
                              (off Big Green)
Little Gregwartha TR16: Four L 4B 120
Little-in-Sight TR11: Mawn S 2B 160
   TR26: S Ives 3C 136
                              (off Pearce's La.)
LITTLE KIRLAND 6D 32
Little La. PL10: King 5E 94
                              (off Fore St.)
   TR27: Hayl 7E 138
Little Laney PL13: Polp 7B 80
Little Mdw. PL31: B'min 3F 33
LITTLE MILL 6E 140
Lit. Mill La. TR27: S Er 6E 140
Little Nangitha TR11: B Wat 2A 132
Little Oaks TR10: P'ryn 5J 127
Lit. Orchard Village TR5: S Agn 1A 96
LITTLE PETHERICK 3D 165
Lit. Point Cres. PL10: M'brk 2D 94
LITTLE POLGOOTH 4D 64
LITTLE PRIDEAUX 5G 51
Little Sinns TR16: Red 6D 102
Lit. Stark Cl. PL26: S Ste 3C 54
Lit. Treginges Caravan & Camp Site
   TR12: S Kev 2D 162
Lit. Trelower Pk. PL26: T'lwth 2B 64
Little Treloweth TR15: Pool 4H 111
Little Trelyn PL27: Rock 2G 23
LITTLE TRETHEWEY 4F 147
Lit. Trethewey Est. TR19: P'cno 4G 147
Little Trethiggey TR8: Q Dow 7C 36
Little Treverrow PL27: Rock 2G 23
LITTLE TREVISCOE 6D 46
Lit. Trevothan Caravan & Camping Site
   TR12: Cover 7B 162
Little Vauxhall TR15: Red 3C 112
Little Western Railway 4G 35
Lit. Woburn Cl. PL15: Laun 5G 17
LIZARD 5G 161 (3A 174)
Lizard Head La. TR12: Lizar 6F 161
Lizard Lifeboat Station, The 5K 161
Lizard Lighthouse 7G 161
Llawnroc Dr. TR14: Camb 1E 118
Llewellyn Rd. PL32: Came 4H 15
Lloyds Rd. TR12: Lizar 6H 161
LOBB'S SHOP 4K 65
Lobster Hatchery 3C 22
LOCKENGATE 2K 43 (1D 169)
Lockyer Ct. PL1: Plym 6G 163
Lockyer St. PL1: Plym 5G 163
                              (not continuous)
Lockyer Ter. PL12: Salt 2J 89
                              (off Elwell Rd.)
Lodenek Av. PL28: Pad 4B 22
Lodge Dr. TR1: Tru 3B 108
LODGE HILL 7K 69
Lodge Way TR9: I Que 1J 45
Loe Bar Rd. TR13: P'ven 6A 156
Loe Beach TR3: Feo 4K 125
Loe Pool & Bar 2D 173
Loe Valley Rd. TR13: Helst 2B 158

LOGGANS 6E 138
Loggans Cl. TR27: Log 6E 138
Loggans Moor TR27: Hayl, Log 6F 139
Loggans Rd. TR27: Con D, Log 6E 138
Loggans Wlk. TR27: Log 6E 138
Loggans Way TR27: Log 6E 138
LOGH 7K 81 (5H 81)
Lois La. PL26: S Ste 4C 54
Lollabury Rd. PL12: Salt 2G 89
Lombarda PL26: Bugl 7G 43
LONDON APPRENTICE 3F 65 (2D 169)
Long Acre PL12: Salt 1D 88
Longacre PL17: Harr 5A 74
Long Acre Est. PL27: Rock 2G 23
Longclose EX23: Stra 4G 9
Longcoombe La. PL13: Polp 5A 80
Long Cross Victorian Gdns. 3D 165
LONGDOWNS 5C 126 (1A 174)
Longdowns Ind. Est. TR10: Longd 5C 126
Longfield TR11: Fal 2C 132
Longfield Cl. PL17: Call 5E 72
Longfield Dr. PL32: Came 4H 15
Longfield Rd. PL32: Came 4H 15
Longhill PL17: Call 4G 73
Longhouse La. PL27: Rock 1G 23
LONGLANDS 4C 88
Longlands La. PL12: Salt 4C 88
Long La. PL26: H St 5E 54
   TR20: Ludg 3H 155
Long Lanes TR20: Gold, S Hil 1B 152
   TR27: S Er 7C 140
Longman's La. PL17: Call 5C 72
Longmeadow Ct. PL12: Salt 2H 89
Longmeadow Rd. PL12: Salt 2G 89
Long Pk. PL15: Laun 5C 16
Longpark Dr. EX23: Wid B 6B 10
Long Pk. Rd. PL12: Salt 3F 89
Longpark Way PL25: S Aus 4K 57
LONGROCK 3B 150 (1C 173)
Long Rock Bus. Pk. TR20: L Roc 3K 149
Long Rock Ind. Est. TR20: L Roc 3K 149
Long Row TR19: Pau 5B 154
Long Steps PL23: Fow 7J 61
                              (off Lostwithiel St.)
LONGSTONE 7F 137
Longstone Cl. TR26: C Bay 7G 137
Longstone Hill TR26: C Bay 7G 137
Longstone Ho. TR26: C Bay 7G 137
Longview Rd. PL12: Salt 2F 89
Longwool Mdw. EX23: March 3G 11
LOOE 7K 81 (2B 170)
Looe Bay Holiday Pk. PL13: S Mar 1K 81
Looe Hill PL11: Seat 6F 79
Looe Lifeboat Station 7K 81 (5H 81)
LOOE MILLS 4G 69
Looe Mus. 6K 81 (5H 81)
Looe Sports Cen. 2H 81
Looe Station (Rail) 4G 81
Looe St. PL4: Plym 5J 163
Looe Workshop Units PL13: Loo 2H 81
Lookout, The TR2: S Jus R 2E 130
   TR11: Fal 7F 129
                              (off High St.)
   EX23: Stra 5H 9
                              (off Fore St.)
Lords Ct. EX23: Stra 5H 9
                              (off Fore St.)
Lords Mdw. TR2: Tregon 6J 99
Loscombe Cl. TR16: Four L 4B 120
Loscombe La. TR16: Four L 3A 120
Loscombe Rd. TR16: Carn, Four L 1A 120
Loscombe Vs. TR16: Four L 3B 120
Lost Gardens of Heligan 2A 134 (3C 169)
LOSTWITHIEL 3E 52 (2A 170)
Lostwithiel Golf Course 1F 53
Lostwithiel Mus. 3E 52
                              (off Fore St.)
Lostwithiel Rd. PL30: B'min 5H 33
   PL31: B'min 5H 33
Lostwithiel Station (Rail) 3F 53
Lostwithiel St. PL23: Fow 7J 61
Lostwood Rd. PL25: S Aus 4J 57
LOSTWYDHYEL 3E 52
Loughboro Rd. PL5: Plym 4K 89
Love La. PL12: Salt 3G 89
   PL23: Fow 6A 60
   PL31: B'min 3H 33
   TR10: P'ryn 4B 128
   TR18: Penz 6D 148
   TR19: Mou 6D 154
   TR26: S Ives 1J 137
                              (off Bunkers Hill)
   TR27: Hayl 7E 138
Lovely La. PL12: S Ger 5D 86
Lovering Rd. PL25: S Aus 3J 57
Lovers La. TR15: Red 4D 112
Lowarth Cl. TR13: Helst 3B 158
Lowarth Elms TR15: Red 3D 112
Lowarthow Marghas TR15: Red 3F 113
Lowenac Cres. TR27: Con D 5K 139
Lowenac Gdns. TR14: Camb 1C 118

Lowen Ct. TR1: Tru 5K **107**
Lowenek Cl. TR11: Fal 7C **128**
Lowenna Gdns. PL13: Loo 4H **81**
Lowenna Mnr. PL27: Rock 1G **23**
Lowen Way TR3: Thre 5K **105**
LOWER AMBLE .3D **165**
Lower Anderton PL10: M'brk 2G **95**
Lwr. Anderton PL10: M'brk 2D **94**
Lower Art Gallery Ter. TR18: Newl 7D **148**
(off Tolcarne Ter.)
LOWER BANNS 6H **97**
Lower Barncoose TR15: I Hig 4B **112**
Lower Bolenna TR6: P'rth 5A **40**
Lwr. Bore St. PL31: B'min 3F **33**
LOWER BOSCASWELL 3B **144**
Lwr. Boscaswell Parc TR19: Pend 3B **144**
Lower Boswyn PL15: Laun 4H **17**
Lwr. Broad La. TR15: I'gan 2J **111**
Lwr. Cardrew La. TR15: Red 2E **112**
Lwr. Castle Rd. TR2: S Mawe 7C **130**
Lwr. Chapel St. PL13: Loo 7K **81**
Lwr. Church St. TR27: Hayl 1J **141**
Lower Cleaverfield PL15: Laun 2G **17**
(off Dutson Rd.)
Lwr. Coronation Ter. PL17: Call 5D **72**
Lwr. Daisy Pk. PL28: S Mer 5D **20**
LOWER DIMSON .1G **75**
LOWER DOWNS .3C **152**
Lower Eastcliffe TR4: P'twn 5C **96**
(off Eastcliff Av. No. 3)
Lwr. East St. TR9: S Maj 4C **30**
Lower Elms PL27: Tred 7G **19**
Lower Fairfield PL12: S Ger 6D **86**
Lwr. Fore St. PL12: Salt 3J **89**
Lwr. Glen Pk. PL14: Pens 1J **67**
Lwr. Goongumpas La. TR16: G Gump 3C **114**
Lower Goonrea PL13: Loo 4F **81**
Lower Greenbanks PL27: Rock 2G **23**
Lower Grn. St. TR18: Newl 2D **154**
Lwr. Gurnick Rd. TR18: Newl 7C **148**
Lower Hillcrest TR6: P'rth 5A **40**
TR13: Helst 3C **158**
Lwr. Hugus Rd. TR3: Thre 6K **105**
Lower Kelly PL18: Cals 6G **75**
LOWER KENNEGGY 5F **155**
Lower Lux St. PL14: Lisk 4B **70**
Lwr. Market St. PL13: Loo 6K **81**
TR10: P'ryn 5A **128**
Lower Meadow TR4: Chac 6E **104**
Lwr. Merritts Hill TR16: I'gan 1K **111**
(off Merritts Hill)
LOWER METHERELL 6C **74**
Lwr. Middle Hill PL14: Pens 3J **67**
LOWER MILL 7F **135**
Lower Molinnis PL26: Bugl 6J **43**
Lower Parc TR12: Gweek 6G **159**
Lower Pk. TR2: Tr'sln 1H **109**
Lwr. Penbeagle Pl. TR26: S Ives 4B **136**
(off Penbeagle Way)
Lower Pengegon TR14: Camb 7F **111**
LOWER PENHALE 5E **44**
Lower Pennance TR16: L'ner 7H **113**
Lwr. Peverell Rd. TR18: Penz 3F **149**
Lwr. Polstain Rd. TR3: Thre 6A **106**
LOWER PORTHPEAN 2K **65**
Lwr. Port Vw. PL12: Salt 3H **89**
Lwr. Pumpfield Row TR15: Pool 4H **111**
Lower Quarter TR20: Crow, Ludg 2J **155**
Lwr. Quay Rd. TR3: Devo 3D **124**
Lower Redannick TR1: Tru 5J **107**
Lower Rd. PL11: Downd 7J **79**
Lwr. Rosewin Row TR1: Tru 4K **107**
(off Rosewin Row)
Lower Row PL10: King 5E **94**
Lwr. Rowes Ter. PL26: Fox 1G **55**
Lower Sheffield TR19: Pau 5B **154**
Lwr. Silver Hill TR13: Helst 3C **158**
LOWER SPARGO .7F **127**
Lower Stennack TR26: S Ives 3H **137**
LOWER STICKER .4K **63**
Lower St. PL4: Plym 5K **163**
PL13: Loo 7K **81**
Lwr. Tamar Ter. PL18: Gun 1H **75**
Lower Ter. TR3: Pons 5F **123**
LOWERTOWN 1B **158** (2D **173**)
Lower Town TR4: Cusg 7G **115**
Lowertown Cl. PL12: Land 6H **83**
Lowertown La. TR13: Helst 2C **158**
LOWER TREGANTLE 6A **92**
LOWER TREGARNE 1A **160**
Lower Tregongeeves PL26: Polg 2D **64**
Lwr. Trelowth Rd. PL26: Polg 3D **64**
LOWER TREMAR .4C **66**
LOWER TREWELLARD 5A **144**
Lower Tywarnhayle TR6: P'rth 4B **40**
Lwr. Well La. TR13: Helst 3C **158**
(off Brixton Ter.)
Lwr. Well Pk. PL26: Mev 7D **134**
Lwr. Wesley Ter. PL14: Pens 1J **67**

Lower Woodside PL25: S Aus 5E **56**
Lowland Point Raised Beach 3B **174**
Low Lee Rd. TR19: Mou 5E **154**
Lowley Rd. PL15: Laun 6E **16**
Lucas Cl. PL31: B'min 5G **33**
LUCKETT 3D **167**
Lucknow Rd. PL31: B'min 6J **33**
Lucknow Rd. Sth. PL31: B'min 7J **33**
LUDGVAN 2H **155** (1C **173**)
LUFFINCOTT 1D **167**
Luffman Cl. PL13: Pely 2C **80**
Lugger, The TR2: P'stho 3K **131**
Lukes Cl. TR1: Tru 4B **108**
Luke's La. TR20: S Hil 3C **152**
LULYNN 1C **154**
Lunar Row TR1: Tru 4K **107**
(off Mitchell Hill)
Lundynart Caravan Site PL27: S Minv 2E **18**
Lundy Rd. PL29: P Isa 2K **19**
LUNEY BARTON .7H **63**
Lusart Dr. TR12: Lizar 5G **161**
Lusty Glaze Rd. TR7: Newq 2H **35**
Luxon Dr. TR7: Newq 5G **35**
Lux Park Leisure Cen. 3B **70**
Luxstowe PL14: Lisk 4B **70**
Luxstowe Dr. PL14: Lisk 4B **70**
Luxstowe Gdns. PL14: Lisk 4B **70**
LUXULYAN 2E **50** (2D **169**)
Luxulyan Rd. PL24: S Bl G 2F **59**
Luxulyan Station (Rail) 1D **50**
Lychgate Dr. TR1: Tru 3H **107**
Lyndhurst Av. PL25: S Aus 5A **58**
Lyndon Ct. PL12: Salt 1F **89**
Lynher Cl. PL12: Salt 4H **89**
Lynher Dr. PL12: Salt 4G **89**
Lynher Way PL17: Call 5E **72**
Lyn Meynek TR15: Red 4E **112**
LYNSTONE 7B **8** (3A **164**)
Lynstone Rd. EX23: Bud, Lyn 7C **8**
Lyn Ter. TR18: Newl 2C **154**
Lynwood Cl. PL31: B'min 4G **33**
Lynwood Cotts. TR19: Mou 5D **154**
Lynwood Flats TR13: P'ven 5F **157**
Lyonesse Apartments TR26: S Ives 4J **137**
Lyons Rd. PL25: S Aus 5B **58**
LYSKERRYS 4B **70**
Lytton Pl. PL25: S Aus 5K **57**

M

Mabbots Ct. TR18: Penz 4G **149**
(off Chyandour Cliff)
MABE BURNTHOUSE 5G **127** (1A **174**)
Mabena Cl. PL30: S Mab 6B **26**
McCauleys Health Club 5F **163**
Macey St. PL11: Tor 3K **93**
McLean Dr. PL26: Fox 2H **55**
Maddever Cres. PL14: Lisk 5B **70**
Madeira Rd. EX23: Wid B 6B **10**
Madeira Rd. PL1: Plym 7H **163**
TR11: Fal 4E **132**
Madeira Wlk. TR11: Fal 3E **132**
MADERS 1A **72**
Madford La. PL15: Laun 4H **17**
Madison Cl. TR27: Hayl 7E **138**
Madison Ter. TR27: Hayl 7E **138**
Madison Vean TR27: Hayl 7E **138**
MADRON 2B **148** (1B **172**)
Madron Rd. TR18: Hea, Penz 3D **148**
TR20: Penz 4E **148**
MAENPORTH 1D **160** (2A **174**)
Maenporth Est. TR11: Maen 7B **132**
Maenporth Rd. TR11: Fal, Maen 6B **132**
TR11: Maen 3C **160**
MAEN VALLEY 4B **132**
Maen Valley Pk. TR11: Fal 4B **132**
MAER 2C **8**
Maer Down Rd. EX23: Flex 3B **8**
Maer Lake Nature Reserve 2C **8**
Maer La. EX23: Flex, Mae 3C **8**
Magic Cove Touring Pk. TR8: M Por 2C **28**
Magistrates' Court
　Bodmin (East Cornwall) 4H **33**
　Plymouth 5H **163**
　Truro 4A **108**
Magnificent Music Machines 1D **78**
Magor Av. TR14: Tro 4G **119**
Magor Hill TR14: Camb, Sth T 2A **110**
Maiden Rd. EX23: Stra 4H **9**
MAIDENWELL 3B **166**
Main Rd. PL11: Downd 6H **79**
PL28: T'one 2G **21**
TR13: Ash . . . . .5K **155** & 1A **156**
(not continuous)
Main St. TR18: Hea 3D **148**
Maker La. PL10: M'brk 2D **94**
Maker Rd. PL11: Tor 4J **93**
Malabar Rd. TR1: Tru 5E **106**

Malakoff, The TR26: S Ives 3J **137**
MALPAS 3B **168**
Malpas Ho. TR1: Tru 6K **107**
Malpas Rd. TR1: Mal, Tru 5A **108**
Malthouse Cl. TR3: Pons 5F **123**
Malt Ho. Ct. TR27: Hayl 1H **141**
(off Sea La.)
Malt Ho. Gdns. TR18: Newl 1C **154**
(off Antoine Cl.)
Malthouse La. PL22: Los 3E **52**
(off Fore St.)
TR17: Mar 4F **151**
MANACCAN 6C **160** (2A **174**)
Manaton Cl. TR13: Helst 1D **158**
Manaton Ct. PL15: Laun 4H **17**
Manaton Dr. PL15: Laun 4H **17**
Maneley Way PL17: Harr 5A **74**
Manewas Way TR7: Newq 2J **35**
Manfield Way PL25: S Aus 5B **58**
Manhattan Ct. PL17: K Bray 2C **72**
Manley Cl. PL14: Lisk 5A **70**
Manley Rd. PL14: Lisk 5A **70**
Manley Ter. PL14: Lisk 5A **70**
Manoa Valley PL26: Treg 1G **65**
Man of War Vw. TR12: Lizar 6G **161**
Manor Cl. PL25: S Aus 4K **57**
TR11: Fal 7C **128**
TR13: Helst 1D **158**
TR18: Hea 3E **148**
TR26: Lel 1E **140**
Manorcombe & Lamerton Bungs. PL17: Harr . . .3D **74**
Manor Cotts. TR11: Fal 1H **133**
Manor Cres. TR11: Fal 7C **128**
Manor Dr. TR9: Fr'don, P'ale 4G **45**
TR26: S Ives 5E **136**
Mnr. Farm Cl. TR20: Gold 4A **152**
Mnr. Farm Rd. PL26: Dup 7A **58**
Manor Gdns. PL10: M'brk 1D **94**
PL32: Came 3J **15**
TR1: Tru 4A **108**
TR15: Red 2D **112**
TR27: S Er 6F **141**
Manor Pk. PL12: Salt 3F **89**
PL14: Duloe 6A **78**
PL26: Penw 4K **49**
MANOR PARSLEY 2F **103**
Manor Pl. TR18: Hea 3E **148**
Manor Rd. EX23: Bud 6E **8**
TR7: Newq 3E **34**
(not continuous)
TR11: Fal 7C **128**
TR14: Camb 7C **110**
TR16: Carh 5K **113**
Manor Vw. PL24: Par 4H **59**
Manor Way TR13: Helst 2D **158**
TR18: Hea 3E **148**
Manse Rd. TR3: C Dow 6D **116**
Manson Pl. PL26: S Den 2F **47**
Maple Av. PL11: Tor 3J **93**
PL32: Came 2K **15**
Maple Cl. PL17: Call 5D **72**
PL26: S Den 2D **46**
PL31: B'min 4D **32**
TR9: S Maj 5A **30**
Maple Gro. PL14: Plym 1H **163**
Maple Leaf Dr. PL27: B'eve 1F **25**
MARAZION 4E **150** (1C **173**)
Marazion Mus. 4E **150**
Marchele Cl. PL31: B'min 4G **33**
Marconi Cl. TR13: Helst 3B **158**
Marconi Monument 3D **173**
Marcus Hill TR7: Newq 3F **35**
Marcwheal TR19: Mou 5D **154**
Margaret Av. PL25: S Aus 6J **57**
Margaret Cnr. PL31: B'min 3E **32**
Margaret Cres. PL31: B'min 4E **32**
Margaret Gdns. PL27: Wade 4G **25**
Margaret Pl. TR11: Fal 2D **132**
Margaret's La. PL29: P Isa 2J **19**
MARGHASYOW 4F **35**
MARHAMCHURCH 3F **11** (3A **164**)
Maria's La. TR19: Senn C 3C **146**
Marina Ct. TR7: Newq 4F **35**
Marine Ct. PL11: Tor 4K **93**
TR6: P'rth 4B **40**
(off Wheal Leisure)
TR11: Fal 2H **133**
(off Pendennis Rd.)
Marine Cres. TR11: Fal 2G **133**
Marine Dr. EX23: Lyn, U'ton, Wid B 3A **10**
PL11: Tor 4K **93**
PL13: Loo 7K **81** (7G **81**)
Marine Pde. TR2: S Mawe 7D **130**
Mariners Ct. PL4: Plym 5K **163**
Marine Ter. PL27: Wade 4E **24**
(off Eddystone Pl.)
PL35: Bosc 1K **13**
TR18: Penz 6F **149**
Maristow La. PL12: Salt 2H **89**

Maritime Studios TR11: Fal 2H **133**
Marjorie Ct. PL12: Salt 1D **88**
Market Av. PL1: Plym 4F **163**
Market Ct. *PL15: Laun* 3H **17**
　　(off Market St.)
　TR27: Hayl 1J **141**
　　(off Market Sq.)
Market Hill PL25: S Aus 5G **57**
Market Ho. Arc. *PL15: Laun* 3H **17**
　　(off Market St.)
Market Jew St. TR18: Penz 5F **149**
Market Pl. PL27: Wade 4E **24**
　PL28: Pad 3B **22**
　PL32: Came 3J **15**
　TR9: S Maj 4C **30**
　TR13: Helst 4B **158**
　TR17: Mar 4E **150**
　TR18: Penz 5F **149**
　TR26: S Ives 2J **137** (2D **136**)
Market Pl. Wlk. *TR18: Penz* 5F **149**
　　(off Market Pl.)
Market Sq. PL1: Plym 4F **163**
　PL17: Call 5C **72**
　PL26: Mev 6C **134**
　　(off River St.)
　TR16: S Da 2K **113**
　TR19: S Jus 3J **145**
　TR27: Hayl 1J **141**
Market Stalls PL1: Plym 4F **163**
Market Strand PL28: Pad 3B **22**
　TR11: Fal 7F **129**
　TR15: Red 3D **112**
　　(off Fore St.)
　TR26: S Ives .2J **137**
Market St. EX23: Stra 5H **9**
　PL10: King 6E **94**
　PL14: Lisk 4B **70**
　PL15: Laun 3H **17**
　PL23: Fow 7K **61**
　PL25: S Aus 6G **57**
　PL31: B'min 3G **33**
　TR3: Devo 2C **124**
　TR11: Fal 1F **133**
　TR19: S Jus 3J **145**
　TR27: Hayl 1J **141**
Market Way PL1: Plym 4F **163**
　TR15: Red 4D **112**
Marks Dr. PL31: B'min 5G **33**
Marks Way *TR7: Newq* 5E **34**
　　(off Holt Cres.)
MARKWELL 4F **87** (2C **171**)
Markwell La. PL12: S Ern 4F **87**
Marlborough Av. TR11: Fal 2D **132**
Marlborough Cl. PL12: Salt 4H **89**
　TR11: Fal 2D **132**
Marlborough Ct. TR11: Fal 2E **132**
Marlborough Cres. TR11: Fal 2E **132**
Marlborough Gro. TR11: Fal 2E **132**
Marlborough Rd. PL4: Plym 2J **163**
　TR11: Fal 2E **132**
Marlborough Way PL26: Stick 3K **63**
Marriotts Av. TR14: Camb 6B **110**
Marrowbone Slip PL4: Plym 5K **163**
Marshall Av. PL27: Wade 4G **25**
Marshall Cl. PL26: Roch 4B **42**
Marshallen Rd. TR4: Mt Hwk 7H **97**
Marshall Rd. PL30: Nans 4A **32**
　PL31: B'min 5F **33**
MARSHGATE .1B **166**
Marsh La. PL18: Cals 7J **75**
　TR27: Hayl 7E **138**
　　(not continuous)
Marthus Ct. *PL14: Lisk* 5B **70**
　　(off Heatlands Rd.)
Martin Cl. TR15: Red 3F **113**
Martin La. PL4: Plym 5K **163**
Martins Cl. *PL14: Lisk* 3D **70**
　　(off Stephens Rd.)
Martin's La. TR15: I'gan 2H **111**
Martin Sq. *PL17: Call* 5D **72**
　　(off Tavistock Rd.)
Martinvale Av. TR15: Red 1G **113**
Martinvale Parc TR15: Red 1G **113**
Martyn's Cl. TR4: Goonh 5H **41**
Marver Camping Park, The TR8: M Por 2C **28**
MARYFIELD 1G **93** (2D **171**)
Mary Newman's Cottage 3J **89**
MARYSTOW 2D **167**
Marys Well TR15: I'gan 1G **111**
　TR16: I'gan 1G **111**
Masons Row PL18: Gun 1G **75**
Matela Cl. TR13: P'ven 7G **157**
Mathew Cl. TR9: I Que 1J **45**
Matthews Buildings *TR26: S Ives* 3H **137**
　　(off Drillfield La.)
Matthews Way PL14: Menh 7J **71**
MAUDLIN 1D **169**
Maudlin Cl. PL14: Lisk 5C **70**
Mawes Cl. TR18: S An Cpl 3C **74**

MAWGAN 2A **174**
MAWGAN PORTH 2C **28** (1B **168**)
Mawgan Porth Holiday Pk. TR8: M Por 2C **28**
Mawgan Vu TR9: Fr'don 4H **45**
MAWLA 3E **102** (3A **168**)
MAWNAN 2A **174**
MAWNAN SMITH 2B **160** (2A **174**)
MAXWORTHY .1C **167**
Maybrook Dr. PL12: Salt 3F **89**
Mayfair Ho. PL4: Plym 3K **163**
Mayfield Cl. PL25: S Aus 5A **58**
　PL29: P Isa 2J **19**
　PL31: B'min 3J **33**
Mayfield Cres. TR7: Newq 4F **35**
Mayfield Dr. PL26: Roch 4B **42**
　PL29: P Isa 2K **19**
Mayfield Rd. PL29: P Isa 2J **19**
　TR7: Newq 4F **35**
　TR11: Fal 1D **132**
Mayfield Ter. *TR26: C Bay* 7F **137**
　　(off Trencrom La.)
Mayflower Sailing Club 6K **163**
Mayflower Stone & Steps 7K **163**
Mayflower St. PL1: Plym 3G **163**
Mayflower Vis. Cen. 6J **163**
May Gdns. TR16: L'ner 1H **121**
May La. PL13: Mill 3K **81**
Maymear Ter. PL30: S Tud 5J **27**
Mayne Cl. PL15: Laun 2G **17**
Maynes Row TR14: Camb 5G **111**
MAYON 4D **146**
Mayon Farm TR19: Senn 4D **146**
Mayon Green TR19: Senn 3E **146**
Mayon Grn. Cres. TR19: Senn 3D **146**
May Pl. PL18: Cals 7J **75**
MEAD 2A **164**
Mead Ho's. TR18: Gul 2G **149**
Meadow, The PL26: Polg 2C **64**
　TR1: Tru 4H **107**
　TR3: P Sta 3J **123**
　TR8: Hol B 2B **38**
　TR16: I'gan 1H **111**
　TR26: S Ives 1H **137**
Meadowbank TR11: M Bri 7E **124**
Meadowbank Rd. TR11: Fal 6E **128**
Meadow Breeze PL22: Los 3E **52**
Meadow Cl. PL12: Salt 2H **89**
　PL23: Polr 7C **60**
　PL25: S Aus 3K **57**
　PL26: S Ste 4C **54**
　TR1: Glo 5C **106**
　TR7: Newq 5H **35**
Meadow Ct. PL28: Pad 4K **21**
　PL30: S Mab 6B **26**
　TR3: Stith 6J **121**
Meadow Dr. EX23: Flex 4E **8**
　PL12: Salt 1F **89**
　PL13: Loo 3H **81**
　PL24: B'vey 4F **59**
　TR14: Camb 6B **110**
　　(not continuous)
Meadow Flats TR26: S Ives 1H **137** (2D **136**)
Meadowhead PL27: Wade 5F **25**
Meadow Lakes Holiday Pk. PL26: Hew W 7G **63**
Meadow La. TR1: Tru 6K **107**
　PL25: T'oon 5D **56**
Meadow Pk. PL14: Lisk 5A **70**
Meadow Pl. PL31: B'min 4F **33**
Meadow Rise PL26: Fox 7H **47**
　PL26: Penw 5J **49**
　TR9: S Maj 5C **30**
Meadows, The PL11: Tor 2G **93**
　PL12: S Dom 3G **77**
　PL26: S Den 3E **46**
　PL30: S Teat 2B **26**
Meadowside PL15: Laun 5F **17**
　PL25: T Mil 3C **58**
　TR7: Newq 5H **35**
　TR15: Red 4B **112**
Meadowside Cl. TR27: Hayl 4F **141**
Meadowside Rd. TR11: Fal 2D **132**
Meadow St. PL26: Mev 6C **134**
Meadowsweet Pk. PL12: Salt 3E **88**
Meadow Ter. PL14: S Cle 4B **66**
Meadow Vw. PL27: Tred 7H **19**
　TR14: Camb 2E **118**
　TR20: Gold 4A **152**
Meadow Vs. *TR18: Newl* 2C **154**
　　(off St Peter's Hill)
Meadow Wlk. PL23: Polr 7C **60**
Meadway PL12: Salt 4G **89**
　PL13: Loo 4H **81**
　PL25: S Aus 4K **57**
MEADWELL 2D **167**
Mearwood La. TR11: Fal 1D **132**
MEAVER 2K **161**
Meaver Rd. TR12: Mull 1J **161**
MEAVY 1D **171**
MEDDON 2A **164**

Medland Gdns. PL25: S Aus 5G **57**
Medrose PL27: Rock 2F **23**
Medrose St. PL33: Dela 2B **14**
Medrose Ter. TR18: Penz 4F **149**
Melbourne Rd. PL14: Lisk 5A **70**
Melbourne Ter. *TR18: Hea* 3D **148**
　　(off Church Rd.)
Mellanear Cl. TR27: Hayl 3G **141**
Mellanear Rd. TR27: Hayl 3G **141**
Mellanvrane La. TR7: Newq 5G **35**
Mellanvrane Rdbt. TR7: Newq 5F **35**
Melliars Way EX23: Flex 4E **8**
Mellingey Mill (Willow Craft Centre) 3D **165**
Melrose St. *TR1: Tru* 4K **107**
　　(off Campfield Hill)
　TR9: Fr'don 3G **45**
Melroy Ter. TR4: Black 3A **104**
Melvill Cl. TR11: Fal 3E **132**
Melvill Cres. TR11: Fal 2F **133**
Melville Rd. TR3: Thre 5K **105**
Melville Ter. PL22: Los 3E **52**
Melvill La. TR11: Fal 3F **133**
Melvill Rd. TR11: Fal 2F **133**
Melyn Cl. TR27: Log 6E **138**
MENABILLY 2D **169**
Menabilly Cl. PL17: Call 7C **72**
Menabilly Rd. PL25: S Aus 3J **57**
Menacuddle Hill PL25: S Aus 5G **57**
Menacuddle La. PL25: S Aus 5G **57**
Menadue Ct. TR27: Reaw 3C **142**
MENAGISSEY .1G **103**
Menague PL27: Rock 1G **23**
Menagwins Ct. PL26: Gorr 1G **135**
Menakarne TR16: Carh 4A **114**
Men-an-Tol 1B **172**
Meneage Ho. TR13: Helst 4C **158**
Meneage Parc TR13: Helst 4C **158**
Meneage Rd. TR13: Helst 5C **158**
Meneage St. TR13: Helst 4C **158**
Meneage Vs. PL25: S Aus 6F **57**
Menear Rd. PL25: S Aus 1A **58**
Menefreda Way PL27: S Minv 6K **19**
Menehay Farm TR11: B Wat 2B **132**
Meneth Gdns. TR12: Gweek 6H **159**
Meneth Rd. TR14: Camb 1F **119**
MENHENIOT 1H **79** (1B **170**)
Menheniot Station (Rail) 4H **79**
MENHENOIT 1H **79**
MENHERION 7E **120**
Menhinick Cl. PL12: Land 7H **83**
Menhyr Dr. TR26: C Bay 6E **136**
MENNA 2C **169**
MENNAYE 6E **148**
Mennaye Field 6E **148**
Mennaye Gdns. TR15: I Hig 3K **111**
Mennaye Rd. TR18: Penz 6E **148**
MENNOR 3A **140**
Mera Pk. PL12: Land 7G **83**
Merbein Cotts. TR8: Tr'grn 6C **28**
Merchant's House Mus. 5H **163**
Merchants Quay PL15: Laun 5E **16**
Meres Valley TR12: Mull 1G **161**
Merlin Golf Course 1E **28**
Merlin Pl. TR19: Mou 6D **154**
Merlins Way PL34: Tin 7C **12**
Mermaid Ct. TR7: Newq 1K **35**
Merrick Av. TR1: Tru 3A **108**
Merrifield Cl. TR1: Tru 4H **107**
Merrill Pl. TR11: Fal 2E **132**
Merritts Hill TR16: I'gan 2K **111**
Merritts Way TR15: Pool 3J **111**
Merry Maidens Stone Circle 2B **172**
MERRYMEET 1G **71** (1B **170**)
MERRYMEETING 1B **122**
Merry Mit Mdw. TR11: B Wat 2A **132**
MERTHER 5G **109** (3B **168**)
Merther Cl. TR13: Sithn 1H **157**
Messack Cl. TR11: Fal 3C **132**
Metha Pk. TR8: S New E 2H **37**
Metha Rd. TR8: S New E 2G **37**
METHERELL 5C **74** (1D **171**)
Methleigh Bottoms TR13: P'ven 5F **157**
Methleigh Parc TR13: P'ven 7F **157**
MEUDON 2D **160**
MEVAGISSEY 6C **134** (3D **169**)
Mevagissey Marine Aquarium 6D **134**
Mevagissey Mus. 6D **134**
Mews, The PL11: Tor 4J **93**
　PL15: Laun 1F **17**
　PL24: S Bla 1H **59**
Mews Ct. PL14: Menh 1H **79**
Mexico La. TR27: Phil 6C **138**
Mexico Ter. TR27: Phil 6C **138**
MICHAELSTOW .3A **166**
Michell Av. TR7: Newq 3F **35**
Michell Ct. TR7: Newq 3E **34**
Mid Cornwall Bus. Pk. PL25: S Aus 5E **58**
Mid Cornwall Galleries 3F **59**
MIDDLE DIMSON 1G **75**

Middlefield Cl. PL12: Salt 2D 88
Middlegates TR5: S Agn 3B 96
MIDDLEHILL 2J 67
Middlehill PL26: Fox 1H 55
Middle Mkt. St. PL13: Loo 6K 81
MIDDLEMOOR 1D 171
Middle Pk. PL14: Pens 1J 67
Middle Rd. TR15: Red 1G 113
Middle Rosewin Row TR1: Tru 4K 107
    (off Rosewin Row)
Middle Row TR13: Ash 1A 156
Middle Stennack Cotts. TR26: S Ives 3G 137
    (off Higher Stennack)
Middle St. PL28: Pad 3B 22
    PL29: P Isa 2J 19
MIDDLE TAPHOUSE 1A 170
Middleton Cres. TR7: Newq 5G 35
Middletons Row TR15: Red 3E 112
Middle Wlk. PL26: Dup 7A 58
Middleway PL24: S Bla 3H 59
Middlewell Parc PL27: Wade 5E 24
Middle Wharf PL26: Mev 6C 134
MIDDLEWOOD 3C 167
Midway Dr. TR1: Tru 3A 108
Midway Rd. PL31: B'min 3C 32
    (not continuous)
Miers Cl. PL5: Plym .5K 89
Milch Pk. PL12: Salt .3E 88
Mildmay St. PL4: Plym 2K 163
Mile Hill TR4: P'twn .1C 102
    TR16: Nanc 1C 102
Milestone Ct. TR3: Thre 4A 106
MILFORD 1A 164
Military Rd. PL10: M'brk 4A 94
Millbank Mdw. TR27: Leeds 7C 142
Millbay Rd. PL1: Plym 5F 163
MILLBROOK 2C 94 (2D 171)
Millbrook Bus. Pk. PL11: M'brk 1A 94
Mill Cl. PL27: Eglo 4H 25
    TR13: P'ven 6F 157
MILLENDREATH 3K 81
Millendreath Holiday Village PL13: Mill 3K 81
Millennium Apartments TR10: P'ryn 3K 127
Millennium Way TR13: Helst 1D 158
Miller Bus. Pk. PL14: Lisk 6A 70
Miller Ct. PL14: Lisk .6A 70
Millet Cl. TR17: Mar .4H 151
Millfield Bungs. TR18: Gul 3G 149
Mill Gdns. PL22: Los 3E 52
    (off Edgecumbe Rd.)
    TR16: S Da 2A 114
Millgrist Mdw. TR15: I'gan 2J 111
Millham La. PL22: Los 2G 53
Millham Rd. PL22: Los 2G 53
Mill Hill PL13: Polp 7B 80
    PL22: Los 3F 53
    TR27: L Dow 4C 140
Millhouse Pk. PL11: Tor 4J 93
Mill La. PL11: Tor 4J 93
    PL12: S Ger 5C 86
    PL30: S B'wd 2J 27
    PL32: Came 2H 15
    TR2: Gram 7A 62
    TR2: Tregon 6H 99
    TR3: Cale 1H 117
    TR13: Helst 3A 158
    TR13: P'ven 6F 157
    TR19: Mou 6D 154
MILL PARK 1G 89
Millpond Av. TR27: Hayl 3G 141
MILLPOOL
    Bodmin 3B 166
    Lostwithiel 2F 53
    Penzance 5F 153
Millpool TR19: Mou .6D 154
Millpool Head PL10: M'brk 2C 94
Millpool Rd. PL10: M'brk 1D 94
Millpool Ter. TR19: Mou 6D 154
    (off Millpool)
Millpool Yd. PL23: Fow 6J 61
Mill Rd. PL10: M'brk .2D 94
    PL12: Tide 1B 86
    PL28: Pad 3B 22
    TR6: Bol 6C 40
    TR12: Cover 6D 162
    TR14: P'nds 3A 118
Mill Sq. PL28: Pad 2B 22
Mills St. TR16: S Da .2A 114
Mill St. PL31: B'min .3G 33
MILLTOWN 7E 52 (2A 170)
Mill Vw. Gdns. PL10: M'brk 2D 94
Mill Vw. Rd. PL10: M'brk 2D 94
Mill Yd. TR3: Pons 5F 123
MILTON ABBOT 3D 167
MILTON COMBE 1D 171
MILTON DAMEREL .2B 164
Minack Theatre 7H 147
Minehead Ter. PL26: Coomb 2G 63
Mine Hill PL14: Menh 7J 71

Mine La. PL30: Lani .6H 31
Miners Ct. TR6: P'rth 5B 40
    TR15: Red 3E 112
Miners Mdw. PL14: Lisk 3C 70
    (off Callington Rd.)
Miners Row TR15: Red 3E 112
Miners Way PL14: Lisk 3C 70
MINGOOSE 4G 97
MINIONS 3C 167
Minions Heritage Cen. 3C 167
Minnie Pl. TR11: Fal .2F 133
Minorca La. PL26: Bugl 5J 43
Minster Av. EX23: Bud 6E 8
Minster Flds. TR12: Mana 6C 160
Minster Ga. EX23: Bud 6E 8
Minster Mdw. TR12: Mana 6C 160
Minton Cl. PL25: S Aus 5A 58
Mission, The TR18: Penz 6G 149
    (off Coinagehall St.)
MITCHELL 2B 168
Mitchell Cl. TR12: Lizar 5H 161
Mitchell Ct. TR1: Tru .4K 107
    (off Mitchell Hill)
Mitchell Hill TR1: Tru 5K 107
Mitchell Hill Ter. TR1: Tru 4K 107
Mitchell La. TR14: Camb 7E 110
Mitchell M. TR1: Tru .4K 107
    (off Mitchell Hill)
Mitchell Rd. PL25: S Aus 5K 57
    TR11: Fal 7E 128
    TR14: Camb 6C 110
Mitchell's Boatyard PL26: P'melln 7C 134
MITHIAN 2A 168
MIXTOW 4K 61
Modus La. PL26: Stick 4K 63
Molenick La. PL12: Tide C 5A 82
Molesworth Ct. PL27: Wade 4E 24
Molesworth St. PL27: Wade 4E 24
    PL34: Tin 7B 12
Molesworth Ter. PL10: M'brk 2D 94
MOLINGEY 3F 65
MOLINNIS 6J 43
Molinnis Cl. PL26: Bugl 6H 43
Molinnis Rd. PL26: Bugl 6H 43
Molteno Pl. TR26: S Ives 3G 137
Monastery Cl. TR12: S Kev 2C 162
Moneycentre Precinct, The
    PL1: N'tyn 3H 163
Mongleath Av. TR11: Fal 2C 132
Mongleath Cl. TR11: Fal 3C 132
Mongleath Rd. TR11: Fal 2C 132
Monkey Sanctuary 2B 170
Monkey Tree Holiday Pk. TR8: H Cft 3K 41
Monks Pk. PL15: Laun 3J 17
Monmouth La. PL22: Los 3F 53
Monroe Gdns. PL3: Plym 1F 163
Montague Av. TR15: Red 2C 112
Montana Vs. PL25: Scre 1H 57
Monterey EX23: Bud .6D 8
Monterey Gdns. TR1: Tru 4A 108
Montgomery Cl. PL12: Salt 2F 89
Montgomery Rd. PL26: Penw 5J 49
Monument Rd. TR13: Helst 4B 158
Monument Way PL31: B'min 4E 32
Moon St. PL4: Plym .4K 163
Moor, The TR11: Fal .1F 133
MOORCROFT 4K 147
Moor Cross EX23: Pou 1E 8
Moorfield TR14: Praze 4K 143
Moorfield Rd. TR15: Pool 4H 111
Moorings, The PL12: Salt 4J 89
    TR19: Pend 3B 144
Moorland Cl. PL14: Lisk 3C 70
Moorland Ct. PL25: S Aus 6G 57
Moorland Mdws. PL26: Roch 4C 42
Moorland Rd. PL15: Laun 5F 17
    PL24: Par 3K 59
    PL25: S Aus 7H 57
    TR9: I Que 1H 45
Moorland Rd. Ind. Est. TR9: I Que 1J 45
Moorland Rd. Ind. Pk. TR9: I Que 1H 45
Moorlands Ind. Est. PL12: Salt 1E 88
Moorlands La. PL12: Salt 1E 88
Moorland Vw. PL12: Salt 1H 89
    PL14: Lisk 3C 70
Moorland Way PL18: Dra 3F 75
Moor La. TR13: Burr .7A 120
Moors, The PL22: Los 4E 52
Moor St. TR14: Camb 7D 110
MOORSWATER 5H 69
Moorswater Ind. Est. PL14: Moo 5H 69
Moorswater Viaduct .6J 69
MOORTOWN 1D 167
Moor Vw. PL11: Tor .3K 93
    PL31: B'min 6H 33
Moor Vw. Ter. PL4: Plym 1K 163
Morcom Cl. PL25: S Aus 4K 57

Morcom's Row TR10: P'ryn 4A 128
    (off Mutton Row)
Moresk Cl. TR1: Tru .4K 107
Moresk Gdns. TR1: Tru 4K 107
Moresk Rd. TR1: Tru .4K 107
Morlaix Av. TR1: Tru .7J 107
Morla La. TR15: Red .2C 112
Morlanow TR18: Penz 6E 148
    (off Alexandra Rd.)
Morleigh Cl. PL25: S Aus 6K 57
Morley Ct. PL1: Plym .4F 163
Morrab Ct. TR7: Newq 3G 35
    (off Pargolla Rd.)
Morrab Gdns. 6F 149
Morrab Pl. TR18: Penz 5F 149
Morrab Rd. TR14: Camb 7C 110
    TR18: Penz 5F 149
Morrab Ter. TR18: Penz 5F 149
Morris Gdns. TR7: Newq 5E 34
    (off Tregunnel Hill)
Mortain Rd. PL12: Salt 1F 89
Mortimore Cl. PL12: Salt 3F 89
MORVAH 1B 172
MORVAL 2B 170
Morven Rd. PL25: S Aus 6K 57
Morven Trad. Est. PL25: S Aus 6K 57
MORWELLHAM 5K 75
Morwellham Cl. PL5: Plym 5K 89
Morwellham Quay 5K 75
Morwenna Gdns. TR6: P'rth 4D 40
Morwenna Ter. EX23: Bud 4C 8
MORWENSTOW 2A 164
Morweth Ct. PL11: Downd 6H 79
Mosquito Cres. PL27: S Eval 2H 31
Moss Side PL17: Call .5F 73
Moss Side Ind. Est. PL17: Call 5E 72
Moss Ter. PL23: Polr .6C 60
Mote Pk. PL12: Salt .2E 88
Mother Ivey's Bay Caravan Pk. PL28: T'vose . . .2B 20
MOUNT
    Bodmin 1A 170
    Truro 7E 38 (2A 168)
Mount, The PL24: Par 4J 59
Mt. Agar Rd. TR3: C Dow 7C 116
MOUNT AMBROSE 1G 113 (3A 168)
Mount Ambrose TR15: Red 2F 113
Mountbatten Cl. TR7: S Mino 2A 36
Mountbatten Rd. PL26: Penw 5K 49
Mt. Bennett Rd. TR3: Tyw 2B 60
Mt. Bennett Ter. PL24: Tyw 2B 60
Mt. Brioni Holiday Apartments PL11: Seat 6F 79
Mount Camel PL23: Tyw 3H 15
Mt. Carbis Gdns. TR15: Red 5E 112
Mt. Carbis Rd. TR15: Red 5E 112
MOUNT CHARLES 6K 57
Mt. Charles Rd. PL25: S Aus 6K 57
Mount Cl. TR7: Newq .5E 34
    (off Tregunnel Hill)
Mount Cres. PL24: Par 4J 59
Mount Edgcumbe Country Park 1K 95
Mount Edgcumbe Country Park Formal Gdns. . . .1J 95
Mount Edgcumbe House 1J 95
Mt. Edgcumber Ter. TR11: Fal 1F 133
    (off Webber Hill)
Mountfield Ter. PL24: Par 3J 59
Mount Folly 4G 33
Mt. Folly Sq. PL31: B'min 4G 33
    (off Fore St.)
Mt. George Rd. TR3: Feo 7H 117
MOUNT HAWKE 7H 97 (3A 168)
Mt. Hawke Holiday Bungs. TR4: Mt Hwk 6F 97
Mount Hawke Skatepark 6K 97
MOUNTJOY 1B 168
Mountlea Country Park 4J 59
Mountlea Dr. PL24: Par 4J 59
Mount Lidden TR18: Penz 6D 148
Mount Madford PL15: Laun 4H 17
Mt. Pleasant PL10: M'brk 2C 94
    PL17: Harr 3B 74
    PL24: S Bla 7H 51
    PL31: B'min 3G 33
    PL35: Bosc 2K 13
    TR11: Fal 3C 132
    TR15: Red 1G 113
    (off Redruth Highway)
    TR16: S Da 3K 113
    (off Carew Rd.)
    TR18: Penz 6C 148
    TR26: Lel 3D 140
    TR26: S Ives 2H 137
    TR27: Hayl 1H 141
Mt. Pleasant Cl. TR14: Camb 2D 118
Mount Pleasant Ecological Park 1D 102
Mt. Pleasant Farm TR14: Camb 2E 118
Mt. Pleasant Gdns. TR27: Hayl 1H 141
Mt. Pleasant Pl. PL22: Los 2E 52
Mt. Pleasant Rd. TR3: Thre 5B 106
    TR13: P'ven 7F 157
    TR14: Camb 1D 118

Mt. Pleasant St. TR19: Mou 6D 154
Mt. Pleasant Ter. TR19: Mou 6D 154
Mount Pleasure TR14: Camb 2E 118
Mt. Prospect Ter. TR18: Newl 7D 148
Mt. Royale Cl. *TR18: Penz* 4G 149
                  (off Chyandour Cliff)
Mounts Bay Caravan Pk. TR17: Mar 3D 150
Mounts Bay Community Sports Cen. 3C 148
Mount's Bay Holiday Flats TR18: Penz 3H 149
Mounts Bay Rd. TR18: Penz 6D 148
Mounts Bay Ter. TR13: Ash 2A 156
   TR13: P'ven 6A 156
MOUNTS BAY VILLAGE 3H 149
Mountside Rd. PL24: Par 3J 59
Mounts Rd. TR13: P'ven 6A 156
Mt. Stamper Rd. PL25: Scre 4G 57
Mountstephen Cl. PL25: S Aus 6E 56
Mt. Stephens La. TR11: Fal 1C 132
Mount St. PL4: Plym 3K 163
   PL26: Mev 6D 134
                    (off Cliff St.)
   TR18: Penz 4F 149
Mount Ter. PL24: S Bl G 3G 59
Mount Vw. TR8: Lane 6J 35
   TR15: C Bre 5B 112
   TR20: Mad 1A 148
Mount Vw. Cl. TR2: Gerr 3J 131
Mount Vw. Cotts. TR20: Mad 1B 148
Mount Vw. Ter. TR17: Mar 4G 151
   TR18: Newl 1C 154
Mt. Whistle Rd. TR14: Sth T 3D 110
Mount Wise PL15: Laun 4H 17
   TR7: Newq 4E 34
Mountwise Cotts. TR7: Newq 4F 35
Mount Zion TR26: S Ives 1J 137
MOUSEHOLE 6D 154 (2B 172)
Mousehole La. TR19: Mou, Pau 4C 154
Mowhay Cl. TR7: Newq 5H 35
Mowhay La. *PL17: Call* 5C 72
                (off Tanyards La.)
Mowhay Mdw. PL11: S John 7D 92
   PL27: Wade 5E 24
   TR9: Fr'don 2G 45
Mowie, The TR9: I Que, S Roa 2G 45
Mowie Cl. TR9: I Que 2H 45
Moyle Rd. PL28: Pad 4C 22
MUCHLARNICK 2B 170
               (off Commercial St.)
Mudges Ter. *PL18: Gun* 1H 75
Mud La. PL11: Ant .6A 92
Mulberry Quay TR11: Fal 7F 129
Mulberry Rd. PL12: Salt 3G 89
Mulfra Quoit 1B 172
Mulgrave St. PL1: Plym 6G 163
MULLION 1H 161 (3D 173)
Mullion Cl. PL11: Tor 2H 93
   PL25: S Aus 2J 57
MULLION COVE 3F 161 (3D 173)
Mullion Cove 3D 173
Mullion Cove Bungs. TR12: Mull 3F 161
Mullion Rural Workshops TR12: Mull 2H 161
MULVRA 2F 65
Murdoch Cl. TR1: Tru 3A 108
   TR15: Red 2D 112
Murdock Rd. PL11: Tor 3H 93
Murtons Ter. TR16: L'ner 7J 113
Museum of Witchcraft 1K 13
Mutley Plain PL4: Plym 1K 163
Mutton Hill TR27: Con D 5H 139
Mutton Row TR10: P'ryn 4A 128
MYLOR BRIDGE 1E 128 (1B 174)
MYLOR CHURCHTOWN 3J 129 (1B 174)
My Lords Rd. TR9: P'ale 4G 45
Myrtle Ct. PL26: Mev 6C 134
Myrtles Ct. PL12: Salt 1F 89
Myrtle Ter. PL18: Dra 3F 75
Mythyon Ct. TR18: Hea 3D 148

N

Nalder's Ct. *TR1: Tru* 5K 107
                (off The Leats)
Nampara Cl. TR26: C Bay 6G 137
Nampara Ct. TR6: P'rth 5B 40
Nampara Way TR1: Tru 5B 108
Nancarrows PL12: Salt 3E 88
NANCEALVERNE 4D 148
NANCEDDAN 1H 155
NANCEGOLLAN 1D 173
NANCEKUKE 2C 102
NANCEKUKE COMMON 2K 101
Nancemellin Cl. TR3: P Sta 1J 123
Nancemere La. TR1: Tru 3A 108
Nancemere Rd. TR1: Tru 3K 107
Nancevallon TR14: Bre 7H 111
NANCHERROW 2J 145
Nancherrow Hill TR19: S Jus 2J 145
Nancherrow Ter. TR19: S Jus 2J 145

NANCLEDRA 1B 172
NANGILES 3H 115
Nangitha Cl. TR11: B Wat 2A 132
Nangitha Pl. *TR11: B Wat* 2A 132
                 (off Chapel Ter.)
Nangitha Ter. TR11: B Wat 2A 132
Nanhayes Row TR8: S New E 2G 37
Nanjivey TR13: S Ives 3B 136
Nanjivey Pl. *TR26: S Ives* 3C 136
             (off Higher Stennack)
Nanjivey Row *TR26: S Ives* 3B 136
              (off Alexandra Rd.)
Nanjivey Ter. TR26: S Ives 3C 136
NANKELLY 7A 30
NANPEAN 5G 47 (2C 169)
Nanpean Barns TR19: S Jus 2F 145
Nanpusker Cl. TR27: Hayl 1K 141
Nanpusker Rd. TR27: Ang, Hayl . . . .7F 139 & 1A 142
NANQUIDNO 7G 145
Nansalsa Ct. TR7: Newq 3H 35
Nansavallon Rd. TR1: Tru 5D 106
Nanscober Pl. TR13: Helst 1B 158
Nans Kestenen TR13: Helst 4B 158
NANSLADRON 7F 65
Nansloe Cl. TR13: Helst 5C 158
Nansmellyn Marsh Nature Reserve 5C 40
Nansmellyon Rd. TR12: Mull 4F 161
NANSTALLON 4A 32 (1D 169)
Nanterrow La. TR27: Con D 2K 139
NANTURRAS 4A 152
Nanturras Parc TR20: Gold 4B 152
Nanturras Row TR20: Gold 4A 152
Nanturras Way TR20: Gold 4B 152
Napier Ter. PL4: Plym 1J 163
Nare Ct. PL26: Mev 6D 134
Nare Head 3C 169
Nare Ho. *TR2: Tregon* 6J 99
              (off Roseland Parc)
NARKURS 2C 171
Narrowcliff TR7: Newq 3G 35
Narrow La. PL12: Bot F 4D 84
   TR8: S Eno 6C 44
   TR9: P'ale 6C 44
NATCOTT 1A 164
Nathan Cl. TR7: Newq 4J 35
National Marine Aquarium 6K 163
National Maritime Mus.
   Cornwall 1G 133
National Seal Sanctuary, The 6H 159
Navy Inn Ct. *TR18: Newl* 2D 154
              (off Higher Grn. St.)
Neeham Rd. TR8: S New E 2G 37
Nelson St. PL4: Plym 2K 163
Neptune Av. PL27: S Eval 3J 31
Netherton Rd. PL28: Pad 4B 22
Netley Mdw. PL26: Bugl 7G 43
Net Lofts, The PL26: Mev 5C 134
Nettell's Hill TR15: Red 3D 112
Nettles Hill *TR13: Helst* 3B 158
             (off Almshouse Hill)
Nettles Row *TR16: I'gan* 1J 111
             (off Trevelyan Rd.)
NETTON 3D 171
Nevada Pl. *TR18: Hea* 3D 148
              (off Nevada St.)
Nevada St. TR18: Hea 3D 148
Nevada Vs. PL24: Par 4J 59
NEWBRIDGE
   Penzance 1B 172
   Truro 6D 106
Newbridge Hill PL18: Gun 1H 75
Newbridge La. TR1: Tru 6D 106
   TR3: Newb 6D 106
New Bridge St. TR1: Tru 5K 107
Newbridge Vw. TR1: Glo 4D 106
Newbridge Way TR1: Tru 5D 106
New Connexion St. TR14: Camb 7D 110
New Ct. *TR11: Fal* .1F 133
                (off New St.)
New Cut TR15: Red 3D 112
New Dairy La. TR17: Mar 2E 150
New George St. PL1: Plym 4F 163
New Guineaport PL27: Wade 4F 25
NEWHALL GREEN .6B 14
NEWHAM 7K 107
Newham Est. TR1: Tru 6K 107
Newham Ind. Est. TR1: Tru 7K 107
Newham La. PL22: Los 5G 53
   TR13: Helst 1A 158
Newham Rd. TR1: Tru 6K 107
New Hill Est. TR2: Gram 7B 62
Newhouses PL17: Meth 1J 77
New La. TR15: Red 1G 113
NEWLYN 1C 154 (2B 172)
Newlyn Art Gallery .7D 148
Newlyn Fish Market TR18: Newl 1C 154
Newlyn Rd. TR19: St Bury 2H 147
Newman Rd. PL12: Salt 2H 89
NEW MILL 1B 172

NEW MILLS 2B 168
NEWMILLS 3F 107
Newmills Cl. TR1: Tru 3H 107
Newmills La. TR1: Tru 3F 107
   TR4: Newm 3F 107
New Molinnis PL26: Bugl 6H 43
New Northernhaye PL15: Laun 3H 17
               (off Tower St.)
New Pk. TR27: Wade 5F 25
New Pk. Rd. PL27: Wade 4F 25
Newperran Holiday Pk. TR8: H Cft 3J 41
NEW POLZEATH 1D 18 (3D 165)
NEWPORT
   Callington 5C 72
   Launceston 2G 17 (2D 167)
Newport Cl. PL12: S Ger 5D 86
Newport Cl. PL17: Call 5D 72
Newport Ind. Est. PL15: Laun 2H 17
Newport Pl. *PL17: Call* 5C 72
               (off Church St.)
New Portreath Rd. TR16: Brid, Red 5K 101
Newport Sq. PL15: Laun 2G 17
Newport St. PL10: M'brk 2C 94
Newport Ter. PL10: M'brk 2C 94
   PL17: Call 5D 72
NEWQUAY 3F 35 (1B 168)
NEWQUAY CORNWALL AIRPORT 6F 29 (1B 168)
Newquay Golf Course 3D 34
Newquay Holiday Pk. TR8: Newq 1D 36
Newquay Rd. PL28: Pad 3K 21
   TR1: Tru 2A 108
   TR4: Goonh 5H 41
   TR9: S Maj 5A 30
   TR9: S Roa 1F 45
Newquay Sports Cen. 3J 35
Newquay Station (Rail) 3G 35
New Quay Ter. PL23: Polr 6C 60
Newquay Zoo 4H 35
New Rd. EX23: Stra 5G 9
   PL10: Caws 4E 94
   PL10: King 5F 95
   PL12: Salt 2F 89
   PL13: Polp 5B 80
   PL14: Lisk 5J 69
   PL17: Call 5C 72
   PL29: P Isa 2J 19
   PL35: Bosc 2K 13
   TR2: Tregon 6J 99
   TR3: Stith 7A 122
   TR6: Bol, P'rth 5C 40
   TR8: P'ale, Sum .6E 44
              (not continuous)
   TR9: P'ale 5F 45
   TR9: S Maj 4C 30
   TR14: Barr 4A 118
   TR14: Bre 7H 111
   TR14: Tro 5G 119
   TR18: Newl, Penz 7D 148
   TR19: S Jus 2J 145
   TR20: Gold, S Hil 4C 152
New Rd. Cl. PL10: Caws 5E 94
New Rd. Hill PL23: Fow 7J 61
New Rd. Ter. PL12: Land 6H 83
New Row TR8: Sum 7B 44
   TR11: M Bri 1E 128
   TR12: Gweek 7G 159
   TR16: Tres 2K 119
New St. PL1: Plym .6J 163
              (not continuous)
   PL10: M'brk 2C 94
   PL26: Bugl 7H 43
   PL28: Pad 3B 22
   TR10: P'ryn 5B 128
   TR11: Fal 1F 133
   TR14: Tro 5G 119
   TR18: Penz 5F 149
New Ter. TR14: Camb 7A 110
NEWTON 6E 74
Newton Ct. PL14: Dob 3D 68
   TR15: Red 2C 112
NEWTON FERRERS 3D 171
NEWTON MOOR 3H 119
Newton Pk. TR2: S Mawe 7D 130
Newton Rd. TR2: S Mawe 6D 130
   TR14: Tro 3G 119
Newton's Margate Ind. Est. PL31: B'min 4K 33
NEWTOWN
   Fowey 5F 61
   Germoe 7F 153
   Launceston 3C 167
   St Just 7J 145
NEWTOWN-IN-ST MARTIN 2A 174
New Town La. TR18: Penz 5F 149
Newtown La. TR20: L Roc 3C 150
New Windsor Ter. TR11: Fal 2E 132
Nicholas Av. TR16: Four L 3B 120
Nicholas Mdw. PL17: Meth 5D 74
Nicholas Parc TR18: Hea 3D 148
Nikita Ter. PL22: Los 2E 52

Niles Ter. TR16: Four L 3C 120
NINE MAIDENS 7A 120
Nine Maidens Stone Circle 1B 172
No Go By Hill TR19: S Jus 2J 145
No Mans' Land Rd. TR11: B Wat 5A 132
Norfolk Rd. TR11: Fal 1F 133
Normandy Hill PL5: Plym 3K 89
Normandy Way PL5: Plym 3K 89
  PL31: B'min 6H 33
  TR14: Camb 1F 119
Normans Way PL30: S Tud 4J 27
NORRIS GREEN 5D 74
North Cliff TR19: Mou 6D 154
North Cl. EX23: Kilkh 1G 7
NORTH CORNER 5D 162
North Cnr. TR12: Cover 5D 162
  TR16: S Da 2A 114
  (off Telegraph Hill)
  TR18: Newl 1C 154
North Cornwall Mus. 3H 15
NORTHCOTT 1D 167
Northcott Mouth Rd. EX23: Pou 1E 8
NORTH COUNTRY 7C 102
North Cross PL1: Plym 2G 163
NORTH DIMSON 1F 75
North Downs TR16: Scor 5J 103
North East Quay PL4: Plym 5K 163
Northey Cl. TR4: Short 6C 98
Northey Rd. PL31: B'min 4F 33
Northfield Cl. TR16: S Da 2A 114
Northfield Dr. TR1: Tru 6K 107
Northgate Pl. PL15: Laun 3H 17
  (off Tower St.)
Northgate St. PL15: Laun 3H 17
  (off Castle St.)
Nth. Grange Ind. Est. TR3: Devo 1C 124
NORTH HILL 3C 167
North Hill PL4: Plym 2J 163
  TR4: Black 2A 104
  TR4: Chac 5D 104
  TR16: Carh 4A 114
North Hill Pk. PL25: S Aus 5G 57
North Pde. TR2: P'stho 3K 131
  TR11: Fal 6D 128
  TR14: Camb 7D 110
  TR18: Penz 5F 149
North Pde. Rear TR14: Camb 7D 110
North Pk. Vs. PL12: Salt 1E 88
NORTH PETHERWIN 2C 167
North Pier 1C 154
North Pier TR18: Newl 1C 154
North Pl. TR26: S Ives 1J 137
North Pool Cl. TR15: I Hig 3J 111
North Pool Rd. TR15: I Hig 3J 111
North Quay PL4: Plym 5K 163
  PL28: Pad 2B 22
  TR27: Hayl 1F 141
North Quay Hill TR7: Newq 2E 34
North Quay Pde. PL28: Pad 2C 22
North Rd. PL11: Tor 4K 93
  PL12: Land 6G 83
  PL12: Salt 2H 89
  PL13: Loo 6J 81 (4G 81)
  PL26: Pent 1D 134
  PL26: W'moor 3J 47
  PL30: S Teat 2B 26
  TR14: Camb 7E 110
  TR16: L'ner 7G 113
  TR20: Gold 4A 152
North Rd. E. PL4: Plym 2G 163
North Rd. W. PL1: Plym 2F 163
North Roskear Mdw. TR14: Camb 5E 110
North Roskear Rd. TR14: Camb 6E 110
North Row TR19: S Jus 2J 145
North Shore TR7: Newq 3G 35
North Sillaton PL12: S Mel 1B 84
North St. PL4: Plym 4K 163
  (not continuous)
  PL15: Laun 1F 17
  PL22: Los 3E 52
  PL23: Fow 7K 61
  PL24: Tyw 2A 60
  PL25: S Aus 5G 57
  TR9: S Maj 4C 30
  TR15: Red 2D 112
  TR17: Mar 4E 150
  TR19: Mou 6D 154
NORTH TAMERTON 1D 167
North Ter. PL26: W'moor 2J 47
  TR26: S Ives 3H 137
NORTH TREVIDDO 2F 79
Northumberland Ter. PL1: Plym 7F 163
North Vw. PL13: Loo 4H 81
North Way TR8: Q Dow 6C 36
Norton Hill TR18: Penz 6E 148
Norton Ter. TR18: Penz 6F 149
  (off Bay Vw. Ter.)
Norway La. TR26: S Ives 1J 137
  (off Back Rd. W.)

Norway Sq. TR26: S Ives 1J 137
NOSS MAYO 3D 171
NOTTER 5K 83
NOTTER BRIDGE 6J 83
Notter Bri. Pk. PL12: Nott 6K 83
Notter Mill Country Holiday Pk. PL12: Nott 5J 83
Notte St. PL1: Plym 6G 163
Nottingham Gdns. PL4: Plym 1K 163
Noweth Pl. TR11: Fal 7C 128
Nunnery Hill PL26: S Ewe 7B 64
Nurseries, The TR11: Fal 7B 128
Nursery Cl. TR24: Tyw 2A 60
  TR1: Tru 4K 107
Nut La. TR27: L Dow 4D 140
Nut Tree Hill PL12: S Ger 5E 86

O

Oak Apple Cl. PL12: Salt 1F 89
Oak Av. PL12: S Mel 5B 76
Oakdene Vs. TR9: Fr'don 3G 45
Oak Dr. PL14: Lisk 5A 70
Oakey Orchard PL17: Meth 6C 74
Oakfield Rd. TR11: Fal 7C 128
Oakland M. TR18: Penz 4F 149
Oakland Pk. TR11: Fal 7B 128
Oaklands Dr. PL12: Salt 2E 88
Oaklands Grn. PL12: Salt 2F 89
Oaklands Ind. Est. PL14: Lisk 4D 70
Oaklands Rd. PL14: Lisk 4D 70
Oak La. TR1: Trel 4C 106
Oakleigh Ter. TR7: Newq 3G 35
Oakleigh Vs. TR8: Sum 6D 44
Oak Pk. PL30: S Tud 4J 27
Oak Pk. Ter. PL14: Lisk 4A 70
Oakridge PL2: S Mel 7B 76
Oaks, The PL24: Par 4J 59
  PL25: S Aus 6F 57
  TR8: Q Dow 6C 36
Oak Ter. PL28: Pad 2C 22
Oak Tree Cl. PL25: S Aus 6B 58
Oak Vale TR2: Gram 7B 62
Oak Vs. TR10: M Bur 7E 126
Oak Way TR1: Tru 4J 107
Oakwood Pk. PL31: B'min 4H 33
Oakwood Ri. PL32: Came 2K 15
Oasis Fun Pool 6K 35
Oates Rd. TR13: Helst 3C 158
  TR17: Mar 4F 151
Observer Cl. TR1: Tru 6J 107
Ocean 1 TR7: Newq 3C 34
Ocean Blue Apartments PL28: Trey 5A 20
Ocean Bowl 2H 133
Ocean Ct. TR4: P'twn 5C 96
Ocean Cove Holiday Pk. PL34: Boss 5C 12
Ocean Cres. TR13: P'ven 6A 156
Oceangate Apartments TR7: Newq 3C 34
Ocean Vw. PL23: Polr 7C 60
  PL25: S Aus 2J 57
  TR7: Newq 4C 34
  TR9: I Que 2H 45
  TR13: P'ven 7F 157
Ocean Vw. Rd. EX23: Flex 3C 8
Ocean Vw. Ter. TR26: S Ives 2G 137 (2C 136)
Officers Mess, The PL10: Mt Ed 3J 95
Okehampton Rd. PL15: Laun 3H 17
Okeltor Wildlife Reserve 7K 75
Old Barn Ct. TR7: Newq 5E 34
Old Barracks, The TR11: Fal 7F 129
  (off The Packet Quays)
Old Boat Yd. PL28: Pad 2C 22
Old Brewery St. TR18: Penz 5F 149
Old Brewery Yd. TR11: Fal 7F 129
Old Bridge St. TR1: Tru 5K 107
Old Cable La. TR19: P'cno 6G 147
Old Callywith Rd. PL31: B'min 2J 33
Old Canal Cl. EX23: March 3F 11
Old Carnon Hill TR3: C Dow 1B 124
Old Chapel Way TR14: M'brk 1D 94
Old Church, The TR18: Penz 6E 148
  (off Mennaye Rd.)
Old Church Rd. TR11: Mawn S 3C 160
Old Coach Rd. PL30: Lani 7F 31
  TR3: P Pla 4G 117
Old Corn Mill, The TR12: Gweek 7G 159
Old Drovers Way EX23: Stra 5H 9
Olde Market Ct. PL27: Wade 4E 24
Old Falmouth Rd. TR1: Tru 1J 117
  TR3: Cale 1J 117
Old Farm Caravan & Camping Site, The TR20: Pra S 5G 155
Old Ferry Rd. PL12: Salt 2H 89
Old Foundry TR19: S Jus 1G 145
Old Foundry Cl. TR19: S Jus 2J 145
Old George St. PL1: Plym 5G 163
Old Grammar School, The TR15: Red 4C 112
Old Grammar School Ct. PL22: Los 3E 52
  (off Shute Hill)

Old Hill TR2: Gram 7A 62
  TR11: Fal 6D 128
  TR13: Helst 3A 158
Old Hill Cres. TR11: Fal 6D 128
OLD KEA 3B 168
Old Kerrow Farm Holiday Pk.
  PL26: Sten 3H 49
Old La. PL26: Roch 4B 42
Old Lawn School La. PL25: S Aus 6F 57
Old MacDonald's Farm 3C 165
Old Market Pl. PL31: B'min 4E 32
OLD MILL 3D 167
Old Mill Herbary 3A 166
Old Mill La. TR14: P'nds 2A 118
Old Mine La. PL18: S An Cpl 2D 74
Old Nursery Cl. TR13: P'ven 6F 157
Old Orchard PL22: Los 3E 52
Old Orchard Cl. EX23: March 3G 11
Old Paul Hill TR18: Newl 7D 148
Old Pilchard Works, The TR18: Newl 7D 148
  (off Creeping La.)
Old Pond La. TR15: Red 3C 112
  (off Treleigh Ter.)
Old Portreath Rd. TR15: Red 7B 102
  TR16: Brid, Red 5K 101
Old Post Office Hill EX23: Stra 5H 9
Old Pound PL26: Nanp 6H 47
Old Quay La. PL12: S Ger 5E 86
Old Railway Yd. PL12: S Ger 6E 86
Old Rectory Dr. TR9: S Maj 4C 30
Old Rectory Mews Residential Homes Pk.
  TR9: S Maj 4B 30
Old Rd. PL14: Lisk, Moo 5J 69
  PL26: Mev 3C 134
  PL35: Bosc 2K 13
Old Roselyon Cres. PL24: S Bla 3H 59
Old Roselyon Rd. PL24: S Bla 3H 59
Old Sandy La. TR16: Red 6F 113
Old School Cl. TR27: Tred 7H 19
Old School Ct. TR27: Wade 4E 24
  PL28: Pad 3B 22
Old Smithy Cl. TR17: Mar 4G 151
Old Station La. TR17: Mar 3C 150
Old Station Rd. PL14: Moo 5J 69
Old Town St. PL1: Plym 4H 163
Old Tram Rd. TR3: Devo 2D 124
Old Vicarage, The TR3: Stith 6A 122
Old Vicarage Cl. TR3: Stith 6A 122
Old Vicarage Pl. PL25: S Aus 6G 57
  (not continuous)
Old Well Gdns. TR10: P'ryn 4A 128
Old Workhouses, The TR16: Red 7D 102
Oliver Ct. PL12: S Mel 5B 76
  PL14: Dob 3D 68
Olivers Quay PL26: Mev 6D 134
  (off Middle Wharf)
Oliver's Ter. TR13: Helst 4C 158
Olivey Pl. TR11: M Bri 7E 124
Omaha Rd. PL31: B'min 5H 33
Omil Ct. PL27: Wade 4E 24
  (off Polmorla Rd.)
Ope's Ct. TR11: Fal 7F 129
Opies La. PL31: B'min 3E 32
Opie's Row TR16: Four L 3C 120
  (Niles Ter.)
  TR16: Four L 4B 120
  (The Lane)
Opie's Ter. TR16: Four L 4B 120
Orange La. TR26: S Ives 2G 137 (2C 136)
Orchard, The PL18: Gun 1H 75
  TR27: S Er 6E 140
Orchard Cl. EX23: Pou 2F 9
  PL12: S Mel 6B 76
  PL12: Tide 1B 86
  PL25: S Aus 5J 57
  TR1: Tru 5F 107
  TR13: Helst 2B 158
  TR14: Barr 4B 118
Orchard Ct. TR18: Penz 5D 148
Orchard Gro. PL25: S Aus 5F 57
Orchard La. TR12: Helf 4A 160
Orchard Pk. PL26: Bugl 6G 43
  (not continuous)
Orchard Pl. TR18: Newl 1C 154
Orchard Ter. TR18: Newl 1C 154
Orchard Va. TR11: Flu 5G 129
Orchard Wlk. PL27: Wade 4E 24
  (off Trevanson St.)
Orchard Way PL26: Dup 7A 58
  TR20: Gold 4A 152
Orford Ho. TR1: Tru 5K 107
Orion Dr. PL27: S Eval 3H 31
Osborne Parc TR13: Helst 3B 158
Osborne Pl. PL1: Plym 7G 163
OTTERHAM 1B 166
Overcliff PL29: P Isa 1J 19
Owen Sivell Cl. PL14: Lisk 4D 70
Oxford Pl. PL1: Plym 3G 163
Oxford St. PL1: Plym 3G 163

Oxford Ter. PL1: Plym 3F **163**
Oxland Rd. TR16: I'gan 7J **101**
Oxley Va. TR7: Newq 4J **35**
Ozzell Bowl 5G **57**

P

Paardeberg Rd. PL31: B'min 6J **33**
Packet La. TR20: Rosu 6C **152**
Packet Quays, The TR11: Fal 7F **129**
Packsaddle TR10: P'ryn 3J **127**
Packsaddle Cl. TR10: P'ryn 3J **127**
Paddock, The PL26: Stick 3J **63**
  TR13: Helst 2C **158**
  TR15: Red 5F **113**
Paddock Cl. PL12: Salt 1F **89**
PADSTOW 3B **22** (3D **165**)
Padstow Harbour Ind. Est. PL28: Pad 3C **22**
Padstow Holiday Pk. PL28: Pad 6K **21**
Padstow Mus. 3B **22**
  (in Library, off Market Pl.)
Padstow Touring Pk. PL28: Pad 6A **22**
PAGE'S CROSS 5J **17**
Pagoda Dr. PL26: Dup 7A **58**
Palace Rd. PL25: S Aus 5H **57**
Palace St. PL1: Plym 5H **163**
Palace Yd. TR26: S Ives 3H **137**
Palm Ct. TR1: Tru 6K **107**
  (off David Penhaligon Way)
Palmers Way PL27: Wade 3G **25**
PANCRASWEEK 3A **164**
Pannier La. TR26: C Bay 6E **136**
PAR .4J **59** (2D **169**)
Parade PL1: Plym 6J **163**
Parade, The PL10: M'brk 2C **94**
  PL14: Lisk 4B **70**
  PL22: Los 3F **53**
  TR1: Tru 5A **108**
  TR13: Helst 4C **158**
  TR19: Mou 5E **154**
Parade Hill TR19: Mou 6D **154**
Parade Ope PL1: Plym 6J **163**
Parade Pas. TR18: Penz 5F **149**
  (off Parade St.)
Parade Sq. PL22: Los 3F **53**
  (off The Parade)
Parade St. TR18: Penz 5F **149**
Paradise Pk. Wildlife Sanctuary 3F **141**
Paradise Rd. PL35: Bosc 3K **13**
PARAMOOR 5J **63**
PAR BEACH 4A **60**
Parbola Holiday Pk. TR27: Reaw 2E **142**
Parc Abnac TR20: Mad 1A **148**
Parc-an-Bal Ct. TR14: Camb 6E **110**
Parc-an-Bre Dr. PL26: S Den 2E **46**
Parc-an-Cady Est. TR19: St Bury 2G **147**
Parc-an-Challow TR10: P'ryn 4K **127**
Parc-an-Creet TR26: S Ives 3B **136**
Parc-an-Dillon Rd. TR2: P'stho 2J **131**
Parc-an-Dix La. TR27: Phil 7C **138**
Parc-an-Dower TR13: Helst 4C **158**
Parcandowr TR2: Gram R 6K **37**
Parc an Forth TR26: S Ives 4B **136**
Parc an Ga. TR19: Mou 5D **154**
Parc an Gew TR13: Helst 1C **158**
Parc an Gonwyn TR26: C Bay 7G **137**
PARC AN GROWES 4A **148**
Parc-an-Ithan TR12: Lizar 5G **161**
Parc-an-Maen TR13: P'ven 7G **157**
Parc an Manns TR11: Mawn S 3B **160**
Parc-an-Peath TR19: St Bury 2G **147**
Parc an Stamps TR26: S Ives 4B **136**
Parc an Yorth TR19: Trew 5B **144**
Parc Bean TR26: S Ives 2G **137**
Parc Behan Ct. TR2: V Grn 5J **135**
Parc Bottom TR12: Gweek 6G **159**
Parcbracket St. TR14: Camb 7E **110**
Parc Brawse TR12: Lizar 6G **161**
Parc Briwer TR10: P'ryn 5B **128**
Parc Dellen PL30: Lux 3C **50**
Parc Eglos PL28: S Mer 6E **20**
  TR13: Helst 3B **158**
PARC ERISSEY 5C **102**
Parc Fer Cl. EX23: Stra 5H **9**
Parc Godrevy TR7: Newq 4D **34**
Parc Holland TR13: Helst 1D **158**
Parc Ledden TR13: Helst 3C **158**
Parc Ledrak TR13: Helst 1B **158**
Parc Letta TR18: Hea 3D **148**
Parc Mellan TR18: Hea 3E **148**
Parc Merys TR2: P'stho 3K **131**
Parc Monga TR11: Const 3H **159**
Parc Monga Dr. TR11: Const 3H **159**
Parc Morrep TR20: Pra S 6H **155**
Parc Owles TR26: C Bay 6F **137**
Parc Peneglos TR11: M Bri 7E **124**
Parc Rowan TR9: Fr'don 4H **45**
Parc Stephney TR11: B Wat 3A **132**

Parc Ter. TR18: Newl 2C **154**
  (off Chywoone Hill)
Parc Vean PL30: Nans 4A **32**
  TR15: Red 4C **112**
Parc Venton Cl. TR14: Camb 1F **119**
Parc Wartha Av. TR18: Penz 4E **148**
Parc Wartha Cres. TR18: Penz 4E **148**
Pargolla Rd. TR7: Newq 3G **35**
Par Grn. TR24: Par 3K **59**
Par Harbour PL24: Par 5K **59**
Park, The TR2: Tregon 5H **99**
  TR10: P'ryn 4K **127**
Parka Cl. TR9: S Roa 1G **45**
  (off Parka Rd.)
Park-an-Bans TR14: Camb 2E **118**
Parkancreeg TR3: C Dow 7D **116**
Park & Float
  Ponsharden 6D **128**
Park an Dreas TR2: Very 6H **135**
Park & Ride
  Eden Project 7D **50**
  Ponsharden 6D **128**
  St Ives 4G **137** (3C **136**)
  Truro 4K **105**
Park an Gorsaf TR14: Camb 1D **118**
Park-an-Gwarry TR3: C Dow 6D **116**
Park-an-Harvey TR13: Helst 2C **158**
Park-an-Mengleth TR15: Red 4E **112**
Park-an-Pyth TR19: Pend 3C **144**
Park-an-Tansys TR14: Camb 1F **119**
Parka Rd. TR9: Fr'don, S Roa, T'ren 1G **45**
  TR9: S Roa 1G **45**
Park Av. TR26: S Ives 3G **137** (3C **136**)
PARK BOTTOM 2H **111** (3A **168**)
Park Cl. TR15: P Bot 2H **111**
Park Cnr. TR18: Penz 5F **149**
Park Cres. TR3: Pons 5F **123**
  TR11: Fal 1E **132**
  TR13: Helst 4B **158**
Park Dr. PL31: B'min 4D **32**
  TR11: Fal 1E **132**
Parkenbutts TR7: S Mino 2A **36**
Parkengear Vean TR2: Pro 3J **99**
  (not continuous)
Parkenhead La. PL28: T'one 3G **21**
Park Enskellaw TR12: Mull 1G **161**
Parken Venton TR12: Mull 1H **161**
Park Erissey Ind. Est. TR16: Red 6C **102**
Parkers Grn. PL18: Gun 1G **75**
Parkesway PL12: Salt 3F **89**
Park Fenton PL14: Lisk 5C **70**
PARKFIELD 1C **171**
Park Gwyn PL26: S Ste 4C **54**
PARKHAM 1B **164**
PARKHAM ASH 1B **164**
Park Hill TR11: Fal 1E **132**
Park Holly TR14: Camb 1A **118**
Park Ho. PL25: S Aus 6F **57**
Parkins Ter. TR1: Tru 4K **107**
Parkland Cl. TR7: S Mino 3A **36**
Parklands PL26: Nanp 4D **54**
  TR5: S Agn 2B **96**
Park La. PL26: Bugl 7G **43**
  TR11: Fal 1E **132**
  TR14: Camb 1E **118**
Park Leven TR16: I'gan 2J **111**
Park Lowen TR26: C Bay 6E **136**
Parknoweth Cl. TR8: S New E 3G **37**
Park Pennkarn PL33: Dela 2B **14**
Park Pl. PL27: Wade 4E **24**
  TR2: Gram R 6K **37**
Park Ri. PL11: Fal 7E **128**
Park Rd. PL11: Tor 3K **93**
  PL12: S Dom 2G **77**
  PL14: Lisk 4B **70**
  PL22: Los 3E **52**
  PL23: Fow 7J **61**
  PL25: S Aus 6G **57**
  PL26: W'moor .3H **47**
  PL27: Wade 4E **24**
  TR3: Pons 5E **122**
  TR14: Camb 7E **110**
  TR15: P Bot 3H **111**
  TR15: Red 4E **112**
  TR18: Newl 2C **154**
Parkryn Rd. TR19: Mou 5E **154**
Park Stenak TR16: Carh 4A **114**
Park Ter. PL4: Plym 4K **163**
  PL13: Loo 5G **81**
  TR11: Fal 1E **132**
Parkvedras Ter. TR1: Tru 5H **107**
Parkventon PL26: Bugl 6H **43**
Park Vw. PL14: Lisk 4B **70**
  PL15: Laun 4H **17**
  TR1: Tru 6J **107**
  TR14: Camb 6D **110**
  TR27: Hayl 7E **138**
Park Vw. Cl. TR3: C Dow 7E **116**

Park Vw. Rd. TR13: Helst 4B **158**
Park Vw. Ter. PL27: Wade 4E **24**
Park Vs. TR3: Pons 5F **123**
Parkway PL25: S Aus 5K **57**
Park Wise TR10: P'ryn 5A **128**
Parkwoon Cl. PL26: Roch 4B **42**
Par La. PL24: Par 3H **59**
Par Moor Rd. PL24: B'vey, Par 4E **58**
  PL25: S Aus 4E **58**
Parnell Ct. PL28: Pad 3B **22**
  (off Mill Rd.)
Par Sands Holiday Pk. PL24: Par 4A **60**
Parsons Ct. PL10: M'bank 1D **94**
Parsons Grn. PL17: K Bray 1C **72**
Par Station (Rail) 2K **59**
Par Track 3K **59**
Pascoe Cl. TR3: Thre 4A **106**
Pasmore Rd. TR13: Helst 3D **158**
Passage Hill TR11: M Bri 1F **129**
Passage La. PL23: Fow 6G **61**
Passage St. PL23: Fow 6K **61**
Passmore Cl. PL14: Lisk 4C **70**
  TR4: Black 2B **104**
Passmore Edwards Ct. PL14: Lisk 4A **70**
Pastimes TR16: L'ner 1H **121**
  (off Lanner Hill)
Paternus Cl. PL15: Sth P 2A **16**
Path Flds. PL11: S John 6E **92**
Pathfields EX23: Bud 5C **8**
  PL14: S Cle 4A **66**
Pathway Flds., The TR27: Hayl 2H **141**
Patna Pl. PL1: Plym 2F **163**
Paton Watson Quadrate PL1: Plym 7J **163**
Pato Point PL11: Wilc 7J **89**
PAUL 4C **154** (2B **172**)
Paul Corin's Magnificent Music Machines 1B **170**
Paull Rd. PL31: B'min 4D **32**
Paulls Row TR15: Red 3E **112**
  (off Jenkins La.)
Paul's Row TR1: Tru 4K **107**
Paul's Ter. TR1: Tru 4K **107**
Pavilion, The PL27: Rock 2G **23**
Pavilion Pk. TR14: Camb 6F **111**
Pavilion Ri. PL26: Dup 7A **58**
Pavilion Wlk. PL26: Dup 7A **58**
Pavillion, The PL11: Seat 6G **79**
Pavlova Cl. PL14: Lisk 5B **70**
Pavlova Ct. PL14: Lisk 5B **70**
PAWL 4C **154**
Paynters La. TR16: I'gan 1J **111**
PAYNTER'S LANE END 7J **101**
Paynter's La. End Est. TR16: I'gan 1H **111**
Peacock Av. PL11: Tor 3J **93**
Peacock La. PL1: Plym 5J **163**
Pearce's Ct. TR26: S Ives 3H **137**
Pearce's La. TR26: S Ives 3C **136**
Pearces Row PL24: Par 3K **59**
Pearl TR7: Newq .2D **34**
PEDNA-CARNE 4H **45**
Pednandrea TR15: Red 4E **112**
  TR19: S Jus 2H **145**
PEDNAVOUNDER 7A **162**
Pedn-Moran TR2: S Mawe 7E **130**
Pednolva Wlk. TR26: S Ives 2J **137** (3D **136**)
Pednolver Ter. TR26: S Ives 3J **137**
Peguarra Cl. PL28: S Mer 5E **20**
Peguarra Ct. PL28: S Mer 5E **20**
PELEAN CROSS 3F **123**
Pellew Cl. PL28: Pad 3A **22**
  TR11: Fal 7E **128**
Pellew Cres. TR13: Helst 4C **158**
Pellew Rd. TR11: Fal 7E **128**
Pellor Flds. TR13: Breag 1D **156**
Pellor Rd. TR13: Breag 1D **156**
PELYNT 2C **80** (2B **170**)
Pembroke Cl. PL24: Par 4J **59**
Pembroke Rd. TR7: S Mino 2B **36**
Pemros Rd. PL5: Plym 3K **89**
Penair Cres. TR1: Tru 3B **108**
Penair Vw. TR1: Tru 4B **108**
Penally Ct. PL35: Bosc 1K **13**
Penally Hill PL35: Bosc 1K **13**
Penally Ter. PL35: Bosc 1K **13**
Penalverne Av. TR18: Penz 5E **148**
Penalverne Cres. TR18: Penz 5E **148**
Penalverne Dr. TR18: Penz 4E **148**
Penalverne Pl. TR18: Penz 5E **148**
Penameyne Ct. TR26: S Ives 1J **137**
Pen an Gwel TR26: S Ives 4C **136**
PENARE 3C **169**
Penare Gdns. TR18: Penz 4F **149**
  (off Penare Rd.)
Penare Rd. TR18: Penz 4F **149**
Penare Ter. TR18: Penz 5F **149**
Penarrow Cl. TR11: Fal 3C **132**
Penarrow Rd. TR11: M Chu 4G **129**
Penarth PL13: Loo 5F **81**
Penarth Rd. TR11: Fal 7E **128**
Penarwyn Cres. TR18: Hea 3C **148**

Penarwyn Rd.—Pensilva

Penarwyn Rd. PL24: S Bla 3G 59
Penarwyn Woods PL24: S Bla 3H 59
PENBEAGLE 4B 136 (1C 173)
Penbeagle Cl. TR26: S Ives 4B 136
Penbeagle Cres. TR26: S Ives 4B 136
Penbeagle Ind. Est. TR26: S Ives 5B 136
Penbeagle La. TR26: S Ives 4B 136
Penbeagle Ter. *TR26: S Ives* *4B 136*
(off Penbeagle Way)
Penbeagle Vean *TR26: S Ives* *4B 136*
(off Penbeagle Way)
Penbeagle Way TR26: S Ives 4B 136
PENBERTH 6K 147 (2B 172)
PENBERTH VALLEY 5K 147
Penberthy Rd. TR13: Helst 4C 158
TR16: Brid, P'ath 4F 101
Penbothidno TR11: Const 3H 159
Pen Brea TR2: S Mawe 6D 130
Penbrea Rd. TR18: Penz 3F 149
Penbugle La. PL31: B'min 1G 33
Pencair Av. PL11: Tor 4G 93
Pencantol TR4: Cusg 7G 115
Pencarn Parc TR16: Four L 3B 120
Pencarrick Cl. TR1: Tru 3H 107
PENCARROW 5J 15 (2B 166)
Pencarrow 3A 166
Pencarrow Cl. PL17: Call 7C 72
Pencarrow Rd. TR16: I'gan 1J 111
Pencavo Hill PL12: Land 7D 82
PENCOYS 4B 120
Pencrebar La. PL17: Call 7B 72
Pendale Sq. TR1: Tru 5H 107
Pendarves TR2: Tr'sln 2G 109
Pendarves Flats TR18: Penz 4E 148
Pendarves Ho. *TR14: Camb* *5E 110*
(off Vyvyans Ct.)
Pendarves Rd. TR1: Tru 3J 107
TR11: Fal 6D 128
TR14: Camb 2C 118
TR18: Penz 4E 148
Pendarves St. TR14: Bea 2F 119
TR14: Camb 6F 111
(not continuous)
TR14: Tro 5G 119
Pendarves St. Rear of *TR14: Camb* *6F 111*
(off Pendarves St.)
Pendarves Vw. TR14: Camb 2C 118
Pendean Av. PL14: Lisk 4A 70
Pendean Cl. PL14: Lisk 4A 70
Pendean Ct. PL14: Lisk 4A 70
Pendean Dr. PL14: Lisk 4A 70
PENDEEN 4C 144 (1A 172)
Pendeen Cl. TR3: Thre 5A 106
Pendeen Cres. TR3: Thre 5A 106
Pendeen Mining Mus. 4C 144
Pendeen Parc TR13: Helst 1C 158
Pendeen Pk. TR13: Helst 1B 158
Pendeen Rd. TR1: Tru 6A 108
TR3: Thre 5A 106
TR13: P'ven 6G 157
Pendennis Castle 3J 133
Pendennis Cl. PL11: Tor 3H 93
TR18: Penz 3F 149
Pendennis Ct. TR11: Fal 2H 133
Pendennis Pl. TR18: Penz 3G 149
Pendennis Ri. TR11: Fal 2H 133
Pendennis Rd. PL13: Loo 3H 81
TR11: Fal 2H 133
TR18: Penz 3F 149
Pender's La. TR15: Red 3D 112
Pendilly Av. PL11: Tor 4H 93
Pendilly Dr. PL25: S Aus 2J 57
Pendinnis Gdns. PL15: Laun 1G 17
PENDOGGETT 3A 166
Pendour Pk. PL22: Los 3G 53
Pendower Beach 1B 174
Pendower Ho. *TR2: Tregon* *6J 99*
(off Roseland Parc)
Pendower Rd. PL13: Loo 4J 81
TR2: Very 6H 135
Pendower Ter. TR14: Camb 2E 118
Pendragon Cres. TR7: Newq 6H 35
Pendragon Rd. PL14: Lisk 5C 70
Pendra Loweth TR11: Fal 4B 132
Pendray Gdns. PL14: Dob 4D 68
Pendrea Cl. TR18: Gul 3G 149
Pendrea Pk. TR14: Camb 5F 111
Pendrea Pl. TR18: Gul 3G 149
Pendrea Rd. TR18: Gul 3G 149
Pendrea Wood TR1: Tru 5F 107
Pendrim Pk. PL13: Loo 4H 81
Pendrim Rd. PL13: Loo 4H 81
Pendruccombe Ct. PL15: Laun 5J 17
Pendruccombe Gdns. PL15: Laun 4J 17
PENELEWEY 7H 117 (3B 168)
Penellen TR27: Phil 6B 138
Pen Enys Ter. *TR26: S Ives* *2C 136*
(off Alexandra Rd.)
Penforth TR14: Camb 1E 118
Penfound Gdns. EX23: Bud 5E 8
Penganne1 Cl. TR7: Newq 5E 34
Pengarth Cl. TR1: Tru 6J 107
Pengarth Ri. TR11: Fal 2E 132
Pengarth Rd. TR5: S Agn 2B 96
TR11: Fal 2E 132
Pengegon Moor TR14: Camb 1F 119
Pengegon Parc TR14: Camb 1F 119
Pengegon Way TR14: Camb 1F 119
PENGELLY 3B 14 (2A 166)
Pengelly PL17: Call 5D 72
PL33: Dela 3A 14
Pengelly Cl. PL11: Wilc 1H 93
Pengelly Hill PL11: Wilc 1H 93
Pengelly La. PL17: Call 4D 72
Pengelly Pk. PL11: Wilc 1H 93
Pengelly Pl. TR11: Fal 7C 128
Pengellys Row TR14: Camb 5G 111
Pengelly Way TR3: Thre 5A 106
Pengeron Av. TR14: Tol D 3F 111
Pengersick Cft. TR20: Pra S 5J 155
Pengersick Est. TR20: Pra S 5J 155
Pengersick La. TR20: Ger, Pra S 6J 155
Pengersick Parc TR20: Pra S 6J 155
Pengover Cl. PL14: Lisk 4C 70
PENGOVER GREEN 3G 71 (1B 170)
Pengover Hgts. PL14: Lisk 4C 70
Pengover Parc TR15: Red 2E 112
Pengover Pk. PL14: Lisk 4C 70
Pengover Rd. PL14: Lisk 4C 70
Pengrowyn PL26: Penw 5J 49
Pengwarras Rd. TR14: Camb 7C 110
Pengwel TR18: Newl 1C 154
PENHALE
Helston 3D 173
St Columb 5F 45 (2C 169)
Torpoint 7F 93
Penhale *TR6: P'rth* *4B 40*
(off Atlantic Bay)
PENHALE CAMP 3A 38 (2A 168)
Penhale Caravan & Camping Pk. PL23: Fow 5E 60
Penhale Cl. PL14: S Cle 4A 66
Penhale Est. TR15: Red 2D 112
Penhale Gdns. TR9: P'ale 5F 45
PENHALE JAKES 2B 156
Penhale Mdw. PL14: S Cle 4A 66
Penhale Rd. PL26: Penw 6J 49
TR11: Fal 4D 132
TR14: Barr, C Grn 1F 143 & 5A 118
Penhaligon Cl. TR15: Red 4F 113
Penhaligon Ct. TR1: Tru 4A 108
Penhaligon Way PL25: S Aus 4K 57
Penhallam Manor 1C 167
PENHALLICK
Helston 5A 162
Redruth 6J 111
Penhallick Rd. TR15: Bosl, C Bre 6J 111
Penhallick Row TR15: C Bre 6J 111
Penhall La. TR4: Mt Hwk 6H 97
PENHALLOW 2A 168
Penhallow TR15: I'gan 2H 111
Penhallow Cl. TR4: Mt Hwk 6H 97
Penhallow Parc PL33: Dela 3A 14
Penhallow Rd. TR7: Newq 2K 35
Penhalls Way TR3: P Pla 4G 117
PENHALURICK 4F 121
PENHALVEAN 5G 121 (1A 174)
Penharget Cl. PL14: Pens 1J 67
Penhaven Cl. TR8: S New E 2G 37
Penhaven Ct. TR7: Newq 3F 35
Penhaven Touring Pk. PL26: Pent 7F 65
Penhellaz Hill TR13: Helst 3B 158
Penhellaz Rd. *TR13: Helst* *3B 158*
(off Almshouse Hill)
Penina Av. TR7: Newq 5G 35
Penjerrick Garden 5A 132
Penjerrick Hill TR11: B Wat 5A 132
Penkernick Cl. TR18: Newl 2B 154
Penkernick Way TR9: S Maj 5C 30
Penkneck Ter. *PL22: Los* *3E 52*
(off Tanhouse Rd.)
Penknight La. PL22: Los 3C 52
Penlean Cl. TR15: Red 1F 113
Penlea Rd. TR10: P'ryn 4K 127
Penlee Caravan Pk. TR19: Mou 5E 154
Penlee Cl. PL17: Call 5D 72
TR2: Tregon 5J 99
TR20: Pra S 5J 155
Penlee Cotts. PL10: Caws 7F 95
Penlee House Mus. 5F 149
Penlee Mnr. Dr. TR18: Penz 6F 149
Penlee Pk. PL11: Tor 2G 93
TR18: Penz 5E 148
Penlee St. TR18: Penz 4F 149
Penlee Vw. Ter. TR18: Penz 6E 148
Penlee Vs. TR3: P Pla 4G 117
Penlu TR14: Camb 5F 111
Penluke Cl. TR16: Four L 3B 120
Penmare Cl. TR27: Hayl 7E 138
Penmare Ct. TR27: Hayl 7E 138
Penmare Ter. TR27: Hayl 7E 138
PENMARTH 1A 174
Penmarth Farm Caravan & Camping Site
TR12: Cover 6C 162
PENMAYNE 1H 23
Penmayne Parc TR16: L'ner 7H 113
Penmayne Vs. PL27: Rock 1H 23
Penmead Cl. PL33: Dela 3B 14
Penmead Rd. PL33: Dela 3B 14
Penmelen PL32: Came 3H 15
Penmellyn Gdns. TR9: S Maj 4C 30
Penmenner Est. TR12: S Kev 2B 162
Penmenner Rd. TR12: Lizar 6G 161
Penmere Cl. TR13: Helst 2B 158
TR18: Penz 3F 149
Penmere Ct. TR11: Fal 2E 132
Penmere Cres. TR11: Fal 2D 132
Penmere Dr. TR7: Newq 4C 34
Penmere Hill TR11: Fal 2D 132
Penmere Pl. TR11: Fal 2D 132
TR18: Penz 3F 149
Penmere Rd. PL25: S Aus 5A 58
TR18: Penz 3F 149
Penmere Station (Rail) 2D 132
Penmerrin Ct. TR7: Newq 4F 35
Penmeva Vw. PL26: Mev 6C 134
Penmorvah TR11: M Bri 2E 128
Penmorvah Pl. TR14: Camb 1E 118
Penmorvah Rd. TR1: Tru 3A 108
Penmount Crematorium TR4: Tru 1A 108
Penmur Rd. *TR7: Newq* *4F 35*
(off Trenance Rd.)
Pennance Hill TR11: Fal 5C 132
Pennance La. TR16: L'ner 7H 113
Pennance Parc TR16: L'ner 7H 113
Pennance Rd. TR11: Fal 4E 132
TR16: Carh, L'ner, T'rth 7G 113
Pennance Ter. PL15: Laun 4H 17
TR16: L'ner 7H 113
Penn an Drea TR13: Helst 1D 158
Penn Kernow PL15: Laun 5K 17
Pennor Dr. PL25: S Aus 6H 57
PENNRYNN 5K 127
PENNSANS 4G 149
PENNTORR 3K 93
PENNYCOMEQUICK 1F 163
Pennycomequick Hill PL3: Plym 1F 163
Pennycomequick Vs. PL4: Plym 1F 163
PENNYCROSS 2D 171
Pennygillam PL15: Laun 5G 17
Pennygillam Ind. Est. PL15: Laun 6E 16
Pennygillam Way PL15: Laun 5D 16
Penny La. EX23: Flex 3D 8
Pennys La. PL24: S Bl G 4F 59
Penoweth TR11: M Bri 2E 128
PENPILLICK 5K 51 (2D 169)
PENPOL
Newquay 5C 34
Truro 2G 125 (1B 174)
Penpol Av. TR27: Hayl 2H 141
Penpol Hill TR3: Devo 2G 125
TR8: Cran 5C 34
PENPOLL 2A 170
Penpol Rd. TR27: Hayl 2G 141
Penpol Ter. TR27: Hayl 2G 141
Penpol Vean TR27: Hayl 2H 141
PENPONDS 2B 118 (1D 173)
Penponds Rd. TR13: P'ven 6F 157
Penpons Cl. TR18: Penz 6D 148
PENPONT 3A 166
Penpont TR8: S Mawg 4G 29
Penpont Rd. TR15: Red 2F 113
Pen Porth Av. TR26: S Ives 3B 136
Penpraze TR16: I'gan, P'ath 5F 101
PENQUITE 4F 83
Penquite Dr. PL31: B'min 3H 33
Penrice Parc PL25: S Aus 6A 58
PENROSE
Bodmin 3G 27
Helston 7J 157
Wadebridge 3C 165
Penrose Ct. TR14: Tol D 3F 111
Penrose Farm Touring Pk. TR4: Goonh 5J 41
PENROSE HILL 7H 157
Penrose Parc TR13: P'ven 6G 157
Penrose Rd. TR11: Fal 1E 132
TR13: Helst 3B 158
Penrose St. PL1: Plym 2F 163
Penrose St. W. PL1: Plym 3F 163
Penrose Ter. TR18: Penz 4G 149
Penruan La. TR2: S Mawe 7E 130
PENRYN 5K 127 (1A 174)
Penryn Mus. 5B 128
Penryn Station (Rail) 4K 127
Penryn St. TR15: Red 4D 112
Penscott La. PL26: Treg 1G 65
PENSILVA 1J 67 (1B 170)
Pensilva TR6: P'rth 5B 40

Pensilva Ind. Est. PL14: Pens 2K 67
Pensilva Rd. TR1: Tru 2A 108
Penstowe Pk. Holiday Village EX23: Kilkh 2F 7
Penstowe Rd. EX23: Kilkh 2F 7
Penstrasse Pl. PL24: Tyw 2B 60
PENSTRAZE 3F 105
Penstraze Bus. Cen. TR4: Chac 2F 105
Penstraze La. PL26: Vict 1B 42
Penstruthal TR16: L'ner, Red 2F 121
Pensylva PL25: S Aus 6J 57
Pentalek Rd. TR14: Camb 1D 118
Pentargon Rd. PL35: Bosc 2K 13
PENTEWAN 1D 134 (3D 169)
Pentewan Hill PL26: Pent 1E 134
Pentewan Rd. PL25: S Aus 3F 65
PL26: Lon A, S Aus 3F 65
Pentewan Sands Holiday Pk. PL26: Pent 2D 134
Pentidna La. TR27: Gwith 1H 139
PENTILLIE 5D 134
Pentillie Gdns. PL17: Call 6C 72
(off Werrington Dr.)
PL25: S Aus .3K 57
Pentillie Way PL26: Mev 5D 134
PENTIRE 4C 34 (1A 168)
Pentire Av. TR7: Newq 4A 34
Pentire Cres. TR7: Newq 4C 34
Pentire Grn. TR8: Cran 6A 34
Pentire Hgts. TR7: Newq 4B 34
Pentire M. TR7: Newq 4C 34
Pentire Rd. PL11: Tor 3H 93
TR7: Newq 3C 34
TR10: P'ryn .4K 127
Pentire Steps to Porth Mear 3C 165
Pentire Workshops PL33: Dela 3A 14
PENTIVALE 7C 42
Pentowan Gdns. TR27: Log 6E 138
Pentowan Rd. TR27: Log, Phil 6D 138
Pentreath Cl. PL23: Fow 6H 61
TR16: L'ner .7J 113
TR18: Penz 3E 148
Pentreath La. TR12: Lizar 5G 161
TR20: Pra S .5G 155
Pentreath Ter. TR16: L'ner 7J 113
Pentrevah Rd. PL26: Penw 5K 49
Pen-Tye TR27: Reaw 2D 142
Pentyre Ct. EX23: Bud 6C 8
Penvale PL14: Pens 1K 67
TR10: P'ryn .1J 127
Penvale Cl. TR14: Barr 4A 118
Penvale Ct. TR11: Fal 1E 132
Penvale Cres. TR10: P'ryn 4K 127
Penvale Dr. TR10: P'ryn 4K 127
Penvean Cl. TR10: M Bur 5G 127
Penvean La. TR11: Fal 7C 128
Penvenen TR6: P'rth 4B 40
(off Atlantic Bay)
Penventinnie La. TR1: Trel 4D 106
(not continuous)
TR4: Newm 2D 106
PENVENTINUE 4H 61
Penventinue La. PL23: Fow 3G 61
PENVENTON 2D 120
Penventon TR15: Red 4C 112
Penventon Ga. TR16: Four L 2D 120
Penventon Ter. TR15: Red 4C 112
TR16: Four L .2C 120
Penventon Vw. TR13: Helst 4B 158
Penview Cres. TR13: Helst 4B 158
Penvorder Cotts. PL30: S B'wd 4J 27
Penvorder La. PL30: S B'wd 4H 27
Penware Parc TR14: Camb 2C 118
Penwarne Cl. TR14: Tol D 3F 111
Penwarne La. PL26: Mev 7C 134
Penwarne Rd. TR11: Mawn S 1A 160
Penwartha TR12: Cover 4C 162
Penwartha Cl. TR7: Newq 2A 36
TR11: Const .3H 159
Penwartha Ct. TR11: Const 3H 159
Penwartha Rd. TR6: Bol 7C 40
TR16: I'gan .1J 111
Penwartha Vean TR16: I'gan 1J 111
Penwerris La. TR11: Fal 6E 128
Penwerris Ri. TR20: Pra S 6H 155
Penwerris Rd. TR1: Tru 5E 106
Penwerris Ter. TR11: Fal 7E 128
Penwethers La. TR1: Tru 6F 107
Penwinnick Cl. TR5: S Agn 3A 96
Penwinnick Parc TR5: S Agn 3B 96
Penwinnick Rd. PL25: S Aus 6F 57
TR5: S Agn 3B 96
Penwith Bus. Cen. TR20: L Roc 3K 149
Penwith Cl. TR26: S Ives 4B 136
Penwith Gallery .1J 137
Penwithian Cl. TR27: Hayl 1K 141
PENWITHICK 5J 49 (2D 169)
Penwithick Pk. PL26: Penw 5K 49
Penwithick Rd. PL26: Penw 6J 49
Penwith Rd. TR26: S Ives 4B 136
Penwith St. TR18: Penz 4F 149

Penwood Cl. TR5: S Agn 3B 96
Penworth Cl. PL15: Laun 4H 17
Penwyth TR12: Gweek 6H 159
PENZANCE 4G 149 (1B 172)
Penzance Astro Pk. 4D 148
Penzance Leisure Cen. 4E 148
Penzance Rd. TR13: Helst 3A 158
TR19: Pend 4D 144
TR19: St Bury 2G 147
Penzance Sailing Club 5G 149
Penzance Station (Rail) 4G 149
Penzance Ter. TR15: Red 1G 113
(off Middle Rd.)
Peoples Pal. TR1: Tru 5J 107
(off Pydar St.)
Pepo La. TR2: Gram 7B 62
Peppers Ct. PL12: S Dom 2F 77
Peppersfield Row TR13: Breag 1D 156
Peppers Pk. Rd. PL14: Lisk 4D 70
PERCUIL 5F 131
Percuil Vw. TR2: S Mawe 7E 130
Percy Davy TR6: P'rth 4B 40
Perhaver Pk. PL26: G Hav 2H 135
Perhaver Way PL26: G Hav 2H 135
Per Kithen TR12: Lizar 5G 161
Permarin Rd. TR10: P'ryn 4A 128
PERRANARWORTHAL 3J 123 (1A 174)
Perran Beach Dunes TR6: P'rth 3C 40
Perran Cl. TR3: Devo 2C 124
Perrancombe Gdn. Ct. TR6: P'mbe 6A 40
PERRANCOOMBE 7A 40
PERRAN DOWNS 4B 152
PERRANPORTH 4B 40 (2A 168)
Perranporth Camping & Touring Pk.
TR6: P'rth 4D 40
Perranporth Golf Course 3D 40
Perran Quay Tourist Pk. TR8: H Cft 2K 41
Perran Sands Holiday Pk. TR6: P'rth 1C 40
Perransdown La. TR20: Rosu 6B 152
Perran Springs Holiday Pk. TR4: Goonh 6K 41
PERRANUTHNOE 6J 151 (2C 173)
PERRANWELL
Goonhavern 7F 41
Perranarworthal 2K 123 (1A 174)
Perranwell Rd. TR4: Goonh 5G 41
PERRANWELL STATION 1K 123
Perranwell Station (Rail) 1A 124
PERRANZABULOE 2A 168
Perranzabuloe Folk Mus. 4B 40
Perrily Mt. EX23: Bud 6D 8
Perry Way TR14: Camb 7F 111
Peters Hill PL26: H St 4H 55
Peter's Wood 1B 166
Petherick Rd. EX23: Flex 3D 8
Pethericks Mill EX23: Bud 6C 8
PETHERWIN GATE 2C 167
Pethybridge Dr. PL31: B'min 5D 32
Petroc Ct. PL18: S An Cpl 2C 74
Peverell Cl. TR14: Praze 4K 143
Peverell Rd. TR13: P'ven 7G 157
TR18: Penz 4F 149
Peverell Ter. TR13: P'ven 7F 157
Phernyssick M. PL25: S Aus 3A 58
Phernyssick Rd. PL25: S Aus 3J 57
Philgray Cl. TR27: Hayl 7E 138
PHILHAM 1A 164
PHILLACK 7D 138 (1C 173)
Phillack Hill TR27: Phil 7D 138
PHILLEIGH 1B 174
Phillimore Ct. PL26: Fox 7G 47
Phillip's Ct. TR17: Mar 4F 151
Phillips Ter. TR16: L'ner 1H 121
Phillips Ter. TR14: Camb 5F 111
(off Boiler Works Rd.)
Phoenix Cinema
Falmouth 1F 133
Phoenix Leisure Cen. 5H 17
Phoenix Wharf TR1: Tru 5K 107
Piala Pl. TR27: Hayl 7E 138
Piazza TR26: S Ives 1J 137
Piazza, The PL31: B'min 3G 33
(off Crockwell St.)
Pickard Way EX23: Flex 3C 8
Pickering Vs. TR4: Chac 6E 104
PIECE 1K 119
Pier La. PL10: Caws 6E 94
Pier St. PL1: Plym 7F 163
Piggy La. PL27: Wade 3D 24
Pigmeadow La. PL14: Lisk 4B 70
(off Dean St.)
Pikes Hill PL23: Fow 7J 61
TR11: Fal 2F 133
Pike St. TR1: Lisk 4B 70
Pilgrim Hall PL4: Plym 3J 163
Pilgrims Way TR27: Fr'ham 7A 142
Pillars Rd. TR11: M Bri 3F 129
PILLATON 1C 171
PILLATONMILL 1F 83
Pill Cotts. PL22: Los 4E 52

Pill La. PL12: Salt 7G 85
TR3: Feo 3K 125
Pillmere Dr. PL12: Salt 1E 88
Pinch Hill EX23: March 2F 11
Pine Cl. TR13: Helst 4D 158
Pine Ct. PL24: S Bl G 3F 59
TR3: P Sta 1K 123
Pine Grn. Caravan & Camping Pk.
PL14: Doubl 4A 68
Pine Lodge Gdns. .5C 58
Pine Rd. TR18: Penz 6C 148
Pine Vw. PL18: Gun 1H 75
PL26: Goth 1H 47
Pinewood Flats PL27: Polz 3D 18
Pinkham Ter. PL12: Cark 6D 84
Pink Moors TR16: S Da, Vog 2J 113
Pin La. PL1: Plym 6J 163
Pinnacle Quay PL4: Plym 4K 163
(off Harbour Av.)
Pinsla Garden & Nursery 1A 170
Pintail Av. TR27: Hayl 4D 140
Pipers Cl. PL15: Laun 5D 16
PIPERS POOL 2C 167
Pipers Standing Stones, The 2B 172
Pipe Well 4B 70
(off Well La.)
Pipewell La. PL14: Lisk 4B 70
(off Well La.)
Piran Cl. PL18: S An Cpl 2C 74
Piran Hgts. EX23: U'ton 1B 10
Pit, The TR16: Red 1D 120
Pitick Ter. TR11: Flu 6F 129
Pit La. TR9: Fr'don 3H 45
Pit Mdw. TR11: Fal 2C 132
Pits La. PL10: Rame 7C 94
PITYME 7F 19 (3D 165)
Pityme Bus. Cen. PL27: Pity 1J 23
Pityme Farm Rd. PL27: Pity 7G 19
Pityme Ind. Est. PL27: Pity 1J 23
Place Parc TR7: S Mino 2A 36
Place Rd. PL23: Fow 7J 61
Place Stables PL23: Fow 7J 61
(off Place Rd.)
Place Vw. PL23: Fow 7J 61
(off Daglands Rd.)
Place Vw. Rd. TR2: S Mawe 7D 130
PLAIDY 4J 81 (2B 170)
Plaidy La. PL13: Loo 4J 81
Plaidy Pk. Rd. PL13: Loo 4J 81
PLAIN-AN-GWARRY .3H 151
Plain-an-Gwarry TR15: Red 3C 112
Plain-an-Gwarry La. TR17: Mar 4G 151
Planet Pk. PL33: Dela 3A 14
Plantation TR14: Tro 7F 119
Plantation La. TR27: Hayl 2G 141
PLASHFORD BRIDGE .7D 78
Plas Newydd Ter. PL31: B'min 5G 33
(off Lostwithiel Rd.)
Platt, The PL27: Wade 4F 25
Playingfield La. TR7: Newq 4E 34
Playing Fld. Ter. PL14: Duloe 6A 78
PLAYING PLACE 5G 117 (3B 168)
Plaza, The 5J 107
Pleasant Pl. TR18: Hea 3D 148
Pleasant Ter. TR19: S Jus 3H 145
Plestin Cl. PL15: Laun 2H 17
Pleyber Christ Way PL22: Los 3E 52
Pleydon Cl. PL13: Polp 5C 80
Plougastel Dr. PL12: Salt 2G 89
Ploughboy M. PL12: Salt 2E 88
Plough Ct. TR10: P'ryn 2G 127
Plough Grn. PL12: Salt 2E 88
Plover Av. TR13: Helst 3E 158
PLUSHABRIDGE 3D 167
PLYMOUTH 4J 163 (2D 171)
Plymouth Arts Cen. 5J 163
Plymouth Athenaeum Theatre, The 5F 163
Plymouth City Museum & Art Gallery 3J 163
Plymouth Pl. PL14: Lisk 5C 70
Plymouth Station (Rail) 1G 163
PLYMPTON 2D 171
PLYMSTOCK 2D 171
Plym St. PL4: Plym 3K 163
Poad's Trust PL14: Menh 1H 79
Pochin Cl. PL25: S Aus 2J 57
Pochin Ho. PL25: S Aus 2J 57
Pocohontas Cres. TR9: I Que 2H 45
POINT 3F 125
Point Green TR3: Devo 3G 125
POINT MILLS 4H 115
Point Rd. TR3: C Dow, Devo 1E 124
POLBATHIC 7B 86 (2C 171)
Polbathic Rd. TR15: Red 2E 112
POLBORDER 7D 76
Polborder Farm Barns PL12: S Mel 7D 76
Polbreen Av. TR5: S Agn 3A 96
Polbreen La. TR5: S Agn 3A 96
POLBROCK 1D 169
Polcoverack TR12: Cover 5A 162

Polcoverack La. TR12: Cover 5C 162
Poldark Gdns. PL24: S Bl G 3G 59
Poldark Mine 1D 173
Poldark Mine Heritage Complex, The 1D 173
Poldark Rd. TR16: I'gan .1J 111
Poldhu Cl. TR26: C Bay 7F 137
Poldhu Rd. PL14: Lisk 4C 70
   TR12: Mull 1F 161
POLDICE 2B 114
Poldice La. TR16: Crof 3B 114
Poldice Ter. TR16: S Da .2B 114
Poldory TR16: Carh 5C 114
Poldory Vw. TR16: Carh .5A 114
Poldrea PL24: Tyw 2B 60
Poldrissick Hill PL12: Land 2H 87
Poldrissick La. PL12: Land 7G 83
Poldue Cl. TR15: Red 2F 113
Polean La. PL13: Loo 4F 81
Polean Trad. Est. PL13: Loo 4F 81
Polgarth TR15: Pool 4J 111
   TR18: Newl 7C 148
Polgarth Cl. TR26: C Bay 7F 137
POLGEAR 7B 120
Polgine Cl. TR14: Tro 4G 119
Polgine La. TR14: Tro 4G 119
Polglase Wlk. TR4: S Erm 3B 98
Polglaze Cl. TR18: Penz .3E 148
Polglaze Holiday Pk. PL23: Fow 4F 61
Polglist PL26: Fox 1G 55
Polgoda Rd. TR4: Goonh 6H 41
Polgoon Cl. TR18: Penz .5D 148
Polgoon Cotts. TR20: Penz 5D 148
POLGOOTH 3D 64 (2C 169)
Polgooth Cl. TR15: Red .2F 113
Polgover Way PL24: S Bla 3H 59
Polgrain Rd. TR14: Tol D 4F 111
Polgrean Pl. PL24: S Bla 2H 59
Polhorman La. TR12: Mull 4G 81
Polisken Way TR4: S Erm 2B 98
POLKANUGGO 5B 126
Polkanuggo La. TR10: Hern 4B 126
POLKERRIS 2D 169
Polkerris Pk. PL24: Par 4J 59
Polkerris Rd. TR16: Carh 4A 114
Polkirt PL26: Mev 7D 134
Polkirt Hgts. PL26: Mev .6C 134
Polkirt Hill PL26: Gorr 1H 135
   PL26: Mev 6D 134
Polkyth Leisure Cen. 5J 57
Polkyth Pde. PL25: S Aus 5J 57
Polkyth Rd. PL25: S Aus 5J 57
Pollard Cl. PL12: Salt 3D 88
Pollard Rd. PL17: Call 5D 72
Pollards EX23: Stra 4G 9
Pollards Cl. PL14: Pens .1K 67
   TR4: Goonh 5H 41
Pollards Way PL12: Salt .1G 89
POLLSYGH 3D 18
Polmanter Touring Pk. TR26: Hal 6C 136
POLMANTER WATER 6A 136
Polmark Dr. PL28: H Bay 3D 20
Polmarth Cl. PL25: S Aus 3K 57
POLMASSICK 3C 169
Polmassick Vineyard 3C 169
POLMEAR 4B 60
Polmear Ct. PL27: Wade 4E 24
                                      (off Fairpark Rd.)
Polmear Hill PL24: Par .4B 60
Polmear Parc PL24: Par 3A 60
Polmear Rd. PL24: Par .3A 60
   PL25: S Aus 6K 57
Polmeere Rd. TR18: Penz 3E 148
Polmena La. PL22: Los .4G 53
Polmennor Dr. TR26: C Bay 1A 140
Polmennor Rd. TR11: Fal 4D 132
   TR18: Hea 2D 148
   TR20: Hea 2D 148
Polmeor Cl. TR26: C Bay 7F 137
Polmewan Flats PL26: Polg 3D 64
POLMORLA 5D 24
Polmorla M. PL27: Wade 4E 24
                                      (off Polmorla Rd.)
Polmorla Rd. PL27: Wade 4E 24
Polmorla Wlk. PL27: Wade 4E 24
                                      (off Polmorla Rd.)
Polmor Rd. TR20: Crow 2K 155
POLPERRO 7B 80 (2B 170)
Polperro Heritage Museum of Smuggling & Fishing
   . . . . .6C 80
Polperro Model Village .6B 80
                                      (off Mill Hill)
Polperro Rd. PL13: Loo .4F 81
Polpey La. PL24: Par, Tyw 3B 60
POLRUAN .7C 60 (2A 170)
Polruan Blockhouse 6B 60
Polruan Ct. TR26: C Bay 1A 140
Polruan Ct. TR1: Tru 7A 108
                                      (off Polruan Rd.)
Polruan Holidays PL23: Polr 7D 60

Polruan Rd. TR1: Tru 6A 108
   TR15: Red 2F 113
Polruan to Lansallos Cliff 2A 170
POLSCOE
   Lostwithiel 1H 53 (1A 170)
   Torpoint 3E 90
Polscoe Rd. PL22: Los 2H 53
Polsethow TR10: P'ryn 5K 127
Polstain Cres. TR3: Thre 5B 106
Polstain Rd. TR3: Thre 5A 106
Polstain Vs. TR3: Thre 5A 106
POLSTRONG 1A 118
Polsue Way TR2: Tr'sln .2G 109
Poltair Av. PL25: S Aus .5J 57
Poltair Cl. TR18: Hea 3D 148
Poltair Ct. PL25: S Aus .5J 57
Poltair Cres. PL25: S Aus 5H 57
Poltair Dr. TR10: P'ryn 5K 127
Poltair Mdw. TR10: P'ryn 5K 127
Poltair Rd. PL25: S Aus .5J 57
   TR10: P'ryn 5K 127
Poltair Ter. TR18: Hea 3C 148
Poltamar PL15: Laun 4J 17
POLTESCO 3A 174
Poltesco & Ruan Minor Coastline 3A 174
Poltisco Cl. TR1: Tru 6A 108
Poltisco Rd. TR10: P'ryn 5K 127
Poltisko Ter. TR10: P'ryn 5K 127
Poltreen Cl. TR26: C Bay 7F 137
Polurrian Cliffs TR12: Mull 3F 161
Polurrian Rd. TR12: Mull 2G 161
Polvarth Est. TR2: S Mawe 7E 130
Polvarth La. TR2: S Mawe 7E 130
Polvarth Rd. TR2: S Mawe 6D 130
Polvean Ter. PL14: Duloe 6A 78
Polvella Cl. TR7: Newq .4C 34
Polvellan Mnr. PL13: Loo 4G 81
Polvellan Ter. PL13: Loo .4G 81
                                      (off North Rd.)
Polvelyn Parc TR27: Hayl 7E 138
Polventon Cl. TR9: S Maj 5B 30
   TR11: Fal 1C 132
   TR15: Hea 3D 148
Polventon Parc TR12: S Kev 2B 162
Polvillion Rd. PL23: Fow .7H 61
Polweath Cl. TR18: Penz 3F 149
Polweath Rd. TR18: Penz 3F 149
Polwhaveral Ter. TR11: Fal 7E 128
                                      (off Glasney Rd.)
Polwheal Rd. TR14: Tol D 4F 111
Polwhele Rd. TR1: Tru 3A 108
   TR7: Newq 6H 35
POLWHEVERAL 3J 159
Polwithen Dr. TR26: C Bay 6E 136
Polwithen Gdns. TR26: C Bay 7E 136
Polwithen Rd. TR10: P'ryn 4K 127
   TR11: Fal 1E 132
   TR18: Penz 5E 148
Polwrath Ter. PL14: Trem 3B 66
Polwyn Cl. TR18: Hea 3C 148
Polyear Cl. PL26: Polg 2C 64
POLYPHANT 2C 167
Polzeath Beach Holiday Pk. PL27: N Pol 2D 18
Pondbridge Hill PL14: Lisk 5B 70
Pondfield Rd. PL12: Salt .2D 88
Pondhu Cres. PL25: S Aus 6F 57
Pondhu Rd. PL25: S Aus 6F 57
Pond La. TR15: Red 2C 112
Pond Lanes End TR15: Red 2D 112
Ponds Hill TR19: Pend 3E 144
Pond Vw. Ter. PL26: Fox 1H 55
Pond Wlk. TR27: Hayl 7D 138
Poniou La. TR20: L Roc .2K 149
                                      (not continuous)
Poniou Rd. TR20: L Roc .3K 149
Poniou Way TR20: L Roc 3A 150
PONJERAVAH 2J 159
Ponsandane Bri. TR18: Penz 3H 149
PONSANOOTH 5F 123 (1A 174)
Ponsharden (Park & Float) 6D 128
Ponsharden (Park & Ride) 6D 128
Ponsharden Cotts. TR11: Fal 6D 128
Ponsharden Ind. Est. TR11: Fal 6C 128
Ponsmere Ct. TR6: P'rth 4B 40
                                      (off Ponsmere Rd.)
Ponsmere Rd. TR6: P'rth 4B 40
PONSNOWYDH 1E 128
PONSONGATH 3A 174
Ponsvale TR3: Pons 5E 122
PONTS MILL 5J 51
Pontsmill Rd. PL24: Penp 6K 51
POOL 4J 111 (3A 168)
Pool Business Pk. TR15: Pool 6H 111
Poole Pk. Rd. PL5: Plym .5K 89
Pool Hall PL14: Menh 2H 79
Pool Ind. Est. TR15: Pool 5K 111
                                      (not continuous)
Pool's Ct. TR27: Hayl 1J 141

Pool St. PL31: B'min 3G 33
Poor Ho. Hill TR10: P'ryn 7K 123
POPESMILL 6F 71
Poplars Ct. TR6: P'rth 4B 40
                                      (off St George's Hill)
Poplar Ter. TR11: Flu 5F 129
PORCUPINE 6K 51
Porcupine La. PL24: L'scot 6K 51
Pordenack Cl. TR26: C Bay 6G 137
Porfell Wildlife Park & Sanctuary 2A 170
Porhan Grn. TR11: Fal 6C 128
PORKELLIS 1D 173
Porspoder Pl. PL10: Caws 5E 94
Portbyhan Rd. PL13: Loo 5F 81
Porteath Bee Cen. 3D 165
Port Eliot Est. PL12: S Ger 3C 86
Port Eliot House 5D 86
Porter Way PL12: Salt 2E 88
PORTGATE 2D 167
PORT GAVERNE 2K 19 (2A 166)
PORTH
   Newquay 1K 35 (1B 168)
   Par 4J 59
PORTHALLOW
   Helston 2A 174
   Looe 5E 80 (2B 170)
Porth Beach Rd. TR7: Newq 1J 35
Porth Beach Tourist Pk. TR7: Newq 1K 35
Porth Bean Rd. TR7: Newq 1K 35
Porthcollum La. TR27: S Er 7G 141
PORTHCOTHAN 3C 165
Porthcothan Beach Cliff .3C 165
PORTHCURNO 6G 147 (2A 172)
Porthcurno Telegraph Mus. 6G 147
Portheast Cl. PL26: G Hav 2H 135
Portheast Way PL26: G Hav 2H 135
Porthenys Pl. TR19: Mou 5D 154
                                      (off Southview Ter.)
PORTHERRAS CROSS .3D 144
Portherras Ter. TR19: Pend 4D 144
Portherras Vs. TR19: Pend 4D 144
Portheyl Pl. TR27: Hayl .1J 141
PORTHGAVRAN 2K 19
PORTHGWARRA 2A 172
PORTHGWIDDEN 1K 137 (2E 136)
Porthgwidden Studios TR26: S Ives 1K 137
PORTHIA 3H 137 (3D 136)
Porthia Cl. TR26: S Ives .4C 136
Porthia Cres. TR26: S Ives 4B 136
Porthia Rd. TR26: S Ives .4B 136
PORTHILLY 3F 23
Porthilly Farm Caravan Site
   PL27: Rock 3F 23
Porthilly La. PL27: Rock .3F 23
Porthilly Vw. PL28: Pad .4C 22
PORTHKEA 3K 117
PORTHLEVEN 7F 157 (2D 173)
Porthleven Rd. TR13: Helst, P'ose 5K 157
Porthmellon Gdns. PL17: Call 5D 72
PORTHMEOR 2D 136 (1B 172)
Porthmeor Hill TR26: S Ives 2G 137 (2C 136)
Porthmeor Rd. PL25: S Aus 6B 58
   TR26: S Ives 1J 137 (2D 136)
Porthmeor Sq. TR26: S Ives 1J 137
PORTHMINSTER 4E 136
Porthminster Point TR26: S Ives 4E 136
Porthminster Ter. TR26: S Ives 4J 137 (3D 136)
PORTH NAVAS 2A 174
PORTHOLLAND 3C 169
PORTHOUSTOCK 1E 162 (2B 174)
Porth Pde. TR7: Newq 1K 35
Porthpean Beach Rd. PL26: P'ean 1K 65
Porthpean Golf Course .3K 65
Porthpean Rd. PL25: S Aus 6K 57
   PL26: S Aus 1K 65
PORTHPYRA 7B 40
PORTHPYRAN 4B 40
Porthreath Tramroad 4F 101
Porthrepta Rd. TR26: C Bay 6G 137
Porth Rd. PL24: Par 4J 59
PORTHRUAN 7C 60
Porth Sands TR7: Newq .1J 35
                                      (off Porth Beach Rd.)
Porth Sawle TR2: P'stho .3K 131
PORTHTOWAN 6C 96 (3A 168)
Porthtowan Tourist Pk. TR4: P'twn 1C 102
PORTHTRETH 4F 101
PORTHUSEK 2J 169
Porth Vale TR4: P'twn 5C 96
Porth Veor Mnr. TR7: Newq 1J 35
Porth Vw. TR2: S Mawe .6E 130
Porth Way TR7: Newq 2J 35
PORTHYNYS 6D 154
PORTHYUST 2J 135
PORT ISAAC 2J 19 (2D 165)
Portland Cl. PL14: Lisk 3B 70
Portland Gdns. TR11: Fal 1D 132
Portland Pl. TR19: Mou .6D 154
Portland Pl. E. PL4: Plym 2J 163

Portland Sq. PL4: Plym .3H 163
    (not continuous)
Portland Sq. La. Nth. PL4: Plym 2H 163
Portland Ter. *PL14: Lisk* *3B 70*
    (off Portland Cl.)
Portland Vs. PL4: Plym .2H 163
PORTLOE 3C 169
PORTMELLON 7D 134 (3D 169)
Portmellon Pk. PL26: Mev 7C 134
Portmellon Rd. PL26: Mev 7D 134
Portmeor Ct. TR26: S Ives 1J 137
Portnadler Bay 2B 170
Port Pendennis TR11: Fal 2G 133
PORT QUIN 2D 165
PORTREATH 4F 101 (3A 168)
PORTSCATHO 3K 131 (1B 174)
Portuan Rd. PL13: Loo 7G 81
Port Vw. PL29: P Isa 2K 19
Port Vw. Ter. *PL12: Land* *7G 83*
    (off Tideford Rd.)
PORTWRINKLE 6D 90 (2C 171)
Posses La. TR18: Gul, Penz 2H 149
Possession La. PL12: Land 7H 83
Post Box Row TR14: Bre 7G 111
Post Office M. TR8: Cube 4F 39
Post Office Row PL26: Fox 1G 55
Post Office Ter. PL26: Nanp 5G 47
    TR16: Carn 1B 120
Potager Garden 2A 174
POTHOLE 3J 63
Potters La. PL35: Bosc 2K 13
Potters M. TR4: Goonh 5H 41
Pottery Est. PL10: M'brk .1C 94
POUGHILL 2F 9 (3A 164)
Poughill Rd. EX23: Flex, Pou 3D 8
Pounda PL14: S Keyn 1C 78
Pound Caravan Site TR16: Crof 4A 114
Pound Dean PL14: Lisk .5K 69
POUNDFIELD 4G 9
Poundfield Cl. EX23: Stra .4G 9
Poundfield La. EX23: Stra .4G 9
Pound Hill PL12: Land 6G 83
Pound La. PL31: B'min 3G 33
    TR3: Baldh, Tru 1A 116
Pound Pk. PL14: Menh 1H 79
Pounds Pk. PL12: Salt 2H 89
POUNDSTOCK 1C 167
Pound St. PL14: Lisk 4B 70
Praa Grn. TR20: Pra S .6H 155
PRAA SANDS 6J 155 (2C 173)
Praa Sands Golf Course 7G 153
Praa Sands Holiday Village
    TR20: Pra S 6H 155
Praed Pl. TR26: Lel 1E 140
Praed's La. TR17: Mar .4F 151
PRAZE 4H 157
Praze, The TR10: P'ryn .4A 128
PRAZE-AN-BEEBLE 4K 143 (1D 173)
Praze-an-Creet TR26: S Ives 3B 136
Praze an Cronor TR9: S Maj 6B 30
Praze Bus. Pk. TR14: Praze 4K 143
Praze Mdw. TR10: P'ryn 4A 128
PRAZE PRAS 6F 141
Praze Rd. TR7: Newq 1J 35
    TR13: P'ven 6G 157
    TR14: Praze 7D 142
    TR27: Leeds 7D 142
Predannack Rd. TR12: Mull 3G 161
Prengarth Cl. PL25: S Aus 2J 57
Presingoll Barns TR5: S Agn 3J 97
Prevenna Rd. TR19: Mou 5D 154
Prian Pl. PL25: S Aus 6G 57
    (off Trinity St.)
Pridaux Cl. PL12: Salt 7E 84
Prideaux PL26: H St 5A 56
Prideaux Place 2A 22
Prideaux Rd. PL24: B'lva, S Bla 7E 50
Pridmouth Rd. PL25: S Aus 3J 57
Priestacott Pk. EX23: Kilkh 2G 7
Priesthood Ter. PL10: M'brk 2C 94
Primative Hill TR14: Camb 5G 111
Primelin Pl. TR10: M Bur 5H 127
Primitive Row TR14: Camb 5G 111
Prim-Raf Theatre *5C 72*
    (off New Rd.)
Primrose Cl. PL11: Tor 2G 93
    PL26: Roch 4C 42
    TR14: Camb 6B 110
    TR20: Gold 4A 152
Primrose Gdns. TR16: I'gan 7G 101
Primrose Hill TR20: Gold 4A 152
Primrose La. TR20: Gold 4A 152
    TR27: Can 6B 140
Primrose Rd. EX23: Bud .5E 8
Primrose Ter. TR1: Tr'sln 2H 109
    TR16: P'ath 4F 101
    TR18: Newl 2D 154
    (off Fore St.)
Primrose Valley TR26: S Ives 4D 136

Primrose Wlk. PL12: Salt 1F 89
Prince Charles Cl. PL15: Laun 2H 17
Prince Charles Ho. PL25: S Aus 4J 57
Prince Charles Pk. PL25: S Aus 4J 57
Prince Charles Rd. PL25: S Aus 4J 57
Prince of Wales Pier TR11: Fal 7F 129
Prince Philip Rd. PL15: Laun 2H 17
Princess Ct. *TR18: Penz* *5F 149*
    (off New St.)
Princess Parc TR9: I Que 2H 45
Princess Pavilion 3G 133
Princes Sq. PL13: Loo 7J 81
Princess Rd. PL14: Bere 1K 67
Princess St. PL1: Plym .5G 163
    TR19: S Jus 3H 145
Princess Ter. Ope PL1: Plym 5H 163
Princes St. EX23: Bud 4C 8
    PL13: Loo 6J 81 (5G 81)
    TR1: Tru 5K 107
    TR18: Penz 5F 149
Princess Way PL1: Plym 5G 163
Prior's Barn PL31: B'min 5H 33
Priors Cl. TR26: S Ives .4B 136
Priory Cl. PL24: Tyw 2K 59
Priory Cotts. PL15: Laun 3G 17
    PL24: Tyw 2A 60
Priory M. PL15: Laun 3G 17
Priory Pk. Rd. PL15: Laun 3G 17
Priory Rd. PL25: S Aus .5G 57
    PL31: B'min 4G 33
    TR7: S Mino 2B 36
    TR8: S Mino 2B 36
Prisks Ter. TR16: L'ner .1H 121
Prislow Cl. TR11: Fal 3C 132
Prislow Flds. TR11: Fal .3C 132
Prislow La. TR11: Fal 3C 132
PROBUS 2H 99 (3C 169)
Promenade TR18: Penz .6E 148
Promenade, The PL1: Plym 7F 163
Promised Land TR5: S Agn 2K 97
Prospect Cl. TR13: Ash .1A 156
    TR27: Hayl 1J 141
Prospect Gdns. TR1: Tru 3A 108
Prospect La. PL12: Salt .2E 88
Prospect Pl. PL1: Plym .6F 163
    PL26: Mev 5C 134
    TR1: Tru 4K 107
    TR11: Fal 7E 128
    TR13: Ash 1A 156
    TR13: Helst 5C 158
    TR13: P'ven 7F 157
    TR18: Penz 4F 149
    TR27: Hayl 1J 141
    (not continuous)
Prospect Row TR13: Ash 1A 156
Prospect St. PL4: Plym .3K 163
Prospect Ter. *PL10: M'brk* *2C 94*
    (off Greenland)
    PL18: Gun 1H 75
    PL18: S An Cpl 3D 74
    PL26: Mev 5C 134
Prospect Wlk. PL12: Salt 2E 88
Prosper Cl. PL26: Trez 6C 42
Prosper Hill TR27: Gwith 1H 139
Prosper Rd. PL26: Trez .6C 42
Prouse Ri. PL12: Salt 3G 89
Prouts Ct. PL15: Laun 3J 17
Prout's La. TR27: Con D 5K 139
Prouts M. PL15: Laun 3J 17
Prouts Way PL15: Treg .5A 16
Providence Pl. *PL18: Cals* *7J 75*
    (off Church St.)
    PL23: Polr *7C 60*
    (off Sydney Hill)
Providence St. PL4: Plym 2K 163
Provis Rd. TR18: Penz 6D 148
Prussia Cove Rd. TR20: Rosu 7B 152
Prynne Cl. PL1: Plym 3F 163
Pryors Row TR13: Ash .1A 156
Prysten House 5H 163
Puckator La. PL14: Trem 5C 66
PUDDLE 1K 51
Puffin Way TR27: Hayl 3D 140
Puggis Hill TR14: Res 5A 110
PULLA CROSS 1E 122
Putnam Cl. PL14: Lisk 5C 70
Pydar Cl. TR7: Newq 4J 35
Pydar M. *TR1: Tru* *5J 107*
    (off The Leats)
Pydar St. TR1: Tru 4J 107
Pyramid Cl. PL25: T'oon .4B 56
PYWORTHY 3B 164

Quakers Rd. TR3: P Sta .1F 123
    TR4: Cusg 1F 123
Quarry Cl. EX23: Flex 3D 8
    PL26: Nanp 6F 47
Quarry Cres. PL15: Laun 5F 17
Quarryfield Holiday Pk. TR8: Cran 5B 34
Quarry Gdns. TR18: Penz 5D 148
Quarry Hill TR11: Fal 1F 133
    TR18: Gul 2H 149
    TR20: Gul 2H 149
Quarry Ho. Flats TR1: Tru 6A 108
Quarry La. PL12: Land 6H 83
    PL12: S Ger 5D 86
    PL18: Gun 2G 75
    TR1: Tru 6A 108
    TR19: Pau 5A 154
Quarrymans Cotts. PL27: Edmon 3A 24
Quarry Parc TR22: Gram .7A 62
Quarry Pk. Rd. TR7: Newq 7J 35
Quarry Pk. Ter. PL31: B'min 3D 32
Quarry Rd. PL14: Pens 1K 67
    TR6: Bol 5D 40
Quarry St. PL11: Tor 3K 93
    PL12: S Ger 5D 86
Quarry Ter. PL24: Par 2J 59
Quarry Vw. PL33: Dela 3B 14
Quarry Wlk. PL26: Dup 1K 65
Quarter Deck Apartments TR7: Newq 1J 35
Quay, The PL12: S Ger 6E 86
    PL13: Loo 6J 81 (5G 81)
    (not continuous)
    PL18: Cals 7J 75
    PL23: Polr 6C 60
    PL26: Mev *6C 134*
    (off Middle Wharf)
    PL26: Pent 1D 134
    TR2: S Mawe 7D 130
    TR5: S Agn 1B 96
    TR10: P'ryn *5B 128*
    (off Commercial Rd.)
    TR18: Penz 5G 149
Quay Hill TR10: P'ryn 5B 128
    TR11: Fal 1F 133
Quay Ho. PL13: Loo 7J 81
Quay La. PL12: T'ton 4J 87
Quay M. *TR1: Tru* *5K 107*
    (off Quay St.)
Quay Rd. PL1: Plym 6J 163
    PL12: S Ger 6E 86
    PL12: Tide 1B 86
    PL13: Loo 6J 81 (4G 81)
    PL13: Polp 7B 80
    PL25: Char 7B 58
    TR3: Devo 2C 124
    TR5: S Agn 1B 96
Quay St. PL13: Loo 6K 81
    PL22: Los 3E 52
    TR1: Tru 5K 107
    TR11: Fal 1G 133
    TR18: Penz 6G 149
    TR19: Mou 6D 154
    TR26: S Ives 1K 137 (2E 136)
Queen Anne Gdns. TR11: Fal 2C 132
Queen Anne Ter. PL4: Plym 2J 163
Queen Elizabeth Rd. PL15: Laun 2H 17
Queen Mary Ct. TR11: Fal 3F 133
Queen Mary Rd. TR11: Fal 3F 133
Queens Clos PL26: Roch 3B 42
Queens Cl. TR9: I Que 2H 45
Queen's Ct. *TR18: Penz* *6F 149*
    (off Daniel Pl.)
Queen's Cres. PL31: B'min 5D 32
Queens Pk. PL27: Wade .5F 25
Queens Rd. PL25: S Aus 6J 57
Queens Sq. *TR18: Penz* *5F 149*
    (off Queen St.)
Queen St. EX23: Bud 4C 8
    PL22: Los 3E 52
    TR18: Penz 5F 149
    TR19: S Jus 3H 145
    TR20: Gold 4K 151
Queen's Way TR20: Gold 5K 151
Queensway TR27: Hayl .2H 141
Queens Way M. TR27: Hayl 1H 141
Queen Ter. PL17: Harr 5A 74
QUENCHWELL 5D 116
Quenchwell Rd. TR3: C Dow 5D 116
Questmap Bus. Pk. TR20: L Roc 2A 150
QUETHIOCK 1C 171
Quillet Rd. TR18: Newl 7C 148
Quilver Cl. PL26: G Hav .3J 135
    (not continuous)
Quimperle Way PL14: Lisk 4D 70
Quintrell Cl. TR8: Q Dow .6D 36
Quintrell Ct. TR7: Newq .3A 36
QUINTRELL DOWNS 6C 36 (1B 168)
Quintrell Downs Station (Rail) 6C 36
Quintrell Gdns. TR8: Q Dow 6D 36

Q

Quadrant, The *TR1: Tru* *4B 108*
    (off Trebartha Rd.)

Quintrell Rd. TR7: Newq, S Mino	.3A **36**
TR8: Q Dow, S Mino	.3A **36**
QUODITCH	.1D **167**
QUOIT	.7E **30**

R

Rabys Row TR16: Scor	.7H **103**
Race Hill PL15: Laun	.4H **17**
TR4: Biss	.5G **115**
Race Hill Ter. PL15: Laun	.4H **17**
Rachel's Way TR9: S Maj	.5C **30**
Radford La. PL10: M'brk	.3B **94**
Radford Rd. PL1: Plym	.7F **163**
RADNOR	.6F **103**
Radnor Cl. PL31: B'min	.4H **33**
Radnor Golf Course	.6G **103**
Radnor Hall PL4: Plym	.3K **163**
Radnor Pl. PL4: Plym	.3K **163**
Radnor Rd. TR16: Red, Scor	.7E **102**
Radnor St. PL4: Plym	.3K **163**
RAF Memorial	.7H **163**
RAF St Mawgan	.7F **29**
RAFTRA	.5F **147**
RAGINNIS	.7C **154**
Raginnis Hill TR19: Mou, Pau	.7B **154**
Railway Cl. PL25: S Aus	.6A **58**
Railway Cotts. TR11: Fal	.2H **133**
Railway Cres. PL14: Dar	.2C **66**
Railway Ter. PL12: S Ger	.5D **86**
PL14: Doubl	.4B **68**
PL30: Lux	.1D **50**
PL31: B'min	.3F **33**
TR16: Carh	.4A **114**
TR16: P'ath	.4F **101**
Railway Vw. PL26: T'vsce	.6C **46**
Railway Vs. TR15: I Hig	.4B **112**
Rainham Cl. TR15: I'gan	.2J **111**
Rainyfields PL28: Pad	.3B **22**
Rainyfields Cl. PL28: Pad	.3B **22**
Raleigh Cl. PL28: Pad	.4A **22**
Raleigh Gdns. PL31: B'min	.5H **33**
Raleigh Pl. TR11: Fal	.1E **132**
Raleigh Rd. PL28: Pad	.3A **22**
Raleigh St. PL1: Plym	.4F **163**
RAME	
Penryn	.5A **126** (1A **174**)
Torpoint	.7D **94** (3D **171**)
Rame La. PL10: Rame	.7D **94**
Rame Vw. PL13: Loo	.3J **81**
Ramoth Way TR6: P'rth	.3C **40**
RAMSGATE	.3C **118**
Ranch Vw. PL15: Laun	.4F **17**
Ranelagh M. PL31: B'min	.3F **33**
Ranelagh Rd. PL25: S Aus	.5J **57**
Raphael Rd. PL13: Polp	.6A **80**
Rapson Rd. PL14: Lisk	.4C **70**
Rashleigh Av. PL12: Salt	.4F **89**
Rashleigh Ct. PL25: Carl	.6C **58**
Rashleigh Gro. PL25: S Aus	.4J **57**
Rashleigh La. PL23: Fow	.7G **61**
Rashleigh M. PL25: S Aus	.6A **58**
Rashleigh Pl. PL25: S Aus	.5K **57**
Rashleigh Vale TR1: Tru	.5A **108**
Ratcliffes La. TR13: Helst, P'ose	.5K **157**
Rattle St. PL26: G Hav	.2J **135**
Rawley La. TR7: Newq	.4F **35**
Rawlings La. PL23: Fow	.6J **61**
Rawlin Homes PL4: Plym	.4K **163**
(off Green St.)	
RAYLE BOTTOMS	.7K **101**
Raymond Rd. TR15: Red	.4E **112**
Read Cl. TR10: P'ryn	.5K **127**
READYMONEY	.6A **60** (2A **170**)
Readymoney Rd. PL23: Fow	.6A **60**
REAWLA	.3D **142**
Reawla La. TR27: Reaw	.3C **142**
Rebecca Cl. PL24: S Bla	.7H **51**
Rebeccas Cl. PL26: Mev	.6C **134**
(off Tregoney Hill)	
Rectory Gdns. PL26: S Ste	.4C **54**
TR14: Camb	.1C **118**
Rectory La. PL17: Call	.6C **72**
PL30: S Mab	.6B **26**
Rectory Rd. PL26: S Den	.1D **46**
PL26: S Ste	.4C **54**
PL30: Lani	.6H **31**
TR14: Camb	.1C **118**
TR19: St Bury	.2H **147**
Redannack TR12: Mull	.1H **161**
Redannack North TR12: Mull	.1H **161**
Redannick Cres. TR1: Tru	.6H **107**
Redannick La. TR1: Tru	.6H **107**
Redbrooke Rd. TR14: Camb	.1E **118**
Redbrooke Ter. TR14: Camb	.1E **118**
(off Redbrooke Rd.)	
Redfern Ct. TR26: S Ives	.3J **137**
REDGATE	.1B **170**
Redgate Ct. TR9: I Que	.1K **45**
Redinnick Gdns. TR18: Penz	.6F **149**
Redinnick Pl. TR18: Penz	.6E **148**
Redinnick Ter. TR18: Penz	.6E **148**
Red La. PL26: Bugl	.6H **43**
TR20: Rosu	.6C **152**
REDMOOR	.1A **52**
Redmoor Cl. PL17: K Bray	.2C **72**
Redmoor Rd. PL17: K Bray	.2B **72**
RED POST	.3A **164**
REDRUTH	.3E **112** (3A **168**)
Redruth Highway TR15: Red	.1G **113**
Redruth Rd. TR13: Helst	.1C **158**
Redruth Station (Rail)	.3E **112**
Redvale Rd. PL30: S Tud	.6J **27**
Redvers Hgts. TR15: Red	.5D **112**
Redwood Cl. EX23: Bud	.5D **8**
Redwood Gro. EX23: Bud	.5D **8**
Reeds Pk. PL22: Los	.3F **53**
Reeds Way TR7: Newq	.4E **34**
Reel Cinema	
Plymouth	.5G **163**
Reen Hill TR6: Bol	.6D **40**
Reen La. TR6: P'rth	.4D **40**
Reen Manor Riding Stables	.4D **40**
Reens Cres. TR18: Hea	.3D **148**
Reens Rd. TR18: Hea	.3D **148**
Rees Ct. TR19: S Jus	.3J **145**
REESHILL	.7B **42**
Reeves Cl. TR13: P'ven	.6G **157**
Regal Cinema	
Redruth	.3D **112**
Wadebridge	.4F **25**
Regan Ct. TR10: P'ryn	.5J **127**
Regent Bldgs. TR18: Penz	.5F **149**
(off Voundervour La.)	
Regent Sq. TR18: Penz	.6F **149**
Regent St. PL4: Plym	.3J **163**
Regent Ter. TR18: Penz	.6F **149**
TR19: Mou	.6D **154**
(off North St.)	
TR19: S Jus	.3H **145**
Rejarne Row TR27: L Dow	.4A **140**
REJERRAH	.7J **39** (2A **168**)
RELEATH	.1D **173**
Relistian La. TR27: Gwinn, Reaw	.1C **142**
Relistian Pk. TR27: Reaw	.3C **142**
RELUBBUS	.1E **152** (1C **173**)
Relubbus Hill TR20: S Hil	.2D **152**
Relubbus La. TR20: S Hil	.3C **152**
Rendle St. PL33: Dela	.2B **14**
RESCASSA	.3C **169**
RESCORLA	
PL26, Penwithick	.2K **49** (2D **169**)
PL26, Sticker	.7A **64** (3C **169**)
Rescorla Ct. TR27: Hayl	.2H **141**
RESKADINNICK	.5B **110**
Reskadinnick Rd. TR14: Camb, Res	.5B **110**
(not continuous)	
RESKIVERS	.7H **99**
Respryn Cl. PL14: Lisk	.4C **70**
Respryn Rd. PL30: B'min, L'ock	.6H **33**
PL31: B'min	.6H **33**
Restormel Castle	.1E **52**
Restormel Ind. Est. PL22: Los	.3F **53**
Restormel Rd. PL4: Plym	.1H **163**
PL13: Loo	.4H **81**
PL22: Los	.1E **52**
TR18: Newl	.7C **148**
Restormel Ter. PL4: Plym	.1H **163**
TR11: Fal	.1F **133**
Restronguet Barton TR11: M Bri	.1H **129**
Restronguet Hill TR11: M Bri	.7F **125**
RESTRONGUET PASSAGE	.6G **125**
RESTRONGUET POINT	.6H **125**
RESTRONGUET WEIR	.7H **125**
RESUGGA	.5C **54**
RESUGGA GREEN	.4K **49**
Resugga Grn. La. PL26: Penw	.4K **49**
RESUGGA LANE END	.7C **54**
Reswythen Wlk. TR14: Tol D	.3F **111**
Retallack Gdns. TR20: Gold	.4K **151**
Retallick Mdws. PL25: S Aus	.4B **58**
Retanning La. PL26: Stick	.3K **63**
RETIRE	.1D **169**
Retorrick Mill TR8: M Por	.3F **29**
Retreat, The TR4: Chac	.6E **104**
Retreat Ct. TR9: S Maj	.4D **30**
Retyn Barns TR8: Sum	.2B **44**
REXON	.2D **167**
Reynolds Gro. PL5: Plym	.5K **89**
REZARE	.3D **167**
Rhind St. PL31: B'min	.3G **33**
Rhubarb Hill TR8: Hol B	.2B **38**
Rialton Barton TR8: St Mino	.3C **36**
Rialton Hgts. TR7: S Mino	.2B **36**
Rialton Rd. TR7: S Mino	.3B **36**
TR8: S Mino	.2C **36**
Rice La. PL26: G Hav	.3H **135**
Richards Cres. TR1: Tru	.5F **107**
Richards La. TR16: I'gan	.1K **111**
Richards Ter. PL10: M'brk	.2C **94**
Richard Taunton Ho. TR1: Tru	.5J **107**
(off Corte Spry)	
Richmond Gdns. TR18: Penz	.4F **149**
(off Richmond St.)	
Richmond Hill TR1: Tru	.5H **107**
Richmond M. TR18: Penz	.4F **149**
(off Tolver Pl.)	
Richmond Pl. TR1: Tru	.5H **107**
TR15: Red	.4E **112**
(off Basset St.)	
TR26: S Ives	.2H **137**
Richmond Rd. PL13: Pely	.2C **80**
Richmond St. TR18: Hea	.3D **148**
TR18: Penz	.4F **149**
Richmond Ter. TR1: Tru	.5H **107**
Richmond Way TR26: C Bay	.7F **137**
Ricketts Rd. PL26: Polg	.3D **64**
Ridgegrove Hill PL15: Laun	.3H **17**
Ridgegrove La. PL15: Laun	.2H **17**
Ridgeo Mill TR18: Gul	.2G **149**
RIDGEOVEAN	.2G **149**
Ridge Pk. Av. PL4: Plym	.1H **163**
Ridgevale Cl. TR18: Gul	.2G **149**
Ridgevale La. TR18: Gul	.2G **149**
Ridgeway PL12: Salt	.4F **89**
TR2: Pro	.2H **99**
TR6: P'rth	.4B **40**
Ridgewell Ter. TR9: Fr'don	.4G **45**
Ridgewood Cl. PL26: S Aus	.1K **65**
RILLA MILL	.3C **167**
Ringway Flats PL31: B'min	.3F **33**
Ringwell Hill TR3: C Dow	.6B **116**
Ringwell Holiday Pk. TR3: C Dow	.6B **116**
RINSEY	.2C **173**
RINSEY CROFT	.2A **156**
Rinsey La. TR13: Ash	.3A **156**
RISING SUN	.3A **74**
Ritz Bingo	
Penzance	.5F **149**
(off Queen St.)	
Rivendell PL27: Wade	.5F **25**
Riverbank PL12: Salt	.2J **89**
River Ct. PL12: Salt	.7F **85**
River Row TR15: I Hig	.4B **112**
Rivers, The PL12: Salt	.4G **89**
Riversdale Pl. PL27: Wade	.4E **24**
RIVERSIDE	.3K **89**
Riverside PL15: Laun	.2G **17**
PL26: Nanp	.6G **47**
PL28: Pad	.3B **22**
PL30: Lani	.6H **31**
TR4: Chac	.5E **104**
(off Chacewater Hill)	
TR20: L Roc	.3A **150**
(off Castle Vw.)	
TR26: Lel	.2E **140**
TR27: Ang	.7G **139**
Riverside Av. TR7: Newq	.4B **34**
Riverside Cl. TR20: Ludg	.2J **155**
Riverside Cotts. PL12: Salt	.4E **88**
Riverside Ct. PL22: Los	.3F **53**
Riverside Cres. TR7: Newq	.4A **34**
Riverside Holdiay Pk. TR8: Lane	.7J **35**
Riverside Ho. TR1: Tru	.1K **117**
Riverside M. PL12: Salt	.2J **89**
Riverside Mills PL15: Laun	.2G **17**
Riverside Vw. TR1: Tru	.6A **108**
River St. PL26: Mev	.6C **134**
TR1: Tru	.5J **107**
TR2: P'stho	.3K **131**
River Ter. PL26: Mev	.6C **134**
(off River St.)	
River Valley Country Pk. TR20: Relu	.1D **152**
River Valley Holiday Pk. PL26: Lon A	.3F **65**
River Vw. PL12: Salt	.2H **89**
PL13: Loo	.4G **81**
PL18: S An Cpl	.3E **74**
TR2: Tr'sln	.3F **109**
TR11: Flu	.5F **129**
Riverview TR11: Fal	.6E **128**
River Vw. Ter. PL23: Gola	.1J **61**
River Wlk. PL25: S Aus	.6F **57**
TR1: Tru	.5K **107**
(off St Mary's Ct.)	
Riviera Apartments TR26: C Bay	.6F **137**
Riviera Cl. TR12: Mull	.2H **161**
Riviera La. TR2: S Mawe	.7C **130**
Riviere Chalet Camp TR27: Phil	.7A **138**
Riviere Sands Holiday Pk.	
TR27: Phil	.6B **138**
RIVIERE TOWANS	.7A **138**
RNAS Culdrose	.2D **173**
RNAS Culdrose TR12: Helst	.7D **158**
RNAS Culdrose Viewing Enclosure	.2D **173**
Roach's Ct. TR26: C Bay	.7G **137**
Roach's Row TR15: Red	.3D **112**

Robartes Ct. PL26: S Den 2E 46
TR1: Tru 5J 107
Robartes Gdns. PL25: S Aus 5J 57
Robartes Pl. PL25: S Aus 5J 57
Robartes Rd. PL26: S Den 2D 46
PL31: B'min 3F 33
TR7: Newq 4G 35
Robartes Ter. PL22: Los 2E 52
TR16: I'gan 7J 101
Robbins Hall PL4: Plym 3J 163
Robert Eliot Ct. PL25: S Aus 6F 57
Robert Hichens Rd. TR11: Fal 7E 128
Roberts Av. PL11: Tor 3K 93
Robin Dr. PL15: Laun 5K 17
Robins Cl. PL24: B'vey 4G 59
Robinsons Dr. TR13: Helst 3E 158
ROBOROUGH 1D 171
ROCHE 5B 42 (1C 169)
Roche Rd. PL26: Bugl 6G 43
PL26: Sten 3G 49
Roche Rock 5C 42
Roche Rural Workshops
PL26: Vict 1C 42
Roche Station (Rail) 2B 42
Rochester Rd. PL4: Plym 1K 163
ROCK 2E 22 (3D 165)
Rock Cl. TR14: Camb 1F 119
Rockhaven Gdns. PL27: Pity 7G 19
ROCKHEAD 1B 14 (2A 166)
Rockhead St. PL33: Dela 1B 14
Rockhill Bus. Pk. PL26: Bugl 2G 49
Rocklands TR7: Newq 3G 35
Rock La. PL31: B'min 4E 32
Rock Lifeboat Station 2D 22
Rock Rd. PL27: Pity, Rock 2D 22
TR18: Penz 7D 148
Rocks, The PL26: Pent 1D 134
Rock Ter. TR18: Hea 3D 148
Rock Towers PL13: Loo 7K 81
Rock Vw. Parc PL26: Roch 3B 42
Rock Vs. PL27: Rock 2F 23
ROCKWENNA 2B 46
Rocky La. TR5: S Agn 1A 96
TR20: Tresc 2J 153
Rocky Pk. Rd. PL25: S Aus 7G 57
Rodda Cl. PL18: Gun 1H 75
Rodda's Rd. TR4: Mt Hwk 7H 97
Rodings, The PL14: Menh 1H 79
Rodwell Cl. TR15: Red 3F 113
Rodwill Cl. TR27: Leeds 7C 142
Roekindale Cl. TR15: I Hig 4K 111
Roeselare Av. PL11: Tor 3J 93
Roeselare Cl. PL11: Tor 3J 93
Rogers Dr. PL12: Salt 1F 89
Roma Ct. TR7: Newq 2K 35
Roman Bri. PL13: Polp 7B 80
Roman Dr. PL31: B'min 6H 33
Ropehaven Cl. PL25: S Aus 3J 57
Ropehaven Rd. PL25: S Aus 3J 57
Rope Wlk. PL4: Plym 6K 163
PL26: Dup 7A 58
(off Pagoda Dr.)
PL28: Pad 3A 22
TR4: Mt Hwk 6G 97
Rope Wlk., The TR2: S Mawe 7D 130
(off Grove Hill)
TR26: S Ives 1J 137
Ropewalk, The TR18: Penz 6D 148
Ropewalk Rd. TR3: Cale 2H 117
ROSCADDON 6D 160
Roscadghill Parc TR18: Hea 3D 148
Roscadghill Rd. TR18: Hea 4C 148
Roscarrack TR15: I'gan 2H 111
Roscarrack Cl. TR11: Fal 3C 132
Roscarrack Rd. TR11: B Wat, Fal 4A 132
Roscarrock Hill PL29: P Isa 2H 19
ROSCROGGAN 4D 110
ROSE 3F 41 (2A 168)
Roseacre Dr. TR15: Red 3E 112
ROSE-AN-GROUSE 5C 140
Rosecliston Campsite TR8: Trevem 7F 35
Rose Cotts. PL17: Harr 5A 74
TR14: Camb 7E 110
Rosecott Pk. EX23: Kilkh 2G 7
Rose Ct. PL25: S Aus 4A 58
Rosecraddoc Holiday Village PL14: Lisk 5E 66
Rosecraddoc Lodge Holiday Bungs.
PL14: Lisk 6E 66
Rosecraddoc Vw. PL14: Trem 5C 66
Rosedale Gdns. PL31: B'min 3J 33
Rosedale Rd. TR1: Tru 4J 107
Rose Eglos TR11: B Wat 3A 132
Rose Eglos Cl. TR11: B Wat 3A 132
ROSEHILL 4C 148
Rose Hill PL22: Los 4E 52
PL23: Fow 7J 61
PL24: S Bla 2H 59
PL26: Stick, T'lwth 3A 64
PL29: P Isa 2J 19

Rose Hill TR4: P'twn 7C 96
TR15: Red 3D 112
Rosehill PL30: Lani 5H 31
TR2: Lad 6F 37
TR11: M Bri 2E 128
TR17: Mar 3E 150
Rosehill Cl. PL22: Los 3E 52
Rosehill Gdns. TR18: Hea 4C 148
Rosehill Lodges TR4: P'twn 7C 96
Rosehill Mdw. TR18: Hea 4C 148
Rose Hill Ter. PL18: Cals 7H 75
ROSELAND 7F 71
Roseland TR2: S Mawe 5D 130
Roseland Ct. TR2: Tregon 6J 99
(off Roseland Parc)
Roseland Cres. TR2: Tregon 6H 99
TR4: Chac 6E 104
Roseland Gdns. PL31: B'min 2G 33
TR2: Very 6H 135
TR15: Red 2E 112
Roseland Parc TR2: Tregon 6J 99
Roseland Pk. TR14: Camb 6D 110
Roseland Rd. PL31: B'min 3G 33
Roseland Vis. Cen. 7D 130
Rose La. TR26: S Ives 1J 137
Roselare Cl. PL25: S Aus 2J 57
Roselidden Parc TR13: Helst 2B 158
Roselyon Pl. PL24: Par 2J 59
Rose Mdw. TR3: Stith 7A 122
Rose Mdws. TR4: Goonh 5H 41
Rosemellen Ter. PL14: Lisk 6A 70
Rosemellin TR14: Camb 6E 110
(not continuous)
ROSEMELLING 3D 50
Rosemergy & Bosportennis 1B 172
Rosemullion TR6: P'rth 4B 40
(off Atlantic Bay)
Rosemullion Gdns. PL17: Call 5D 72
TR14: Tol D 3F 111
Rosemullion Head 2A 174
Rosemundy TR5: S Agn 3B 96
ROSENANNON 1C 169
Rosenannon TR11: Mawn S 2B 160
Rosenannon La. TR15: I'gan 2H 111
Rosenannon Rd. TR15: I'gan 2H 111
ROSENITHON 2E 162
Rose Row TR15: Red 3D 112
Roserrow PL27: S Minv 4F 19
Roserrow Golf Course 5F 19
Rose Ter. PL18: S An Cpl 3E 74
PL28: S Mer 6E 20
TR12: Gweek 6H 159
TR18: Penz 4F 149
(off Rosevean Rd.)
Rosevale TR18: Penz 6E 148
Rosevale Cres. TR14: Camb 6C 110
Rose Va. Dr. TR14: Camb 6C 110
Rosevale Gdns. PL30: Lux 2D 50
Rose Valley TR10: M Bur 7F 127
Rosevalley TR3: Thre 5A 106
Rosevallon La. PL31: B'min 4E 32
ROSEVEAN 1J 49 (2D 169)
Rosevean TR18: Penz 4F 149
Rosevean Av. TR14: Camb 7E 110
Rosevean Cl. TR14: Camb 7E 110
Rosevean Rd. TR18: Penz 4F 149
Rosevean Ter. TR18: Penz 4F 149
ROSEVEAR 1J 49
Roseveare Dr. PL26: Goth 1H 47
Roseveare Pk. PL26: Goth 1H 47
Rosevear Rd. PL26: Bugl 7H 43
Rosevear Rd. Ind. Est. PL26: Bugl 7H 43
Roseville Holiday Pk. TR4: Goonh 4H 41
ROSEVINE 1K 131
Rosewall Cotts. TR26: S Ives 4G 137
Rosewall Ter. TR26: S Ives 3G 137 (3C 136)
ROSEWARNE
Camborne 6D 110
Hayle 2E 142
Rosewarne TR13: P'ven 7F 157
Rosewarne Cl. TR14: Camb 6C 110
Rosewarne Cotts. TR14: Camb 6A 70
Rosewarne Downs TR14: Camb 5D 110
Rosewarne Farm Caravan Pk.
TR14: Camb 6D 110
Rosewarne Gdns. TR14: Camb 7D 110
Rosewarne Ga. TR14: Camb 5D 110
Rosewarne Mdws. TR14: Camb 5D 110
Rosewarne Pk. TR14: Camb 6D 110
Rosewarne Rd. TR14: Camb 7D 110
TR27: Gwinn 2E 142
Rosewarne Ter. TR14: Camb 5D 110
Rosewater Caravan Pk. PL30: S Teat 2A 26
ROSEWEEK 2H 65
Rosewin M. TR9: S Maj 4C 30
Rosewin Row TR1: Tru 4K 107
TR9: S Maj 4C 30
Rosewithian Cl. TR27: Con D 5K 139

ROSEWORTHY
Camborne 1D 173
Truro 7A 98
Rosina Way PL26: Penw 5K 49
Roskear TR14: Camb 7E 110
Roskear Cft. TR14: Camb 4E 110
Roskear Flds. TR14: Camb 6E 110
Roskear Parc TR14: Camb 5F 111
Roskear Rd. TR14: Camb 7E 110
Roskilling TR13: Helst 2D 158
Roskilling Wartha TR13: Helst 2D 158
Roskilly La. TR14: Barr, P'nds 3A 118
Roskilly's 3C 162
ROSKORWELL 2A 174
Roskrow Cl. TR16: Four L 3B 120
Roskruge Cl. TR13: Helst 1D 158
Ros Lyn TR26: C Bay 7E 136
Roslyn Cl. PL25: S Aus 3A 57
(not continuous)
Rosparc TR2: Pro 2J 99
Rosparvah Gdns. TR18: Hea 3D 148
Rospeath Ind. Est. TR20: Crow 2K 155
Rospeath La. TR20: Crow . . . . .2K 155 & 1F 151
Rossett Gdns. PL31: B'min 4J 33
Rostalek PL30: S B'wd 4H 27
ROSUDGEON 6B 152 (2C 173)
ROSUDGEON COMMON 6C 152
Rosudgeon Downs TR20: Rosu 7C 152
Rough La. TR3: Pons 5F 123
Rough St. TR16: L'ner, Red 2F 121
Rough Tor 2B 166
Roughtor Dr. PL32: Came 4H 15
Rough Tor Hut Circles 2B 166
Roughtor Rd. PL32: Came 3K 15
Roughtor Vw. PL33: Dela 3A 14
Roundhouse Business Park, The
PL24: Par 3J 59
Round Ring TR10: P'ryn 3A 128
(not continuous)
Round's La. PL34: Tin 7C 12
Roundwood Settlement 3B 168
Rous Rd. PL12: S Dom 2F 77
ROW 3J 27 (3A 166)
Row, The TR2: V Grn 4K 135
Rowan Cl. PL31: B'min 4D 32
Rowan Ct. PL12: Salt 3E 88
Rowans, The EX23: Bud 6D 8
PL12: S Mel 6A 76
Rowe Bowl 7D 110
Rowe Cl. PL14: Dob 3D 68
Rowe's La. TR13: Helst 2E 158
Rowes Ter. PL26: Fox 1G 55
Rowe St. PL11: Tor 3K 93
Row Hill PL30: S B'wd 2H 27
Rowse Gdns. PL18: Cals 7J 75
Royal Albert Ct. PL12: Salt 2F 89
Royal Cinema
St Ives 3H 137 (3D 136)
Royal Citadel, The 7J 163
Royal Corinthian Yacht Club 7J 163
Royal Cornwall Mus. 5J 107
Royal Cornwall Showground 4A 24
Royal Cornwall Yacht Club 7F 129
Royale Ct. TR18: Penz 4G 149
Royal Fowey Yacht Club 7K 61
Royalist Ct. TR11: Fal 2G 133
(off Tregunter M.)
Royal Naval War Memorial 7G 163
Royal Pde. PL1: Plym 5G 163
Royal Sq. TR26: S Ives 3H 137
Roydon Cl. PL15: Laun 1G 17
Roydon La. PL15: Laun 1G 17
Roydon Rd. PL15: Laun 1G 17
RUAN HIGH LANES 5F 135 (3C 169)
RUAN LANIHORNE 3B 168
RUAN MAJOR 3A 174
RUAN MINOR 3A 174
Rubble La. TR7: Newq 4C 34
RUDDLEMOOR 7F 49
RUMFORD 3C 165
Rumps Cliff Castle, The 2D 165
Rundle Ct. PL14: Lisk 6A 70
Rundles Ct. TR1: Tru 6A 108
Rural Workshops EX23: Kilkh 1H 7
PL26: S Den 2D 46
RUSHFORD 3D 167
Rush Pk. Ter. PL18: Gun 1G 75
Ruskin Ct. TR9: S Maj 6B 30
Russell Cl. PL12: Salt 2E 88
PL18: Gun 1H 75
Russell Pl. PL4: Plym 1G 163
Russell St. PL14: Lisk 5B 70
Russell Way TR10: P'ryn 5A 128
RUTHERNBRIDGE 1D 169
RUTHVOES 1C 169
Ruthy's La. PL28: Pad 3B 22
Rye Hill PL12: Salt 3E 88
TR3: Pons 5F 123
Rylands Ter. PL30: S B'wd 2J 27

RYSKAMMEL 3J 15
RYSRUDH 3E 112

S

Saffron Cl. PL23: Fow 7J 61
Sail Loft Studios TR26: S Ives 1J 137
ST AGNES 2B 96 (2A 168)
St Agnes Beacon Caravan Site TR5: S Agn 1F 97
St Agnes Mus. .3A 96
ST ALLEN 2B 168
St Ambrusca Rd. TR8: Cran 6B 34
St Andrews Cl. PL12: Salt 3E 88
  PL18: Cals 7J 75
  TR3: Pons 5F 123
St Andrews Cross PL1: Plym 5H 163
St Andrew's Pl. PL10: Caws 6E 94
St Andrew's Rd. EX23: Stra 5G 9
  PL24: Par 2J 59
St Andrew's St. PL10: Caws 6E 94
  TR26: S Ives 2J 137 (3D 136)
St Andrews Ter. PL24: Par 1J 59
  TR3: Pons 5F 123
  (off Park Rd.)
St Andrew St. PL1: Plym 5H 163
  PL10: M'brk .2B 94
St Annes TR11: Mawn S 3B 160
St Annes Cl. TR26: Lel 2E 140
St Annes Hill EX23: Bud 1D 10
St Annes La. TR7: Newq 3H 35
St Annes Rd. PL12: Salt 2G 89
  PL24: B'vey .4G 59
  PL25: T'oon .5C 56
  TR7: Newq 2H 35
ST ANN'S CHAPEL 3D 74 (3J 167)
St Anta Rd. TR26: C Bay 7G 137
ST ANTHONY 1B 174
St Anthony Ho. TR2: Tregon 6J 99
  (off Roseland Parc)
ST ANTHONY-IN-MENEAGE 2A 174
St Anthony Pl. TR18: Penz 6F 149
  (off Under Chapel Yd.)
St Anthony Rd. TR12: Mana 6C 160
St Anthony Way TR11: Fal 3E 132
St Aubyn Cres. TR7: Newq 3H 35
St Aubyn Est. TR14: Praze 4K 143
St Aubyns TR20: Gold 4K 151
St Aubyns Cl. TR14: Praze 3K 143
St Aubyn's Rd. TR1: Tru 6K 107
St Aubyns Ter. TR4: Cusg 1E 122
St Aubyn's Vean TR1: Tru 6K 107
  (off Strangways Ter.)
ST AUSTELL 6H 57 (2D 169)
St Austell Arts Centre & Theatre 7E 56
St Austell Bay Bus. Pk. PL25: S Aus 5E 58
St Austell Brewery 5H 57
St Austell Enterprise Pk. PL25: S Aus 1J 57
St Austell Golf Course 1D 64
St Austell Rd. PL24: S Bl G 4E 58
  TR2: Pro 2H 99
St Austell Row TR2: S Mawe 7D 130
St Austell Station (Rail) 5H 57
St Austell St. TR1: Tru 5K 107
  TR8: Sum 7B 44
St Benedicts Pl. PL24: Tyw 2A 60
St Benets Cl. PL30: Lani 7H 31
ST BLAZEY 1H 59 (2D 169)
ST BLAZEY GATE 3G 59 (2D 169)
St Blazey Rd. PL24: Par 2J 59
St Breaca Cl. TR13: Breag 2D 156
St Breock Downs Monolith 1C 169
ST BREOCK (VILLAGE) 5C 24 (3D 165)
ST BREOCK (WADEBRIDGE) 4F 25
ST BREWARD 2J 27 (3A 166)
ST BUDEAUX 2D 171
ST BURYAN 2G 147 (2B 172)
St Buryan Hill TR19: Penb 5K 147
St Carantoc Way TR8: Cran 6A 34
St Catherine's Castle 7A 60
St Catherines Ct. PL23: Fow 6A 60
St Catherines Cove PL23: Fow 6A 60
St Catherines Hill PL15: Laun 4F 17
St Clare Flats TR18: Penz 4E 148
St Clare St. TR18: Penz 4E 148
St Clare Ter. TR18: Penz 4E 148
  (off St Clare St.)
ST CLEER 4A 66 (1B 170)
St Cleer Dr. PL27: Wade 3G 25
St Cleer Holy Well 4A 66
St Cleer Rd. PL14: Lisk 3B 70
ST CLEMENT 7E 108 (3B 168)
St Clement's Cl. TR1: Tru 5A 108
St Clement's Hill TR1: Tru 5A 108
St Clements Parc TR1: Tru 5A 108
St Clements Ter. TR1: Tru 4K 107
  TR19: Mou 6D 154
St Clement St. TR1: Tru 4K 107
St Clement Vean TR1: Tru 3B 108

ST CLETHER 2C 167
St Columb Bus. Cen. TR9: S Maj 5C 30
ST COLUMB MAJOR 4C 30 (1C 169)
St Columb Major Bus. Pk. TR9: S Maj 6C 30
St Columb Major Ind. Est. TR9: S Maj 6B 30
ST COLUMB MINOR 2A 36 (1B 168)
St Columb Rd. Ind. Workshops TR9: S Roa . . .1G 45
  (off Newquay Rd.)
St Columb Road Station (Rail) 1G 45
St Cuthbert Cl. PL15: Laun 2G 17
St Cuthbert's Rd. TR7: Newq 3E 34
St Cyriac PL30: Lux 1D 50
ST DAY 3K 113 (3A 168)
St Day Rd. TR15: Red 3E 112
  TR16: Tref 5F 113
ST DENNIS 2E 46 (2C 169)
St Dennis Workshop Units PL26: S Den 2D 46
ST DOMINICK 2G 77 (1C 171)
St Dominic Pk. PL17: Meth 6A 74
St Dominics Cl. PL31: B'min 3G 33
St Dominic Sq. TR1: Tru 5J 107
St Dominic St. TR1: Tru 5J 107
  TR18: Penz 4F 149
  (off St Michael's St.)
St Edmunds La. PL28: Pad 3B 22
St Eia St. TR26: S Ives 1K 137 (2E 136)
St Elvan Cres. TR13: P'ven 5F 157
St Elvan's Courtyard TR13: P'ven 7F 157
  (off Commercial Rd.)
ST ENDELLION .3D 165
ST ENODER 6C 44 (2B 168)
St Enodoc Cl. PL27: Wade 3G 25
St Enodoc Golf Course 1D 24
ST ERME 3C 98 (3B 168)
ST ERNEY 2G 87 (2C 171)
ST ERTH 6F 141 (1C 173)
St Erth Hill TR27: S Er 7F 141
St Erth Ind. Est. TR27: Can 4D 140
St Erth La. TR27: S Er 6F 141
ST ERTH PRAZE 6K 141 (1C 173)
St Erth Station (Rail) 5D 140
ST ERVAN 3C 165
ST EVAL 3H 31 (1B 168)
St Eval Kart Circuit 1B 168
ST EWE 3C 169
St Fimbarrus Rd. PL23: Fow 6B 60
St Francis Rd. TR9: I Que, S Roa 1G 45
St Francis St. TR18: Penz 4F 149
  (off St Michael's St.)
ST GENNYS 1B 166
St George's Arc. TR11: Fal 1F 133
St Georges Ct. PL13: Loo 6H 81
St George's Cres. PL31: B'min 4E 32
St George's Hill TR6: P'rth 5A 40
St Georges Hill Cl. TR6: P'rth 5A 40
St George's Pk. PL22: Los 2E 52
St Georges Rd. PL12: Salt 2F 89
  PL13: Loo 4H 81
  PL26: Nanp 6G 47
  TR1: Tru 4H 107
  TR7: Newq 3E 34
  TR27: Hayl 2H 141
St Georges Sq. PL26: Mev 6C 134
ST GERMANS 5D 86 (2C 171)
St Germans Rd. PL17: Call 6D 72
St Germans Station (Rail) 6E 86
St Giles Dr. PL27: Wade 3F 25
St Giles M. PL27: Wade 3F 25
ST GILES ON THE HEATH 1D 167
St Gluvias Parc TR10: P'ryn 4B 128
St Gluvias St. TR10: P'ryn 5B 128
St Golder Rd. TR18: Newl 7C 148
St Grace's Ct. TR2: Pro 2J 99
St Henry St. TR18: Penz 4F 149
  (off St Michael's St.)
ST HILARY 3B 152 (1C 173)
ST ISSEY 3D 165
ST IVE 1C 171
St Ive Rd. PL14: Pens 1K 67
ST IVES 2J 137 (1C 173)
St Ives Bay Holiday Pk. TR27: Log 5E 138
St Ives Holiday Village TR26: Lel 4A 140
St Ives La. TR27: Gwith 2G 139
St Ives Leisure Cen. 4G 137 (3C 136)
St Ives Mus. 1K 137 (2E 136)
St Ives (Park & Ride) 4G 137 (3C 136)
St Ives Rd. TR19: Pend 3D 144
  TR26: C Bay, Lel, S Ives 5E 136
St Ives Society of Artists Gallery 1J 137
St Ives Station (Rail) 4J 137 (3D 136)
St Ives Theatre .3H 137
St James Ct. PL11: Tor 3K 93
  TR26: S Ives .3G 137
St James Pl. TR13: Helst 3B 158
  (off Church St.)
St James Pl. E. PL1: Plym 6F 163
St James Pl. W. PL1: Plym 6F 163

St James Rd. PL11: Tor 4K 93
St James's Ter. TR10: P'ryn 5K 127
St James' St. TR18: Penz 4F 149
St James Vw. TR9: P'ale 4F 45
ST JIDGEY 1C 169
ST JOHN 6D 92 (2D 171)
St Johns Bus. Pk. TR13: Helst 4B 158
St Johns Cl. PL10: M'brk 2C 94
  TR13: Helst 3A 158
St Johns Gdns. TR11: Flu 6F 129
St Johns La. PL11: Ant, S John 5C 92
St Johns Rd. PL10: M'brk 1C 94
  PL15: Laun 5F 17
  TR7: Newq 3E 34
  TR13: Helst 3B 158
St John's St. TR27: Hayl 1J 141
St John's Ter. TR3: Devo 2C 124
  TR18: Penz 4F 149
  (off Leskinnick Ter.)
  TR19: Pend 4C 144
St Johns Wlk. TR26: S Ives 3B 136
St Joseph's Rd. PL15: Laun 1G 17
St Julitta PL30: Lux 1D 50
ST JUST
  Penzance 3J 145 (1A 172)
  Truro 2D 130 (1B 174)
ST JUST IN ROSELAND 2E 130 (1B 174)
ST KEVERNE 2C 162 (2A 174)
St Keverne Rural Workshops TR12: S Kev 3B 162
ST KEW 3A 166
ST KEW HIGHWAY 3A 166
ST KEYNE 1C 78 (1B 170)
St Keyne Cl. TR1: Tru 3J 107
St Keyne Wishing Well Halt Station (Rail) 1E 78
ST LAWRENCE 5B 32 (1D 169)
St Lawrence M. PL4: Plym 1J 163
St Lawrence Rd. PL4: Plym 1J 163
  PL30: B'min 5B 32
  PL31: B'min 5B 32
St Leonards PL31: B'min 4E 32
St Leonard's Rd. PL15: Laun 1G 17
St Leonards Ter. PL31: B'min 3E 32
ST LEVAN 7G 147 (2A 172)
St Levan Cl. TR17: Mar 4G 151
St Levan Rd. TR17: Mar 4G 151
St Lukes Ter. PL12: Tide 1B 86
  (off Church Rd.)
ST MABYN 6C 26 (3A 166)
St Mabyn Holiday Pk. PL30: S Mab 6E 26
St Margarets La. PL26: Polg 2D 64
St Margarets Pk. PL26: Polg 2D 64
ST MARTIN
  Helston 2A 174
  Looe 1J 81 (2B 170)
St Martins Cl. PL13: Loo 3H 81
  TR14: Camb 1C 118
St Martins Ct. PL14: Lisk 5D 70
St Martins Cres. TR14: Camb 7C 110
St Martins Rd. EX23: Stra 6G 9
  PL13: Loo, S Mar 3G 81
St Martin's Ter. TR14: Camb 7C 110
St Marwenne Cl. EX23: March 3E 10
St Mary's PL13: Loo 7K 81
St Mary's Cl. PL31: B'min 4E 32
  TR18: Penz 5F 149
  (off St Mary's Ter.)
St Mary's Ct. TR7: Newq 4E 34
  (off St Mary's Rd.)
St Mary's Cres. PL31: B'min 4E 32
St Mary's Gdns. PL31: B'min 4E 32
St Mary's Pl. TR18: Penz 5F 149
  (off St Mary's Rd.)
St Marys Rd. PL15: Laun 1H 17
  PL24: B'vey 4F 59
  PL31: B'min 5D 32
  TR7: Newq 4E 34
St Mary's St. TR1: Tru 5K 107
  TR18: Penz 4F 149
St Mary's St. M. TR1: Tru 5K 107
  (off St Mary's St.)
St Mary's Ter. TR1: Tru 4J 107
  TR18: Penz 5F 149
St Matthews Hill PL27: Wade 3G 25
St Matthews Mdw. PL14: Lisk 4D 70
  (off Pengover Rd.)
ST MAWES 7D 130 (1B 174)
St Mawes Castle 7C 130
ST MAWGAN 5G 29 (1B 168)
St Mawgan Cl. PL31: B'min 3H 33
St Mellans Ter. TR12: Mull 2G 161
ST MELLION 6D 76 (1C 171)
St Mellion Cotts. PL12: S Mel 7D 76
St Mellion Golf Course 6C 76
ST MELLION PARK 6A 76
St Meriadoc Rd. TR14: Camb 7C 110
ST MERRYN 6E 20 (3C 165)
ST MEWAN 7D 56 (2C 169)
St Mewan La. PL25: S Mew, T'oon 5D 56
  PL26: S Mew .5D 56

ST MICHAEL CAERHAYS 3C 169
ST MICHAEL PENKEVIL 3B 168
St Michael's Cl. TR27: Hayl 3G 141
St Michael's Mount 6D 150
St Michael's Rd. EX23: Stra 5G 9
TR3: Pons .5F 123
TR6: P'rth .5B 40
TR7: Newq .4E 34
St Michael's St. TR18: Penz 4F 149
St Michael's Ter. TR18: Penz 4E 148
St Michael's Ter. La. PL4: Plym 2G 163
St Michael's Way PL26: Roch 5B 42
ST MINVER 6K 19 (3D 165)
St Minver Holiday Pk. PL27: S Minv 7K 19
St Moritz Cl. PL27: Treb 4C 18
St Moritz Vs. PL27: Treb 4C 18
ST NEOT 1A 170
ST NEWLYN EAST 2G 37 (2B 168)
St Newlyn East Golf Course 4J 37
St Nicholas Cl. TR27: Gwith 4G 139
St Nicholas Ct. TR26: S Ives 1J 137 (1D 136)
St Nicholas M. PL31: B'min 4G 33
St Nicholas Pk. PL22: Los 2D 52
St Nicholas's Chapel 1D 136
St Nicholas St. PL31: B'min 4G 33
TR1: Tru 5K 107
St Olaf's Rd. EX23: Stra 5G 9
St Peters Hill TR11: Flu 5F 129
TR18: Newl 2C 154
St Peters Rd. EX23: Stra 5G 9
TR11: Flu .5F 129
TR13: P'ven 7G 157
St Peters St. TR26: S Ives 1J 137 (2D 136)
St Peters Way TR13: P'ven 7G 157
St Petroc Church .3G 33
St Petrocs Cl. PL28: Pad 4B 22
PL31: B'min 4G 33
St Petrocs Mdw. PL28: Pad 3A 22
St Petry TR20: Gold 4K 151
St Philip St. TR18: Penz 4F 149
(off St Michael's St.)
ST PINNOCK 7A 68 (1B 170)
St Piran Cl. PL31: B'min 4D 32
St Pirans Cl. PL25: S Aus 3J 57
TR1: Tru 5K 107
St Pirans Ct. TR7: Newq 4E 34
TR14: Camb 1F 119
(Vivian Pk.)
TR14: Camb 7D 110
(Wellington Rd.)
TR18: Penz 5F 149
(off Jennings St.)
St Piran's Hill TR3: P Sta 3K 123
St Pirans Pde. TR6: P'rth 4B 40
St Pirans Parc TR13: P'ven 7G 157
St Pirans Rd. TR6: P'rth 4B 40
TR7: Newq 3D 34
St Pirans Way TR4: Short 6B 98
TR20: Perran 6J 151
St Pol-de-Leon Vw. TR19: Pau 4C 154
ST RUAN 3A 174
St Sampsons Cl. PL24: Tyw 1B 60
St Sampsons Ter. PL23: Gola 1J 61
St Saviour's Hill PL23: Polr 7B 60
St Saviour's La. PL28: Pad 2B 22
St Saviour's Ter. PL23: Polr 7C 60
(off St Saviour's Hill)
Saints Health & Fitness Cen. 1K 65
ST STEPHEN 4C 54 (2C 169)
ST STEPHENS
Launceston 1F 17 (2D 167)
Saltash 4F 89 (2D 171)
St Stephens Ct. PL15: Laun 2G 17
St Stephen's Hill PL12: Salt 4E 88
PL15: Laun 1G 17
St Stephens Rd. PL12: Salt 4F 89
PL26: Stick 2J 63
St Sulien PL30: Lux 1D 50
ST TEATH 2B 26 (2A 166)
St Teresa Ho. PL4: Plym 4K 163
St Therese Cl. PL17: Call 6D 72
St Thomas Cl. TR1: Tru 5F 107
St Thomas Ct. PL4: Plym 4K 163
St Thomas Hill PL15: Laun 3H 17
St Thomas Rd. PL15: Laun 2G 17
TR7: Newq 3F 35
St Thomas St. TR10: P'ryn 5B 128
ST TUDY 5J 27 (3A 166)
St Uny Cl. TR26: Lel 3D 140
St Uny Cres. TR15: C Bre 5B 112
ST VEEP 2A 170
St Warren St. TR18: Penz 4F 149
(off St Michael's St.)
ST WENN 1C 169
ST WINNOLLS 3A 90 (2C 171)
St Winnolls Pk. PL13: Loo 4H 81
ST WINNOW 2A 170
Salamanca St. PL11: Tor 3K 93

SALEM 6B 104
Salisbury Rd. TR1: Tru 5H 107
Salmon Row TR1: Tru 5K 107
(off Mitchell Hill)
SALTASH 3H 89 (2D 171)
Saltash By-Pass PL12: Salt 1D 88
Saltash Heritage Mus. 3J 89
Saltash Ind. Est. PL12: Salt 1E 88
Saltash Leisure Cen. 3G 89
Saltash Parkway Ind. Est.
PL12: Salt 1D 88
Saltash Rd. PL3: Plym 1F 163
PL17: Call .6D 72
Saltash Sailing Club 3J 89
SALTASH SERVICE AREA 7E 84
Saltash Station (Rail) 3J 89
Saltbox Cl. TR11: M Bri 2E 128
Saltbox Rd. TR11: M Bri 2E 128
Salt Cellar Hill TR13: P'ven 7F 157
Saltings, The TR26: Lel 3D 140
Saltings Ct. TR26: Lel 3D 140
Saltings Reach TR27: Hayl 4D 140
Saltmill Cl. PL12: Salt 2H 89
Saltmill Rd. PL12: Salt 1H 89
Saltponds TR19: Mou 6D 154
Salubrious Pl. TR26: S Ives 2J 137
Salubrious Ter. TR26: S Ives 2J 137
(off Fore St.)
SAMPFORD SPINEY 1D 171
Sampson Cl. PL18: S An Cpl 2D 74
Sampson Gdns. TR3: Pons 5E 122
Sampson's Ct. TR27: Con D 5J 139
Sampson Way TR3: Thre 5A 106
Sampys Hill TR11: Mawn S 2B 160
Samuel Bone Cl. PL14: Lisk 4C 70
SANCREED 2B 172
Sanctuary Cl. TR14: Camb 1C 118
Sanctuary La. EX23: Stra 4H 9
TR13: Helst 3C 158
Sanctuary La. Flats TR13: Helst 3C 158
(off Sanctuary La.)
Sand Bay TR11: Fal 3G 133
Sand Bay Holiday Flats TR6: P'rth 4B 40
Sand Cotts. TR3: Devo 2C 124
Sandfield Cres. TR14: Camb 1C 118
Sand Hill PL18: Dra, G'thy 3G 75
Sand Hill Pk. PL18: Dra 2G 75
Sandhurst Ter. TR1: Tru 4J 107
(off Higher Trehaverne)
Sand La. PL18: Cals 6G 75
Sandows La. TR26: S Ives 3G 137 (3C 136)
SANDPLACE 2B 170
Sandplace Rd. PL13: Loo 1G 81
Sand Quay La. PL12: Salt 3J 89
(off Old Ferry Rd.)
Sandra Way PL31: B'min 3E 32
SANDWAYS 5G 75
Sandyacres TR27: Log 6E 138
SANDY BOTTOM .5K 57
Sandy Cl. PL14: S Keyn 2C 78
Sandy Comn. PL28: Cons B 5A 20
Sandy Ct. TR8: M Por 2C 28
Sandy Cove TR4: P'twn 6D 96
Sandy Hill PL25: S Aus 5K 57
Sandyhills PL27: Rock 2G 23
SANDYLAKE 2H 53
Sandylake La. PL22: Los 2H 53
Sandy La. PL25: S Aus 5F 57
(off Blowing Ho. Cl.)
PL28: H Bay 3D 20
PL28: T'one 2G 21
TR15: Red .4F 113
TR16: Red, Tref 4F 113
Sandy Rd. TR4: P'twn 6C 96
(not continuous)
Sango Ct. PL10: M'brk 1D 94
Sango Rd. PL11: Tor 4J 93
Santos Ter. PL24: Tyw H 7J 51
Saracen Cres. TR10: P'ryn 5A 128
Saracen Cl. TR10: P'ryn 5A 128
Saracen Pl. TR10: P'ryn 5A 128
Saracen Way TR10: P'ryn 5A 128
Sarahs Cl. PL28: Pad 4B 22
Sarahs Ct. PL28: Pad 4B 22
Sarah's La. PL28: Pad 4A 22
Sarahs Mdw. PL28: Pad 4B 22
Sarahs Vw. PL28: Pad 4B 22
Saunders La. PL11: Craft, P'wkle 5D 90
SAVEOCK 5G 105
Savoy Cinema
Penzance .5F 149
Sawles Rd. PL25: S Aus 6H 57
Sawmills La. TR16: Scor 6K 103
Scarcewater Vean TR1: St C'mt 5C 108
Scarletts Well Pk. PL31: B'min 2E 32
Scarletts Well Rd. PL31: B'min 2D 32
Scarne Ct. PL15: Laun 6J 17
Scarne Ind. Est. PL15: Laun 6H 17
Scholar's La. TR13: Sithn 1K 157

School Cl. PL24: B'vey 4G 59
TR7: S Mino 3B 36
School Hill PL15: Sth P 2A 16
PL23: Gola .1J 61
PL26: H St .5J 55
PL26: Mev .5C 134
PL28: Pad .3B 22
TR3: P Sta .3J 123
TR4: Short .7B 98
TR12: S Kev 2C 162
School La. PL17: Harr 5A 74
PL23: Polr .7C 60
PL25: T Mil .3C 58
TR1: Tru 6J 107
TR11: B Wat 2A 132
TR12: Cover 6D 162
TR14: Tro .5G 119
TR15: Red .3E 112
TR17: Mar .4F 151
TR18: Gul .2H 149
TR20: S Hil .3C 152
TR27: S Er .6F 141
School Rd. PL12: Land 6G 83
PL14: Pens .1J 67
PL17: Harr .5A 74
PL30: S Tud 5J 27
TR8: Sum 7B 44
TR14: Praze 4K 143
TR27: Leeds 7C 142
School Wlk. PL27: Wade 3G 25
Schooners Bus. Pk. PL27: Wade 3H 25
Sconner Rd. PL11: Tor 3J 93
Scoria Cl. TR16: Scor 6J 103
SCORRIER 6J 103 (3A 168)
Scorrier Ho. Workshops TR16: Scor 7J 103
Scorrier Rd. TR16: Red 7G 103
Scorrier St. TR16: S Da 2A 114
Scott Av. PL5: Plym 5K 89
Scott Cl. PL14: Pens 1K 67
Scowbuds TR14: Camb 5F 111
Scrations La. PL22: Los 3E 52
SCREDDA 1H 57
Screech Owl Sanctuary 1C 169
Sea Front TR16: P'ath 4E 100
Sea Front Cl. PL13: Loo 7K 81
Sea La. TR27: Hayl 1H 141
Sea Meads TR20: Pra S 7J 155
SEA MILLS 6C 22
Seapoint Apartments TR7: Newq 3F 35
Sea Rd. PL25: Carl 6C 58
Seaspray Leisure Flats TR4: P'twn 5C 96
SEATON 5F 79 (2C 171)
Seaton Ct. PL11: Seat 6G 79
Seaton Pk. PL11: Seat 5F 79
Seaton Valley Countryside Pk. 2C 171
Sea Vw. TR8: Cube 3D 38
Sea Vw. Cotts. TR20: L Roc 3A 150
(off Beech Ter.)
Seaview Cotts. TR11: Fal 7F 129
Sea Vw. Ct. TR11: Fal 3F 133
Sea Vw. Cres. TR2: S Mawe 7D 130
Sea Vw. Holiday Pk. TR19: Senn 5D 146
Sea Vw. La. TR8: Cube 3D 38
Sea Vw. Pl. TR26: S Ives 1K 137
Sea Vw. Rd. TR2: S Mawe 7D 130
TR11: Fal 3E 132
Sea Vw. Ter. PL13: Loo 5G 81
(off Chapel Ground)
PL18: S An Cpl 3E 74
PL24: S Bla 7H 51
PL26: Penw 5J 49
TR13: Helst 3B 158
TR14: Camb 1E 118
TR15: Red .4E 112
TR18: Newl 2C 154
TR20: Rosu 7E 152
TR26: S Ives 3H 137 (3D 136)
Seawall Rd. EX23: Flex 3E 8
Sefton Ho. TR14: Camb 5E 110
(off Vyvyans Ct.)
Seleggan Hill TR16: Red 7C 112
Sellon Cl. PL1: Plym 4F 163
SEN DAY 3K 113
Seneschall Pk. TR13: Helst 1D 158
SEN KLER 4A 66
SEN KOLOMM VEUR 4C 30
SEN MOWGAN 5G 29
SENNEN 4D 146 (2A 172)
Sennen Cl. PL11: Tor 2H 93
SENNEN COVE 3C 146 (2A 172)
Sennen Hgts. TR19: Senn C 3B 146
SEN OSTELL 6H 57
Sergeants Cl. TR4: Chac 6D 104
Sethnoe Way TR13: Breag 2D 156
Seton Cotts. TR14: Camb 7B 110
SEVENSTONES 2K 73
Seven Trees Ct. PL4: Plym 1K 163
SEWORGAN 1A 174
Seymour Av. TR7: Newq 3F 35

Seymour Cl. TR3: Thre 5K **105**
Seymour St. PL4: Plym 3K **163**
Shackleton Cres. PL27: S Eval 3J **31**
Shackleton Dr. TR7: Newq 4J **35**
Shaft Downs La. TR27: Reaw 2E **142**
Shaftesbury Cotts. PL4: Plym 1K **163**
Shaftesbury Ct. PL4: Plym 2K **163**
Shaftesbury Pl. *PL4: Plym* *2K 163*
       (off Shaftesbury Cotts.)
Sharaman Cl. PL25: S Aus 4A **58**
Sharlands Rd. EX23: March 4G **11**
Sharrow Point & Sharrow Cliffs 2C **171**
SHAUGH PRIOR 1D **171**
Sheep Fair Mdw. PL17: Call 5D **72**
SHEFFIELD 5B **154**
Sheila's Ct. TR26: C Bay 7F **137**
Shelburne Ct. TR11: Fal 2D **132**
Shelburne Rd. TR11: Fal 1D **132**
Shelley Rd. PL25: S Aus 5A **58**
SHERWELL 1K **73**
Sherwell Arc. PL4: Plym 2J **163**
Sherwell La. PL4: Plym 2J **163**
Sherwood Dr. PL31: B'min 3D **32**
SHEVIOCK 3G **91** (2C **171**)
Sheviock La. PL11: Craft, Shev 5F **91**
Shilson Ter. PL15: Laun 4H **17**
Shipbuilder Cl. PL26: Mev 4C **134**
Ships & Castle Leisure Cen. 2H **133**
Shipwreck Rescue & Heritage Cen. 7B **58**
Shipyard, The TR13: P'ven 7F **157**
Shire Hall Court Room Experience 4G **33**
       (off Mount Folly)
Shire Horse Centre & Carriage Mus. 3J **119**
Shires Way PL26: Roch 4B **42**
Shoemaker's La. PL12: Salt 3G **89**
Shoot Row TR15: Red 3E **112**
SHOP
   Bude 2A **164**
   Holsworthy 2B **164**
   Padstow 6D **20** (3C **165**)
Shop Hill TR17: Mar 4G **151**
Shopside TR15: C Bre 5B **112**
Shores La. PL27: Rock 1G **23**
Shortacross PL14: Trem 5C **66**
Short Cotts. PL11: Tor 3J **93**
Short Cross M. TR4: Mt Hwk 7G **97**
Short Cross Rd. TR4: Mt Hwk 7G **97**
SHORTLANESEND 6C **98** (3B **168**)
Shorts Hill TR14: Kill, Tresl 3D **118**
Shrubberies Hill TR13: P'ven 7G **157**
Shute Hill PL13: Pely 2C **80**
   PL22: Los 3E **52**
   TR11: Mawn S 3B **160**
   TR13: Breag 2D **156**
   TR13: Helst .3C **158**
   TR16: Carh 5K **113**
Shute La. PL14: Pens 1K **67**
   TR10: P'ryn 4A **128**
   TR13: P'ven 7F **157**
Shute Mdw. TR2: P'stho 3K **131**
   TR10: P'ryn 5A **128**
SHUTTA 3H **81**
Shutta Rd. PL13: Loo 6K **81** (4G **81**)
Siding PL4: Plym 1G **163**
Sidings, The PL25: S Aus 6J **57**
   PL26: Bugl .6H **43**
   PL33: Dela .3B **14**
Sidney Ter. TR15: Red 3E **112**
Silvanus Jenkin Av. PL14: Lisk 5D **70**
Silverbow Pk. TR4: Goonh 6G **41**
Silver Ct. TR15: Red 4D **112**
Silverdale Ct. *TR7: Newq* *3F 35*
       (off Mount Wise)
Silverdale Rd. TR11: Fal 2D **132**
Silver Hill TR3: P Sta 1J **123**
Silvershell Rd. PL29: P Isa 2J **19**
Silvershell Vw. PL29: P Isa 2J **19**
Silver St. PL12: Salt 3J **89**
Silver Ter. PL10: M'brk 1E **94**
Silverton Cl. EX23: Bud 5D **8**
Silverton Parc PL26: Bugl 2H **49**
Silverton Rd. EX23: Bud 5D **8**
Silver Way TR3: Thre 5K **105**
Sims Ter. PL18: Gun 2H **75**
Singlerose Rd. PL26: Sten 4G **49**
SINNS COMMON 5F **103**
Sir Arthur Quiller-Couch Memorial 7K **103**
SITHNEY 1H **157** (2D **173**)
SITHNEY COMMON 2K **157**
Sithney Common Hill TR13: Helst, Sithn . .2K **157**
SITHNEY GREEN 1K **157**
Sithney Old Hill TR13: Helst, Sithn 2K **157**
Skardon Pl. PL4: Plym 2J **163**
Skidden Gdns. TR26: S Ives 3J **137**
Skidden Hill TR26: S Ives 3J **137** (3D **136**)
Skinnard La. PL18: Alb 4F **75**
SKINNER'S BOTTOM 2J **103**
Skinner's Brewery 6K **107**
       (off Newham Rd.)

Skitta Cl. PL17: Call 4D **72**
Slade Pk. Rd. PL14: Pens 1K **67**
SLADESBRIDGE 5K **25** (3A **166**)
Slades La. TR10: P'ryn 4A **128**
Slades Rd. PL25: S Aus 3J **57**
Slate Cl. PL33: Dela 3A **14**
SLAUGHTERBRIDGE 2B **166**
Slipway PL27: Rock 2E **22**
Smallridge La. EX23: Stra 5J **9**
Smeaton's Tower 7G **163**
Smithfield Ct. TR8: Lane 6J **35**
Smithfield Dr. PL12: Salt 2D **88**
Smithick Hill TR11: Fal 1F **133**
Smiths Way PL12: Salt 2D **88**
Smithy Cl. PL12: Salt 1E **88**
Smithy Ct. PL32: Came 4J **15**
Smithy La. TR3: C Dow 7D **116**
Smugglers Cove TR16: P'ath 4E **100**
Smugglers Row *TR11: Fal* *7F 129*
      (off The Packet Quays)
Snappers La. PL26: Coomb 1E **62**
Snell Dr. PL12: Salt 2D **88**
Snells Ct. PL17: Call 5D **72**
Snowdrop Cres. PL15: Laun 5K **17**
Snowland Leisure Pk. PL24: Par 3K **59**
Socotra Dr. PL25: T'oon 5D **56**
Solar Row *TR1: Tru* *4K 107*
      (off Mitchell Hill)
SOLDON CROSS 2B **164**
Somerville Rd. TR6: P'rth 5B **40**
Sona Merg Cl. TR18: Hea 3D **148**
Sound Vw. PL18: S An Cpl 3E **74**
South Albany Rd. TR15: Red 5E **112**
Southbourne Cl. PL26: Fox 7J **47**
Southbourne Rd. PL25: S Aus 7H **57**
SOUTH CARN BREA 7B **112**
South Cliff TR19: Mou 6D **154**
Southcliff TR11: Fal 3G **133**
SOUTHDOWN 1F **95**
Southdown Cl. PL26: Stick 3K **63**
Southdown Quay 1F **95**
Southdown Rd. PL10: M'brk 1D **94**
   PL26: Stick .3K **63**
South Downs TR15: Red 6F **113**
Sth. Down Ter. PL10: M'brk 1E **94**
South Dr. TR14: Sth T 1E **110**
   TR15: Red .6F **113**
Southernhaye PL15: Laun 4H **17**
Southern Rd. PL17: Call 7C **72**
Southern Way PL27: Wade 4F **25**
Southfield PL12: Salt 3E **88**
Southfield Pl. TR26: S Ives 3G **137** (3C **136**)
Southfield Rd. EX23: Bud 5D **8**
Southgate Cl. *PL15: Laun* *3H 17*
      (off Southgate St.)
Southgate Pl. PL15: Laun 3H **17**
Southgate St. PL15: Laun 3H **17**
   TR15: Red .5E **112**
South Harbour *TR10: P'ryn* *5B 128*
      (off Eastwood Rd.)
SOUTH HILL 3D **167**
South Hill Rd. PL17: Call 2A **72**
SOUTH HOLE 1A **164**
Southlea Ter. TR3: Stith 1A **126**
South Pde. *TR18: Penz* *5F 149*
      (off Parade St.)
South Pde. M. *TR18: Penz* *5F 149*
      (off Parade St.)
South Pk. TR9: S Maj 5C **30**
   TR15: Red .4B **112**
South Pk. Cl. TR15: Red 4C **112**
Southpark Rd. PL24: Tyw 2K **59**
SOUTH PETHERWIN 2A **16** (2D **167**)
SOUTH PILL 1G **89**
South Pl. *TR18: Penz* *6F 149*
      (off Under Chapel Yd.)
   TR19: S Jus 3H **145**
South Pl. Folly TR18: Penz 6F **149**
South Pl. Gdns. TR19: S Jus 3H **145**
South Quay PL28: Pad 3B **22**
Sth. Quay Hill TR7: Newq 3E **34**
South Rd. TR3: Stith 1A **126**
   TR20: Gold 5K **151**
South Roskear Ter. TR14: Camb 6F **111**
Southside Quay PL1: Plym 6J **163**
Southside St. PL1: Plym 6J **163**
South St. PL22: Los 3E **52**
   PL23: Fow .7K **61**
   PL25: S Aus 6G **57**
   TR2: Gram R 7K **37**
SOUTH TEHIDY 3E **110**
South Ter. TR14: Camb 1D **110**
   TR18: Penz 6F **149**
South Towan TR4: P'twn 6D **96**
SOUTH TREVIDGE 3F **79**
South Turnpike *TR15: Red* *5E 112*
      (off Buckett's Hill)
South Vw. PL14: Lisk 3C **70**
   TR10: P'ryn 4A **128**

South Vw. TR13: P'ven 6F **157**
   TR16: I'gan *1J 111*
      (off Trevelyan Rd.)
Southview PL10: M'brk 1E **94**
Southview Dr. PL31: B'min 3G **33**
South Vw. Parc TR4: P'twn 7B **96**
Southview Rd. PL24: B'vey 4G **59**
South Vw. Ter. TR4: Black 2A **104**
Southview Ter. TR19: Mou 6D **154**
South Wlk. PL26: Goth 2H **47**
South Way TR8: Q Dow 6C **36**
Southway PL28: Win 3G **21**
Sth. Wheal Towan TR4: P'twn 5D **96**
SOUTH WHEATLEY 1C **167**
South Winds Caravan & Camping Pk.
   PL27: S Minv 2F **19**
Spargo Ct. TR10: M Bur 6G **127**
Spargo's La. *TR1: Tru* *4A 108*
      (off Tregolls Rd.)
Spar La. TR15: I'gan 1G **111**
Sparnock Gro. TR1: Tru 5D **106**
Sparnon Cl. PL25: S Aus 5F **57**
   TR15: Red .4E **112**
Sparnon Ct. *TR15: Red* *4E 112*
      (off Sparnon Cl.)
SPARNON GATE 7B **102**
Sparnon Hill TR15: Red 4E **112**
Sparnon Ter. TR15: Red 4E **112**
SPARRY BOTTOM 5B **114**
Sparry La. TR16: Carh 5A **114**
Spaven Mor TR14: Camb 5F **111**
Speares, The PL12: Salt 3D **88**
Spear's Ter. TR11: Fal 3D **132**
Speech La. TR3: Pons 6G **123**
Speedwell Cl. EX23: Bud 5E **8**
   PL10: M'brk 2D **94**
Spencer Gdns. PL12: Salt 4G **89**
Spernen Cl. TR26: C Bay 6E **136**
Spernen Wyn Rd. TR11: Fal 3E **132**
Spicers La. EX23: Stra 5H **9**
Spinnakers, The TR11: Fal 3C **132**
Spire Hill Pk. PL12: Salt 3E **88**
Spires, The TR1: Tru 3J **107**
Spitfire Row PL27: S Eval 3J **31**
Splash Leisure Pool 5E **8**
SPLATT
   Launceston 2C **167**
   Wadebridge 1G **23**
Sportsmans Cl. PL32: Came 3H **15**
Sportsmans Rd. PL32: Came 4G **15**
Springfield TR2: P'stho 3K **131**
Springfield Apartments PL26: Bugl 6H **43**
Springfield Bus. Pk. PL15: Laun 5E **16**
Springfield Cl. PL14: Dob 4D **68**
   PL22: Los 3F **53**
   PL25: S Aus 4K **57**
   PL26: Polg .2C **64**
   PL27: Phil .7D **138**
Springfield Ga. *PL13: Loo* *3H 81*
      (off Springfield Rd.)
Springfield Pk. TR11: M Bri 7E **124**
   TR14: Barr .4A **118**
Springfield Pl. TR9: S Maj 5B **30**
Springfield Rd. PL13: Loo 3H **81**
   PL14: Lisk .4D **70**
   TR7: Newq .3F **35**
   TR11: Fal .1C **132**
   TR20: Gold 4A **152**
Springfields PL26: Bugl 6H **43**
Springfield Way PL26: Roch 4B **42**
   TR3: Thre .5K **105**
   TR16: S Da 2K **113**
Spring Gdns. PL27: Wade 3F **25**
Springwell Vw. PL31: B'min 3H **33**
Spurway Rd. PL14: Lisk 4C **70**
Square, The EX23: Kilkh 2G **7**
   PL10: Caws 6E **94**
   PL12: Salt .2E **88**
   PL18: Gun .1H **75**
   PL18: S An Cpl 2D **74**
   PL26: Pent 1D **134**
   PL26: S Ste 4D **54**
   PL30: S Teat 2B **26**
   TR2: Gerr .3J **131**
   TR2: Gram R 6K **37**
   TR2: Pro 2H **99**
   TR2: P'stho 3K **131**
   TR2: S Mawe 7D **130**
   TR2: Tregon 6H **99**
   TR3: Stith .7A **122**
   TR4: Chac .6E **104**
   TR7: S Mino 2B **36**
   TR10: P'ryn 5B **128**
   TR11: Mawn S 2B **160**
   TR12: Lizar 5G **161**
   TR12: S Kev 2C **162**
   TR13: P'ven 7F **157**
   TR14: Praze 4K **143**
   TR16: Four L 3B **120**

Square, The TR16: P'ath 4F 101
　TR17: Mar 4E 150
　TR19: Pend 4C 144
　TR20: Ludg 2G 155
　TR27: Leeds 7C 142
Square Ind. Units, The TR2: Gram R 6K 37
Square Sail Shipyard .7B 58
Squire La. TR16: Carh 5A 114
Squires La. TR13: Helst, P'ose 3J 157
Stable Ct. PL27: Wade 3F 25
Stable Hobba TR20: Newl 7B 148
Stable Hobba Ind. Est. TR20: Newl 7C 148
Stables, The TR14: Sth T 1D 110
Stables Caravan Park, The TR9: I Que 2J 45
Stablys Dolcoath TR14: Camb 1F 119
STADDISCOMBE 2D 171
STADDON 3B 164
Staddon Ter. La. PL1: Plym 2F 163
Stafford Cl. TR7: S Mino 3A 36
Staggy La. TR3: C Dow 7D 116
Stamford Hill EX23: Pou, Stra 3G 9
Stamp Hill PL26: S Den 3K 45
Stamps, The PL17: Harr 4B 74
Stamps Hill TR9: I Que 2J 45
　　　　　　　　　　　　　　　　　　(not continuous)
Stamps La. TR15: I Hig 4K 111
Stanford Cl. TR18: Penz 5E 148
Stanford M. TR9: S Maj 5C 30
Stanford Ter. TR18: Penz 5E 148
Stanharver Cl. TR7: S Mino 3B 36
Stanhope Rd. PL5: Plym 3K 89
Stanlake Cl. PL12: Salt 3F 89
Stanley Maggs Way PL14: Lisk 5D 70
　　　　　　　　　　　　　(off Silvanus Jenkin Av.)
Stanley Ter. TR15: Red 3D 112
　　　　　　　　　　　　　(off Plain-an-Gwarry)
Stanley Way TR15: Red 2E 112
Stannary Rd. PL26: Sten 4G 49
Stannon Stone Circle 3B 166
Stantons Row PL14: Trem 4C 66
Stanways Rd. TR7: S Mino 2A 36
Stapleton Rd. EX23: Bud 6E 8
Star Pk. PL18: Gun .1H 75
Statham Rd. PL31: B'min 4E 32
Station App. PL14: Lisk 6A 70
　TR7: Newq 3G 35
　TR9: S Roa 1G 45
　TR27: S Er 5D 140
Station Hill TR4: Chac 4B 104
　TR14: Praze 4K 143
　TR15: Red 4D 112
　TR26: Lel 2E 140
　TR27: Hayl 2G 141
Station La. PL18: Cals 7J 75
Station Pde. TR7: Newq 3G 35
Station Rd. PL12: Salt 3J 89
　PL13: Loo 3G 81
　PL14: Lisk 6A 70
　PL15: Laun 3H 17
　PL17: K Bray 1D 72
　PL18: Dra 3G 75
　PL23: Fow 6K 61
　PL24: S Bla 1H 59
　PL26: Bugl 6H 43
　PL28: Pad 3B 22
　PL30: S Mab 5A 26
　PL32: Came 1G 15
　TR1: Tru 5G 107
　TR2: Gram R 7K 37
　TR3: P Sta 2K 123
　TR4: Chac 4C 104
　TR6: P'rth 4B 40
　TR8: S New E 2G 37
　TR9: S Maj 5C 30
　TR9: S Roa 1G 45
　TR10: P'ryn 4K 127
　TR13: Helst 2C 158
　TR14: C Grn 1F 143
　TR15: Pool 6H 111
　TR15: Red 3E 112
　TR18: Penz 4G 149
Station Yd. PL14: Lisk 6A 70
　TR14: Camb 1D 118
　　　　　　　　　　　　　(off Mt. Pleasant Rd.)
Steamers Hill TR27: Ang 7G 139
Steamers Mdw. TR27: Ang 7G 139
Steeple Cl. TR26: S Ives 5D 136
Steeple La. TR26: S Ives 6D 136
Steeple Vw. Ct. TR26: C Bay 7E 136
Stenagwyns Ct. PL26: Fox 7G 47
STENALEES 4G 49 (2D 169)
Stenalees Hill PL26: Sten 4G 49
STENCOOSE 3G 103
STENNACK 5F 119
Stennack, The TR26: S Ives 3G 137 (3C 136)
Stennack Gdns. TR26: S Ives . .3G 137 (3C 136)
Stennack Parc TR19: Trew 5B 144
　　　　　　　　　　　　　　　　　　(not continuous)
Stennack Rd. PL25: S Aus 5B 58

STEPASIDE 2C 54
Stepaside Cnr. PL26: Treth 2C 54
Stephens Rd. PL14: Lisk 3D 70
Stephney Cl. TR11: B Wat 3A 132
Stepland Hill PL22: Los 2G 53
Steppy Downs Rd. TR27: S Pra 7H 141
Stevens Ct. PL26: Bugl 6H 43
Stewarts Bldgs. TR18: Penz 5F 149
　　　　　　　　　　　　　　　　　　(off Morrab Rd.)
STIBB 3A 6 (2A 164)
STICKENBRIDGE 4J 123
STICKER 3K 63 (2C 169)
Sticklers Cnr. TR3: Thre 4K 105
　　　　　　　　　　　　　　　　　(off Chyvelah Rd.)
Stiles, The TR8: S New E 2G 37
Stillman Ct. PL4: Plym 5J 163
Stillman St. PL4: Plym 5J 163
Stippy Stappy TR5: S Agn 2B 96
STITHIANS 7B 122 (1A 174)
Stithians Row TR16: Four L 3C 120
Stockadon Barns PL12: S Mel 1D 84
Stocks La. PL14: S Keyn 5B 78
STOKE 1A 164
Stoke Rd. PL17: K Bray 1C 72
Stokes La. PL1: Plym 6J 163
Stokes Rd. TR1: Tru .4J 107
Stoke Ter. PL17: K Bray 1C 72
Stone Chair La. TR19: Senn C 3C 146
Stone Hill EX23: Bus, Pou 2G 9
Stoney Hill PL25: G Val, T'oon 5D 56
Stoney Lands PL12: Land 6H 83
Stoney La. PL25: S Aus 5G 57
　PL26: Polg 2D 64
Stony La. PL18: Dra, G'thy 3G 75
　PL30: Nans 4B 32
　PL31: B'min 4B 32
STOPTIDE 2G 23 (3D 165)
STOURSCOMBE 5K 17
Stourscombe Wlk. PL15: Laun 5K 17
Stourscombe Wood PL15: Laun 5K 17
STOWFORD 2D 167
Stracey Rd. TR11: Fal 3F 133
Strafford Cl. EX23: Lyn 7B 8
Strand, The EX23: Bud 5C 8
　PL28: Pad 3B 22
　TR11: Fal 3G 133
　TR18: Newl 1C 154
Strand St. PL28: Pad 3B 22
Strangways Ter. TR1: Tru 6J 107
Strangways Vs. TR1: Tru 6K 107
　　　　　　　　　　　　　　　(off Strangways Ter.)
Strasburg Ter. PL18: Gun 1H 75
　　　　　　　　　　　　　　　　　　(off King St.)
STRASNEDH 5H 9
Stratside Art Cen. 5G 9
STRATTON 5H 9 (3A 164)
Stratton Footpath EX23: Bud, Stra 5E 8
　　　　　　　　　　　　　　　　　　(not continuous)
Stratton Pl. TR11: Fal 7E 128
Stratton Rd. EX23: Bud 6D 8
Stratton Ter. TR1: Tru 5H 107
　TR11: Fal 6E 128
Strawberry Cl. TR15: Red 2D 112
Strawberry Cres. TR15: Red 2D 112
Strawberry Flds. TR16: L'ner 7G 113
　TR20: Crow 2J 155
Strawberry Gdns. TR16: L'ner 7G 113
Strawberry La. TR15: Red 2D 112
　TR26: Lel 2D 140
　TR27: Hayl 4H 141
Stray Pk. Ct. TR14: Camb 1F 119
Stray Pk. Rd. TR14: Camb 1E 118
Stray Pk. Way TR14: Camb 1F 119
Straythe, The 3C 169
STREET 1C 167
Street-an-Garrow TR26: S Ives 3H 137 (3D 136)
Street-an-Pol TR26: S Ives 3J 137 (3D 136)
Stretyn TR3: C Dow .6D 116
STRICKSTENTON 7B 52
Stringers Hill TR20: T'gvrh 5A 148
Stripple Stones Henge & Circle 3B 166
Stuart Rd. PL3: Plym 1F 163
Stuarts Way PL12: Hatt 3A 84
Stucley Rd. EX23: Bud 5F 9
Summer Cl. PL28: S Mer 6E 20
SUMMERCOURT 7B 44 (2B 168)
Summerfield Cl. PL26: Mev 6B 134
Summerfields PL12: Salt 4E 88
Summerheath TR10: M Bur 5H 127
Summerhill Rd. PL15: Laun 4F 17
Summerhill Ter. PL10: M'brk 1F 95
Summer La. PL13: Pely 1C 80
Summer La. Pk. PL13: Pely 2C 80
Summerleaze Av. EX23: Flex 3C 8
Summerleaze Cres. EX23: Bud 4C 8
Summer Lodge Holiday Resort TR8: W Cros 1B 44
Summers St. PL22: Los 3E 52
Summer Valley Touring Pk. TR4: Allet 6B 98

Sun Cotts. PL14: Trem 2B 66
Suncrest Est. TR9: I Que 2H 45
Sunderland Av. PL27: S Eval 2J 31
Sundew Wlk. PL15: Laun 5K 17
Sun Girt La. PL14: Lisk 5B 70
Sun Haven Valley Holiday Pk. TR8: M Por 3E 28
Sunhill TR11: B Wat 2A 132
Sunley TR1: Tru 5K 107
Sunningdale TR1: Tru 5G 107
Sunningdale Rd. PL12: Salt 3E 88
Sunny Bank PL30: B'min 6K 33
Sunnybank TR13: P'ven 6A 156
Sunnybanks PL12: Hatt 4A 84
SUNNY CORNER 6E 114
Sunny Cnr. TR12: Cover 6D 162
　TR16: P'ath 4G 101
Sunny Cnr. La. TR19: Senn 2E 146
Sunny Mdws. Touring Pk. TR4: Goonh 4G 41
Sunnyside PL11: Polb 7B 86
　PL14: Menh 1H 79
　　　　　　　　　　　　　　　　　　(off East Rd.)
　PL17: Harr 5A 74
　TR2: P'stho 3K 131
　　　　　　　　　　　　　　　　　(off North Pde.)
　TR4: Black 2B 104
　TR6: P'rth 5B 40
　TR15: I'gan 2J 111
　TR15: Red 4D 112
Sunnyside Mdw. PL32: Came 3J 15
Sunnyside Parc TR15: I'gan 2J 111
Sunnyside Ter. TR16: L'ner 7H 113
Sunnyvale Cl. TR16: P'ath 4F 101
Sunnyvale Rd. TR16: P'ath 4F 101
Sunrising PL13: Loo .3H 81
Sunset Dr. TR13: P'ven 7G 157
Sunset Gdns. TR13: P'ven 7G 157
Sun Valley Holiday Pk. PL26: Pent 7E 64
Sun Valley Pk. TR9: S Maj 5C 30
Sunwell La. PL11: Ant, S John 6B 92
Surf Vw. TR7: Newq .3B 34
Sussex Pl. PL1: Plym 6H 163
Sussex St. PL1: Plym 6H 163
SUTCOMBE 2B 164
Sutherland Rd. PL4: Plym 1K 163
Sutton Harbour 6K 163
Sutton Rd. PL4: Plym 5K 163
Sutton Vw. PL4: Plym 4K 163
Sutton Wharf PL4: Plym 5K 163
Swallow Cl. EX23: Bud 6C 8
Swallowfield Cl. PL24: Tyw 2A 60
Swallow Ho. TR11: Fal 2G 133
　　　　　　　　　　　　　　　(off Bosloggas M.)
Swan Cl. PL10: M'brk 1E 94
SWANPOOL 4D 132
Swanpool Ct. TR11: Fal 4E 132
Swanpool Gdns. TR11: Fal 3D 132
Swanpool Hill TR11: Fal 3E 132
Swanpool Rd. TR11: Fal 3E 132
Swanpool St. TR11: Fal 2G 133
Swan's Reach TR11: Fal 4D 132
Swanvale Rd. TR11: Fal 2D 132
Sweet Briar Cres. TR7: Newq 5H 35
SWEETS 1B 166
SWEETSHOUSE 1D 169
Sycamore Av. PL25: S Aus 4J 57
Sycamore Cl. PL26: Polg 2D 64
　PL27: Rock 1H 23
　PL31: B'min 4D 32
　TR14: Praze 5K 143
Sycamore Ct. PL26: Fox 2H 55
Sycamore Dr. PL11: Tor 3H 93
　TR15: I'gan 3K 111
　TR15: Red 3F 113
Sycamore Gdns. TR8: Sum 7B 44
Sycamore Rd. PL12: Salt 2D 88
Sycamores, The PL25: S Aus 5H 57
SYDENHAM DAMEREL 3D 167
Sydney Cl. PL25: S Aus 6G 57
Sydney Hill PL23: Polr 7C 60
Sydney Rd. PL11: Tor 3J 93
　TR7: Newq 3E 34
Sydney St. PL1: Plym 2F 163
Sylvan Cl. PL25: S Aus 3J 57
Sylverton Pl. TR18: Hea 3D 148
Symons Cl. PL25: S Aus 4A 58
　TR4: Black 2B 104
Symon's Hill TR11: Fal 7E 128
Symons Rd. PL12: Salt 3H 89
Symons Ter. TR15: Red 3D 112

T

Tabernacle St. TR1: Tru 5K 107
Talgos Cl. TR16: Red .7G 103
Talland Hill PL13: Polp 6B 80
Talland Rd. TR26: S Ives 4J 137 (3D 136)
Talland St. PL13: Polp 6B 80
Tally Ho TR20: Mad .1B 148

Talmena Av. PL27: Wade 4D **24**
TALSKIDDY .1C **30** (1C **169**)
Talveneth TR14: Camb 7F **111**
  TR15: Red 2E **112**
  TR19: Pend 4D **144**
Tamar & St Ann's Cotts. PL17: Harr 4D **74**
Tamar Bri. PL12: Salt 3J **89**
Tamar Bri. Rd. PL5: Plym 3K **89**
Tamar Bus. Pk. PL15: Laun 5F **17**
Tamar Cl. EX23: Bud .5F **9**
  PL17: Call 5E **72**
Tamar Ct. PL12: Salt .3H **89**
Tamar Estuary Nature Reserve 5H **85**
Tamarisk La. TR7: Newq 5H **35**
Tamar Lakes 2A **164**
Tamar Otter & Wildlife Cen. 2C **167**
Tamar Pk. PL18: Cox .1B **74**
Tamar Pl. PL18: Cals .7J **75**
                     (off The Quay)
Tamar River Sailing Club 4J **89**
Tamar St. PL11: Tor 3K **93**
  PL12: Salt 3J **89**
Tamar Ter. PL12: Salt .3J **89**
  PL15: Laun 4J **17**
  PL18: Cals 7H **75**
               (off Commercial Rd.)
Tamar Valley Centre, The 3F **75**
Tamar Valley Donkey Pk. 3D **74**
Tamar Vw. PL12: S Dom 3H **77**
  PL15: Laun 4J **17**
Tamar Vw. Ind. Est. PL12: Salt 7F **85**
Tamar Way PL18: Gun .1H **75**
Tamblin Av. PL14: Dob 4D **68**
TAMERTON FOLIOT .1D **171**
Tangye Cl. TR16: I'gan 6J **101**
Tangye Rd. TR15: Pool 4J **111**
Tanhouse Rd. PL22: Los 3D **52**
Tanners La. TR3: P Sta 3H **123**
Tannery Ct. PL12: Salt 3E **88**
Tanwood La. PL31: B'min, Dun 2B **32**
Tanwood Vw. PL31: B'min 3E **32**
Tanyard La. TR13: Helst 3B **158**
                    (off Lady St.)
Tanyards La. PL17: Call 5C **72**
Taranto Rd. TR13: Helst 5D **158**
Tarovoer Rd. TR18: Penz 4F **149**
Tarovoer Ter. TR18: Penz 4F **149**
Tarrandean Bungs. TR3: P Sta 1A **124**
Tarrandean La. TR3: Devo, P Sta 1A **124**
TARTENDOWN CROSS 5E **82**
Tate Gallery 1H **137** (2D **136**)
Tavern Barn PL23: Fow 6H **61**
Taverners Halt TR6: P'rth 5B **40**
Tavistock Pl. PL4: Plym 3J **163**
Tavistock Rd. PL15: Laun 4J **17**
  PL17: Call 5D **72**
Tavy Rd. PL12: Salt 2J **89**
Tayberry Dr. TR16: L'ner 7H **113**
Taylor Cl. PL12: Salt .2E **88**
Taylor Ct. TR13: Helst 3D **158**
Taylor Rd. PL12: Salt .2E **88**
Taylors Ct. TR16: Red .6C **102**
Teagues Ter. PL30: S Teat 2B **26**
Tedder Rd. PL26: Penw 5K **49**
Teetotal St. TR26: S Ives 1K **137**
Tehidy Cl. TR14: Sth T 3F **111**
Tehidy Copse TR14: Sth T 1D **110**
Tehidy Country Pk. 7C **100**
Tehidy Gdns. TR14: Sth T 3F **111**
Tehidy Holiday Pk. TR16: Red 1A **102**
Tehidy Pk. TR14: Sth T 1D **110**
Tehidy Pk. Golf Course 7E **100**
Tehidy Rd. PL24: Tyw .2A **60**
  TR14: Camb 6D **110**
Tehidy Ter. TR11: Fal .6E **128**
Telcarne Cl. TR27: Con D 5J **139**
Telegraph Hill TR16: S Da 2A **114**
Telegraph St. TR16: S Da 2K **113**
Telephone La. PL26: Sten 3G **49**
TEMPLE 3B **166**
Tenacres La. PL14: Pens 2K **67**
Tencreek Av. TR18: Penz 5F **149**
Tenderah Ct. TR13: Helst 3C **158**
Tenderah Rd. TR13: Helst 3C **158**
Terrace, The PL11: Craft 5F **91**
  PL11: Polb 7B **86**
  PL11: P'wkle 6D **90**
  PL17: Harr 4B **74**
  PL22: Los 3E **52**
  PL26: Pent 1E **134**
  PL27: Rock 2E **22**
  PL29: P Isa 2J **19**
  TR4: Chac 6D **104**
  TR10: P'ryn 5A **128**
  TR18: Penz 5F **149**
  TR26: S Ives 3J **137** (3D **136**)
Terrapins TR18: Penz .3H **149**
TERRAS 4B **54**
Terras Hill PL22: Los .2E **52**

Terras Rd. PL26: S Ste 4B **54**
Terrills Ct. TR27: Hayl .3G **141**
TETCOTT 1D **167**
Tethadene PL30: S Teat 2B **26**
Tewington Pl. PL25: S Aus 5F **57**
TEWYNN PLEUSTRI 3F **35**
Teyla Tor Rd. TR26: C Bay 7F **137**
Thanckes Cl. PL11: Tor 3J **93**
Thanckes Dr. PL11: Tor 3J **93**
The . . . .
  Names prefixed with 'The' for example 'The Adits'
  are indexed under the main name such as 'Adits, The'
Theatre Royal
  Plymouth 5G **163**
Thetis Pl. TR11: Fal 1F **133**
              (off Wodehouse Ter.)
Theydon Rd. TR11: Fal 2D **132**
Thomas Bullock Cl. PL30: Lanl 4A **52**
Thomas St. TR13: P'ven 7G **157**
Thomas Ter. TR13: P'ven 7G **157**
Thornberry Ter. TR18: Penz 4G **149**
THORNE 7E **8**
Thorn La. PL12: Salt .2E **88**
Thornpark Rd. PL25: S Aus 4J **57**
Thorn Pl. PL14: Lisk .5A **70**
                  (off Varley La.)
Thorn Ter. PL14: Lisk .5A **70**
Thornton Cl. PL26: Roch 4A **42**
Thornwell La. PL12: T'ton 2A **88**
THREE BURROWS 1D **104** (3A **168**)
Three Corners Cl. PL32: Came 5G **15**
THREEMILESTONE 4A **106** (3A **168**)
Threemilestone Ind. Est. TR4: Thre 5J **105**
Threemilestone Retail Pk.
  TR4: Thre 4J **105**
Threeways PL11: Downd 6H **79**
THRUSHELTON 2D **167**
THURDON 2A **164**
Tiddy Cl. PL12: S Ger .6E **86**
TIDEFORD 1B **86** (2C **171**)
TIDEFORD CROSS 5A **82** (1C **171**)
Tideford Cross La. PL12: Tide C 6A **82**
Tideford Dr. PL12: S Ger 1C **86**
Tideford Rd. PL12: Land 7G **83**
Tillie St. PL17: Call 5C **72**
Timber Cl. PL25: S Aus 5F **57**
Time Wells La. PL15: Laun 3H **17**
                 (off Castle Dyke)
Tincombe PL12: Salt 3E **88**
Tincombe Nature Reserve 3F **89**
Tincroft Rd. TR15: C Bre 7H **111**
TING TANG 5K **113**
TINHAY 2D **167**
Tinkers Hill PL23: Polr .7C **60**
Tin La. PL4: Plym 5K **163**
Tinners Cl. PL27: N Pol 2D **18**
Tinners Dr. PL27: N Pol 2D **18**
Tinner's Wlk. TR11: Fal 2H **133**
Tinners Way PL17: Call 4E **72**
  PL27: N Pol 2D **18**
  TR26: S Ives 4B **136**
Tinney Dr. TR1: Tru 4B **108**
Tinside Lido 7G **163**
TINTAGEL 7B **12** (2A **166**)
Tintagel Castle 5A **12**
Tintagel Hgts. PL34: Tren 7D **12**
Tintagel Old Post Office 7B **12**
Tintagel Rd. PL35: Bosc 3J **13**
Tintagel Ter. PL29: P Isa 2J **19**
Tintagel Toy Mus. 6B **12**
Tiny Mdws. PL15: Sth P 1B **16**
Tippett Mdws. TR9: S Maj 5B **30**
Tippetts Backlet TR1: Tru 5J **107**
                  (off River St.)
TIPWELL 3D **76**
TITCHBERRY 1A **164**
TITSON .7K **11** (3A **164**)
Tobruk Rd. PL12: Salt .2G **89**
Toby Way TR7: Newq 2E **34**
Toddington Lea PL26: Fox 1J **55**
TODPOOL 1C **114**
TOKENBURY CORNER .1G **67**
TOLCARNE
  Camborne 3F **119**
  Penzance 7D **148**
  Redruth 3K **113**
Tolcarne Cl. PL25: S Aus 7J **57**
Tolcarne M. TR7: Newq 3G **35**
Tolcarne Pl. TR18: Newl 7D **148**
Tolcarne Rd. TR7: Newq 3G **35**
  TR14: Bea 3F **119**
  TR16: Vog 3J **113**
Tolcarne St. TR14: Camb 1D **118**
Tolcarne Ter. TR18: Newl 7D **148**
Tolcrows Ct. TR7: Newq 2K **35**
TOLDISH 1J **45**
Tolgarrick Rd. TR14: Camb 5F **111**
TOLGULLOW 1K **113**
Tolgullow Ho. TR16: S Da 1K **113**

Tolgus Hill TR15: Red .3C **112**
Tolgus La. TR15: Red .2K **111**
TOLGUS MOUNT 2B **112**
Tolgus Pl. TR15: Red 2C **112**
Tolgus Vean TR15: Red 3C **112**
                   (not continuous)
Tolgus Wartha TR15: Red 2C **112**
Tollgate Cl. PL14: Lisk .6A **70**
Tollgate Farm Caravan & Camping Pk.
  TR6: P'rth 3E **40**
Tollgate Rd. PL31: B'min 5J **33**
Toll Point & Parson's Beach 2A **174**
Tollyfrank Hill TR2: Very 6H **135**
Tolmen Centre, The 2H **159**
Tolpedn Flats TR26: C Bay 6G **137**
                (off Headland Rd.)
Tolponds Rd. TR13: P'ven 5F **157**
Tolroy Mnr. Holiday Pk. TR27: S Pra 5H **141**
Tolroy Rd. TR27: S Pra .5H **141**
Tolskithy La. TR15: I Hig 4A **112**
Tolticken Hill TR16: P'ath 4J **101**
Toltuff Cres. TR18: Penz 6D **148**
Toltuff Rd. TR18: Penz .6D **148**
TOLVADDON DOWNS .3F **111**
Tolvaddon Downs TR14: Tol D 4F **111**
                (off Polgrain Rd.)
Tolvaddon Energy Pk. TR14: Tol D 3G **111**
Tolvaddon Rd. TR14: Camb 5G **111**
TOLVER 1K **149**
Tolver Pl. TR18: Penz .4F **149**
Tolver Rd. TR18: Penz .4F **149**
Tolverth Ter. TR20: L Roc 3A **150**
Tolview Ter. TR27: Hayl 3G **141**
Tom Lyon Rd. PL14: Lisk 5D **70**
Tom Nicolls Cl. PL14: S Cle 4A **66**
TOMPERROW 6J **105**
Tonkins Ope TR1: Tru .5K **107**
                  (off The Leats)
Top Hill TR2: Gram R 6K **37**
Top Rd. PL11: Downd 6J **79**
Torbridge Cl. PL12: Salt 3F **89**
Tor Cl. TR13: P'ven 6G **157**
TORFREY 1G **61**
Tor La. PL12: Salt 4E **88**
Torleven Ri. TR13: P'ven 6G **157**
Torleven Rd. TR13: Helst, P'ven 6G **157**
Torleven Vw. TR13: P'ven 6G **157**
TORPOINT 3K **93** (2D **171**)
Torpoint & Rame Community Sports Cen. 2H **93**
Torpoint Mosquito Sailing Club 4K **93**
Tor Rd. TR7: Newq 3F **35**
Tors Vw. Cl. PL17: Call .5D **72**
Tor Vw. PL15: Treg 5A **16**
  PL26: Bugl 6H **43**
  PL32: Came 5H **15**
Torwell TR13: P'ven 7G **157**
                  (off Forth Scol)
Torwood Cl. PL31: B'min 4F **33**
Tourist Info. Cen.
  Bodmin 4G **33**
  Boscastle 1K **13**
  Bude 5C **8**
  Camelford 3H **15**
  Fowey 7K **61**
  Hayle 1H **141**
  Helston 4B **158**
  Launceston 3H **17**
  Liskeard 4B **70**
  Looe 6J **81** (5G **81**)
  Lostwithiel 3E **52**
  Mevagissey 6C **134**
               (off St Georges Sq.)
  Newquay 3F **35**
  Padstow 2B **22**
  Perranporth 4B **40**
  Plymouth, The Barbican 6K **163**
  St Agnes 3A **96**
  St Austell 7J **57**
  St Just 3H **145**
  St Mawes 7D **130**
  Tintagel 7B **12**
  Truro 5K **107**
TOWAN
  Padstow 5C **20**
  St Austell 5G **65**
Towan Blystra Rd. TR7: Newq 4H **35**
Towan Ct. PL28: S Mer .6D **20**
TOWAN CROSS 5F **97**
Towan Head 1C **34**
Towan Prom. TR7: Newq 3F **35**
Towan Rd. PL26: P'ean .5H **65**
  TR4: P'twn 5D **96**
TOWANS, THE 6B **138** (1C **173**)
Towans, The PL28: S Mer 5C **20**
Towans, The 2D **173**
Towan Vs. PL28: S Mer .6D **20**
TOWEDNACK 1B **172**
Towednack Rd. TR26: S Ives 3A **136**

Tower Cl. PL13: Pely 2C **80**
   TR19: Senn 5D **146**
Tower Ct. PL12: Salt 3E **88**
Tower Hill PL13: Loo 6K **81**
   PL27: Eglo 4H **25**
Tower Mdws. TR19: St Bury 2G **147**
Tower Pk. PL13: Pely .2C **80**
   PL23: Fow 6A **60**
   PL30: Lani 6H **31**
Tower Pk. Camping & Caravan Pk.
   TR19: St Bury 2G **147**
Tower Rd. TR4: S Erm 3C **98**
   TR7: Newq 3D **34**
Tower St. PL15: Laun 3H **17**
Tower Ter. PL30: S Teat 2B **26**
Tower Vw. PL12: Salt 4F **89**
Town Arms Pas. *PL31: B'min* *3G 33*
(off Bell La.)
TOWN END **3E 32**
Town End *PL31: B'min* *3E 32*
(off Tranquil La.)
   TR10: P'ryn 3K **127**
Town Farm TR15: Red 5E **112**
Townfield TR15: Pool 4J **111**
Town Hill TR5: S Agn 2B **96**
Town Mills Cl. PL15: Laun 2G **17**
Town Quay PL23: Fow 7K **61**
   PL27: Wade 3F **25**
   TR1: Tru 5K **107**
TOWNSEND **4H 9**
Townsend PL23: Polr 7C **60**
TOWNSHEND **1C 173**
Townswell Cl. PL12: T'ton 1A **88**
Townswell La. PL12: T'ton 1A **88**
TRABOE **2A 174**
Tracey Ct. PL1: Plym 3F **163**
Trafalgar Flds. TR20: Mad 1B **148**
Trafalgar Row *TR1: Tru* *5A 108*
(off Malpas Rd.)
Trafalgar Sq. *PL23: Fow* *7K 61*
(off Market St.)
   TR1: Tru 5K **107**
Trafalgar St. PL4: Plym 4K **163**
Trafalgar Ter. PL17: K Bray 1D **72**
Traly Cl. EX23: Bud .6E **8**
TRAMAGENNA **6G 15**
Tram La. TR16: L'ner 7G **113**
Tram Rd. TR16: Nanc 4B **102**
Tram Track, The TR7: Newq 3F **35**
Trannack Ter. *TR18: Penz* *3F 149*
(off Coombe La.)
Tranquil La. PL31: B'min 3E **32**
Trasdeves Orchard PL17: Call 5D **72**
Travail Bus. Pk. PL31: B'min 6H **33**
Travellers Rest TR15: I'gan 1G **111**
Travers Cl. PL14: Lisk 4K **69**
Treago Farm Caravan & Camping Pk. TR8: Cran 6A **34**
TREAMBLE **1H 41**
Treamble Valley Caravan Pk. TR4: Rose 1H **41**
Trease TR19: Pend .3C **144**
Treassowe M. TR20: Ludg 1F **155**
Treassowe Riding TR20: Ludg 1F **155**
Treassowe Rd. TR18: Penz 4F **149**
Treasure Pk. 6B **102**
TREATH **4C 160**
TREATOR . . . .**3K 21 (3D 165)**
Trebah Garden 2A **174**
Treban Rd. TR18: Penz 6D **148**
TREBARBER **1B 168**
TREBARTHA **3C 167**
Trebartha Rd. TR1: Tru 4B **108**
Trebarthen Ter. TR4: Goonh 4G **41**
Trebarva Cl. TR15: Red 2C **112**
TREBARVAH **7K 151**
Trebarvah Cl. TR11: Const 2G **159**
Trebarvah La. TR11: Const 2G **159**
   TR20: Perran, Rosu 7K **151**
Trebarvah Rd. TR11: Const 2G **159**
TREBARWITH **2A 166**
Trebarwith Cres. TR7: Newq 3F **35**
Trebarwith Rd. PL33: Dela 1A **14**
Trebellan Pk. TR8: Cube 5G **39**
Treberran Gdns. TR14: Tol D 4F **111**
TREBETHERICK . . . .**4B 18 (3D 165)**
TREBOST **4D 122**
Treboul Way PL12: S Ger 6E **86**
TREBUDANNON **1B 168**
Trebullan PL26: T'lwth 2B **64**
TREBULLETT **3D 167**
Treburdon Dr. PL26: Roch 3B **42**
TREBURGIE WATER **4B 68**
TREBURLEY **3D 167**
TREBURRICK **3C 165**
Trebursye Rd. PL15: Laun 4E **16**
TREBYAN **1D 169**
Trebyhan Parc TR3: Stith 7B **122**
Trecan Cl. PL15: Laun 4G **17**

Trecarne TR11: Fal 7C **128**
Trecarne Cl. PL25: S Aus 4B **58**
   PL26: Polg 2D **64**
   TR1: Tru 4A **108**
Trecarne Gdns. PL33: Dela 1B **14**
Trecarne Vw. PL14: S Cle 4A **66**
Trecarrack Rd. TR14: Camb 7F **111**
Trecarrell PL15: Laun 5H **17**
Trecarrell Cl. PL15: Laun 5H **17**
Trecerus Ind. Est. PL28: Pad 4K **21**
Treclago Vw. PL32: Came 5H **15**
Tredanek Cl. PL31: B'min 3D **32**
Tredarvah Dr. TR18: Penz 5D **148**
Tredarvah Rd. TR18: Penz 5D **148**
TREDAULE **2C 167**
TREDAVOE . . . .**1A 154 (2B 172)**
Tredavoe La. TR18: Newl 2B **154**
Tredenham Cl. PL24: Par 3J **59**
Tredenham Rd. TR2: S Mawe 7D **130**
TREDETHICK **5G 53**
TREDHINAS **2E 46**
TREDINNICK
   Liskeard **1A 170**
   Looe **2B 170**
   Wadebridge **3D 165**
Tredinnick La. PL12: S Ern 1D **86**
Tredinnick Way TR6: P'rth 5A **40**
Tredinnick Wood Cl. TR13: Helst 1D **158**
TREDIS **2C 90**
Tredis Ct. PL11: Shev 2B **90**
Tredis Vw. PL11: Craft 4E **90**
Tredour Rd. TR7: Newq 5F **35**
Tredova Cres. TR11: Fal 3E **132**
Tredragon Cl. TR8: M Por 2C **28**
Tredragon Rd. TR8: M Por, T'nce 1C **28**
Tredrea Gdns. TR3: P'hal 3J **123**
Tredrea La. TR27: S Er 7C **140**
TREDRIZZICK **7G 19**
Tredrizzick Cl. PL27: Tred 7G **19**
Tredruston Rd. PL27: S Bre, White 5A **24**
Tredydan Rd. PL15: Laun 3G **17**
Tredynas Rd. TR11: Fal 2H **133**
Tredyson Pl. TR11: Fal 2E **132**
Tre-El-Vern Cl. TR1: Tru 5G **107**
TREEN
   Penzance . . . .**5J 147 (2A 172)**
   St Ives **1B 172**
Treen Hill TR19: Treen 5J **147**
Treetop Cl. PL12: Salt 1F **89**
Treetops Hill PL13: Looe 5F **81**
Treeve Farm Ind. Units TR27: Con D 4H **139**
Treeve La. TR27: Con D 4G **139**
Trefewha TR14: Praze 3K **143**
Treffry Ct. TR1: Tru .3K **107**
   TR7: Newq *3E 34*
(off Crantock St.)
Treffry Rd. TR1: Tru .2A **108**
Treffry Way PL24: B'vey 4G **59**
Trefleur Cl. PL35: Bosc 2K **13**
Trefloyd Cl. PL17: K Bray 2C **72**
TREFORDA **1E 26**
Treforda Rd. TR7: Newq 5G **35**
Treforest Rd. PL27: Wade 3D **24**
Treforthlan TR16: I'gan 1J **111**
Treforthlan Cl. TR16: I'gan 1J **111**
Trefresa Farm Caravan Site PL27: Rock 2H **23**
TREFREW . . . .**1J 15 (2B 166)**
Trefrew Rd. PL32: Came 3J **15**
TREFULA **3H 113**
TREFULLOCK MOOR **7D 44**
Trefusis Cl. TR1: Tru 4B **108**
Trefusis Rd. TR11: Fal 3C **132**
   TR11: Flu 4E **112**
   TR15: Red 4E **112**
Trefusis Sq. TR15: Red 3E **112**
Trefusis Ter. PL10: M'brk 1C **94**
   TR15: Red 3E **112**
TREGADA **2D 167**
TREGADGWITH **2K 147**
TREGADILLETT . . . .**5A 16 (2D 167)**
Tregaer TR11: Fal 2G **133**
Tregainlands Pk. PL30: Wash 1A **32**
TREGAJORRAN **6J 111**
Tregalister Gdns. PL12: S Ger 6E **86**
Tregaller Cl. PL15: Sth P 6D **16**
Tregaller La. PL15: Sth P 7D **16**
TREGAMERE **2E 30**
Treganoon Rd. TR15: Red 1F **113**
Tregargus TR16: Scor 5K **103**
Tregargus Vw. PL26: S Ste 3C **54**
Tregarland Cl. TR14: Camb 2E **118**
TREGARNE **2A 174**
Tregarne Ter. PL25: S Aus 5G **57**
Tregarrek Cl. PL26: Roch 4A **42**
Tregarrian Rd. TR14: Tol D 3F **111**
Tregarrick Cl. TR13: Helst 2B **158**
Tregarrick La. PL13: Pely 2B **80**
Tregarrick Rd. PL26: Roch 4B **42**

Tregarrick Way PL13: Pely 2C **80**
Tregarth PL26: Penw 5J **49**
Tregartha Way PL14: Lisk 4C **70**
TREGARTHEN **1A 150**
Tregarthen TR26: S Ives 3C **136**
Tregarth Pl. TR18: Penz 6D **148**
Tregaskes Parc EX23: Bud 5E **8**
Tregassack Rd. TR20: Ludg 3F **155**
Tregassick Rd. TR2: Gerr 4J **131**
TREGATILLIAN **5E 30**
Tregatillian Homes Pk. TR9: S Maj 5E **30**
Tregatreath TR11: M Bri 2F **129**
TREGAVARAH **5A 148**
TREGAVETHAN **1K 105**
Tregavethan Vw. TR3: Thre 4K **105**
Tregavone Farm Touring Pk.
   PL28: S Mer 7H **21**
Tregay La. PL14: Lisk 3B **70**
TREGAYS **7J 53**
Tregeagle Way PL26: Roch 5B **42**
Tregea Hill TR16: P'ath 4E **100**
TREGEAR **2B 168**
TREGEARE **2C 167**
Tregear Gdns. TR1: Tru 5J **107**
Tregease Rd. TR5: S Agn 2A **96**
Tregea Ter. TR16: P'ath 4E **100**
(not continuous)
Tregella Farm Cotts. PL28: Pad 6J **21**
Tregella La. PL28: Pad 6J **21**
Tregellas Cl. TR5: S Agn 2A **96**
Tregellas Rd. TR12: Mull 2H **161**
Tregellast Cl. TR12: S Kev 2C **162**
Tregellast Parc TR12: S Kev 2C **162**
Tregembo Hill TR20: Relu 2E **152**
Tregender La. TR20: Crow 1K **155**
Tregender Rd. TR20: Crow 2K **155**
TREGENNA **6C 64**
Tregenna Castle Golf Course 5E **136**
Tregenna Ct. TR11: Fal 2G **133**
   TR14: Camb 1C **118**
Tregenna Flds. TR14: Camb 1C **118**
Tregenna Hill TR26: S Ives . . . . .3J **137 (3D 136)**
Tregenna La. TR14: Camb 1D **118**
Tregenna Parc TR26: S Ives 1C **118**
Tregenna Pl. TR26: S Ives . . . . .3H **137 (3D 136)**
Tregenna Ter. TR26: S Ives . . . . .3H **137 (3D 136)**
Tregenver La. TR11: Fal 1D **132**
Tregenver Rd. TR11: Fal 1D **132**
Tregenver Ter. TR11: Fal 1D **132**
Tregenver Vs. TR11: Fal 1D **132**
TREGESEAL . . . .**2J 145 (1A 172)**
Tregeseal Hill TR19: S Jus 2K **145**
Tregeseal Row TR19: S Jus 2J **145**
Tregeseal Ter. TR19: S Jus 2J **145**
Tregew Cl. TR11: Flu 5F **129**
Tregew Mdw. TR11: Flu 5F **129**
Tregew Rd. TR11: Flu 3D **128**
Tregian Cl. TR1: Tru 4B **108**
Tregie TR18: Newl 7C **148**
Tregiffian Burial Chamber 4A **148**
TREGISKEY . . . .**3C 134 (3D 169)**
Tregisky La. TR12: Cover 5D **162**
Treglenwith Rd. TR14: Camb 6C **110**
Treglyn Cl. TR18: Newl 2B **154**
Tregoddick Cl. TR20: Mad 1B **148**
TREGOLE **1B 166**
TREGOLLS **2A 126**
Tregolls Cl. TR1: Tru 4A **108**
Tregolls Rd. TR1: Tru 5A **108**
TREGONCE **6D 22**
TREGONETHA **1C 169**
Tregoney Ct. *PL26: Mev* *6C 134*
(off Tregoney Hill)
Tregoney Hill PL26: Mev 6B **134**
Tregoneggives La. PL26: Polg, S Aus 1D **64**
TREGONHAWKE . . . .**4A 94 (2D 171)**
Tregoniggie Ind. Est. TR11: Fal 1B **132**
Tregoning Dr. PL25: S Aus 2J **57**
Tregoning Rd. PL11: Tor 4H **93**
Tregonissey Cl. PL25: S Aus 4H **57**
TREGONISSEY LANE END **3J 57**
Tregonissey Rd. PL25: S Aus 5H **57**
Tregonning Cl. TR13: Ash 1A **156**
Tregonning Ct. *TR6: P'rth* *4B 40*
(off St Pirans Rd.)
Tregonning Pk. TR12: S Kev 2B **162**
Tregonning Rd. TR3: Stith 7B **122**
Tregonning Vw. TR13: P'ven 7G **157**
TREGONWELL **7B 160**
TREGONY . . . .**6J 99 (3C 169)**
Tregony Hill TR2: Tregon 6H **99**
Tregony Ind. Est. TR2: Tregon 7G **99**
Tregony Rd. TR2: Pro 7H **99**
TREGOODWELL . . . .**3K 15 (2B 166)**
TREGORRICK . . . .**1G 65 (2D 169)**
Tregorrick Rd. PL26: S Aus, Treg 1G **65**
Tregos Rd. TR26: C Bay 6E **136**
TREGOSS **1C 169**
Tregoss Rd. TR7: Newq 3G **35**

Tregothnan Rd. TR1: Tru 6A 108
   TR11: Fal 7D 128
TREGOWRIS 2A 174
Tregoyne TR4: P'twn 5D 96
Tregrea TR14: Bea 2E 118
TREGREENWELL 3D 26
Tregrehan Garden 4E 58
TREGREHAN MILLS 3D 58 (2D 169)
TREGRILL 7H 71
Treguddock Dr. PL27: Wade 4G 25
Tregullan TR16: I'gan 2J 111
Tregullan Vw. PL31: B'min 5F 33
TREGULLON 1D 169
Tregullow TR16: Scor 1K 113
Tregullow Rd. TR11: Fal 7C 128
Tregundy Cl. TR6: P'rth 4A 40
Tregundy Ct. TR6: P'rth 4A 40
   (off Tregundy La.)
Tregundy La. TR6: P'rth 4A 40
Tregundy Rd. TR6: P'rth 4A 40
Tregundy Ter. TR6: P'rth 4A 40
TREGUNNA 1A 24
Tregunna Cl. TR13: P'ven 6G 157
Tregunnel Hill TR7: Newq 4E 34
   (not continuous)
Tregunnel Pk. TR7: Newq 4D 34
Tregunnick La. PL11: Seat 6F 79
Tregunnus La. PL11: Downd 7K 79
Tregunter M. TR11: Fal 2G 133
Tregurra La. TR1: Tru 3A 108
TREGURRIAN 6C 28 (1B 168)
Tregurrian Hill TR8: Tr'grn 7A 28
TREGURTHA DOWNS 3J 151
Tregurtha Vw. TR20: Gold 4K 151
Tregurthen Cl. TR14: Camb 1C 118
Tregurthen Rd. TR14: Camb 1C 118
Tregustick Holiday Pk.
   TR8: Newq 1C 36
Treguth Cl. TR8: Hol B 2B 38
Tregwary Rd. TR26: S Ives 3C 136
Tregye Rd. TR3: C Dow, Feo 7E 116
Tregynsa TR3: Stith 6K 121
Trehaddle TR4: Cusg 7E 114
TREHAN 4C 88 (2D 171)
Trehane Rd. TR14: Camb 7B 110
Trehannick Cl. PL30: S Teat 3B 26
Trehannick Rd. PL30: S Teat 3B 26
Trehaverne La. TR1: Tru 4J 107
Trehaverne Pl. TR1: Tru 4J 107
   (off Rosedale Rd.)
Trehaverne Ter. TR1: Tru 4J 107
   (off Rosedale Rd.)
Trehaverne Vean TR1: Tru 4J 107
Trehawke La. PL14: Merry 1G 71
Trehayes Mdw. TR27: S Er 6E 140
Trehayes Parc TR27: Hayl 7E 138
   (off Trelee Cl.)
Treheath Rd. PL14: Dob 4D 68
Trehellan Hgts. TR7: Newq 4B 34
Trehelles TR8: T'nce 1C 28
TREHEMBORNE .7C 20
Trehill Cross PL12: S Dom 3F 77
Trehill La. PL10: Rame 7C 94
TREHUNIST 1C 171
Trekeen Rd. TR10: P'ryn 4K 127
TREKENNER 3D 167
TREKENNING 6B 30 (1C 169)
Trekenning Point TR9: S Maj 5C 30
   (off Trekenning Rd.)
Trekenning Rd. TR9: S Maj 6B 30
Trekestle Caravan Pk.
   PL15: Treg 5A 16
TREKNOW 2A 166
Trekye Cl. TR16: Four L 3C 120
Trekye Cove TR4: P'twn 6C 96
Trelake Rd. PL25: S Aus 5F 57
TRELAN 3A 174
Trelan TR14: Camb 7F 111
Trelander Barton TR1: Tru 4A 108
   (not continuous)
Trelander East TR1: Tru 5B 108
Trelander Highway TR1: Tru 5A 108
Trelander Nth. TR1: Tru 5A 108
Trelander Sth. TR1: Tru 5B 108
Trelander Vean TR1: Tru 5B 108
   (off Trelander Nth.)
Trelantis PL28: S Mer 5E 20
TRELASH 1B 166
TRELASSICK 2B 168
TRELAVOUR 1E 46
Trelavour Rd. PL26: S Den 2E 46
Trelavour Sq. PL26: S Den 2E 46
Trelawne Cl. TR3: C Dow 7D 116
Trelawne Rd. TR3: C Dow 7C 116
Trelawney Av. EX23: Pou 1E 8
   TR11: Fal 2F 133
   TR15: Red 1G 113
   TR26: S Ives 3G 137 (3B 136)
Trelawney Bus. Pk. PL17: Call 5E 72

Trelawney Cl. PL11: Tor 3G 93
   PL31: B'min 4E 32
   TR11: Maen 2D 160
Trelawney Cotts. PL15: Laun 4J 17
Trelawney Ct. PL27: Pity 7F 19
Trelawney Est. TR4: Cusg 7F 115
   TR20: Mad 2B 148
Trelawney Flats TR26: S Ives 3G 137
Trelawney Gdns. PL14: Pens 1H 67
Trelawney Hgts. PL17: Call 6D 72
Trelawney Ho. PL25: S Aus 6G 57
   (off Trinity St.)
Trelawney Parc TR9: S Maj 6B 30
Trelawney Pl. TR10: P'ryn 4A 128
   TR27: Hayl 1H 141
Trelawney Ri. PL11: Tor 3G 93
   PL17: Call 6D 72
Trelawney Rd. PL12: Salt 3G 89
   PL17: Call 6D 72
   PL25: S Aus 4J 57
   PL28: Pad 4B 22
   PL31: B'min 5E 32
   TR1: Tru 4H 107
   TR2: S Mawe .7C 130
   TR3: Pons 6F 123
   TR4: Chac 6E 104
   TR5: S Agn 2A 96
   TR7: Newq 4F 35
   TR11: Fal 1F 133
   TR13: Helst 4C 158
   TR14: Camb .6D 110
   TR26: S Ives 3G 137 (3C 136)
Trelawney Ter. PL13: Loo 4G 81
   (off Polperro Rd.)
   PL14: Pens 1K 67
   (off Fore St.)
Trelawney Way PL11: Tor 3G 93
   TR27: Hayl 1H 141
Trelawny Ct. TR14: Camb 7C 110
Trelawny Rd. PL14: Menh 7J 71
Trelawson Pk. TR14: Camb 1E 118
Trelay Farmpark PL13: Pely 4D 80
Treleaver Way TR1: Tru 6F 107
Trelee Cl. TR27: Hayl 7E 138
TRELEIGH 7E 102
Treleigh Av. TR15: Red 2C 112
Treleigh Ind. Est. TR16: Red 1E 112
Treleigh Ter. TR15: Red 3C 112
Trelevan Cl. PL25: S Aus 6G 57
Treleven Rd. EX23: Bud 6E 8
TRELEW 3G 129
Trelew Gdns. TR19: S Jus 3H 145
   (off Cape Cornwall St.)
TRELIDDON 4K 79
Treliddon Hill PL11: Downd, Nark 6J 79
Treliddon La. PL11: Downd 6J 79
Treliever Rd. TR10: M Bur, P'ryn 5G 127
   TR10: P'ryn .4K 127
TRELIGGA 2A 166
Treligga Downs Rd. PL33: Dela 3A 14
TRELIGHTS 3D 165
Trelil Caravan Pk. TR13: Helst 1E 158
TRELILL 3A 166
Trelil La. TR11: B Wat 3A 132
Trelindon PL15: Sth P 2A 16
Trelinnoe Cl. PL15: Sth P 2A 16
Trelinnoe Gdns. PL15: Sth P 2A 16
TRELION 5A 54
TRELISKE 3D 106
Treliske Ind. Est. TR1: Trel 4C 106
Treliske La. TR1: Tru 5E 106
   TR4: Newm, Tru 5E 106
Treliske Rd. TR15: Red 2F 113
Trelispen Caravan & Camping Pk.
   PL26: Gorr 1G 135
Trelispen Pk. PL26: G Hav 2G 135
Trelispen Pk. Dr. PL26: G Hav 2H 135
TRELISSICK 1B 174
Trelissick Apartments PL25: S Aus 6A 58
   (off Waterwheel Cl.)
Trelissick Flds. TR27: Hayl 4G 141
Trelissick Garden 1B 174
Trelissick Gdns. PL17: Call 7C 72
   (off Werrington Dr.)
Trelissick Ho. TR27: Hayl 2H 141
Trelissick Rd. TR11: Fal 7D 128
   TR27: Hayl 4G 141
Treloan Coastal Holidays TR2: P'stho 4J 131
Treloan La. TR2: Gerr 3J 131
Treloar Ter. PL15: Laun 3G 17
Treloggan TR7: Newq 6J 35
Treloggan Ind. Est. TR7: Newq 5J 35
Treloggan La. TR7: Newq 4H 35
Treloggan Rd. TR7: Newq 5H 35
Trelowarren Ct. PL17: Call 7C 72
   (off Werrington Dr.)
Trelowarren St. TR14: Camb 7D 110
Treloweth Cl. TR27: S Er 6E 140

Treloweth La. TR27: S Er 5D 140
Treloweth Rd. TR15: Pool 4J 111
Treloweth Ter. TR15: P Bot 3H 111
Treloweth Way TR15: Pool 3J 111
TRELOWTH 2C 64
Trelowth Rd. PL26: Polg, T'lwth 2B 64
TRELOYAN 1E 162
Treloy Golf Course 1E 36
TRELOYHAN 5D 136
Treloyhan Cl. TR26: S Ives 5E 136
Treloyhan Mnr. Dr. TR26: S Ives 5E 136
Treloyhan Pk. Rd. TR26: S Ives 5E 136
TRELUSWELL 1H 127
Trelyn PL27: Rock 1G 23
Trelyn Rd. TR12: S Kev 2C 162
TRELYON 5D 136
Trelyon Av. TR26: S Ives 4E 136
Trelyon Cl. TR19: St Bury 2H 147
Tremabe La. PL14: Dob 4D 68
Tremabe Pk. PL14: Dob 4D 68
Tremadart Cl. PL14: Duloe 6A 78
Tremadart Farm Barns PL14: Duloe 7A 78
Tremadart La. PL14: Duloe 7A 78
TREMAIL 2B 166
TREMAINE
   Launceston 2C 167
   Looe 1A 80
Tremaine Cl. TR18: Hea 3D 148
Tremanor Way TR11: Fal 7B 128
TREMAR 5C 66 (1B 170)
Tremar Cl. PL14: Trem 5C 66
TREMAR COOMBE 3B 66
Tremar La. PL14: S Cle, Trem 4A 66
Tremarle Home Pk. TR14: Camb 5F 111
Tremarne Cl. TR3: Feo 4J 125
Tremarren Rd. PL27: Wade 4D 24
Tremar Rd. TR26: S Ives 3B 66
TREMATON 1A 88 (2C 171)
Trematon Cl. PL11: Tor 2G 93
Tremayne Cl. TR3: Devo 2C 124
Tremayne Ho. PL31: B'min 4D 32
Tremayne Pk. TR14: Camb 1F 119
Tremayne Quay 2A 174
Tremayne Rd. PL25: S Aus 5J 57
   TR1: Tru 4J 107
   TR16: Carh 4A 114
Trembath Cres. TR7: Newq 4F 35
Trembear Rd. PL25: S Aus 5E 56
Trembel Rd. PL12: Mull 1H 161
TREMBRAZE 3C 70
TREMBROATH 5K 121
Tremeadow Ter. PL14: Lisk 3C 70
   TR27: Hayl 3G 141
Tremear Grn. TR9: S Roa 1G 45
Tremearne Rd. TR13: P'ven 7G 157
Tremeddan Ct. PL14: Lisk 4B 70
   (off Tremeddan La.)
Tremeddan La. PL14: Lisk 4B 70
Tremeddan Ter. PL14: Lisk 6A 70
Tremeer La. PL30: S Tud 5H 27
Tremellin La. TR27: S Er 7F 141
Tremena Gdns. PL25: S Aus 5G 57
Tremena Rd. PL25: S Aus 5G 57
Tremenheere Av. TR13: Helst 1D 158
Tremenheere Rd. TR18: Penz 4E 148
TREMETHICK CROSS 4A 148
Tremewan PL25: T'oon 4C 56
   (not continuous)
Tremodrett Rd. PL26: Roch 4B 42
Tremoor Ct. TR2: Pro 2H 99
TREMORE 1D 169
Tremore Rd. TR15: Red 2F 113
Tremorva TR27: Hayl 1H 141
Tremorvah Barton TR1: Tru 4A 108
Tremorvah Ct. TR1: Tru 4A 108
   TR11: Fal 4D 132
Tremorvah Cres. TR1: Tru 4A 108
Tremorvah Pk. TR11: Fal 4D 132
Tremorvah Wood La. TR1: Tru 4A 108
Tremough Barton Cotts. TR10: P'ryn 4H 127
TREMOUGH DALE 4K 127
TRENALE 7D 12
Trenale Ct. PL34: Tren 7D 12
Trenale La. PL34: Tin, Tren 7C 12
Trenalt Ter. TR1: Tru 4H 107
TRENANCE
   Helston 1E 162
   Mawgan Porth 1C 28 (1B 168)
   Newquay 4F 35
   Wadebridge 3D 165
Trenance Av. TR7: Newq 4F 35
Trenance Caravan & Chalet Pk.
   TR7: Newq 4G 35
Trenance Cl. TR13: Helst 2B 158
Trenance Ct. TR7: Newq 5F 35
   TR12: Mull 2G 161
Trenance La. TR7: Newq 5F 35
   TR12: Mull 2G 161
Trenance Leisure Pk. 4G 35

Trenance Mill *PL25: S Aus* 5F **57**
    (off Blowing Ho. La.)
Trenance Pl. PL25: S Aus 5F **57**
    (not continuous)
Trenance Rd. PL25: S Aus 4E **56**
  TR7: Newq 4F **35**
  TR14: Camb 6E **110**
TRENANS 1C **28**
TRENANT
  Liskeard 4K **71**
  Wadebridge 3G **25**
Trenant TR16: S Da 2K **113**
Trenant Cl. PL27: Polz .3E **18**
Trenant Ind. Est. PL27: Wade 3G **25**
    (not continuous)
Trenant Point 4G **81**
Trenant Rd. PL13: Loo .3H **81**
  PL24: Tyw 2B **60**
Trenant Steading Pk. PL27: S Minv 1F **19**
Trenant Va. PL27: Wade 4G **25**
TRENARREN 3D **169**
Trenarren Vw. PL25: S Aus 3A **58**
Trenarth TR10: P'ryn .4A **128**
Trenarth Rd. TR7: Newq 4F **35**
Trenawin La. TR27: Con D 5K **139**
TRENCREEK 4J **35** (1B **168**)
Trencreek Cl. TR4: S Erm 2B **98**
Trencreek Holiday Pk. TR8: Newq 5J **35**
Trencreek La. TR8: Newq 5J **35**
Trencreek Rd. TR8: Newq 5J **35**
Trencrom Hill 1C **173**
Trencrom La. TR26: C Bay 1A **140**
Trendale Ind. Pk. PL26: Trez 7C **42**
TRENDEAL 2B **168**
Trendeal Gdns. *TR18: Penz* 5F **149**
    (off Clarence St.)
Trendreath Cl. TR26: Lel 3D **140**
TRENEAGUE
  St Austell 3B **54**
  Wadebridge 6E **24**
Treneague Pk. PL27: Wade 5E **24**
TRENEAR 1D **173**
Trenear Cl. TR15: Red 2F **113**
TRENEERE 3E **148**
Treneere La. TR18: Hea 3D **148**
Treneere Rd. TR18: Penz 4E **148**
TRENEGLOS 2C **167**
Treneglos TR4: Cusg .7G **115**
Treneglos Ter. TR18: Gul 2H **149**
  TR18: Newl 7D **148**
Trenerry Cl. TR1: Tru .3K **107**
TRENERTH 4B **142**
Trenerth Rd. TR27: Leeds, Reaw 4C **142**
Trenethick Av. TR13: Helst 1D **158**
Trenethick Bus. Pk. TR13: Helst 1C **158**
Trenethick Cl. TR13: Helst 2D **158**
Trenethick Parc TR13: Helst 2D **158**
TRENEWAN 2A **170**
Trengove PL26: Bugl .7H **43**
Trengrouse Av. PL11: Tor 3H **93**
Trengrouse Way TR13: Helst 4C **158**
TRENGUNE 1B **166**
TRENGWAINTON 3B **148**
Trengwainton Garden 3A **148**
Trenhayle La. TR27: Hayl, S Er 5G **141**
TRENINGLE HILL . . . . .7B **32** & 4K **31**
Treningle Vw. PL31: B'min 5E **32**
TRENINNICK 5G **35**
Treninnick Hill TR7: Newq 4G **35**
Treninnow La. PL10: M'brk 3B **94**
Trenissick Rural Pk. TR8: Cube 4J **39**
Trenithick Mdw. TR4: Mt Hwk 7H **97**
Trennal La. TR20: Ger 5J **153**
Trennick La. TR1: Tru .5A **108**
Trennick Row TR1: Tru 6A **108**
Trennick Vs. TR1: Tru 6A **108**
TRENOUTH 3D **66**
Trenouth Cl. PL14: S Cle 4B **66**
Trenovissick Rd. PL24: S Bl G 3G **59**
Trenowah Rd. PL25: S Aus 4B **58**
  PL25: T Mil 4C **58**
TRENOWETH
  Camborne 3K **143**
  Penryn 6F **127**
Trenoweth Av. TR14: Camb 7B **110**
Trenoweth Ct. TR12: Lizar 6G **161**
Trenoweth Cres. TR18: Penz 6C **148**
Trenoweth Est. TR16: Red 7C **102**
Trenoweth La. TR10: M Bur 6E **126**
Trenoweth Mdw. TR12: Lizar 6G **161**
Trenoweth Mill TR12: S Kev 1D **162**
Trenoweth Rd. TR11: Fal 4D **132**
  TR18: Penz 6C **148**
Trenoweth Ter. TR10: M Bur 7F **127**
Trenoweth Vean TR10: M Bur 5F **127**
Trenow La. TR20: Perran 5H **151**
Trenowth Ter. TR2: Gram R 7K **37**
Trenwith Bri. *TR26: S Ives* 3B **136**
    (off Higher Stennack)

Trenwith La. TR26: S Ives 3C **136**
Trenwith Pl. TR26: S Ives 3H **137** (3D **136**)
Trenwith Rd. TR14: Camb 7B **110**
Trenwith Sq. TR26: S Ives 4G **137** (3C **136**)
Trenwith Ter. TR26: S Ives 3G **137**
Trenython Rd. PL24: B'vey 4G **59**
Tre-Pol PL26: T'lwth .2B **64**
Tre-Pol-Pen *TR17: Mar* 4G **151**
    (off Turnpike Rd.)
TRERAGIN 6B **74**
TRERAMMETT 7B **12**
Treraven La. PL27: S Bre 6F **25**
Trereife Bus. Pk. TR20: Penz 6B **148**
Trerew Rd. TR18: Penz 6D **148**
TRERICE 3A **46**
Trerice 2B **168**
Trerice Ct. PL17: Call .6C **72**
Trerice Dr. TR7: Newq 4H **35**
Trerice Flds. TR14: Praze 4K **143**
Trerice Pl. TR26: S Ives 3C **136**
Trerice Rd. TR26: S Ives 3C **136**
Trerice Ter. PL26: S Den 2B **46**
Trerieve PL11: Downd 6H **79**
Trerise Rd. TR14: Camb 7C **110**
Treroosel Rd. PL30: S Teat 1A **26**
Trerose Coombe PL11: Downd 6J **79**
Treruffe Hill TR15: Red 4D **112**
Treruffe Pl. *TR15: Red* 4D **112**
    (off Sparnon Cl.)
Treruffe Ter. TR15: Red 4D **112**
TRERULEFOOT 2C **171**
Treryn Cl. PL24: S Bla 3H **59**
Tresaddern Holiday Pk. TR16: S Da 3A **114**
TRESADERNS HILL 3B **114**
Tresaderns Hill TR16: S Da 4A **114**
Tresaderns Rd. TR15: Red 2C **112**
Tresahar Rd. TR11: Fal 2E **132**
TRESAMBLE 1F **123**
Tresamble Hill TR3: Pons 1E **122**
  TR4: Cusg 1E **122**
TRESAVEAN 1J **121**
Tresavean Est. TR16: L'ner 1J **121**
Tresavean Gdns. *TR16: L'ner* 1J **121**
    (off Tresavean Hill)
Tresavean Hill TR16: L'ner 1J **121**
Tresavean Ter. TR16: L'ner 1J **121**
Tresawla Ct. *TR14: Tol D* 4F **111**
    (off Boswithian Rd.)
Tresawle Rd. TR11: Fal 6D **128**
Tresawls Av. TR1: Tru 5D **106**
Tresawls Rd. TR1: Trel, Tru 4C **106**
Tresawna Ter. TR11: Fal 7F **129**
Tresawya Dr. TR1: Tru 5J **107**
Trescobeas Rd. TR11: Fal 7B **128**
Trescoe Rd. TR20: L Roc 2A **150**
TRESCOLL 1K **43**
Tresco Pl. TR11: Fal .1D **132**
TRESCOWE 4G **153** (1C **173**)
TRESCOWE COMMON 2H **153**
Trescowe Rd. TR20: Gold 4B **152**
Tresdale Parc TR27: Con D 5K **139**
TRESEAN 2E **38**
Treseder's Gdns. TR1: Tru 4K **107**
TRESEVERN 6G **121**
Tresevern Hill TR3: Stith 5G **121**
Tresidder Cl. TR11: Fal 1C **132**
TRESILLIAN 2G **109** (3B **168**)
Tresillian Bus. Pk. TR2: Pro 1K **109**
Tresillian Rd. TR11: Fal 6D **128**
TRESINNEY 7H **15** (2B **166**)
Tresithney Rd. TR16: Carh 5B **114**
Treskerby TR15: Red .1G **113**
  TR16: Red 1H **113**
Treskewes Est. TR12: S Kev 2B **162**
Treskewes Ind. Est. TR12: S Kev 3B **162**
TRESKILLARD 2J **119** (1D **173**)
TRESKILLING 2B **50**
TRESKINNICK CROSS 1C **167**
Tresleigh Gdns. TR2: Gram R 7K **37**
TRESLOTHAN 5E **118**
Treslothan Rd. TR14: Tro 5F **119**
TRESMEER 2C **167**
Tresooth Ct. *TR10: P'ryn* 5B **128**
    (off Anchor Quay)
Tresooth La. TR10: P'ryn 4A **128**
TRESOWES 7K **153**
TRESOWES HILL 1A **156**
Tresowgar La. TR2: Pro 2F **99**
TRESPARRETT 1B **166**
TRESPARRETT POSTS 1B **166**
Tresprison Bus. Pk. TR13: Helst 4E **158**
Tresprison Ct. TR13: Helst 4E **158**
Tressa Dowr La. TR1: Tru 3B **108**
TRESWITHIAN 7A **110** (1D **173**)
TRESWITHIAN DOWNS 5A **110**
Treswithian Downs Crematorium TR14: Res 5A **110**
Treswithian Pk. Rd. TR14: Camb 7B **110**
Treswithian Rd. TR14: Camb 7A **110**
Trethannas Gdns. TR14: Praze 4K **143**

TRETHEAGUE 1A **126**
Trethellan TR16: L'ner 4H **121**
Trethellan Hill TR7: Newq 4D **34**
TRETHELLAN WATER 3H **121**
TRETHEM 1F **131**
Trethem Mill Touring Pk. TR2: S Jus R 1F **131**
Trethern Cl. TR14: Tro 5G **119**
Tretherras TR7: Newq 3H **35**
Tretherras Rd. TR7: Newq 3H **35**
TRETHEVEY
  Par 3H **51**
  Tintagel 5F **13**
Trethevy Cl. PL14: S Cle 4A **66**
Trethevy Quoit 3C **66**
TRETHEW 1J **51**
TRETHEWELL 2F **131**
Trethewell TR9: S Maj 5C **30**
Trethewey Way TR7: Newq 4E **34**
Trethew Gdns. TR14: Camb 6E **110**
TRETHIGGEY 7C **36**
Trethiggey Cres. TR8: Q Dow 6C **36**
Trethiggey Touring Pk. TR8: Q Dow 7C **36**
TRETHILL 5H **91**
Trethill La. PL11: Craft 6G **91**
TRETHILLICK 2J **21**
Trethorne Leisure Farm 2C **167**
Trethorns Ct. TR20: Ludg 2G **155**
TRETHOSA 1C **54** (2C **169**)
Trethosa Rd. PL26: S Ste 3C **54**
Trethowan Hgts. TR1: Tru 6F **107**
TRETHOWEL 3G **57**
Trethurffe TR2: Lad 6G **37**
Trethurffe Ter. TR9: S Maj 5C **30**
Trethurffe Vs. TR2: Lad 6G **37**
TRETHURGY 7B **50** (2D **169**)
Trethurgy Gdns. PL17: Call 6C **72**
Tretoil Vw. PL31: B'min 6G **33**
Tretorvic TR18: Hea 3D **148**
TREVADLOCK 3C **167**
TREVAIL 3E **38**
Trevail Way PL25: S Aus 5J **57**
Trevale TR18: Penz 5D **148**
TREVALGA 3G **13** (1A **166**)
Trevalga Cl. TR6: P'rth 5B **40**
Trevallack Parc TR12: S Kev 2B **162**
Trevallack Vw. TR12: S Kev 2B **162**
Trevallion Pk. TR3: Feo 3G **125**
Trevallyn Rd. PL15: Laun 5G **17**
TREVANCE 3D **165**
Trevance TR10: P'ryn 4J **127**
Trevance Pk. PL24: Tyw 2A **60**
TREVANGER 6H **19** (3D **165**)
Trevanion Barns PL27: Wade 5E **24**
Trevanion Cl. PL27: Wade 5E **24**
Trevanion Ct. TR1: Tru 5F **107**
Trevanion Culverhouse 5E **24**
Trevanion Hill PL25: T'oon 5D **56**
Trevanion La. PL25: T'oon 4C **56**
Trevanion Pk. PL27: Wade 5E **24**
Trevanion Rd. PL14: Lisk 5B **70**
  PL25: S Aus 7G **57**
  PL25: T'oon 5C **56**
  PL27: Wade 5E **24**
Trevanion Ter. PL27: Wade 5E **24**
  TR15: C Bre 5B **112**
TREVANSON 3C **24** (3D **165**)
Trevanson Rd. PL27: Trev, Wade 3C **24**
Trevanson St. PL27: Wade 3E **24**
TREVARGH 5C **66**
Trevarner Way PL27: Wade 4F **25**
Trevarno Cl. PL25: T'oon 5D **56**
Trevarno Gardens 1D **173**
Trevarnon Cl. TR27: Con D 5K **139**
Trevarnon La. TR27: Con D 5J **139**
TREVARRACK 2H **149** (1B **172**)
Trevarrack Cl. TR18: Gul 2G **149**
Trevarrack Cotts. *TR18: Gul* 2G **149**
    (off Trevarrack Rd.)
Trevarrack La. TR26: C Bay 7E **136**
Trevarrack La. TR18: Gul 2G **149**
Trevarrack Noweth TR18: Gul 2H **149**
Trevarrack Rd. TR18: Gul 2G **149**
Trevarrack Row TR18: Gul 2H **149**
TREVARREN 1C **169**
Trevarren Av. TR16: Four L 3B **120**
TREVARRIAN 4C **28** (1B **168**)
Trevarrian Ct. TR8: Trev'rn 4C **28**
Trevarrian M. TR8: Trev'rn 6A **28**
Trevarrian Holiday Pk. TR8: Trev'rn 4C **28**
Trevarrian M. TR8: Trev'rn 4C **28**
TREVARRICK 3C **169**
Trevarrick Dr. PL25: S Aus 5F **57**
Trevarrick Rd. PL25: S Aus 5F **57**
TREVARTH 6K **113**
Trevarthen Cl. TR27: Con D 5J **139**
Trevarth Est. PL26: Mev 5B **134**
Trevarth Holiday Pk. TR4: Black 1C **104**

Trevarthian Rd. PL25: S Aus 5G **57**
(not continuous)
Trevarth Rd. TR11: Fal 7C **128**
TR16: Carh, T'rth 7K **113**
Trevarth Ter. TR16: T'rth 7K **113**
Trevarweneth Rd. PL24: S Bl G 3G **59**
Trevassack Ct. TR27: Hayl 1J **141**
Trevassack Hill TR27: Hayl 1J **141**
Trevassack Parc TR27: Hayl 1K **141**
Trevaunance Cl. TR5: S Agn 1A **96**
Trevaunance Cove TR5: S Agn 1B **96**
Trevaunance Rd. TR5: S Agn 1A **96**
Trevaylor Cl. TR1: Tru 3A **108**
Trevaylor Rd. TR11: Fal 7D **128**
Treveague Farm Camping & Caravanning Site
PL26: Gorr 3G **135**
Treveal 1B **172**
Trevean Cl. TR14: Camb 7B **110**
Trevean Gdns. TR18: Penz 5E **148**
Trevean La. TR20: Rosu 7B **152**
Trevean Rd. TR1: Tru 5E **106**
TR18: Penz 5E **148**
Trevean Way TR7: Newq 4D **34**
TR20: Rosu 6B **152**
Trevear Cl. PL25: S Aus 6H **57**
Trevear Rd. PL26: S Ste 4D **54**
Trevecca Cotts. PL14: Lisk 2B **70**
TREVEGEAN 7H **145**
Treveglos TR27: Hayl 1G **141**
Treveglos Ct. TR12: Mull 1H **161**
Treveglos Rd. TR11: Fal 4C **132**
TREVEIGHAN 3A **166**
Trevelgue Holiday Pk. TR8: Newq 1B **36**
Trevelgue Rd. TR7: Newq 1K **35**
TR8: Newq 1K **35**
Trevella La. TR4: Trisp 1B **98**
Trevellance La. TR6: Bol 7C **40**
Trevellan Rd. TR11: M Bri 1E **128**
Trevella Pk. TR8: Cran 7D **34**
Trevella Rd. EX23: Flex 3D **8**
TREVELLAS 2A **168**
Trevella Vean TR4: S Erm 2C **98**
TREVELMOND 6B **68** (1B **170**)
Trevelthan Rd. TR16: I'gan 1K **111**
Trevelva Rd. TR1: Tru 6A **108**
Trevelveth Rd. TR8: Cran 5B **34**
Trevelyan Cl. TR20: Gold 4A **152**
Trevelyan Rd. TR15: I'gan 2H **111**
TR16: I'gan 2H **111**
Trevelyan Way TR20: Gold 4A **152**
TREVEMPER 6G **35**
Trevemper Rd. TR7: Newq 5G **35**
TREVEN 7B **12**
Trevena Cl. TR18: Penz 6D **148**
Trevena Dr. PL34: Tin 7B **12**
Trevena Gdns. TR11: Mawn S 2B **160**
Trevena Rd. TR18: Penz 6D **148**
Trevena Ter. TR7: Newq 3E **34**
Trevenen Rd. TR13: Helst 4C **158**
Treveneth Cres. TR18: Newl 2C **154**
Treveneth Pl. TR18: Newl 3C **154**
Treven La. TR27: S Pra 7K **141**
TREVENNA CROSS 5H **29**
Trevenner Cotts. TR17: Mar 4G **151**
(off Trevenner La.)
Trevenner La. TR17: Mar 4G **151**
Trevenner M. TR15: Red 3D **112**
(off Blight's Row)
Trevenner Sq. TR17: Mar 4G **151**
Trevenson Campus TR15: Pool 4G **111**
Trevenson Ct. TR15: Pool 4H **111**
Trevenson La. TR14: Camb 1D **118**
TR15: Pool 4G **111**
TREVENSON MOOR 3G **111**
Trevenson Rd. TR7: Newq 3J **35**
TR8: Newq 3J **35**
TR15: Pool 5G **111**
Trevenson St. TR14: Camb 1D **118**
Treventon Cl. TR2: P'stho 3J **131**
TR11: Fal 1C **132**
Treventon Ri. TR9: S Maj 5C **30**
Treventon Rd. TR2: P'stho 3J **131**
Trevoor PL14: Lisk .4C **70**
(off Pengover Rd.)
TREVERBYN 3H **49**
Treverbyn Cl. PL14: Lisk 4D **70**
Treverbyn Gdns. PL25: S Aus 5K **57**
Treverbyn Ri. TR10: P'ryn 4J **127**
Treverbyn Rd. PL25: S Aus 1J **57**
PL26: Sten 3H **49**
PL28: Pad 3B **22**
TR1: Tru .3A **108**
TR11: Fal 4C **132**
TR26: S Ives 3G **137** (3C **136**)
Trevere Cl. TR27: Con D 5H **139**
Treverno Rd. TR14: Camb 4D **110**
TREVERVA 1A **174**
Treveryn Parc TR11: B Wat 3A **132**
TREVESCAN 6C **146** (2A **172**)

TREVETHAN 4J **113**
Trevethan Cl. TR6: Bol 6C **40**
TR11: Fal 1E **132**
Trevethan Ct. TR11: Fal 7E **128**
Trevethan Gdns. TR11: Fal 1E **132**
Trevethan Hill TR11: Fal 7F **129**
Trevethan Ri. TR11: Fal 1E **132**
Trevethan Rd. TR11: Fal 1E **132**
Trevethenick Rd. TR1: Tru 6A **108**
Treveth La. TR13: Helst 1D **158**
TREVETHOE 2B **140**
Treveth Tean TR9: Fr'don 4H **45**
Trevethylyn TR14: Camb 5F **111**
TREVIA 3G **15** (2A **166**)
TREVIADES 3K **159**
Trevia La. PL32: Came, T'via 3G **15**
Trevian Cl. TR6: P'rth 5B **40**
Trevia Pk. Ter. PL32: Came 4G **15**
Treviglas Cl. TR7: Newq 2A **36**
Treviglas La. TR2: Pro 2G **99**
Treviglas Ri. TR2: Pro 2G **99**
TREVIGRO 1C **171**
TREVILLA 2K **125**
Trevilla Hill TR3: Feo 2K **125**
Trevilla Rd. TR3: Feo 1J **125**
Trevilledor Caravan Site TR8: S Mawg 1K **29**
TREVILLEY 6D **146** (2A **172**)
Trevilley La. PL30: S Teat 2B **26**
PL33: Dela 2B **26**
TREVILLICK 5B **62**
Trevilling Rd. PL27: Wade 2E **24**
Trevillis Pk. PL14: Lisk 6A **70**
TREVILSON 3K **37**
Trevilson Ct. TR8: S New E 2H **37**
Trevince Parc TR16: Carh 5A **114**
Trevince Woods TR16: Carh 6A **114**
Trevine Mdws. TR9: I Que 1J **45**
Trevingey Cl. TR15: Red 5C **112**
Trevingey Cres. TR15: Red 5C **112**
Trevingey La. TR15: Red 5C **112**
(off Trevingey Rd.)
Trevingey Parc TR15: Red 4C **112**
Trevingey Rd. TR15: Red 5C **112**
TREVISCOE 5C **46** (2C **169**)
Trevisker Dr. TR13: P'ven 6G **157**
TREVISKEY 1K **121**
TREVISSOME 4D **128**
Trevissome Ct. TR11: Fal 6D **128**
(off Dracaena Av.)
TR11: Flu 5D **128**
Trevithick PL28: S Mer 7E **20**
Trevithick Av. PL11: Tor 2G **93**
Trevithick Cl. PL28: S Mer 6E **20**
TR1: Tru .4A **108**
TR7: Newq 5G **35**
Trevithick Cottage 2B **118**
Trovithick Ct. TR1: Tru 3A **100**
TR14: Camb 7C **110**
TR15: I Hig 4J **111**
Trevithick Cres. TR27: Hayl 2J **141**
Trevithick Rd. PL25: S Aus 6J **57**
TR1: Tru .3A **108**
TR4: Chac 6E **104**
TR11: Fal 7C **128**
TR14: Camb 7D **110**
(not continuous)
TR15: Pool 4J **111**
TREVIVIAN 2B **166**
Trevoarn TR27: Hayl 2G **141**
Trevol Bus. Pk. PL11: Tor 3F **93**
TREVOLLARD 4K **87**
Trevollard La. PL12: T'ton 4K **87**
Trevol Pl. PL11: Tor 4G **93**
Trevol Rd. PL11: Tor 3D **92**
TREVONE 2G **21** (3C **165**)
Trevone Cres. PL25: S Aus 5E **56**
Trevone Rd. PL28: T'one, Win 2G **21**
Trevoney TR11: B Wat 3A **132**
Trevonnenn Rd. TR3: Pons 5F **123**
TREVOOLE 1K **143**
Trevor Cl. PL28: Cons B 5B **20**
Trevorder Cl. PL11: Tor 4H **93**
Trevorder Dr. PL25: S Aus 2J **57**
Trevorder Rd. PL11: Tor 4H **93**
Trevornick Holiday Pk. TR8: Hol B 2D **38**
Trevose Av. TR7: Newq 3D **34**
Trevose Cl. TR5: S Agn 1A **96**
Trevose Ct. TR7: Newq 3D **34**
Trevose Est. PL28: Cons B 4C **20**
Trevose Golf Course 4B **20**
Trevose Rd. TR1: Tru 4E **106**
TREVOTHEN 7B **162**
Trevowah Mdws. TR8: Cran 6B **34**
Trevowah Rd. TR8: Cran 7B **34**
Trevu Rd. TR14: Camb 1D **118**
Trevurvas La. TR13: Ash 6K **155**
TREW 2D **173**
TREWALDER 6B **14** (2A **166**)
TREWALL 5K **79**

Trewall Hill PL11: Downd, Nark 6J **79**
Trewans Ter. TR15: Red 2C **112**
TREWARDREVA 1G **159**
Trewardreva Cross TR11: Const 1G **159**
TREWARLETT 2D **167**
TREWARMETT 2A **166**
Trewarne La. TR8: Q Dow 6C **36**
TREWARTHA 5K **135**
Trewartha Cl. TR26: C Bay 7F **137**
Trewartha Ct. PL14: Lisk 4B **70**
(off Pound St.)
Trewartha Est. TR26: C Bay 7F **137**
Trewartha Flats TR26: C Bay 7F **137**
Trewartha Rd. TR20: Pra S 6J **155**
Trewartha Ter. TR18: Penz 4F **149**
Trewarton Rd. TR10: P'ryn 3J **127**
Trewarveneth St. TR18: Newl 2C **154**
TRE WAR VENYDH 7B **12**
TREWASSA 2B **166**
Trewavas Cres. TR13: Helst 4C **158**
Trewavas Rd. TR18: Newl 2C **154**
Treweath Rd. TR18: Penz 3E **148**
Trewedna La. TR3: P Sta 2G **123**
TREWEDNA WATER 2G **123**
Treweeks Rd. TR19: Pend 3C **144**
TREWEEN 2C **167**
TREWELLARD 5B **144** (1A **172**)
Trewellard Hill TR19: Trew 5B **144**
Trewellard Ind. Est. TR19: Trew 5B **144**
Trewellard Rd. TR19: Trew 5B **144**
Trewelloe Rd. TR20: Pra S 6J **155**
Trewelm La. TR16: S Da 3A **114**
TREWEN 2C **167**
TREWENNACK 2D **173**
TREWENNAN 1B **26**
Trewennan Rd. PL30: S Teat 1B **26**
Trewen Rd. TR11: B Wat 3A **132**
TREWETHA 3K **19** (3A **166**)
Trewetha La. PL29: P Isa 2J **19**
TREWETHER 5H **53**
Trewethett Farm Caravan Club
PL34: T'thvy 4E **12**
TREWHELA 6G **45**
Trewhella La. TR20: Gold, S Hil 1C **152**
Trewhiddle Holiday Est. PL26: S Aus 1F **65**
Trewhiddle Rd. PL25: S Aus 7G **57**
TREWIDDEN 6A **148**
Trewidden Cl. TR1: Tru 4A **108**
Trewidden Ct. TR1: Tru 4A **108**
Trewidden Garden .6A **148**
Trewidden Rd. TR26: S Ives 4G **137** (3C **136**)
TREWIDLAND 4E **78** (1B **170**)
TREWILLIS 7C **162**
Trewince Farm Touring Site TR2: P'stho . . .6H **131**
Trewince Holiday Lodges TR2: P'stho 6H **131**
Trewince La. PL22: Los 2E **52**
TR2: Gram R 7K **37**
Trewince Ter. TR18: Newl 2C **154**
Trewinnard Ct. TR1: Ken 3H **107**
Trewinnard Gro. TR1: Tru 3H **107**
Trewinnard La. TR27: S Er 7C **140**
Trewinnard Rd. TR3: P Sta 3J **123**
TREWINNEY 4C **134**
TREWINNOW 4E **62**
Trewin Pl. TR3: Thre 5K **105**
TREWINT
Bude 1B **166**
Liskeard . . . . .7K **71** & 1K **79**
Trewint Cres. PL13: Loo 4H **81**
Trewint Est. PL14: Menh 1J **79**
Trewint La. PL12: S Ern 1F **87**
PL27: Rock 1G **23**
Trewint Rd. PL14: Menh 1H **79**
PL27: Rock 7D **18**
Trewirgie Gdns. TR15: Red 4D **112**
Trewirgie Hill TR15: Red 5D **112**
Trewirgie Rd. TR15: Red 4D **112**
Trewirgie Vean TR15: Red 4D **112**
Trewiston La. PL27: Pity 6E **18**
Trewithan Parc PL22: Los 3F **53**
Trewithen 3C **169**
Trewithen Gardens 2K **99**
Trewithen Parc TR8: S New E 2G **37**
Trewithen Rd. TR18: Penz 5E **148**
Trewithen Ter. TR13: Ash 4K **153**
TREWITHIAN 1B **174**
Trewithick Rd. TR13: Breag 3A **156**
TREWITHIEN LANE-END 2J **63**
TREWOEN 5G **119**
Trewollock Cl. PL26: G Hav 2H **135**
Trewollock La. PL26: G Hav 1H **135**
TREWOOFE 2B **172**
Trewoolsta Ter. PL14: Pens 1K **67**
TREWOON
Helston .1J **161**
St Austell 5C **56** (2C **169**)
Trewoon Rd. TR12: Mull 1J **161**
Treworden Cl. EX23: Stra 5H **9**
Treworder La. PL27: Eglo 4H **25**

Treworder Rd. TR1: Tru 5H **107**
Treworgan Ct. TR4: S Erm 2B **98**
Treworgans Holiday Pk. TR8: Cube 2F **39**
Treworgan Vw. TR4: Trisp 2B **98**
Treworlis Ct. TR13: Helst 1D **158**
Treworrick La. PL14: S Cle 4A **66**
TREWORTHAL 1B **174**
Treworthal Cl. TR4: Goonh 5G **41**
Treworthal Rd. TR3: P Sta 3J **123**
Treworvenneth Dr. TR17: Mar 4G **151**
Trewrickle La. PL11: Craft 5D **90**
Trewyn Flats TR26: S Ives 2H **137**
TREYARNON 7A 20 (3C **165**)
Treyarnon Bay Caravan Pk. PL28: Trey 5A **20**
Treyarnon La. PL28: S Mer 7B **20**
Treyew Pl. TR16: Carh 4B **114**
Treyew Rd. TR1: Tru 5G **107**
TREZAISE 6C **42**
Trezaise Av. PL26: Trez 6C **42**
Trezaise Cl. PL26: Trez 6C **42**
Trezaise Est. PL26: Roch 6B **42**
Trezaise Rd. PL26: Roch, Trez 5B **42**
Trezaise Sq. PL26: Trez 6C **42**
Treza Rd. TR13: P'ven 5F **157**
Trezela Rd. TR18: Penz 4E **148**
Triangle, The PL10: Caws 6E **94**
Trinity Pl. PL1: Plym 7F **163**
Trinity Row TR12: Lizar 6G **161**
Trinity St. PL25: S Aus 6G **57**
Trinity Watch TR26: S Ives 4H **137** (3D **136**)
TRISPEN 2B **98** (2B **168**)
Tristan Rd. TR1: Tru 4B **108**
Tristram Caravan Pk. PL27: Polz 3C **18**
Tristram Cliff PL27: Polz 3C **18**
TROAN 4C **44**
Trolver Cft. TR3: Feo 4G **125**
Trolver Hill TR3: Feo 2G **125**
Trolvus Vean TR10: Longd 5C **126**
TROON 5G **119** (1D **173**)
Troon Moor TR14: Tro 5G **119**
Troon Row TR13: Breag 2C **156**
Troubridge Rd. TR13: Helst 5C **158**
Troy Ct. PL23: Fow 7J **61**
Truck Hill TR2: Pro 2F **99**
Trungle TR19: Pau 4C **154**
Trunglemoor Cotts. TR19: Pau 4C **154**
Trungle Parc TR19: Pau 4C **154**
Trungle Ter. TR19: Pau 4C **154**
TRURO 5K **107** (3B **168**)
Truro (Park & Ride) 4K **105**
Truro Bowl 4J **107**
Truro Bus. Pk. TR4: Thre 5J **105**
Truro Cathedral 5K **107**
Truro City FC 6G **107**
Truro Golf Course 4E **106**
Truro Hill TR10: P'ryn 3A **128**
Truro La. TR10: P'ryn 4A **128**
Truro Lanes *TR1: Tru* *5J 107*
                               (off Kenwyn St.)
Truro Lawn Tennis Club 6D **106**
Truro Leisure Cen. 4C **106**
Truro Rd. PL25: S Aus 6F **57**
   PL26: S Aus, S Mew 7D **56**
   PL30: B'min, Lani 7H **31**
Truro Station (Rail) 5H **107**
Truro Technology Pk. TR1: Tru 7A **108**
Truro Vean Ter. TR1: Tru 4K **107**
TRURU 5K **107**
TRUTHWALL
   Plain-an-Gwarry 1G **151**
   St Just 1H **145**
Truthwall La. TR19: S Jus 1H **145**
Tryelyn PL31: B'min 6H **33**
Tryhornek TR26: C Bay 1B **140**
TRYTHOGGA 2G **149**
Trythogga Hill TR18: Gul 3G **149**
Trythogga Rd. TR18: Gul 2G **149**
Tubbon Hill TR3: Stith 6C **122**
Tuckers Cl. TR8: Newq 5J **35**
TUCKINGMILL 7G **111** (3A **168**)
Tucoyse La. TR11: Const 2F **159**
Tudor Ct. PL12: Salt 3J **89**
Tudor Lodge Holiday Pk. TR20: Crow 1G **151**
Tuke Cl. TR11: Fal 7C **128**
Tunnels Through Time 4F **35**
Turbot Point 3D **169**
Turfdown Rd. PL30: Carm 7K **33**
Turf St. PL31: B'min 4G **33**
Turnavean Rd. PL25: S Aus 4E **56**
Turnaware Ho. *TR2: Tregon* *6J 99*
                           (off Roseland Parc)
Turnaware Rd. TR11: Fal 3C **132**
TURNCHAPEL 2D **171**
Turnpike PL18: S An Cpl 3D **74**
   TR13: Helst 2C **158**
Turnpike, The TR19: S Jus 2J **145**
Turnpike Hill TR17: Mar 4F **151**
Turnpike Pl. PL14: Lisk 6A **70**
Turnpike Quarry TR15: Red 2F **113**

Turnpike Rd. TR17: Mar 4G **151**
   TR27: Con D 5J **139**
TUTWELL 3D **167**
TWELVEHEADS 3G **115** (3A **168**)
Twelvewoods PL14: Dob 3C **68**
Twelvewoods Cl. PL14: Dob 3D **68**
Twelvewoods Pl. PL14: Dob 3D **68**
Twinbrook Caravan Pk. TR11: Fal 5C **132**
TWO BURROWS .1A **104**
Two Chimneys Holiday Pk. TR20: Pra S . . .5H **155**
Two Hills Pk. PL12: Salt 3E **88**
Two Trees PL27: Wade 5E **24**
Two Trees Rd. PL22: Los 4G **53**
Tyacke Rd. TR13: Helst 4B **158**
Tybesta TR2: Gram 7B **62**
Tye Hill Cl. PL25: T'oon 5D **56**
Tyland Rd. PL32: Came 3K **15**
Tynance Ct. PL26: S Den 2E **46**
Tyringham Pl. TR26: Lel 2D **140**
Tyringham Rd. TR26: Lel 2D **140**
Tyringham Row TR26: Lel 2D **140**
Tyshute La. PL26: Polg 3C **64**
TYWARDREATH 2B **60** (2D **169**)
TYWARDREATH HIGHWAY 7K **51** (2D **169**)
Tywardreath Hill PL24: Par 2B **60**
Tywarnhaile Way TR4: P'twn 6C **96**
Tywarnhayle Rd. TR6: P'rth 4A **40**
Tywarnhayle Sq. TR6: P'rth 4B **40**

U

Uglow Cl. TR14: Camb 7C **110**
Ulalia Rd. TR7: Newq 3G **35**
Umfula Pl. TR26: S Ives 3H **137**
Under Chapel M. *TR18: Penz* *6G 149*
                          (off Under Chapel Yd.)
Under Chapel Yd. TR18: Penz 6G **149**
Undercliff TR27: Phil 7D **138**
Underhayes La. PL15: Laun 1F **17**
Underhill EX23: Kilkh 1F **7**
Under La. PL15: Laun 3A **16**
Underlane EX23: March 3F **11**
Under Rd. PL18: Gun 1H **75**
   PL35: Bosc 2J **13**
UNDERWOOD 2D **171**
Uneedus Pk. TR1: Tru 7K **107**
Union Hill EX23: Stra 5G **9**
   TR1: St C'mt, Tru 3B **108**
   TR9: S Maj 4C **30**
Union Pl. PL23: Fow 7K **61**
   TR1: Tru 5K **107**
Union Rd. TR11: Fal 6B **128**
   TR9: S Maj 4C **30**
Union Sq. TR9: S Maj 4C **30**
Union St. PL1: Plym 5F **163**
   TR1: Tru 4J **107**
   TR14: Camb 1D **118**
   TR18: Penz 5F **149**
UNITED DOWNS .4D **114**
United Downs Ind. Pk. TR16: S Da 4C **114**
                             (not continuous)
United Downs Raceway 5D **114**
United Rd. TR16: Carh 4A **114**
Unity Pl. *TR19: Mou* *6D 154*
                          (off Southview Ter.)
Unity Rd. TR13: P'ven 7G **157**
University College Falmouth
   Tremough Campus 4H **127**
   Wellington Terrace Annexe 1F **133**
   Woodlane Campus 2F **133**
University of Exeter in Cornwall
   Tremough Campus 4H **127**
University of Plymouth
   Constantine St. .4K **163**
   Gibbon St. 3J **163**
   Portland Sq. 2H **163**
University of Plymouth Squash & Fitness Complex
    . . . . .2J **163**
Upland Cl. TR1: Tru 3B **108**
Upland Cres. TR1: Tru 4A **108**
Uplands PL12: Salt 4G **89**
Uplands, The PL22: Los 3D **52**
Uplands Vean TR1: Tru 4B **108**
Up. Castle Rd. TR2: S Mawe 7C **130**
Upper Chapel PL15: Laun 5F **17**
Up. Dobbin Cl. PL28: T'one 3G **21**
Up. Dobbin La. PL28: T'one 3G **21**
Up. Eastcliffe Rd. PL24: Par 3A **60**
Upper Hillcrest TR6: P'rth 5A **40**
Up. Lynstone Camping & Caravan Pk. EX23: Bud 7B **8**
Upper Mdw. *TR26: S Ives* *1H 137*
                            (off The Meadow)
Up. School La. TR1: Tru 6J **107**
Upper Tredrea TR3: P'hal 3K **123**
UPTON
   Bude 1B **10** (3A **164**)
   Liskeard 3C **167**
UPTON CROSS 3C **167**
Upton Mdws. EX23: Lyn 7B **8**

Upton Slip TR11: Fal 1F **133**
UPTON TOWANS 4G **139**
Urban Ter. PL17: Call 5D **72**
Uzella Pk. PL22: Los 3E **52**

V

Valency Row PL35: Bosc 1K **13**
Valentine Pl. *PL17: Call* *5C 72*
                          (off Valentine Row)
Valentine Row PL17: Call 5C **72**
Valletort Ho. PL1: Plym 2F **163**
Valley, The TR3: C Dow 6C **116**
   TR19: P'cno, S Lev 5G **147**
   TR26: C Bay 6F **137**
Valley Bungs. PL13: Mill 3K **81**
Valley Caravan Pk. PL27: Polz 3D **18**
Valley Cl. TR1: Tru 5E **106**
   TR4: Goonh 7F **41**
Valley Gdns. TR16: I'gan 1K **111**
Valley La. TR3: C Dow 6D **116**
Valley Lodges PL17: Harr 4D **74**
Valley Pk. La. PL26: Mev 6C **134**
Valley Rd. EX23: Bud 6D **8**
   PL12: Salt 3G **89**
   PL26: Mev 4B **134**
   TR26: C Bay 6E **136**
VALLEY TRUCKLE 4H **15** (2B **166**)
Valley Truckle Caravan Club Site PL32: Came . . .5G **15**
Valley Vw. PL14: S Keyn 1B **78**
   PL27: Wade 5F **25**
   PL30: S Teat 3B **26**
   PL31: B'min 5G **33**
   TR16: I'gan 1K **111**
   TR16: L'ner 7G **113**
Valley Vw. Dr. TR1: Tru 5E **106**
Valley Vw. Est. TR16: L'ner 7G **113**
Valley Vw. Pk. PL26: Bugl 6H **43**
   PL31: Dun 3B **32**
Valley Vw. Ter. TR3: Pons 4F **123**
Valley Vw. Touring Pk. TR4: Black 2A **104**
Vancouver Pl. PL15: Laun 3G **17**
Varfell La. TR20: L Roc 1B **150**
Varley La. PL14: Lisk 5A **70**
Varley Ter. *PL14: Lisk* *5A 70*
                               (off Dean St.)
Vauxhall Ct. PL4: Plym 5J **163**
Vauxhall Quay PL4: Plym 5K **163**
Vauxhall St. PL4: Plym 6J **163**
Vauxhall St. Flats PL4: Plym 5K **163**
Vean Rd. TR14: Camb 1E **118**
Vean Ter. TR14: Camb 1E **118**
Vellan Cl. TR14: Barr 4B **118**
Vellan Dreath TR19: Senn 2E **146**
Vellandrucia TR3: Stith 7B **122**
Vellanhoggan M. *TR18: Gul* *3H 149*
                        (off Trevarrack La.)
VELLANOWETH 2H **155**
Vellan Parc Av. TR27: Ang 7G **139**
Vellan Vrane TR27: Ang 7H **139**
Vell La. PL33: Dela 3A **14**
VELLY 1A **164**
Venetian Views TR9: P'ale 4F **45**
Venland Cl. PL14: Trem 4C **66**
VENNGREEN 2B **164**
Venslooe Hill PL14: Lisk 1A **70**
VENTERDON 3D **167**
Ventnor Ter. TR26: S Ives 2G **137** (2C **136**)
Venton East Hill TR19: S Jus 2J **145**
Venton East Sq. TR19: S Jus 2J **145**
Venton Lace Rd. TR2: Gram R 6K **37**
Ventonleague Hill TR27: Hayl 7E **138**
Ventonleague Row TR27: Hayl 7E **138**
Ventonraze TR16: I'gan 7J **101**
Ventonraze Ter. TR16: I'gan 7J **101**
Venton Rd. TR11: Fal 1C **132**
   TR26: S Ives 5E **136**
Ventonvaise *TR6: P'rth* *4B 40*
                          (off Atlantic Bay)
Venton Vision Ri. TR26: S Ives 3B **136**
Veor Ho. TR14: Camb 1D **118**
Veor Rd. TR7: Newq 2K **35**
Verdun Ter. PL14: Lisk 5A **70**
Vernon Pl. TR11: Fal 1F **133**
Vernon Vs. PL24: S Bl G 3G **59**
Vernon Way TR10: P'ryn 5K **127**
VERYAN 5J **135** (3C **169**)
VERYAN GREEN 4J **135** (3C **169**)
Viaduct Hill TR27: Hayl 1K **141**
Viaduct La. TR14: P'nds 2A **118**
Vibert Pl. TR19: Mou 6D **154**
Vicarage Cl. PL14: Menh 1H **79**
   TR11: B Wat 2A **132**
Vicarage Gdns. PL5: Plym 3K **89**
Vicarage La. TR27: S Er 6F **141**
Vicarage Hill PL25: S Aus 6G **57**
   PL26: Mev 5C **134**
   PL34: Tin 7A **12**

Vicarage Hill TR11: B Wat 2A **132**
  TR16: S Da 3A **114**
Vicarage La. PL24: Tyw 2A **60**
  TR4: Black 1D **104**
  TR12: Mana 6C **160**
  TR12: Mull 1H **161**
  TR26: Lel 2E **140**
Vicarage Mdw. PL23: Fow 7J **61**
  (not continuous)
Vicarage Rd. EX23: Bud 5C **8**
  PL11: Tor 4K **93**
  PL24: Tyw 2K **59**
  TR5: S Agn 3B **96**
  TR13: P'ven 6F **157**
Vicarage Row TR13: Breag 2D **156**
Vicarage Ter. TR11: Const 2G **159**
VICTORIA
  Lostwithiel 3E **52**
  St Austell 1C **42** (1C **169**)
Victoria Bus. Pk. PL26: Vict 1C **42**
Victoria Cl. PL14: Lisk 4B **70**
Victoria Commercial Cen. PL26: Vict 2C **42**
Victoria Cotts. PL12: Salt 2G **89**
  TR11: Fal 2F **133**
Victoria Ct. TR18: Penz 4F **149**
  (off Victoria Sq.)
Victoria Gdns. TR3: Thre 5A **106**
  TR9: S Roa 1G **45**
Victoria Interchange PL26: Vict 1D **42**
Victoria La. PL12: Salt 3H **89**
Victoria M. TR18: Penz 4F **149**
  (off Victoria Sq.)
Victoria Pk. PL27: Wade 3F **25**
Victoria Pl. PL14: Lisk 5B **70**
  (off Russell St.)
  PL25: S Aus 6G **57**
  TR3: Pons 5F **123**
  TR18: Penz 5F **149**
  (off Parade St.)
  TR26: S Ives 1J **137** (2D **136**)
Victoria Quay TR11: Fal 7F **129**
Victoria Rd. EX23: Flex 3C **8**
  PL12: Salt 3H **89**
  PL25: S Aus 6J **57**
  PL26: Roch, Vict 4B **42**
  PL32: Came 3J **15**
  TR3: Thre 5A **106**
  TR26: S Ives 1J **137**
Victoria Row TR19: S Jus 3H **145**
Victoria Sq. PL31: B'min 5H **33**
  TR1: Tru 5J **107**
  TR18: Penz 4F **149**
Victoria St. PL11: Tor 3K **93**
  TR9: S Maj 4C **30**
  TR14: Camb 1D **118**
Victoria Ter. PL4: Plym 1H **163**
  PL12: S Dom 2K **77**
  PL14: Lisk 5A **70**
  (off Station Rd.)
  PL26: Nanp 6G **47**
  TR2: P'stho 3K **131**
Victoria Trad. Est. PL26: Vict 1C **42**
Victory Hill TR2: S Mawe 7D **130**
Village, The PL14: Duloe 6A **78**
  PL14: S Keyn 1C **78**
  PL26: T'lwth 2B **64**
Village Farm Cl. EX23: March 3G **11**
VILLATON 3K **83**
Vincent Way PL12: Salt 3H **89**
Vinefield Ct. TR11: Flu 5F **129**
Vine Pl. PL24: Tyw 2B **60**
Vinery Mdw. TR10: P'ryn 4A **128**
Vineyard, The TR3: Stith 7A **122**
Vingoe's La. TR20: Mad 1B **148**
Virgin Hill TR17: Mar 3E **150**
Virgin Pl. TR19: Mou 6D **154**
VIRGINSTOW .3D **167**
Virgin St. TR26: S Ives 1J **137** (2D **136**)
Visicks Works TR3: P'hal 2B **124**
Vista, The TR7: Newq 4D **34**
Vista-Del-Mar TR15: Red 2F **113**
Vivian Cl. TR7: Newq 4F **35**
Vivian Ct. TR1: Tru 6K **107**
Vivian Pk. TR14: Camb 1F **119**
Vivian Pl. TR19: Mou 6D **154**
  (off Millpool)
Vivian Rd. PL31: B'min 4D **32**
Vivian Ter. TR19: Mou 6D **154**
  (off Millpool)
VOGUE 3J **113**
VOGUE BELOTH 1K **111**
Vogue Hill TR16: Vog 3J **113**
Vogue Ter. TR16: S Da 3K **113**
Vogus La. PL12: S Dom 2G **77**
  PL17: Meth 2H **77**
Vollard's La. PL12: Hatt 4J **83**
Vorfield Cl. TR15: Red 2D **112**
VORVAS 7D **136**
Vosporth Hill TR8: Cran 6B **34**

Voss Rd. PL12: Salt, T'ton 7A **84**
Vounder Glaze TR19: S Jus 3H **145**
Voundervour La. TR18: Penz 5F **149**
Vyvyan Dr. TR8: Q Dow 6D **36**
Vyvyan Pl. TR13: Helst 4C **158**
Vyvyans Ct. TR14: Camb 5E **110**
Vyvyan's Ter. TR14: Praze 4K **143**
Vyvyan St. TR14: Camb 7D **110**

W

WADEBRIDGE 4F **25** (3D **165**)
Wadebridge Rd. PL30: S Mab 6B **26**
  PL30: S Tud 4J **27**
Wadebridge Sports Cen. 2F **25**
Wadeland Ter. PL14: Lisk 5J **69**
Wadham Cl. PL14: Lisk 5B **70**
Wadham Dr. PL14: Lisk 5C **70**
Wadham Rd. PL14: Lisk 5B **70**
Wagg La. TR2: Pro 2H **99**
WAINHOUSE CORNER 1B **166**
Wainsway TR6: P'rth 5B **40**
Wake St. PL4: Plym 1F **163**
Walk, The PL15: Laun 3H **17**
  (off Dockacre Rd.)
Walker Lines Ind. Est. PL31: B'min 6H **33**
  (not continuous)
WALKHAMPTON 1D **171**
Walk Ter. PL23: Polr 7B **60**
  (off West St.)
WALL 2D **142** (1D **173**)
Wallace Rd. PL31: B'min 3F **33**
Walled Garden, The TR10: P'ryn 6J **127**
Wall Gdns. TR27: Reaw 2D **142**
Wall Rd. TR27: Reaw 2D **142**
Wall Vean TR27: Reaw 3D **142**
Walsingham Pl. TR1: Tru 5K **107**
Wansford Mdw. PL26: G Hav 2H **135**
WARBSTOW 1C **167**
Warburton Gdns. PL5: Plym 4K **89**
Ward Cl. EX23: Stra 5G **9**
Warehouse, The TR10: P'ryn 5B **128**
  (off Anchor Quay)
Warfelton Cres. PL12: Salt 3G **89**
Warfelton Gdns. PL12: Salt 3G **89**
Warfelton Ter. PL12: Salt 3G **89**
WARLEGGAN .1A **170**
Warleigh Vs. PL12: Salt 3J **89**
  (off Culver Rd.)
Warne Cl. TR2: Tregon 6H **99**
Warraton Cl. PL12: Salt 2F **89**
Warraton Grn. PL12: Salt 2F **89**
  (off Warraton Rd.)
Warraton La. PL12: Salt 2F **89**
Warraton Rd. PL12: Salt 2F **89**
Warren, The PL13: Polp 7B **80**
  TR26: S Ives 3J **137** (3D **136**)
Warren Cl. TR13: P'ven 7G **157**
Warren Ct. PL26: Sten 3H **49**
Warren Rd. TR9: I Que 1J **45**
Warrens Fld. PL32: Came 3J **15**
Warren Way TR27: Hayl 2H **141**
Warwick Av. TR16: I'gan 7H **101**
Warwick Cl. PL28: S Mer 6E **20**
Warwick Cres. PL27: S Eval 2J **31**
Warwick Dr. PL25: S Aus 4B **58**
Warwick Rd. EX23: Bud 6D **8**
  TR16: I'gan 7H **101**
WASHAWAY 1D **169**
WATERGATE 6K **101**
Watergate Bay Holiday Pk. TR8: Tr'grn 6C **28**
Watergate La. PL30: S Mab 6B **26**
Watergate Rd. TR7: Newq 1K **35**
  TR8: Newq 7A **28**
Watering Hill Cl. PL25: S Aus 6J **57**
Waterings Rd. TR11: M Bri 1E **128**
Water La. PL23: Gola 1J **61**
  PL33: Dela 2B **14**
  PL35: Bosc 1K **13**
  TR5: S Agn 2B **96**
  TR8: Curr 6B **34**
  TR27: Hayl 4F **141**
WATERLOO 3B **166**
Waterloo TR1: Tru 5A **108**
Waterloo Cl. TR2: S Mawe 6D **130**
Waterloo Pl. TR11: Fal 1F **133**
  (off Waterloo Rd.)
Waterloo Rd. TR11: Fal 1F **133**
Waterloo St. PL4: Plym 2K **163**
Waterloo Ter. PL17: K Bray 1D **72**
Water-Ma-Trout TR13: Helst 1C **158**
Water-Ma-Trout Ind. Est. TR13: Helst 1C **158**
Waters Edge PL28: Pad 2C **22**
Watersedge Cl. PL25: S Aus 5F **57**
Waterside TR10: P'ryn 5C **128**
Watersmead Parc TR11: B Wat 2A **132**
Waterwheel Apartments PL25: S Aus 6A **58**
  (off Charlestown Rd.)

Waterwheel Cl. PL25: S Aus 6B **58**
Waterworld
  Newquay 4H **35**
Watery La. PL31: B'min 2F **33**
Waves TR8: Newq 6A **28**
Wavish Pk. PL11: Tor 3G **93**
Wayfield Rd. TR11: M Chu 3H **129**
Wayside Folk Mus. 1B **172**
WEARDE 4H **89**
Wearde Rd. PL12: Salt 3F **89**
Webber Hill TR11: Fal 1F **133**
Webber St. TR11: Fal 1F **133**
Webb St. PL23: Fow 7K **61**
Wedgewood Ct. PL14: Lisk 4B **70**
  (off Lower Lux St.)
Wedgewood Rd. PL25: S Aus 5A **58**
WEEK GREEN .1C **167**
WEEK ST MARY 1C **167**
Weeks Ri. PL32: Came 5G **15**
Weeks Row PL18: Gun 1H **75**
Weeth Cl. TR14: Camb 7C **110**
Weethes Cotts. TR18: Penz 5E **148**
Weeth La. TR14: Camb 7C **110**
Weeth Rd. TR14: Camb 6B **110**
Weir Head PL18: Gun 3H **75**
Welbeck Av. PL4: Plym 1H **163**
WELCOMBE 2A **164**
Welcome Cl. TR4: Trisp 2B **98**
Weller Ct. TR11: Fal 2F **133**
Well Gdns. PL1: Plym 3F **163**
Wellington Cl. TR14: Camb 7C **110**
Wellington Gdns. TR11: Fal 1F **133**
  (off Wellington Ter.)
Wellington Pl. PL27: Wade 5F **25**
  TR11: Fal 1F **133**
  (off Clare Ter.)
  TR13: P'ven 7G **157**
  TR18: Penz 5E **148**
Wellington Plantation TR3: Feo 7H **117**
Wellington Rd. PL26: S Den 2D **46**
  PL27: S Eval 2H **31**
  TR13: P'ose, P'ven 6G **157**
  TR14: Camb 7D **110**
Wellington St. PL4: Plym 2K **163**
  PL11: Tor 3K **93**
Wellington Ter. TR1: Tru 5J **107**
  (off George St.)
  TR2: P'stho 3K **131**
  TR11: Fal 1F **133**
  TR13: P'ven 6G **157**
  TR18: Penz 5E **148**
  (off Wellington Pl.)
Well La. PL13: Loo 5F **81**
  PL14: Lisk 4B **70**
  PL14: S Cle, Trem 4A **66**
  TR2: Gerr 3J **131**
  TR2: Tregon 6H **99**
  TR11: Const 2H **159**
  TR11: Fal 1F **133**
  TR12: S Kev 2B **162**
  TR16: I'gan 1K **111**
  (Forth End)
  TR16: I'gan 6H **101**
  (Langwedth)
  TR20: Gold 4B **152**
WELLMORE 7F **157**
Well Pk. Rd. PL11: Tor 3K **93**
Wellpark Rd. PL18: Alb, Dra 4G **75**
Wells Ct. PL10: M'brk 3C **94**
Well St. PL17: Call 5C **72**
  PL24: Tyw 2B **60**
  PL33: Dela 2B **14**
  TR2: Tregon 6H **99**
WELLTOWN 3H **13**
Well Way TR7: Newq 2K **35**
Welman Rd. PL10: M'brk 1D **94**
Welsby Ter. PL14: S Cle 4A **66**
WELSFORD 1A **164**
Welway TR6: P'rth 5B **40**
WEMBURY 3D **171**
WENDRON 1D **173**
Wendron St. TR13: Helst 3C **158**
Wendron Ter. TR16: Four L 4C **120**
WENFORDBRIDGE 3A **166**
Wentworth Cl. EX23: Lyn 7B **8**
  PL27: Polz 3D **19**
  TR15: Red 5E **112**
Wentworth Way PL12: Salt 3E **88**
WERRINGTON .2D **167**
Werrington Dr. PL17: Call 7C **72**
Wesley Cl. PL17: K Bray 1C **72**
  PL26: Sten 3H **49**
Wesley Cottage .2C **167**
Wesley Ct. PL1: Plym 6F **163**
  PL11: Tor 3K **93**
  (off Tamar St.)
  PL14: Pens 1J **67**
  PL26: Mev 6C **134**
  (off Meadow St.)

Wesley Ct. *TR13: P'ven* 7F *157*
    (off The Gue)
    TR15: Red 3E *112*
    (off Wesley St.)
Wesley La. PL12: Salt 3H 89
Wesley Pas. TR26: S Ives 3H 137
Wesley Pl. PL25: S Aus 6K 57
    TR18: Newl 1C 154
    TR26: S Ives 3H 137 (3D 136)
Wesley Rd. PL12: Salt 3H 89
    PL14: Pens 1J 67
    TR8: Cube 4F 39
Wesley Sq. *TR19: Mou* 6D *154*
    (off The Wharf)
Wesley St. TR14: Camb 7E 110
    TR15: Red 3E 112
    TR18: Hea 3D 148
Wesley Ter. PL12: Land 7G 83
    PL13: Loo 4H *81*
    (off Shutta Rd.)
    PL26: Bugl 5H 43
Wesley Yd. TR7: Newq 3E 34
West Bay TR11: Maen 1E 160
W. Beach Rd. TR4: P'twn 6C 96
Westborne Hgts. TR15: Red 5D 112
    (not continuous)
Westborne Rd. TR14: Camb 6B 110
Westbourne Dr. PL25: S Aus 6F 57
Westbourne La. PL14: Lisk 4A 70
Westbourne Ter. PL12: Salt 2H 89
    TR9: P'ale 4F 45
Westbridge Rd. PL15: Laun 2G 17
    PL25: T'oon 5C 56
West Burraton PL12: S Dom 3J 77
Westby Rd. EX23: Bud 5D 8
W. Camps Bay PL11: Downd 7J 79
W. Charles St. TR14: Camb 1D 118
West Cliff TR4: P'twn 6C 96
West Cl. TR13: Helst 2D 158
West Corner TR3: C Dow 6D 116
West Cornwall Golf Course 1E 140
W. Cornwall Shopping Pk. TR27: Hayl 7F 139
WESTCOTT 1A 76
Westcott PL27: Wade 3D 24
Westcott Mdw. PL27: Wade 3D 24
Westcotts Ct. TR26: S Ives 3J 137
Westcott's Quay 3J 137 (3D 136)
West Ct. TR7: Newq 3D 34
WEST CURRY 1C 164
W. Darite Ter. PL14: C Nes 2D 66
Westdown Rd. PL33: Dela 4A 14
WESTDOWNS 2A 166
WEST DOWNS 6G 31
West Downs Ct. *PL13: Loo* 4G *81*
    (off Downs Rd.)
WEST END 3A 104
West End PL26: Pent 1D 134
    TR2: Pro 2G 99
    TR4: Chac 6D 104
    TR10: P'ryn 4K 127
    TR13: P'ven 7F 157
    TR15: Red 4C 112
    TR16: S Da 2K 113
    TR17: Mar 4E 150
    TR20: Gold 4K 151
West End Cl. TR10: P'ryn 4A 128
West End Ind. Est.
    TR10: P'ryn 4K 127
West End Sq. *PL17: Call* 5C *72*
    (off Liskeard Rd.)
West End Ter. PL10: M'brk 3C 94
Westend Ter. *TR10: P'ryn* 4A *128*
    (off West St.)
Westerlands Rd. PL27: Wade 3E 24
Western App. PL1: Plym 4F 163
Western Av. PL14: Lisk 5J 69
Western Pl. TR10: P'ryn 4K 127
Western Rd. PL15: Laun 5G 17
Western Ter. PL15: Laun 4G 17
    PL31: B'min 4E *32*
    (off St Leonards)
    TR11: Fal 2E 132
W. Fairholme Rd. EX23: Flex 3D 8
Westgate *PL15: Laun* 4H *17*
    (off Westgate St.)
Westgate M. *PL15: Laun* 4H *17*
    (off Dockey)
Westgate St. PL15: Laun 4H 17
Westgate Ter. PL15: Laun 4H 17
Westground Way PL34: Tin 6C 12
Westhead Rd. PL10: Rame 7C 94
Westheath Av. PL30: B'min 6B 32
    PL31: B'min 6B 32
Westheath Rd. PL31: B'min 5D 32
West Hill PL25: S Aus 6G 57
    PL27: Wade 4B 24
West Hoe Pk. 7F 163
West Kitty TR5: S Agn 2A 96
Westlake Cl. PL11: Tor 3H 93

West La. PL11: Craft 5F 91
    PL12: Land 6E 82
    PL33: Dela 3B 14
WEST LOOE 5G 81 (2B 170)
W. Looe Hill PL13: Loo 5F 81
W. Looe Sq. PL13: Loo 7J 81
Westmoor Cres. TR3: P Sta 2J 123
Westover Rd. PL17: Call 6C 72
WEST PANSON 1D 167
West Pk. PL12: Tide 7B 82
    PL27: Wade 4G 25
    TR3: P Sta 2J 123
    TR9: S Maj 5C 30
    TR15: Red 4B 112
West Pk. Rd. EX23: Flex 3C 8
    PL27: Eglo 5G 25
WEST PENTIRE 1A 168
W. Pentire Rd. TR8: Cran 6A 34
West Pl. TR11: Fal .2E 132
    TR19: S Jus 3H 145
    TR26: S Ives 2H 137 (2D 136)
W. Polmear Ct. PL25: Char 7B 58
WEST PUTFORD 2B 164
West Quay *PL10: M'brk* 2C *94*
    (off Dawes La.)
    PL28: Pad 3B *22*
    (off The Strand)
West Ri. TR11: Fal .2D 132
West Rd. PL13: Loo 4G 81
    TR8: Q Dow 6C 36
WEST SETON 5E 110
West St. EX23: Kilkh 2G 7
    PL10: M'brk 3C 94
    PL14: Lisk 4A 70
    PL23: Polr 6B 60
    TR9: S Maj 5C 30
    TR10: P'ryn 4A 128
WEST TAPHOUSE .1A 170
West Tehidy TR14: Tol D 3F 111
West Ter. *TR18: Newl* 7D *148*
    (off Creeping La.)
    TR27: Hayl 1G 141
WEST TOLGUS 2K 111
West Tolgus TR15: Red 2K 111
West Trevingey TR15: Red 4C 112
W. Trewirgie Rd. TR15: Red 4D 112
West Vw. PL28: T'one 2G 21
    TR13: P'ven 6F 157
Westward Flats PL27: Polz 3G 59
Westward Rd. TR26: S Ives 2G 137 (2C 136)
West Wharf PL26: Mev 6D 134
Westwood PL14: Lisk 4A 70
Westwood Holiday Parc *TR27: Hayl* 7E *138*
    (off Caroline Row)
WEST YOULSTONE 2A 164
Wetherham La. PL30: S Tud 6H 27
WHALESBOROUGH 3D 10
Whalesborough Parc EX23: Bud 5E 8
Wharf, The EX23: Bud 5C 8
    TR19: Mou 6D 154
    TR26: S Ives 1J 137 (2D 136)
Wharf Rd. TR18: Penz 5G 149
    TR26: S Ives 2J 137 (2D 136)
Wharfside Shop. Cen. TR18: Penz 5G 149
Wheal Agar TR15: Pool 4J 111
Wheal Alfred Rd. TR27: Hayl 1K 141
Wheal Anna TR4: Goonh 6G 41
Wheal-an-Wens TR17: Mar 4F 151
Wheal Ayr Ct. *TR26: S Ives* 3C *136*
    (off Alexandra Rd.)
Wheal Ayr Ter. *TR26: S Ives* 3C *136*
    (off Alexandra Rd.)
WHEAL BADDON 4K 115
Wheal Brake Lodge PL26: Nanp 6F 47
Wheal Bull PL26: Fox 1G 55
WHEAL BULLER 1D 120
Wheal Busy La. TR4: Chac 5C 104
Wheal Butson Rd. TR5: S Agn 2K 97
Wheal Catherine Cl. TR6: P'rth 4C 40
WHEAL CLIFFORD .4F 115
Wheal Cunning TR19: S Jus 2G 145
Wheal Damsel Rd. TR16: Carh 4K 113
Wheal Dance TR15: Red 5F 113
Wheal Dream TR26: S Ives 1K 137 (2E 136)
Wheal Eliza Cl. PL25: S Aus 4B 58
Wheal Fire La. TR5: S Agn 3K 97
Wheal Fortune La. TR15: I Hig 4K 111
WHEAL FRANCES .7H 41
Wheal Friendly La. TR5: S Agn 1A 96
Wheal Gerry TR14: Camb 6E 110
Wheal Golden Dr. TR8: Hol B 2B 38
Wheal Gorland Rd. TR16: S Da 2K 113
Wheal Harmony TR15: Red 1D 112
Wheal Harmony Bungs. TR15: Red 1D 112
Wheal Harmony Ter. TR15: Red 1D 112
WHEAL HARRIET 2F 119
WHEAL HENRY 2E 114
WHEAL HOPE 3H 41

Wheal Jane Mdws. TR3: Thre 5K 105
Wheal Jewel TR16: Crof 3B 114
Wheal Kitty TR5: S Agn 1C 96
Wheal Kitty La. TR5: S Agn 2B 96
Wheal Kitty Workshops TR5: S Agn 1B 96
Wheal Leisure TR6: P'rth 4B 40
Wheal Leisure Cl. TR6: P'rth 4B 40
Wheal Margery TR26: C Bay 5E 136
WHEAL MONTAGUE 7C 102
Wheal Northey PL25: S Aus 4B 58
Wheal Oak TR13: Helst 1D 158
WHEAL PLENTY 4F 103
WHEAL PROSPER .1E 114
Wheal Prosper Engine House 2C 173
Wheal Quoit Av. TR5: S Agn 2A 96
Wheal Ramoth *TR6: P'rth* 4B *40*
    (off Atlantic Bay)
Wheal Regent Pk. PL25: Carl 6D 58
Wheal Rodney Holiday Pk. TR17: Mar 3F 151
WHEAL ROSE 4H 103
Wheal Rose TR13: P'ven 7G 157
Wheal Rose Caravan & Camping Pk.
    TR16: Scor 5H 103
Wheal Silver TR15: Red 3D 112
Wheal Speed TR26: C Bay 6E 136
Wheal Speed Rd. TR26: C Bay 7E 136
Wheal Sperries Way TR1: Tru 5D 106
Wheal Tehidy La. TR15: I Hig 4A 112
Wheal Trefusis TR15: Red 6E 112
Wheal Trelawney TR15: Red 5F 113
Wheal Uny TR15: Red 5D 112
Wheal Venture Rd. TR26: S Ives 5E 136
Wheal Vw. PL26: S Ste 3C 54
Wheal Vlow TR6: P'rth 2D 40
Wheal Vor TR15: Red 5F 113
Wheal Vrose Bus. Pk. TR13: L'twn 1C 158
Wheal Vyvyan TR11: Const 2H 159
Wheal Whidden TR26: C Bay 6E 136
Wheatfield Cres. TR7: Newq 5H 35
Wheeler Higman Cl. PL26: Sten 4G 49
Wherry Pl. *PL23: Polr* 7C *60*
    (off School La.)
WHERRY TOWN 6E 148
Wherry Way PL14: Dob 4D 68
Whieldon Rd. PL25: S Aus 5A 58
WHIMBLE 3B 164
Whimple St. PL1: Plym 5H 163
WHIPSIDERRY 1K 35
Whipsiderry Cl. TR7: Newq 1K 35
WHITCHURCH 1D 171
Whitcross Hill TR15: Bosl 1J 119
Whitecroft Way EX23: Kilkh 1H 7
WHITE CROSS
    Helston 2D 173
    Newquay 1C 44
WHITECROSS
    Penzance 7A 140
    Wadebridge 4A 24 (3D 165)
White Cross Ct. PL4: Plym 3K 163
Whitecross Ind. Est. TR8: W Cros 1B 44
Whitefield Ter. PL4: Plym 2K 163
Whiteford Cl. PL17: Call 6C 72
White Friars La. PL4: Plym 4K 163
Whitegate PL26: S Den 2D 46
Whitegate Mdws. PL26: S Den 2D 46
Whitegate Rd. TR7: Newq 3H 35
Whitegate Shop. Complex
    TR7: Newq 2H 35
WHITEHALL 6K 103
White Hart Arc. *PL15: Laun* 3H *17*
    (off Broad St.)
Whitehill Ter. *TR13: Helst* 5C *158*
    (off Bullock La.)
Whitehouse PL23: Fow 6B 60
White Ho. Cl. TR26: C Bay 6E 136
White La. PL1: Plym 6J 163
WHITEMOOR 2J 47 (2C 169)
White River Cinema 6G 57
White River Pl. PL25: S Aus 6G 57
Whiterock Rd. PL27: Wade 4E 24
Whiterock Cl. PL27: Wade 4E 24
Whiterock Rd. PL27: Wade 4E 24
Whiterocks Pk. PL18: S An Cpl 2C 74
    (not continuous)
Whitethorn Ter. PL27: Wade 4E 24
Whites Cl. TR5: S Agn 2A 96
White Smock Mdw. PL35: Bosc 2K 13
Whitestone Cres. PL31: B'min 5E 32
Whitestone Rd. PL31: B'min 5E 32
Whitewater TR7: Newq 2H 35
WHITEWELL 3A 26
Whitewell Rd. PL30: S Teat 3B 26
Whitford Yd. PL23: Fow 7K 61
WHITLEIGH 2D 171
Whitley Cl. TR1: Tru 5K 107
Whitley Grange PL14: Lisk 4K 69
Whitport Hill PL12: S Ger 5B 86
Whitsand Bay Golf Course 5E 90
Whitsand Bay Holiday Pk. PL10: M'brk 3A 94

Whitsand Bay Vw. PL11: P'wkle 6D **90**
WHITSTONE 1C **167**
Whittington St. PL3: Plym 1F **163**
Whitworth Cl. TR5: S Agn 3A **96**
Whym Kibbal Ct. TR15: Red 3E **112**
WIDEGATES 2B **170**
WIDEMOUTH BAY 6A **10** (3A **164**)
Widemouth Bay Holiday Village EX23: Wid B 7B **10**
Widemouth Fields Touring Pk. EX23: Bud 7E **10**
Widgeon Way TR27: Hayl 4D **140**
WILCOVE 7H **89** (2D **171**)
Wilcove La. PL11: Wilc 1G **93**
Wildebeest Rd. PL27: S Eval 2J **31**
Wildflower La. TR7: Newq 3H **35**
(not continuous)
Wilkes Wlk. TR1: Tru 5K **107**
Wilkinson Cl. PL17: K Bray 2C **72**
Wilkinson Gdns. TR15: Red 5F **113**
Willapark Vw. PL35: Bosc 2J **13**
William Edwards Cl. EX23: Flex 4D **8**
William Laundry Cl. PL14: Menh 1J **79**
Williams Cl. TR11: Fal 7E **128**
Williams Ct. TR1: Tru 5J **107**
(off Union St.)
Williams Ho. PL31: B'min 4D **32**
William St. TR1: Tru 6K **107**
TR14: Camb 1D **118**
William Young M. PL14: Lisk 5D **70**
(off Silvanus Jenkin Av.)
Willis Vean TR12: Mull 2H **161**
Willoughby Pl. PL17: Call 5C **72**
Willowbank TR9: Fr'don 3G **45**
Willow Cl. PL17: Call 5D **72**
TR8: Q Dow 6D **36**
TR11: M Bri 1E **128**
Willow Dr. TR14: Camb 6B **110**
Willowfield TR18: Penz 5D **148**
Willow Grn. PL12: Salt 3F **89**
Willows, The PL12: S Dom 2F **77**
PL26: Bugl 7H **43**
TR7: Newq 1K **35**
Willows M. TR13: Helst 3B **158**
Willow Valley Holiday Pk. EX23: Bus 1H **9**
Willow Way PL14: Lisk 5A **70**
Wills La. TR26: S Ives 2H **137**
Willsmoor PL26: G Hav 3H **135**
Will's Row TR15: P Bot 2J **111**
Wilson Way PL24: B'vey 4G **59**
TR15: I Hig, Pool 5J **111**
Wilton Ter. PL13: Pely 2C **80**
Winding Ter. TR10: Longd 5C **126**
WINDMILL 3H **21**
Windmill PL23: Fow 7J **61**
Windmill Hill PL12: Salt 3G **89**
PL15: Laun 4H **17**
TR2: S Jus R 3D **130**
Windmill Hill Ter. PL15: Laun 4H **17**
Windmill La. PL15: Laun 4H **17**
Windsor Ct. TR7: Newq 4E **34**
TR11: Fal 1F **133**
Windsor Dr. PL25: Carl 6C **58**
Windsor Gro. PL31: B'min 3H **33**
Windsor Hill TR26: S Ives 3H **137** (2C **136**)
Windsor La. PL12: Salt 3G **89**
PL17: K Bray 1C **72**
Windsor M. PL31: B'min 3G **33**
Windsor Pl. PL1: Plym 6G **163**
PL14: Lisk 5B **70**
TR18: Penz 4F **149**

Windsor Quarry TR11: Fal 1F **133**
(off Windsor Ter.)
Windsor Ter. PL11: Tor 3K **93**
(off King St.)
TR11: Fal 1E **132**
TR18: Penz 4E **148**
TR26: S Ives 3G **137** (3C **136**)
Windsor Vs. PL1: Plym 6G **163**
Windsworth PL24: S Bl G 2F **59**
Windy Ridge PL26: Goth 2H **47**
Windyridge PL12: Land 6G **83**
(off Tideford Rd.)
Wingfield PL31: B'min 3J **33**
Winifred Baker Ct. PL4: Plym 2J **163**
WINNARD'S PERCH 1C **169**
Winsor Est. PL13: Pely 3D **80**
Winston Av. PL4: Plym 1H **163**
Winstowe Ter. TR8: Cran 6B **34**
Winwell Fld. PL27: Wade 3G **25**
Witheybrook Ct. PL17: Call 5E **72**
(off Lynher way)
WITHIEL 1C **169**
Withnoe La. PL11: M'brk 7D **92**
Woburn Rd. PL15: Laun 5G **17**
Wodehouse Ter. TR11: Fal 1F **133**
Wolcocke Cl. TR17: Mar 4H **151**
Wolseley Rd. PL5: Plym 3K **89**
WOODACOTT 3B **164**
Wood Acre PL12: Salt 1D **88**
Woodacre Ct. PL12: Salt 1D **88**
Wooda Farm Pk. EX23: Stib 2G **9**
Wooda La. PL15: Laun 3G **17**
Wooda Rd. PL15: Laun 3H **17**
Woodbine Farm Bus. Cen. TR3: Thre 5J **105**
Woodbine La. TR16: I'gan 1G **111**
Wood Cl. PL12: Salt 2D **88**
PL26: Penw 5J **49**
Woodcock Cl. PL10: M'brk 1E **94**
Wood Dr. PL12: S Mel 6B **76**
Woodfield Rd. EX23: Flex 3D **8**
WOODFORD
EX23 ....2A **164**
PL7 ....2D **171**
Woodgate Rd. PL14: Lisk 4K **69**
Woodgrove Pk. PL26: Polg 2C **64**
Woodhill TR10: P'ryn 2E **126**
Woodland Av. PL24: Tyw 2A **60**
TR10: P'ryn 5K **127**
Woodland Cl. PL18: Gun 1G **75**
PL25: S Aus 6J **57**
PL30: Lani 6H **31**
Woodland Ct. TR1: Tru 4A **108**
Woodland Glade PL30: Lani 6H **31**
Woodland Hgts. TR1: Tru 4A **108**
Woodland Ri. TR10: P'ryn 5K **127**
Woodland Rd. PL25: S Aus 6J **57**
Woodlands PL24: Par 4J **59**
TR12: Mull 1H **161**
Woodlands, The TR14: Sth T 1C **110**
Woodlands La. PL26: Coomb 7E **54**
Woodlands Ter. TR16: L'ner 7H **113**
Woodlands Vw. PL13: Loo 4F **81**
Woodland Vw. PL26: Coomb 7E **54**
PL26: Dup 1K **65**
(off Bay Vw. Rd.)
PL30: Lani 7H **31**
TR15: P Bot 2H **111**
Woodland Way PL11: Tor 3H **93**
PL18: Gun 1H **75**

Wood La. PL12: Land 1H **87**
PL24: Tyw 1A **60**
TR1: Tru 6K **107**
(off Hurland Rd.)
Woodlane TR11: Fal 2F **133**
Woodlane Cl. TR11: Fal 2F **133**
Woodlane Cres. TR11: Fal 2F **133**
Woodlane Dr. TR11: Fal 2F **133**
Woodley Cl. EX23: Stra 5G **9**
Woodman's Cnr. TR11: Fal 7B **128**
Wood Parc PL25: S Aus 6K **57**
Woodridge Cl. TR27: Leeds 7C **142**
Woodsbrowning Ind. Est.
PL31: B'min 6H **33**
Woodside TR10: P'ryn 5K **127**
Woodside Paddock TR4: Chac 6D **104**
Wood St. TR18: Penz 4F **149**
(off Market Jew St.)
Woodvale Ter. PL15: Laun 4H **17**
Wood Vw. TR10: P'ryn 5K **127**
Woodway TR10: P'ryn 6K **127**
Woolcocks Ct. TR13: Helst 4C **158**
(off Meneage St.)
WOOLFARDISWORTHY 1B **164**
WOOLLEY 2A **164**
WOOLSERY 1B **164**
Woolster Ct. PL1: Plym 5J **163**
WOOLWELL 1D **171**
Woon La. TR3: C Dow 6D **116**
Woon Mill Cotts. PL26: Roch 6F **43**
Worcester Rd. PL25: S Aus 5A **58**
World of Model Railways 6C **134**
(off Meadow St.)
WOTTON CROSS 5F **83**
Wreford Cl. TR9: S Maj 5B **30**
Wren Ind. Est. TR1: Trel 4C **106**
Wrey Av. PL14: Lisk 3B **70**
Wych Hazel Way TR7: Newq 5G **35**
Wyndhurst Orchard PL27: Wade 4E **24**

Y

Yellow Tor Ct. PL12: Salt 3E **88**
Yellow Tor La. PL12: Salt 3E **88**
(off Fairmead Rd.)
Yellow Tor Rd. PL12: Salt 2D **88**
YELLOW-WORT 7E **120**
YELVERTON 1D **171**
YEOLMBRIDGE 2D **167**
Yeomans Cl. PL14: Lisk 5C **70**
Yeoman's Ct. PL26: Roch 4B **42**
Yeoman Way TR7: Newq 3H **35**
Yewberry Ter. PL31: B'min 3G **33**
Yew Tree Ct. TR1: Tru 3B **108**
York Rd. PL11: Tor 3K **93**
York St. TR18: Penz 4E **148**

Z

Zaggy La. PL17: Call 5C **72**
ZELAH 2B **168**
Zenith TR7: Newq 1K **35**
ZENNOR 1B **172**
Zennor Head 1B **172**
Zennor Quoit 1B **172**
Zinc TR7: Newq 2E **34**
Zion St. PL1: Plym 6H **163**

HOSPITALS, HOSPICES and selected HEALTHCARE FACILITIES covered by this atlas.

N.B. Where it is not possible to name these facilities on the map,
the reference given is for the road in which they are situated.

BODMIN COMMUNITY HOSPITAL 4D **32**
Boundary Road
BODMIN
PL31 2QT
Tel: 01208 251300

BODMIN NHS TREATMENT CENTRE 4C **32**
Bodmin Community Hospital
Boundary Road
BODMIN
PL31 2QT
Tel: 01208 262520

CAMBORNE REDRUTH COMMUNITY HOSPITAL . . .4B **112**
Barncoose Terrace
REDRUTH
TR15 3ER
Tel: 01209 881688

DUCHY PRIVATE HOSPITAL 3D **106**
Penventinnie Lane
Treliske
TRURO
TR1 3UP
Tel: 01872 226100

EDWARD HAIN MEMORIAL HOSPITAL . . .4J **137** (3D **136**)
Albany Terrace
ST. IVES
TR26 2BS
Tel: 01736 576100

FALMOUTH AND DISTRICT HOSPITAL 1D **132**
Trescobeas Road
FALMOUTH
TR11 2JA
Tel: 01326 434700

FOWEY HOSPITAL 6J **61**
Green Lane
FOWEY
PL23 1EE
Tel: 01726 832241

HELSTON COMMUNITY HOSPITAL 6D **158**
Meneage Road
HELSTON
TR13 8DR
Tel: 01326 435800

LAUNCESTON GENERAL HOSPITAL 5H **17**
Link Road
LAUNCESTON
PL15 9JD
Tel: 01566 765650

LISKEARD COMMUNITY HOSPITAL 3D **70**
Clemo Road
LISKEARD
PL14 3XD
Tel: 01579 335600

LITTLE HARBOUR HOSPICE 3K **65**
Porthpean Road
ST. AUSTELL
PL26 6AZ
Tel: 01726 871 800

MOUNT EDGCUMBE HOSPICE 1K **65**
Porthpean Road
ST. AUSTELL
PL26 6AB
Tel: 01726 65711

NEWQUAY HOSPITAL 4G **35**
St Thomas Road
NEWQUAY
TR7 1RQ
Tel: 01637 893600

NHS WALK-IN CENTRE (CARDREW) 2E **112**
60 Cardrew Industrial Estate
Redruth
REDRUTH
TR15 1SS
Tel: 01209 340997

POLTAIR HOSPITAL 2C **148**
Madron Road
PENZANCE
TR20 8SR
Tel: 01736 575570

PROBUS SURGICAL CENTRE 3J **99**
Tregony Road
TRURO
TR2 4JZ
Tel: 01726 885104

ROYAL CORNWALL HOSPITAL (TRELISKE) 4D **106**
Treliske
TRURO
TR1 3LJ
Tel: 01872 250000

ROYAL EYE INFIRMARY 1J **163**
Apsley Road
PLYMOUTH
PL4 6PL
Tel: 0845 1558094

ST AUSTELL COMMUNITY HOSPITAL 1K **65**
Porthpean Road,
ST. AUSTELL
PL26 6AD
Tel: 01726 291100

ST BARNABAS HOSPITAL .3H **89**
Higher Port View
SALTASH
PL12 4BU
Tel: 01752 857400

ST JULIA'S HOSPICE 3G **141**
Trelissick Road
HAYLE
TR27 4HW
Tel: 01736 759070

ST MICHAEL'S HOSPITAL .3G **141**
Trelissick Road
HAYLE
TR27 4JA
Tel: 01736 753234

STRATTON HOSPITAL 5G **9**
Hospital Road
Stratton
BUDE
EX23 9BR
Tel: 01288 287700

WEST CORNWALL HOSPITAL 4E **148**
St Clare Street
PENZANCE
TR18 2PF
Tel: 01736 874000

FSC
www.fsc.org

MIX
Paper from
responsible sources
FSC® C006021

The representation on the maps of a road, track or footpath is no evidence of the existence of a right of way.

The Grid on this map is the National Grid taken from Ordnance Survey® mapping with the permission of the
Controller of Her Majesty's Stationery Office.

Copyright of Geographers' A-Z Map Company Ltd.

No reproduction by any method whatsoever of any part of this publication is permitted without the prior consent of
the copyright owners.

Printed and bound in the United Kingdom by Polestar Wheatons Ltd., Exeter.